STUDIES ON THE CIVILIZATION
AND CULTURE OF
NUZI AND THE HURRIANS

Volume 5

Studies on the Civilization and Culture
of Nuzi and the Hurrians

Edited by

David I. Owen

Published by Eisenbrauns

1. *In Honor of Ernest R. Lacheman on His Seventy-fifth Birthday, April 29, 1981*. Edited by M. A. Morrison and D. I. Owen. 1981.
2. *General Studies and Excavations at Nuzi 9/1*. Edited by D. I. Owen and M. A. Morrison. 1987.
3. *Joint Expedition with the Iraq Museum at Nuzi VII: Miscellaneous Texts*. By Ernest R. Lacheman† and Maynard P. Maidman. 1989.
4. *The Eastern Archives of Nuzi and Excavations at Nuzi 9/2*. Edited by D. I. Owen and M. A. Morrison. 1993.
5. *General Studies and Excavations at Nuzi 9/3*. Edited by D. I. Owen. 1995.

Published by CDL Press

6. *JEN VII: A Commentary on Two Hundred Nuzi Texts from the Oriental Institute of the University of Chicago*. By Maynard P. Maidman. 1994.
7. *The Edith Porada Memorial Volume*. Edited by D. I. Owen and G. Wilhelm. 1995.

GENERAL STUDIES

edited by

David I. Owen

and

EXCAVATIONS AT NUZI 9/3

by

Ernest R. Lacheman† and David I. Owen

EISENBRAUNS
WINONA LAKE, INDIANA
1995

Library of Congress Cataloging-in-Publication Data

General studies / edited by David I. Owen ; and, Excavations at Nuzi 9/3 / [compiled] by Ernest R. Lacheman and David I. Owen.
p. cm. — (Studies on the civilization and culture of Nuzi and the Hurrians ; v. 5)
English and German.
Includes index.
ISBN 0-931464-67-6
1. Nuzi (Extinct city) 2. Hurrians. 3. Akkadian language—Texts. 4. Hurrian language. I. Owen, David I. II. Lacheman, Ernest René, 1906– . III. Excavations at Nuzi 9/3. IV. Series.
DS70.5.N9G46 1995
935—dc20 95-18828
CIP

The paper used in this publication meets the minimum requirements of the American National Standard for Information Sciences—Permanence of Paper for Printed Library Materials, ANSI Z39.48-1984.♾™

CONTENTS

PART 1
GENERAL STUDIES

PART 2
TEXTS IN THE HARVARD SEMITIC MUSEUM
EXCAVATIONS AT NUZI 9/3
E. R. LACHEMAN† AND D. I. OWEN

Preface

It is with a combination of pride and relief that I present herein the final installment of "Excavations at Nuzi 9." For me it represents the fulfillment of a promise I made to Professor Lacheman not long before his death to see to the complete publication of his copies. It also represents the culmination of the first and most demanding stage of the Nuzi Publication Project, the collation and publication of the tablets in the Harvard Semitic Museum and in the Oriental Institute copied by Lacheman. In this and in the preceding four volumes, more than 750 tablets have been published in copies, nearly all by Lacheman. In total they nearly exceed in number the copies published by him during his lifetime.

We can now proceed with the second phase of the "Nuzi Publication Project," the publication of specific studies based on the cumulative evidence of the Nuzi archives as they are now more fully understood. Not only will earlier studies be revised in the light of the new evidence at our disposal, but entirely new approaches to the archives may now be undertaken. Clarification of the language of the tablets can proceed apace because the lexicographical base has been greatly expanded. The discovery of a long Hurrian-Hittite bilingual epic, *Kirenzi* ("Epic of Manumission"), at Boğazköy will certainly add to our understanding of Hurrian grammar and lexicon and will provide additional insights into the Hurro-Akkadian dialect of Nuzi. Computerization of the Nuzi corpus has begun, and this new resource will allow for more sophisticated analyses to be undertaken. Preliminary results from the partially completed data base already have demonstrated the benefits of the computer.

The accompanying articles in Part I of *SCCNH* 5 continue to reveal the diverse research possibilities to which the Nuzi archives lend themselves. Some already incorporate the use of texts from *EN* 9/1–2. Others represent new assessments of Nuzi archives and related materials. One presents new data from the Hurrian-Hittite bilingual and another some observations on Nuzi ware.

Already published are two additional volumes in this series. They are *JEN VII: A Commentary on Two Hundred Nuzi Texts from the Oriental Institute of the University of Chicago* (*SCCNH* 6 [1994]), by Maynard P. Maidman, and *The Edith Porada Memorial Volume* (*SCCNH* 7 [1995]), edited by D. I. Owen and G. Wilhelm. *The Richard F. S. Starr Memorial Volume* (*SCCNH 8* [1996]) is in preparation and will appear early next year.

Volume 7 and subsequent volumes of *Studies on the Civilization and Culture of Nuzi and the Hurrians* will be co-edited by David I. Owen (Cornell University) and Gernot Wilhelm (Julius-Maximilians-Universität Würzburg) and will appear annually in March as a publication of CDL Press, Bethesda, Maryland. The editors will consider articles submitted on historical, philological, archaeological, and art historical topics relating to the general topics of Nuzi, Hurrians, Hurrian, Hurro-Akkadian, Hurro-Hittite, and Urartian in their widest chronological and geographical contexts. In addition, book-length manuscripts will also be considered for publication. Accompanying photos must be printed on gloss paper and clearly labeled. Charts and line drawings should be made so that they can be accommodated in the format size of this volume. Manuscripts from Europe should be sent directly to Professor Gernot Wilhelm, Institut für Orientalische Philologie der Julius-Maximilians-Universität Würzburg, Ludwigstraße 6, D-97070 Würzburg, Germany. Those from North America and Asia should be sent to Professor David I. Owen, Near Eastern Studies, Rockefeller Hall 360, Cornell University, Ithaca, NY 14853-2502 USA. Inquiries may also be made by electronic mail to DIO1@CORNELL. EDU or EXIT@VAX.RZ.UNI-WUERZBURG.D400.EDU; by facsimile to 011-607-255-1345 (USA) or 049-931-57-22-61 (Germany). Preferably, manuscripts should be submitted in electronic form (IBM or Mac format), with the name and version of the word processor used accompanied by a printed copy made on a laser or equivalent printer. Abbreviations should follow either the *Chicago Assyrian Dictionary, the Akkadisches Handwörterbuch*, the *Handbuch der Keilschriftliteratur*, or the *Chicago Hittite Dictionary.* Closing date for manuscripts each year will be July 15. Contributors will be provided with 30 free offprints of their articles. The printing of additional offprints will not be possible.

Studies on the Civilization and Culture of Nuzi and the Hurrians volumes 1–5 and following may be obtained from Eisenbrauns, POB 275, Winona Lake, IN 46590 USA. Volumes 6 and following may be obtained directly from CDL Press, P. O. Box 34454, Bethesda, MD 20827 USA.

Acknowledgments

The publication of this fifth volume of Studies on the Civilization and Culture of Nuzi and the Hurrians fourteen years after the appearance of Volume 1, the *Lacheman AV*, comes with a sense of great personal pride and accomplishment. On the one hand it brings to a close the publication of Lacheman's monumental work, *Excavations at Nuzi* 9, while on the other it has demonstrated the continuing interest in Nuzi studies and the enormous amount of information that this unique corpus continues to reveal to students of the ancient Near East.

I would like to acknowledge my debt to Cornell University, the Department of Near Eastern Studies, the Faculty Research Committee, and the Provost. Over the years I have been the recipient of a number of faculty research grants that have facilitated my work in Assyriology. The secretarial staff of the Department of Near Eastern Studies has been particularly helpful, and the former chair of the department, Professor Ross Brann, has been most supportive of my work. I would also like to thank Professor Martha A. Morrison, with whom I began this endeavor and with whom I worked closely on the production of the first four volumes. Professor Maynard P. Maidman has been particularly helpful, with his careful reading of certain manuscripts, suggestions for improvement, and references to unpublished data. Jim Eisenbraun and his staff have assured the highest standards of book design and publication. They have been a pleasure to work with all these years. To these individuals and institutions, named and unnamed, go my sincerest thanks.

David I. Owen
Ithaca, New York
April 24, 1995

PART 1
GENERAL STUDIES

edited by

David I. Owen

Gesellschaftsformen im Königreich Arrapḫe (*aḫḫūtu*) (II)

Gudrun Dosch
Universität Heidelberg

Die Gesellschaftsverträge, Verbrüderungen

Im ersten Teil[1] wurde bei der Untersuchung des Formulars der Verträge, die in den Nuzi-Texten Verbrüderungs- und Gesellschaftsverhältnisse widerspiegeln, auf Grund philologischer Aspekte das gleiche legale und soziale Verhältnis der beteiligten Personen nachgewiesen: Gleichberechtigung der einzelnen Parteien. Als deren Auflösung wurde die *ṭuppi zitti* gedeutet. Hier sollen nun die bisherigen Interpretationen der *aḫḫūtu* und die Urkunden in ihren typischen Passagen noch einmal vorgestellt werden; denn aus ihnen ergibt sich, daß Gesellschaftsformen und ihre Begründungen im Königreich Arrapḫe nachgewiesen werden können.

Jankowska[2] meint, daß die *aḫḫūtu* und *mārūtu*-Transaktionen die gleichen legalen Geschäfte beinhalten, im Grunde dasselbe bedeuten. Der Unterschied bestehe nur darin, daß sie Rückschlüsse auf die ursprünglich vorhandenen Hausgemeinschaften böten (sie geht von Koschakers Interpretation der Hausverbände aus): Ob das Land innerhalb der Familie vorher geteilt oder ungeteilt gewesen sei, also persönlich oder gemeinschaftlich besessen worden sei, drücke sich in den Verträgen aus, die abgeschlossen würden. *JEN* 87 sei deshalb ein *aḫḫūtu*-Vertrag, weil er Kurpa-saḫ in ungeteiltes Land aufnehme, und nur von einem Partner abgeschlossen werde. “Had the transaction with Kurpa-zaḫ been concluded not by Punni-ḫarapa alone, but by all the partners in their joint ownership it would have been worded as adoption of the former as ‘son’ and not as ‘brother’.” Es finden sich jedoch keine Hinweise, wie Jankowska annimmt, daß das betreffende Land der Familie Kizzuk sich schon vor dem Vertragsabschluß bei jenem bestimmten Bruderpaar befand und Kurpa-saḫ, der andere Bruder, keinen Anteil daran hat. Der weiter unten besprochene Text *JEN* 59 zeigt z.B., daß diese Interpretation von *mārūtu* und *aḫḫūtu* nicht standhält. Aus diesen Verträgen läßt sich m.W. ablesen,

Verfaßers Anmerkung: Ich benutzte die Dossiers des Heidelberger Seminars und danke allen, die daran mitgearbeitet haben. (Außer den bekannten Nachschlagewerken wurden folgende Arbeiten benutzt, Nuzi-Literatur wird nach dem Erscheinungsjahr zitiert, wie in den Nuzi-Bibliographien üblicherweise angegeben.)

[1] Teil I, s. Dosch 1987 in *Mesopotamia* 21: Parva Assyriologica Karolo Henrico Deller Dedicata, 191–207.

[2] Jankowska 2 1969 S. 240ff.

daß das Familienland normalerweise nach dem Tod des Familienvorstandes nach den Erbbräuchen des Königreiches Arrapḫe geteilt wird und daß sich die Brüder danach z.T. zusammentun und erklären, die Verbrüderung fortbestehen zu lassen, wie sie vor dem Tod des Vaters unter ihnen bestanden hat (nur standen sie als solche damals unter der Autorität des Vaters), oder daß Nicht-Verwandte eine Gemeinschaft gründen, die für die Zukunft gelten soll, wahrscheinlich um besser wirtschaften zu können.

Paradise[3] sieht in den Bruderschaftstafeln eine formale Anerkennung der Rechte eines Miterben, der kein leiblicher Sohn sei, durch die Söhne des Erblassers, damit dieser an der Teilung teilhaben könne. Er stützt sich dabei hauptsächlich auf Lewy und Gadd:[4] einer Bruderschaftsurkunde sei immer eine Adoption vorausgegangen. Nur in Testamenten der Kategorie "chief heir adoption," wie HSS 19,65 in dem die Teilung bis zur Reife der Enkel aufgeschoben sei, würde die Teilung einige Zeit lang hinausgeschoben und die Erben wirtschafteten bis dahin gemeinsam. In dieser Hinsicht behandelt er Gadd 29; *JEN* 87; 221; 204; HSS 19,140; 62; 65. Zwei Texte, die er dazu stellt, *JEN* 392 und 19,71 haben m.E. mit Verbrüderung nichts zu tun. Seine Annahme, in *JEN* 392 sei ein Bruderschaftsverhältnis deshalb nicht passend, weil der Erbe Taja ein Bruder des verstorbenen Erblassers sei, so daß der Adoptierte rechtlich sein Neffe sei und nicht im korrekten Verhältnis stünde für eine Bruderschaft ("brotherhood"), beruhen auf dem Irrtum, es komme bei Verbrüderungen immer auf den Verwandtschaftsgrad an. Paradises Begründung geht zu einseitig von den Testamenten aus und ist nur möglich, wenn man auch die "künstlichen Bruderschaften" als bloße Anerkennung bereits bestehender Beziehungen auffaßt. Die gleichen Bedingungen, die für eine *aḫḫūtu* festgelegt werden, finden sich natürlich auch in den Testamenten, wo bestimmt wird, daß Erbengemeinschaft fortbestehen soll, besonders wenn *abbūtu* gegeben wird, d.h. wenn der Zustand, wie er unter dem Vater bestand unter dem Vormund fortbestehen soll; dort wo die Söhne noch keine individuelle inteile verteilt bekamen, sondern gemeinsam unter seiner Autorität wirtschaften (gemeinsam teilen), wobei jeder gleichberechtigt ist. Es ist dabei nützlich, daß in Nuzi Normen bestanden. Die Schreiber bedienen sich für bestimmte rechtliche Beziehungen oder für Strafen des gleichen Vokabulars. Dies ist auch von Nuzi-Gelehrten für einige Vertragstypen untersucht worden, zuletzt von Paradise für die Testamente. So scheint es, daß es in Arrapḫe einen Rechtskodex gab, dessen Regeln für bestimmte Verhältnisse benutzt werden, und der von daher überliefert ist. Schwierig für unser Verständnis scheint es nur, zwischen "teilen" und Anteile "zer/aufteilen" richtig zu unterscheiden.

Koschaker[5] legte den Begriff einer fratriarchalischen Familie zu Grunde, die keine Gleichberechtigung kenne, und sah daher in den Bruderschaften eine Art Subordination. Stohlman[6] bestritt Lewys Auslegung der Texte *JEN* 87, 204 und

[3] Paradise 1972 S. 372.

[4] Gadd 1926 55ff., siehe besonders Bemerkungen S. 148; H. Lewy 2 1940 S. 362ff.

[5] Koschaker 1933 S. 45.5.

[6] Stohlman 1971 S. 208ff.

604, in der sie meinte, Kurpa-saḫ and Mat-tešup seien Söhne einer Konkubine, die mit diesen Urkunden Erbberechtigung bekämen. Er wies elf *aḫḫūtu*-Urkunden nach, die in der folgenden Besprechung berücksichtigt werden: Vier faßt er als Verkaufsurkunden auf, sieben als "real adoption," deren Hauptzweck es sei, dem "adoptierten" Bruder einen bestimmten Anteil zu geben. Er unterscheidet gegenseitige und nicht-gegenseitige Adoptionen. Zuerst sollen die schon oft in der Literatur besprochenen Verbrüderungen in der Familie Kizzuk behandelt und die betreffenden Personen beschrieben werden, damit der gesellschaftliche Rahmen abgesteckt wird: *JEN* 87 stammt aus dem Archiv der Familie Kizzuk.[7]

Zu diesem Text gehören *JEN* 204 und auch *JEN* 498 woraus die rechtlichen Verpflichtungen der *aḫḫūtu* abgeleitet werden können. In der fünften Generation dieser Familie ist Ḫilpiš-šuḫ als Abkömmling des Streitwagenfahrers Kiliške bekannt.[8] Nach Kiliške waren dessen sohn Kirzija/Kirzam-pula und einer dessen Söhne Ḫuti-ḫamanna S. Kirzija, Onkel des Ḫilpiš-šuḫ, Streitwagenfahrer (erschlossen aus HSS 16,331/332), also jeweils ein Sohn der nächsten Generation. Ḫilpiš-šuḫs Bruder Aittara und dessen Sohn Ianzi-mashu, sind oft Zeugen für MÍTulpunnaja. Sie sind außer in dem Prozeß *JEN*u 423, den Aittara mit seinem Bruder Ḫilpiš-šuḫ wegen eines Hauses zu führen scheint, (der Text ist sehr fragmentarisch) und den er verliert, nur als Zeugen belegt. Ḫilpiš-šuḫ wird einmal adoptiert von Akkul-enni S. Itḫ-apu und bekomt Häuser als seinen Anteil (*JEN*u 854). Er tauscht in *JEN*u 348 ein Objekt mit einem Zi . . . ja/da (*NPN* 179a) S. Zilip-tilla—der Text ist auch sehr zerstört—und ist Feldnachbar des Kel-tešup S. Ḫutija (aus der gleichen Familie aber Abkömmling des Ariḫ-ḫamanna, des Bruders von Kiliške. Kel-tešup ist höchstwahrscheinlich der Oberbefehlshaber des linken Flügels und Streitwagenfahrer) und nach Feldtausch (*JEN* 616 unter Verwandten) Feldnachbar der Söhne seines Kousins Eḫlutil und Zikte(-pukasu) S.e Šeštep-iašu in URU Uluawe. Zwischen diesen beiden Familienzweigen finden aber auch in der vorherigen Generation schon Immobilientauschgeschäfte statt: Kiliške tauscht mit seinem Neffen Kuššija Häuser, Garten und Brunnen (*JEN* 241) und Kiliškes Sohn Kirzija tauscht in *JEN*u 730 Felder mit Kuššijas Enkel Kel-tešup S. Ḫutija.

Ḫilpiš-šuḫ hatte vier Söhne: Punni-ḫarpa/Punnija, Mat-tešup, Kurpa-saḫ und Tupki-tilla. In *JEN* 87 nun nimmt Punnija seinen eigenen Bruder Kurpa-saḫ zur Bruderschaft, wie *CAD* A/1 187b bereits vermerkte. Kurpa-saḫ erhält als seinen Anteil, ein in der Größe nicht spezifiziertes A.ŠÀ *tab-ri-e* (Z. 5) und gibt dem Punnija 9 BÁN Gerste und 3 BÁN Weizen (die Z. 15 ist leider in der Mitte weggebrochen). In *JEN* 204 nimmt der andere Bruder Tupki-tilla S. Ḫilpiš-šuḫ ebenfalls Kurpa-saḫ zur Bruderschaft, gibt ihm einen genau bemessenen Garten als seinen Anteil und bekommt dafür als Anteil drei Schafe. *JEN* 604 ist wegen der Unsicherheit der Namen der Väter hier bei der Familie Kizzuk nicht aufgenommen und wird später besprochen (die Spuren von Mat-tešups Vater ergeben nicht

[7] S. Dosch-Deller 1981 in Morrison-Owen 1981 S. 91ff.; Dosch, "Zur Struktur der Gesellschaft des Königreichs Arrapḫe" (Diss. Heidelberg, 1987) Kap. 1.2–1.2.4.4 (jetzt in Heidelberger Studien zum Alten Orient, Band 5, 1993).

[8] H. Lewy 2 1940 S. 367; Jankowska 2 1969 S. 241.

Ḫilpiš-šuḫ wie Lewy annimmt). *JEN* 498 übersetzt *CAD* I/J 75b "PN" (Kurpa-saḫ) "is stationed in the town where he performs (his) *ilku*-duty, and his brothers are stationed with the chariotry (and are well)." Sollte dieser Bericht auf die abgeschlossenen Bruderschaften ein Licht werfen, dann ist das von *CAD* in Klammern gesetzte (his) auf jeden Fall zu streichen, wie es *CAD* A/1 203a auch übersetzt: "PN is said to be in the village where he does *ilku*-duty and his comrades are said to do service with the chariots"; denn wie sich bei der genauen Betrachtung der *aḫḫūtu*-Urkunden herausstellen wird, sind diese auch zum Teil zur Arbeitsteilung abgefaßt worden. *JEN* 498 läßt sich dann interpretieren: Kurpa-saḫ war in der Stadt geblieben und erfüllt die *ilku*-Arbeiten, während die Brüder den Kriegsdienst versehen. Daß *ilku* nicht Kriegsdienst bedeutet, verdeutlichen HSS 19,62 und 140.

In die gleiche Richtung scheinen wohl auch *JEN* 311 und 315 zu weisen, in denen Punni-ḫarpa S. Ḫilpiš-šuḫ seinem Bruder Felder für eine begrenzte Zeit *ana titennūti* gibt. Nach *JEN* 498 wäre es denkbar, daß er diese wegen des Kriegsdienstes nicht selbst bestellen kann. Kurpa-saḫ, der in der Stadt geblieben ist, kann die Felder weiter bewirtschaften und die Interessen seiner "Brüder" vertreten. Kurpa-saḫ regelt die Angelegenheiten des Gartens des in Bruder-/Partnerschaft stehenden Bruders Tupki-tilla (*JEN* 204), wie *JEN* 124 zeigt, wo fremde Schafe geweidet hatten (Hayden 1962, S. 40 scheint zu der Auffassung zu kommen, daß die beiden Brüder gegeneinander prozessieren). Es scheint aber eine Affaire zwischen Tamar-tae und Kurpa-saḫ zu sein, denn es könnte auch folgendermaßen gedeutet werden: In den Eiden Z. 7–8 und Z. 14 sagen beide Brüder aus, daß Kurpa-saḫ die Verantwortung mit dem Anteil mit übernommen hat, weshalb er als einziger bejaht, die Schafe in Gewahrsam genommen zu haben (Z. 16–17). Da in den Z. 18–20 weder Sache noch Personen genannt sind, kann auch Kurpa-saḫ mit Tamar-tae zum Ordal gehen—dessen Schafe er genommen hatte, weil sie dort geweidet hatten (Z. 3–7/16–17). Denn der Abschnitt Z. 1–8 kann die Erklärung sein, daß Kurpa-saḫ in dieser Angelegenheit zuständig ist, während der durch Querstrich abgetrennte Abschnitt Z. 18–20 berichtet, daß die Angelegenheit durch Ordal entschieden wird.

Ein ebensolches Gesellschaftsverhältnis hatte in dieser Familie bereits zwischen den Brüdern Ḫanatu und Ḫutija S.e Kuššija bestanden wie aus *JEN* 59:3 hervorgeht (Tutija S. Kuššija passim in dem Archiv der Familie). Ḫutija war LÚ.TAB-šu des eigenen Bruders, also Sozius, Partner, der diese Partnerschaft aber nun auflöst und seine Besitztümer dem ehemaligen Kompagnon ganz überträgt (Z. 10–11, in totaler, echter Adoption, wobei er ihm die Testamentstafeln, auf denen sein Besitz eingetragen ist, übergibt in Z. 24–25). Er selbst wird also auf dem Land nicht mehr arbeiten, dafür aber jährlich versorgt und bekleidet mit 5 ANŠE Gerste, 2 ANŠE Weizen und einem Kleid/Stoff. Der Text lautet: *JEN* 59 *JEN*u 708 113 × 73 × 28 Room 11 Dossier Šuriniwe, geschr. in *āl ilāni* (= Paradise Nr. 9)

Vs 1 *ṭup-pí ma-ru-ti ša*
2 ᴵ*Ḫa-*⌈*na*⌉*-du* DUMU *Ku-uš-ši-ja*
3 ᴵ*Ḫu-*⌈*ti*⌉*-ja* LÚ.TAB-*šu-ma*

4 *a-na ma-ru-ti i-te-pu-uš*
5 *um-ma* ^{I}*Ḫa-na-du-ma*
6 *mi-nu-um-*⸢*me-e*⸣ A.ŠA. MEŠ É.ḪI.A.MEŠ
7 *mi-im-ma* ⸢*šu-un*⸣*-šu* ḪA.LA-*ja*
8 ^{I}*Ku-uš-ši-ja a-bi-ja*
9 *ša ja-ši ša id-dì-nu ù i+na-an-na*
10 *a-na-ku* GÌR-*ja u*[*š*]-⸢*te*⸣-[*li*]
11 *a-na* ^{I}*Ḫu-ti-*⸢*ja*⸣ [TAB bzw. ŠEŠ-*ja at-ta-di*]*n-šu-nu-ti*
12 *a-di-i* ^{I}*Ḫa* -[*na*]-⸢*du ba-al*⸣*-tù*
13 ^{I}*Ḫu-di-ja i-pal-la-aḫ-šu*
14 *ù* ^{I}*Ḫu-di-ja i+na* MU *ù i+na* MU
15 1 TÚG *ki-ma lu-bu-ši-šu*
16 5 ANŠE ŠE 2 ANŠE GIG
17 *ki-ma* ŠE.BA-*šu*
Rd 18 *a-na* ^{I}*Ḫa-na-du i+na-an-dì-nu*
19 *im-ma-ti-mé-e*
Rs 20 ^{I}*Ḫa-na-du im-tù-ut*
21 *ù* ^{I}*Ḫu-di-ja*
22 *i-bá-ak-ki-šu-ma*
23 *ù uq-te-bi-ir-šu*
24 *um-ma* ^{I}*Ḫa-na-du-ma ṭup-pu*
25 *ša ši-im-ti-ja a-na* ^{I}*Ḫu-di-ja-ma at-ta-din*
26 *ma-an-nu-um-me-e ša i+na* DAL.BA.NA-*šu-nu*
27 KI.BAL-*at* 2 MA.NA KÙ.BABBAR 2 MA.NA GUŠKIN DIRI
28 *ṭup-pu* EGIR *šu-du-ti ina* KA É.GAL-*lì*
29 *i+na* URU DINGIR.MEŠ *šá-tì-ir*

Es folgen sechs Zeugen oder Beisitzer, ein Schreiber und die Siegel der sieben Personen (vgl. *AHw* 1321b s.v. *tappû* "Genosse, Gefährte, Kompagnon," "Geschäftspartner," nennt aber keine Nuzi-Belege).

Genau so ist HSS 19,41 zu deuten, ein Text, der aus der gleichen Familie stammt. Hier adoptiert Kuššija S. Ariḫ-ḫamanna einen wesentlich jüngeren Verwandten aus der Linie des Kiliške, den Ḫupitaja S. Ḫasija und vererbt ihm nach dem Tod einen Teil seines Besitzes. Bis zu diesem Zeitpunkt aber gelten folgende Bedingungen: HSS 19,41:28–32:

Rd 28 . . . . *a-dì-i* ^{I}⸢*Ku*⸣*-uš-ši-ja*
29 *ù* ^{I}*Ḫu-bi-ta-a+a ba-al-tú*
30 A.ŠA.MEŠ-*ti-šu-nu ša ki-la-le-šu-nu*
Rs 31 *it-ta-ḫa-mi-iš a-na šu-ta-pu-ti*
32 *i-ru*!(LI)-*šu ù* ŠE.MEŠ *mi-it-ḫa-ri-iš i-zu-z*[*u*]

Solange es Kuššija und Ḫupitaja gut geht (die Ubersetzung dieses Ausdruckes ist von der in *CAD* I/J 75b sub e) angegebenen übernommen), bestellen sie die dazugehörigen Felder beide gemeinsam in Partnerschaft/Genossenschaft (vgl. *AHw*

1291 s.v. *šutāpūtu* "Genossenschaft, gemeinsame Arbeit") und teilen die Gerste zu gleichen Teilen. Das Vokabular, worauf es ankommt, ist also hier: *ittaḫamiš—ana šutāpūti—mitḫāriš izzuzzū*.

Im Zusammenhang dieses Archives betrachtet, bekommt Kuššija Hilfe bei der Feldarbeit und Ḫupitaja, der wahrscheinlich aus dem Zweig der Nichterbsöhne kommt, die Existenzgrundlage. In Temtena(š)-Šuriniwe, d.h. in kassitischem Milieu treten Gesellschaftsbedingungen gehäuft auf. In der folgenden Besprechung der anderen Verbrüderungen zeigt sich jedoch, daß sie sich auch in nichtkassitischer Umgebung oft finden. Welches sind nun die hervortretenden juristischen und sozialen Merkmale solcher *aḫḫūtu*-Verhältnisse? Denn in der folgenden Besprechung dieser Verträge zeigt sich deutlich, daß die Partner zu juristisch und sozial Gleichberechtigten werden—wie es Eilers und Ries[9] für das Alt- und Neubabylonische nachwiesen. Dabei stellt sich heraus, daß *aḫḫūtu* und *mārūtu* zwei verschiedene Urkundentypen sind: *aḫḫūtu* bezieht sich auf Gleichberechtigung personenrechtlicher Art, auf Gleichberechtigung bei Erwerbsteilung und Arbeit, während *mārūtu* sich auf Nichtgleichberechtigung, auf keine Gleichberechtigung bei Arbeit und Erwerbsteilung bezieht. Gemeinsam ergeben sich aus diesen Urkunden nur gewisse Erbansprüche bei dem Tod des einen Partners, falls keine anderen Erben vereinbart wurden.

Erkennbar sind hier erstaunliche Parallelen zu dem altrömischen Recht, wie es Kaser[10] auf S. 98 beschrieb:

> Eine Berechtigung mehrerer Eigentümer an derselben Sache kennt das altrömische Recht bei der Gemeinschaft *ercto non cito*, wie sie bei der Erbengemeinschaft und bei der ihr nachgebildeten Verbrüderung besteht, die den Vorläufer des Gesellschaftsverhältnisses bildet.

Bei der Besprechung der Gesellschaft sagt er auf S. 180:

> Nach altrömischem Recht konnte das Rechtsverhältnis, das nach dem Tod des "*paterfamilias*" unter mehreren Hauserben ("*sui heredes*") als fortgesetze Hausgemeinschaft besteht, auch künstlich durch Rechtsakt geschaffen werden . . . Der Rechtsakt, mit dem dieses Verhältnis nachgestaltet wurde, eine förmliche "*legis actio*", führte nicht nur eine Vergemeinschaftung der gesamten Vermögen der Genossen herbei . . . sondern auch eine familienrechtliche Verbrüderung, die den Genossen personenrechtlich die gleiche Stellung gab . . . "*Sui heredes*" sind die Personen, die beim Tod des "*paterfamilias*" unter seiner Hausgewalt gestanden haben. Sie werden daher erst mit seinem Tod vermögensfähig, und die Erbschaft, die ihnen zufällt, ist zunächst ihr einziges Vermögen, das ihnen als ungeteiltes Gesamtgut gehört. Es ist darum nur folgerichtig, daß auch bei der künstlichen Verbrüderung alles Vermögen der Genossen vergemeinschaftet wird, obschon man bei ihr wie bei der Erbengemeinschaft die

[9] W. Eilers, *Gesellschaftsformen im abab. Recht* (Leipziger rechtswissenschaftliche Studien 65; Leipzig 1931); G. Ries, *Neubab. Bodenpachtformulare* (Münchener Universitätsschriften, Jur. Fak., Band 16; Berlin 1976) S. 85ff.

[10] M. Kaser, *Römisches Privatrecht. Ein Studienbuch* (München 1981, 12. Auflage) o 23,IV 1. und o 43,I 1.a.

> Bildung von Sondergütern, die dem einzelnen gehörten, daneben allmählich zugelassen hat.

Diese hat Shaffer in Arrapḫe als *kitru* nachgewiesen:[11]

> Doch konnte auch jeder Genosse jederzeit die Aufhebung herbeiführen, indem er . . . die Aufteilung des Vermögens betrieb. Der Zweck der Verbrüderung lag vielleicht darin, die Erbengemeinschaft, die durch einen dieser Umstände aufgehoben worden war, unter den übrigen Genossen wiederherzustellen; doch war sie auch in anderen Fällen möglich.

Weiter erklärt Kaser, diese nachgeformten Bruderschaften seien durch erklärte Einverständnisse begründet worden, wobei die Sachen der Genossen gemeinschaftliches Vermögen würden, doch bedürfe es zur Übertragung der Anteile unter den Genossen einer (allenfalls auch stillschweigend) vollzogenen "*traditio*" in den Mitbesitz der Gesellschafter, sei es durch Eingehung der Gesellschafter an allen ihren gehörenden Sachen, sei es nachher an denen, die sie später erwerben, sei es an bestimmten erwähnten einzelnen Sachen, (später als Gelegenheitsgesellschaften für begrenzte Einzelzwecke bekannt). Auf S. 181(3) fährt er fort:

> Die Beiträge der Gesellschafter bestehen zumeist in Vermögenswerten, zuweilen auch in Arbeitsleistung. Die Anteile am Gewinn und Verlust aus den gemeinschaftlichen Unternehmungen sind, wenn nichts anderes vereinbart ist, gleich groß.

Beendet werde das Gesellschaftsverhältnis durch den Tod, Verurteilung oder Konkurs eines Gesellschafters oder aber durch Willenskundgebung. Es könne jedoch durch eine voraus getroffene Abrede, es solle nach dem künftigen Tod eines Gesellschafters fortbestehen, verlängert oder abgeändert werden.

Auch in der klassischen griechischen Zeit kennt man Miteigentum und Gemeinschaft—oft ausgedrückt mit κοινωνία oder dem verb κοινωνεῖν—wie bei Biscardi[12] beschrieben. Biscardi nennt Beispiele für Vermögensgemeinschaft unter Geschwistern, Onkel und Neffen (verwandtschaftliches Miteigentum) und unter Nichtfamilienangehörigen, das durch Verbrüderung geschlossen werde. Es könne 1. durch stillschweigendes Einverständnis entstehen. (Wenn hier die Quellen auf einen Entstehungsakt hinwiesen, dann meist durch indirekten Bezug) 2. durch Abschluß eines entsprechenden Vertrages, wenn es darum gehe, die Rechtswirsamkeit der Vermögensgemeinschaft wiederherzustellen, die einmal durch die Forderung auf Herausgabe eines Anteils aufgehoben worden sei. Die Nutznießung sei dabei proportional zu den Vermögensbeiträgen, wie auch die Ertrags- oder Verlustverteilung. Interessant ist nun, daß i.a. als Vorbild der Verbrüderung orientalische Einrichtungen angesehen werden.

[11] Shaffer 1964 S. 181ff.

[12] A. Biscardi, "Über die Regelung des Milteigentums im attischen Recht" in *Zur griechischen Rechtsgeschichte* (hrsg. v. E. Berneker; Wege der Forschung, Band 45; Darmstadt 1968).

Es lassen sich durchaus dafür mehrere Parallelen in arrapḫäischen *aḫḫūtu*-Urkunden finden: HSS 19,63 hat jedoch außer der Überschrift *ṭuppi* ŠEŠ-*ḫu-ti* und der Bemerkung in Z. 4 *a-na* ŠEŠ-*hu-ti i-pu-us-sú* keine der für Bruderschaften typischen Merkmale. Der Gegenwert für das Baugrundstück des Unap-tae wird von Teḫip-apu als *qištu* gegeben, das nicht typisch für *aḫḫūtu* ist, auch das ilku wird einseitig von Unap-tae getragen. Es ist anzunehmen, da beide Wantija als Vater haben, daß es sich um leibliche Büder handelt (*AAN* 144a).

In *JEN* 99 nehmen zwei Personen Teḫip-tilla S. Puḫi-šenni *ana aḫḫūti* und erhalten für 4 (nicht 5 wie bei Cassin 1938 S. 148–49) *a-mi-ḫa-ri* Feld in Tašenniwe, die ihm als sein Anteil gegeben werden, 30 SU KÙ.BABBAR als ihren Anteil—die Spuren weisen in Z. 12 eher auf *ki-ma* Ḫ[A.LA] als auf *ki-ma* N[ÍG.BA] hin (wie z.B. *JEN* 204:15,17)—und das entspricht den anderen Verbrüderungsverträgen.

Betrachtet man danach die von Stohlman auf S. 208ff. und 215ff. behandelten *aḫḫūtu*-Urkunden (auf die anfangs zurückgegriffen wird), dann lassen sich Grundzüge einer künstlichen Verbrüderung, eines Gesellschaftsverhältnisses, erkennen. In *JEN* 570 (aus Zizza) nehmen drei Personen Pakla-piti zur Verbrüderung. Stohlman setzt in die Lücke in Z. 1 Pakla-piti, das ergäbe Pakla-piti S. Ḫili(p-šarri), *NPN* jedoch nicht, ebenso liest Stohlman den Namen in Z. 3 ^{I}*Si-il-me-ia-bi-šu*, den *NPN* 120b *Si-il-me-ia* liest. (Könnte die abgebrochene Lücke DUMU XX-*šu* gelesen werden?) Da die Verwandtschaftsverhältnisse unklar bleiben, werden die bei *NPN* 161a und 60b verzeichneten Namen eingesetzt: Silmeja, Dûdu-abušu und Enna-mati S. Ḫilip-šarri. Die entscheidenden Zeilen sind Z. 9–10 und 14–17:

9 *a-na aḫ-ḫu-ti il-qú-uš*
10 *a-na zi-it-ti it-ta-*⸢*du*⸣*-uš*
. . . .
14 *uš-tu* u_4-⸢*mi an-ni*⸣-(*i*)
15 *zi-i-iz ta-a-ru*
16 *ù da-ba-bu*
17 *ja-a-nu*

AHw 1534b liest die Z. 15 fälschlicherweise *zi-i-iz-ta* A.SÀ s.v. *zīztu* "Teilung" als einzigen Beleg dafür, ebenso *CAD* 109a und D 3b und übersetzt s.v. *ziʾiztu*: "From this day on there shall be no (further) division of the field or (any more) claims." Stohlman liest dagegen *zi-i-iz ta-a-ru* und übersetzt sicher richtig: "From this day it is shared. There is no turning back or speaking (against it)." Diese Lesung ist in Anbetracht des nA *tuāru u dabābu laššu* vorzuziehen. Der Text ist lückenhaft und kann nur schwer ergänzt werden, klar geht nur hervor, daß bei Verbrüderung "geteilt" werden soll.

JEN 604 *Dossier Temtena*(*š*) ist wieder einseitig und ähnlich wie *JEN* 570 formuliert. (Text auch bei Lewy, *Or* 9 [1940] 367, cf. Skaist, *JAOS* 89 [1969] 11). Teḫija nimmt Mat-tešup (s.o.) zur Bruderschaft zu seinem Anteil an Garten und Häusern. Die wichtigsten Zeilen sind *JEN* 604:3–9:

3 . . . . .*a-na aḫ-ḫu-ti*
4 *a-n*[*a* Ḫ]A.LA-*šu a-na* GIŠ.SAR *ù* [*a-n*]*a*
5 É.ḪI.A.MEŠ *i-te*$^{!}$ (SUM)-*pu-uš*
6 *im-ma-ti-mé-e* ^{I}*T*[*e-ḫ*]*i-ja*
7 *i+na* URU *Te-em-te-n*[*a*]*-aš*
8 *it-ta-la-ak ù it-ti*
9 ^{I}*M*[*a-a*]*t-te-šup i+na* É-*ti i-zu-zu*

Der interessante Hinweis in Z. 6–8, daß beide das Gebiet, Anwesen (Haus im Singular, cf. Stohlman: "that which belongs to the estate") dann teilen, wenn Teḫija "aus Temtenaš weggeht (Prs. Gt)," läßt darauf schließen, daß dieser Verbrüderungsvertrag aus ähnlichen Gründen abgefaßt wurden, wie oben *JEN* 498,204 und 87, damit der Genosse bei Abwesenheit des anderen die Arbeiten und Interessen des anderen wahrt und vertritt.

HSS 19,64 Dossier Hurazina ṣeḫru

Dieser Test ist sehr zerstört und nur schwer lesbar. Urte nimmt Šerta-m(a)-ilu als Bruder auf. Nach dem Formular des Textes in Z. 16–17 und 19 zu urteilen, soll Šerta-m(a)-ilu die Pflichten eines Sohnes mit Urte gemeinsam übernehmen, wobei ^{MÍ}*Dam-ḫurāsi abbūtu* hat (*AAN* 138b Tamḫurazi)(?). Die Z. 28, die Stohlman S. 22 als unbekannt *ḫu-wa-mu-la-ma* erklärt, läßt sich unschwer emendieren zu *ḫu-ud-du*$^{!}$ (AŠ)-*mu-um-ma*, der Strafe, die dem ungehorsamen Sohn droht.[13] Zu Z. 19 bemerkt Stohlman: "The *itti* in this sentence is probably *ittiḫamiš* as also in line 5 and 21." Diese gemeinsamen Pflichten sind, soweit verständlich, in den Z. 5, 19, 21, und 34 aufgezählt und sind

1. Pflichten, die mit dem Streitwagen zusammenhängen
2. dienstbar sein
3. Pflichten, die das Feld betreffen
4. Schulden abbezahlen

HSS 19,62:18–27 Dossier Zizza

Dies sind die wesentlichen Zeilen für einen Partnervertrag; am Anfang wird gesaagt, daß Niḫri-tešup S. Tarmija und Kitenni S. Nutkupa untereinander Bruderschaft ausmachen:

18 *ù i+na mi-it-ḫa-ri-iš*
19 *ni-iz-za-az-mi* GAL *ù* TUR
20 *ja-nu il-ku ù dì-ku-tu*$_{4}$
21 *i+na mi-it-ḫa-ri-iš-ma*

[13] Dosch 1987 in Owen-Morrison 1987 *SCCNH* 2.

22 *na-ši-ma šum-ma* ^{I}*Ki-te-ni*
23 ⸢BA⸣.ÚŠ *ù* ^{I}*Ni-iḫ-ri-t[e-šup]*
Rd 24 *e-wu-ru-um-ma* DÙ-*uš*
25 *šum-*⸢*ma*⸣ ^{I}*Ni-iḫ-ri-te-šup*
26 ⸢BA⸣.ÚŠ *ù* ^{I}*Ki-te-ni*
Rs 27 *e-wu-ru-um-ma* DÙ-*uš*

d.h. der Konsens ist beidseitig, aber der Anteil wird einseitig von Niḫri-tešup gegeben, offensichtlich sein ganzer Besitz, den er geerbt hatte (doch nicht von seinem Vater). Sie teilen zu gleichen Teilen, es gibt keinen Bevorrechtigten (die Zeile 19 hat mit erben nichts zu tun, wie Stohlman dies vermutet), sie teilen aber auch zu gleichen Teilen die Pflichten, die auf dem Land liegen: *ilku* und *dikûtu*. Wie in *JEN* 498 (s.o.) vermutet, werden *ilku*-Verpflichtungen von dem Kriegsdienst unterschieden. Dazu kommt die Übereinkunft, daß das Gesellschaftsverhältnis über den Tod eines Genossen hinausgehen soll und sie sich gegenseitig zum Erben machen, wobei man erkennt, daß *ewuru* sowohl Erbe des Besitzes als auch Erbe der Verpflichtungen dieses Besitzes bedeutet, wie Paaradise dies bewies.[14]

HSS 19,65 aus Nuzi

Dies ist eine beidseitige Erklärung der Verbrüderung zwischen Arip-tilla S. Niḫrija und Zikaja S. Ḫuziri. Beider Besitzungen werden miteinander verschmolzen und solange beide leben, wohnen sie miteinander, sie trennen die Hausgemeinschaft nicht, und sie tragen ilku zusammen (wörtlich zusammen wie Brüder). Wieder endet die Urkunde mit der Abmachung daß bei ihrem Tod die Söhne beider gemeinsam teilen (letzteres erg.). Die wesentlichen Zeilen sind HSS 19,65:9–18 und 32–35:

9 *i+na be-ri-ni us-sé-*⸢*em*⸣*-[mi-ḫu]*
10 *a-du-ú ni-[nu k]i-la-al*$^{!}$*-l[e-e]-ma*
11 *bal-tu*$_4$ *[it-ti]-ḫa-mi-iš a-ši-ib*
12 *m[a-an-nu] š[u-m]i* ḪA.LA *la i-qáb-bi*
13 *il-k[a*$_4$*-n]i i[t-t]i-ḫa-mi-iš na-ša-ku-mi*
14 *im-m[a-t]i-me-[e]* ^{i}*Zi-qa-a+a*
15 *ù* ^{I}*[A-r]i-ip-{*TA*}-til-la* BA.ÚŠ
16 *ù* ⸢*e-*⸣*-[wu-u]r-ru-[u]m-ma* DUMU.MEŠ *ša*
17 ^{I}*Z[i-qa-a]+a ù [ša]* ^{I}*A-[ri-i]p-til-la*
18 *i-z[u*$^{?}$*-uz-zu]x x[ ]-šu*

. . . .

32 *um-ma* ^{I}*A-ri-ip-til-la mi-nu-u[m-me-e]*
33 A.ŠÀ.MEŠ É.MEŠ *ša* [^{I}]*Ur-ḫi-ja*
34 *it-ti* A.ŠÀ.MEŠ É.MEŠ *ša*
35 ^{I}*Zi-qa-a+a us-sé-mì-ḫu*

[14] Paradise 1972 S. 242ff.

JEN 221 Dossier Hurazina ṣeḫru

"This tablet is not a *ṭuppi aḫḫūti* text but it seems to presuppose that relation" sagt Stohlman über diesen Text auf S. 226. Hier wird in der Tat nichts anderes ausgesagt, als daß Mušuja und Šukrija S.e Pui-tae allen Anteil an Feldern im offenen Land (*ṣēru*, cf. *AHw* 1093b) ihrem Genossen Mušeja S. Ḫašija übergeben (Z. 5: *a-na* ^{I}*Mu-še-ja* DUMU *Ḫa-ši-ja* ŠEŠ-[*šu*]-*nu*), der dafür Rechte und Pflichten des Feldes übernimmt und ihnen 1,8 ANŠE Gerste entsprechend ihres Anteiles gibt. Dies ist eine Erklärung der Auflösung einer ursprünglichen Verbrüderung und als solche unter den Auflösungen der Erbengemeinschaften/Verbrüderungen unter *ṭuppi zitti* aufgenommen.

Cassin[15] bezeichnet diesen Text zwar als *ṭuppi zitti*, behandelt ihn aber gleich wie die *ṭuppi mārūti* als fingierte Verkaufsurkunde, während ihn Paradise als Teilungstext deutet, in dem zwei Brüder ihr Erbe mit einem Mann mit anderem Patronym teilten, der als "ihr Bruder" bezeichnet sei (s.o.). Der Text sei ähnlich wie Gadd 29 zu betrachten, den er unter "brotherhood" auf S. 348 interpretiert. In Kritik zu Cassin sagt Paradise, der Preis (gift) scheine viel zu gering für das Land und man müsse ihn wohl symbolisch deuten. Er nimmt an, der adoptierte Sohn habe einen bestimmten Besitz versprochen bekommen, deshalb erklärten die Brüder, sich ihm nicht zu nähern und gäben alle Ansprüche auf; der adoptierte Bruder trage das ilku. Mušuja und Šukrija sagen sich hier aber m.E. von den Verpflichtungen des Vertrages los und geben das Feld auf.

HSS 19,66 (aus Nuzi?)

Die rechte Hälfte dieses Textes ist abgebrochen. Nach Z. 3 ist er ein *aḫḫūtu*-Vertrag (*a-na aḫ-ḫu-*[*ti*]), aber es ist nicht zu erkennen, ob die Beträge einseitig oder zweiseitig gegeben wurden. Doch ergänzen sich die Z. 8–10 so, daß die Hauptmerkmale der Verbrüderungsverhältnisse erkennbar werden:

8 *ù it-t*[*i-ḫa-mi-iš*] oder wie Stohlman *it-t*[*i* ^{I}Wantija]
9 *ma-al-*[*la-ha-mi-iš*]
10 *i-zu-*[*uz-zu*]

VS 1,110

Diesen Text gibt Stohlman S. 229 als eventuellen *aḫḫūtu*-, wahlweise *mārūtu*-Vertrag an, während Paradise Nr. 17 *mārūtu* ergänzt und ihn als solchen interpretiert. Die Z. 6, 10 und 11 tragen aber, soweit sie rekonstruierbar sind, die für die Verbrüderung typischen Merkmale:

6 [PN *sú*]-*um-mu-uḫ*
9 . . . . *it-ti*

[15] Cassin 1938 S. 28; Paradise 1972 S. 349.

10 [PN *mi*]-*it-ḫa-ri-iš i-zu-*⸢*uz-zu*⸣-*mi*
11 [GAL.MEŠ ù TUR].MEŠ *i+na be-ri-ni j*[*a-nu*]

Denn es ist wieder "Anteilgeben am Besitz" (cf. *AHw* 1017a s.v. *samāḫu* D 6) im Stativ, vgl. zu der Form aber HSS 19,23:18 *i-sú-um-mu-ḫu* und Stohlmans Ergänzung auf S. 229 und s.u. HSS 19,44:9), "zu gleichen Teilen Teilen" und außerdem die Versicherung ausgedrückt, daß es keinen Bevorrechtigten geben soll (erg. nach den anderen Urkunden): d.h. beide Partner sollen die gleichen Rechte haben. Daher wird *VS* 1,110:1 und 4 ergänzt: Z. 1 [*ṭup-pí aḫ-ḫu-ti*] *ša* und Z. 4 [*a-na aḫ-ḫu-t*]*i i-te-ep-pu-uš*. Da in dieser Urkunde keine Söhne erwähnt werden, zwischen denen Verbrüderungsverhältnis mit einem adoptierten Bruder bestehen solte, kann es sich m.E. nur um zwei gleiche Partner und um eine Verbrüderung handeln; ein *mārūtu*-Vertrag mit Verbrüderungsverhältnissen könnte nur vom Standpunkt des Vaters aus abgeschlossen worden sein.

Außer diesen bei Stohlman wiedergegebenen Urkunden lassen sich noch folgende Texte aufführen:

HSS 19,140 Dossier Zizza

Diese am Anfang abgebrochene Tafel beinhaltet mit großer Wahrscheinlichkeit ein *ṭuppi aḫḫūti*. Einer der Partner ist Kitenni S. Tarmija, an den nach einer Adoptionsauflösung in HSS 19,31 von Taukkanni S. Tae die Immobilien eines Ipša-ḫalu S. Malija gegeben werden. Dieser Ipša-ḫalu S. Malija könnte der in diesem Text Z. 10′, 13′ und 16′ genannte Ipša-ḫalu sein, der hier als Partner des Kitenni hervorgeht (vgl. dazu noch HSS 19,131). Für die Verbrüderung typische Merkmale enthält HSS 19,140:5′–9′:

5′ *ù it-ti* ^{I}*Ki-te-ni*
6′ DUMU *Tar-mi-ja ni-iz-za-az-*[*mi*]
7′ GAL ⸢*ù*⸣ TUR *i+na* [*lìb*]-*bi-*[*ni*]
8′ *ja-nu il-*⸢*ku ù*⸣ *dì-ku-*⸢*tu*$_{4}$⸣
9′ *ma-al-la-ḫ*[*a*]-*mi-iš na-ši-ni*

Sie teilen gemeinsam und haben die gleichen Rechte, ilku und dikûtu tragen sie gemeinsam (wie Brüder, s.o. zu HSS 19,62, wo auch ilku und dikûtu getrennt genannt und *ina mitḫāriš* "zu gleichen Teilen" getragen wurden. Vgl. Paradise S. 351, Bemerkungen zu diesem Text).

Gadd 29 aus āl ilāni (RA 23,107–9 und 148b)

Gadd 29 gibt zwei Prozesse wieder, von denen nur der erste hier interessant ist (vgl. zu diesem Text Paradise S. 348). Ein *Na-na-*[ ] sagt, Eḫlija habe ihn nicht adoptiert, sondern er schwöre, daß Enna-pale, Kelip-šarri und Nai-teja mit ihm ein Verbrüderungsverhaltnis abgeschlossen und ihm Anteil gegeben hätten an ihren Feldern und Häusern, und er dafür ein ANŠE Gerste gegeben habe. Der eine Genosse habe gesagt: "Wenn ich deine Felder im offenen Lande und die Häuser in der Stadt nicht gebe, darfst du alle meine Felder und Häuser behalten" (übersetzt).[16] Für beide Prozesse fällen die Richter das Urteil, die Felder zu teilen (Z. 17–20). Hier sind wieder *samāḫu* D und *zâzu* gebraucht, die Immobilienanteil scheinen einseitig von den drei Personen gegeben worden zu sein, aber über die Größe der Anteile der drei gibt der Text keine Auskunft. Die entscheidenden Zeilen sind Z. 5–10:

5 *ù šum-ma i+na ar-ka-nu*
6 ^{I}*E-en-na-ba-li ù* ^{I}*Ge-li-ip-šarri*
7 *ù* ^{I}*Na-i-te-ja a-na aḫ-ḫu-ti*
8 *la i-te-ep-šu-un-ni-ma*
9 *ù a-na* A.ŠÀ.MEŠ-*šu-nu ù a-na* É.ḪI.A.MEŠ-*šu-nu*
10 *la us-sé-em-mi-ḫu-un-ni-ma*

HSS 19,44 Ort unbekannt

Dieser stark zerstörte Text scheint einer der seltenen Lehverträge zu sein (Z. 22 *a-na* U[Š.BA]R?.MEŠ *ú-la-am-ma-ad-šu-nu-ti*) und ist wahrscheinlich als *mārūtu* abgefaßt (vgl. Paradise Nr. 31 A. 129ff.), da der Aufgenommene mit den Söhnen des Vertragsabschließenden ein Gesellschaftsverhältnis bilden soll. Der Anfang der Z. 9 kann wieder verschieden ergänzt werden: wie in *VS* 1,110:6 oder wie in HSS 19,23:18 (s.o. *VS* 1,110) also [*la/i-*]*summuḫ* (vielleicht wäre [*u-*] vorzuziehen), je nachdem ob Mul-tešup auch in dem väterlichen Erbe Anteil bekommen soll, oder ob die väterlichen von den gekauften Feldern unterschieden werden sollen und er nur an letzteren einen Anteil bekommt. Die wichtigsten Zeilen für eine Verbrüderung sind: HSS 19,44:8–14

8 [*a-na*] DUMU.MEŠ-*ia na-ad-nu ù* ^{I}*Mu-ul-te-šup*
9 [*la/i-*]*sú-um-mu-uḫ mi-nu-um-me-e* A.ŠÀ[.MEŠ]
10 É.ḪI.A.MEŠ *ša a-na ši-mi el-qú-ú*
11 (Rasur) *ma-na-ḫa-tu*$_4$ *mar-ši-it-tu*$_4$ *mi-im-mu šu-un-šu* ^{I}Z[*i-líp-še*]-*en-*[*ni*]
12 *a-na* ^{I}*Mu-ul-te-šup ù a-na* DUMU.MEŠ-*ia* {*na-ad-nu*}
13 *na-ad-nu* ⸢*ù*⸣ *mi-it-ḫa-ri-iš i-zu-uz-zu*
14 GAL *ù* TUR [*i+n*]*a lìb-bi-šu-nu ja-nu*

Auch hier sind die wesentlichen Merkmale: er soll Anteil bekommen, sie sollen zu gleichen Teilen teilen, und sie sollen die gleichen Rechte haben, d.h. gleichberechtigte Gesellschafter sollen sie sein.

Hinweise darauf, daß Verbrüderungverhältnisse bestanden, ohne sie ausdrücklich zu benennen, finden sich in folgenden Texten.

[16] Wilhelm 1970 S. 60 Z. 17–20.

HSS 5,99 aus Nuzi

Dies ist ein *ṭuppi tamgurti*.[17] Ein Enkel und ein Sohn des Tajuki, Mannija S. Tultukka und Ilanu S. Tajuki (A 34) kommen überein: der "angesammelte" (Grund)besitz (*AHw* 876a s.v. *puḫḫuru* 2) des Tajuki wird nach den Gesetzmäßigkeiten des Erbrechts geteilt; demnach bekommt Mannija zwei Anteile (wahrscheinlich die Anteile des verstorbenen Vaters, der GAL war), Ilanu einen. Alles was sie aber jeweils hinzuerworben haben, wurde zu gleichen Teilen geteilt. (*CAD* Z 81a: "We have divided equally whatever (assets) we had acquired"; *AHw* 811b Dtn *pḫr* "jeweils sammeln"). Die für ein Gesellschaftsverhältnis entscheidenden Z. 10–14 lauten:

10 *ù i+na* EGIR-*ki* ^{I}*Ta-a-i-ú-ki*
11 *mi-nu-um-me-e ša nu-up-te-eḫ-ḫi-ru*
12 *a-na-ku ù* ^{I}DINGIR-*a-nu*
13 *mi-it-ḫa-ri-iš*
14 *ni-iz-zu-uz*. . . .

Daß ein Kompagnon (ŠEŠ) für die Pflichten seines Partners aufkommt, besonders wenn er ewuru (Z. 12 und 27) geworden war, zeigt noch AASOR 16,38: Utḫap-še S. Kalija ŠEŠ (nach Z. 27) des inzwischen verstorbenen Tae S. Akawatil vertritt seinen Kompagnon bei dessen Prozessen und wird zu dessen Gerichtsschulden verurteilt, mit dem Nachsatz:

34 . . . . .*ki-mé-e* A.ŠÀ.MEŠ-*šu* É.MEŠ-*šú*
35 [*ša*]$^{?}$ ^{I}*Ta-e* ^{I}*Ut-ḫáp-še il-te-qè*

Das Verbrüderungsverhältnis muß danach mit gegenseitiger Beerbung abgeschlossen gewesen sein, und es wird hier besonders deutlich, daß damit sowohl die Rechte als auch die Pflichten des Verstorbenen gemeint sind, wie Paradise es nachgewiesen hatt).

Außergewöhnlich, aber wahrscheinlich die Bedingungen eines Verbrüderungsvertrages erfüllend, ist HSS 5,65:1–5a abgefaßt (A34 (II), aus Nuzi):

1 *ṭup-pí* DUMU
2 *ša* ^{I}*A-ku-*⌜x⌝*-ja* (über Rasur) *a-na* DUMU *i-pu-šu*
3 ^{I}*A-ri-ja a-na* DUMU *i-pu-sú*
4 *i+na* A.ŠÀ ù GIŠ.MEŠ (Fehler für É?) *ù-sé-mi-ḫu-eš*$^{!}$ (*AHw* 1017a)
5 ^{I}*A-ku-ja ù ma-ra-sú ma-la-ḫa-mi-iš*
5a *i-zu-zu*

Die beiden Partner adoptieren sich hier gegenseitig und geben einander an den Besitzungen teil. Akkuja und seine Tochter (gemeint ist Tulpun-naja die Tochter des

[17] Koschaker 2 1944 S. 169,1.

Arija, wie in HSS 9,116:3 aus den Spuren ergänzt werden kann, denn beide Texte gehören zusammen; nachzutragen in *NPN* 157a) teilen gemeinsam zu gleichen Teilen. Der Text ist früh von Sin-ibnī (vgl. *NPN* 121b) geschrieben, vielleicht erklären sich so die Schreiberungeschicklichkeiten. Eventuell ist der frühe Zeitpunkt auch der Grund, warum sich die beiden Partner hier gegenseitig adoptieren, eine Form, die sonst für diese Vertragsart in Nuzi unüblich ist, aber doch so etwas wie Verbrüderung bedeutet haben muß, mit der Tochter jedenfalls Partnerschaft war bis diese Akkuja in HSS 9,166 in Immobilienadoption adoptierte.

Hierzu ist auch IM 10522[18] zu zählen. Ipša-ḫalu S. Ṭamanna gibt diese Erklärung ab (umma): Die Tafel der zwei ANŠE Feld hat Kipaja S. Aka[ ] dem Ṭamanna gegeben und jetzt habe ich diese Tafel der zwei ANŠE Feld dem Ḫašip-tilla S. Erwi-šarri gegeben und

10 ᴵ*Ḫa-ši-*[*ip-t*]*il-la* 2 ANŠE A.ŠÀ *ša-*[*a-šu*]
11 *it-ti* ᴵ*Ip-šá-ḫa-lu*
12 *i+na mi-it-*⌜*ḫa-ri*⌝*-iš i-zu-u*[*z-zu*]

Ein zu diesem Thema interessanter Prozess ist *JEN* 340 aus Šuriniwe. Aus ihm geht hervor, daß Kuari A. Akip-tašenni ein Feld, obwohl er es *ana titennūti* gegeben hatte, von seinem Partner (Širinta ŠEŠ-*šu ša* Kuari Z. 17–18) für drei Jahre bearbeiten ließ und dafür verurteilt wird. In *JEN* 111 zahlt er sowohl die Strafe als auch die *titennūtu*-Schuld, indem er eine seiner Sklavinnen übergibt. Daß ŠEŠ hier nicht leiblicher Bruder ist, ist aus der Liste *JEN* 514:19–20 (ebenfalls aus Šuriniwe, s. oben, Anm. 7, s. S. 105 und Kap. 1.2.3.) zu sehen, in der unmittelbar nach Kuari S. Akija ein Širinta S. Šukrija aufgezählt ist. Sie sind mit großer Wahrscheinlichkeit identisch mit den beiden ŠEŠ aus *JEN* 340.

Kaser sagt (s.o.), die altrömischen Verbrüderungen seien der Erbengemeinschaft nachgebildet. Vergleichbar mit dem Assyrischen (*ina aḫḫē lā zīzûte*) finden sich auch in Nuzi gleiche Merkmale in manchen Testamenten wie in den *aḫḫūtu*-Verträgen. Aus A34 ist das Testament der Frau des Akap-šenni ᴹᴵPekušḫe überliefert (HSS 5,74). Sie hatte wohl keine Kinder, denn sie adoptiert ihre Nichte ᴹᴵAzuli (HSS 13,15) und Akap-šenni hatte seinen Bruder Šelluni adoptiert an Sohnes Statt (HSS 5,7). Nun sollen Šulluni und Akawatil (wahrscheinlich Sohn des Bruders Elli und nach HSS 5,74:22 Ehemann der Azuli), also Adoptivsohn und Ehemann der Adoptivtochter gemeinsam erben:

14 ᴵ*Še*! (LU)*-el-lu-ni it-ti-ḫa-mi-iš*
15 ᴵ*A-qa-wa-til mi-it-ḫa-ri-*⟨*iš*⟩
16 *i-zu-uz-zu*

d.h. das Erbe des Akap-šenni wird nach den Richtpunkten der Verbrüderung weitergegeben. (Zu dem Text vgl. Paradise Nr. 48.)

[18] Lacheman 2 1976 S. 128 und 143ff., Nr. 8.

In zahlreichen anderen Testamenten finden sich Hinweise, daß so verfahren werden soll wie in einem Gesellschaftsverhältnis. Es fällt auf, daß das immer auftritt, wenn eine Frau *abbūtu* (Vaterschaft) ausübt: in anderen Worten, solange sie lebt, darf der Besitz nicht aufgeteilt werden, soll Erbengemeinschaft bestehen bleiben, was mit dem gleichen Vokabular bestimmt wird wie in den Verbrüderungverträgen. Für den Besitz werden den vier Adoptivsöhnen aus HSS 19,18 (aus A34 und Nuzi) folgende Bestimmungen auferlegt:

14 . . . . .GAL *ù* [TUR *ja-nu*]
15 *mi-it-ḫa-ri-iš i-zu-u*[*z-z*]*u*

Die Mutter des Erblassers, die diesmal die Vormundschaft erhält, müssen die vier Partner ehren. Dies ist ausgedrückt mit.[19]

22 4 LÚ.MEŠ ŠEŠ.MEŠ *an-nu-*[*t*]*i i-pal-*[*la-aḫ-ša*]

HSS 19,17 ist das Testament des Arip-papni S. Šilwa-tešup ⸢DUMU LUGAL⸣ (ergänzbar in Z. 2, vgl. Z. 40, nicht in *AAN* 28B), bei dem die Tochter *abbūtu* über ihre bekommt; auch hier wird bestimmt:

13 DUMU.MEŠ-*ia* GAL ⸢*ù*⸣ TUR [*j*]*a-nu*

Zu diesem Testament gehört HSS 19,37, eine Urkunde, in der Arip-papni S. Šilwa-tešup (ergänzbar in Z. 2) einen Šekar-tilla, der ihn aus einem fremden Land befreit hatte, (Z. 39–42, cf. Paradise Nr. 14) adoptiert und ihn zum Miterben bestimmt, in einer Gemeinschaft, die auch über den Tod Arip-papnis und seiner Ehefrau Šašuri hinaus bestehen soll (Z. 7–11), wenn die Tochter ^{MÍ}Ukke *abbūtu* über alle bekommt. Dies wird in den Z. 12–15 folgendermaßen festgesetzt:

12 *it-ti* DUMU.MEŠ *A-ri-ip-pa-ap-ni-ma*
13 *a-ši-ib il-*ka_4 *it-ti-šu-nu-ma na-ši*
14 *ù šu-mi* ḪA.LA *la i-qáb-bu-ú*
15 *ma-am-ma sí-ki-il-ta la* TUK

Dasselbe wird auch für die nächste Generation vorbestimmt (Z. 18–10). Erst wenn die Söhne erwachsen sind, kann geteilt werden nach den allgemeinen arrapḫäischen Erbgesetzmäßigkeiten, wobei die Söhne des Šekar-tilla mit den jüngeren Söhnen den restlichen Anteil erhalten, nachdem die beiden ältesten ihre Anteile bekommen haben. Es ist hier also besonders vermerkt, daß bis zu dem Zeitpunkt der Aufteilung zwischen den Söhnen und dem Adoptivsohn und dessen Söhnen eine Erbengemeinschaft bestehen soll.

[19] Vgl. R. Albertz, *Persönliche Frömmigkeit und offizielle Religion* (Calwer Theologische Monographien, Reihe A, Band 9; Stuttgart 1978).

HSS 19,23 (Anfang abgebrochen) ist wahrscheinlich auch ein Testament, bei dem ^{MÍ}Minen-naja *abbūtu* innehatte, nach den dafür üblichen Klausl zu schließen (Z. 12–14) und weil die Erbenden ihr dienstbar sein sollen (Paradise Nr. 39). Wieder lauten die Z. 4–6:

4 *i+na mi-it-⟨ḫa⟩-ri-iš i-zu-*[*uz*$^{?}$*-zu*]
5 *i+na lìb-bi-šu-ni* GAL-*bi* [*ù* TUR-*ri*$^{?}$]
6 *ja-nu*. . . . .

In dem Testament HSS 13,465 (Paradise Nr. 12, Shaffer 1964 S. 188) sagt Galwa, daß Abiduran Häuser und Felder *ana kiterri* bekomme, für die Galwa von Ḫuišša (und) Nai-šeri zum Erben (*ewurumma*) gemacht wurde (die Z. 3–5 beziehen sich dann auf ein vorheriges Verbrüderungsverhältnis), die restlichen Felder und Häuser solle er:

9 [*it*]-*ti* ŠEŠ.MEŠ-*šu ša* ^{I}*Gal-wa*
10 *it-ti-ḫa-*⟨*mi*⟩*-iš mi-it-ḫa-*[*ri-iš*]
11 [*i-zu*]-*uz-zu-ú*

gemäß eines Verbrüderungsverhältnisses teilen. Die Partner (ŠEŠ in Z. 9) sind höchstwahrscheinlich die aus dem Gesellschaftverhältnis der vorherigen Generation.

HSS 19,19 (Paradise Nr. 16) ist das Testament eines Tarmija S. [ ]ja. Es ist stark abgebrochen; Wilhelm[20] lieferte dazu ein Anschlußstück. ^{MÍ}Tieš-naja übt *abbūtu* aus. Wegen des fragmentarischen Zustandes sind Einzelheiten schwer zu erkennen. Die Bestimmungen der Erbengemeinschaft zeigen sich ab der Z. 19 auf der Rückseite und können ungefähr so gelesen werden: [DUM]U.MEŠ-*ia šu-*[*mi* ḪA.LA] *la i-qàb-bu-ú*. . . . .Z. 34 *ù a-n*[*a*] *mi-it-ḫa-ri-iš* [*i-zu-uz-zu*]. Z. 35. . . . . GAL.GAL ⌜*ù*⌝ TUR.TUR *a-na x*[*ja-nu*$^{?}$] und Z. 55: *i*[*l-ku-ša* A.ŠA-*i*]*a* DUMU.MEŠ-*ia an-nu-tu*$_{4}$ [*a-n*]*a mi-it-ḫa-ri-i*[*š na-šu*]-*ú*.

Gadd 51 ist eine echte Adoption, in der Našwe S. Ar-šenni seinen Schwiegersohn Wullu adoptiert, ihm Felder und Häuser gibt (Z. 22ff.) und ihn bei seinem Tod zum Erben macht (*ewurumma*). Falls aber noch ein Sohn des Našwe geboren werden sollte, dann soll er mit diesem nach den Regeln der Erbengemeinschaft verfahren, beide sollen brüderlich teilen (*mi-it-ḫa-ri-iš i-zu-uz-zu* Z. 12–13).

HSS 19,1 (Paradise Nr. 13) ist das Testament des Zike S. Tamar-tae, bei dem die Frau ^{MÍ}Tataja *abbūtu* erhält (erg.). Der Text ist lückenhaft und muß an den Zeilenenden wahrscheinlich länger ergänzt werden, als Paradise auf S. 65–67 vorschlägt. So ist in Z. 10 analog zu den anderen Testamenten mit *abbūtu* die Beerdigungsklausel zu erwarten. Außerdem ist die Schreibung am Anfang der Zeile mit I ^{MÍ}Tataja interessant. War es ein Schreiberversehen oder soll es den besonderen Status der Frau, die die Stellung ihres Mannes einnimmt hervorheben? (Paradise läßt den Personenkeil weg, ohne es anzugeben.) In Z. 8 wäre noch der Name des

[20] Wilhelm 1981 in Morrison-Owen 1981, S. 343.

Tešup-erwi zu erwarten und die Namen in Z. 5 scheinen nicht ganz in Ordnung. Dennoch ist die bei *abbūtu* zu erwartende Erbengemeinschaft in Z. 13–14 ausgedrückt: *it-ti-ḫa-me-iš i-zu-zu*.

In den anderen Testamenten, in denen *abbūtu* gegeben wird, finden sich zwar Hinweise auf Erbengemeinschaft, sie ist jedoch nicht mit den Wendungen ausgedrückt, die hier als typisch für die *aḫḫūtu* festgestellt wurden. So ist z.B. in HSS 19,7:10–17 ausdrücklich erwähnt, daß die Söhne erst nach dem Tod der Mutter ihre Anteile zugeteilt bekommen.

Es finden sich demnach dieselben Merkmale in Erbengemeinschaften wie in den Verbrüderungen, das gleiche legale und soziale Verhältnis entsteht, alle davon betroffenen Parteien sind gleichberechtigte Partner.

Sur la characteristique typologique de l'Hourrite et l'Ourartéen

M. L. KHAČIKYAN
Yerivan, Armenia, USSR

Pour charactériser une langue du point de vue de la typologie contensive, c'est-à-dire celle qui traîte les langues en termes des différences existant dans les moyens de rendre les relations du sujet/objet de la réalité, il est nécessaire de tenir compte du lexique, de la syntaxe, de la morphologie et parfois de la morphonologie. Cela crée des difficultés sérieuses quand on a affaire aux langues mortes, puisqu'il est impossible de faire leur analyse complète, ayant des données linguistiques restreintes.

C'est justement le cas des langues hourrite et ourartéenne: nous ne disposons pas d'un liste exhaustif du lexique, symptomatique pour la charactéristique typologique, de plus, nos connaissances de la syntaxe et de la morphologie de ces langues sont très schématiques.

Tout de même, un essai d'une charactéristique pareille de l'hourrite et de l'ourartéen n'est pas tout à fait désespéré, surtout que la différence chronologique des textes en ces langues nous permet de suivre l'évolution de leur typologie.

1. Typologiquement l'état des langues hourro-ourartéennes, excepté les dialectes hourrites les plus archaïques, peut être charactérisé comme celui de l'ergativité avancée.

Dans les langues ergatives, selon les données récentes, les verbes sont divisés non pas en transitifs : intransitifs, mais en agentifs : factitifs. Les verbes agentifs expriment une action allant du sujet à l'objet et transformant le denier ("briser", "couper", "arracher"), tandis que les factitifs expriment l'état du sujet ou bien son influence superficielle sur l'objet ("aller", "croître", "éternuer", "crier", "mordre", "pincer").[1]

En hourrite et ourartéen, cependant, une opposition pareille n'est pas fixée. Les verbes sont opposés dans ces langues selon l'indice de la transitivité : intransitivité.

Malheureusement, le lexique accessible à notre compréhension ne permet pas de juger, si l'opposition de l'agentivité : factitivité nous échappe à cause de la modicité des données linguistiques ou bien si elle n'était pas propre à l'hourrite et à l'ourartéen par suite de la nominativisation considérable de ces langues.

L'ergativité avancée de l'hourrite et de l'ourartéen est affirmée particulièrement par le fait d'une quantité insignifiante des verbes diffuses, fonctionnant dans

[1] Cf. G. A. Klimov, *Les principes de la typologie contensive* (Moscow, 1983) 95 [en russe].

les langues ergatives en qualité d'une quasi-implication, ascendant à l'époque active de l'hourro-ourartéen (hour. *ûn-* 'venir/ apporter', ourart. *nah-*, de même sens,[2] par l'existence de tels lexèmes, typiques à la formation nominative ou ergative avancée, comme "prendre" et "donner",[3] par la présence du copule.[4]

Les verbes de possession, propres aux langues nominatives, mais pas ergatives n'étaient pas connus en hourrite et ourartéen. La possession en hourrite était exprimée, apparemment par le verbe "exister".[5]

2.1. Pour la proposition hourrite et ourartéenne sont propres les constructions suivantes:

a) construction ergative, étant le modèle de la proposition transitive avec le prédicat exprimé par un verbe transitif, le sujet—par un nom/pronom en cas ergatif et l'objet direct en cas absolutif
b) construction absolutive, étant le modèle de la proposition intransitive, avec le prédicat, exprimé par un verbe intransitif et le sujet—en cas absolutif

A part des constructions ergative et absolutive, typique à la syntaxe de langues ergatives, en hourrite et ourartéen est attestée aussi une construction équative. La construction équative se compose du sujet en absolutif, du prédicat nominal/participial et du copule, parfois omis:[6] hour. *unduman šênif·e-n faš·ôzi* 'Ainsi mon frère a expédié' (*-n-* copule), Mit. III_{107}; *iyenamanin Manez̄ Keliyal·ân kadil·eda urγal·ân yaldal·ân* 'ceux (les mots) que Mane et Keliya diront, sont justes et sont vrais' (*-l·a-* copule), Mit. IV_{21-23}; *šēnif· fas·ozi* 'mon frère a expédié' (sans copule), Mit. I_{49-50}; ourart. *qəwranəquldinəmâno* 'la terre était aride' (*mâno-* copule), UKN, passim; *Tariria̯hinelə tinə* 'son nom est Taririahinelə' (sans copule),[7] Mit. $III_{3,6}$.

Il est remarquable, que dans la lettre mittannienne, représentant un dialecte assez avancé vers le type nominatif, le copule se présente dans un nombre des propositions avec un verbe intransitif (ce dernier coïncide formellement avec le participe): *adinin tâz̄e-n it·ôz̄-t-a* 'ainsi le don est allé' (*-n-* copule), Mit. I_{90}; *adinin Mane-n-ân . . . ûna* 'ainsi Mane vient' (*-n-* copule), Mit. II_{13-14}.

[2] Cf. G. A. Klimov, *L'essai de la théorie générale de l'ergativité* (Moscow, 1973) 119 [en russe]; idem, *La typologie des langues de la formation active* (Moscow, 1977) 140 [en russe].

[3] Klimov, *L'essai*, 153.ə

[4] En hourrite le rôle du copule est accompli par le pronom personnel de l'objet de la 3me personne (*-n* au singulier, *-l·a* au pluriel) En ourartéen comme copule fonctionne le verbe *mân-* 'etre'.

[5] Sur le verbe *tup·-* 'exister' en hourrite cf. G. Wilhelm, "Der hurritische Ablativ-Instrumental /ne/," *ZA* 73 (1983) 100–101.

[6] Les propositions avec le prédicat, exprimé par un participe transitif, sont traitées par H.-J. Thiel dans *Das hurritologische Archiv, Corpus der hurri(ti)schen Sprachdenmäler der Freien Universität Berlin* (1975) 202, comme antipassives. Cependant la présence du copule dans ces propositions nous permet de les interpréter comme constructions équatives.

[7] Le fait que le copule, absent dans une phrase qui exprimait le présent, était employé dans les contextes avec le sens du passé, montre que *mâno* exprimait l'aspect perfectif (le passé).

Il est possible, que dans ces exemples on a affaire aux constructions équatives et non pas absolutives. Ce fait nous permet de supposer que dans le dialecte mittannien le volume des propositions ergatives et absolutives se réduit pour le compte de la construction équative avec un prédicat participial transitif ou intransitif. Peut-on interpréter ce fait comme résultat de l'unification de la construction de la proposition, indépendamment de la transitivité : intransitivité, ce qui est propre aux langues nominatives?

2.2. En hourrite et ourartéen domine l'ordre des mots, typique pour les langues ergatives: S_{erg}(sujet)—O_{II} (objet indirect)—O_I (objet direct)—V_{tr} (verbe transitif) dans la construction ergative, et S_{abs} (sujet)—V_{intr} (verbe intransitif) dans la construction absolutive, bien que des cas d'inversion expressive soient dans ces langues assez fréquents.

3.1.0. Comme il est dit plus haut (§1.), les verbes en hourrite et ourartéen sont divisés en trasitifs et intransitifs.

3.1.1. Les verbes transitifs sont conjugués d'après le type ergatif (conventionnellement II conjugaison), avec les signes personnels du sujet de même origine que les suffixes possessifs.

3.1.2. Le verbe intransitif dans les deux langues est conjugué d'après le type abasolutif (conventionnellement I conjugaison). Ce dernier est formé par l'adjonction au thème verbal de l'indice de l'intransitivité/état et des signes personnels du sujet, coïncidant avec ceux de l'objet du verbe de la II conjugaison, par l'exception de l'indice de la 3me persone du sg., voir cidessous (§6.1.2).

3.1.3. En hourrite, contrairement à l'ourartéen, où le verbe transitif est conjugué exclusivement d'après le type ergatif, il y a des cas de la conjugaison du verbe transitif d'après le type absolutif (thème verbal + indice de la transitivité *-i-* (aspect neutre)/ *-u-* (perfectif) + indices personnels absolutifs). Dans les formes pareilles, pourtant, le signe de la 3me personne du sg. est *-b* dans les dialectes "babylonien" et de Bogazköy et dans les noms propres et *-m* dans le dialecte d'Urkeš, au contraire aux verbes intransitifs où le rôle de l'indice du sujet est accompli par -Ø: *faš·-i-b* 'il expédie', Mari $1_{3,\ 6}$; *ûn-u-b* 'il (le dieu Kumarbi) mit au monde', KUB 47 78 I 14′ *Ar-i-b-* 'il donne-'; *pahašt-u-m* 'il constrisit', Urk. 6.

Il est intéressant, que dans le dialecte "babylonien" et dans les noms propres ce même indice *-b* est présent aussi dans les verbes intransitifs: *šidil-a-b*, du sens inconnu, Mari 1_{10}; *Ûn-a-b-* 'il vient/il vint'.

Ainsi l'élément *-b/-m* exprimait également le sujet du verbe transitif et intransitif, autrement dit celui du verbe actif (dynamique) des langues actives.

Cela signifie que la fonction primaire de *-b* était l'expression du sujet du verbe actif et que la conjugaison absolutive remonte à l'état actif de l'hourro-ourartéen. Plus tard, par suite de l'ergativisation et de la formation de la conjugaison ergative, l'indice du sujet d'action *-b/-m* en hourrite sort de l'usage, tandis que celui du sujet d'état -Ø, commence à fonctionner comme signe du sujet du verbe intransitif, y compris le verbe d'état.

En ourartéen, par contre, le signe *-b*, ayant déplacé l'indice du sujet d'état -Ø, prend le rôle de celui du sujet du verbe intransitif. L'exception fait le verbe *mân-* 'être', où en qualité du signe personnel fonctionne l'indice du sujet d'état -Ø (*mân-o-Ø*).

3.2. L'opposition actif : passif n'est pas propre au verbe hourrite et ourartéen, ce qui est typique aux langues non-nominatives.[8] En font l'exception les participes ourartéen, en *-u/orə*, voir ci-dessous (§3.5).

3.3. La catégorie de version, propre aux langues actives,[9] n'est pas connue en hourrite et en ourarteen non plus. Les survivances de cette catégorie, pourtant, sont observées dans un seul dialecte de l'hourrite, présenté par la bilingue suméro-hourrite.[10]

Il est difficile de juger, si le suffixe *-tə* en ourartéen, remontant à l'indice de la version introverte en hourrite, mais réinterprété par suite de la nominativisation considérable de cette langue fonctionne comme indice de la version subjective ou comme pronom réfléchi. En tout cas la présence dans une langue quelquonque de l'un ou de l'autre indique à l'état fort nominativisé de cette langue.

3.4. La catégorie aspectuelle-temporelle, assez développée dans les langues ergatives avancées, au contraire aux langues actives,[11] est propre à l'hourro-ourartéen.[12]

Le grand nombre des suffixes, changeant d'une telle ou telle manière la sémantique de la racine verbale, parle de l'expansion des gradations d'Aktionsart dans la période préergative de l'hourro-ourartéen.

3.5. En hourrite et ourartéen sont connus des participes adverbiaux, formés à l'aide du suffixe polifonctionnel *-aə/-e*,[13] et des infinitifs, formés par l'adjonction des suffixes *-aə/-ê* et *-um·ə*.

En ourartéen n'est attesté qu'un infinitif de but, formé à l'aide de la désinence *-edə/-ydə*, ascendant à l'indice du cas directif.

Ces deux classes de mots sont assez répandues dans les langues ergatives, contrairement aux langues du type actif.[14]

3.6. Pour l'hourrite et l'ourartéen il est propre aussi la classe des participes, présentés assez modestement dans les langues ergatives, mais développés dans les langues nominatives.[15]

Les participes coïncident formellement avec le thème des verbes de la I conjugaison.

En ourartéen, à côté des participes adjectivisés d'état (*agun-o-nə* 'fortifié'), il y a des participes avec le suffixe *-u/orə*, employés dans les constructions équatives

[8] Cf. Klimov, *L'essai*, 104, et idem, *La typologie*, 139.

[9] Cf. Klimov, *La typologie*, 140.

[10] Cf. M. L. Khačikyan, "Towards the Categories of Aspect and Version in Hurro-Ourartian," *ZA* 74 (1984) 92–95.

[11] Cf. Klimov, *L'essai*, 180, et idem, *La typologie*, 144.

[12] Cf. Khačikyan, *ZA* 74 (1984) 95–97.

[13] Ce même suffixe était employé pour exprimer les modes terminatifs, pour former des adverbes, des nomina actionis et des adjectifs qualitatifs.

[14] Cf. Klimov, *L'essai*, 118.

[15] Ibid., 118.

négatives. Il est remarquable, que ces derniers sont opposés selon l'indice actif : passif et non pas transitif : intransitif (*oyə . . . ag/yu/orə* 'personne . . . n'a conduit', UKN 136_5; *oyə . . . ušt-u/orə* 'personne . . . n'y est allé', UKN $155E_{43}$; mais *oyə . . . šid-a-(y)u/orə* 'rien n'est été construit', UKN passim.

L'analyse typologique des niveaux différents de l'ourartéen nous permet d'interpréter cette opposition non pas comme une survivance de l'opposition action : état, particulière aux langues actives, mais comme une diathèse de voix, propre aux langues nominatives, surtout que c'est justement dans ce fragment de la langue (les participes), que la diathèse de voix se forme en premier lieu.[16]

3.7. Le pluriel dans la conjugaison ergative et dans les formes modales est exprimé en hourrite et en ourartéen soit par le suffixe verbal -(*i*)*d*- (hour.), -(*i*)*t*- (ourart.), soit par la désinence -*ža* (hour.), -*šə* (ourart.), de même origine que l'indice du pluriel dans les substantifs.

Il est probable, si l'on juge de la place du suffixe -(*i*)*d*-, -(*i*)*t*- dans la forme verbale (dans le thème verbal et non pas à côté de l'indice du sujet), que ce suffixe exprimait originellement la pluralité de l'action, ce qui est propre aux langues actives.[17] Plus tard, ayant perdu sa fonction primaire, il a pris celle du pluralisateur du sujet.

4.0. Les substantifs en hourrite et ourartéen ne forment pas de classes typologiquement significatives.

En dehors des cas positionnels, ceux de l'ergatif, cas du sujet de la proposition transitive, et l'absolutif, cas du sujet de la proposition intransitive et de l'objet de la propositon transitive, le système casuel des deux langues comprend le génitif, le datif, l'instrumental et quelques cas circonstanciels.

4.1. Comme on le sait, le génitif, le datif et l'instrumental ne sont complètement formés que dans les langues nominatives, tandis que leur présence dans les langues non-nominatives parle de la nominativisation considérable de ses langues.[18]

Le génitif en hourrite et ourartéen joue le rôle d'attribut. Il n'y a qu'un seul exemple du génitif subjectif: *tâžene-wəit·um·ə* 'le départ du don', Mit. I_{92-93}. On n'a pas fixé de cas du génitif objectif, qui est propre seulement aux langues nominatives.

Le datif en hourrite et ourartéen accomplit le rôle du directif general.[19]

L'instrumental en hourrite et ourartéen est formé sur la base de l'ablatif circonstanciel.[20]

4.2. Dans les langues ergatives l'ergatif comprend deux fonctions, celle du cas d'agent et du cas oblique (datif ou instrumental). La présence dans une langue

[16] Ibid., 175.

[17] Cf. Klimov, *La typologie*, 100.

[18] Cf. Klimov, *Les principes*, 45–48.

[19] Il est à remarquer, que dans les combinaisons postpositionnelles le substantif/pronom en cas datif s'accorde avec la postposition, mise en directif: *ak·už agu-wa edi-ye-da* 'l'un pour l'autre' (Mit. I_{82}) et *ênif·u-wa ayi-ye-da* 'devant ma déesse' (Mit. III_{97-99}), etc.

[20] Sur l'ablatif-instrumental hourrite cf. Wilhelm, *ZA* 73 (1983) 96–113.

d'un ergatif spécial, aussi que des cas datif et instrumental, parle d'un progrès considérable de cette langue vers le type nominatif.[21] C'est justement le cas de l'hourrite et de l'ourartéen, qui disinguent des cas spéciaux ergatif, datif et instrumental.

L'origine de la désinense de l'ergatif dans ces langues n'est pas tout à fait claire. Cependant, son emploi dans l'expression archaïque *Kumarvene-ẕ ûn-u-b* '(le dieu) Kumarvə(t') a mis àjour', KUB 47 78 I 14′, avec le verbe diffuse *ûn-* (voir §1) en fonction transitive en I conjugaison et le signe du sujet d'action *-b* (voir §3.1.2), ascendant à l'état actif de l'hourro-ourartéen, nous permet de supposer que l'indice de l'ergatif remonte à celui du cas actif.

En ce rapport il est à remarquer que dans les langues nakh-daghestaniennes il y a un ergatif spécial en *-a*(*s*), à côté des cas en *-w* et d'autres, fonctionnat comme cas ergatif et oblique à la fois.[22] Le dernier cas (en *-w*) nous présente aussi un intérêt particulier. Il est vraisemblable, que les indices du génitif *-wə* (hour.), *-eyə* (ourart.) et du datif *-wa* (hour.), *-yə* (ourart.) y remontent. Ainsi, si notre supposition est juste, l'hourrite et l'ourartéen, ayant perdu la fonction d'agent du cas daghestanien en *-w*, ont gardé celle du cas oblique.

Quant à l'élément *-a* du datif hourrite, il fait partie de plusieurs cas circonstanciels en hourrite.[23]

5. En hourrite et ourartéen, contrairement aux langues actives, où l'adjectif n'est pas formé et coïncide formellement avec le thème du verbe d'état, l'adjectif constitue une classe complètment formée.

Cependant dans un texte de Mari, représentant un dialecte archaïque ("babylonien"), it est attesté un adjectif qualitatif en forme du thème du verbe d'état, sans aucune désinence: *muz êni-yuẕ* 'ton dieu juste', Mari 6, *muẕ êne-ra* 'avec le dieu juste', Mari 19.

Il est possible, que cette forme soit interprétée comme survivance de la période active de la langue. Tout de même, il n'est pas exclu, qu'on a affaire ici aux formes à la voyelle thématique élidée.

6.1.0. Les pronoms personnels en hourrite et ourartéen se divisent en deux groupes: indépendants et dépendants.

6.1.1. Les pronoms indépendants, employés d'ordinaire emphatiquement, se déclinent par analogie avec les substantifs.

6.1.2. Les pronoms dépendants expriment le sujet du verbe de la I conjugaison et l'objet du verbe de la II (ces pronoms-là ne coïncident pas seulement à la 3me personne du sg.).

Dans les dialectes archaïques de l'hourrite sont attestés deux différents pronoms sujets de la 3me personne du sg.: *-b*, exprimant le sujet d'action et employé avec les verbes transitifs et intransitifs d'action, et *-ə*, exprimant le sujet d'état.

Ce fait-là parle de la présence dans ces dialectes de l'oppostion sujet d'action : sujet d'état, propre aux langues du type actif.

[21] Cf. Klimov, *L'essai*, 186.
[22] Ibid., 188.
[23] Cf. Thiel, *Archiv*, 221–22.

La fonction du pronom objet de la II conjugaison dans les deux langues est accomplie de l'élément *-n(·a)* (hour.), *-nə* (ourart.).

Ainsi un fragment de l'hourro-ourartéen, celui des pronoms personnels dépendands, révèle la division du cas absolutif, exprimant le sujet du verbe intransitif et l'objet du verbe transitif, en deux cas différents: en cas du sujet et celui de l'objet, ce qui est une preuve évidente de la nominativisation de l'hourro-ourartéen.

6.1.3. Dans le systéme des pronoms personnels dépendants en hourrite, contrairement au substantifs, les formes d'objet direct et d'objet indirect ne se distinguent pas. Ainsi, on a affire ici aux traces du complément proche des langues actives, dont la notion est plus large que celle du complément direct des langues nominatives et partiellement ergatives.[24]

En ourartéen, par contre, une partition du complément proche en compléments direct et indirect est fixée, ce qui est une autre manifestation de la nominativisation considérable de l'ourartéen.

6.2. Un autre trait, symbolisant la nominativisation de l'ourartéen est la présence dans cette langue du pronom réfléchi (ou, peut-être, de la version subjective?), remontant à l'indice de la version introverte en hourrite.

6.3. Les deux langues connaissent des pronoms possessifs suffix aux de même origine que les indices ergatifs du verbe de la II conjugaison.

La catégorie de la possession, avec la corrélation de possession aliénable : inaliénable, qui est propre aux langues actives, n'est pas connue en hourrite et ourartéen.

Cependant il y a des faits, prouvant la présence de cette catégorie pendant la période préergative de ces langues.

Il s'agit de la bilingue suméro-hourrite, où la fonction du pronom possessif de la 3me personne du sg. est accompli par la grammème *-di* (graph.), qui ne se rencontre autre part.

Il est vraisemblable, que cette grammème, étant l'ancien indice de la possession inaliénable, par suite de la neutralisation de cette catégorie, ait déplacé dans ce dialecte l'indice de la possession aliénable *-ya-/-yə*.

Les traces de l'opposition des formes de la possession aliénable et inaliénable sont obserées dans certaines langues nakh-daghestaniennes, particulièrement en darghinien, où un groupe de substantifs dénotant des parties du corps, est employé constamment en forme possessive, se variant selon les classes des hommes, des femmes, des animaux et générale, conformément avec les indices *v-, r-, b-, d-*.[25] Il est possible, qu'il y a un lien génétique entre le dernier et le pronom *-di* de la bilingue.

7. Tout ce qui précède permet de charactériser l'hourrite et l'ourartéen comme des langues du type ergatif avancé, avec quelques traits survivants du type actif, surtout dans les dialectes archaïques, et tout une série de traits, propres aux langues nominatives, surtout dans les dialectes plus tardifs de l'hourrite et en ourartéen.

[24] Cf. Klimov, *La typologie*, 119.

[25] Cf. Klimov, *L'essai*, 195.

Getreideertragsabgaben an den "Palast" im hurritischen Staat Arrapḫe

Manfred Müller
Universität Leipzig

In der Einleitung zu seinem Buch über *Das Getreide im alten Babylonien* schrieb Bedřich Hrozný im Jahre 1913:

> Die Assyriologie leidet trotz der glänzenden Fortschritte, die sie besonders in der letzten Zeit gemacht hat, noch immer an manchen Mängeln. Als ein besonders fühlbares Übel möchte ich den Umstand bezeichnen, daß von Seiten der Assyriologen bis jetzt so wenig Aufmerksamkeit der materiellen Kultur der alten Babylonier gewidmet wurde. Man hat sich bis jetzt aufs Intensivste mit der politischen Geschichte, mit der Geisteskultur, Literatur, Religion und Mythologie der alten Babylonier beschäftigt, während die vielen Fragen der wirtschaftlichen Kultur dieses uralten Kulturlandes fast unbeachtet geblieben sind. Und doch kann es keinem Zweifel unterliegen, daß nicht nur der geistige, sondern auch der materielle Besitz der alten Babylonier unsere vollste Aufmerksamkeit verdient.

Und er konstatiert:

> Für die allgemeine Kulturgeschichte muß die Kenntnis der wirtschaftlichen Verhältnisse des alten Babyloniens, eines der ältesten Kulturländer, von größtem Werte sein.

Dabei sei es ein selbstverständliches Erfordernis, daß entsprechend "dem überwiegend agrarischen Charakter" der altmesopotamischen Staaten im "Mittelpunkt einer wirtschaftsgeschichtlichen Betrachtung des alten Babyloniens der Ackerbau und die Viehzucht stehen muß."[1]

Editor's note: This article is a completely revised and expanded version of a paper delivered to the "Conference in Honor of the Centenary of Bedřich Hrozný" at Charles University, Prague, Czechoslovakia, 5 May 1979.

[1] B. Hrozný, *Das Getreide im alten Babylonien* (Sitzungsberichte der Kaiserl. Akad. d. Wiss. in Wien. Phil.-hist. Kl., Bd. 173 1; Wien 1913) S. 3.

Mit der Aufforderung an seine Fachkollegen, sich verstärkt der Erforschung der materiellen Grundlagen der altmesopotamischen Kultur zu widmen, dürfte Bedřich Hrozný umittelbar vor dem ersten Weltkrieg mehr abschätziges Lächeln erregt als Verständnis und Zustimmung gefunden haben. Sie erweist ihn als einen weitsichtigen Gelehrten, der—auch später—wesentliche wissen—schaftliche Aufgaben und Probleme, die einer Bearbeitung harrten, als solche erkannte und ihre Lösung zu befördern versuchte. Das wird schlaglichtartig erhellt durch den Umstand, daß noch ein reichliches halbes Jahrhundert später der bekannte amerikanische Assyriologe I. J. Gelb es als notwendig erachtete, in seinem Beitrag zur Festschrift für Benno Landsberger[2] in ähnlicher Weise wie vor ihm Hrozný noch einmal nachdrücklich auf die Notwendigkeit der vorrangigen Erforschung der materiellen Kultur der Völker des alten Vorderasiens hinzuweisen.

Gewiß sind solche grundsätzlichen Mahnungen heute nicht mehr notwendig, sind seither die Bemühungen um die Erschließung der altmesopotamischen Landwirtschaft und damit unsere Kenntnisse auf diesem Gebiet ganz erheblich angewachsen. In den letzten 25 Jahren erschienen mehrere grundlegende und weiterführende Arbeiten, von denen hier nur einige größere erwähnt seien: A. Salonens *Agricultura Mesopotamica*,[3] die Untersuchungen zur Dattelwirtschaft von B. Landsberger[4] und D. Cocquerillat,[5] zur alt- und neusumerischen Landwirtschaft von K. Maekawa[6] und G. Pettinato,[7] die Studien von F. R. Kraus zur staatlichen Viehwirtschaft in altbabylonischer Zeit[8] und von M. de J. Ellis zu Problemen des Besitzes, der Bearbeitung und der Abgabenerhebung von landwirtschaftlichen Nutzflächen[9] sowie J. Zabłockas Analyse der Agrarverhältnisse im Reich der Sargoniden.[10] Besondere Beachtung verdienen auch die anregenden und vielfach grundlegenden Bemühungen von Kilian Butz um das Verständnis der altmesopotamischen Landwirtschaft.[11] Aber noch immer ist die Forderung Hroznýs, daß die unüberschaubare Menge keilschriftlicher Rechts- und Wirtschaftsurkunden,

[2] *Studies in Honor of Benno Landsberger* (AS 16; Chicago 1965) S. 62.

[3] Annales Academiae Scientiarum Fennicae B149 (Helsinki 1968).

[4] *The Date Palm and its By-products according to the Cuneiform Sources* (AfO Beiheft 17; Graz 1967).

[5] "Aperçus sur la phéniculture en Babylonie à l'époque de la 1ère dynastie de Babylone," *JESHO* 10 (1967) 161–223; *Palmeraies et cultures de l'Eanna d'Uruk (559–520)* (Berlin 1968).

[6] "Agricultural Production in Ancient Sumer," *Zinbun* 13 (1974) 1–61; ders., "The Rent of the Tenant Field (gán-APIN.LAL) in Lagash," *Zinbun* 14 (1977) 1–54.

[7] *Untersuchungen zur neusumerischen Landwirtschaft, I. Die Felder, 1. und 2. Teil* (Napoli 1967).

[8] *Staatliche Viehhaltung im altbabylonischen Lande Larsa* (Mededelingen der Koninklijke Nederlandse Akademie van Wettenschappen, AFD. Letterkunde N.R. 29,5; Amsterdam 1966); grundlegende Untersuchungen zu einzelnen Problemen von Ackerbau und Viehzucht des "Palastes" in altbabylonischer Zeit auch im Zusammenhang mit der Bearbeitung des Edikts Ammi-saduquas in SD 5 und 11.

[9] *Agriculture and the State in Ancient Mesopotamia: An Introduction to Problems of Land Tenure* (Philadelphia 1976).

[10] *Stosunki agrarne w państwie Sargonidów* (Poznań 1971).

[11] Vgl. "Ur in altbabylonischer Zeit als Wirtschaftsfaktor," *OLA* 5 (1979) 257–409 und den Artikel "Landwirtschaft," *RlA* 6 (1983) 470–86.

die sich auf die Landwirtschaft bezieht, bearbeitet und ausgewertet werden möge, erst zu einem kleineren Teil und—notwendigerweise—fast nur für ausgewählte, chronologisch und geographisch meist eng begrenzte Teilbereiche erfüllt. Viele wichtige Probleme der altmesopotamischen Landwirtschaft sind noch ungeklärt. Dazu zählen nicht nur offene oder umstrittene landwirtschaftliche, gartenbautechnische und spezielle botanische Fragen, sondern auch solche, die für die Aufhellung der ökonomischen und sozialen Verhältnisse und Strukturen auf dem Lande in den unterschiedlichen Regionen und während der verschiedenen Perioden altvorderasiatischer Geschichte von Bedeutung sind: Fragen zu den Eigentums- und Besitzverhältnissen an Grund und Boden, den Formen und der Technik der Bodenbearbeitung, der Erhebung von Naturalabgaben, Pachten und Steuern sowie zu weiteren wirtschaftlichen, verwaltungs- und organisationstechnischen Problemen.

Mit den folgenden Ausführungen soll ein kleiner Beitrag zu einem speziellen Problem der altmesopotamischen Landwirtschaft erbracht werden: der Bewirtschaftung staatlichen Ackerlandes. Im Mittelpunkt steht dabei der Nachweis, daß im Staat Arrapḫe, einem vom Mitanni-Reich abhängigen hurritischen Kleinkönigtum (15. bis Mitte 14. Jh. v.u.Z.) im heutigen Nordirak, über die Festlegung der Getreideertragsabgaben von bestimmten, individuell bewirtschafteten Grundstücken an den "Palast" spezielle Urkunden ausgefertigt wurden, in denen die einzelnen Grundstücksinhaber Art und Umfang der festgesetzten Abgabenleistung durch Untersiegelung des Dokuments verbindlich anerkannten.

Grundlage für diese Mitteilung zur arraphäischen Landwirtschaft[12] sind einige kurze, unscheinbare Urkunden, die aus Tell al-Faḫḫār, einem kleinen Ruinenhügel etwa 45 km südwestlich von Kirkūk, stammen, wo von einer irakischen Expedition in den Jahren 1967–69 ein lokaler Palast ausgegraben wurde.[13] Die betreffenden Dokumente gehören überwiegend zu der Gruppe von Texten aus Tell al-Faḫḫār, deren Veröffentlichung durch Frau Dr. Bahija Khalil Ismail und den Verf. erfolgen wird.[14]

[12] Neuere Untersuchungen zur Landwirtschaft und zum Grundbesitz im Land Arrapḫe: C. Zaccagnini, "The Yield of the Fields at Nuzi," *OA* 14 (1975) 181–225; G. Wilhelm, "Zur Rolle des Grossgrundbesitzes in der hurritischen Gesellschaft," *RHA* 36 (1978) 205–13; C. Zaccagnini, *The Rural Landscape of the Land of Arraphe* (Roma 1979); M. A. Morrison, "Evidence for Herdsmen and Animal Husbandry in the Nuzi Documents," SCCNH 1 (1981) 257–96; C. Zaccagnini, "Land Tenure and Transfer of Land at Nuzi (XV–XIV Century B.C.)," in: T. Khalidi (Hrsg.), *Land Tenure and Social Transformation in the Middle East* (Beirut 1984) S. 79–94. Wertvolle Zusammenstellungen zu Ackerbau, Gartenwirtschaft und Viehzucht in einzelnen Ortschaften enthalten die *Studien zur Topographie und Prosopographie der Provinzstädte des Königreichs Arrapḫe* von A. Fadhil (Mainz 1983). Die Struktur einer Gutswirtschaft im Gebiet von Arrapḫe wird erstmalig durch G. Wilhelm in seinem Werk *Archiv des Šilwa-teššup* (Wiesbaden 1980ff.) umfassend dokumentiert und analysiert werden. Siehe Nachtrag, p. 43.

[13] Y. Mahmoud, "Tell al-Fakhar. Report on the First Season's Excavations," *Sumer* 26 (1970) 109–26, Pl. 2–27; Y. Mahmoud al-Khalesi, "Tell al-Fakhar (Kurruḫanni), a *dimtu*-Settlement," *Assur* 1/6 (Malibu 1977).

[14] Auch an dieser Stelle sei der irakischen State Organization of Antiquities und ihrem Generaldirektor herzlich gedankt für die Erlaubnis, diese Texte publizieren und auswerten zu dürfen.

Die Texte dieses Urkundentyps sind nach folgendem Grundschema stilisiert:

x [ANŠE.A.ŠÀ *ša* PN (DUMU PN_2) x ANŠE . . . ŠE/GIG/ZÍZ.AN.NA ŠU(*-tù*) *ša* É.GAL(*-lì*) (*i-lu-ú*).[15] NA_4 PN.

[15] Die Deutung der Verbalform *i-lu-ú* bereitet morphologische und semantische Schwierigkeiten. Ob es sich um die 3. Pers. pl. des Präteritums oder des Stativs handelt, ist im Einzelfall nicht sicher zu entscheiden. Wegen der überwiegend stativischen Formulierungen vergleichbarer Verwaltungsaufzeichnungen aus dem Gebiet von Arrapḫe, vor allem aber dem Gebrauch des Stativs *šūlû* in analogem Kontext (s. S. 34 nach Anm. 19), dürfte die fragliche Verbalform im vorliegenden Zusammenhang grundsätzlich als Stativ aufzufassen sein. Auch eine dritte in ähnlichen Verwaltungsnotizen über Getreide begegnende Form von *elû*, *e-te-la-a*, ist aller Wahrscheinlichkeit nach ein Stativ (*etellâ* = Stativ des Gtn-Stamms + Ventiv), s. G. Wilhelm, *AdŠ* 3, S. 198.

Problematischer ist die Bedeutungsbestimmung. Hierbei empfiehlt es sich, alle im Zusammenhang mit Getreideabgaben in Verwaltungsurkunden aus Arrapḫe belegten Stativformen (G, Gtn und Š) in die Untersuchung einzubeziehen:

Mit dem Stativ *ilû* "sie (= die genannten Getreidemengen) sind aufgekommen/angefallen" wird in den vorliegenden Urkunden aus Tell al-Faḫḫār zum Ausdruck gebracht, daß sich bei der Abgabenfestlegung bzw. -feststellung von der genannten Feldfläche eine Getreideabgabe in der angegebenen Höhe ergeben hat, wobei die Erfüllung dieser zu erbringenden Leistung, wie die Untersiegelung ausweist (s. dazu S. 33), noch aussteht.

Außerhalb dieser Textgruppe sind dem Verf. aus arraphäischen Texten für *ilû* in Verbindung mit Getreide nur wenige weitere Belege bekannt: In CT 51,5 (bearbeitet von W. Mayer, *UF* 8 [1976] 198f.), einer Notiz über die erfolgte Abrechnung und Einlieferung von vier Gerstebeträgen aus vier verschiedenen Siedlungen durch einen Gesamtverantwortlichen, ist bei jeder Einzelsumme vermerkt, daß es sich um die aus der betreffenden Ansiedlung "aufgekommene" (*ša i-lu-ú*, Z. 3, 10, 17; Z. 22 fehlt diese Verbalform) Gerstemenge handelt. Eine ähnliche Formulierung begegnet in HSS 16,237, einer Urkunde über die Ausgabe von Gerste als Saatgut. Dort lauten die Teilsummationen (Z. 12–14 und 35–39): x ANŠE ŠE.MEŠ (*iš-tù ma-aq-ra-at-ti*) *iš-tù* x ANŠE A.ŠÀ *ša/i-na* ON *i-lu-ú* 'x Homer Gerste (von der Tenne) (sind es), von x Homer Feld in der Ortschaft ON sind sie aufgekommen/angefallen.' In beiden Texten bezieht sich die Verbalform *ilû* auf Gersteaufkommen von bestimmten Feldflächen (dies ist nur in HSS 16,237 ausdrücklich vermerkt, für CT 51,5 aber vermutlich zu postulieren) in verschiedenen Siedlungen, die mengenmässig festgestellt worden waren und über die nunmehr bei ihrer Einlieferung (CT 51,5) bzw. Ausgabe (HSS 16,237) abgerechnet worden ist. Ob die abgelieferten Gerstebeträge analog den genannten Urkunden aus Tell al-Faḫḫār als Ernteertragsabgaben oder etwa als gesamtes Ernteertragsaufkommen zu verstehen sind, läßt sich allein aufgrund des Wortlauts der einzelnen Urkunden nicht entscheiden. Einen weiteren Beleg, leider in unklarem Gesamtzusammenhang, bietet die Prozessurkunde *JEN* 643, wo der Kläger(?) zu Protokoll gibt: 2 *ma-ti* ANŠE ŠE.MEŠ*-ja ša i-na ma-aq-ra-at-tu i-lu-ú* (Z. 2) '200 Homer mir gehöriger Gerste (sind es), die auf der Tenne "aufgekommen" sind.'

Die Form *etellâ* wird in den Getreidelisten HSS 9,66; 13,428 und 14,598 (= Wilhelm, *AdŠ* 3, Nr. 173–75) in ähnlichem Kontext wie ilû gebraucht: "Getreide (*ša* PN/*ša* PN *ištu* ON/*ša qāt* PN/ *ištu* ON) *ša e-te-la-a*" bzw. "Getreide *ša* ON *e-te-la-a ša qāt* PN." G. Wilhelm hat *AdŠ* 3, S. 198 diese Verbalform und ihre möglichen Bedeutungen in den drei Texten besprochen. Seinem negativen Ergebnis, daß sie keinesfalls einen Transport der beträchtlichen Getreidemengen an einen einzigen Ort bedeuten kann, ist voll zuzustimmen. Vermutlich kommt *etellâ* dieselbe Bedeutung wie *ilû* zu, wobei sich die Verwendung der Gtn-Form zwanglos dadurch erklären ließe, daß sich die in diesen Sammellisten verbuchten Getreideaufkommen verschiedener Orte aus jeweils mehreren Einzelposten zusammensetzte.

Am besten bezeugt ist die Verwendung des Stativs *šūlû*: Er wird in Texten aus Nuzi in der Bedeutung "sie sind herausgenommen, entnommen, abgezogen" u.a. mit Bezug auf Vieh (aus der Herde) und Zählsteine gebraucht. Mit Getreide als Objekt bieten die Wörterbücher für diese Bedeu-

(Betrifft) x Homer Feld, gehörig dem PN (,dem Sohn des PN_2): x Homer . . . Gerste/Weizen/Emmer sind als Anteil)[16] des Palastes (erhoben [= festgesetzt/festgestellt] worden). Siegel des PN. (Es folgt die Siegelabrollung des PN.)

Belege: 1. IM 70917 (= Nr. 48 der in Vorbereitung befindlichen Publikation), 2. IM 70915 (= Nr. 49), 3. IM 70905 (ohne Siegelbeischrift und Siegelabrollung),[17] 4. IM 73279 (= A. Fadhil, *Rechtsurkunden und administrative Texte aus Kurruḫanni* (= *RATK*), Magister-Arbeit, Heidelberg 1972, Nr. 24; ohne Siegelbeischrift und Siegelabrollung), 5. IM 70783 A (= Nr. 50).[18]

Die Untersiegelung der Mehrzahl der überlieferten Texte durch den jeweiligen Inhaber des Feldgrundstücks erweist diese Dokumente als individuelle Verpflichtungen zur Lieferung der jeweils angegebenen Getreidemenge. Die Erhebung dieses Getreides in Abhängigkeit vom Besitz bestimmter Feldgrundstücke und die Bezeichnung der Leistung als "Anteil des Palastes" qualifiziert sie als Feldertragsabgabe.

---

tung des Verbums *šūlû* nur Belege aus mittelbabylonischen Urkunden sowie die spätbabylonische Wendlung *tēlītu šūlû* 'Ertragsabgabe aufbringen und abführen' (*AHw* 209b 6f). Aber auch die Belege für "Getreide *šūlû*" aus arraphäischen Urkunden sind dieser Bedeutung zuzuordnen. Aus den oben im folgenden (S. 34) besprochenen Getreidelisten HSS 15,231; 16,190 und 417 ergibt sich, daß die als *šūlû* bezeichneten Getreidemengen jeweils "(als Ertragsabgabe) erhoben und abgeliefert worden sind." Einen weiteren Beleg bietet HSS 16,24. In dieser Gersteausgabeliste lautet die Summation (Z. 25–27): 27 ANŠE ŠE.MEŠ *ša le-qú-ú ša* ON *ša šu-lu-ú* '27 Homer Gerste (sind es), die in Empfang genommen und (zuvor) aus der Ortschaft ON (als Abgabe) erhoben und abgeliefert worden sind'; vgl. auch HSS 16,33: 99 ANŠE ŠE.MEŠ *ša ma-aq-ra-at-ti ša ú-še-el⟨-lu⟩-ú a-na* ŠU PN *ù a-na* PN_2 *na-ad-nu*. NA_4 PN. '99 Homer Gerste, die auf der Tenne (als Abgabe) erhoben und abgeführt werden, sind zur Verfügung des PN und des PN_2 gegeben. Siegel des PN.'

Versuchsweise sei im folgenden das bisherige Ergebnis zur Bedeutung der Stative *ilû*, *etellâ* und *šūlû* mit Bezug auf Getreide zusammengestellt, das auf der Grundlage der Verpflichtungen zur Lieferung festgesetzter Getreideertragsabgaben aus Tell al-Faḫḫār und der Verbuchungen über erfolgte Ablieferungen derartiger Abgaben aus Nuzi gewonnen wurde:

Getreide *ilû*:	"(x Homer) Getreide sind (als zu leistende Ertragsabgabe[/als Ernteertrag?] bei der Abgabenfestlegung bzw.-feststellung aufgekommen/angefallen (= erhoben, aber noch nicht abgeführt worden)."
Getreide *etellâ*:	"(x Homer) Getreide sind insgesamt (als Abgabe) aufgekommen/angefallen (= erhoben, aber noch nicht abgeführt worden)."
Getreide *šūlû*:	"(x Homer) Getreide sind 'hochgelassen' = sind (als zu leistende Ertragsabgabe[/als Ernteertrag?]) erhoben und abgeliefert worden."

[16] Die Übersetzung des Schlüsselbegriffs *qātu ša ekalli* mit "Anteil des Palastes" unterliegt keinem Zweifel. Das Nomen *qātu* ist in der Bedeutung "Anteil" für das Hurro-Akkadische von Arrapḫe ausreichend bezeugt, s. *AHw* S. 910b C3 und *CAD* Q S. 197a oben, vgl. auch HSS 5,46, 18: 2 *qà-ta-tù* '2 Teile' und 74,9: 1-*en* ŠU *ša mu-ti-ja* 'ein Anteil meines Ehemannes'. Der Begriff *qātu ša ekalli* ist auch in den Getreidelisten HSS 15,231 und 16,190 (s. dazu S. 34) belegt. Zu *qātu ša šarri* vgl. HSS 14,147,4, zu *qātu ša* PN HSS 9,66 (= Wilhelm, *AdŠ* 3, Nr. 175). Die Wortverbindung *qātu ša* PN/Institution ist bisher nicht immer konsequent von der Wendung *ša qāt* (bzw. *ana qāti*) PN 'zur Verfügung des PN' unterschieden worden.

[17] Die Kenntnis dieses Textes verdanke ich einer freundlichen Information durch Frau Dr. B. Kh. Ismail.

[18] Gelegentlich fehlt die Angabe der Feldfläche (Nr. 3, 6–10; Nr. 5); besonders stark verkürzt ist Nr. 5.

Unter den publizierten Keilschrifttexten aus Nuzi und Kirkūk gibt es keine gleichartigen Urkunden. Das ist auch nicht verwunderlich, handelt es sich doch um einen Urkundentyp, der nur für die kurze Zeit von der Festlegung der Abgabe bis zur Ablieferung des Getreides aufbewahrt wurde. Es lassen sich jedoch drei Dokumente unter den veröffentlichten Verwaltungstexten aus Nuzi nachweisen, die zu dem durch die genannten Urkunden aus Tell al-Faḫḫār bezeugten Vorgang der Festlegung und Erhebung von staatlichen Getreideabgaben von bestimmten Feldern gehören. Es sind die Texte HSS 16,190; 15,231 und 16,417.[19] Die einzelnen Eintragungen in diesen Verwaltungsurkunden folgen dem Schema:

> x ANŠE (. . .) GIG(.MEŠ)/*ku-ni-šu*$^{(\text{MEŠ})}$ *it-ti* PN (ŠU-*ti/tù ša* É.GAL-*lì*)[20] *iš-tu* x ANŠE/GIŠ.APIN A.ŠÀ (*ša*) *šu-lu-ú*. (NA$_4$ PN$_2$).
>
> x Homer (. . .) Weizen/Emmer sind (es, die) von[21] PN (als Anteil des Palastes) y von x Homer/*awiḫaru* Feld erhoben (= festgesezt) und abgeführt[22] worden (sind). (Siegel des PN$_2$).[23]

Es handelt sich also um—zum Teil vom Empfänger bestätigte—Verbuchungen erfolgter Ablieferungen von Getreideabgaben offensichtlich der Art, wie sie durch die soeben vorgestellten Abgabeveranlagungen mit Lieferungsverpflichtung aus Tell al-Faḫḫār bezeugt sind. Die inhaltlichen und formulärmaßigen Parallelen sind evident.

C. Zaccagnini hat die beiden erstgenannten Urkunden in einer Untersuchung über die Felderträge in Nuzi in *Oriens Antiquus* 14 (1975) 187–91 bearbeitet. Auf Grund seines philologischen Verständnisses der einzelnen Verbuchungsvermerke[24] sieht er in den Personen, die in diesen Texten genannt werden, die Empfänger,[25] nicht die Ablieferer des Getreides und betrachtet die aufgeführten Getreidemengen als die Gesamterträge der betreffenden Feldflächen. Dadurch kommt er im Ergebnis seiner Untersuchungen zu sehr niedrigen Felderträgen im Gebiet von Nuzi. Der

[19] Die Transliteration dieses Textes ist an den beschädigten Anfängen der Z. 3, 5 und 7 entsprechend HSS 15,231 und 16,190 zu emendieren.

[20] In dem Text HSS 15,231 wird der Vermerk *qātu ša ekalli* nur jeweils beim ersten Eintrag der aufgelisteten Weizen- bzw. Emmerbeträge notiert (Z. 2 und 25), gilt aber zweifellos für alle Verbuchungen.

[21] Der Gebrauch von *itti* in separativer Bedeutung ist im Hurro-Akkadischen von Arrapḫe selten, da dort dafür in der Regel die Präposition *ašar* verwendet wird; vgl. jedoch z.B. HSS 5,29, 11: 10 GÍN KÙ.BABBAR . . . *itti*(KI)-*ja ana* PN *inandin* '10 Sekel Silber . . . von mir werde ich(!) dem PN geben', ähnlich Z. 14 und 19.

[22] Zur Bedeutung von *šūlû* im vorliegenden Zusammenhang s. oben Anm. 15.

[23] HSS 16,190. Der Siegelnde, Eḫlip-apu, ist vermutlich ein Angestellter des betreffenden Palastmagazins in Nuzi. Seine Siegelung der Empfangsnotiz verleiht der Tafel den Charakter eines Empfangsbelegs für den Ablieferer. HSS 15,231 ist demgegenüber eine Verwaltungsliste; sie verzeichnet Getreideeingänge von mehreren Personen.

[24] Zaccagnini übersetzt die einzelnen Eintragungen mit "x *imērū* . . . of wheat/emmer are with PN, at the Palace's disposal, which have been brought from x *imērū* of field" (*OA* 14 [1975] 189, 191). Vgl. dazu oben die Anm. 16, 21 und 23.

[25] Zaccagnini, *OA* 14 (1975) 189, Bemerkung zur Übersetzung.

Zusammenhang dieser Texte mit den hier beschriebenen Urkunden über erfolgte Ernteertragsabgaben-Veranlagungen, in denen es sich eindeutig um die Verpflichtung zur Abgabe nur eines Teils des Ernteertrags, nicht der gesamten Ernte handelt, spricht jetzt gegen diese Interpretation.

Zu dem hier vorliegenden System der Festsetzung von Feldertragsabgaben in Urkunden mit individueller Lieferungsverpflichtung des Veranlagten und der Verbuchung der erfolgten Leistungen in zusammenfassenden Listen gibt es "buchhaltungstechnische" und inhaltliche Parallelen, von denen hier die in der Viehverwaltung des Gutes des Königssohnes Šilwa-Tešup und bei der Verbuchung von Rückständen an Getreideabgaben an den "Palast" erwähnt seien. In beiden Fällen wurden über Fehlbestände[26] an Vieh bzw. über Fehlbeträge an Getreideabgaben zu Lasten der jeweiligen Hirten bzw. Bauern Urkunden ausgestellt, in denen die Betreffenden durch Untersiegelung die Schuld anerkennen und sich zu deren Leistung verpflichten.[27] Diese "Außenstände" sind dann von der jeweiligen Verwaltungszentrale in Listen erfaßt worden.[28] Schließlich wurde auch über deren Eingang exakt "Buch geführt."[29]

Die Urkunden über die Festsetzung der Höhe von Getreideertragsabgaben von bestimmten Feldflächen mit Lieferungsverpflichtung der Veranlagten und die Listen, in denen derartige Getreideabgaben an den "Palast" als Eingänge verbucht sind, werfen eine Vielzahl weiterführender Fragen auf. Dazu gehören die Probleme: In wessen Eigentum befinden sich die abgabepflichtigen Feldgrundstücke, wer sind die Bebauer, welche soziale Stellung nehmen sie ein und in welchem juristischen Verhältnis stehen sie zu dem von ihnen bebauten Boden, welcher Art sind die Abgaben und wie hoch sind sie, gemeßen am Ernteertrag, und schließlich, wann und in welchem Zusammenhang wurden die Höhe der Ertragsabgaben festgelegt und darüber Urkunden zu Lasten der Grundstücksinhaber ausgestellt? Kaum eine der genannten Fragestellungen kann zur Zeit mit Sicherheit beantwortet werden. Voraussetzung dafür wären umfassendere Untersuchungen zu Fragen des Ackerbaus und der Grundbesitzverhältnisse[30] im Staat Arrapḫe auf der Grundlage aller zur Verfügung stehenden Dokumente und unter durchgängiger Berücksichtigung prosopographischer und archivmässiger Zusammenhänge. Aber selbst dann wird die begrenzte Aussagefähigkeit des zur Verfügung stehenden einschlägigen Quellenmaterials und die quellenmäßig nur ganz unzureichende Information über den Umfang und die Bewirtschaftung des Kronlandes im Staat Arrapḫe[31] nicht zur sicheren Beantwortung aller offenen Fragen ausreichen.

Was die Eigentumsverhältnisse an den fraglichen Grundstücken anbetrifft, so darf davon ausgegangen werden, daß diese Felder Eigentum des "Palastes" waren,

[26] Zu dem in diesem Zusammenhang gebrauchten Terminus "*muddu*" s. den Exkurs S. 39ff.

[27] Zu den betreffenden Urkunden über Vieh vgl. unten S. 40 mit Anm. 55 und 56 und zu der Urkunde IM 70778 über Gerste den Exkurs S. 39ff.

[28] Vgl. die Listen über Viehaußenstände HSS 13,389; 14,590, 14,596,22ff.; 14,637; 16,304 und zu Gersteaussenständen die Anm. 53 genannten Belege.

[29] Kleinvieh: HSS 13,400; 14,596,1–21; zu Gerste s. Anm. 54.

[30] S. dazu zuletzt Zaccagnini, "Land Tenure" (s. Anm. 12), S. 79–94.

[31] S. dazu Zaccagnini, "Land Tenure," S. 80 mit Anm. 7.

da die Abgaben von den einzelnen Produzenten direkt an den "Palast" geleistet und von diesem unter Angabe der Feldfläche und des Bebauers verbucht wurden[32] und die Höhe der Abgaben[33] eine Art Steuer ausschliesst. Es kann sich vielmehr nur um eine Ertragsabgabe von—möglicherweise verstreut gelegenen—Grundstücken handeln, die vom "Palast" zur individuellen Bewirtschaftung, etwa in Form einer Grundstückspacht oder eines vererblichen "Lehens"[34] vergeben wurden. Eine Parallele dazu bietet die Bewirtschaftung von Feldgrundstücken des "Palastes" in altbabylonischer Zeit durch Angehörige verschiedener Personengruppen gegen Leistung einer Ertragsabgabe (*miksum*).[35] Die entsprechenden Feldgrundstücke, die im Gebiet von Arrapḫe individuell bewirtschaftet wurden, könnten zu dem nur durch HSS 13, 212 und 300 bezeugten *iškaru*(= Abgaben)-Land des "Palastes"[36] gehören.

Über die Inhaber solcher Kronländereien im Gebiet von Arrapḫe läßt sich, allein von den besprochenen Texten ausgehend, die sich vorläufig kaum in größere archivmäßige Zusammenhänge einordnen lassen, nichts Allgemeingültiges sagen ausser der Feststellung, daß es sich—soweit nachprüfbar—um juristisch freie Personen handelt. Leider besitzen wir in der Regel keine soliden Voraussetzungen für prosopographische Untersuchungen zu den namentlich bekannten Inhabern solcher Grundstücke, vor allem deshalb, weil diese nur in Ausnahmefällen mit Filiation[37] oder Berufsbezeichnung[38] genannt sind. Bei letzteren dürfte es sich um Spezialisten in Diensten des "Palastes" handeln. Diese näher bestimmten Personen verfügen in den uns vorliegenden Texten über die größten Feldflächen (2 × 5 ANŠE, 1 × über 6 ANŠE), während sonst der Durchschnitt je Bebauer bei etwa 2 Homer (ANŠE) Feld liegt. Allerdings handelt es sich dabei nicht unbedingt um die Gesamtfläche an Kronland, die der jeweiligen Person zur Verfügung stand, sondern nur um die in den einzelnen Texten genannten ein oder zwei von einem bestimmten Bebauer mit Getreide bestellten und mit einer Abgabe belegten Feldflächen. Dennoch deuten bereits diese Unterschiede auf einen differenzierten Vergabemodus hin, wobei vermutlich die größeren Feldkomplexe von deren Inhabern nicht

---

32 Vgl. dazu die oben besprochenen Texte HSS 16,190; 15,231 und 16,417.

33 Vgl. dazu die Erwägungen zur prozentualen Höhe der Abgaben unten S. 37f.

34 Zur Vergabe von Feldern auf Pachtbasis in der Gutswirtschaft des Šilwa-Tešup s. Wilhelm, *AdŠ* 3, S. 206; zur Vererblichkeit von Palastland in Privatbesitz vgl. *SCCNH* 1 (1981), S. 386, YBC 5142,13–15 (*ṭuppi šīmti*).

35 Vgl. dazu *CAD* M/2 S. 64b s.v. *miksu* lb 1′ ("share of the yield of a field paid to the palace as the owner of the field"), *CAD* M/1 S. 127f. s.v. *makāsu* lc 1′ und S. 129b s.v. *mākisu* la 2′, §15 des Edikts Ammi-saduqas und die Diskussion damit zusammenhängender Probleme zuletzt bei F. R. Kraus, *Königliche Verfügungen in altbabylonischer Zeit* (SD 11; Leiden 1984) S. 244–48 sowie S. 332–44 zu *nāši biltim* und *iššakkum* als Bewirtschaftern von Kronland, ebd. S. 241–44 auch zu *mākisum* und *makāsum*.

36 Vgl. Zaccagnini, "Land Tenure," S. 80. Mit *iškaru* werden in den Wirtschaftsurkunden aus Nuzi u. a. von Gärtnern zu erbringende Abgaben von Gewürzen (HSS 14,239[= 601]), in anderen Fällen angefertigte und abgelieferte Kleidungsstücke und Streitwagen (s. *CAD* I/J S. 247 a d) und aus Holz hergestellte Gegenstände (HSS 13,101) bezeichnet.

37 IM 73279,2 in: Fadhil, *RATK*, S. 97.

38 Der Zimmermann (*nagāru*) Taḫirišti (HSS 16,190,2f.) und der Arzt(?) (*asû* oder *azû*, letzteres *CAD* A/2 S. 528b) Teḫip-apu (HSS 15,231,24).

persönlich bearbeitet wurden, sondern mit Hilfe von Abhängigen, durch (Unter-) Verpachtung oder Miete freier Arbeitskräfte.

Die Tatsache, daß in Tell al-Faḫḫār neben den Getreideabgaben-Veranlagungen mehrere Empfangsbelege über Saatgetreide, zum Teil unter Angabe der damit zu bestellenden Aussaatfläche, gefunden wurden,[39] legt es nahe, daß an Inhaber von Feldgrundstücken des "Palastes" bei Bedarf Saatgut ausgegeben wurde. Ein direkter Nachweis dieses vermuteten Zusammenhangs ist auf prosopographischer Grundlage—zumindest bisher—allerdings nicht möglich.

Das Verhältnis von Abgabenhöhe zu Anbaufläche unterliegt bei gleicher Feldfrucht bereits innerhalb einer Liste—also in ein und demselben Jahr und vermutlich ein und derselben Flur oder Ortschaft—erheblichen Schwankungen.[40] Das läßt den Schluß zu, daß die Berechnung der Abgabe nicht unmittelbar oder undifferenziert nach der Größe der bewirtschafteten Fläche, sondern dem darauf tatsächlich erzielten oder zu erzielenden Ernteertrag erfolgte. Dabei dürfte mit hoher Wahrscheinlichkeit davon auszugehen sein, daß die absolute Höhe der Abgabe auf der Grundlage eines normativen Bruchteils des Ernteertrags dieser Grundstücke, eben jenes "Anteils des Palastes" (*qātu ša ekalli*), jährlich individuell festgesetzt wurde. Diese Quote angesichts der geringen Zahl von Belegen bestimmen zu wollen, ist fragwürdig. Dennoch sei ein Versuch gewagt: Die oben genannten Urkunden über Ernteertragsabgaben-Veranlagungen aus Tell al-Faḫḫār zugrundegelegt, beträgt das Verhältnis von Aussaatfläche zu Abgabenmenge—jeweils in Homer (ANŠE) gemessen, was annähernd dem Verhältnis von Aussaatmenge zu Abgabenmenge entspricht[41]—bei Gerste 1 : 4,[42] bei Emmer 1 : 3,43 und 1 : 3,9,[43] bei Weizen 1 : 2,6 und 1 : 4,3.[44] Wenn man das in Prozessen übliche Strafmaß für widerrechtliche einjährige Bebauung eines Feldes in Nuzi zur Grundlage für die Bestimmung des durchschnittlichen Ernteertrages nimmt, so kommt man auf ein Verhältnis von Saatgut zu Ernteertrag bei Getreide von etwa 1 : 10.[45] Danach würden die Abgaben

[39] Aufschlußreich dafür ist die Textgruppe IM 70330–70333 (= Nr. 42–45 unserer in Vorbereitung befindlichen Publikation), deren Grundschema folgendermaßen lautet: x ANŠE (. . .) ŠE/GIG *a-na* NUMUM (*a-na* x ANŠE A.ŠÀ) *a-na* PN *na-ad-nu*. NA_4 PN. 'x Homer Gerste/Weizen sind zur Aussaat auf x Homer Feld dem PN gegeben worden. Siegel des PN.' (Es folgt die Siegelabrollung des PN.)

[40] In HSS 15,231 schwankt z.B. das Verhältnis von (Homer) Feld zu (Homer) Ertragsabgabe bei den Z. 23–43 gebuchten Emmerbeträgen zwischen 1 : 3,2 und 1 : 7 bzw., ergänzt, 1 : 7,5 (Z. 29) bei einem Durchschnitt von 1 : 5,4.

[41] Vgl. Zaccagnini, *OA* 14 (1975) 217f.

[42] IM 73279 (= Fadhil, *RATK*, Nr. 24): 1 ANŠE A.ŠÀ—4 ANŠE ŠE.

[43] IM 70917 (= Nr. 48 der in Vorbereitung befindl. Publ.): 7 GIŠ(.APIN)A.ŠÀ—2 ANŠE 4 BÁN ZÍZ.AN.NA; IM 70915 (= Nr. 49): 2 ANŠE A.ŠÀ—7 ANŠE 1 (PI) 2 BÁN [ZÍ]Z.AN.NA.

[44] IM 73279 (= Fadhil, *RATK*, Nr. 24): 4 ANŠE A.ŠÀ—10 ANŠE 4 BÁN 3 SÌLA GIG.MEŠ; IM 70905: 1 ANŠE A.ŠÀ—4 ANŠE 3 BÁN GIG.

[45] Vgl. die instruktive Übersicht bei Zaccagnini, *OA* 14 (1975) 204. Seine Annahme, daß die Quote 1 : 10 an sich bereits Strafcharakter besitzt (ebd. S. 205), dürfte allerdings kaum zutreffen. In den diesbezüglichen Prozessurkunden wird der zu zahlende Naturalbetrag vielmehr ausdrücklich als der dem Eigentümer während der Dauer des widerrechtlichen Feldbesitzes entgangene "Feldertrag" (*išpikū*) bezeichnet. Danach dürfte die regelmäßige Verurteilung des unrechtmäßigen Bebauers zur Zahlung des Zehnfachen der Aussaatmenge an den Grundstückseigentümer die volle Erstattung für den entgangenen Ernteertrag—ohne Berücksichtigung des erfolgten Saatgut- und Arbeitsaufwands durch den Bebauer—bedeuten. Die dieser Erstattung zugrundegelegte Ertragshöhe entspricht allerdings

an den "Palast" bei etwa einem Drittel liegen. Berücksichtigt man jedoch die Möglichkeit, daß alle Abgabenveranlagungen aus einem nur mäßig guten oder gar schlechten Ertragsjahr stammen und daß es sich bei der Quote von 1 : 10 wohl eher um ein gutes[46] als um ein durchschnittliches Ertragsergebnis handelt und zieht schließlich vergleichend und ergänzend die Getreide-Abgabenverbuchungen HSS 15,231; 16,190 und 417 hinzu, verschiebt sich das Bild. In letzteren betragen bei einer Schwankung der einzelnen Raten zwischen 1 : 2,375 und 1 : 7 bzw., ergänzt, 1 : 7,5 die durchschnittlichen Quoten der Ertragsabgaben bei Emmer 1 : 5,77 und bei Weizen ca. 1 : 3.[47] Das läßt eher an Abgaben von oder bis zu 50% denken. Aber das sind bei den genannten Unsicherheiten und ohne eine statistisch relevante Datengrundlage vorläufig noch—wie bereits angedeutet—kaum mehr als Zahlenspielereien. Außerdem könnte die Abgabenquote in Abhängigkeit von möglichen Zusatzleistungen des "Palastes" wie Gestellung von Saatgut, Zugvieh und Pflug, falls diese nicht separat abgerechnet wurden, unterschiedlich hoch gewesen sein. Insgesamt dürfte davon auszugehen sein, daß die anteiligen Abgaben an den Grundstückseigentümer bei Getreide im Gebiet von Arrapḫe nach den vorliegenden Daten mindestens ein Drittel, möglicherweise aber auch (nur bei Zusatzleistungen des "Palastes"?) die Hälfte der Ernte betrugen.

Über Zeitpunkt, Ort und alle sonstigen Umstände der jährlich durchzuführenden mengenmäßigen Festlegung der Getreideertragsabgaben von den einzelnen Parzellen und der Ausstellung von Urkunden über den "Anteil des 'Palastes'" besitzen wir in Anbetracht des grundsätzlichen Fehlens von Datierungen in arrapḫäischen Urkunden und der Kargheit der Angaben in den betreffenden Urkunden und Verwaltungslisten leider keine Informationen. Grundsätzlich bestehen dafür jedoch zwei Möglichkeiten: Entweder ist der zu erwartende Ernteertrag "auf dem Halme," also noch vor der Ernte, geschätzt und die Abgabe danach mengenmäßig festgelegt worden, oder das ausgedroschene und geworfelte Getreide wurde auf der Tenne anteilmäßig aufgeteilt. Letzterenfalls dürfte sich die Ausfertigung individueller Lieferungsverpflichtungen nur dann notwendig gemacht haben, wenn der "Anteil des 'Palastes'" aus irgendwelchen Gründen noch im Besitz des Grundstücksinhabers verblieben war. Das dürfte aber die Ausnahme gewesen sein. Bei Abgabefestlegungen aufgrund von Ertragsschätzungen waren hingegen Aufzeichnungen über die Höhe der von den einzelnen Grundstücksinhabern zu erbringen-

---

eher einem optimalen als einem durchschnittlichen Ernteergebnis (s. Anm. 46). Eine Bestätigung scheint diese Deutung durch die Strafklausel der Urkunde *JEN* 550 (Z. 11–13) zu finden, wonach ein gemieteter Erntearbeiter je Homer nicht abgeernteter Feldfläche strafweise 20 Homer Gerste zu entrichten hat. Die Höhe dieser Strafe entspricht dem Duplum der normierten Ertragsquote 1 : 10. Damit liegt hier offensichtlich die in den Urkunden aus dem Land Arrapḫe häufige Strafandrohung vor, im Übertretungsfall das Doppelte des vertraglich Vereinbarten leisten zu müßen (vgl. dazu B. Kh. Ismail und M. Müller, *WO* 9 [1977] 21f.).

[46] Zum Verhätnis von Saatgutmenge zu Ernteertrag bei Gerste vgl. zuletzt K. Butz, *RlA* 6 (1983) 482–84. Danach bedeutet die Relation 1 : 10 nicht nur für Nuzi (§11.3.2.2), sondern auch für das alte Ägypten, das antike Palästina und Italien sowie den modernen Irak (§11.3.1) ein gutes Ernteergebnis. Siehe Nachtrag, S. 43.

[47] Angaben in HSS 15,231 z.T. weggebrochen.

den Abgaben unabdingbar. Solche Ernteertragsschätzungen mit Festlegung der zu liefernden Abgaben sind für Babylonien belegt und betreffen dort vorwiegend Datteln und Gerste. Die altbabylonischen Texte verwenden für diesen Vorgang den Begriff *šukunnûm*,[48] die neu- und spätbabylonischen den Terminus technicus *imittu*.[49] In beiden Perioden wurden über die zu leistenden Abgaben, die spezielle Kommissionen kurz vor der Ernte festsetzten, Schuldurkunden zu Lasten der einzelnen Ablieferungspflichtigen ausgestellt. Die Urkunden aus Tell al-Faḫḫār, in denen der "(Ernteertrags-)Anteil des 'Palastes'" mengenmäßig festgesetzt und als zu erbringende Leistung von den Grundstücksinhabern anerkannt wurde, entsprechen jenen Schuldurkunden. Ob sie allerdings das Ergebnis von Ertragsschätzungen "auf dem Halme" sind, bleibt ungewiß, zumindest bisher zichere Zeugnisse für die Durchführung derartiger Ertragsschätzungen im hurritischen Siedlungsgebiet fehlen. Andererseits ist erwiesen, daß die Praxis der Ertragsschätzung vor der Ernte im alten Vorderasien nicht auf Südmesopotamien beschränkt war. Nach dem Zeugnis tradierter Briefe Mohammeds wurde sie auf der Arabischen Halbinsel noch bis in frühislamische Zeit bei Datteln[50] zur Festsetzung der jeweiligen Höhe der Naturalabgabe angewendet und bei Getreide[51] im Zusammenhang mit dem Verkauf des zu erwartenden Feldertrags "auf dem Halme." Der Prophet hat beides als ungerecht abgelehnt und vorgeschrieben, den Zehnt von den tatsächlich geernteten Früchten zu erheben.[52]

Exkurs: Zu IM 70778 und dem Begriff "muddu"

In der *Welt des Orients* 9 (1977) 28–34 war von Bahija Khalil Ismail und dem Verf. der Text IM 70778 (= Nr. 47 der in Vorbereitung befindlichen Publikation) bearbeitet worden. Die drei gleichartigen Eintragungen auf dieser Tafel folgen dem Schema:

x ANŠE.MEŠ (*ša*) *iš-pí-ki-šu mu*-UD-DU-*šú ša* PN.

x Homer Gerste seines Feldertrags sind "*muddu*" des PN. (Anschließend folgen die Siegelbeischriften (NA_4 PN) und die Siegelabrollungen der drei Personen.)

[48] Die einschlägigen Texte sind, insbesondere soweit sie Datteln betreffen, von Landsberger (*Date Palm*, S. 56–60) und Cocquerillat (*JESHO* 10 [1967] 175–78, 188–90, 212–22) untersucht worden. Mit der Bewirtschaftung von Dattelpalmengärten während der altbabylonischen Zeit auf der Basis von Abgaben, die durch Ertragsschätzungen vor der Ernte festgelegt wurden, befaßt sich der Beitrag von J. Renger zur Festschrift für F. R. Kraus, *Zikir Šumim* (Leiden 1982) S. 290–97. Belege für Gerste s. *AHw* 1266 s.v. *šukunnû(m)* 2.

[49] Zur neubabylonischen *imittu*-Pacht vgl. die zusammenfassende Darstellung von H. Petschow, *RlA* 5 (1976) 68–73 (mit Lit.) und G. Ries, *Die neubabylonischen Bodenpachtformulare* (Berlin 1976) S. 90–113.

[50] J. Wellhausen, *Skizzen und Vorarbeiten* IV (Berlin 1889) S. 130f. Nr. 69.

[51] Ibid., S. 131, Nr. 71. Vgl. auch *Lisān al-ᶜarab*, s.v. *al-muhāqala* (freundlicher Hinweis meines Kollegen Holger Preißler).

[52] Vgl. Anm. 50; im Irak hat sich die Besteuerung nach dem tatsächlich erzielten Ernteertrag im Verlauf des 7. und 8. Jh. durchgesetzt, s. M. G. Morony, in: T. Khalidi (Hrsg.), *Land Tenure and Social Transformation in the Middle East* (Beirut 1984) S. 210.

Die Siegelung der Tafel durch die drei im Text genannten Männer bedeutet, daß sie die Feststellung des Dokuments als zutreffend und für sich verpflichtend anerkennen, wonach ein Teil ihres Ernteertrags an Gerste—11, 12 bzw. 16 Homer (ANŠE)—ihr "*muddu*" ist. Daß einzelne Personen dem 'Palast' Gerste als ihr "*muddu*" schulden[53] oder abgeliefert hatten,[54] wird durch Verwaltungsnotizen aus Nuzi bestätigt. Als ein "*muddu*"-Anerkenntnis" über Gerste ist die vorliegende Urkunde jedoch bisher singulär. "*Muddu*"-Anerkenntnisse," die sich auf Kleinvieh beziehen,[55] sind dagegen in großer Zahl überliefert, vereinzelt auch solche über Rinder,[56] Textilien,[57] Metalle,[58] Holz,[59] sowie Gegenstände aus Metall und aus Holz,[60] wobei gelegentliche Zusätze[61] eindeutig bestätigen, daß es sich um das Anerkenntnis von Lieferungsverpflichtungen handelt. Welcher Art diese Lieferungsverpflichtungen sind, ist abhängig von der Deutung des Begriffs "*muddu*."

Nachdem dieser problematische Terminus sehr unterschiedliche Interpretationen—u.a. als "quota," "share," "etwa 'Verantwortung'?," "Zuteilung"—erfahren hatte,[62] ist er im Zusammenhang mit der Bearbeitung des Textes IM 70778 von uns in *WO* 9:30–33 besprochen worden. Dabei hatten wir die Vermutung geäußert, daß das nur in Urkunden aus dem Gebiet von Arrapḫe sicher[63] bezeugte Wort ein nach dem Nominalschema purs gebildetes, von der akkadischen Verbalwurzel *mdd* abgeleitetes Abstraktum mit der Grundbedeutung "Vermessung, Abmessung" sein könnte. Vom Kontext des Wortes in IM 70778 und der postulierten Ableitung von *mdd* ausgehend, hatten wir die Meinung vertreten, daß der Terminus in individuellen "*muddu*"-Lieferungsverpflichtungen (= "*m.*-Anerkenntnissen") und in Verwaltungslisten und -notizen über "*muddu*"-Außenstände bzw. -Eingänge von Vieh und Gerste eine für den jeweiligen Fall speziell bemessene, auferlegte Abgabe(nmenge), eine "Abgabenauflage" oder ein "Ablieferungssoll," im Zusammenhang mit Getreide- und Materialausgaben dagegen eine gewiße abgemessene, zugeteilte Menge des jeweiligen Stoffes bezeichne.

Im gleichen Jahr erschien *CAD* M/2 (1977), das den Terminus als "*muddû* (*mundu*, or *muṭṭû*)" ansetzte, ihn als "outstanding balance, delivery dur, deficit, leftover" deutete und eine Ableitung von der Wurzel *mṭī* "gering sein/werden" erwog.[64] Auch M. A. Morrison, die 1981 in der Festschrift für E. R. Lacheman (= SCCNH 1) eine Analyse der "*muddu*"-Texte aus der arraphäischen Vieh-

[53] HSS 16,97; vgl. 15,263 (mit teilweiser Personenidentität) und die Gerste-"*muddu*"-Liste HSS 16,109.

[54] HSS 16,99, 16–20.

[55] *WO* 9 (1977) 31; Morrison, SCCNH 1 (1981) 277–85 und 294–96.

[56] *WO* 9; 31, Anm. 38; Morrison, SCCNH 1 (1981) 285 mit Anm. 167.

[57] HSS 15,177 und 176.

[58] HSS 14,256 (= 612), vgl. HSS 13,449.

[59] HSS 14,243 (= 576).

[60] HSS 15,129.

[61] Vgl. *WO* 9:31.

[62] Vgl. *WO* 9:30.

[63] Zu einem möglichen mittelassyrischen Beleg s. unten S. 42 mit Anm. 77.

[64] *CAD* M/2 S. 161f.

wirtschaft vorlegte,[65] definierte die Bedeutung des Lexems in diesem Zusammenhang als " 'outstanding balance' or 'deficit' of the herdsman."[66] Andererseits wies K. Deller[67] in einer Rezension zu *CAD* M/2 auf die semantische Verwandtschaft dieses Wortes mit *iškaru* hin und regte eine neue parallele Untersuchung aller Belege für beide Termini an. Unlängst hat schließlich G. Wilhelm[68] die vorgeschlagenen Ableitungen von *mdd* bzw. *mṭī* einer kritischen Analyse unterzogen, ohne entscheidende Argumente für oder gegen die eine oder andere Möglichkeit beibringen zu können. Er hat aber in Aussicht gestellt, den Gebrauch des Wortes "*muddu*" in den Dokumenten der Viehwirtschaft des Šilwa-Tešup in Heft 5 seines *Archivs des Šilwa-teššup* zu analysieren, denn "gerade in diesem Bereich lassen die beiden vorgeschlagenen Ableitungsmöglichkeiten (*mdd* oder *mṭī*) unterschiedliche Interpretationen des Sachverhalts zu, die erst nach gründlicher Rekonstruktion der Textgruppe gegeneinander abgewogen werden können."[69]

Ohne der zu erwartenden Untersuchung von G. Wilhelm vorgreifen zu wollen, sei hier, angeregt durch die Behandlung des Lemmas in *CAD* M/2, auf einige für die Bestimmung der Semantik des Wortes entscheidende Belege außerhalb der Viehwirtschaft des Šilwa-Tešup hingewiesen, die uns bei der Besprechung des Begriffs in *WO* 9 zum Teil entgangen waren:[70]

1. In der Prozeßurkunde *JEN* 386[71] wird der Angeklagte, nachdem er des Einbruchs in den ihm unterstehenden Getreidespeicher überführt und zu einer hohen Strafe verurteilt wurde, durch die Richter zur Ersatzleistung verpflichtet mit den Worten (Z. 40–43): ŠE.MEŠ *ša* É *qa-ri-ti i-ma-an-dá-du-ma ù mu*-UD-DU-*šu ša* ŠE.MEŠ PN *a-na* PN_2 *ú-ma-al-la* 'Die Gerste des Speichers (, die noch vorhanden ist,) soll man ausmessen und dann wird PN (= der Einbrechen dem PN_2 (= der Eigentümer) den "*muddu*" der Gerste voll ersetzen.' Anschließend (Z. 44f.) gibt der Eigentümer die ursprüngliche Füllmenge des Speichers zu Protokoll, offensichtlich als Grundlage zur Bestimmung der Differenz zwischen der eingelagerten und der nach dem Diebstahl noch vorhandenen Gerste, die der Angeklagte als "*muddu*," als "Fehlbetrag," zu ersetzen hat.
2. Der Text HSS 15,129 enthält eine Aufstellung verschiedenster Metall- und Holzgegenstände, die "verschwunden" (*ḫaliq, ša ḫalqū*), "nicht vorhanden" (*jānu*) oder "zu wenig" (*ša maṭû*) sind. Der abschließende Vermerk lautet (Z. 31–33): *an-nu-*tu_4 *mu*-UD-DU *ša* PN_1 PN_2 *ù* PN_3 *inandinū*(SUM-*nu*)[72] 'Diese (Gegenstände) sind "*muddu*," die $PN_{1\text{-}3}$ geben werden.' Anschließend folgen die Siegelbeischriften und die Siegelabrollungen der drei Personen. Es handelt sich also um ein "*muddu*"-Anerkenntnis" über fehlende Gegenstände, für die die Genannten verantwortlich sind, mit ausdrücklich vermerkter Lieferungsverpflichtung. Der Begriff "*muddu*" hat hier, wie sich aus dem Kontext

[65] SCCNH 1 (1981) 277–88 und 294–96.

[66] Ibid., S. 277f. mit Anm. 139.

[67] *Or* 53 (1984) 104f.

[68] *AdŠ* 3 (1985) 97f.

[69] Ibid., S. 98.

[70] Das betrifft die im folgenden behandelten Texte *JEN* 386 und HSS 15,129.

[71] Vgl. dazu *CAD* M/2 162 zu Beginn des Abschnitts c und Wilhelm, *AdŠ* 3, S. 97.

[72] In *CAD* M/2 161b ist das Logogramm SUM-*nu* als *nadnu* aufgelöst, der gesamte Kontext erfordert jedoch Präsens-Futur.

zweifelsfrei ergibt, die Bedeutung "Fehlbestand" oder—modern ausgedrückt—"Inventurdifferenz."

3. Weitere Hinweise bieten Texte über die Ausgabe von Gerste als Pferdefutter: In HSS 16, 96 werden für 17 Pferde für eine Dauer von 12 Tagen 21 BÁN Gerste "als sein (= des Empfängers) "*muddu*" (*ki-ma mu*-UD-DU$_4$-*šú*)" ausgegeben, je Pferd pro Tag also fast genau 1 SÌLA (wenn wir, wie zu erwarten, das große BÁN-Maß zu 10 SÌLA zugrundelegen). Andererseits wird in diesem Text Z. 6–8 ausdrücklich festgestellt, daß an jedes Pferd täglich 2 SÌLA Gerste zu verfüttern seien. Es handelt sich also offensichtlich um die Nachlieferung eines "Fehlbetrags," eines "Lieferungsrückstands." In anderen Notierungen über die Ausgabe von Gerste als Futter für Pferde erscheinen die "*muddu*"-Beträge immer am Schluß der Aufzeichnungen und betreffen in der Regel geringe bzw. geringere Mengen.[73]

Die angeführten Texte erlauben es, die Bedeutung des fraglichen Lexems in der vom *CAD* M/2 angegebenen Richtung zu bestätigen und und zu präzisieren: "*muddu*" ist in diesen signifikanten Belegen ein zu leistender oder beglichener "Fehlbetrag," "Fehlbestand" bzw. "Lieferungsrückstand." Das entspricht den in *CAD* M/2 und von M. A. Morrison angegebenen Bedeutungen "outstanding balance" und "deficit." Auch wenn diese Bedeutung noch der Überprüfung für die Dokumente der Viehwirtschaft bedarf, ist sie doch auch hier nicht unwahrscheinlich, auch bei einem Vergleich mit der staatlichen Viehwirtschaft in altbabylonischer Zeit.[74] Die von uns ursprünglich angesetzte Bedeutung "Abgabe," "Ablieferungssoll" scheint vielmehr dem Begriff *iškaru* zuzukommen.[75]

Aus semantischer Sicht ist die Entwicklung der Bedeutung "Fehlbetrag" aus einem postulierten Abstraktum *muddu* "Vermessung" zwar nicht auszuschließen, andererseits ist es auffällig, daß diese Bedeutung im Akkadischen sonst dem insbesondere aus assyrischen Texten gut bezeugten, im Hurro-Akkadischen aber nach den Wörterbüchern nicht belegten Nomen *muṭāʾu/muṭû* zukommt. Unser Lexem könnte daraus möglicherweise durch eine Quantitätsmetathese (*muṭṭu* < *muṭû*), wie sie für das Spätbabylonische bezeugt ist,[76] oder analog *GAG* §20e entstanden sein, was durch den mittelassyrischen Beleg *a-na mu-uṭ-ṭa-e*[77] nahegelegt wird. Eine Neubildung *muṭṭû* (Inf. des D-Stamms) innerhalb des Akkadischen von Arrapḫe ist dagegen weniger wahrscheinlich,[78] obwohl grundsätzlich nicht auszuschließen, da das Verbum *maṭû* zum Wortschatz der Texte von Nuzi gehört. Bei Abwägung der dargestellten Ableitungsmöglichkeiten erscheint es am wahrscheinlichsten, daß der besprochene Terminus das hurro-akkadische Pendant

[73] Vgl. HSS 14,83; 16,99 und 149.

[74] Zu Fehlbeständen bzw. Lieferungsrückständen der Hirten in altbabylonischer Zeit vgl. F. R. Kraus, *Ein Edikt des Königs Ammi-Ṣaduqa von Babylon* (Leiden 1958) S. 94; ders., *Staatliche Viehhaltung*, S. 61–63; J. N. Postgate, *JSS* 20 (1975) 6 und 9; zu Vieh- und Wollnachlieferungslisten s. K. Butz, *WZKM* 65–66 (1973–74) 20 und ders., *OLA* 5 (1979) 359f. mit Anm. 271.

[75] Vgl. oben Anm. 36.

[76] Vgl. aA *burāʾum*, bab. *burû*, spB auch *burru* 'Rohrmatte' und m/nA *mūsāʾu*, bab. *mūsû*, spB auch *mussû* 'Ausgang'.

[77] *VS* 19,56, 54; vgl. dazu K. Deller, *Or* 53 (1984) 104f.

[78] Wilhelm, *AdŠ* 3, S. 97.

zu gemeinakkadischem *muṭā'u/muṭû* ist und als *muṭṭu* oder als *muṭṭû* angesetzt werden muß.

Für die Interpretation des Textes IM 70778 bedeuten die Ausführungen zur Semantik dieses Lexems, daß er kein Zeugnis für die Praxis der individuellen Festlegung von Getreideabgaben auf Grund des geschätzten oder tatsächlich erzielten Ernteertrags darstellt. Die Urkunde ist vielmehr als ein Anerkenntnis von Lieferungsrückständen an Gerste zu verstehen. Vermutlich handelt es sich dabei um Rest-Außenstände der Ernteertragsabgaben-Verpflichtung der im Text genannten drei Personen, die noch von dem erzielten Feldertrag der Bebauer zu begleichen sind.

Nachtrag (23. 3. 1993): Das Manuskript des vorliegenden Beitrags war am 2. 4. 1987 an den Herausgeber abgeschickt worden. Seither sind einige Untersuchungen erschienen, die für einzelne Aspekte dieses Artikels von Bedeutung sind, aber nicht mehr eingearbeitet werden konnten. Dazu gehören vor allem B. Scholz, Bodentechnik und Ertragssteigerung in Mesopotamien, in: Grazer Morgenländische Studien 2 (1989), S.331–341 [wichtig zur Frage des Verhältnisses von Saatgutmenge zu Ernteertrag]; B. Hruška, Tradiční Obilnářství Staré Mezopotámie. Der traditionelle Ackerbau im Alten Mesopotamien. Praha 1990; C. Zaccagnini, Again on the yield of the fields at Nuzi, in : BSAg 5 (1990), S.201–217.

Miscellanea Hurritica

Erich Neu
Ruhr-Universität Bochum

0. Die über mehrere Tontafeln verteilte hurritisch-hethitische Bilingue aus Ḫattuša[1] stellt hinsichtlich ihrer Thematik und Kompositionsweise ein bisher einzigartiges Literaturdenkmal des Alten Orients dar. Mit seiner hethitischen Übersetzung liefert das zweisprachige Textensemble zugleich einen Schlüssel, der es ermöglicht, tiefer in Grammatik und Lexikon des Hurritischen einzudringen. Der Bitte von Herrn Kollegen David I. Owen um einen hurritologischen Beitrag für diesen Sammelband bin ich um so lieber nachgekommen, als die Bilingue u.a. auch schon bei der Deutung hurritischen Sprachmaterials aus Nuzi hat hilfreich sein können.[2] Meine Ausführungen lassen sich folgendermaßen gliedern:

1. Die hurritische Bezeichnung für "Finger"
2. Hurritische Entsprechungen zu hethitisch *uttar*
3. Hurritische Wörter für "Weide, weiden"
4. Zu hurritischen Partizipialbildungen
5. Das hurritische Negationssuffix *-ma*

1. *Die hurritische Bezeichnung für "Finger"*

1.1 Im Hethitischen wird für "Finger" und "Zehe" das Wort *k/galulupa-*[3] gebraucht. Zur Verdeutlichung können die hethitischen (heth.) Wörter für "Hand" bzw. "Fuß" im Genitiv hinzugefügt werden. Für die Verwendung von *k/galulupa-* in der Bedeutung "Zehe" sei hier beispielhaft der Vokabulareintrag GÌR-*aš ka-lu-lu-p*[*a-aš*] angeführt, dem in der akkadischen Spalte [*ú-ba-nu ša*] GÌR entspricht (KBo 1 51 Rs. III 10′).[4] In dem althethitischen Ritual für das Königspaar (StBoT 8: IV 26f.) wurde das erläuternde Genitivattribut (akkadographisch) *ŠA QA-TI-ŠU-NU* 'ihrer Hände' betont an das Satzende gestellt: *ta ka-lu-lu-pu-uš-mu-uš*

[1] Vgl. H. Otten, *Blick in die altorientalische Geisteswelt. Neufund einer hethitischen Tempelbibliothek* (Jahrbuch 1984 der Akademie der Wissenschaften in Göttingen; Göttingen 1985) 50ff.; E. Neu, *Das Hurritische: Eine altorientalische Sprache in neuem Licht* (Abhandlungen der Geistes- und Sozialwissenschaftlichen Klasse der Akademie der Wissenschaften und der Literatur zu Mainz, Jahrgang 1988, Nr. 3); idem, *Neue Wege im Hurritischen* (ZDMG Supplement 7; Stuttgart 1989) 293ff. (mit weiteren Literaturhinweisen, S. 303).

[2] Vgl. G. Wilhelm, *ZA* 78 (1988) 281f.

[3] Vgl. J. Friedrich, *HW* 96b; J. Tischler, *HEG* (Innsbruck 1983) 1:470f.

[4] Zu akkad. *ubānu*(*m*) 'Finger, Zehe' s. W. von Soden, *AHw* 3:1398f.

ga-a-pí-ni-it ḫu-la-a-li-e-mi ŠA QA-TI-ŠU-NU ‘dann umwickele ich mit einem Faden ihre Finger’. Demgegenüber steht in der Bilingue KBo 32 13 II 30 das Genitivattribut *kišraš* ‘der Hand’ (bzw. ‘der Hände’) betont am Satzanfang: *ki-iš-ra-aš-ma-aš-ši ga-lu-lu-pé-e-eš-še-eš ta-lu-ga-e-*[*eš*][5] ‘ihre Finger aber (waren) ihr lang (ausgestreckt)’, gemeint sind die Finger der Allani, der Sonnengöttin der Erde. Sie feierte in ihrem Palast “an den Riegeln der Erde” ein großartiges Fest, zu dem Teššub, der oberste Gott des hurritischen Pantheons, als Ehrengast geladen war. Wie ein Mundschenk[6] tritt Allani vor den Wettergott Teššub (heth. ^{d}IM-*unni piran* = ^{d}*Tarḫunni piran*). In diesem Zusammenhang heißt es dann beschreibend, daß ihre Finger lang (ausgetreckt) seien und daß vier Finger sich unter dem Rhyton befinden, aus welchem sie ihrem Gast zu trinken anbietet (II 31ff.): *na-at-kán mi-i̯a-u-e-eš-pát*[7] *ga-lu-lu-pé-e-eš* [*A-NA*? *B*]*I-IB-RI kat-ta-an-ta ki-an-ta-ri.*

1.2. Der eingangs zitierte heth. Satz. *kišraš=ma=šši galulupeš=šeš talugae*[*š*] gibt den aus nur zwei Wörtern bestehenden hurritischen (hurr.) Satz. *u̯u*$_{u}$*-ku-ga-ri ki-re-e-et-te* wieder. Daraus ergibt sich für “Finger” die hurr. Bezeichnung *u̯u*$_{u}$*-ku-ga-ri*, wohl kollektivisch zu verstehen (vgl. dtsch. **Gefingere*);[8] so dürfte auch in *kirette* (zu *keri* “long” s. E. Laroche, *GLH* 143) eine kollektivische Abstraktbildung, und zwar auf *-te* (*-ti*) vorliegen. Ebenso stellt das im nächsten Satz auftretende, mit “Artikel” versehene Zahlwort *tumnati* “vier” eine Abstraktbildung dar, wie überhaupt Abstraktbildungen für den Bereich des hurr. Zahlworts typisch sind. Auf das Prädikatsnomen *kirette* (s. oben) folgt ein neuer Satz: *tu-um-na-ti-ne-el-la* (*tumnati=ne=lla*)[9] *ḫu-ú-ru-ub-u̯e*$_{e}$*-ni*[10] *tu-u-um-u̯a*$_{a}$ (wörtlich:) ‘sie (Plur.), die Vier, (befinden sich) unter dem Rhyton’. Ob heth. *kiantari* in der hurr. Vorlage eine lexikalische Entsprechung hatte, läßt sich nicht ausmachen, da die auf *tu-u-um-u̯a*$_{a}$ folgende Zeile bis auf einige unklare Zeichenspuren weggebrochen ist.[11] Die äußerlich wie ein Dativ aussehende Wortform *tu-u-um-u̯a*$_{a}$ dürfte heth. *kat-*

[5] Dieses Adjektiv ist bereits ab *-lu-* über den Rand geschrieben, so daß dahinter kaum noch ein weiteres Wort gestanden hat. Daher dürfte es sich bei dem hier zitierten Wortlaut um einen Nominalsatz handeln.

[6] Hurrit. *tabšaḫa* (Essiv) = heth. ^{LÚ}SAGI-*aš iu̯ar*; vgl. E. Neu, *Hethitica* 9 (1988) 161f.

[7] Zum heth. Zahlwort für “vier” s. E. Neu, *IBS* 52 (1987) 176f. Möglicherweise liegt das den nicht-anatolischen indogermanischen Sprachen eigene Zahlwort für “vier” (vgl. altind. *catvāraḥ*, griech. *téttares*, lat. *quattuor* usw.) in heth. *kutruan-* ‘Zeuge’ (zur Stammbildung s. N. Oettinger, *GsKronasser* 1982, 164f.) vor; vgl. diesbezügliche Literaturhinweise bei Tischler, *HEG* 1:682.

[8] In dem wortauslautenden *-i* dürfte auch noch das Possessivpronomen der 3. Pers. Sing. stecken.

[9] Das hurr. pluralische Pronomen *-lla* dürfte in der heth. Übersetzung zur Verwendung des Pronomens *-at* (in: *na-at-kán*) geführt haben, das von der heth. Grammatik her dort nicht erforderlich gewesen wäre.- Zum Zahlwort *tumni* ‘vier’ s. F. W. Bush, “A Grammar of the Hurrian Language” (Ph.D., Brandeis University, 1964) 108; E. Laroche, *GLH* 271.

[10] Zu *ḫuruppi-* (Friedrich, *HW* 77a) ‘Rhyton’ s. bereits Neu, *Das Hurritische*, 15,43; idem, *Neue Wege im Hurritischen*, 297.

[11] In der heth. Übersetzung wird man zwei der drei auf *kiantari* folgenden bruchstückhaften Zeilen vielleicht folgendermaßen ergänzen und übersetzen dürfen (II 33–34): [*iš-ru ḫal-u̯a-n*]*i-it-ma ku-e-ez a-ku-u̯a-an-na* / [*pí-iš-ki-zi a-pé-e-d*]*a*?*-ša an-da aš-šu-u̯a-a-tar ki-it-t*[*a*(-) ‘Aus welchem Rhyton auch immer (sie, d.h. Allani) dann zu trinken [gibt], in jenen (d.h. in den mit Getränken gefüllten Rhyta) aber liegt Güte (im Sinne von guter Qualität)’.

tanta entsprechen und ist etymologisch wohl mit hurr. *du-ú-ri*[12] zu verbinden, das auf der gleichen Tafel (KBo 32 13 I 10) durch heth. *kattanta* im Sinne von "hinab" wiedergegeben wird.[13]

Die hier behandelte Textstelle aus der Bilingue erweist für hurr. *u̯u*$_{u}$*-ku-ga-ri*, lautlich wohl [*fugugari*], die Bedeutung "Finger" (auch in kollektivischem Sinne).[14]

2. *Hurritische Entsprechungen zu hethitisch uttar*

In der hurritisch-hethitischen Bilingue gibt heth. *uttar* 'Wort, Sache, Angelegenheit' drei verschiedene hurr. Wörter wieder, die jedoch alle auf einer gemeinsamen Wurzel beruhen.

2.1. Die schon bekannte Gleichsetzung von heth. *uttar* mit hurr. *tiu̯e*$_{e}$ (s. Laroche, *GLH* 268) läßt sich in der Bilingue z.B. durch folgenden Satz belegen: ^{m}*Me-e-ki-né-e ti-bé-e-na* ^{d}IM*-ub-u-ta ku-un-zi-ma-i qa-ti-i̯a* KBo 32 15 IV 12f. = heth. ^{m}*Me-e-ke-eš ud-da-a-a̯r a-ru-u̯a-an-za* IM*-un-ni me-mi-iš-ki-iz-zi* 'Meki spricht kniefällig (folgende) Worte zum Wettergott . . . ' (hurr. *Teššub*).[15] Hieraus ergibt sich die Gleichsetzung der Pluralformen hurr. *ti-bé-e-na* = heth. *ud-da-a-ar* 'Worte (sprechen)'. Auf *kadii̯a* bzw. *memiškizzi* folgt die Rede des Meki. Für *ti-bé-e-na* begegnet in der Bilingue auch die Graphie *te-u̯e*$_{e}$*-na*, ebenfalls in Verbindung mit [*qa-*]*ti-i̯a* KBo 32 11 Rs. (IV) 12′, 16′. In diesem Zusammenhang lassen sich heth. *uddār* und die hier aufgezeigte hurr. Entsprechung als "Worte" im Sinne von "Wortlaut", also als sprachliche Äußerung verstehen.

---

[12] Zu *turi* 'inférieur' s. Laroche, *GLH* 273. Die Ausdrücke *du-ú-ri* und *tu-u-um-u̯a*$_{a}$ lassen sich bei Annahme einer Wurzel **du-* miteinander verbinden.

[13] Zu der hurr. Wendung *ti-me-er-re-e* (**timeri=ne*) *e-še-ni du-ú-ri* = heth. *kattanta tankuu̯ai takni* 'hinab zur dunklen Erde' und zu den damit verbundenen Implikationen s. Oettinger, *WO* 20/21 (1989/90) 83ff.

[14] Wohl nur äußerlich klingt die Verbalform *pu-ku-ka-ri-id-du-le-e-eš* KUB 27 42 Rs. 16′ an *fugugari* an, das wortbildungsmäßig eine nominale *-ugar*-Ableitung darstellen könnte; vgl. E. A. Speiser, *Introduction to Hurrian* (New Haven 1941) 136f. -Zu KBo 32 13 II 28–33 s. auch H. Otten, *FsÖzgüç* (Ankara 1989) 368.

[15] Zur vergleichenden Analyse dieses Satzes s. E. Neu, *FsThomas* (München 1988) 506f. Da zuvor im Text erwähnt wurde, daß Meki dem Wettergott wiederholt zu Füßen fiel (*na-aš* ^{d}[I]M*-un-ni* GÌR$^{HI.A}$*-aš kat-t*[*a-an*] *ḫa-li-iš-ki-it*[*-ta-a*]*t*), hat man *aruu̯ai-* hier vielleicht eher mit "sich niederwerfen" zu übersetzen, weshalb wir das hurr. Gerundium *kunzimai* mit dem Ausdruck "kniefällig" wiedergeben. Zur Diskussion um die Bedeutung von *aruu̯ai-* vgl. *StBoT* 2 (1989) 155 oben. Die heth. Wendung GÌR$^{HI.A}$*-aš kattan ḫalii̯a-* 'zu Füßen niederfallen, niederknien' ist in der Bilingue (KBo 32 15 III 10f.) zwar nicht als Grußgestus, sondern konkret als Unterwerfungsgeste zu verstehen, ihr Auftreten in der Bilingue aber, deren hurr. Text in Nordsyrien entstanden sein dürfte, könnte die Auffassung bestätigen, wonach die gleichlautende Huldigungsformel aus dem nordsyrischen Raum entlehnt wäre; vgl. A. Hagenbuchner, *THeth* 15 (1989) 61 (doch s. dort auch Anm. 66). Zum Namen *Me-e-ki* (=*Megi* ?) s. D. I. Owen and R. Veenker, "*MeGum*, the First Ur III Ensi of Ebla," in L. Cagni (Hrsg.), *Ebla 1975–1985. Dieci anni di studi linguistici e filologici* (Atti del Convegno Internazionale; Napoli, 9–11 ottobre 1985; Napoli 1987) 263ff.; vgl. H. Otten, "Ebla in der hurritisch-hethitischen Bilingue aus Boğazköy," in H. Hauptmann und H. Waetzoldt (Hrsg.), *Wirtschaft und Gesellschaft von Ebla* (Heidelberger Studien zum Alten Orient 2, 1988) 292 Anm. 17.

2.2. Eine weitere lexikalische Gleichung stellt heth. *uttar* = hurr. *ti(-i)-ib-ša-a-ri* dar (KBo 32 14 I/II 23 et passim; KBo 32 12 I 18, IV 21′), die innerhalb der Bilingue in folgendem engeren Kontext auftritt: hurr. *ku-u-le-eš an-ti ti(-i)-ib-ša-a-ri u-la-ab-u̯a*$_a$ *(uli=ppa) qa-du-ul-li* = heth. *ar-ḫa da-a-le-eš-tén a-pa-a-at ut-tar nu-uš-ma-aš ta-ma-i ut-tar me-mi-iš-ki-mi* 'laßt jene Geschichte beiseite! Ich werde euch eine andere Geschichte erzählen'.[16] Die beiden Sätze sind Teil einer Übergangspassage zwischen gleichnisartigen Erzählungen mit anschließender Nutzanwendung für konkrete Fälle aus dem täglichen Leben. Statt "Geschichte" oder "Erzählung" wäre in diesem Kontext für *tibšāri* (heth. *uttar*) auch die Übersetzung "Fall, Fallbeispiel" zu erwägen. Hurr. *tibšāri* dürfte etymologisch mit hurr, *tiu̯e*$_e$ zusammengehören, indem nämlich beiden Ausdrücken die Wurzel *tif-* (bzw. *tef-*) zugrundeliegt. Wortbildungsmäßig ist *ti(-i)-ib-ša-a-ri* vergleichbar u.a. mit *e-en-za-a-ri* 'Gottheit' (mit *-z-* aus *-s-* nach *-n-*; vgl. *eni* 'Gott').[17]

2.3. Schließlich ist aus der Bilingue die lexikalische Gleichsetzung von heth. *uttar* mit hurr. *ti-u̯u*$_ú$*-uš-ḫi-ni* (mit "Artikel" *-ni*) zu erwähnen (KBo 32 15 III/IV 8). Voraus geht eine längere Rede, auf die im Hurritischen wie folgt Bezug genommen wird: *ti-u̯u*$_ú$*-uš-ḫi-ni ḫa-ši-im-ma* (*ḫaš=i=mma*) = heth. *nu maḫḫan* ᵐ*Mēki[š ki] uttar išt[amašta]* "und als Meki [diese] Rede hö[rte] . . . " Der heth. Adverbialsatz wie auch vergleichbare Textstellen der Bilingue lassen allerdings statt *ḫaš=i=mma* eher gerundiales *ḫaš=i=mai* erwarten (s. FsThomas 1988, 504f.). Aus dem Kontext bietet sich für hurr. *ti-u̯u*$_ú$*-uš-ḫi* am ehesten die Bedeutung "Rede" an.[18] Auch diesem Ausdruck liegt die Wurzel *tif-* (bzw. *tef-*) zugrunde. Somit ergeben sich für diese Wurzel folgende Ableitungselemente: *-e* (Stammvokal; 2.1),[19] *-šāri* (2.2), *-(u)šḫi* (2.3).

3. *Hurritische Wörter für "Weide, weiden"*

Für "Weide" überliefert uns die Bilingue zunächst den hurr. Ausdruck **nau̯ni*; er ist in der mit Possessivsuffix der 3. Pers. Sing. versehenen Genitivform *na-ú-ni-i-e* 'seiner Weide' enthalten (KBo 32 14 I 5; vgl. Xenia 21 [1988] 102;

[16] Zur Analyse dieser beiden Sätze s. E. Neu, *Xenia* 21 (1988) 106f. Im Gegensatz zu hurr. *uli* 'andere(r)' bedarf heth. *tamai* eines Stützwortes. Entsprechendes gilt etwa auch für heth. *ta-a-an*, das vorhergehendes *telipuri* als Stützwort zu sich nimmt, während in der hurr. Vorlage das Zahlwort *šinzi* (wohl Abstrakbildung) ohne *ḫalzi* stehen kann; vgl. Neu, *Hethitica* 9 (1988) 169 Anm. 32.

[17] Vgl. V. Haas bei E. Neu, *Xenia* 21 (1988) 115 Anm. 28 Daß das konsonantische Element der komplexen Zeichen *u̯a*$_e$, *u̯e*$_e$, *u̯i*$_i$ usw. im Hurritischen den Reibelaut [*f*] bezeichnet, erscheint mir noch nicht endgültig gesichert.

[18] Im Keššе-Epos (KUB 47 1 I 7) ist der Essiv *ti-u̯u*$_u$*-uš-ḫa* bezeugt.

[19] Ob man als Stammbildungsvokal *-e* oder *-i* anzusetzen hat, erscheint mir noch nicht endgültig geklärt. Für *-i* spricht z.B. die Graphie *ti-i-u̯i*$_i$*-na* KUB 47 1 I 8; vgl. auch die unterschiedlichen Graphien bei Laroche, *GLH* 268. Zu *ti-u̯e-e-e*ᴹᴱŠ 'choses' (Mitt. I 80) s. W. L. Moran, *Les Lettres d'El-Amarna. Correspondance diplomatique du pharaon* (Traduction de W. L. Moran avec la collaboration de V. Haas et G. Wilhelm; traduction française de D. Collon et H. Cazelles; Paris 1987) 140.

hier auch zum engeren Kontext). Gemeint ist an der Belegstelle konkret das Weideland auf einem Berg. Mit "Artikel" erscheint das Wort für "Weide" in der Form *na-a-ú-un-ne* bzw. *na-a-ú-un-né* (vgl. Laroche, GLH 180 sub *naunni*). Die Verbalwurzel *nau̯-*[20] liegt der prädikativen intransitiven Partizipialform *na-a-u̯a*$_a$ 'weidet' (KBo 32 14 I 26) zugrunde.

Jüngst hat G. Wilhem (SMEA 29, 1992, 247) überzeugend in einem Text aus Nuzi ein hurritisches Substantiv *suḫrušše bzw. suġrošše* in der Bedeutung "Wiese" erschlossen (Etwa auch "Weide"?, E.N.).

In der Pluralform *na-i-ḫé-e-na* (mit "Artikel")[21] überliefert uns die Bilingue ein weiteres Wort für "Weide": *naiḫe* (KBo 32 14 I 27). Im Kontextzusammenhang bezeichnet es aus der Sicht eines Rehbockes besonders saftiges, daher von ihm erstrebtes, jedoch nicht erreichbares Weideland jenseits eines Flusses. Wortbildungsmäßig ist eine etymologische Verknüpfung mit *nau̯-* "weiden" (s. oben) naheliegend, jedoch lautlich schwierig.

4. *Zu hurritischen Partizipialbildungen*

Im Gegensatz zum indogermanischen Hethitischen verfügt die hurritische Grammatik über eine große Anzahl infiniter Verbalformen.[22] Zur Wiedergabe hurr. Gerundien oder Partizipien behilft sich das Hethitische oft mit Adverbial- oder Attributivsätzen.

4.1. Zu der hurr. Verbalwurzel *pa-* 'bauen' überliefert uns die Bilingue das prädikative transitive Partizip *pa-a-aš-tu-u-um* (*pa=ašt=u=m*) = heth. *ú-e-te-et* '(er) baute' (KBo 32 14 Rs. 35 bzw. 41).[23] Demgegenüber wird das hurr. Partizip *pa-i-ri* (*pa=i=ri*) 'der gebaut hat' aus folgendem Kontext im Hethitischen durch einen Relativsatz (*ú-e-te-et-ma-an ku-iš* 'wer aber sie, scil. Mauer, gebaut hat . . . ') wiedergegeben: *pa-i-ri-ma u-bi-né-eš ši-da-a-ra* (*šid=ar=a*) *šu-ḫu-un-né-eš* KBo 32 14 Rs. 36 "und die törichte Mauer verflucht den, der (sie) gebaut hat".[24] Passivisch hat man dagegen die im Ergativ auftretende Partizipialform *pa-i-li-i̯a-né-eš* in folgendem Satz zu verstehen: *i-i̯a-at pa-i-li-i̯a-né-eš* [*ši-d*]*a*[*-a-r*]*a* *šu-ḫu-un-né-eš* KBo 32 14 Rs. 38f. "warum (*ii̯a* = heth. *ku̯at*) verflucht mich

[20] Möglicherweise besteht ein etymologischer Zusammenhang mit akkad. *nawûm* 'Weidegebiet; Steppe' (*AHw* II, 771). Zu *na-a-u̯a*$_a$ 'weidet' in seinem engeren Kontext wie auch zu dem vielleicht zur gleichen Wurzel gehörigen 'Glossenkeilwort' *na-ú-i-la-aš* (Genitiv) s. bei H. Otten, *StBoT*, Beiheft 1 (1988) 40. Zu akkad. *nawûm* und Verwandtem vgl. A. Malamat, in *Biblical Archaeology Today*, 240f.

[21] Dazu gehört attributiv die pluralische Pronominalform *i-ša-a-u̯e*$_e$*-na*, die mit abweichender Graphie ibid. I 29 im Singular auftritt (*e-ša-a-bé-e*) und im Hethitischen durch neutrisches *ki* 'dieses' (zu *ka-*) wiedergegeben wird. Hurr. *e/išau̯e* "jenseitig", *agabe* "diesseitig".

[22] Vgl. Wilhelm, SCCNH 2:331ff.; Neu, *FsThomas*, 503ff.

[23] Vgl. Neu, *Das Hurritische*, 7 mit Anm. 15.

[24] Zur Bildungsweise dieser hurr. Partizipien, auch im Urartäischen, s. Wilhelm, *Xenia* 21 (1988) 50ff. Zu der Vorstellung, daß Gegenstände zu ihrem Verfertiger sprechen, vgl. Neu, *Das Hurritische*, 27, dort auch zur Gleichung hurr. *u-u̯e*$_e$*-né-eš* bzw. (wie hier) *u-bi-né-eš* = heth. *marlanza* 'töricht, einfältig, tumb'.

(*-tta*, hier *-t*) die (von mir) gebaute Mauer?" Die heth. Übersetzung dieses Satzes zeigt folgenden Wortlaut (KBo 32 14 Rs. 45): *ku-u̯a-at ú-e-te-nu-un ku-in ku-ut-ta-an nu-mu ḫu-u-ur-za-ki-zi* 'warum verflucht mich die Mauer, die ich gebaut habe?'[25] Die auf der partizipialen Basis **pa=ili* beruhende Weiterbildung *pailii̯ani* (hier im Ergativ) wird in der heth. übersetzung durch einen Relativsatz im Aktiv(!) umschrieben.

4.2. Von der hurr. Verbalwurzel *tab/w-* 'gießen'[26] sind in der Bilingue die gleichen Partizipialbildungen wie von der Wurzel *pa-* 'bauen' (§4.1) bezeugt. Da ist zunächst wieder das prädikative Partizip *ta-u̯a*$_{a}$*-aš-tu-u-um* (*taw=ašt=u-m*) = heth. *la-a-ḫu-uš* '(er) goß' (KBo 32 14 I 43 bzw. II 42, 43) zu nennen. Dem Partizip *pairi* 'der gebaut hat' entspricht wortbildungsmäßig *ta-bi-ri*(*-i*) 'der gegossen hat' (KBo 32 14 I 46, 47),[27] und zu der ergativischen Partizipialform *pa-i-li-i̯a-né-eš* bildet *ta-bi-li-i̯a-ni-iš* (KBo 14 32 I 53) die morphologische Entsprechung: *i-i̯a-a*(-)*ta-bi-li-i̯a-ni-iš*[28] *ši-ta-a-ra ka-bal-li-iš* 'warum verflucht mich das (von mir) gegossene Kupfer?'

Zur Wurzel *tab/w-* 'gießen' gehört die Berufsbezeichnung *tabli* '(Kupfer-)Gießer', in der Bilingue nur im Ergativ mit "Artikel" bezeugt: *ta-bal-li-iš* (KBo 32 14 I 42, 55), in der hethitischen Übersetzung sumerographisch durch ᴸᵁ́SIMUG (geschrieben: E.DÉ; DÉ 'gießen') wiedergegeben. Dem gleichen Sumerogramm entspricht in der hurr. Vorlage auch der mit "Artikel" versehene Absolutiv *tab-re-e-in-ni* (KBo 14 32 I 50, 52), dem die Partizipialbildung *tabiri/e* (s. oben) zugrundeliegen könnte, die vielleicht infolge Akzentverlagerung ihren Zweitsilbenvokal *-i-* durch Synkopierung eingebüßt hat: **taw=ire=ni=ni* (mit sogenanntem Individualisierungsmorphem *-ni* und "Artikel" *-ni* bzw. *-né*).

4.3. Erwähnung verdient auch das partizipiale Nebeneinander von *ši-i̯a-lu-u-šu-um* (*šii̯al=uš=u=m*; prädikativ), *ši-i̯a-le-e-ri* bzw. *ši-i̯a-li-ri* (*šii̯al=e/iri*) und *ši-i̯a-li-i-e-né*[*-eš*][29] (KBo 32 14 Rs. 56, 57, 60). Hurr. *šii̯al-*, das vielleicht noch weiter zu zerlegen ist,[30] hat man wohl mit heth. *titnu-* 'hinstellen, errichten' gleichzusetzen (Die heth. Übersetzung ist für diesen Textabschnitt weitgehend weggebrochen).

4.4. Isoliert steht bisher die im Ergativ bezeugte passivische Partizipialform *še-e-du-i-li-i̯a-ni-iš* (KBo 32 14 I 10), aus der im Vergleich mit den unter §4.1 und §4.2 behandelten, wortbildungsmäßig entsprechenden Formationen ein hurr. Verbum **šedu̯-* zu gewinnen ist, dem auf Grund der heth. Übersetzung die Bedeutung

[25] Die heth. *-šk-*Form **ḫurt=sk=i=zi* gebe ich nicht eigens durch Adverbien wie "immer wieder, wiederholt, mehrfach" oder "dauernd" wieder, da mit dem *-šk-* Formans (hurr. *-ar-*) hier doch wohl lediglich angezeigt werden soll, daß die Verfluchung aus mehreren Flüchen besteht.

[26] Vgl. Neu, *Das Hurritische*, sub *tab/w-*.

[27] Damit dürfte sumerisch tabira, tibira zusammenzubringen sein; s. Wilhelm, *Xenia* 21 (1988) 50ff.; E. Neu, *Das Hurritische*, 27 Anm. 83.

[28] Die vorliegende Schreibung beruht auf Haplographie für zu erwartendes *i-i̯a-at ta-bi-li-i̯a-ni-iš* (vgl. §4.1).

[29] Auffallend ist die Schreibung *-li-i-e-* (von mir am Original 1989 kollationiert) gegenüber *-li-i̯a-* in den unter §4.1 und §4.2 behandelten Partizipialformen *pa-i-li-i̯a-né-eš* und *ta-bi-li-i̯a-ni-iš*.

[30] Zu einer Verbalwurzel *ši-* bzw. *ši-* s. Wilhelm, *Xenia* 21 (1988) 56.

heth. *u̯arganu-* ‘fett machen, mästen’ zugeordnet werden darf: hurr. *i-i̯a-a-at še-e-du-i-li-i̯a-ni-iš ši-ta-a-ra* (*šid=ar=a*) *na-a-al-li-iš* (Ergativ von **nāli=ni*) ‘warum verflucht mich der (von mir) gemästete Rehbock?’ In der heth. Übersetzung wird der Fragesatz der hurr. Vorlage durch einen Aussagesatz wiedergegeben: *a-li-i̯a-na-an ku-in u̯a-ar-ga-nu-nu-un ki-nu-na-mu a-ap-pa ḫu-ur-za-ki-zi* (vgl. §4.1) ‘der Rehbock, den ich gemästet habe, verflucht mich jetzt aber hinterher’.[31] Die Abfolge strukturell vergleichbarer Textabschnitte legt jedoch die Vermutung nahe daß das heth. Frageadverb *kuu̯at* ‘warum?’ (= hurr. *ii̯a*) hier irrtümlicherweise ausgelassen wurde; man hätte es sich syntaktisch dann vor *alii̯anan* zu denken.

5. *Das hurritische Negationssuffix -ma*

5.1. In “Kleine Beiträge zur churritischen Grammatik” (MVAeG 42/2, Leipzig 1939) hatte J. Friedrich hurr. Verbalformen auf *-iāma* als negierte Futura verstehen wollen. Seine diesbezügliche Auffassung stützte er u.a. auf folgendes Satzgefüge des Mittani-Briefes (IV 54–55): *a-i-ma-a-ni-i-in* ᵐ*Ma-né-en še-e-ni-iu̯-u̯u-uš pa-aš-ši-a-a-ma u-u-li-ma-a-an pa-aš-še-e-ta* ‘wenn mein Bruder aber (den) Mane nicht schicken wird, sondern einen anderen schicken wird . . . ’[32] Friedrich bemerkt dazu: “Ich suche also in *paššiāma* einen dem positiven *paššeta* ‘er wird schicken’ entsprechenden negativen Ausdruck ‘er wird nicht schicken’.”

E. A. Speiser (*Introduction to Hurrian* [New Haven 1941] 164f.) hat Friedrichs Interpretation von *-i-a-a-ma* als “3 p. of the negated future” übernommen, zugleich aber auf die Problematik deren morphologischer Analyse hingewiesen. In seiner Dissertation “A Grammar of the Hurrian Language” (Brandeis University 1964, 205f.) buchte F. W. Bush *paššiāma* und andere damit vergleichbare Verbalformen unter der Kapitelüberschrift “The negative suffix *-ma*”, sah also die eigentliche Negation im auslautenden Suffix *-ma*, doch kommentiert er (ibid. 368 Anm. 132) diese Auffassung mit den Worten: “ . . . but this is problematical”. In der 1987 von W. L. Moran (in Zusammenarbeit mit G. Wilhelm) vorgelegten Übersetzung des Mittani-Briefes[33] wird *paššiāma* im Sinne von Friedrich übersetzt, wenn es dort nämlich heißt: “Si mon frère n’envoie pas Mane et envoie quelqu’un d’autre. . . . ”

5.2. Die hurritisch-hethitische Bilingue bietet nun zwei klare Beispiele für die hier angesprochene negierte Verbalbildung. An zwei Textstellen nämlich wird hurr. *a-ri-i̯a-am-ma* (zum Verbum *ar-* ‘geben’ s. Laroche, *GLH* 52) jeweils mit heth. *Ú-UL pa-a-i* ‘er gibt nicht/wird nicht geben’ übersetzt. Beide Sätze, von denen einer im folgenden zitiert sei, weisen vom Kontext her auf futurische Interpretation dieser Verbalform: hurr. ᵐ*Za-a-za-al-la-aš* (Ergativ) *ki-re-en-zé a-ri-i̯a-am-ma*

[31] Zu hurr. *nāli* s. Neu, *IBS* 52 (1987) 177.

[32] J. Friedrich hatte in seiner deutschen Übersetzung u.a. hinter “wenn” ein Fragezeichen und die betreffende negierte Verbalform in Sperrdruck gesetzt. Zu dieser Textstelle s. auch J. Friedrich, *Handbuch der Orientalistik*, I. Abteilung, 2. Band, 1. und 2. Abschnitt, Lieferung 2 (Leiden/Köln 1969) 19 (§49 c 2), 29 (als “noch unklar” bezeichnet).

[33] Moran, *Les Lettres d’El-Amarna*, 149 (§31).

KBo 32 15 IV/III 17f. = heth. ᵐ*Za-a-za-al-la-aš* (Nominativ) *pa-ra-a tar-nu*[*-mar*] *Ú-UL pa-a-i* (wörtlich:) 'Zazalla wird Freilassung nicht geben'.[34] Die Bilingue bestätigt also aufs beste die Richtigkeit Friedrichs Auffassung bezüglich *paššiāma* des Mittani-Briefes (oben §5.1).

Allerdings fällt die unterschiedliche Schreibweise zwischen *a-ri-i̯a-am-ma* der Bilingue und den entsprechenden Verbalformen des Mittani-Briefes (*pa-aš-ši-a-a-ma* IV 55, *gu-li-a-a-ma* II 105, 106, IV 21, 27) auf. Da die Bilingue als die frühere Überlieferung keine Pleneschreibung des vorletzten *a* zeigt, besteht wenig Anlaß, diese als phonematische Länge zu werten, näherliegend wäre vielleicht, sie als Markierung des Wortakzentes zu verstehen. Inwieweit die Doppelschreibung des *m* etwas mit der Unterscheidung von Fortis und Lenis zu tun hat, müßte noch in größerem Zusammenhang geprüft werden. Die Verbalform *a-ri-i̯a-am-ma* scheint mir aus transitivem *arii̯a* (3. Pers. Sing. "Präs.") und dem eigentlichen Negationssufix -(*m*)*ma* zu bestehen; entsprechend sind die oben genannten Verbalformen des Mittani-Briefes als *pašši*(*i̯*)*a=ma* (vgl. Laroche, *GLH* 197) und *guli* (*i̯*) *a=ma* (vgl. Laroche, *GLH* 151) zu verstehen, so daß sich aus dem Vergleich der zweifachen Überlieferung tatsächlich ein Negationssuffix /-ma/ ergibt (vgl. Bush, "Grammar of Hurrian," 205). Die betreffenden negierten Verbalformen (bisher sicher nur für die 3. Pers. Sing. nachgewiesen) scheinen (auch) futurische Konnotation zu haben.

6. Überschaut man abschließend noch einmal die hier behandelten fünf Themenbereiche, dürfte deutlich werden, daß die hurritisch-hethitische Bilingue uns nicht nur eine Fülle an neuem hurritischen Sprachmaterial überliefert, das dank der beigefügten hethitischen Übersetzung erschlossen werden kann, sondern auch bisher an anderen Texten Erarbeitetes zu bestätigen bzw. für bisher noch Problematisches Entscheidungshilfen zu geben vermag.

[34] Zu hurr. *kirenzi* = heth. *para tarnumar* s. Neu, *Das Hurritische*, 13f.

The Scribes of Nuzi and Their Activities Relative to Arms According to Palace Texts*

PAOLA NEGRI SCAFA

General Aspects

One interesting aspect of the Nuzi texts is that they provide sufficiently articulated documentation on the presence of scribes in the various sectors of social and economic life, outside their primary function. Elsewhere,[1] we have already attempted to provide a preliminary view of textual occurrences in which there is an indication that the scribes had activities other than drawing up documents. It was also ascertained that about one-fourth of the scribes that we know about had a responsibility in another area of activity.

Beyond a panoramic view of these activities, it should also be very useful if we could evaluate to what degree the scribes participated in these tasks,[2] whether they shared them with others or held them exclusively. This work proposes to respond to such questions pertaining to one sector for which, as is seen in the article cited above, the documentation is sufficiently large: arms and materials for military use (with the exclusion, for the time being, of barley rations, wagons and horses).[3]

The weapons cited in the Nuzi texts are:[4] *arītu* ("shield"), *gurpisu* ("helmet"[5] to which *kalku* "visor, brim" is connected), *ḫaṣṣinnu* ("battleaxe"), *iltuḫḫu* ("whip"), *išpatu* ("quiver," to which the terms *ḫillu*, *illakkannu* and *ilmû*[6] are connected), *paṭru* ("sword"), *qaštu* ("bow"), *sariam* ("cuirass" to which the term

* Translated from the Italian by C. Faith Richardson.

[1] Cf. P. Negri Scafa, "Gli scribi di Nuzi in funzioni diverse da redattori di testi," *Mesopotamia* 21 (1986), 249–59.

[2] What was considered the principal activity of a scribe is shown by the use of the professional adjective in the witness lists.

[3] With the expression "arms and materials for military use" we want to indicate both real offensive and defensive weapons (bows and arrows, etc.) and objects such as metal plates that are included in their construction.

[4] Cf. E. Salonen, *Die Waffen der Alten Mesopotamier*, Helsinki 1965, as well as T. Kendall, "The Helmets of the Warriors at Nuzi" in D. I. Owen and M. A. Morrison, eds., *Studies on the Civilization and Culture of Nuzi and the Hurrians* (= *SCCNH*) 1, Winona Lake 1981, pp. 201–31. Kendall is also author of "Warfare and Military Matters in the Nuzi Tablets" (unpublished thesis, Brandeis University, which I have been unable to consult).

[5] Kendall, *SCCNH* 1 (1981), op. cit.: "helmet"; E. Salonen, *Waffen*, op. cit., pp. 101 and 103: "coat of mail in leather with metal plates"; Salonen's definition is also repeated by *AHw* 929 and *CAD* G 139 whereas *CAD* A/2 has "helmet" as the meaning for *gurpisu*.

[6] *Ḫillu* is a "synonym for quiver" and the other two words are "decorations on the quiver": cf. Salonen, *Waffen*, op. cit., pp. 77 and 80.

kurṣimadu [*kurṣindu*] "metal plates"[7] is connected), *šukitu* ("spear" or "wagon"[8]), *tutiwa* ("breast-plates"). To the weapons cited above are to be added the arrows for which the texts report an abundant terminology: *qanû* ("arrows" or "reeds for arrows"), *šukudu*, *šiltaḫu* and *ḫurḫutūtu* ("arrows"), *šulu* (type of reed for arrows).

Texts relative to this subject come from rooms L1, L14, L27, L29, M79, M89, N120, R76 and R81 of the Palace; most of them come from rooms M79, M89, N120, R76 and R81. Materials coming from rooms L14 and L27 are secondary and less specific inasmuch as they are lists of various objects. However, this does not exhaust the documentation in this respect. In fact, texts with regard to arms also come from areas outside the Palace. It is necessary to take particular notice of material found in rooms D3 and D6 which have been recognized as having a close connection with Palace documents.[9] Tablets found in rooms C28, F24, F25, G29 and G73 are to be added to the texts from rooms D3 and D6.

Even the surrounding area has provided texts on the subject as in the case of the archive of Šilwa-Tešup (rooms A23 and A26) as well as rooms A16 and A34 (the archive of Akawatil s. Zike) from the same complex A (eastern suburban area). Even complex T (western suburban area) produced texts in which weapons are cited: two contracts of Teḫip-Tilla and two lists of arms that came from room T12 and consequently concern the cities of Šuriniwe-Purulliwe and belong to the archive of Kel-Tešup s. Ḫutija.[10] There are also texts relative to weapons for which no provenance is recorded.

However, documentation relative to the scribes and their responsibility in this chosen sector comes primarily from the Palace. Hence it will be documentation of "palatine" origin to which we will give our attention in order to arrive at our predetermined goal. Therefore we intend to:

(1) identify and analyze activities relative to weapons registered in the Palace texts;

(2) identify officials and different categories of persons concerned with the various processes (production; distribution, etc.) registered by the documents;

(3) seek to clarify the role of the scribes within these processes.

Then, with regard to the use of documentation from outside the Palace found both in other parts of the citadel and in the suburban area, it is going to be pointed out that the extra-palatine documentation is of particular interest because it pro-

[7] Kendall, *SCCNH* 1 (1981), op. cit., p. 322, n. 61.

[8] Cf. W. Mayer, *UF* 8, p. 212, who proposes a parallel between the term *suḫitu* of the EA texts and the Nuzi word *šukitu.* The context in which the word appears at Nuzi would seem to confirm Mayer's interpretation (HSS XV 167:117: 1 *šu-ki-tu*$_4$ *ù 1* ANŠE.KUR.RA). Also see G. Wilhelm, *Das Archiv des Šilwa-teššup*, III Heft. Wiesbaden 1986.

[9] For this room's connection to the Palace, see E. R. Lacheman in *Le Palais et la Royauté* (= RAI 19), 359–71. For information about the rooms where the texts were found, see the data provided by publications of the texts. For texts coming from the Palace also see W. Mayer, *Nuzi-Studien. I. Die Archive des Palastes und die Prosopographie der Berufe.* AOAT 205/1, Neukirchen Vluyn 1978.

[10] For the connection between the texts of room T12 and the archive of Kel-tešup and his family, see G. Dosch and K. Deller, "Die Familie Kizzuk. Sieben Kassitengenerationen in Temtena und Šuriniwe," *SCCNH* 1 (1981), 92, n. 2.

vides data both on a "circulation" of arms between persons whose connection with the Palace was somewhat indirect (archives of Teḫip-Tilla s. Puḫi-šenni and Akawatil s. Zike) and on the existence of archives outside the Palace characterized by a complex organization (archives of Šilwa-tešup *mār šarri* and Kel-tešup s. Ḫutija). Consequently, although the subject of the present study is the process relative to the Palace and registered in documents from that provenance, in case we recognize in these external archives some analogy with the palatine ones, it will be useful to take note of the possible comparative data obtainable from them—especially in the archive of Šilwa-Tešup—in order to clarify and complete, where necessary, the information received from the texts coming from the Palace.

Apart from the subject at hand, these documents can be classified as to type and structure as follows:

(1) *Registrations of distributions or allotments of (completed) weapons.* The Palace areas that have produced texts of this kind are rooms M79 (HSS XIII 60, HSS XIII 74, HSS XIII 85, HSS XIII 175, HSS XIV 222, HSS XIV 224, HSS XIV 225, HSS XIV 228, *EN* IX/1 335), M89 (HSS XIV 221) and R76 (HSS XIII 71, HSS XIV 220=626, HSS XV 17). With regard to the subject of the registrations found in rooms M79, M89 and R76, they are primarily arrows (with the exception of HSS XV 17). However, from documentation outside the Palace we know there were also allocations of outfits of armor (cf. HSS XV 6, room C28) and swords (HSS XIV 263b).[11]

(2) *Registrations of distributions or allotments of materials for the making of weapons.* Under this type are texts rather similar to those indicated in point 1). These texts come principally from room M79 (HSS XIII 99, HSS XIII 100, HSS XIII 103, HSS XIII 206, HSS XIV 223 and HSS XIV 227) to which we add a text coming from room L29 (HSS XIII 116). Note that even in this case we are dealing almost exclusively with arrows or materials related to arrows.[12]

(3) *Lists of various objects among which are weapons or materials for their construction.* One text comes from room M79 (HSS XIV 283=608). Three other texts come from rooms L27, R76, R81 (HSS XV 130, HSS XIV 235=529 and HSS XIII 436). The rest of the Nuzi documentation is from outside the Palace.[13]

4) *Lists of persons and the condition of their respective weapons or outfits of armor.* Texts of this type come from room N120 (HSS XV 2, HSS XV 3, HSS XV 12, HSS XV 14, HSS XV 15, HSS XV 16, HSS XV 18, HSS XV 20, HSS XV 21, HSS XV 37, HSS XV 39, HSS XV 50, HSS XV 305). The objects cited are of various kinds: from armor to metal plates, helmets, bows (and a statement about their condition).[14]

[11] Texts of this kind have been found outside the Palace in room C28 (HSS XV 6) and room A16 (HSS XIV 226), A23 (HSS IX 55, HSS XIII 421) and A26 (HSS XIII 354).

[12] Texts of this kind from outside the Palace have been found in rooms C28 (HSS XV 5), F25 (HSS XV 9), A23 (HSS XV 9b, HSS XV 208) and A26 (HSS XV 11).

[13] Materials have been found outside the Palace in rooms F24 and F25 (HSS XIV 163 and HSS XV 142), A26 (HSS XIII 195 and HSS XV 81) and A34 (HSS V 106).

[14] Texts of this kind have been found outside the Palace in rooms D6 (HSS XV 7), G29 (HSS XV 8) and G73 (HSS XV 10) of the citadel and T12 (JEN 527 and JEN 533) of the western suburban area. For a few texts of this kind, the provenance is unknown (HSS XV 4, HSS XV 23).

(5) *Contracts or certificates.* There are a limited number of tablets in which weapons are the subject of a contract or certificate. All have been found outside the Palace,[15] except for one (HSS XV 38) found in room L1.

If we consider the family of Teḫip-Tilla as a model for Nuzi chronology,[16] the texts go back over a span of time from the third to the fifth generations of Teḫip-Tilla. The fact that the material is both heterogeneous by typology and refers primarily to a specific period of time does not hinder the reconstruction of a general picture of Palace activities in this sector. In fact, we are interested here in identifying the procedures adopted to administer and coordinate the arms sector. Because of the repetitiveness and typical crystallization of any bureaucracy, these procedures included within the administrative and bureaucratic sphere of Palace life persisted over time (especially when, as in this case, they did not cover an extremely long period) and are not influenced by incidental facts. Particular external events (threats in border areas, the final crisis) can affect the quantity of documents relative to specific phases of the procedure (see, for example, the number of texts from room N120) but not cause the appearance of a process. Besides, the arms sector was too vital for the very survival of the kingdom of Arrapḫa for it not to have been necessary to administer it throughout the whole history of the kingdom.

Analyzing the texts under the profile of activities described in them, it is possible to observe how in some way the various types of texts correspond to different phases in the whole process that begins with the Palace distributing the materials necessary for the construction of arms and continues with the distribution of completed items to those who may be described as the "ultimate consumers." Finally, the texts listed under number 4 provide data on a further form of control by the Palace with regard to the use of materials by the so-called "ultimate consumers."

Phases of the Process

(A) Distribution of materials for the construction of arms

Although some texts from the Palace give us a glimpse, among other things, of a few methods for acquiring materials and primary resources, those that have been recovered up to this time do not identify the weapons (with the exception perhaps of HSS XVI 450 where there is reference to 4 minas of copper for arrows). However, the distribution of materials for the construction of arms is documented.

The most linear type of transaction relative to this is registered in HSS XIII 99, HSS XIII 100, HSS XIII 103, HSS XIII 116, HSS XIII 206, HSS XIV 223, where some persons (who seal the text) take (*ilqū/ilteqū*) or receive (*nadnū*) materials to manufacture (*ana epēši*) weapons. Sometimes (HSS XIII 103, HSS XIII

[15] *JEN* 196, *JEN* 519, HSS V 44, HSS V 93, Genava 15 (1967), 10, no. 3.

[16] Cf. most recently A. H. Friedmann, "Toward a Relative Chronology at Nuzi," *SCCNH* 2 (1987), 109–30.

206) a person is indicated from whom the material is consigned (*ašar* PN). In texts dealing with the manufacture of arrows, the material used is cane.

The Palace performed the function of supplying materials even for use in other localities, as is shown by HSS XIV 227 in which the *ḫazannu* of Lupti, Puitae, is said to have received 10 minas of copper for arrowheads from Erwi-šarri (*šakin bīti* of the Nuzi Palace) to be delivered to the *geltuḫle* of that city.

In summary the actions that characterize this phase are: (a) delivery of materials "inside the Palace" for the manufacture of weapons, presumably for the Palace storehouse; (b) delivery of materials "outside the Palace," presumably for the needs of other localities (which, however, come to the Palace storehouses in some way) provided with local labor.

(B) Distribution of weapons

With regard to the distribution of complete weapons, the Nuzi Palace set forth duties of storehouse and center for circulation of goods; these are duties quite consistent with its typical functions and already recognizable in the section on the distribution of materials. Even in this case, texts were recovered from rooms M79, from which came many texts regarding the activities of the *šakin bīti*, and R76 which, among others, has provided administrative texts of various kinds.

As in the case of the distribution of materials, the documents deal primarily with arrows (HSS XIII 71, HSS XIII 74, HSS XIII 75, HSS XIII 85, HSS XIII 175, HSS XIV 224, HSS XIV 225), although texts coming from various areas outside the Palace speak specifically of armor provided by it.[17] Moreover, HSS XV 17 (room R76) describes which outfits of armor went in and out of the storehouses.

A particular type of activity with regard to keeping track of arrows is documented in HSS XIII 60 where 50 arrows are consigned to Kimil-Tešup s. Šenni—a Ḫanigalbatian of the *emantu* of Ilaja s. Ḫapiru—and given back to the Palace by him.[18] Likewise, in a similar situation to which HSS IV 220=626 (room R76) seems to make reference, it is said that the *šakin bīti*, Erwi-šarri, consigned thousands of arrows "on loan" to the scribe Aril-lumti.[19] Moreover, arms from the Palace were also sent to other cities such as Erḫaḫḫe (HSS XIV 224), Šauawe (HSS XIII 71), Ḫurasina rabu (HSS XIV 225), Tarbašḫe (HSS XIII 175) and Tarmike (EN 9/1 335).

In summary, Palace activities expected in this phase are:

(a) Distribution of arms (and armor) for the needs of the cities of Nuzi, similar to what happened in the manufacturing phase;

[17] Cf. HSS XV 6, room C28.

[18] Similarly in HSS XIV 263b (of unknown provenance) Ḫutip-apu s. Tešup-nirari takes four swords from the Palace which must be returned.

[19] The use of the expression *ana ḫubulli* is particularly interesting. It is clear both from what is "borrowed" and the structure of the text that it was not a "normal" loan and hence the term here is used with a slightly different meaning than what is attested even in dictionaries.

(b) Distribution of arms to cities dependent in some way on the Nuzi Palace and its administration;

(c) Specific distributions in which weapons are perhaps consigned in an extremely short time, probably not for combative (offensive or defensive) intentions, but for symbolic reasons to persons who assume the responsibility for resupply. It is interesting to note in this regard that even foreigners like the Ḫanigalbatian Kimil-Tešup s. Šenni had the right to come to the Palace storehouses to withdraw and return weapons. We know that foreigners came there even for withdrawals of longer duration.[20]

(C) Audit of supplies of weapons

There were two types of activities in the "audit phase": (1) meticulous verification of agreement between written registrations and activity in the storehouse; (2) an interest in tracking the whereabouts of the weapons even after they were distributed.

Actually the real "audit" would have been the first type which was the administrative verification so necessary within a well-organized bureaucracy, whereas the second type of "audit" included special oversight of the storehouse. However, documentation on the first type is extremely poor and elusive, actually only brief notes on written registrations, as is shown by HSS XIV 263=608 and, from outside the Palace although related to it, HSS XV 6.

The second type of "audit" is better documented. Evidence of it comes from lists of persons and individual supplies of weapons that principally came from room N120. The impressive number of tablets from a single area and the fact that they belonged to the last generations of Nuzi have attracted the attention of scholars who have analyzed these texts from a "historic" perspective in order to draw as much information as possible about the end of the city and kingdom of Arrapḫa. However, what interests us here is that the Palace was preoccupied with meticulous descriptions of the condition of the armor of the men and horses, carefully listing the names of the persons who came to the arms section of the Palace administration.

The registrations include:

(1) The condition of weapons consigned to different individuals (HSS XV 21, HSS XV 37, HSS XV 18). Sometimes also registered is the name of whomever has taken the goods on consignment and is responsible for its distribution to others;

(2) Persons who put back their armament after having lost their equipment in a "campaign" (HSS XV 3);

(3) List of persons who "did not go" (to Zizza) and their respective weapons that consequently were not taken out of the storehouse (HSS XV 10, HSS XV 14, HSS XV 15, HSS XV 16, HSS XV 20, HSS XV 305). Persons are indicated both individually and under the name of the one responsible for the group;

[20] On relations between Nuzi and Ḫanigalbat, cf. C. Zaccagnini, *Le rapports entre Nuzi et Hanigalbat*, *Assur* 2/1 (1979), 1–34.

(4) Lists of persons remaining in the Palace and the condition of their cuirasses (HSS XV 12, HSS XV 39).

In a certain sense these detailed registrations concluded the process that was begun with the distribution of materials for the manufacturing of arms. Yet, the fact that by this means they intended to keep track of the condition of weapons, even after delivery to persons concerned (the "ultimate consumers"), leaves us to understand again that the Palace could take part in restoring armaments in poor condition, confirming once more its function as storehouse/center for the distribution of goods.

Actors in the Process

(A) Those in charge of distribution

As we have seen previously, there was more than one phase or time when the Palace was called upon to allocate weapons or goods connected to them: typically a phase relative to the manufacture of weapons (with the distribution of the materials), a phase for the distribution of completed weapons and, as has been pointed out, also a time for restoring weapons and armor that had deteriorated in some way. It is most appropriate to begin by dealing with the actors in the process, starting with those employed in distribution.

It must be emphasized that the structure of the text tends to give prominence not so much to the person who consigns as to the person who receives, inasmuch as the latter is considered responsible to the Palace. Consequently in expressions with the verb *nadānu* or *leqû*, the emphasis is always on the one who receives and not on the one who consigns.

To indicate who has the function of consigning weapons or materials for their manufacture, the texts refer both to *ša ekalli* (HSS XIII 99, 100, 116; HSS XIV 223) and to *šakin bīti* (HSS XIII 103, 206; HSS XIV 227). In HSS XIII 102 (whose evidence is corroborated by HSS XIII 85 where completed weapons are delivered and not just materials to construct them) both terms *šakin bīti* and *ša ekalli* appear. In this text it is specified that *mār šipri* Akap-tae s. Ariwakali and Unap-Tešup s. Arik-kaja receive materials from the Palace in order to make arrows, and *šakin bīti* Erwi-šarri is to deliver them. This leads to the conclusion that in such contexts *šakin bīti* and *ša ekalli* may be considered equivalents in some way, in the sense that when the Palace is mentioned it is plausible to consider that *šakin bīti* is intended. Mention of the *šakin bīti* in this function is not surprising since it confirms his position (drawn from other texts) as the one responsible for the movement of goods in and out of the Palace, which may have had Nuzi itself or some other city as a destination.

With regard to those receiving material, they belong in three different categories: (1) those employed in construction; (2) *mār šipri* (Akap-tae s. Ariwakal); (3) *ḫazannu* (Pui-tae *ḫazannu* of Lupti). Unap-Tešup s. Arik-kaja surely belongs in the first group, about which we will dwell at length below, as well as Ḫerikaja s. Šilwaja and Enna-mati s. fPuḫu-menni, as it is possible to infer from the structure of the text. The presence of a *mār šipri* and a *ḫazannu*, the first traditionally tied to activities of the transfer and movement of goods (see below) and the second also responsible for the administration of another city (Lupti is a case in point), confirms the function of the Palace as the source of provisions for the entire region. The text relative to *mār šipri* (HSS XIII 103) mentions that *sasinnu* Unap-Tešup s. Arik-kaja also received materials but reports that only Unap-Tešup affixed his seal. Was this an oversight or a clear indication of a difference of status and function? The presence of *mār šipri* leads us to assume that Unap-Tešup must have traveled outside of Nuzi (and hence happened to be the "one responsible" at the time of said removal). All things considered, was it always the *sasinnu* who was obliged to respond? The answer to this question is positive; we have two situations: (a) Nuzi artisans who served cities and other centers lacking attachés; (b) centers provided with their own employees (like Lupti), if the interpretation of "Bogenhersteller" as *geltuḫle*[21] is correct.

The situation with regard to the distribution of finished weapons is more difficult to describe. Although, even in this case, the emphasis is placed more on who withdraws than on who distributes, yet it is possible to perceive that the distribution function does not seem to be exclusively the prerogative of the *šakin bīti*. At least three texts refer to him or, more generally, to the Palace (also in this case meant to be equivalent?): HSS XIII 74, HSS XIV 220, HSS XIII 85. Moreover, we note the presence of *mār šipri*: Akap-urḫe, scribe and *mār šipri* of *šakin māti* Wantija,[22] withdrew weapons (HSS XIII 175); Tatip-Tešup, identified as a *mār šipri*, shipped weapons to the city of Šauawa (HSS XIII 71).

Yet, with regard to the distribution of completed arms, unlike what is attested for the distribution of materials for production—in which there is no mention that the materials are delivered for the work of an *iškaru*—the *iškaru* of a particular artisan appears as another possible source of supply. He was a *sasinnu* by the name of Unap-tae from whose work quota, according to the evidence of HSS XIV 221 (room M89), HSS XIV 228 (room M79) and EN 9/1 335 (room M79), (confirmed also by evidence outside the Palace in HSS IV 226, room A16), arrows were ordered for different persons: Apuška (HSS XIV 228), Puhi-šenni, a *ḫazannu* of a city whose name is lost (HSS XIV 221), WA[. . .] (HSS XIV 226) and Ḫašip-Tilla s. [. . .]-ja, whose professional title can be completed as [LÚ *la*]-*sī-mu*, who shipped arrows to the city of Tarmike. The evidence of EN 9/1 335, corroborated by the presence of a *ḫazannu* as recipient in HSS XIV 228, shows that Unap-tae's products were sent outside of the Palace and the city.

In most of the texts in this small group, it seems that an artisan's products were distributed directly to persons without inspection by an official. Hence, of great interest is EN 9/1 335 from which it is clear that operations were carried out

[21] According to M. Dietrich and O. Loretz, *WO* 3 (1966), 203, *geltuḫle* are understood as "Bogenhersteller."

[22] For the identification of Wantija with the *šakin māti*, cf. Mayer, *Nuzi-Studien* I, p. 203, and P. Negri Scafa, *Mesopotamia* 21 (1986), 256.

under the aegis of the *šukallu* Akija. We are dealing with a functionary different from a *šakin bīti* who elsewhere we have seen as a superintendent of envoys. Consequently, should we assume that there was an official, possibly different from a *šakin bīti*, even in other cases where the text indicates a direct order from an artisan? Or is the situation to which EN 9/1 335 refers different because the arrows concerned production (or allotment)[23] for the previous year (cf. l. 5: [. . .] *ša ša-ad-dá-aq-dá*)? Moreover, what is the relationship between *šukallu* and *lāsimu*?

With regard to persons who order or receive weapons on consignment, it would seem from an analysis of the documents that almost certainly an intermediary played a role between the Palace (or the *šakin bīti*) and those who were the final users. In fact:

(1) The great quantities taken on consignment without any mention of transport outside Nuzi (cf., e.g., HSS XIII 74, HSS XIII 85) show that even in cases where the weapons remained in the city, there was someone responsible for ordering and then distributing them. Indirect confirmation of there being someone in charge comes from HSS XIII 60 and HSS XIV 220 in which a delivery of weapons is registered in transit. Whoever the person who took them on consignment, the following names are registered: Šekar-Tilla s. Enna-mati, Wirraḫḫe, the scribe Aril-lumti, foreigners like Kimil-Tešup s. Šenni.

A prospographic analysis with regard to these persons would be of extreme importance since it would better illuminate the function of the scribe Aril-lumti within the process, but this is not particularly easy. In fact:

(a) The name of Šekar-Tilla s. Enna-mati (HSS XIII 74) is a *hapax*. Even an examination of texts that mention a Šekar-Tilla without the family name (about fifteen) is of no particular help. For example, it is possible to identify a Šekar-Tilla connected to the transport of barley (HSS XIV 233=580 and HSS XIV 579). There are certainly other Šekar-Tillas related to military activities (see Šekar-Tilla of the city of Zallu in HSS XV 18, or Šekar-Tilla who is under the responsibility (*ša* ŠU) of Tarmi-Tilla in HSS XV 15, HSS XV 39 and HSS XV 40). However, at the moment nothing emerges from an examination of the texts that would allow us to connect Šekar-Tilla s. Enna-mati with one of these other Šekar-Tillas.

(b) No family name is given to Wirraḫḫe (HSS XIII 85). Even in this case, at this stage of our studies, it is not possible from an examination of the texts in which this name occurs to connect the Wirraḫḫe of HSS XIII 85 with any other. He was very close to the king and his *entourage* (e.g., receives rations: HSS XIV 46, HSS XIV 48, HSS XIV 49, HSS XIV 53, HSS XIV 55, HSS XIV 57, HSS XIV 94).[24] Another Wirraḫḫe is connected with the movement of goods (barley, cf. HSS XV 264). There is also a Wirraḫḫe connected with military tablets: among these HSS XV 39 (the same one in which a Šekar-Tilla appears), HSS XV 34 (interesting for the presence of a *šukallu*, Akija, who in HSS XIV 135 is connected to *šakin māti* Wantija and now to a Wirraḫḫe). Hence, we have a series of

[23] This can only be conjecture because of gaps in the text.

[24] Can he be linked to the Wirraḫḫe *mār šarri*?

very allusive and suggestive elements but none clearly convincing in the present state of study.

(c) As we saw above, even the distribution of weapons to foreigners was taken for granted; from the context it would seem that these were obtained to deal with goals of short duration. The scribe, Aril-lumti, ties into this picture. He is known for having affixed his seal, together with the *šukallu* Tiltaššura and Akija and eleven other person, at the bottom of *JEN* 321, a process overcome by Kel-Tešup s. Ḫutija.

(2) In case arms were shipped to other cities, similar to what happened in the distribution of materials for the production of armaments, it was the *ḫazannu* who took delivery of the completed weapons (cf. HSS XIV 224). Moreover, HSS XIII 71 and HSS XIII 175 document that a shipment could take place under the supervision of a *mār šipri*. A scribe is cited in this role. In fact, besides the *mār šipri* Tatip-Tešup (HSS XIII 71) there is a reference in HSS XIII 175 to the scribe Akap-urḫe who is described as *mār šipri ša Wantija.* Consequently, both from the evidence of the documentation relative to arms and from what is generally known about *mār šipri*, it may be concluded that any time they are mentioned it concerns the transport of goods. Less clear is the method of shipping the materials described in HSS XIV 222. Yet one scribe, Ḫupita s. Šeršija, takes arrows from the Palace on consignment; to deliver them to him is Tišam-mušni[25] who, besides being mentioned in texts that register movements of the queen's barley and other goods from the Palace, reappears in EN 9/1 335 where he plays a role that a lacuna does not allow us to clarify. Turning to HSS XIV 222, it is not specifically said that the material had to be transported outside Nuzi, although the use of *ištu* allows us to take this for granted. Among persons charged with transport outside the city there is a *lāsimu* as well as a *mār šipri.*

However, from a study of those employed in distribution, it is possible to reconstruct the following course of action: the one responsible at the Palace (*šakin bīti*)—intermediary (in case of transport outside the city: *mār šipri* and *lāsimu* + *ḫazannu*)—final users. According to EN 9/1 335, where a *sukkallu* is indicated, there is also the possibility that there was a different itinerary, activated by an official "from the outside," so to speak. Thanks to the prosopography we can suppose that intermediaries did not belong strictly to the Palace administration, but were connected to it "from outside." This would allow the conclusion that, at least with regard to the scribes involved in this type of activity, they might not be in the

[25] The figure of Tišam-mušni is somewhat elusive. There are texts in which he acts as an official of the Nuzi Palace (cf. HSS XIV 262, HSS XIV 623) employed in the movement of goods coming in and going out. In others (cf. HSS XIV 63, HSS XIV 163) he controls the movement of barley of the queen of Arrapḫa and Nuzi or seals personnel lists of the Nuzi Palace. Then the name of Tišam-mušni reappears associated with Ezira and Pai-Tilla. The triad, Tišam-mušni, Ezira and Pai-Tilla, is closely tied to Turša. In HSS XIII 17 Tišam-mušni is called *ḫazannu* of Turša and in HSS XIII 352 with the other two men seals a document, again from Turša concerning Palace slaves. The three are also specifically mentioned in relation to Ansukalli (HSS XIV 232=HSS XIV 605) and Nuzi (HSS XV 182). This association with Nuzi suggests a connection with the Tišam-mušni of HSS XIV 262, HSS XIV 323, HSS XIV 22, HSS XIV 18. Certainly an analysis of the seals would contribute to the solution of this prosopographic puzzle.

category of Palace personnel. Finally, it seems possible to conclude that some of the intermediaries in charge were included in the category of ultimate users.

(B) Those employed in production

The artisans employed in the production of arms belong in the category of workers in leather (*aškāpu*) and metal (*nappāḫu*). To these is to be added the artisan specializing in the production of bows and arrows (the *sasinnu*). The Nuzi texts mention a number of them by name, primarily in lists of rations or witnesses. Besides these artisans, the Nuzi texts twice use the term *geltuḫle* which, as is seen, should be interpreted as "Bogenhersteller" according to Loretz and Dietrich. From what has emerged in the preceding point, the production of weapons might have taken place in the *iškaru* of a specific artisan from whom, as we have seen, products could be directly ordered.

The Palace texts, however, also mention others engaged in this activity yet without specifying in what area it took place. From an examination of HSS XIII 99, HSS XIII 100, HSS XIII 103, HSS XIII 116, HSS XIII 206 and HSS XIV 223 we get the name of one of these employees: Unap-Tešup s. Arik-kaja, a specialist in the production of arrows, who sometimes is accompanied by Ḫerik-kaja s. Silwaja (HSS XIII 99, HSS XIII 100, HSS XIII 206), Enna-mati s. Puḫu-menni (HSS XIII 116) or *mār šipri* Akap-tae s. Ariwa-kali. In one case (HSS XIV 223) Unap-Tešup alone is to receive the material.

That Unap-Tešup is one of the principal ones responsible for the production of arrows is shown by his almost constant presence in documents on the subject. The quantity of reeds that is entrusted to him leaves us to assume that he is assured of what is necessary from the Nuzi Palace. Other than in texts relative to arrows, his name with the relative patronym appears in one other tablet, HSS XIII 220, whose provenance is unknown. This text relating to the distribution of barley (and also wheat in a very limited way) allows us to connect Unap-Tešup to other persons and hence to better describe him. Among others, those associated with him are: the *atuḫlu* Arnija s. Akap-tukke, Unap-Teššup s. Teḫi-šenni—known, among other things, to be witness in a transaction relative to horses concerning Tarmi-tilla s. Šurki-Tilla (*JEN* 108)—and the *nappāḫu* Turar-Tešup. This is not the place to analyze the list of persons and to draw possible conclusions about the criteria that influenced their composition. Yet, it does not seem totally accidental that a group of persons who through professional services (like the *nappāḫu*) or their connection with chariots (like the *atuḫlu*) can be thought to be tied, directly or indirectly, to the military. If such a conclusion is correct, we would have further, although indirect, confirmation that the primary activity of Unap-Tešup s. Arik-kaja is tied to the production of arrows. At this point it seems sufficiently justifiable to connect Unap-Tešup s. Arik-kaja with the *sasinnu* Unap-Tešup of HSS XV 71 (room F24).

Mention of Akap-tae s. Ariwa-kali in association with Unap-Tešup s. Arik-kaja in HSS XIII 109 is of particular interest. It is the only reference to the former. Yet in this text Akap-tae is described as *mār šipri*. Since, as we have seen above, it is evident from the Nuzi texts that *mār šipri* are always attached to the control of transferring property and goods,[26] a well-grounded conjecture can be advanced—on the basis of HSS XIII 103—that Unap-Tešup s. Arik-kaja must also have carried on his activities outside the Palace and that Akapa-tae s. Ariwa-kali pursued the further movement of materials. This assumes that the Palace was able to act not only as the source of supplies but also as a point of departure for itinerant artisans who went forward to carry out their activities in localities that did not have their own artisans.

It is more difficult to describe Šilwaja s. Ḫerik-kaja and Enna-mati s. Puḫu-menni whose names do not appear outside materials examined here. Unlike what has been deduced about the *iškaru* of Unap-tae, which documents indicate had its own method of distribution, it seems legitimate to consider that at least part of Unap-Tešup's production of weapons (and also that of Ḫerik-kaja s. Šilwaja and Enna-mati s. Puḫu-menni, and possibly other artisans and associates who remain nameless) went to replenish the Palace storehouses.

Finally, we would also include the *geltuḫle* of the city of Lupti among those employed in the work cited in the texts. As is to be expected, there are no scribes among those employed in production.

(C) The recipients of weapons ("ultimate consumers")

We have already mentioned the so-called "temporary" distribution of weapons about which there is even a reference to redelivery to the Palace in a short time (HSS XIII 60, HSS XIV 220=626, and also HSS XIV 263b). Moreover, in dealing with the phase of distribution, we have already made reference to the final users of arms.

In discussing the topic, not so much from an action (=distribution) point of view as the actors (=recipients), it may be observed that the recipients of arms can be divided into three categories:

(a) Those attached to a military unit belonging to the city of Nuzi who are cited individually by name (HSS XV 3, HSS XV 18, HSS XV 21, HSS XV 37), at times with an indication of belonging to the "left" or the "right,"[27] at times also mentioned under the name of the one responsible for the group (*ša* ŠU PN). Although the lists are not arranged according to "military" criteria[28] but from an "administrative" view of storehouse accounting, it is still possible to glean information on the composition of these groups within which appear *rakib narkabti* (as would be expected), artisans (*ēpû*, HSS XV 3; *nuḫatimmu*, HSS XV 18), *warad ekalli* (HSS XV 12). In these lists two scribes are quoted, Nanna-igi.du (HSS XV 18) and Kanaja (HSS XV 37); these references may be of some interest, even if

[26] Cf. C. Zaccagnini, "The Merchant at Nuzi," *Iraq* 39 (1977), 171–89. The *mār šipri* also seems to be involved in "transfers" of real estate. Moreover, the title is often accompanied by further indications such as: *ša ekalli, ša šarri, ša šukkalli.*

[27] For the sign for "right" and "left" also C. Zaccagnini, *Assur* 2/1 (1979), 1–34.

[28] However, belonging to the "right" or "left" may be specified at times.

they are scarcely connected to the subject of this work (the presence of scribes in the administrative process relative to arms).[29]

(b) Military personnel belonging to other cities, as is shown not only by texts cited previously relative to the shipment of arrows and other weapons to various cities, but also by HSS XV 6 (room C28) which, although not having been found in the Palace, makes specific reference to it as a "storehouse for replenishing" the men of Tašenniwe who had lost their cuirasses.[30] In this case it is more difficult to identify the social category to which these persons belonged since they are cited collectively.

(c) To these two groups can also be added foreigners such as the Ḫanigalbatians who went directly to the Nuzi Palace. In fact the Nuzi texts—especially the lists of rations—reveal a conspicuous presence of Ḫanigalbatian military personnel[31] whose permanence in the kingdom of Arrapḫa was more or less brief and tied to a few military contingents (cf., e.g., HSS XIV 171, HSS XIV 249). For the most part these persons are described as *rakib narkabti* and not infrequently with the function of *emantuḫlu*. Among texts with regard to them: HSS XV 14, HSS XV 26, HSS XV 40, HSS XV 82, HSS XV 99, HSS XV 114, etc. Certainly Kimil-Tešup s. Šenni was boss of one of these groups (see above).

(D) Those attached to audit control

As has been said before, the most authentic phase relative to audit control, the verification of materials in relation to written registrations, is poorly documented. The few and sparse references in the texts allow us to establish that it was done (cf. HSS XV 6) but do not enlighten us as to employees or methods.

With regard to employees, the fact that in HSS XIV 263=608, for example, the goods mentioned on the list (among which there are even arrowheads) are taken on consignment by the *šakin bīti* may be a casual statement simply indicating that these were goods charged to the Palace and hence were properly "taken" by the *šakin bīti*. However—taking into account ll. 9–13 "*an-nu-tu*$_4$ *ú-nu-tu*$_4$ *ša* É.GAL-*lì i+na tup-pí la-be-ri ša ú-nu-ti la i-ša-at-tar*"—it may also mean that the latter had a connection with the process of verification.

With regard to the arms, written documentation also provides another form of audit which concerns the performance of an *iškaru*; see, for example, the fragmentary text HSS XVI 441, from unknown provenance although probably found in the Palace,[32] in which the *tutiwa* are cited specifically as "*iškaru ša lā*

[29] A Wirrahhe appears in lists; is he connected to the Wirrahhe of HSS XIII 85?

[30] It is interesting to observe that it makes mention of a written registration of the transaction.

[31] Cf. C. Zaccagnini, *Assur* 2/1 (1979), 1–34.

[32] This conclusion seems plausible because the texts with the seal of Ezira (see below, n. 34) come from the Palace area (level L1, R81; "C2": Palace area on the main mound within streets 4, 5 and 12, cf. Starr, *Nuzi*, vol. II, plate 13), although the sequence of SMN numbers has no particular value. However, note that HSS XV 178 (SMN 1503) and HSS XV 175 (SMN 1508)—rather close in the list to SMN 1504 = HSS XVI 441—come from room R76.

ipšu."[33] Ezira and Tarmija sealed the text and thanks to the seals it is possible to describe the figures in a more positive way. In fact, Ezira's seal in HSS XVI 441 is identical to the seal in HSS XIII 17, HSS XIII 352, HSS XIII 435, HSS XIV 232 and HSS XV 182, while the seal of Tarmija in HSS XVI 441 is identical to the seal of Tarmija s. Unap-tae which appears in many texts (*JEN passim* but in particular see *JEN* 166, *JEN* 175, *JEN* 176, *JEN* 183, *JEN* 479).[34]

Ezira seems to be closely connected with the city of Turša and with the *ḫazannu* of Tišam-mušni. As to Tarmija, thanks to his patronym, it is possible to reconstruct his connections with the *mār šarri* Teššuja and the city of Turša. The fragmentation and destruction of documentation have not allowed us to place these figures specifically and satisfactorily into our reconstruction of Palace procedures relative to arms. However, they may be considered examples of a certain type of attached to audit. At this stage of studies no scribe has been identified as employed in audit control.

Comparisons and Conclusions

The situation relative to the Palace described above has partial confirmation in documents coming from other parts of Nuzi and in documents for which the provenance is not known. However, on the whole, they provide information on the production of other types of arms (cuirasses, *tutiwa*, metal plates). Except for HSS XV 9 (room F25), which is simply a posting of small and large metal plates, most of the texts are receipts or registration of a consignment of materials.

The most intelligible documentation comes from the archive of Šilwa-Tešup. These texts confirm the existence of specialized workers, often mentioned together in the same text. This is the case of Akkul-enni, an *aškāpu* often associated with Tultukke, Kupa-šaḫ (HSS XV 196, HSS XV 208) and Ḫutip-Tilla. With regard to its specialization, this group seems to be connected in some way with the administrator of Šilwa-Tešup, Pai-Tešup. Ḫutip-Tilla is usually connected with the production and maintenance of *gurpisu* (HSS XV 9b, HSS XV 24, HSS XV 196, HSS XV 208), Kupa-šaḫ and Tultukka with chariots. Female personnel are also registered; they are employed in the wool industry in the production of *tutiwa* (cf. HSS XV 212). With regard to Kupa-šaḫ there is explicit mention that material was delivered to him for his *iškaru.*

Moreover, still in the archive of Šilwa-Tešup, HSS XV 11 seems to suggest the existence of another group employed for the production of weapons; making up part of it are Ḫutija and Aḫ-illika who from the former receives metal plates for the construction of cuirasses. Along with wool and skins registered as materials distributed for the production of arms there are oils and fats for the working of leather.

[33] Cf. what K. Deller writes in connection with HSS XV 2 and its envelope in K. Deller and W. R. Mayer, "Akkadische Lexicographie: CAD M," *Orientalia* NS 53 (1984), 101.

[34] Cf. E. R. Lacheman, *Excavations at Nuzi*, 5 (HSS XIV; Cambridge, Mass.: Harvard University Press, 1950), p. xiii.

From room C28, another area of the citadel, comes text HSS XV 5. Although it has a structure unlike other texts described earlier relative to the distribution of materials for the production and maintenance of weapons, it is interesting because it allows us to calculate the number of metal plates in a cuirass on the Arrapḫa model and on the Ḫanigalbat model.

HSS XIV 253 has a structure very similar to the Palace texts, yet its provenance is unknown. In it is registered a delivery made to Katiri of skins died red for the making of *tutiwa*.

Even with regard to the distribution of arms, a comparison with texts coming from outside the Palace adds little to the picture described so far nor modifies it substantially. In this case as well the evidence comes essentially from the archive of Šilwa-tešup and room C28.

The texts of the archive of Šilwa-Tešup are primarily concerned with the movement of arms taken by the various *bīt nakkamti*. In HSS XIII 354, Ḫašip-apu, Šilwa-Tešup's administrator, consigns to the latter's son two bows, one from Nuzi and one from Arrapḫa, while in HSS XIII 421 he delivers arrows to Intertaja. Šilwa-Tešup himself was interested in the movement of bows and arrows (HSS IX 55). Then HSS XIV 616 registers the delivery of a whole group of weapons from Ḫutija to Aḫ-illika. As we see, these are records of traffic in accumulated goods which generally have many similarities with what is derived from the Palace documents. Upon examination, one difference that is found between the texts coming from the latter and those of a similar topic from Šilwa-Tešup's archive is their lack of a figure similar to the *mār šipri*.

Of particular interest is the previously cited HSS XV 6 in which it is said that the Palace is due to replace the cuirasses that the men of Tašenniwe have lost. This is evidence which, as we have seen, helps us to better delineate one of the Palace's functions.

Lists of persons and individual supplies of arms have also been found outside the Palace although in smaller number. A more specific parallel is with texts of the archive of Kel-Tešup s. Ḫutija[35] (*JEN* 527 and *JEN* 533). Texts found in rooms G73 and G29 (HSS XV 8 and HSS XV 10), to which HSS XV 4 from unknown provenance is to be added, are very similar to those of the Palace levels and probably are to be put in relation with them. Moreover, movement of goods, including weapons, is recorded in texts found outside the Palace, as in HSS XV 183 (room F24) and HSS XV 142 (room F25), which constitute the small archive of Itḫip-Tilla s. Ibašši-ilu and record the movement of goods with regard to father and son.

Another kind of documentation outside the Palace (with the exception of HSS XV 38 found in room L1) is that relative to trials and contracts of the *ṭuppi mārūti* type, for example; see HSS V 44, a text coming from room A34 in which the name of a type of arrow (*ḫurḫutūtu*) is handed down. Of particular interest are three texts,

[35] Elements that indicate some connection if not with the Palace certainly with the king are derived from HSS XIII 363 where there is reference to the father of Kel-Tešup, Ḫutija s. Kuššija, with the title of *mār šipri ša šarri*. Moreover, Kel-Tešup is interested in shipping a very large quantity of barley into Kassite territory.

JEN 196, *JEN* 519 and MAH 18566 = *Genava* NS 15 (1967), no. 3, in which arrows and quivers undoubtedly have a symbolic meaning.[36]

In summary, it is evident that, even though the textual material is different in typology (receipts, lists of objects, lists of persons, etc.) and hence different with regard to the functions within the Palace administration, it is possible to trace the basic outline of a procedure which was put in place to guarantee the management of the arms sector. An analysis of the texts found in the Palace relative to arms, compared with material coming from other parts of Nuzi, allows us to conclude the following:

(1) Once the material first arrived in the Palace area it was the task of the *šakin bīti* to distribute it to those in charge of production, artisans connected to the Palace who could also be sent into regions which had no attachés and where their work was necessary;

(2) The Palace acted as the source of raw materials even for other cities. Included among the tasks of the *šakin bīti* was to prearrange the delivery of requested materials which were taken on consignment by a local official (in this case, the *ḫazannu*) who took care of further distribution to those concerned;

(3) Documentation indicates that weapons were made other than at the workplace of a specified group of artisans (who also acted as itinerant workers), even within an *iškaru*;

(4) The Palace also acted as a storehouse for the distribution of previously made arms according to a procedure similar to that described for the delivery of materials;

(5) Transport to the outside was primarily under the control of a *mār šipri*;

(6) Management of a storehouse also meant audit control for which, however, few indications remain;

(7) The Palace could provide arms even for brief periods and to foreigners;

(8) Some groups of users were also assured by verification of the condition of the armament and replacement when necessary.

Along with this so-called "primary" procedure it is also possible to get a glimpse of the presence of other functionaries such as the *šukallu* (who seems to activate the "secondary" or "external" procedure) or, more indirectly, the *šakin māti*. This second type of procedure seems to be concerned particularly with the shipment of goods to other cities and to require the employment of *mār šipri* and *lāsimu*.

As we have seen, documentation relative to the arms sector allows us to reconstruct for the Palace primarily a passive role as storehouse for withdrawals and not so much an active role as an autonomous central office for distribution. Foremost in this process is the figure of the *šakin bīti* who assures the operation of the storehouse and controls its various activities. A series of other figures come to him in their intermediary capacity, both those attached to production and those

[36] Cf. A. Fadhil, *Studien zur Topographie und Prosopographie der Provinzenstädte des Königreiche Arraphe*, 1983, pp. 280–81.

concerned with the successive movements of the goods. The latter is the role displayed by the *mār šipri* and it is in this role that we find the names of scribes.

From an examination of the identified "primary" procedure, it emerges that those with "intermediary responsibility," among which even the scribes are counted, do not seem to be included in Palace personnel (obviously intended in this context as a storehouse from which to take things away). Rather they seem to be responsible for completed withdrawals or for the transport and delivery of goods both to the Palace and to other concerned persons. An indirect confirmation seems to come from Akap-urḫe who appears to act in the double capacity as Wantija's envoy (*mār šipri ša Wantija* and hence the one acting as his agent) and the one responsible for withdrawals at the Palace (and in this capacity seals HSS XIII 175).

Hence, whatever may be deduced from the procedure reconstructed here, especially that belonging to the arms sector, the time for shipment and transport seems to be structured as an autonomous segment with its own responsible person; with respect to this also text EN 9/1 132,[37] relative to the scribe Ḫupita.

Within this area of yet indistinct boundaries is placed the function of the scribes. Further studies in this direction will allow us to get a better picture of it.

One last point remains to be considered: besides the Palace there were autonomous centers for production (and distribution). Some were attached to the Palace itself (maybe even as a source of supplies); others, however, were included within organizations similar and parallel to it (for example, see the archive of Šilwa-Tešup).

This means circulation existed outside the Palace and in a certain sense outside of its control, as is also shown by reference to arms in contracts. This indication of the existence of a traffic in arms connected to and only partially controlled by the Palace is something to keep in mind in studies focused on the reconstruction of the organization of the kingdom of Arrapḫa.

[37] Now published in *SCCNH* 2 (1987). I thank D. I. Owen for making me aware of this text, as well as EN 9/1 335, in advance of publication. It deals with a letter written by Ḫupita concerning a shipment of barley, among other things.

Ein neuer Text zum Ordal in Nuzi (*JEN* 659 + SMN 1651)

GERNOT WILHELM
Julius-Maximilians-Universität Würzburg

Unsere Kenntnis der Prozedur des Flußordals ist durch die jüngste Publikation einschlägiger Texte aus Mari durch J.-M. Durand wesentlich gefördert worden.[1] Nach den Darlegungen Durands fand das Flußordal, soweit die Texte eine Aussage hierüber zulassen, in Hīt am Euphrat statt, wo dieser Brauch möglicherweise seinen Ursprung hatte. In Mari waren beim Ordal offenkundig auch Stellvertreter zulässig. Durands Auffassung zufolge verlangte das Ordal von dem Probanden, eine zeitlang oder eine bestimmte Strecke unter Wasser zu schwimmen, wobei es vorkommen konnte, daß er ertrank.

Das Flußordal in Nuzi[2] dagegen setzt voraus, daß zwar eine eindeutige Entscheidung erfolgt, dabei aber der durch das Ordal als schuldig Befundene keineswegs ertrinkt, sondern danach hingerichtet oder dem königlichen Urteilsspruch überantwortet wird, einmal auch seinen Grundbesitz verliert.[3] Über den Ablauf des Ordals in Nuzi liegen keine Informationen vor. Seine Voraussetzung war die Unmöglichkeit, eine richterliche Entscheidung auf der Grundlage positiver Evidenz herbeizuführen. Dies war der Fall, wenn Urkunde und Zeugen fehlten und Aussage gegen Aussage, oft in eidlicher Form, stand.

[1] J.-M. Durand, *Archives Epistolaires de Mari* I/1 (ARM 26; Paris 1988) 509–39.

[2] Zum Flußordal in Nuzi cf. H. Liebesny, "Evidence in Nuzi Legal Procedure," *JAOS* 61 (1941) 130–42, besonders 138–40; R. E. Hayden, "Court Procedure at Nuzi" (Ph.D. Diss., Brandeis University 1962) 39–52; A. Lieberman, "Studies in the Trial-by-River Ordeal in the Ancient Near East during the Second Millennium B.C.E." (Ph.D. Diss., Brandeis University 1969); T. Frymer-Kensky, "The Judicial Ordeal in the Ancient Near East" (Ph.D. Diss., Yale University 1977); eadem, "Suprarational Legal Procedure in Elam and Nuzi," in SCCNH 1:115–31, besonders 122ff. Cf. noch G. Cardascia, "L'ordalie par le fleuve dans les 'lois assyriennes'," in *Fs. Wilhelm Eilers* (Wiesbaden 1967) 19–36; J. Bottéro, "L'ordalie en Mésopotamie ancienne," *Ann. Pisa*, Ser. III, 11/4 (1981); O. R. Gurney, *The Middle Babylonian Legal and Economic Texts from Ur* (Oxford 1983) 10–12.

[3] *aššum awâti annâti ina* ᶠᴰ*ḫuršan illakū ša ikkallû idukkū-š* 'Wegen dieser Angelegenheit werden sie zum Flußordal gehen. Denjenigen, der zurückgehalten wird, den wird man töten' (AASOR 16 74:24–26; cf. AASOR 16 75:29–31).

[*u ašš*]*um awâti annâti* [*ina* ᶠ]ᴰ*ḫuršan illakū* [*ša i*]*kkallû šarru ṭēma* [*iš*]*akkan* 'Und wegen dieser Angelegenheit werden sie zum Flußordal gehen. Über denjenigen, der zurückgehalten wird, wird der König eine Entscheidung treffen' (HSS 9 7:23–26; cf. HSS 13 422:35–38, 14 8:16–18).

ša ikkallû ištu eqlēti šaššumma eppušū-š 'Denjenigen, der zurückgehalten wird, wird man aus seinen Feldern ausweisen' (*RA* 23 Nr. 29:43–44).

Es kam vereinzelt vor, daß eine Partei vor dem Ordal zurückschreckte und es vorzog, ihre Rechtssache verloren zu geben.[4] Bisher nicht bekannt war dagegen der im folgenden Text bezeugte Fall, daß eine Partei in einem Rechtsstreit, in dem sie Tafel und Zeugen nicht beibringen kann, von sich aus ein Ordal anbietet. Hierdurch und durch eine zusätzliche Verfügung, die leider aufgrund des an dieser Stelle fragmentarischen Zustands der Tafel unverständlich bleibt,[5] wird die gegnerische Partei veranlaßt, das Ordal zu verweigern, auf den weiteren Rechtsweg zu verzichten und ihre Ansprüche aufzugeben.

Der Zusammenhang ergibt sich durch den Join einer wohlbekannten Tafel aus dem Archiv der Söhne des Teḫip-Tilla (*JEN* 659 = *JEN*u 841)[6] mit dem bisher unveröffentlichten Fragment SMN 1651.[7]

Vs. 1 ᵐ*Šur-ki-til-la* DUMU *Te-*[*ḫi-i*]*p-til-la*
2 *it-ti* ᶠ*A-ḫa-*⸢*ḫu*⸣-[*i*]*a* [DUMU.MUNUS ᵐ]*A-*⸢*ta*⸣*-a+a*
3 *ù it-ti* ᵐ*Ta-e* DUMU ⸢ᶠ*A*⸣*-ḫa-ḫu-ia*
4 *aš-šum* 1 ANŠE 2 APIN A.ŠÀ *ši-qí-i*
5 *ša* URU *Ši-ni-na ša* ⸢*ge*⸣*-er-ri zu-*⸢*ur*⸣*-ri-id-d*[*u-e*]
6 *ge-er-ru š*[*a*] ⸢URU *Tar*⸣-[*ku*]*-ul-*⸢*li*⸣
7 *tù-bu-uq-q*[*a*]*-a*[*s-s*]*ú ik-ki-is*
8 *i+na di-ni a-na pa-n*[*i*] DI.KU$_5$.ME[Š] *i-te-lu-ma*
9 *um-ma* ᵐ*Šur-ki-til-la-ma* 1 AN[Š]E 2 [API]N ⸢A.ŠÀ⸣ *š*[*a*]*-*⸢*a-šu*⸣
10 ᵐ*A-ta-a+a* DUMU *Ku-uk-ku-ia a-na a-b*[*i-i*]*a*
11 ᵐ*Te-ḫi-*⸢*ip*⸣*-til-la id-din* ⸢*ù*⸣ *a-na*
12 *m*[*a-r*]*u-*[*ti*] *i-pu-uš ù i+na-an-na*
13 A.⸢ŠÀ⸣ *ša-*⸢*a*⸣-[*š*]*u* ᶠ*A-ḫa-ḫu-ia ù* ᵐ*Ta-e*
14 *iš-tu qà-ti-ia il-te-qú-ú*
15 *ù* DI.KU$_5$.MEŠ ⸢*a*⸣*-na* ᵐ*Šur-ki-til-la* ⸢*iq*⸣*-ta-bu-ú*
16 *i-bá-aš-ši-mi-*⸢*i*⸣ *ṭup-pa-ka$_4$ ù š*[*i*]*-bu-ti-ka$_4$*
17 *ù le-qa-aš-š*[*u-nu*]*-ti-mi ki-me-e*
18 ᵐ*A-ta-*⸢*a*⸣*+a* ᵐ*Te-*[*ḫi-i*]*p-*⸢*til*⸣*-la a-na*
19 *ma-r*[*u-ti*] ⸢*i*⸣-[*pu-uš-mi* E]ME*-šu*
20 *š*[*a* ᵐ*Šur-ki-til-la i+na pa-ni* DI.KU$_5$.MEŠ *i*]*q-ta-bi*
21 ⸢*ṭup-pí*⸣ ⸢*ù*⸣? *š*[*i-bu-tu-ia ia-nu*]?
22 A.ŠÀ *ki-ma* A.ŠÀ ⸢*a*⸣*-š*[*a*?-]

[4] Cf. *JEN* 467:26–30: [*lišān-šu*] *ša* PN *ana pāni šībūti iqtabi ana* [ÍD *ḫuršān*] *ana alāki qabâku ù lā allak* '[Aussage] des PN; vor Zeugen sagte er: "Zum [Flußordal] zu gehen ist mir befohlen, aber ich werde nicht gehen!"'

[5] Zeile 21 etwa *aš*[*akkan-mi*]? oder *aš*[*addad-mi*]?

[6] Für die Zeilen 4–7 und 38–41 cf. A. Fadhil, *Studien zur Topographie und Prosopographie der Provinzstädte des Königreichs Arrapḫe* (Baghdader Forschungen 6; Mainz 1983) 151.

[7] Für die Erlaubnis, das Fragment einsehen und publizieren zu dürfen, danke ich den zuständigen Herren des Semitic Museum der Harvard University, Professor F. M. Cross und Professor W. L. Moran sowie ihren Nachfolgern im Amt, Professor L. Steger und Professor P. Steinkeller. Für stete Unterstützung bin ich insbesondere auch Dr. Carney E. S. Gavin verpflichtet. Auf den Zusammenschluß einer anderen Tafel des Teḫip-Tilla-Archivs (*JEN* 13) mit einem Fragment der SMN-Sammlung hat M. P. Maidman, in: SCCNH 2:345–49, hingewiesen.

23 *it-ti* ^{f}*A-ḫa-ḫu-ia* [*ù it-ti*]
24 ^{m}*Ta-e i+na* ^{ÍD}*ḫur-š*[*a-an a-la-ak-mi*]
25 *ù* EME-*šu-nu ša* ^{f}[*A-ḫa-ḫu-ia ù*]
26 ⸢*ša*⸣ ^{m}*Ta-e i+na pa-ni*
U. Rd. 27 ⸢DI.KU$_5$.MEŠ⸣ *iq-ta-bu-*[*ú it-ti*]
28 ^{m}*Šur-ki-til-la i+na* ^{ÍD}[*ḫur-ša-an*]
29 *la ni-la-ak-mi di-*[*na*]
Rs. 30 *it-ti* ^{m}*Šur-*⸢*ki*⸣*-til-l*[*a*]
31 [*l*]*a* [*n*]*i-ip-p*[*u-uš-mi*]
32 *ù* A.ŠÀ *ša-*[*a-šu a-na*]
33 ^{m}*Šur-ki-til-l*[*a*]
34 *ú-me-eš-ši-i*[*r-m*]*a-mi i+na*
35 EGIR-*ki-šu la* ⸢*ni*⸣*-ša-as-sí-mi*
36 *ki-ma* EME-*šu-nu-ma ša* ^{f}*A-ḫa-ḫu-ia*
37 *ù ša* ^{m}*Ta-e* ^{m}*Šur-ki-til-la*
38 *i+na di-ni il-te-e-ma ù* DI.KU$_5$.MEŠ
39 1 ANŠE 2 AP[IN] ⸢A⸣.ŠÀ *ša-a-šu ša* URU *Ši-ni-na*
40 *ša ge-e*[*r-r*]*i ša zu-ur-ri-id-du-e*
41 *ša* [*t*]*ù-bu-qa-as-sú* (Rasur) *ge-er-ru*
42 *š*[*a* U]RU *Tar-ku-ul-li ik-ki-sú*
43 [*a*]*-na* ^{m}*Šur-ki-til-la*
44 [*i*]*t-ta-ad-nu*

(Siegelabrollung Porada Nr. 857)
45 ⸢NA$_4$ ^{m}*Tar-mi-ik*⸣*-k*[*u-du*] DUMU *Pu-ru-sa*
(Siegelabrollung Porada Nr. 480)
46 [N]A$_4$ ^{m}*Šúk-ri-te-šu*[*p* DUMU *Ḫ*]*a-ip-*LUGAL
47 NA$_4$ ^{m}*Ta-i-til-l*[*a* DUM]U [*Š*]*a-ri-*⸢*iš*⸣*-še*
u. Rd. (Siegelabrollung Porada Nr. 465)
l. Rd. 48 [NA$_4$ ^{m}DINGIR]*-ni-šu* DUB.SAR DUMU ^{d}30-*náp-šer*$_{10}$ ⸢NA$_4$ ^{m}⸣[x(x)]x-*ma-al-li*
[(Siegelabrollung)] (Siegelabrollung Porada Nr. 458) (Siegelabrollung)
49 NA$_4$ ^{m}*Ḫa-ši-ip-a-ra-aš-ši-iḫ* : DUMU *Ša-ma-aš-še*

Šurki-Tilla, der Sohn des Teḫip-Tilla, trat mit Aḫaḫuja, der Tochter des Ataja, und mit Tae, dem Sohn der Aḫaḫuja, wegen 1 ANŠE 2 APIN bewässerten Feldes der Stadt Šinina am Wege des *surrittu*—der Weg nach Tarkulli schneidet seine Ecke—im Gericht vor den Richtern auf, und Šurki-Tilla (sagte) so: "Diese 1 ANŠE 2 APIN Feld gab Ataja, der Sohn des Kukkuja, meinem Vater Teḫip-Tilla und adoptierte ihn. Und jetzt haben Aḫaḫuja und Tae dieses Feld aus meinem Besitz weggenommen." Und die Richter sagten zu Šurki-Tilla: "Sind deine Tafel und deine Zeugen vorhanden, so nimm sie her, daß Ataja Teḫip-Tilla adoptiert hat!" Aussage des Šurki-Tilla; vor den Richtern sagte er: "Meine

Tafel und(?) [*meine Zeugen sind nicht vorhanden*](?). Ein Feld *s*[*telle*(??)] ich für ein Feld. Mit Aḫaḫuja [und mit] Tae [werde ich] zum Flußord[al gehen.]" Und die Aussage der [Aḫaḫuja und] des Tae; vor den Richtern sagten sie: "[Mit] Šurki-Tilla gehen wir nicht zum Fluß[ordal]! Einen Proz[eß] ma[chen] wir nicht mit Šurki-Tilla! Und dieses Feld überlassen wir dem Šurki-Tilla. Wir werden ihn nicht verklagen." Gemäß der Aussage der Aḫaḫuja und des Tae siegte Šurki-Tilla im Prozeß, und die Richter gaben diese 1 ANŠE 2 APIN Feld der Stadt Šinina am Wege des *surrittu*, dessen Ecke der Weg nach Tarkulli schneidet, dem Šurki-Tilla.
(Siegelbeischriften).

The Origin of Nuzi Ware: A Contribution From Tell Hamida

PAUL ZIMANSKY
Boston University

In the otherwise rather dreary and artistically uninspired corpus of Mesopotamian pottery dating to early historic periods, Nuzi ware stands out as something very special. With its elegant vessel forms and intricate patterns of white paint on a dark background, its appearance in the archaeological record has often been treated as a phenomenon crying out for explanation. In the 1920s and 1930s the standard response to the question of its origin tended to be an invasion hypothesis tinged with ethnic corollaries. This approach has long since fallen out of favor, not just because we have come to know more about the diversity of cultural manifestations of Hurrians and Indo-Aryans, but also because modern archaeological theory no longer comfortably equates ancient ethnicity with potsherd distributions. Other explanations have been sought for the emergence of this striking style of decoration at widely scattered sites, such as Nuzi, Tell Brak, Alalaḫ, and Tell Billa, but all of these are contingent on understanding where, and how rapidly, the new ware emerged.

The current status of the problem was reviewed by Diana Stein,[1] whose general conclusion, based on a review of excavations conducted in the 1930s and 1940s, was that the appearance of Nuzi ware was an indigenous development in northern Mesopotamia, in which a unique decorative scheme, primarily defined by the appearance of white paint, was applied to vessel forms that had clear antecedents in the Mesopotamian corpus of the Ur III and Isin-Larsa periods. While she did not commit herself on the source of inspiration for new decorative schemes, she noted that

> the technique of a white on black design has been derived from a number of sources ranging from black-impressed ware to the mural painting at Mari, and the alternating black and white patterns which occur on dark painted sherds from Brak level 3 all of which are Mesopotamian. . . . As there are no two examples of Nuzi Ware with exactly the same white painted design, nor are there two sites where Nuzi Ware decoration is conceived in exactly the same way, it is probable that not one but several diverse influences contributed directly or indirectly to the Nuzi style of decoration.[2]

[1] D. Stein, "Khabur Ware and Nuzi Ware: Their Origin, Relationship, and Significance," *Assur* 4/1 (Malibu: Undena, 1984) 1–64.

[2] Ibid., 27.

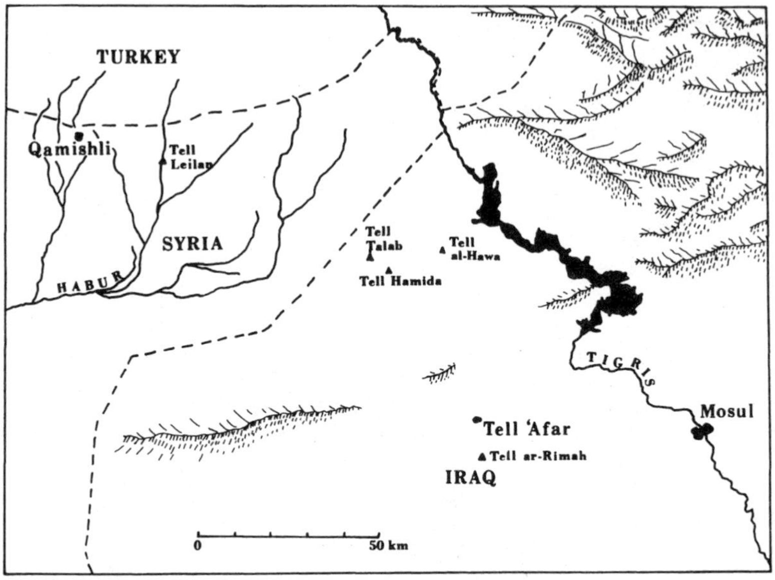

FIGURE 1. *Map locating Tell Hamida in North Jazira.*

One of the difficulties in penetrating this thicket of uncertainty is the comparative rarity of Nuzi ware, particularly from sites excavated with any degree of stratigraphic precision. On surveys it hardly ever turns up, despite its conspicuous attributes. Given this paucity of information, the materials discovered at Tell Hamida are not without value in the discussion of the origins of Nuzi Ware, although only one short season of survey and excavation has as yet been conducted there.

Tell Hamida is a twenty-three hectare site located midway between the towns of Uwainat and Rabiyah in Iraq's North Jazira. Although larger in surface area than Chagar Bazar, the volume of settlement debris here is considerably less; at its maximum elevation the tell rises less than seven meters above the level of the plain, in a gentle slope unmarked by any feature that would indicate the presence of a city wall or fortifications.

In 1986, the rapid development of irrigation projects in the plain immediately north of the Jebel Sinjar prompted Iraq's Department of Antiquities and Heritage to invite foreign archaeologists to undertake rescue projects. The author and Elizabeth Stone, as directors of a Boston University/SUNY Stony Brook expedition to Iraq, were interested in finding a site that would shed some light on the internal workings of the Kingdom of Mitanni, the least well known of the great empires that dominated the Near Eastern world in the Late Bronze Age. The opening of the North Jazira provided us with a welcome opportunity to pursue this goal and between Christmas and New Year's Day we conducted a brief survey to locate a suitable tell for our project. Tell Hamida, where we eventually conducted a program of surface survey and excavation between June 15 and August 11, seemed

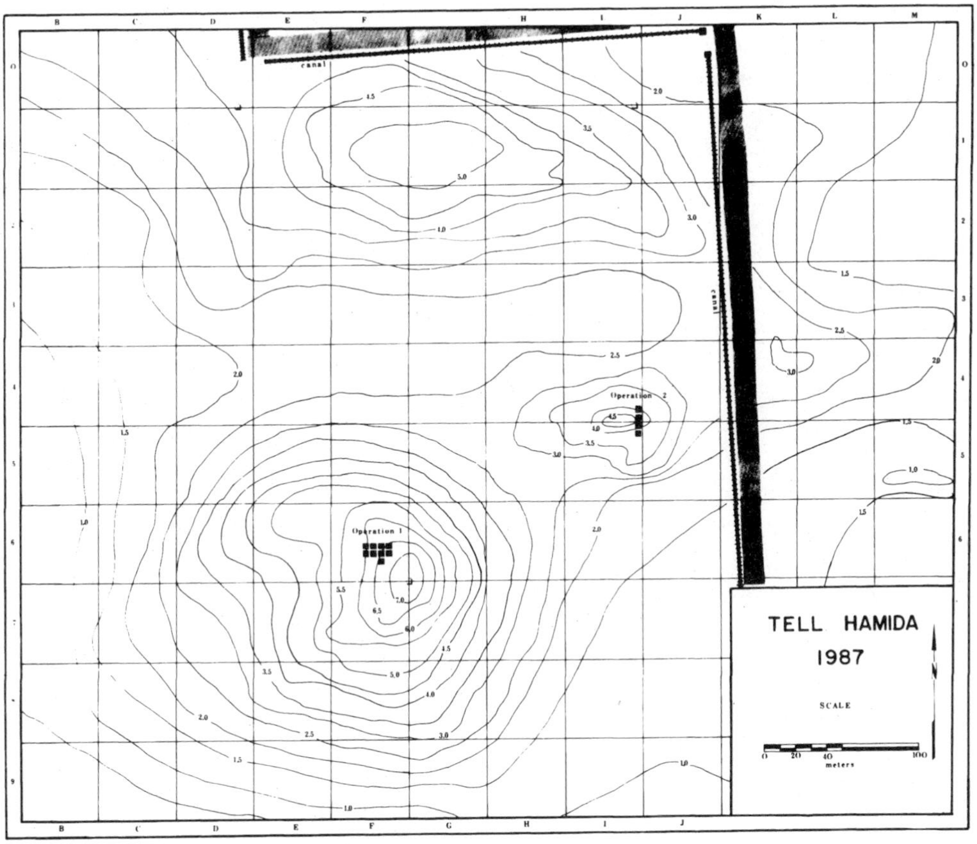

FIGURE 2. *Contour plan of Tell Hamida showing locations of operations 1 and 2, and irrigation channel in which Nuzi ware was found.*

ideally suited to our objectives because surface remains indicated that mid-second millennium remains would be relatively accessible.[3]

There are three eminences on the site, the largest of which is a nearly conical mound on its southern side. Two hundred meters northeast of this there is a smaller and lower rise separated from the large mound by a shallow saddle. North of both there is another rise with gentle contours forming an east–west ridge that covers an area of slightly more than four hectares. The entire site has been under cultivation in recent times and because of plowing there are no sharp breaks in its topography. At the time of our arrival, the grain harvest had already been completed and the surface was clearly exposed, with the exception of isolated areas covered by accumulations of chaff.

[3] A preliminary report of this field season has been submitted to *Sumer*. A more-extensive monograph on Tell Hamida is currently in preparation and will appear in Undena's *Syro-Mesopotamian Studies* series.

In the first phase of our work we mapped the site, laying out a grid of 50 × 50 meter squares along a magnetic north–south/east–west axis. From ten-by-ten meter subunits in the southwest corner of each of these squares, we collected all surface sherds. These surface collections confirmed our first impressions of the chronology of occupation. Although Hassuna and Halafian assemblages are well represented in the North Jazira, no sherds of these were found at Tell Hamida. There were rare examples of Ubaid pottery, and, equally rare, both incised and painted Ninevite 5. We also found incised wares that we associated with the Akkadian period. The greatest number of identifiable sherds, however, belonged to the middle of the second millennium. There was also some pottery of the first millennium B.C., but virtually nothing glazed or manifestly later than the first century or so. In all of our survey, I should note, we found not a single piece of white-on-dark Nuzi ware.

We did know, however, that such pottery was to be found at the site, because it had been discovered previously in the bulldozer cut for the channel on the eastern side of the site by Salim Yunis, then of the Tell ᶜAfar Department of Antiquities. This is what had brought us to the site in the first place. We assumed that Nuzi ware would be the most specific chronological indicator for the period in which we were interested, the floruit of Mitanni, and wanted to excavated levels in which it would be found.

We were torn, however, on where to locate our trenches in order to reach the Mitannian period most efficiently. The surface survey showed little significant variation between the squares in terms of quantity of pottery, although the low area between the northern and southern tells yielded very few sherds and some of the squares to the east of the irrigation channel produced unexpectedly high numbers of sherds, given that the tell was hard to distinguish from the surrounding plain. There was much more significant clustering of the squares showing the highest percentage of painted wares. As noted above, painted pottery was characteristic of more than one period in which the site was occupied, but since the vast majority of identifiable painted sherds belonged to what has been called "younger Ḫabur ware," we assume this distribution speaks for a concentration of second-millennium occupation. The northern tell showed a very thin presence of painted ware, whereas the southern one was dominated by high concentrations. It would appear, therefore, that the actual focus of mid-second millennium occupation was the relatively small area of the conical southern tell, but there was a chance that this was all earlier than the Mitannian period. Salim had actually found Nuzi ware northeast of this on the lower eminence, but it might not be near enough the surface for us to reach easily.

The Director of Antiquities had specified that excavations on the North Jazira project were to be confined to a single chronological period, insofar as possible, and that continuous horizontal exposure was to be the primary objective. With our surface survey pointing in one direction and Salim's discoveries in another, we eventually compromised and opened two separate excavation areas with the understanding that one would be shut down in favor of the other after a brief period of work. Ultimately, our uncertainty produced unexpected dividends with regard to the question of the origin of Nuzi ware.

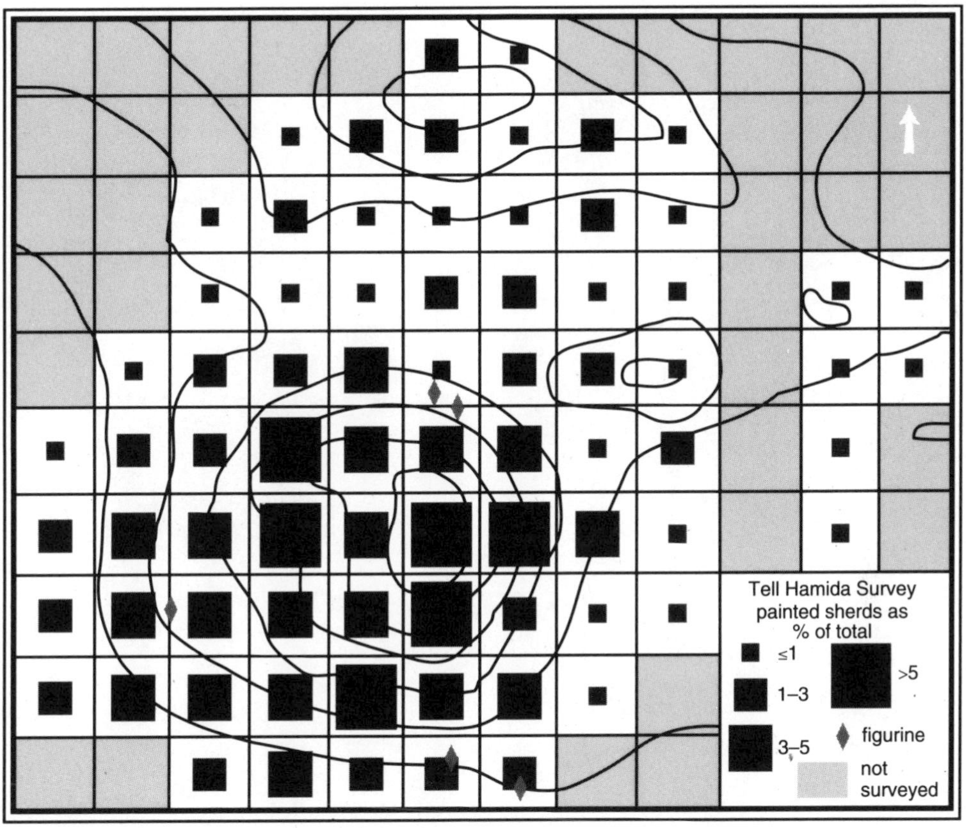

FIGURE 3. *Distribution of painted pottery found in surface survey (the grid from fig. 2 has been shifted to the southwest, so that the 10 × 10 m squares from which collections were made now lie in the center of each 50 × 50 m square of the plan).*

We opened two rows of five-by-five meter squares: one on the south tell running east–west and termed "operation 1," and the other, called "operation 2," going north–south on smaller hillock near the bulldozer cut. In operation 2, the foundations of a fairly substantial building were discovered quite near the surface, associated with Seleucid and early Parthian pottery. Since this was obviously not what we were looking for, this was the area we decided to close, but not before we had found one sherd of rather highly developed Nuzi ware in the mixed fill below the building.

In operation 1 none of this later material was found and the sherds from the plow zone to the lowest points we reached this year, about 1.5 m below the modern surface, were consistently in the mid-second millennium tradition. We eventually expanded the operation to nine five-by-five meter squares, and, broadly speaking, were able to distinguish seven relative sequential phases, although it would be inaccurate to specify these as major building levels. Architectural preservation everywhere on the site was poor, although it improved as we went farther below

FIGURE 4. (a) *Late Ḫabur ware shoulder vessel from operation 1;* (b) *Late Ḫabur ware cup from operation 1.*

the modern plow zone. There was nothing at all spectacular about the small finds; all seemed to be associated with simple domestic life. There were numerous animal figurines, pieces of model chariots, metal pins, and an assortment of spindle whorls. What is of interest is that almost nothing modern—or even from the last three millennia—was found in any level of operation 1. The later occupation of the site evidenced in operation 2 must have been modest indeed to leave so little imprint only two hundred meters away.

All phases of operation 1 were characterized by continuity of ceramic styles—there were no abrupt breaks in the sequence and in all probability it represents only a short period of time. There did appear to be an interestingly high percentage of painted wares in the late Ḫabur tradition as we went down, but, with the exposures of the earliest phases limited to only part of one square, it would be premature to make much of this. The late Ḫabur ware tradition is customarily dated from 1650 to 1550 B.C.[4] In our case, shoulder vessels with thin bands of paint on their rims and upper bodies were common, as were cups, chalices, and pedestal bases. In most cases the paint was a reddish brown, sometimes deepening to a dark purple. Simple bands of monochrome paint were by far the most-common form of decoration. Open bowls with an internal ledge rim painted in deep crimson were also characteristic of this sequence. Also in evidence, but relatively rare, were representations of birds in black and red paint. In short, what we see in operation 1 at

[4] David Oates, "Excavations at Tell al-Rimah, 1971," *Iraq* 34 (1972) 85.

FIGURE 6. (a) *Nuzi ware sherd from operation 2;* (b) *Sherd with birds' feet from operation 1;* (c, f) *White painted spots on dark red bands from operation 1;* (d–e) *"Union Jack" decorations of white paint on black background from operation 1;* (g–i) *Bowls with red painted ledge rims from operation 1.*

FIGURE 9. *General view of excavations in operation 1.*

Tell Hamida is an assemblage of pottery that corresponds to Chagar Bazar level 1 phase E, Tell Billa stratum 3, Tell Brak HH level 3, and very early Alalaḫ 4.

Whether Nuzi ware was present here depends on what one calls Nuzi ware. There are certainly painted vessel forms—specifically shoulder vessels—which are regarded by Stein and others as part of the Nuzi ware corpus. Some white paint was used in all phases of operation 1, and every sherd on which it appears is wheel-made, so there can be no doubt that these belong to the second millennium rather than, for example, the Halafian period. In some cases this was a white horizontal band flanked by thicker black bands. There were many instances in which white spots were applied on top of dark red bands. There were also a few "Union Jack" patterns of thin white diagonal lines on a black background. However, the really ornate Nuzi ware of floral patterns, rolling spirals, etc., was not found in operation 1.

The relevance of this to the question of the origin of Nuzi ware is that it shows that there was a period of experimentation when all of the elements that were to converge to create intricate, mature Nuzi ware were in place, but the ware itself did not yet exist. Having excavated, typed, photographed, and counted tens of thousands of sherds from operation 1, we can offer the "negative evidence" for this conclusion with some confidence. The white paint, the vessel forms, the bird decorations, can all be seen in operation 1, but not the fully developed style, which is found elsewhere on the site.

One might argue that the absence of Nuzi ware in operation 1 had more to do with function than chronology. Nuzi ware has been regarded as a luxury ware, or palace ware, on the grounds of its esthetic appeal and comparative luxury. If the area of operation 1 was never occupied by élites, there would be no particular reason for it to appear there. This remains a possibility, but it is hard to see why it would then be found in the area of operation 2, which, in view of its low elevation is unlikely to have been the site of a major structure. The evidence from sites such as Tell al-Faḫḫār suggests that, even at small sites in rural areas, massive building was characteristic of élite establishments.[5] The overwhelming association of standard late Ḫabur ware sherds with the early white painted wares in operation 1, and the general scarcity of such sherds in the area of operation 2 insofar as we can judge from the surface survey, would also suggest a chronological distinction between the two areas.

Thus the evidence from Tell Hamida, at least as it stands in this preliminary stage of investigation of the site, would appear to be in accord with Stein's conclusion that Nuzi ware evolved locally in northern Iraq and Syria, rather than being introduced suddenly from elsewhere. Its evolution took place over a time span of uncertain length in the sixteenth, and perhaps fifteenth, century. In the interval between the inception of its primary elements and the emergence of the elaborate style, the focus of settlement at Hamida moved from one locus to another a few hundred meters away. More-precise chronological definitions and an evaluation of the circumstances of this shift must await more-precise contextual information, which can only come from further excavation.

[5] Yasin Mahmoud Al-Khalesi, "Tell al-Fakhar (Kurruḫanni), a dimtu-Settlement: Excavation Report," *Assur* 1/6 (Malibu: Undena, 1977).

PART 2

TEXTS IN THE HARVARD SEMITIC MUSEUM

Excavations at Nuzi 9/3

by

E. R. Lacheman† and D. I. Owen

Introduction

This, the third and final part of *Excavations at Nuzi* 9, is published with certain reservations and not as originally planned. It was my intention from the outset to collate each tablet against Lacheman's copies before publishing them. This has been possible for nearly all the texts in Parts 1 and 2. It has not been possible for much of this section. At the pace that developed over the years, it became apparent that it was going to take much more time to complete all the collations than I had anticipated. It was thus, reluctantly, that I decided to publish Lacheman's remaining copies as received. Nevertheless, given the experience with earlier published texts, I concluded that the overall accuracy of the copies I had examined for Parts 1 and 2 strongly indicated that the remaining copies were likely to be equally accurate and reliable. Furthermore, between the notations on the copies and the notes and transliterations left by Lacheman, it appears that he had actually checked all or nearly all of the tablets included in *Excavations at Nuzi* 9. In most instances where errors were found, they were along edges where signs were left out. This was due to Lacheman's technique of copying directly on enlarged photos of tablets where edges and their accompanying signs were often obscured by the curvature of the tablets. He would add these signs later when collating the copies.[1] In most cases he had completed this task. But, as indicated elsewhere, he left no indication as to which texts were not completed. Thus, I plan, over the years ahead and as time and circumstances permit, to complete the collations and to communicate the results as "Nuzi Notes."

The final section of *Excavations at Nuzi* 9 contains the usual mix of documents. It concludes the publication of the major segment of the best preserved texts excavated at Nuzi. With its completion we can now enter the second phase of the "Nuzi Publication Project" which is to include the reevaluation of previous analyses of Nuzi institutions and culture. It will also allow for new approaches in the study of the Nuzi archives based on a much expanded data base (now being completely computerized) and on a greatly enhanced knowledge of the language and lexicon of Nuzi Akkadian and of Hurrian. It is my hope that this series will provide a major vehicle for these studies while, at the same time, continue to include new texts, especially the many hundreds of substantial fragments in the Harvard Semitic Museum and the Oriental Institute and the important groups of texts and fragments in the British Museum[2] and in the Staatliche Museum in Berlin.[3]

[1] See the relevant description by M. P. Maidman of Lacheman's technique in *SCCNH* 3 (1989), 4–10.

[2] See now M. P. Maidman, *ZA* 76 (1986), 254–88.

[3] According to information provided by M. Müller, Leipzig.

To facilitate the use of this and the previous two parts of *Exacavtions at Nuzi* 9, I have compiled cumulative indexes of SMN numbers, room numbers, and scribes. Each SMN number has been checked against published numbers and duplications eliminated wherever noted. This final compilation corrects and supersedes the lists published with the previous parts. In addition, and with the help of Paola Negri Scafa, I have included a cumulative index of scribes with additions and corrections to previous entries. A cumulative catalogue has also been prepared, with numerous additions and corrections. It should facilitate the use of the three parts.

Finally, I wish to note my debt to Professor Maynard P. Maidman who carefully read through this catalogue and offered numerous corrections and suggestions for improvements, to Professor Martha A. Morrison with whom I began this project, and to Professor Gernot Wilhelm for the collations of some of the texts which he generously shared with me.

Cumulative Catalogue to *Excavations at Nuzi* 9

DAVID I. OWEN

This cumulative catalogue includes the two previously published catalogues originally prepared by D. I. Owen and M. A. Morrison in *SCCNH* 2 and 4. They have been revised and integrated by the editor with the catalogue for *EN* 9/3 that he had compiled for this volume. Every effort has been made to incorporate corrections and clarifications made by the editor, those pointed out in reviews or communicated to the editor by Professors M. P. Maidman and G. Wilhelm. Descriptions have often been rewritten and have been kept brief. They do not attempt to be thorough but only to provide general descriptions of text type and contents. There remain numerous problems with SMN and room numbers. The confusion in the records left by Lacheman is extensive, with frequently conflicting data. In a number of cases, selection of SMN number was based on what was perceived to have been the best choice at the time. It should also be noted that although the highest number in the plates is 529, there exist only 526 copies. The discrepancy lies in the necessity to remove three copies that turned out to be duplicates of others in the volume. As was already indicated in my 1979 Brandeis University dissertation (*LDN*), Lacheman had changed text numbers around in his preliminary manuscript of *EN* 9. In the catalogue I have noted the *EN* 9 numbers in *LDN* and their final publication numbers in square brackets where they were changed. Furthermore, Lacheman had planned to add copies of additional fragments, of which there remain several hundreds. His sequence has been retained to preserve references to *EN* 9 texts in the Lacheman papers, in dissertations and in other places where they may occur. Those *EN* 9 texts that have been treated in dissertations and in A. Fadhil's *STPPKA* have also been provided with the appropriate references, although no exhaustive search of the dissertation literature has been attempted.

* * *

EN 9/1 1 SMN 3082 C 28
Ṭuppi mārūti by which Zikuya son of Keliya adopts Zike and "his brother" Ari(p)-šatuya gives Zike a 9 *a-mi-a-ri* field in exchange for 18 shekels of silver. Apil-Sîn the scribe.

EN 9/1 2 SMN 3094 C 28
Ṭuppi mārūti by which Zike son of Ar-tirwi receives 1 ANŠE sown field from Akip-apu son of Keliya in return for 1 ox and 40 ANŠE of grain. Apil-Sîn the scribe.

EN 9/1 3 SMN 3101 C 28
Ṭuppi mārūti by which Zike son of Ar-tirwi receives a 2 ANŠE sown field from ^{f}Ḫumeri in return for 2/3 MA.NA of silver. Apil-Sîn the scribe.

EN 9/1 4 SMN 2684 *SCTN* 2:222
Ṭuppi mārūti by which Eḫliya son of Ezira receives the *dimtu* [. . . .] from Teḫip-apu son of [Wa]ntiya in return for a number of goods including tin, grain and livestock. Tablet written in Nuzi.

EN 9/1 5 SMN 3595 G 29
Ṭuppi mārūti by which Šekar-Tilla son of Urḫiya receives a new *dimtu* from Elḫip-Tilla son of Šukriya in return for 1 ox, 4 MA.NA of bronze and 1 BÁN of grain. Tablet written in Nuzi by Turar-Tešup son of Itḫ-apiḫe.

EN 9/1 6 SMN 3560 F 25
Ṭuppi mārūti wherein Attilammu son of Ni[ḫriya] is adopted by Šellapai, Ḫairni, Arim-matka, and Teḫip-Tilla, four sons of Ipša-ḫalu. ^{d}UTA.AN.GAL the scribe.

EN 9/1 7 SMN 2630 K 32 *SCTN* 2:197
Ṭuppi mārūti by which Beliya son of Rabšeya acquires property in Ḫurazina ṣeḫru from Arip-apu son of Eniš-tae in return for 22 MA.NA of copper, 2 ANŠE 5 BÁN of grain and a full *kuduktu* of wool.

EN 9/1 8 SMN 2015
Ṭuppi mārūti by which Zikatu son of Akip-šarri receives all his property in Nuzi as his inheritance share from Ar-šaḫala son of Šann-apu. Turar-Tešup [son of] Kel-Tešup the scribe.

EN 9/1 9 SMN 906
Ṭuppi mārūti wherein ^{f}Mi[-x-..]-a daughter of Eniya adopts Kawinnanni son of Ar-teya and receives houses in Anzugalli. Sîn-iqiša (^{d}30-qí-ša) the scribe.[1]

EN 9/2 10 SMN 2390 S 132 *SCTN* 2:112–13
Statement of Ḫerši and Urḫi-Tilla sons of Naniya by which they adopt Utḫap-tae son of Ar-tura and give him houses in the *kirḫu* of the city of Nuzi. [Arip]-šarri [the scribe].

EN 9/1 11 SMN 1168 A 30
Ṭuppi mārūti weherein Ziliya adopts Keliya and Šummi-ilu sons of Kupiya. Sîn-aḫḫa-iddina (^{d}30-ŠEŠ-SUM-na) the scribe.

EN 9/1 12 SMN 1090
Fragmentary [*ṭuppi mārūti*] text.

EN 9/1 13 SMN 1109
Fragmentary [*ṭup*]*pi mārūti* text of [Namḫea] son of Arzipni [and ^{f}]Tarmennaya M[Í.LUGAL].

[1] In the catalogue to *EN* 9/1, the scribes in texts 9 and 11 were reversed. Note also the reading Sîn-aḫḫa-iddina instead of Sîn-nadin-aḫe for *EN* 9/1 11.

EN 9/1 14 SMN 1454
Ṭuppi mārūti by which [I]tḫiya son of Akkuya is adopted by Utḫapše son of Eḫliya and [f]Akamme and receives houses in Nuzi in return for 15 shekels of silver. [d]NANNA.MA.AN.SUM the scribe.

EN 9/1 15 SMN 2613 P 401 *SCTN* 2:185
Ṭuppi mārūti by which Zilim-ninu *amat ekalli* receives houses in Nuzi from Tešup-erwi *warad ekalli* in return for 30 MA.NA of copper and 2 sheep. Arim-matka the scribe.

EN 9/2 16 SMN 2128 S 151
Ṭuppi mārūti by which Wantiš-šenni son of [. . . .] adopts Tarmiya son of [Ḫuya] and gives him [4[?]+]3 GIŠ.APIN of fields west of the road of the city of Tarkulli. Tablet written at the Tiššа gate. Turar-Tešup son of [Kel-Tešup] the scribe.

EN 9/2 17 SMN 2302 S 124 *SCTN* 2:78
Ṭuppi mārūti by which Ḫanie son of Teḫip-apu adopts Muš-apu son of Purna-zini and gives him a 3 ANŠE field in the *ugāru* of Unapšewe. Amum-miya the scribe.

EN 9/2 18 SMN 2700+1780 S 113 *SCTN* 2:233
Ṭuppi mārūti by which Eḫli-apu son of [Abeya] adopts Muš-apu son of Purna-zini and gives him a 3 ANŠE field. [See now G. Wilhelm, *SCCNH* 7 (1995) 147.]

EN 9/2 19 SMN 2007+2957 S 124
Ṭuppi mārūti by which Ḫanukka son of Zilip-Tilla adopts Puḫi-šenni son of Muš-apu and gives him a field in the *ugāru* of Unapšewe. Tablet written in Unapšewe by Elḫip-Tilla. [See now G. Wilhelm, *SCCNH* 7 (1995) 148.]

EN 9/2 20 SMN 2083 S 112
Ṭuppi mārūti by which Nai-te son of Ḫanaya adopts Puḫi-šenni son of Muš-apu and gives him property on the canal (*ḫirītu*) of Unapšewe. Tablet written in Unapšewe by Elḫip-Tilla.

EN 9/2 21 SMN 2095 S 129
Ṭuppi mārūti by which Nai-te son of Ḫanaya adopts Puḫi-šenni son of Muš-apu and gives him property in the *ugāru* of Unapšewe. Tablet written in Unapšewe by Elḫip-Tilla.

EN 9/2 22 SMN 2091 S 129
Ṭuppi mārūti by which anakka son of Milkiya adopts Puḫi-šenni son of Muš-apu and gives him property in the *ugāru* of Unapšewe. Tablet written in Unapšewe by Elḫip-Tilla.

EN 9/2 23 SMN 2307+2433 S 124 *SCTN* 2:80
Ṭuppi mārūti by which Ḫatarte son of [Atanaḫ-ili] and Nai-te son of Ḫanaya adopt Puḫi-šenni son of Muš-apu and give him property in the *ugāru* of Unapšewe. Tablet written in Unapšewe by Elḫ[ip-Tilla].

EN 9/1 24 SMN 2629 K 465 *SCTN* 2:267
Ṭuppi mārūti by which Teḫiya and Ḫutiya sons of Kip-tae receive property *ina ṣērīti* of the city of Nuzi from Šennaya son of Ar-nuzu in return for livestock and moveable property. [. . . .]-sa the scribe.

EN 9/1 25 SMN 723 A 26
Ṭuppi mārūti by which Pai-Tešup son of Ḫanaya receives an orchard from Atal-Tešup and Tarmi-Tešup sons of Enna-mati in return for 2 ANŠE of grain. Tablet written at the Zizza gate by ^{d}AK-DINGIR.RA son of Sîn-napšir.

EN 9/1 26 SMN 1415+1708
Ṭuppi mā[rūti] by which Puḫiya son of IBILA$^{!}$-^{d}[. . . .] is adopted by and receives property from Pai-Tešup and Eḫli-Tešup sons of Ma[. . . .] for 10 MA.NA of tin, bronze and barley. Text written in Anzugalli.

EN 9/2 27 SMN 2193 S 113 *SCTN* 2:19
[*Ṭuppi mārūti*] of Akkul-enni son of [Eḫliya] adopts ^{f}Tulpunaya and provides an orchard in Temtenaš to her. Taya the scribe. Lines 1–4 may be restored as follows:

(1) [*ṭup-pí ma*]-⌈*a-ru*⌉-*te* (2) [*ša* ^{I}*ak-ku-le-en-ni* DUMU] *eḫ-li-ia* (3) [*ù*] ⌈^{f}⌉*tù-ul-*⌈*pu*⌉*-un-na-a-a* (4) [*a-na* DUMU]-*ti* DÙ-*sú-ma*

EN 9/2 28 SMN 2168+? S 112 *SCTN* 2:10.
[*Ṭuppi mārūti*] by which Eḫlip-apu son of [Apeya] adopts Muš-apu son of Purna-zini and gives him houses and *paiḫu* land. Tablet written in Unapšewe by [. . .]-*ia*.

EN 9/2 29 SMN 2133 S 151
Ṭuppi mārūti by which Unap-tae son of Akkul-enni adopts Bel-šaduni *wardu* of [. . . .]. Šamaš-uraššu son of Ṣilliya the scribe.

EN 9/1 30 SMN 2068 N 120
Declaration before witnesses concerning the real estate adoption of Tul-[. . . .] daughter of Meli[. . . .]. ^{d}AK-DINGIR.RA the scribe.

EN 9/2 31 SMN 2362 S 132 *SCTN* 2:97.
Ṭuppi mārūti by which Ennaya son of Ete[š-šenni$^{?}$] adopts Arikkaya his brother. Arik-kaya gives Ennaya 15 sheep. Tablet written in Al-Ilani by [^{d}AK-DINGIR.RA] son of Sîn-napšir.[2]

EN 9/2 32 SMN 2366 S 132 *SCTN* 2:99
Ṭuppi mārūti by which Ennaya son of Eteš-šenni adopts Ḫuziri son of Arikkaya and gives him property. Taya son of Apil-sîn the scribe.

EN 9/2 33 SMN 2376 S 152 *SCTN* 2:105
[*Ṭuppi mārūti*] by which Tae son of [. . . .] adopts Pašši-Tilla and gives him an orchard. ŠU-^{d}IŠKUR the scribe.

[2] So according to the analysis of Paola Negri Scafa, and not Taya as in the catalogue to *EN* 9/2.

EN 9/2 34 SMN 2485 S 151 *SCTN* 2:132
Statement of Tenteya, Umpiya, Iwišti, Ennike and Puḫiya sons of Keliya by which they adopt Ḫanukka son of Tarmiya and give him houses in the city of Nuzi. Ar-purusa the scribe.

EN 9/2 35 SMN 2488 S 151 *SCTN* 2:134
Ṭuppi mārūti by which Wantip-šarri and Makuya sons of Zike adopt Ḫuya son of Šimika-atal and give him houses in the city of Nuzi. Arim-matka the scribe.

EN 9/2 36 SMN 2497 S 151*SCTN* 2:141–42
[*Ṭuppi mārūti*] by which Ḫaniu-šaḫari son of [. . . .] adopts Tarmiya son of Ḫuya and gives him two parcels of land, one in the *dimtu* of Kazzi-buzzi. Tablet written in Nuzi.

EN 9/1 37 SMN 3610 G 29
Damaged [*ṭuppi m*]*ārūti* by which [Zilip-apu son of Zi]nkuya is adopted by [Puḫiya and] Šamaḫul, sons of Zi[patu].

EN 9/2 38 SMN 2474 S 151 *SCTN* 2:127 (not transliterated)
Fragmentary [*ṭuppi mārūti*]? in which Muš-apu receives property in Unap-šewe. *SCTN* 2:127 assigns the text to Room 133.

EN 9/2 39 SMN 2517 S 151 *SCTN* 2:152–53
[*Ṭuppi mārūti*] by which Pai-Tilla and Teḫip-Tilla [sons of Šukriya] adopt Tarmiya son of Ḫuya and give him a ANŠE field in the *ugāru* of Nuzi.

EN 9/2 40 SMN 2501 S 151 *SCTN* 2:144
Statement (*lišānu*) of Ennike son of [. . .] by which he adopts Tarmiya and gives him *paiḫu* land in the *kirḫu* of Nuzi. [Šiman]ni son of Nabu-ila the scribe.

EN 9/1 41 SMN 2580 P 380[3] *SCTN* 2:168–69
Ṭuppi mārūti by which Zilip-apu son of Zinkuia adopts Puia and Šamahu sons of Zipatu. Kinniya the scribe.

EN 9/1 42 SMN 2584 P 382 *SCTN* 2:171
Ṭuppi mārūti by which Ḫampizi son of Ar-š[atuya] receives fields in Nuzi as their inheritance shares from Elḫip-šarri, [Ḫa]manna, and Kipaya sons of [Šellaya].

EN 9/1 43 SMN 2650 P 466 *SCTN* 2:207
Sammelurkunde recording *ṭuppi mārūti* arrangements by which Taya son of Arim-matka receives real estate. Balṭu-kašid [TI.LA.KUR] son of Apil-Sîn the scribe.

EN 9/1 44 SMN 2720 *SCTN* 2:243–44
[*Ṭupp*]*i mārūti* wherein Kilta-muli son of Ḫalutta adopts Kikkiya and Ḫašip-Tilla sons of Akikka and receives property in the *dimtu* of [. . . .] and buildings for 9 MA.NA 30 GÍN of bronze. Tablet written in Nuzi by Sîn-šaduni.

[3] Not P 382, as published in *EN* 9/1.

EN 9/2 45 SMN 2733 *SCTN* 2:253
Ṭuppi mārūti by which Nai-šeri adopts Paya, Ar-zizza and Alki-Tešup sons of Elḫip-šarri and gives them a 5 ANŠE field in the *dimtu* of Kurriawe. Tablet written in the city of Akip-apu. [*x*]-*a-gal*? son of Sîn-iluya the scribe.

EN 9/2 46 SMN 3483 F 24
Ṭuppi mārūti by which Iluya son of Ipša-ḫalu and Waraduya son of Warḫi-šenni adopt Arik-kaya son of Eteš-šenni and give him property. Taya the scribe.

EN 9/1 47 SMN 2645 P 466 *SCTN* 2:203
Ṭuppi mārūti by which Eḫli-Tešup son of Taya receives 1 ANŠE 4 GIŠ.APIN of fields from Kindutti and Šekaru sons of Unnuki in return for 1 ANŠE 5 BÁN of grain and 1 sheep. Zini [son of Kiyanipu] the scribe.

EN 9/1 48 SMN 3666 G 73
Ṭuppi mārūti of Pui-tae son of [Uki]atal who adopts Kerip-šeri [son of Šer-Tešup] and provides him with a [field] in the city of Kipri on the [road] to the city of Anzukalli.

EN 9/2 49 SMN 2323 S 124 *SCTN* 2:85
[*Ṭuppi mārūti*] by which Eḫlip-apu son of [Abeya] adopts Muš-apu son of Purna-zini and gives him a *n* GIŠ.APIN field in the *ugāru* of [Unapšewe].

EN 9/3 50 SMN 2716[4]
Ṭuppi mārūti wherein Taizunni son of Ḫalutta probably adopts fTarmennaya daughter of Teḫip-Tilla. Her share in the *ugāru* of the city of Atakkal is mentioned. [*Šuk*?-]*ri*-Tešup the scribe. See also nos. 52A, B, C and 53.

EN 9/3 51 SMN 3606 G 29
Ṭuppi mārūti wherein Kinzi son of Ṭab-šarru from the land of [. . . .] is adopted Katiri son of Aka[ya].

EN 9/3 52A, B, C SMN 2775+2779+?
Fragmentary [*ṭuppi mārūti*] wherein fTarmennaya MÍ.LUGAL, daughter of Teḫip-Tilla is adopted by Elḫip-apu son of Šanḫari. Tablet written after the *šudutu* at [the gate of the city of Atakal]. See also nos. 50 and 53. May be restored as follows.

A: (1) [*ṭup-pi ma-ru*]-*ti ša* I[*eḫ-li-pa-pu*] (2) [DUMU *Ša-an*]-*ḫa-ri* (3) [f*tar-mé*]-*en-na-a-a* (4) [DUMU.MÍ *te*]-*ḫi-ip-til-la* [*a-na*] (5) [*ma-ru-ti*] *i-te-pu-uš* (6) [*ki-ma* ḪA.LA]-*šu* 7 GIŠ.APIN [A.ŠÀ *ši-qú-ú*] (7) [*i-na ú-ga*]-*ri ša* URU *a*-[*tak-kál i-na*] (8) [*su-ta-an* A].ŠÀ *ša* I*na*-[. . . . *i-na*] (9) [*šu-pa-al* A].ŠÀ *sa* I*pu*-[. . . .] (10) [*i-na* . . .-*n*]*i* A.ŠÀ *ša* I[. . . .] (11) [*i-na e-le*]-*en* A.ŠÀ *ša* I*ú*-[. . . .]

B: (1) [. . . .]-*šu*-[. . . .] (2) [I*eḫ-l*]*i-pa-pu* A.[ŠÀ *ša-a-šu*] (3) [*ú-z*]*a-ak-ka*$_4$*-mi a*-[*na*] (4) [f]*tar-mé-en-na-a-a* [*i-na-an-din*] (5) [*šum*]-*ma* A.ŠÀ GAL *ù la i*-[*na-ak-ki-is/sú*] (6) *ù* I*eḫ-li-pa-pu ka*$_4$-[*ás-ka*$_4$] (7) [*i*]*š-tu* A.ŠÀ *an-nu-ú ù* (8) [*la i-na-ak-ki-is m*]*a-am-ma-ma la i*-[*na-an-din*]

[4] According to Lacheman's handwritten annotation in *SCTN* 2 241, the tablet SMN 2716 transliterated in *SCTN* 2 241 was renumbered as SMN 2761 and the tablet published here was given the number 2716. No explanation was provided for the change.

C: (1) ù [. . . .] l.e. (2) *il-ku ša* [A.ŠÀ [I]*eḫ-li-pa-pu*] (3) *na-ši ù* [f]*t*[*ar-mé-en-na-a-a*] (4) *la na-ši ma-an-nu-um-*[*me-e*] rev. (5) *i-na be-ri-šu-nu ša* K[I.BAL-]/*ak-ka*$_4$*-tu*$_4$ 1 MA.NA KÙ.BABBAR (6) 1 MA.NA KÙ.SI$_{18}$ *ú-ma-a*[*l-la*] (7) *ṭup-pi i-na* EGIR-*k*[*i šu-du-ti i-na*] (8) [*ba-ab a*]-⌈*bu-ul*⌉-[*li ša* URU *a-tak-kál*] 9) [*ša-ṭi-ir*] (remainder destroyed)

EN 9/3 53 SMN 2774
Fragmentary [*ṭuppi mārūti*], [f]Tarmennaya mentioned. See above nos. 50 and 52A, B, and C. Fields on the road to the city of Ulamme are involved.

EN 9/3 54 SMN 2782
Ṭuppi [*mārūti*] wherein Paratta [so]n of Akip-šar[ri] is adopted.

EN 9/3 55 SMN 3622 G 29
[*Ṭuppi*] *mārūti* wherein Minaš-šuk son of Enna-mati is adopted by Tarmiya son of Teššuya and provided with a 1 ANŠE 2 GIŠ.APIN *kumānu* field (and other fields?) in the city of Ḫaminaš. Tablet written after the *šudutu* at the gate of the city of Ḫaminaš. [Day]yan-beli the Ḫapiru scribe.

EN 9/3 56 SMN 3491 F 24
Ṭuppi mārūti wherein Teḫip-šarri son of Šelwiḫu and Ḫinziku son of Ar-Tešup adopt Zilip-apuḫe son of Ṭab-šarri. Iniya the scribe.

EN 9/3 57 SMN 3589 G 29
Ṭuppi mārūti wherein Nal-tuka son of A[rmanni] and Ḫašuar son of Itḫ-amurri adopt Itti-šarri son of Turari and provide him with a 3 ANŠE field on the road to Nuzi. Tablet written after the *šudutu* of the palace at the gate of the city of Nuzi[!]. A[kipta-š]enni the scribe son of Tešup-atal. Collated.

EN 9/3 58 SMN 3591 G 29
Ṭuppi mārūti wherein Tešup-nirari, Šimikatal, Itḫi-Tilla, and Šurki-Tilla sons of Teḫip-Tilla adopt Kelip-šarri son of Ḫut-Tešup and a 1 ANŠE field in the city of Kipri is provided. Tablet written after the *šudutu*. Taika the scribe.

EN 9/1 59 SMN 3150 C 28
Ṭuppi mārūti by which Šilaḫi-Tešup son of Ḫašuar adopts [Ḫu]tiya son of Alki-Tešup and a field on the road to Artiḫḫe is provided. E[ḫe]l-Tešup the scribe.

EN 9/3 60 SMN 3475 F 16
Ṭuppi mārūti wherein [f]Ur-iyaše daughter of A[. . . .] is adopted by [Zike] son of Kawinni and Ḫutanni son of Turar-Tešup. Tablet written after the *šudutu* at the western/lower gate of the city of Nuzi. Arip-šarri the scribe.

EN 9/3 61 SMN 3619 G 29
Ṭuppi mārūti wherein Tešup-atal and Ḫaniku sons of Tulpiya are adopted by Itti-šarri son of Turari and a 1 ANŠE 1+n [GIŠ].APIN field on the road to the city of Subari is provided. Tablet written after the *šudutu* of the palace of Nuzi at the Great Gate. Akipta-šenni the scribe son of Tešup-a[tal].

EN 9/3 62 SMN 3760
Fragmentary *Ṭuppi mārūti* wherein Ḫampizi probably adopts Alki-Tilla. [Šeršiya the scribe.]

EN 9/3 63 SMN 3652 G 53
Ṭuppi mārūti wherein Kirip-šeli son of Un-Tešup adopts [Ar-ša]nta son of Šennaya and a 1 ANŠE 5 GIŠ.APIN field in the ci[ty of Nuzi] is provided. [Tur]-šenni the scribe.

EN 9/3 64 SMN 3628 G 29
Ṭuppi šupeʾʾulti wherein Kinzi son of Ṭab-šar-beli exchanged [1] ANŠE of barley in the city of Ṣilliyawe with Ḫupita son of Kel-Tešup and in Nuzi with Kiwatae son of Makuya to be paid back in the month of Ululi. Ḫupita the scribe.

EN 9/3 65 SMN 2136 P 470
[Declaration (*lišānu*)] before witnesses by [. . . .] concerning land, houses and tin loaned(?) to/exchanged(?) with Utḫap-tae son of Artura. Tablet written after the *šudutu* at the gate of the city of Nuzi. [*Ni-ra*]-*ri* son of Taya the scribe.

EN 9/3 66 SMN 1421
Statement (*umma*) of Akip-šenni son of [. . . .] concerning a *mārūtu* agreement between Akip-šenni and Itḫa[. . . .]. [^{d}UTA]-ḪE.GAL the scribe.

EN 9/2 67 SMN 2114 N 120
Statement (*umma*) of Ar-tašenni son of Arik-kewar concerning property in the *ugāru* of Nuzi that he has given to Utḫap-tae son of Ar-tura for six years. They will share the produce of the field. Tablet written by Ḫeltip-kuš⟨uḫ⟩.

EN 9/3 68 HM 8401
Ṭuppi mārūti and a declaration (*lišānu*) whereby Pal-Tešup son of Mat-Tešup and Alkiya son of Il-Tešup adopt Ḫašuar son of Šimi-katal and *kirḫu* land in the city of Lubti is involved. Tablet written at the Great Gate. [^{d}UTA/^{d}IŠKUR]-MA.AN.SUM the scribe.

EN 9/3 69 SMN 721 A 30
Ṭuppi šupeʾʾulti by which two brothers, Enna-mati and Ḫutanni-Tešup sons of Ewara-kale, exchange houses that they obtained through inheritance. Kabtu-beli the scribe.

EN 9/3 70 SMN 1083 A 26
[*Ṭuppi šu*]*peʾʾulti* whereby Ḫutanni-Tešup son of Ewar[a-kale] and Tešup-nirari son of Ewara-kale exchange *paiḫu* structures. Kabtu-[bel]i the scribe.

EN 9/3 71 SMN 905+1779(no copy) A 30
Ṭuppi šupeʾʾulti whereby houses and inheritance shares belonging to Arteya son of Takurr-ampi and Teḫiya son of Urḫital are exchanged. Arteya receives houses in the *ṣēritu* of Anzukalli and an inheritance share of an orchard in the same city. Teḫiya receives an inheritance share of houses in the city of Arrapḫe and of land in the city of Ellazi. Taya son of Apil-Sîn the scribe. Collated, joined and transliterated by G. Wilhelm.

(1) [ṭup]-*pí šu-pé-ul-ti ša* (2) ⸢^{I}*ar*⸣-*te-ia* DUMU *ta-kùr-ra-a-pí* (3) *ù ša* ^{I}*te-ḫi-ia* DUMU *ú-ri-ri* (4) ⸢É⸣.MEŠ.ḪÁ ḪA.LA-*šú ša* Á É.MEŠ *ša* (5) ⸢^{I}⸣*te-ḫi-ia um-mu-du* ^{I}*ar-te-ia i-na* (6) [UR]U *ar-ra-ap-ḫe a-na* ^{I}*te-ḫi-ia id-dì-i-in*$_6$ (7) [*ù*] ^{I}*te-ḫi-ia*

a-na [I]*ar-te-ia* (8) [É].MEŠ *i-na* URU *an-zu-gal-li* 2-*šu* (9) [*ú-k*]*a*$_4$-*al-la-a-ma ù i-na-an-din* (10) [É.MEŠ *i-n*]*a* Á É.MEŠ *ša* [I]*ar-te-ia* (11) [. . .]-*ti i-ga*$_{14}$-*ri-šu um-mu-du* (12) A.ŠÀ.M[EŠ Ḫ]A.LA-*šú* AŠ URU-*ki el-la-zi šu-pa-li-ia* (13) [I]*ar-te-ia a-na* [I]*te-ḫi-ia id-dì-in*$_6$ (14) *ù* [I]*te-ḫi-ia a-na* [I]*ar-te-ia* (15) ⌜É⌝.MEŠ AŠ URU *an-zu-gal-li i-na le-et* (16) É.MEŠ ⌜*ša*⌝ [I]*pur-ni-ia* AŠ *ṣé-ri-ti ù* GIŠ.KIRI$_6$ ḪA.LA-*šu* (17) *i-na* URU *a*[*n-z*]*u-*[*g*]*al-li ki-ma* [I]*te-ḫi-ia* (18) *a-na* [I]*a*[*r-t*]*e-ia id-dì-in*$_6$ (19) *ma-an-nu š*[*a*] BAL 1 MA.NA KÙ.BABBAR (20) 1 MA.NA KÙ.SI$_{18}$ *i-na-din* (21) IGI *bal-ṭù-ka*$_4$-*ši-id* DUMU-IBILA-DINGIR.30 (22) ŠU DUB.SAR-*rù* (lower edge) (23) IGI *ta-a-a* DUMU IBILA-DINGIR.30-*ma* (24) DUB.S[AR]-*ri-ma* (reverse) (25) IGI *ta-ku-ú-ia* DUMU [x]-*lu-še-en-ni* (26) ⌜*na*⌝-*gi*$_5$-*ru* (27) IGI *ar-nu-ur-ḫe* DUMU *ḫa-ma-an-na* (28) IGI *kè-el-te-šup* DUMU *ni-íḫ-ri-ia* (29) IGI *en-na-ma-ti* DUMU ⌜*zi*⌝-*li-ia* (30) ⌜IGI⌝ [*t*]*e-ḫi-ip-til-la* DUMU *na-ki-pu* (31) [IG]I *tup-ki-ia* DUMU *a-ri-ip*-LUGAL LÚ (32) UŠ.BAR {Seal impression} {Seal impression} (upper edge) 33) NA$_4$.KIŠIB [I]DUB.SAR-*ri* {Seal impression} (lower edge) {Seal impression}

EN 9/3 72 SMN 2010
Statement (*umma*) of Akkulenni concerning a field which was not *ḫišūru* belonging to [Akap]-taema and which had not been given to Ariḫ-ḫarpa.

EN 9/2 73 SMN 2337 S 129 *SCTN* 2:88–89
*Ṭuppi šupe*ʾʾ*ulti* by which Paya son of Elḫip-šarri and Pai-Tešup son of Arteya exchange *paiḫu* fields. Tablet written in the city of Akip-apu.

EN 9/2 74 SMN 2314 S 124 *SCTN* 2:82–83
*Ṭuppi šupe*ʾʾ*ulti* by which Utḫap-tae son of Enna-mati and Puḫi-šenni son of Muš-apu exchange fields in the *ugāru* of Unapšewe. El[ḫip-Tilla] the scribe.

EN 9/1 75 SMN 2627 P 465 *SCTN* 2:194
*Ṭuppi supe*ʾʾ*ulti* by which Taya son of Arim-matka and Šeḫala son of Akkuya exchange 8 GIŠ.APIN of fields. Arim-matka the scribe.

EN 9/2 76 SMN 2498 S 151 *SCTN* 2:142–43
*Ṭuppi šupe*ʾʾ*ulti* by which Šukriya son of Ḫuya and Šekar-Tilla son of Tarwaza exchange fields. Šukriya receives property north of the *dimtu* of Ḫuya. Rim-Sîn the scribe.

EN 9/2 77 SMN 2173+2316 S 124 *SCTN* 2:12; 83–84
*Ṭuppi šupe*ʾʾ*ulti* by which Ḫutip-Tilla son of Ḫuya and Puḫi-šenni son of Muš-apu exchange fields in Unapšewe. Elḫip-Tilla the scribe.

EN 9/3 78 SMN 1042 A 10
Statement (*umma*) of Elḫip-Tilla son of Ḫui-Tilla concerning an exchange of fields with his brother Keliya in the city and environs of Nuzi. Tablet written after the *šudutu* in Nuzi at the palace gate. Akap-šenni the scribe.

EN 9/3 79 SMN 3753
[*Ṭuppi šupe*ʾʾ*u*]*lti* whereby Ḫaniu [son of Arip-š]elli and Ennaya son of Irkipa exchange fields. Ḫaniu obtains land bordering on the Nirašše and Ardammaru canals in the district of Ḫalbaeniwe in exchange for land in Zaradanni? and an additional payment of *mobilia*.

EN 9/3 80 SMN 843+1293 A 26
Ṭuppi šu[*pe*ʾʾ*ul*]*ti* whereby Apukka son of Ḫak[. . . .] and Tupki-šenni [son of A]r-Tešup exchange female personnel. Tupki-šenni obtains Arim-ninu and Ḫaši-belt-ekalli from Apukka in exchange for Alani[. . .] and Petiya. Sîn-mušal the scribe.

EN 9/2 81 SMN 2706 *SCTN* 2:236
*Ṭuppi šupe*ʾʾ*ulti* by which Ḫuziri son of Arik-kaya and Ennaya son of Eteš-šenni exchange fields. dNANNA.MA.AN.SUM the scribe.

EN 9/3 82 SMN 2100 N 120
Statement (*umma*) of Akap-taema son of Arimmuiya concerning fields and houses which he had given to Ḫutiya son of Šimi-katal. Unuku the scribe.

EN 9/2 83 SMN 2126 S 130
Statement (*umma*), perhaps in court, of Akkul-enni concerning fields given to Ariḫ-ḫarpa and Kiziri.

EN 9/3 84 SMN 3576 F 26
*Ṭuppi šupe*ʾʾ*ulti* whereby Šar-Tešup son of Utḫap-tae and Kannaya son of Ikkiya exchange 1 *sariyannu ḫarari*. Tablet written after the *šudutu* at the gate of the city of [. . .]taḫḫe. Wur-Tešup the scribe.

EN 9/1 85 SMN 3107 C 28
List of fields owned by various individuals.

EN 9/3 86 SMN 2052 N 120
Declarations (*lišānu*) of Kupaya and Šumalla before the men of Temtenaš concerning fields, houses, and orchards about which Zaziya and Šamaš-dayyanu impressed their hems in clay. Long list of witnesses. Tablet written after the *šudutu* at the gate of the city of Temtenaš. Sîn-iqiša the scribe.

EN 9/3 87 SMN 3464 D 20
[Declaration (*lišānu*)] of [. . . .]-Tešup before [. . . .].MEŠ involving [Na]nip-Tešup son of Urḫiya.

EN 9/3 88 SMN 835 T 19
List of 30 ANŠE of fields for harvesting of various crops (wheat, barley, etc.) in the city of Arrapḫe and the districts of Ki[. . . .], Šiki[. . . .], Zula, and Ḫalani.

EN 9/3 89 SMN 1158 A 26
Statement (*umma*) concerning a field on the road to Apenaš which Akip-tašenni gave to his wife fPuḫati.

EN 9/3 90 SMN 822 R 76
Three fields which had been given to individuals from the city of Zimḫalše were taken (back?) by Apiḫe.

EN 9/3 91 SMN 2242 N 120 *SCTN* 2:68
Record concerning a field of Šaḫluya son of Tuliya which was taken by the palace (authorities) for *ilku* obligations.

EN 9/3 92 SMN 2614 V 428 *SCTN* 2:202
Record of a 2 ANŠE field of Erwi-šarri and Tišenna sons of Arta-šenni along with quantities of bronze, wool, barley, and wheat given to Utḫap-tae.

EN 9/2 93 SMN 2354 S 132 *SCTN* 2:93–94
List of fields for harvesting and individuals who hold them. Declaration (*umma*) of Ḫanaya and Teḫiya.

EN 9/1 94 SMN 3105 C 28
List of real estate (*nakkatu*) and houses owned by various individuals.

EN 9/1 95 SMN 2137 P 466
Wage contract between Eḫli-Tešup son of Taya and Utḫap-tae son of Enna-milka. Šar-Tilla son of Iluya the scribe.

EN 9/2 96 SMN 2512 S 151 *SCTN* 2:149–50
List of *tarbie* fields owned by certain individuals. Totaled as 2 ANŠE 2 GIŠ.APIN *tarbie ša* ZAG.

EN 9/2 97 SMN 2439 S 133 *SCTN* 2:125
Tin loan of Pašši-Tilla son of Pula-ḫali. Mukiya the scribe.

EN 9/3 98 SMN 3004
Record of 12 ANŠE of fields on the road to the city of Karanna which Ḫaš[iya son] of Warḫabi! gave to Mušeya.

EN 9/1 99 SMN 2579 P 382 *SCTN* 2:168
Letter from Wantiyama to Tuni-lenna concerning his trip to the city of Šuri-niwa and his transactions over grain and straw.

EN 9/3 100 SMN 845
Record of barley and wheat seed provided by Ḫašip-Tilla son of [. . . .] to Nan-Tešup son of Kirip-Til[la] for sowing a 1 ANŠE 5 GIŠ.APIN field.

EN 9/2 101 SMN 2487 S 151 *SCTN* 2:133
Statement of Eniš-tae son of Tauka concerning grain, the grain yield (*išpikū*) to be given to Tarmiya son of Ḫuya. Tablet written after the *šudutu* at the Great Gate in the city of Ar-šalipe by Enna-mati the scribe.

EN 9/2 102 SMN 2380 S 132 *SCTN* 2:107
Letter to Teḫip-šarri from Akip-tašenni SUKKAL concerning Kipal-enni son of Pula-ḫali.

EN 9/2 103 SMN 2510 S 151 *SCTN* 2:148
List of 25 men from the city of Nuzi to whom Pai-Tilla provides water.

EN 9/3 104 SMN 363(2?)1 G 29
Ṭuppi mārūti and statement (*umma*) of Takip-Tilla, who gave his son for adoption to Kinzi. Belam-nirari the scribe.

EN 9/3 105 SMN 3179 C 36
Record of 8 containers of oil (DAL Ì.MEŠ) given to the MÍ.LUGAL of Nuzi.

EN 9/2 106 SMN 2504 S 151 *SCTN* 2:146
[*Ṭuppi mārūti*] by which Akawatil, Tai-Tilla, and Šelluni [sons of Akap-šenni?] adopt Tarmiya son of Ḫuya. Tablet written after the *šudutu* in Nuzi at the Great Gate. Witnessed by 7 *mušalmu*.

EN 9/3 107 HM 8402
Statement (*umma*) of Akip-apu son of Taya relinquishing claim to houses that he had [given?] to Turarteya, Nuzza, and Niḫriya, sons of Ekeke. Tablet written at the Great Gate. ᵈIŠKUR-MA.AN.SUM the scribe.

EN 9/3 108 SMN 3001?
Ṭuppi mārūti whereby Untea son of Ma[t]eya adopts Ziliya son of [. . . .]ya. A 4 GIŠ.APIN field is provided.

EN 9/3 109 SMN 3506 F 24
Letter to ᶠŠunšunnaya from Ḫutip-uraše concerning one woman whom Tarmi-Tešup son of Mutaya took as a price for horses in Al-Ilani.

EN 9/2 110 SMN 2438 S 133 *SCTN* 2:125
Beginning of text lost. Lacheman notes read:

(x+1) *um-ma* [ᴵ*wa-an-ti-ia-ma*] (x+2) *a-nu-u*[*um-ma* . .] (x+3) ᴵ*šur-k*[*i-til-la* . .] (x+4) LÚ [. . . .] (x+5) *ša* [. . . .] (x+6) 6 ANŠE.MEŠ-*šu* (x+7) 4 LÚ.MEŠ [. .] (x+8) *i-na* KUR *nu-ul-*[*lu-a-ú*] (x+9) DU-*ak* (x+10) *a-na* ŠU-*t*[*i*] (x+11) *bi-ki-is-*[*mi*] (x+12) *ù li-qè-*[*mi*] (x+13) NA_4 ᴵ*wa-an-ti-*[*ia*] (x+14) NA_4 ᴵ*te-ḫi-ip-til-la* DUMU *pu-ḫi-še-en-ni*.

EN 9/2 111 SMN 2361 S 132 *SCTN* 2:97
Fragmentary letter. Nanna-adaḫ the scribe.

EN 9/1 112 SMN 3356 D 6 *CPN*, p. 23
Letter from Ḫeltip-Tešup to Ipša-ḫalu concerning a legal case of Teḫip-apu.

EN 9/1 113 SMN 2737 *SCTN* 2:254–55
[Letter] to Pišaqu?? of Tabriu concerning water and canals.

EN 9/1 114 SMN 2572 P 357 *SCTN* 2:165
Letter to Zil-Tešup from Akiya.

EN 9/1 115 SMN 3582? F 38
Letter to Tišam-mušni from Akiya.

EN 9/1 116 SMN 1045 A 34
Letter from Šar-Tešup, the *ḫalzuḫlu* to Zike, the mayor of Zizza.

EN 9/1 117 SMN 3083 C 28 Chow, *KQN*, 177
Letter to the SUKKALs from the judges concerning a lawsuit between Ḫutiya son of Arip-sarri and Qištiya son of Šennaya. Kel-Tešup the scribe.

EN 9/2 118 SMN 3657 G 73
Statement of Ila-nišu son of Ḫabira concerning the transfer of Tarmiya and Taika sons of Kulaḫubi to Eḫlip-apu son of Apeya. The two men were debtors of Ila-nišu, and Eḫlip-apu paid their debt to him. Tablet written in Nuzi by Muš-Tešup son of Ḫupita.

EN 9/1 119 SMN 3567 F 25
Letter from Ḫutip-uraššе to Aril-lumti concerning the status of some property.

EN 9/1 120 SMN 3489 F 24
Letter to Tupki-Tilla from *Na-bi*$^{?}$-[. . . .].

EN 9/1 121 SMN 858
Letter to ^{f}Aštaḫuta from Ar-Tešup.

EN 9/1 122 HM 8400+1696 *SCCNH* 1, p. 374
Statement (*umma*) of Ikkiri son of Šarukke concerning real estate. Turari the scribe. [See now G. Wilhelm, *SCCNH* 7 (1995) 146.]

EN 9/1 123 SMN 1999
[Declaration (*lišānu*)] before witnesses of Akapše, Akawatil and [. .]kerḫe, sons of Elli regarding the harvesting of fields in the *dimtu* of Akkuya. ^{d}AK-DINGIR.RA the scribe.

EN 9/1 124 SMN 3175$^{?}$ C 28
[Declaration (*lišānu*)] before witnesses of Akkul-enni son of Zilip-apu whereby he states that Amur-atal son of Tulpi-šenni gave him the *kaška* (feudal rights) to his field and that he has given that field *ana titennūtu* to Amur-atal son of Tulpi-šenni for ten years. Seal of the scribe.

EN 9/2 125 SMN 2208 N 120 *SCTN* 2:28.
Record of a total of 3 ANŠE 8 GIŠ.APIN of fields in the city of [. . . .], the inheritance share of Utḫap-tae, which he gave to his "brother" Šeḫal-Tešup. [. . . .] the scribe.

EN 9/1 126 SMN 2587 P 382 *SCTN* 2:172
Statements (*umma*) of Taya son of Ninu-atal, Eḫli-Tešup son of Ṣupr-Adad, and Urḫiya son of Ṣupr-Adad concerning the division of property belonging to Ṣupr-Adad in Nuzi. Sîn-iqiša the scribe.

EN 9/1 127 SMN 2088+? N 120
Ṭuppi tamgurti between ^{f}Awišnaya and (her husband) Šešwaya son of Arzizza and Arip-enni *wardat* ^{f}Tulpan-naya. Top of tablet joined to fragment of unknown SMN number. Šeršiya the scribe.[5]

EN 9/2 128 SMN 1684
Part of a transaction whereby fields are given to Muš-apu and Šeḫliya.

EN 9/2 129 SMN 2475 S 136 *SCTN* 2:127–28
Letter to Eḫli[ya] from Šurki-Tilla concerning the Tišša gate, the gathering of scribes and the people of Nuzi, and their dispatch to Anzugalli.

EN 9/2 130 SMN 2505 S 151 *SCTN* 2:146–47
Declaration (*lišānu*) before witnesses of Tai-Tilla son of Utḫap-še concerning the 10 ANŠE barley yield (*išpikū*) from a 5 ANŠE field which he promises to provide.

[5] According to graphemic analysis, Šarwiya in this text is an error for Šar/Šer-ši!-ia.

EN 9/1 131 SMN 2264x[6] N 120
[*Ṭupp*]*i* [*m̥* *.ā*]*rūti* wherein Taya [son of I]pnuša adopts Urḫiya, Urpatta and [Ak]kuya son of Ninu-atal. Ila-nišu the scribe.

EN 9/1 132 SMN 3375? D 6
Letter from Ḫupi[ta the scribe] to Utḫa[ya].

EN 9/1 133 SMN 3650 G 53
Letter from Urḫi-Tešup to Wantari.

EN 9/1 134 SMN 2385 S 132 *SCTN* 2:134
Letter from Erwi-šarri to Elḫi[p-Tilla?].

EN 9/1 135 SMN 2642 P 460–66 *SCTN* 2:202
Letter to Šeršiya from Šar-Tešup concerning Eḫli-Tešup son of Taya of Nuzi.

EN 9/1 136 SMN 3517 F 24
Letter to Killi from Akip-Tilla, the scribe, "I am not your slave!"

EN 9/1 137 SMN 3564? F 24
Damaged letter perhaps dealing with temple personnel.

EN 9/1 138 SMN 1154 A 34
Letter to ᵈIŠKUR.MA.AN.SUM and to Ar-Tešup from Puitae.

EN 9/1 139 SMN 755
Damaged real estate transaction. ᵈAK-DINGIR.RA son of Sîn-napšir the scribe.

EN 9/1 140 SMN 3557 F 25 *CPN*, p. 41
Statements (*umma*) by Naiteya son of Ikkinna and Puḫi-šenni son of Paliya, each claiming ownership of the same segment of land in the west tract. Ar-Tešup son of Turari the scribe.

EN 9/1 141 SMN 1593
Declaration (*lišānu*) before witnesses of Ariya [son of Š]ukr-apu concerning a dispute over a 5 ANŠE field. Seal of the scribe.

EN 9/2 142 SMN 2179 S 112 *SCTN* 2:14–15
Statement (*umma*) of Unnuni son of Waqar-beli concerning the renewal of a real estate *titennūtu* with Muš-apu son of Purna-zini made previously by his father. Dayyan-beli [the scribe?].

EN 9/2 143 SMN 2313 S 124 *SCTN* 2:82
Ṭuppi titennūti whereby Akap-šenni son of Purna-zini gives a 3 ANŠE field in the *ugāru* of Unapšewe to Muš-apu son of Purna-zini. Tablet written in Unapšewe by [. . . .] the scribe.

EN 9/2 144 SMN 2803 *IN*, Text 11
[Statement (*umma*)] of Akip-tašenni who enters the house of Muš-apu son of Purna-zini *ana titennūti* for three years. 20 MA.NA of copper and 2 ANŠE 50 SÌLA of barley are provided.

[6] SMN 2264, a different text, is published as HSS 15 47.

EN 9/2 145 SMN 2519 S 132 *SCTN* 2:154
Ṭuppi titennūti by which Wantiya son of Ar-nu[zu] gives a 9 GIŠ.APIN field in the *ugāru* of the city of Unapšewe to Muš-apu son of Purna-zini for four years.

EN 9/2 146 SMN 2319+2321 S 124 *SCTN* 2:84–85
[*Ṭuppi mārūti*] by which Amarša adopts Puḫi-šenni. Tablet written in Unapše by [Elḫip?]-Tilla.

EN 9/1 147 SMN 1418 A 30 *IN*, pp. 136–37
Ḫanaya son of Apiššeya receives 3 GUN of copper from Kainanni and Ennaya *ana titennūti* and remains in the house of Ar-teya until he returns the copper. Turari the scribe.

EN 9/1 148 SMN 1635
Fragmentary [declaration (*lišānu*)] concerning real estate.

EN 9/1 149 SMN 1592 *IN*, p. 112
[*Ṭuppi titennūtu*] in which Zirra places his son Pal-Tešup with Pai-Tešup, *šellintannu* of Šilwa-Tešup, as surety for a loan of wheels and asses for two years. Document written after proclamation in the Tišša gate in Nuzi. Scribe Ḫašip-[x son of x]-enni.

EN 9/1 150 SMN 2778
Fragmentary *ṭuppi* [*titennūṭi*] real estate transaction. Dayyan-beli the scribe.

EN 9/1 151 SMN 2047 N 120 *IN*, p. 137
Ṭuppi titennūtu in which Kip-talili places his sons as surety with Tai-Tilla for a tin loan to Ipša-ḫalu son of Te[ḫu]ya. Ancillary real estate clause not entirely legible. Ipša-ḫalu the scribe.

EN 9/2 152 SMN 2102 *IN*, Text 35
Ṭuppi titennūti whereby Matip-apu and Akip-Tešup sons of Tarmiya receive bronze from Utḫap-tae son of Ar-tura in return for Akip-Tešup's working for Utḫap-tae for four years. Pui-tae the scribe.

EN 9/2 153 SMN 2493 S 151 *SCTN* 2:137; *IN*, Text 13
Declaration (*lišānu*) before witnesses of Ay-abaš whereby he places his son Wantišše *ana titennūti* with Tarmiya son of [Ḫuya] for *n* years. Tablet written after the *šudutu* at the Great Gate in Nuzi.

EN 9/1 154 SMN 2144
Statement of Akkul-enni son of Tuniya by which he enters the house of Tešup-mati son of Šerta-ma-ilu *ana titennūti* in return for 50 MA.NA of tin. Tablet written after the *šudutu* at the gate in Ḫurazina ṣeḫru (GUŠKIN-*na*-TUR) by Iriri the scribe.

EN 9/1 155 SMN 3587 G 29 *IN*, p. 110
Titennūtu in which Iluya and Ḫasse, sons of Adad-eriš, give their brother Kaniya as surety to Kirip-šeri son of Ḫut-Tešup on a loan of grain, tin, livestock, and cloth. Utḫap-tae the scribe.

EN 9/2 156 SMN 2013 S 113 *IN*, Text 6
Ṭuppi ti⟨te⟩nnūti by which Minaš-šuk son of Keliya and ᶠUnuš-kiaše wife of Keliya give Appuzizi son of Keliya to Šeḫal-Tešup son of Teḫup-šenni for four years. Tablet written in Nuzi. [. . . .] the scribe.

EN 9/2 157 SMN 2367 S 132 *SCTN* 2:100.
Fragmentary [statement (*umma*)] describing a *titennūtu* arrangement between Ḫane son of Teḫip-apu and Muš-apu [son of Purna-zini]. A previous arrangement is mentioned. Tarmi-Tilla the scribe.

EN 9/2 158 SMN 2338 S 129 *SCTN* 2:89.
Statement (*umma*) of Šurki-Tilla son of Tampi-kutati who gives his inheritance share to Urḫi-šarri son of Ḫanaya.

EN 9/3 159 SMN 2240 N 120 *SCTN* 2:67
Statement (*umma*) of Arip-šeriš concerning something of Zilip-Tilla which Artura had received.

EN 9/1 160 SMN 3492 F 24
Fragmentary [statement (*umma*)] of Taika son of [. . . .] who gives a field *ana titennūti* for five years. Tablet written after the *šudutu* in Nuzi by Nirari son of Taya the scribe.

EN 9/3 161 SMN 2815
Declaration (*lišānu*) of Ešukru son of Turari before witnesses concerning 3 GIŠ.APIN of land belonging to his father which had been given *ana titennūtu*. ᵈUTA-AN.DÙL son of Taya [the scribe].

EN 9/1 162 SMN 825 A 26
Ṭuppi titennūti by which Ḫupita son of Tente receives 1 ANŠE 5 GIŠ.APIN of field in Tašenni from Ḫabira and Ar-tirwi sons of Šenniya in return for 10 MA.NA of copper, 4 sheep, and 12 ANŠE of grain.

EN 9/2 163 SMN 2194 S 113 *SCTN* 2:20
[*Ṭuppi*] *titennūtu* by which Akaya son of Kuššiya gives property in the *ugāru* of the city of Unapšewe to Puḫi-šenni son of Muš-apu for five years. Elḫip-Tilla the scribe.

EN 9/3 164 SMN 1062
Ṭuppi titennūti wherein fields in the *dimtu* of Šešatu and Tamkariwe belonging to Eraši son of Zilip-apu and Ekeke son of Paiš-kummi were given to Akip-šenni son of Ku[la-ḫupi] for four years. 7 witnesses are (*m*)*ušelwu*. Zini the scribe.

EN 9/1 165 SMN 1067 *IN*, p. 130; *STPPKA*, p. 255
Ṭuppi titennūtu in which Šullum-Adad son of Tuḫmi-Tešup becomes surety to Ipša-ḫalu son of Unaya on a livestock and metal loan. Prior *ilku* obligation to Kirip-šarri by the borrower passed to Nula-zaḫi and Wur-te. Written at the gate of the city of Dur-ubla after the *šudutu*. Ḫurpi-Tešup scribe.

EN 9/2 166 SMN 2245 N 120 *SCTN* 2:69–70
Ṭuppi titennūti by which Teḫup-šenni son of Urḫiya enters the house of Paya son of Elḫip-šarri. [Tablet written after the *šudutu* in the city of Nuzi] by A[kipta]-šenni the scribe.

EN 9/3 167 SMN 1707
[Declaration (*lišānu*)] of Urḫitea son of Šilwaya before witnesses concerning 3 GIŠ.APIN of field on the road to Nuzi belonging to his brother, Kilenni. Tablet written at the Great Gate of the city of Kipri by Tae the scribe.

EN 9/2 168 SMN 2821 *SCTN* 2:258
[*Ṭuppi titennūtu*] by which Teḫip-Tilla [son of Šukriya] gives property to Tarmiya. Tablet written after the *šudutu* [in the city of . . . .] by SAG.AN.[KI] the scribe.

EN 9/3 169 SMN 1043 A 11
Ṭuppi titennūti wherein Tupki-šarri son of Kuzzu gave 1 ANŠE 5 GIŠ.APIN of field in the *ugāru* of the city of Nuzi to Pai-Tešup servant of Šilwa-Tešup for n years. Ipša-ḫalu the scribe.

EN 9/1 170 SMN 3472 F 16
[Statement (*umma*)] of Ḫutanni son of [. . . .] who gives 1 fine, twice-plucked ewe *ana titennūti* to Šimi-Tilla in exchange for a wheel. Arip-šarri the scribe.

EN 9/2 171 SMN 2312 S 124 *SCTN* 2:81–82.
Declaration (*lišānu*) of Attilammu son of Tur-šenni before witnesses whereby he gives a field in the *ugāru* of the city of Unapšewe to Puḫi-šenni son of Muš-apu *ana titennūti* for three years. Elḫip-Tilla son of Kel-Tešup the scribe.

EN 9/2 172 SMN 2132 S 152
Ṭuppi titennūti by which Keliya son of Tampuya gives a 1 ANŠE field in Nuzi to Gimil-abi son of Akip-apu for five years. SAG.AN.KI the scribe.

EN 9/3 173 SMN 998
Statement (*umma*) of Teḫip-Tilla son of Šekari concerning 6 ANŠE of barley which he borrowed from Šukraya son of Utḫap-tae.

EN 9/3 174 SMN 1300
Fragment of an interest-bearing loan.

EN 9/2 175 SMN 2311 S 124 *SCTN* 2:80–81
Ṭuppi titennūti by which Šeḫliya son of Purna[-zini] and Ḫašip-Tilla son of Šeḫliya provide a 9 GIŠ.APIN field to Ḫanaya son of Tae. Three witnesses are [*mušalmu*]. Tablet written after the *šudutu* in the city of Unapšewe.

EN 9/2 176 SMN 2125+2476 S 136 *SCTN* 2:128
Ṭuppi titennūti by which Kelteya son of Ḫuziri gives a 1 ANŠE 2 GIŠ.APIN field to Zikaya son of Ḫu[ziri] for six years. Tarmiya the scribe son of Kuari.

EN 9/2 177 SMN 2511 S 151 *SCTN* 2:149
Declaration (*lišānu*) of [Ḫupita] son of Šuk[riya] before witnesses by which he gives a 5 [GIŠ.APIN] field bordering the road to the city of Unapšewe to Šar-Tešup *ana titennūti* for 2 years. Tablet written after the *šudutu* in the Great Gate of the city of Nuzi by Akap-šenni the scribe son of Šukriya.

EN 9/1 178 SMN 1542
Declaration (*lišānu*) of Šekar-Tilla before witnesses concerning a loan from Ḫašuar. ^{d}IŠKUR.MA.AN.SUM son of ^{d}UTA.[AN.DÙL] the scribe.

EN 9/3 179 SMN 3629 G 29
[*Ṭuppi ti*]*tennūti* whereby Warad-Ištar son of Ḫani[e] gives a field for 3 years to Kirip-šeri [son of . . . .]. Six witnesses are *mušelwu*. [Ak]ap-tae the scribe.

EN 9/3 180 SMN 3665 G 53
Ṭuppi ti[*tennu*]*ti* wherein Ḫuiya son of [. . . .] provides a 2 ANŠE field to Kanaya [son of . . . .] in the *dimtu* of Belu. Iniya the scribe.

EN 9/1 181 SMN 2568 P 357 *SCTN* 2:163a
Declaration (*lišānu*) of Enna-mati son of Ḫamanna before witnesses concerning the release of 4 ANŠE field belonging to Ḫampizi son of Ar-šatuya in the city of Nai-šerriwe which had previously been given *ana titennūti*. Ilarabi the scribe.

EN 9/3 182 SMN 3601 G 29
[*Ṭuppi*] *titennūti* wherein [Aru]m-atal son of ^{d}[. . . .] provides a field for four years to Ilaya son of Ḫabira. Sîn-šaduni son of Amur-šarri the scribe.

EN 9/1 183 SMN 2608 P 401 *SCTN* 2:181
Ṭuppi titennūti by which Unap-tae son of Akkul-enni gives 3 GIŠ.APIN of fields to Puḫiya son of Maši for three years in return for 1 ANŠE of grain and 3 MA.NA of tin. Tablet written after the *šudutu* in Nuzi by Arip-šarri the scribe.

EN 9/2 184 SMN 2004
[*Ṭuppi titennūti*] by which Šeḫal-Tešup son of Teḫup-šenni receives a field in the *ugāru* of the city of Ḫušri from Marru [son of . . . .]. Tablet written after the *šudutu* in the city of Ḫušri by Abi-ilu the scribe.

EN 9/2 185 SMN 2518 S 151 *SCTN* 2:153
[Declaration (*lišānu*) before witnesses] by Tarmiya and by [. . . .] sons of [. . . .] concerning goods and fields of Tarmiya which they had received. Tablet written in the Great Gate by [Šim]anni the scribe.

EN 9/2 186 SMN 2112 S 112
Declaration (*lišānu*) of Kula-ḫubi son of Ḫuya by which he gives goods (barley, wheat, sheep, goats, garments, etc.) along with a 3 GIŠ.APIN field to Tarmiya son of Ḫuya *ana titennūti* for four years. Tablet written after the *šudutu* in Nuzi by Arip-šarri the scribe.

EN 9/2 187 SMN 2479 S 151 *SCTN* 2:128–29
Ṭuppi titennūti by which Teḫip-Tilla son of Šukriya and Warḫi-Nuzu wife of Šukriya give property in the *dimtu* of Šimika-atal to Tarmiya son of Šukriya *ana titennūti* for five years. Four witnesses are *mušalwu.* Tablet written in Nuzi by Arip-šarri.

EN 9/2 188 SMN 2002
Ṭuppi titennūti by which Ḫatarte son of Atanaḫ-ili gives a 1 ANŠE 8 GIŠ.APIN field in the *ugāru* of the city of Unapšewe to Puḫi-šenni son of Muš-apu. Tablet written after the *šudutu* in the Great Gate of the city of Unapšewe by Elḫip-Tilla the scribe.

EN 9/2 189 SMN2301 S 124 *SCTN* 2:76–77
[*Ṭuppi titennūti*] by which Ḫatarte son of [Atanaḫ-ili] gives a field to Ḫašip-Tilla son of Šeḫliya. Tablet written in Unapšewe. Tablet written after the *šudutu* at the Great Gate of the city of Unapšewe by Enna-mati son of Puḫi-šenni the scribe.

EN 9/3 190 SMN 3499
Fragmentary text.

EN 9/1 191 SMN 2138 P 465
[Declaration (*lišānu*)] before witnesses by which Še-[. . . .] son of Šurukka gives a 1 ANŠE of field to Eḫli-Tešup son of Taya for five years. Tablet written after the *šudutu* at the gate of the city of Nuzi by Šamaš-nuri the scribe.

EN 9/1 192 SMN 2139
Ṭuppi titennūti by which Puḫi-šenni son of Zike gives a 2 ANŠE field on the road to the city of Ulamme to Eḫli-Tešup son of Taya for four years in return for livestock and other goods. Tablet written after the *šudutu* in the Great Gate in the city of Nuzi by Tarmiya the scribe son of Kuari. See *EN* 9/1 199.

EN 9/1 193 SMN 2591 P 400 *SCTN* 2:173
Ṭuppi titennūti by which Eḫli-Tešup son of Taya receives 1 ANŠE of fields from Inkari son of Kipal-zukki for three years in return for 8 ANŠE of grain, 1 ANŠE wheat, and 1 ANŠE of emmer. Three witnesses are *mušalwu.* Tablet written after the *šudutu* at the Great Gate in the city of Nuzi by Šar-Tilla the scribe son of Iluya.

EN 9/1 194 SMN 2622 P 465 *SCTN* 2:190
Ṭuppi titennūti by which Eḫli-Tešup son of Taya receives a 1 ANŠE field in the *dimtu* of Ḫašari from Eḫli-Tešup and Ḫašip-Tilla sons of [Ar]-teya for three years in return for 1 ANŠE of grain and 2 BÁN wheat. Naniya son of Keliya guarantor. Four witnesses are *mušelmu.* Zinni son of Kiyanipu [the scribe].

EN 9/1 195 SMN 2649 P 466 *SCTN* 2:206
Ṭuppi titennūti by which Eḫli-Tešup son of Taya receives 1 ANŠE 3 GIŠ.APIN of field for eight years from Ḫawinnaya son of [Keliya] in return for 8 ANŠE of grain and 20 MA.NA of copper. Tarmiya the scribe.

EN 9/1 196 SMN 2574 U374/365! *SCTN* 2:166
Ṭuppi titennūti by which Eḫli-Tešup son of Taya receives 2 ANŠE of fields from Ḫawinnaya and Katiri sons of Ke[liya] in return for 10 MA.NA of copper and 7 ⟨ANŠE⟩ 10 SÌLA of grain. Tablet written after the *šudutu* by Nanna-adaḫ the scribe. See *EN* 9/1 198 and 225.

EN 9/1 197 SMN 2582 P 382 *SCTN* 2:169
Ṭuppi titennūti by which Puḫiya son of Maši receives 1 ANŠE 2 GIŠ.APIN of fields from Unap-tae son of Akkul-enni for four years in return for 18 MA.NA of tin and 4 twice-sheared ewes with their wool. Two witnesses are *mušelwu*. Tablet written after the *šudutu* in the Great Gate of the city of Nuzi.

EN 9/1 198 SMN 2628 P 465 *SCTN* 2:195
[Declaration (*lišānu*)] before witnesses of Šimika-[atal son of Tarmiya?] who gives a 1 ANŠE of field *ana titennūti* to Eḫli-Tešup son of Taya for five years in return for 1 ox, 2 sheep, and 3 ANŠE of grain. Tablet written after the *šudutu* in the Great Gate of the city of Nuzi by Šar-Tilla the scribe son of Iluya. See *EN* 9/1 196 and 225.

EN 9/1 199 SMN 2646 P 466 *SCTN* 2:204
Declaration (*lišānu*) before witnesses of [Puḫi-šenni] son of Zike who gives a 2 ANŠE of field on the road to [Pananumma] *ana titennūti* to Eḫli-Tešup son of Taya in return for 9 ANŠE of grain, 1 ANŠE of wheat, 1 ANŠE of emmer and 1 she goat. Tablet written after the *šudutu* in the Great Gate in the city of Nuzi by Šar-Tilla the scribe. See *EN* 9/1 192.

EN 9/2 200 SMN 2143
[*Ṭuppi titennu*]*ti* of Ḫaiš-Tešup whereby he agrees to redeem property that Tarmiya [son of Ḫuya] holds *ana titennūtu* from Zaziya son of Aittara. Tablet written after the *šudutu* in the [Great Gate] of the city of Nuzi. Seal of the scribe.

EN 9/1 201 SMN 2696 *SCTN* 2:228
Declaration (*lišānu*) before witnesses of Turari son of N[ullu] who gives a 1 ANŠE field *ana titennūti* for two years to Eḫli-Tešup son of Taya in return for 6 ANŠE of grain. Three witnesses are *mušalmu*. Tablet written after the *šudutu* at the Great Gate of the city of Nuzi. Seal of the scribe.

EN 9/3 202 SMN 3614 G 29
Declaration (*lišānu*) of [Šurk]i-Tilla s[on of . . . .] before witnesses concerning 3 ANŠE of wheat which fŠurkuya daughter of Itḫip-ukur had received along with a 2 ANŠE field in the *dimtu* of Zukirwe which he had given to her for 5 years *ana titennūtu*. Three witnesses are [*mušelmu*]. Tablet written after the *šudutu* at the Great Gate by [. . . . the scribe].

EN 9/1 203 SMN 2631 P 465 *SCTN* 2:196
Ṭuppi titennūti by which Katiri son of Keliya gives a 1 ANŠE 5 GIŠ.APIN field in the *dimtu* of Ekeke to Eḫli-Tešup son of Taya for six years in return for 10 ANŠE of grain and 20 MA.NA of copper. In addition there is a declaration (*lišānu*) of Katiri before witnesses concerning silver that Eḫel-Tešup had received. Tablet written after the *šudutu* in the Great Gate by Tarmiya the scribe.

EN 9/2 204 SMN 2500 S 151 *SCTN* 2:144
[*Ṭuppi tamgurti*] concerning the division of various goods (oxen, barley, straw, a table [*makrattu*], etc.) between Zime and Eḫli-Tešup. Probably belongs to the southwest archives.

EN 9/3 205 SMN 2251 N 120 *SCTN* 2:72
Ṭuppi mārūti wherein Erwin-atal son of Iliya is adopts Utḫ[ap-tae] son of N[a. . .]. Kel-Tešup the scribe son of Sîn-ibni. Lacheman's collations read as follows:

(1) *ṭup-pí ma-ru-ti ša* ^{I}*er-wi-na-tal* (2) DUMU DINGIR-*ia ù* ^{I}*Ut-ḫ*[*ap-ta-*]*e* (3) DUMU *n*[*a-. . . . a-na ma-ru-ti i-te*]*-pu-ús-sú* (4) [. . . .]-*tù* (5) *a*-[. . . .] (6) [. . . .] A.ŠÀ-*šu* (remainder of obverse destroyed; beginning of reverse destroyed) (7) IGI [. . . . DUMU . . . .] (8) IGI *a-kap-ta-e* DUMU *kè-el-*[. . . .] (9) IGI *kè-el-te-šup* DUB.SAR (10) DUMU ^{d}*sîn-ib-ni* (11) NA$_4$ ^{I}*a-ki-ia* (upper edge) (12) NA$_4$ ^{I}*kè-el-te-šup*

EN 9/2 206 SMN 2520 S 151 *SCTN* 2:154
Akkul-enni and Ar-teššе sons of [Ar-tirwi] give a 2 ANŠE field to Ḫuya son of [Šimital] *ana titennūti* for [n] years. [Seal] of the scribe.

EN 9/2 207 SMN 2377 S 132 *SCTN* 2:106
Fragmentary commercial text involving Ḫašip-Tilla son of Kip-ukur and Kipa-lenni [son of Pula-ḫali?]. Šamaš-naṣir the scribe.

EN 9/3 208 SMN 1596
[*Ṭuppi titennūti*] involving Ḫašip-Tilla and Eḫilip-apu involving property for four years. Tablet written after [the *šudutu*] at the palace gate in the city of Nuzi. [. . . . the scribe].

EN 9/2 209 SMN 2368 S 132 *SCTN* 2:100
Declaration (*lišānu*) before witnesses of Ṣilli-Šamaš son of [. . .]ip-šarri concerning the receipt of tin which he loaned to Pula-ḫali LÚ.DAM.GÀR. Maliya the scribe.

EN 9/3 210 SMN 3580
Fragment with a list of witnesses.

EN 9/3 211 SMN 2557 K 197 *SCTN* 2 158
[*Ṭuppi titenn*]*ūti* wherein Zike son of ^{f}Ka[. . . .] receives a field from Unap-Tešup son of Itḫiki for 3 years in exchange for 20 MA.NA of tin and 1 ANŠE of grain. Mukiya the scribe.

EN 9/2 212 SMN 2426 S 133 *SCTN* 2:119–20
Ṭuppi titennūti by which Ḫutin-nawar son of [Šuk]ri-Tešup and Nul-aḫḫe son of Killate give a field to Šamaš-iluni son of Bel-aḫḫe for three years. Qaqqadu the scribe.

EN 9/1 213 SMN 2660 P 485 *SCTN* 2:211
Ṭuppi titennūti by which Eḫli-Tešup son of Taya receives 1 ANŠE 1+n GIŠ.APIN of fields from Melmaššuk son of Puraya for 8 years in return for 6 ANŠE of grain and 1 MA.NA of tin. Four witnesses are (*m*)*ušelwu*. Tarmiya the scribe son of Kuari.

EN 9/1 214 SMN 3476 F 16
[Declaration (*lišānu*)] before witnesses by Elḫip-šarri where he provides Katiri son of Ar-šawa a 2 year old ox *ana titennūti* for three years along with a field in Nuzi. Four witnesses are *mušelwu*. Tablet written after the *šudutu* in Nuzi by [. . . .-a/i]p-apu the scribe son of [. . . .]-šenni.

EN 9/3 215 SMN 3609 G 29
[*Ṭuppi t*]*itennū*[*ti*] wherein [Kinnuya son of] Ḫatarte provides a 6 GIŠ.APIN field to Mušaya son of Eka[. . .] in exchange for 5 ANŠE of grain and 2 MA.NA 30 SU of silver. Tablet written after the *šudutu* in the city of [. . . .] by [. . . . the scribe].

EN 9/3 216 SMN 3594 G 29
Ṭuppi titennūti wherein Teḫup-šenni and Tulpi-šenni sons of Šekarum provide a 2 ANŠE field for 5 years to Šurkuya daughter of Teḫip-ukur in exchange for 20 ANŠE of grain. Utḫap-tae the scribe.

EN 9/3 217 SMN 3613 G 29
[*Ṭuppi titennūti*] wherein Zike [son of . . . .] provides a 1 ANŠE field to Ḫašip-Tilla son of Keliya for 3 years in exchange for 2 ANŠE 10 SÌLA of grain and 5 MA.NA of tin. Four witnesses are (*m*)*ušelminu*!. Amu[mi-Tešup] the scribe.

EN 9/3 218 SMN 2041
Fragmentary loan? text. [Sîn-šaduni? the scribe].

EN 9/1 219 SMN 3495 F 24
Ṭuppi titennūti by which Ṣill-apuḫe son of Ṭab-šarri receives 1 ANŠE 2 GIŠ.APIN of field for six years from Šellapai son of Puḫiya in return for 2 GUN of copper. Bi[. . .]e/ia son of Sa?[. . .]pu the scribe.

EN 9/3 220 SMN 3597 G 29
Ṭuppi titennūti wherein Tupki-Tilla son of Uke provides a 2 ANŠE field in the *ugāru* of the city of It[tuḫḫe] along the road to the city of Ululiyama for 5 years to Kirip-šeri son of Ḫut-Tešup in exchange for 7 ANŠE of grain. [. . . . the scribe].

EN 9/3 221 SMN 3590 G 29
Ṭuppi titennūti wherein Teššuiya, Šimika-atal, and Šurki-Tilla provide a 1 ANŠE 5 GIŠ.APIN field on the road to Nuzi and a 5 GIŠ.APIN field on the road to the city of Ḫamena for 5 years to Kirip-šeri son of Ḫut-Tešup in exchange for 16 ANŠE of grain. Utḫap-tae the scribe.

EN 9/3 222 SMN 3599 G 29
Ṭuppi t[*ite*]*nnūti* wherein Ḫanaya and Ipšaḫalu sons of Ak[iya] provide a field in the city of Kipri for 6 years to Kirip-šeri son of Ḫut-Tešup in exchange for 10 MA.NA of tin and 3 ANŠE 4 SÌLA of grain. Five witnesses are *mu*⟨*še*⟩*lwu*. Utḫap-tae son of En-šukru the scribe.

EN 9/3 223 SMN 3600 G 29
[*Ṭuppi titennūti*] wherein Kerip-šeri [son of Ḫut-Tešup] provides [a field] for 5 years to Arip-apu [son of . . . .] in exchange for 15 ANŠE of grain for five years. Five witnesses are *mušalwu*. Utḫap-tae the scribe.

EN 9/2 224 SMN 2443 S 133 *SCTN* 2:126.
Ṭuppi titennūti by which Šurukka son of Arip-urikke gives a field in the *ugāru* of the [city of Tupšarrini]we to Pašši-Tilla son of Pula-ḫali for two years. Tablet written after the *šudutu* in the Great Gate of the city of Tupšarrini(we) by Šamaš-naṣir the scribe son of Akiya.

EN 9/1 225 SMN 2596 P 400 *SCTN* 2:175
Statement (*umma*) of Šimika-atal son of Tarmiya who gives a 1 ANŠE field *ana titennūti* for five years in return for 1 ANŠE of grain, 5 BÁN of wheat, and 5 BÁN of emmer to Eḫli-Tešup son of Taya. Tablet written after the *šudutu* in the Great Gate of the city of Nuzi by Akap-šenni the scribe.

EN 9/1 226 SMN 3485 F 24
Declaration (*lišānu*) of Ḫašip-Tilla son of Akip-tašenni by which he gives 2 ANŠE 6 GIŠ.APIN of field *ana titennūti* to his brother Ulmi-Tilla for four years in exchange for 25 head of small cattle and 5 ANŠE of grain. Also contains a declaration (*lišānu*) of Zime. Tablet written after the *šudutu* in the Great Gate of the city of Anzugalli by Tampi-Tilla the scribe.

EN 9/3 227 SMN 3585 G 29
Statement (*umma*) of Utḫap-tae son of Šukriya concerning a 4 ANŠE field, 1 talent of copper, and 20 ANŠE of barley which he had given *ana titennūti* to Kirip-šeri son of Ḫut-Tešup. Utḫap-tae the scribe.

EN 9/3 228
No text.

EN 9/3 229 SMN 3627 G 29
[*Ṭuppi titennūti*] wherein Kirip-šeri [son of Ḫut-Tešup] provides a field for n years to Šimika-atal and Šurki-Tilla. Utḫap-tae the scribe. See *EN* 9/3 227.

EN 9/3 230 SMN 2719 *SCTN* 2:242
[Statement (*umma*)] wherein Puḫi-šenni and Pula-ḫali provide a field in the *ugāru* of Tupšarriniwe for 6 years to Tupki-Tilla and Ḫašiya sons of [. . . .] *ana titennūti* in exchange for some fine, young animals, and 2+n MA.NA of copper for five years. Tablet written at the gate of the city of Tupšarriniwe by Šamaš-[naṣir] son of Akiya the scribe.

EN 9/3 231 SMN 798
[*Ṭuppi titennūti*] wherein Šatu-[šenni] son of Awiš-[tuni] provides a 5 GIŠ.APIN field for three years to Elḫip-šarri son of [Ari-]mattiki in exchange for 2 ANŠE of grain. Ar-puruša the scribe.

EN 9/3 232 SMN 1176
Ṭuppi titennūti wherein [Ḫui-/Šukri]-Tešup son of Tur-šenni provides a field in the vicinity of Nuzi for six years. [Ḫa]šip-tašenni the scribe.

EN 9/1 233 SMN 2388 S 132[!] *SCTN* 2:110
Ṭuppi titennūti by which Šerta-ma-ilu son of [. . . .] receives a field from Pilmašše for six years in return for four shekels of silver and four MA.NA of tin. Tablet written after the *šudutu* in the city of Ḫurazina ṣeḫru (GUŠKIN-[*ru*]) by Iriri the scribe.

EN 9/2 234 SMN 2490 S 151 *SCTN* 2:135
[*Ṭuppi tamgur*]*ti* in which Teḫip-Tilla son of Šukriya and Kaya and Zimmari sons of Qišteya agree to the fact that Teḫip-Tilla paid off a large loan debt of Šukriya amounting to 18 ANŠE of barley and 10 ⟨GÍN⟩ of *ḫašaḫušenni*-silver. Tablet written after the *šudutu* at the Tišša gate by Kaluppani son of Aḫu-šini the scribe.

EN 9/2 235
No text.

EN 9/2 236 SMN 2345 S 130 *SCTN* 2:90
Fragmentary record of a *titennūti* by which a Ḫašip-Tilla receives a field from Ḫanie son of Alki-Tilla.

EN 9/1 239 SMN 2994
Ṭuppi titennūti by which [f]Šarum-elli receives a field from Katiri and will keep it when she has paid [n+]4 MA.NA of copper and 10 ANŠE of grain to Eḫel-Tešup and Šilwe. [n] witnesses are *mušelwu*.

EN 9/1 240 SMN 1212 A 34
Ṭuppi titennūti by which Tae provides real estate.

EN 9/1 241 SMN 2925
Fragment of a transaction in which Tae and another individual receive silver. A Teš-tae is named *ewuru* if Tuppiya does not have a son. Perhaps to be related to HSS 19 34.

EN 9/1 242 SMN 3645 G 29
Fragmentary statement (*umma*) by Mi[na]š-šuk son of Enna-ma[ti] concerning the daughter of [f]Awiš-kipaḫe who was living in Minaš-šuk's house.

EN 9/1 243 SMN 1849
Ṭuppi titennūti by which Pai-Tešup receives from [. . . .] son of Ḫanaya a 1 ANŠE field for four years adjacent to properties of which one belongs to Šilwa-Tešup.

EN 9/1 244 SMN 2712 *SCTN* 2:239
[*Ṭuppi mārūti*] by which Ḫašip-Tilla receives houses from Tupki-Tilla. [n] witnesses are *mušalwu*. Arip-šarri the scribe.

EN 9/1 245 SMN 1025 A 23
Fragment of a transaction whereby Ḫabira commits his son Eḫliya who will be redeemed by the substitution of a hireling or 4 GUN of copper.

EN 9/3 246 SMN 3762
[*Ṭuppi ti*]*tennū*[*ti*] wherein Ḫaište [son of . . . .] provides a field to Akip-tašenni son of Elni[?][. . .]. Utḫap-tae the scribe.

EN 9/1 247 SMN 2732 *SCTN* 2:252
Record of deliveries of grain from the palace to singers from the city of Zizza.

EN 9/1 248 SMN 2633 P 465 *SCTN* 2:199
Damaged legal text concerning the repayment[?] of a loan of 30 MA.NA of tin.

EN 9/2 250 SMN 2221 N 120 *SCTN* 2:42.
Damaged sale by which Ḫašiya son of Bel-aḫḫe sells fine sheep to Paššiya. Tablet written at [the Great Gate] of the city of Tupšarriniwe by Šamaš-naṣir son of Akiya the scribe.

EN 9/1 251 SMN 2703 *SCTN* 2:234–35
Ṭuppi titennūti by which Puḫi-šenni son of Zike gives a 2 ANŠE 7 GIŠ.APIN field in the vicinity of the city of Atagal for 3 years to Eḫli-Tešup son of Taya in return for 36 ANŠE of grain, 3(?) BÁN of wheat, 7 MA.NA of tin, a number of sheep and a bronze dagger. Three witnesses are *(m)ušelwu*. Tablet written after the *šudutu* by Tarmiya the scribe son of Kuari.

EN 9/1 252 SMN 2658 P 485 *SCTN* 2:210
Ṭuppi titennūti by which Paik-kerḫe son of Arip-api gives houses in Nuzi to Unap-Tešup son of Arillu for five years in return for goods totaling 2+n MA.NA of bronze. Tablet written in Nuzi.

EN 9/1 253 SMN 3497 F 24
[Declaration (*lišānu*) before] witnesses by [Tar]mi-Tilla son of Akip-tašenni which annuls an earlier tablet that concerned his brothers in the city of Šurina. Tablet written after [the *šudutu*] at the palace gate by Akiya son of Šumu-libši the scribe.

EN 9/3 254 SMN 2109
Ṭuppi titennūti wherein Enamati son of En[naya] provides a 1 ANŠE field in the *ugāru* of Nuzi for 6 years to Ari-ḫamanna son of Ḫatarte in exchange for 8 ANŠE of barley. Tablet written after the *šudutu* at the great *šupali* gate of the city of Nuzi. Tarmi-Tešup son of Šarru-muštal the scribe.

EN 9/3 255 SMN 1451
Ṭuppi titennuti wherein Ḫanie [son of . . . .] provides a 10 ANŠE field to Ḫutie son of Šurteiya for 6 years. Tablet written after the [*šudutu*] in the city of [Nuzi]. [. . . .]-RI the scribe.

EN 9/1 256 SMN 2920
Fragmentary record of a *titennūtu* contract involving Mušapu.

EN 9/1 257 SMN 2818
[Declaration (*lišānu*)] before witnesses of Taya son of [. . . .]-*ta*-[. . . .] concerning the receipt of goods (a fine ox, tin, and ewes) from Ar-tašenni son of Nanaya-eriš as wages.

EN 9/1 258 SMN 3129 C 28
Declaration (*lišānu*) before witnesses of Aḫiya son of Ḫabur-[. . . .] concerning an exchange of fields with Utḫap-tae son of [. . . .] which were given *ana titennūti*. Ila-nišu the scribe son of Ašt[ena]?

EN 9/3 259 SMN 3586 G 23
Fragmentary *ṭuppi titennūti*? involving Akip-[. . .], Šekaru and Eḫlip-apu, whose statement (*umma*), is partially preserved. It concerns a n+2 ANŠE field in the *ugāru* of the city of Ḫamina.

EN 9/1 260 SMN 3719 *IN*, p. 115

Titennūtu contract in which Iluya son of Adad-eriš gives his son Unteya to Kirib-šeri son of Ḫut-Tešup as surety for six years on a loan of one twice-plucked ewe, 2 ANŠE of grain and one cloth weighing 4 *kuduktu*. Tukulti-beli the scribe.

EN 9/3 261 SMN 1711

Fragmentary [*ṭuppi titennūti*] mostly lost. Tablet written after the *šudutu* in the city of [. . . .]. Seal of Arip-šarri scribe.

EN 9/2 262 SMN 2107 N 120

Statement of Eḫli-Tešup son of Kipaya concerning the *paiḫu* property in the city of Nuzi which he agreed to give to Utḫap-tae son of Ar-tura. Arip-šarri the scribe. Compare *AASOR* 16, pp. 40–41 no. 58 (SMN 2085).

EN 9/3 263 SMN 3617 G 29

[Statement (*umma*)] wherein Kilip-šeri [son of . . . .] provides a field to Kelip-šeri *ana titennūti*. Tablet written after the *šudutu* before the gate of the city of Kipri. Eḫli-Tešup the sc[ribe] son of Tešup-[. . . .].

EN 9/2 264 SMN 2708 *SCTN* 2:236–237

Ṭuppi titennūti by which [Ḫupi]ta son of Arip-ḫurra gives property to Tarmiya. Sîn-šaduni the scribe.

EN 9/1 265 SMN 1598 *IN*, p. 127 Text 33; *STPPKA*, p. 45

Ṭuppi titennūtu in which Teḫip-zizza son of Ḫanaya becomes surety to Pai-Tešup son of Za-[. . . .] for a loan with additional security of land in the city of Ḫ[ušr]i above the *dimtu* of Mamiaḫḫe in case of death or disappearance. Taki the scribe.

EN 9/3 266 SMN 2996

[*Ṭuppi ti*]*tennūti* wherein Niḫir-Tilla son of Ḫamanna takes a 1 ANŠE 7 GIŠ.APIN field in the *ugāru* of the city of Zalmanue for five years. [. . . the scribe].

EN 9/2 267 SMN 2773

Fragmentary *titennūtu* agreement by which Šurki-Tilla and possibly one other person gives a field to Šurki-Tilla, Paššі-Tilla and Kipa-lenni sons of Pula-ḫali. Three witnesses are *mušelwu*. Tablet written after the *šudutu* at the gate of the city of Tupšarriniwe. [. . . . the scribe].

EN 9/2 268 SMN 2428 S 133 *SCTN* 2:121

Fragmentary *titennūtu* agreement by which a field with an orchard, well, and threshing floor is given by Šekaru to Paššiya son of Pula-ḫali for three years.

EN 9/1 269 SMN 3510 F 24

Statement (*umma*) of Tae son of Tae son of Ṣill-apuḫe who gave his son as surety to Turarteya son of Ipšaya but the latter sold him in another land. Teḫip-ri took the matter to court on his behalf to free his son. [. . .]-*a-ka* the scribe.

EN 9/3 270 SMN 2997
Fragmentary [*titennūtu*] agreement Turar-Tešup provides fields to [. . . .] sons of Itḫi[. . .] who promise to pay Turar-Tešup 10 female Nullu slaves if the agreement is not fulfilled. [Tur]ar-Tešup the scribe.

EN 9/3 271 SMN 1089 A 14
Aššatu contract where Pai-Tešub gives ᶠḪinzuri as a wife to Ḫašip-Tilla. Amumi-Tešup son of Sin-nadin-šumi the scribe.

EN 9/3 272 SMN 3755
Ṭuppi titennūti wherein Naltuya son of Še[. . . .] is provided with a 2 ANŠE field in the *dimtu* of Ka[. . . .] for 5 years by Dan-ili son of Niniš-še for 7 ANŠE of barley. Five witnesses are *(m)ušelwu*. Kip-talili the scribe.

EN 9/2 273 SMN 2499 S 151 *SCTN* 2:143
[*Ṭuppi tam*]*gurti* whereby Puḫi-šenni son of [. . . .]e and Tarmiya agree concerning the payment of grain, livestock, and metals. Tablet written after the *šudutu* at the gate. Niḫriya the scribe.

EN 9/3 274 SMN 2769
Fragmentary [*ṭuppi titennūti*] wherein a field is provided to Akukul-enni for six years. The city of Zizza is mentioned. Amumi-Tešup the scribe son of [Sîn-nadin-šumi].

EN 9/2 275 SMN 2777 *SCTN* 2:258 (not transliterated)
Fragmentary *titennūtu* by which Akaya son of Ka[. . . .] gives property to Puḫi-šenni son of Muš-apu previously given to him by his father?.

EN 9/3 276 SMN 739 A 11
Ṭuppi titennūti wherein Ar-zizza and Teḫip-zizza sons of Wardiya provide a 1 ANŠE field for 3 years to Kulpi-Tilla son of Šukr-[apu] for 1 *naḫlaptu*, 20 *qa* of grain, and 20 *qa* of malt. Tablet written after the *šudutu* at the Tiššae gate in the city of Nuzi. Sîn-šaduni the scribe son of Amur-šarri.

EN 9/3 277 SMN 3527
Ṭuppi titennūti wherein Ḫabira provides a 4 GIŠ.APIN field in Tašenniwe to Akap-tukke in exchange for 2 ANŠE of grain and 2 sheep. Beliya-utu the scribe.

EN 9/3 278 SMN 2823
[*Ṭuppi titennūti*] wherein [. . . . son of . . . .] provides a 1 ANŠE 1[+n] GIŠ.APIN field in the *dimtu* of Šimika-atal in the city of Nuzi to Arip-šarri son of Itti-šarri for 10 years.

EN 9/2 279 SMN 2513 S 151 *SCTN* 2:151
Record of a *titennūtu* agreement by which Ḫašip-Tilla and Zigi sons of Arteya give a 1 ANŠE 2 GIŠ.APIN field to Eḫli-Tešup. Perhaps belongs to the southwest archives. ᵈNANNA-MA.AN.SUM the scribe.

EN 9/3 280 SMN 2950
Fragmentary text concerning compensation payments (*ḫiššumaku*) to Akip-šenni. The city of Temtena is mentioned. Šukriya the scribe.

EN 9/3 281 SMN 2998
Fragmentary [*titennūtu*] agreement concerning *ilku* obligations. City of Temtena mentioned.

EN 9/3 282 SMN 2999
Fragmentary [*titennūtu*] agreement wherein Puta son of Kailu provides a field on the road to the city of Mezu[ra]e to Marteya for two years.

EN 9/2 283 SMN 2401 S 132 *SCTN* 2:117
Statement (*umma*) of Taika son of Akap-šenni by which he sells a pair of doors (GIŠ.IG) from his father's house to Paššši-Tilla son of Pula-ḫali for 6 MA.NA of tin. Šamaš-naṣir the scribe.

EN 9/3 284 SMN 3157 C 36
Record of a sale? of 2 ewes for the *awelūti ubarūti* of Aššur and 1 goat and 4 ewes for the NIN-DINGIR.RA of the city of Apenaš.

EN 9/1 285 SMN 2644 P 466 *SCTN* 2:203
Statement (*umma*) of Ḫerrika son of Šarriya concerning 2 *umpani* GIŠ.MAR.GÍD.DA which belonged to Nanteya son of Ḫutiya and Ḫerrika son of Šarriya and which had been given to Eḫli-Tešup son of Taya but which he had not returned to Nanteya son of Ḫutiya. Š[im]anni the scribe.

EN 9/1 286 SMN 3113 C 28
An order to dispatch barley to the city of Erami.

EN 9/3 287 SMN 1998
Fragmentary [*titennūtu*] agreement. Tablet written after the *šudutu* at the gate of the city of [. . . .].

EN 9/3 288 SMN 2051
Fragmentary [*titennūtu*] agreement. Tablet written after the *šudutu* at the great gate of the city of Nuzi. Šar-Tilla son of Iluya the scribe.

EN 9/2 289 SMN 2418 S 132 *SCTN* 2:119 (not transliterated)
Fragmentary statement of Ḫa/Za[ ] son of Šerši[ya] concerning Tulpi-šenni [the . . . . of the] MÍ.LUGAL and Šeḫal-[Tešup] son of Ar-tura the shepherd (*kuzallu*). Possibly a dispute concerning the queen's sheep.

EN 9/3 290 SMN 3528
Fragmentary text of declaration (*lišānu*) before witnesses. Ḫutiya the scribe.

EN 9/2 291 SMN 2370 S 132 *SCTN* 2:102.
Declaration (*lišānu*) of [A]kip-Tilla before witnesses concerning repayment of a missing (*ḫalqu*), fine male donkey belonging to Ḫašip-Tilla son of Kip-ukur. He repaid Ḫašip-Tilla 1 cow for its loss.

EN 9/2 292 SMN 2365 S 132 *SCTN* 2:98–99.
Statement (*umma*) of Zunna son of Urḫiya who borrowed an ass from Paššši-Tilla son of Pula-ḫali for a journey of the palace. Tablet written in Ulamme by Ḫut-Tešup.

EN 9/3 293 SMN 3515 F 24
Statement (*umma*) of Paip-purni son of Nulzaḫi concerning 5 MA.NA of tin, the price of a donkey, which he received from Teḫip-šarri. Ḫutiya the scribe.

EN 9/3 294 SMN 3529
Fragmentary text concerning an interest-bearing loan of pitchforks for straw (gišḫ*arwaraḫḫu ša* I[N.NU]).

EN 9/3 295 SMN 3238 D 3
Declaration (*lišānu*) of Nanip-ukur son of Ḫalutta and Unap-še son of [. . . .] before witnesses concerning Ḫerri the lú*nakiru* from Nuzi.

EN 9/1 296 SMN 3519 F 24
Statement (*umma*) of Ḫur-šenni son of Tau-[. . . .] and Akkul-enni son of Naya who declare that they have received the prices for their donkeys from Teḫip-šarri son of [. . . .]-ti-šarri. dAK-DINGIR.RA the scribe.

EN 9/2 297 SMN 2124 S 130
Šekar-Tilla son of Šelwiya borrows a shekel of gold from Ari-ḫamanna son of Ḫamutta. Teḫip-Tilla the scribe.

EN 9/2 298 SMN 2011 S 113
Statement (*umma*) concerning a herding contract by which Ipša-ḫalu son of [. . . .] and Paya son of Ni[. . . .] receive sheep from Šeḫal-Tešup son of Teḫup-šenni. The 10 sheep were received and will be returned in Nuzi in the month of Impurtanni. SAG.AN.KI the scribe.[7]

EN 9/2 299 SMN 2681 P 485 *SCTN* 2:219
Ṭuppi martūti by which Uante son of Enna-mati gives his sister Elwi[ni] *ana martūti* to Paššі-Tilla son of Pula-ḫali. Paššі-Tilla then married her to a man from Arrapḫe. Her *terḫatu* was 40 shekels of silver. Šamaš-naṣir the scribe.

EN 9/1 300 SMN 1705 *LDN*, p. 98; *STPPKA*, pp. 134, 159, 344
List of grain allotments to various individuals.

EN 9/2 301 SMN 2620 P 428! *SCTN* 2:188.
Multiple grain loan text of Puḫi-šenni son of Muš-apu. Teḫiya the scribe.

EN 9/1 302 SMN 3602 G 29 *LDN*, pp. 99–100
Declaration (*lišānu*) by Urḫi-tirwi son of Eḫel-Tešup, Akiya son of Šukriya, and Teḫip-Tilla son of Enšukru concerning a loan of 10 ANŠE of barley which they had borrowed from Akip-tašenni and which they promise to repay after the harvest in the city of Kipri.

EN 9/1 303 SMN 780 A 26 *LDN*, p. 100
Record of various interest-bearing loans of barley between different individuals to be repaid after the harvest.

EN 9/1 304 SMN 679 A 14 *LDN*, pp. 100–101; *STPPKA*, p. 334
Statement (*umma*) by Ḫašip-apu son of Taḫiri[šti] concerning a loan of barley from the towns of Zuyawa and Ṣilliyawa lent to him by Šilwa-Tešup DUMU LUGAL.

[7] Misread as Kase in the previously published catalogue.

EN 9/1 305 SMN 662 A 26 *LDN*, p. 101
Record of barley loans to various individuals by Šilwa-Tešup DUMU LUGAL in the city of Tašenniwe.

EN 9/1 306 SMN 657 *LDN*, pp. 101–2
Record of barley loans to various individuals by Šilwa-Tešup DUMU LUGAL in the city of Tašenniwe.

EN 9/1 307 SMN 954 A 14 *LDN*, p. 102
Barley loan from Šilwa-Tešup to Ni[. . . .-Te]šup.

EN 9/1 308 SMN 776 A 26 *LDN*, pp. 102–3
Record of barley loans to various individuals by Šilwa-Tešup in the city of Tašenniwe.

EN 9/1 309 SMN 1204 A 26 *LDN*, p. 103
Record of barley loans to various individuals by Šilwa-Tešup DUMU LUGAL in the city of Tašenniwe.

EN 9/1 310 SMN 1237 A 26 *LDN*, pp. 103–4
Record of barley loans to various individuals by [Šilwa-Tešup DUMU LUGAL] in the city of Tašenniwe. [Elḫip]-Tilla the scribe.[8]

EN 9/1 311 SMN 2910 *LDN*, p. 104
Record of barley loans to various individuals by Šilwa-Tešup DUMU LUGAL in the city of Tašenniwe.

EN 9/1 312 SMN 1245 A 26 *LDN*, pp. 104–5
Record of barley loans to various individuals by Šilwa-Tešup DUMU LUGAL.

EN 9/1 313 SMN 1219 *LDN*, p. 105
Record of barley loans to various individuals by Šilwa-Tešup in the city of Tašenniwe.

EN 9/1 314 SMN 914 T 19 *LDN*, pp. 105–6
Loan of wheat belonging to Uzna wife of Enna-mati to Ukur-atal son of Apukka and Teḫiya son of Arip-šerri in the city of Tašenniwe to be returned after the harvest in Nuzi. Turar-Tešup the scribe.

EN 9/3 315 SMN 1263 T 19
Fragmentary text concerning wheat belonging to Ḫutiya.

EN 9/3 316 SMN 3562 F 25
Fragmentary letter to Wur-šenni from Ḫutip-uraššе.

EN 9/1 317 SMN 879 A 33 *LDN*, p. 106
Loan of barley by ᶠŠašuri in the *dimtu* of Terriwe to Šukriya son of Wunnukiya to be returned after the harvest in Nuzi. Akaya the scribe.

EN 9/3 318 SMN 1010
Fragmentary [*titennūtu*]? text. [. . .]-*i*?-Tilla the scribe.

[8] In Owen, *LDN*, p. 99, this text is assigned to Teḫiya. But DUB.SAR in rev. 45 is written close to both Teḫiya and [Elḫip]-Tilla. It is assigned to the latter as a result of graphemic analysis.

EN 9/1 319 SMN 1435 A 26 *LDN*, pp. 106–7
Loan of copper by Biriaš-šura son of [. . . .]-Tilla to Kuš-kipa son of Kušte the merchant. Sîn-šarri the scribe.

EN 9/1 320 SMN 1247 T 18 *LDN*, p. 107
Loan of barley by Nai-Tilla son of Teššuya to Tiyampera son of Puza and Akip-šenni son of Kaya. Urḫi-Tešup the scribe.

EN 9/2 321 SMN 2167 S 112 *SCTN* 2:10; *LDN*, p. 107
Ḫaniani son of Makuya borrows grain from Urḫi-kušuḫ DUMU LUGAL. Taknak-ilu the scribe.

EN 9/2 322 SMN 2157 S 110 *SCTN* 2:5; *LDN*, p. 108
Statement (*umma*) of Enna-mati son of Ḫabira by which he gives his son Belani to Utḫap-tae son of Ar-tura in exchange for an ox. [Ipša]-ḫalu the scribe.

EN 9/2 323 SMN 2334 S 129 *SCTN* 2:87; *LDN*, p. 108 *EN* 9 323 [= *EN* 9/2 490]
Tai and Šekaru sons of Ḫašip-apu borrow grain from Puḫi-šenni son of Muš-apu. Elḫip-Tilla the scribe.

EN 9/2 324 SMN 2358 S 132 *SCTN* 2:96; *LDN*, p. 108 *EN* 9 324 [= *EN* 9/2 323]
Teḫup-šenni son of Šekaru borrows grain from Minaš-šuk. Bel-ili the scribe.

EN 9/2 325 SMN 2387 S 132 *SCTN* 2, pp. 109–10; *LDN*, pp. 108–9
[. . . .]wiya son of [. . . .] borrows tin from Muš-Tešup son of Akip-tašenni. The following transliteration, based on an early Lacheman file, contains parts of the tablet no longer preserved when the tablet was copied.

(1) [12] MA.NA *a-[na-ku ša]* (2) [^{I}. .]*-wi-ia* DUMU [. . . .] (3) ^{I}*mu-uš-te-šup* (4) DUMU *a-kip-ta-še-en-ni* (5) *a-na* UR_5.RA *il-[te-qè]* (6) *i-na* EGIR*[-ki* EBUR *i-na* (7) ITI *ḫi-in-zu-[ri it-ti]* (8) *ṣí-ip-ti-šu* (9) 12 MA.NA *a-na-ku* (10) ^{I}*mu-uš-te-šup ù* (11) [. . . . *ši*]*-ka* (12) [*ú-ta*]*-ar* (13) [*šum-ma i-na*] ITI *ḫi-in-zu-ri ši-im-*[*ta-mu*] (14) [. . .] *ša* MÁŠ *ša* [. . . .] rev. (15) [NA_4] *tar-mi-te-šup* (16) NA_4 *še-en-nu-un-mi* (17) DUMU *ša-li-ia* (18) NA_4 *pa-i-til-la* DUMU *ar-te-šup* (19) [NA_4 *šu*]*-ur-kip-til-la* DUMU [. . . .]

EN 9/2 326 SMN 2674 P 465! *SCTN* 2:216; *LDN*, p. 109
Statement (*umma*) of Tupki-Tilla son of Unaya concerning the return of the grain he loaned to Muš-apu son of Purna-zini in Unapšewe. Kel-Tešup the scribe.

EN 9/2 327 SMN 2303 S 124 *SCTN* 2:78–79; *LDN*, p. 109
Kuari son of Kuššiya borrows grain from Puḫi-šenni son of Muš-apu.

EN 9/3 328 SMN 3748 T 18 *LDN*, pp. 109–10 *EN* 9 328 [= *EN* 9/2 333]
Fragmentary text concerning the fashioning of a wagon. Penalty for not completing the wagon on time is four sheep.

EN 9/2 329 SMN 2077 S 132 *LDN*, p. 110
Akip-Tilla son of Ḫurpu and Ḫutik-kewar son of Artapai borrow grain from Puḫi-šenni son of Muš-apu. Elḫip-Tilla the scribe.

EN 9/3 330 SMN 3085
Declaration (*lišānu*) of Enna-mati son of Šar-Tešup concerning wheat given (loaned) to Ḫutil-enni son of Uzimpalitu to be returned at the end of the month of Mitirunni. Tešup-nirari the scribe.

EN 9/2 331 SMN 2350 S 132 *SCTN* 2:92; *LDN*, pp. 110–11
Declaration (*lišānu*) before witnesses of Tultukka son of Akitte concerning silver he received from Eteš-šenni son of Ḫabira. Ari-ḫamanna the scribe.

EN 9/1 332 SMN 2635 P 465 *SCTN* 2:201; *LDN*, p. 110
Barley loan by which Turari son of Ḫalutta and Ippaya son of Ḫutiya borrow barley from Šekar-Tilla son of Sîn-šarri.

EN 9/2 333 SMN 2680 P 480! *SCTN* 2:218; *LDN*, pp. 110–11 *EN* 9 328 [= *EN* 9/2 333]
Loan of Ḫatarte son of Ata⟨na⟩ḫ-ili and Akip-tašenni son of Kawinni who borrow grain from Puḫi-šenni son of Muš-apu.

EN 9/2 334 SMN 2315 S 124 *SCTN* 2:83; *LDN*, p. 111 *EN* 9 334 [= *EN* 9/3 454]
Loan of Eteš-šenni son of Atanaḫ-ili and Nai-Tešup son of Ḫanaya who borrow barley and wheat, respectively, from Puḫi-šenni son of Muš-apu.

EN 9/1 335 SMN 1167 M 79
Reed account.

EN 9/2 336 SMN 2113 N 120 *LDN*, p. 111
Loan of Akapše son of Kartiya, Matte son of Enna-mati, and Taika son of Maliya who borrow wheat from Puḫi-šenni son of Muš-apu. Elḫip-Tilla the scribe.

EN 9/2 337 SMN 2363 S 132 *SCTN* 2:98; *LDN*, pp. 111–12
Loan of Ḫutip-apu son of [E]ḫliya who borrows tin from Taika son of A[kap-šenni]. Šamaš-naṣir the scribe.

EN 9/2 338 SMN 2162 S 112 *SCTN* 2:7; *LDN*, p. 112
Loan of Puḫi-šenni son of [Ar-ta]šenni[9] who borrows grain from Puḫi-šenni son of Muš-apu. Kelteya the scribe.

EN 9/2 339 SMN 2359 S 132 *SCTN* 2:98; *LDN*, pp. 112–13
Statement (*umma*) of Nur-kubi son of [. . . .]šu concerning the copper and bronze which he had loaned to Pula-ḫali his son for interest and commercial profit. Mušteya the scribe. *SMN* 2369 in *LDN* is a typographical error.

EN 9/2 340 SMN 2079 S 132 *LDN*, p. 113
Loan of Ḫutip-apu and Tarmi-Tilla sons of Eḫliya who borrow grain from Pašši-Tilla son of Pula-ḫali. Šamaš-naṣir the scribe.

EN 9/2 341 SMN 2180 S 112 *SCTN* 2:15; *LDN*, pp. 113–14
Loan of Kušuniya son of K[ank]eya who borrows tin from Pašši-Tilla son of Pula-ḫali. Šamaš-naṣir the scribe.

[9] Lacheman restored [*a-kip-ta-š*]*e-en-ni*. Our restoration is suggested on the basis of the name in line 24, although it is spelled differently.

EN 9/2 342 SMN 2081 S 132 *LDN*, p. 114
Loan of Ḫupita son of Akitta who borrows tin from Paššī-Tilla son of Pula-ḫali. Tarmi-Tilla the scribe.

EN 9/2 343 SMN 2142 *LDN*, pp. 114–15
Loan of Ḫellu [son of . . . .] who borrows copper from Paššī-Tilla son of Pula-ḫali. Tarmi-Tilla the scribe.

EN 9/2 344 SMN 2381 S 132 *SCTN* 2:107; *LDN*, p. 115
Loan of Taika son of Akap-šenni who borrows tin from Paššī-Tilla son of Pula-ḫali. Šamaš-naṣir the scribe.

EN 9/2 345 SMN 2690 *SCTN* 2:225: *LDN*, p. 115
Loan of Zime son of Ziliya who borrows tin from Paššī-Tilla son of Pula-ḫali. Šamaš-naṣir the scribe.

EN 9/2 346 SMN 2384 S 132 *SCTN* 2:108–9; *LDN*, pp. 115–16
Loan of Zil-Tešup son of Šennaya who borrows bronze from Paššiya son of Pula-ḫali. Seal of the scribe.

EN 9/2 347 SMN 2832 S 132 *SCTN* 2:108; *LDN*, p. 116
Loan of Ḫalutta son of Akiya who borrows tin from Waḫḫura son of Paššiya.

EN 9/2 348 SMN 2434 S 133 *SCTN* 2:123; *LDN*, pp. 116–17 *EN* 9 348
[= *EN* 9/2 349]
Declaration ([*lišānu*]?) of Zike son of Akiya concerning repayment of grain loan of Kipa-lenni son of Pula-ḫali.

EN 9/2 349 SMN 2445 S 133 *SCTN* 2:127; *LDN*, p. 117 *EN* 9 349
[= *EN* 9/2 348]
Loan of Šurukka son of Arip-urikke who borrows grain from Paššiya son of [Pula-ḫali]. Abi-ilu the scribe son of ᵈA[K-DINGIR.RA].

EN 9/1 350 SMN 2392 S 132 *SCTN* 2:113–14
Fragmentary record concerning a transaction of horses and chariots.

EN 9/1 351 SMN 2160 S 110 *SCTN* 2:6; *LDN*, p. 117 *EN* 9 351 [= *EN* 9/2 118]
Barley loan by Ar-tura to Inki-Tilla son of Ḫutip-erwe and Arim-matka son of Ḫašip-Tilla. Turar-Tešup the scribe.

EN 9/2 352 SMN 2349 S 132 *SCTN* 2:91–92; *LDN*, p. 118
Loan of Eḫliya son of Akkuya who borrows tin from the sons of Pula-ḫali. Šamaš-naṣir the scribe.

EN 9/2 353 SMN 2116 N 120 *LDN*, pp. 118–19
Šurukka son of Arip-urikke borrows tin from the sons of Pula-ḫali. Šamaš-naṣir the scribe. SMN 2216 in *LDN* is a typographical error.

EN 9/2 354 SMN 2158 S 110 *SCTN* 2:5–6; *LDN*, p. 119 *EN* 9 354
[= *EN* 9/1 379]
Statement (*umma*) of Pal-Tešup son of Ḫutiya concerning the sale of a slave girl for 30 MA.NA of tin to Utḫap-tae son of Ar-tura. [. . .]-*nu* the scribe.

EN 9/1 355 SMN 3496 F 24 *LDN*, p. 120
Loan of copper by Pu[rusa?] son of Niḫriya to [A?]riḫ-mušni son of Ta[ya]. Scribe dUTA.AN.DÙL son of Taya.

EN 9/2 356 SMN 2414 S 132 *SCTN* 2:119; *LDN*, p. 120
Loan of Arikku son of Šamaš-ilu, who borrows tin from Tupkiya.

EN 9/2 357 SMN 2352 S132 *SCTN* 2:93; *LDN*, pp. 120–21
Declaration (*lišānu*) of Ḫašip-Tilla son of Tiantukku before witnesses concerning his borrowing of grass seed (*abšu*) and a fine garment (*qatnu*) from Ḫašip-Tilla son of Kip-ukur.

EN 9/2 358 SMN 2336 S 129 *SCTN* 2:87–88
Loan of Ḫanne son of Šukriya, who borrows tin from Puḫi-šenni son of Muš-apu. El[ḫip-Tilla the scribe].

EN 9/2 359 SMN 2161 S 112 *SCTN* 2:7: *LDN*, p. 121
Statement (*umma*) of Šeḫal-Tešup son of Teḫup-šenni concerning grain which he owes to Ḫeltip-apu. Ḫutip-apu the scribe.

EN 9/2 360 SMN 2001 S 113 *LDN*, pp. 121–22
Declaration (*lišānu*) of Šekar-Tilla son of Mušte before witnesses concerning his borrowing a fine, twice-plucked sheep from Šeḫal-Tešup son of Teḫup-šenni. Šamaš-naṣir the scribe.

EN 9/3 361 SMN 1074 A 23
Record of grain loan from Šilwa-Tešup DUMU LUGAL to four individuals.

EN 9/2 362 SMN 2335 S 129 *SCTN* 2:87; *LDN*, p. 122 *EN* 9 362 [= *EN* 9/2 452]
Loan of Kinni son of Ḫaniu who borrows grain from Puḫi-šenni son of Muš-apu. Elḫip-Tilla the scribe.

EN 9/2 363 SMN 2108 S 110 *LDN*, p. 122
Loan of Utḫiya son of [Kelte]ya who borrows tin from Utḫap-tae son of Artura. Aḫa-ay-amši the scribe.

EN 9/2 364 SMN 2393 S 132 *SCTN* 2:114; *LDN*, pp. 122–23 *EN* 9 364 [= *EN* 9/1 351]
Loan of [. . . .] who borrows [grain] from Paššiya [son of Pula-ḫali]. Urḫi-Tešup the scribe.

EN 9/1 365 SMN 817 T 19 *LDN*, p. 123; *STPPKA*, p. 118
Loan of Akiya son of Eḫli-Tešup who borrows grain from Ḫašuar son of Šimika-atal. dIŠKUR.MA.AN.SUM the scribe.

EN 9/1 366 SMN 1071 A 14 *LDN*, p. 123–24; *STPPKA*, p. 119
Declaration (*lišānu*) of Inkir-abuya son of Uke before witnesses concerning a loan of grain taken from Ḫašuar son of Šimika-atal. Written at the gate by dIŠKUR.MA.AN.SUM the scribe.

EN 9/1 367 SMN 1166 A 14 *LDN*, p. 124
Loan of Zikkami son of Ḫutiya and Kušši-tae son of Enna-pali who borrow grain from Ḫašuar son of Šimika-atal to be repaid in the *dimtu* of Arikanni. Teḫiya the scribe.

EN 9/1 368 SMN 793[10] A 14 *LDN*, p. 124; *STPPKA*, p. 119
Declaration (*lišānu*) by Ḫumpape son of Tupki-Tilla before witnesses concerning a loan of barley from Ḫašuar son of Šimika-atal. ᵈIŠKUR.MA.AN.SUM the scribe.

EN 9/1 369 SMN 929 A 14 *LDN*, p. 125
Loan of Urḫi-šarri son of Ar-tirwe who borrows grain from Ḫašuar son of Šimika-atal to be repaid in the city of Lubdi. ᵈIŠKUR.MA.AN.SUM the scribe.

EN 9/1 370 SMN 753 A 26 *LDN*, p. 125
"Tablets of interest-bearing barley loans of the 'other side' (*eberta*)." Elongated tablet, possibly a school text.

EN 9/2 371 SMN 2358A S 132 *LDN*, p. 125 *EN* 9 371 [= *EN* 9/2 324]
Fragmentary grain loan of Šeḫal-Tešup son of Teḫup-šenni. [. . .]-*ni*-[. . .] the scribe.

EN 9/1 372 SMN 2446 *LDN*, p. 125
Damaged record of two wheat loans. SMN 2358 number recorded in Owen, *LDN* for *EN* 9 372 belongs to *EN* 9/2 291.

EN 9/1 373 SMN 2593 P 400 *SCTN* 2:174–75; *LDN*, p. 125 *EN* 9 373 [= *EN* 9/3 412]
Statement (*umma*) of Ḫerri concerning the loan of a male sheep, three fine metal scraps (*ḫušu*) and four MA.NA of tin to Zilip-apu by Mutta. All the goods have been returned. Tumiya the scribe.

EN 9/2 374 SMN 2379 S 132 *SCTN* 2:106–7; *LDN*, pp. 126–27
List of individuals with whom tin was deposited. Pašši-Tilla son of Pula-ḫali and Akkul-enni son of Akitte are included. Tablet written in the city of Tilla. Ninkiya the scribe.

EN 9/1 375 SMN 1276 A 23 *LDN*, p. 127 *EN* 9 375 [= *EN* 9/2 450].
Barley account.

EN 9/1 376 SMN 773 A 23 *LDN*, p. 127 *EN* 9 376 [= *EN* 9/3 451].
Various quantities of [t]in loaned? by Wariae.

EN 9/1 377 SMN 3104 C 28 *LDN*, p. 128
Record of various loan transactions between ᶠNanawa and Ḫumpape son of Muš-Tešup. Statements (*umma*) and a declaration (*lišānu*) are made by Ḫumpape. SAG.AN.KI the scribe.

EN 9/3 378 SMN 3481 F 24
Record of a transaction of Tae son of Šila-apuḫe and Wur-tuluk son of Ḫannaya. Note syllabic writing, *wa-ar-dá-aḫ-ḫi-šu* for ÍR-ŠEŠ-*ḫi-šu*. Arip-šarri the scribe.

EN 9/1 379 SMN 2212 N 120 *SCTN* 2:31; *LDN*, p. 119 *EN* 9 354
Loan of 1 three-year-old oxen, 1 three-year-old jenney, and 15 MA.NA of tin by Tai-Tilla son of Ninu-atal to Pazizu son of Akkul-enni the merchant to be repaid in the month of Tammuz. Niḫi-Tilla the scribe.

[10] Published as SMN 973 in *EN* 9/1.

EN 9/3 380 SMN 3508 F 24
Tešup-šarri son of Urḫiya provides 20 copper items to various individuals.

EN 9/1 381 SMN 2217 N 120 *SCTN* 2:37; *LDN*, pp. 128–29
Statement (*umma*) by Aršuḫ son of Ḫui-Tilla concerning his borrowing of barley and wheat from ᶠTuppel-enna daughter of Ḫiar-elli. Tablet written at the Great Gate of the city of Nuzi.

EN 9/3 382 SMN 1633
Statement (*umma*) of Kašma-tae son of Šimika-atal concerning a horse belonging to Tešup-nirari son of Turar?-Tešup. Emuqa son of Balṭu-kašid the scribe.

EN 9/3 383 SMN 1218 A 14
Record of a sale of 5 ANŠE of grain belonging to Šimika-atal son of Nanaya. ᵈIŠKUR-MANSUM son of ᵈUTA-AN.DÙL the scribe.

EN 9/2 384 SMN 2075 S 132
Record of Awiluti son of Šennatati who owes Irašu son of Akitte a cow. [T]eḫip-Tilla the scribe.

EN 9/3 385 SMN 3056 S 19
Record of a dispute of Šurkip-šarri son of Akip-šarri concerning 23 TÚG.MEŠ and Enna-ma[ti] the *ḫalzuḫlu* and Beliya the shepherd. [. . *a*]-*it*-[*ta*]-*ra* [the scribe]. Transliteration, *EN* 7 452.

EN 9/1 386 SMN 3520 F 24 *LDN*, p. 129
Statement (*umma*) by Šekaya son of Akip-šenni concerning his borrowing of a donkey from Teḫip-šarri son of Itti-šarri. A fine male donkey is to be returned in Al-ilani during the month of Kinunati. Ḫutiya the scribe.

EN 9/2 387 SMN 2371 S 132 *SCTN* 2:102; *LDN*, pp. 129–30
Statement (*umma*) of Teḫip-Tilla son of Taya concerning a fine ox owed to him by Utḫap-tae and its transfer (*ana wurubatḫam*) by Utḫap-tae to Šamaš-dayyanu. Tablet written in Nuzi by Ḫašip-Tilla.

EN 9/1 388 SMN 2150 M 91 *SCTN* 2:1; *LDN*, p. 130 *EN* 9 389
Record of outstanding silver loans owed by various individuals to Akap-šenni.

EN 9/1 389 SMN 2583 P 382 *SCTN* 2:170; *LDN*, p. 130 *EN* 9 389
[= *EN* 9/1 388]
Declaration (*lišānu*) of Akawatil son of Pui-tae before witnesses concerning his debt of grain to Muka the *asu* to be repaid after the harvest. Eḫli-Tešup the scribe.

EN 9/1 390 SMN 2618 P401/456! *SCTN* 2:187–88
Deposition before judges of Alkiya son of [. . . .] concerning a 5 ANŠE 1 [GIŠ.APIN] field in the *dimtu* of Ar-Tešup given *ana titennūti* to ᶠKunziya daughter of [. . . .]. [Ḫa]šip!-Tilla the scribe.

EN 9/2 391 SMN 2246 N 120 *SCTN* 2:70
Contract by which Paššі-Tilla son of Pula-ḫali agrees to pay Arnukka son of Elḫip-Tilla wages (*igru*) and food (*akalu*) for making bricks.

EN 9/2 392 SMN 2481 S 151 *SCTN* 2:130; *LDN*, p. 130
Statement (*umma*) of Šata son of Itḫ-apiḫe concerning Tarmiya [lú]*gugallu* son of Ḫuya who is the guarantor for the interest on a loan received from Matip-Tešup son of Muš-Tešup. Balṭu-kašid the scribe.

EN 9/2 393 SMN 2012 S 113
Loan of Ḫutiya son of Šimika-atal who borrows bricks from Arip-šeriš. Nabu-ila the scribe.

EN 9/3 394 SMN 934
Statement (*umma*) of Kel-Tešup concerning a receipt of bricks from the palace.

EN 9/2 395 SMN 2495 S 151 *SCTN* 2:140–41
Deposition in court of Irwa-ḫuta *warad* Ḫašuar who testifies before judges concerning Ḫalutta's presence without permission in Ḫašuar's orchard. Šer-šiya the scribe.

EN 9/1 396 SMN 3109 *CPN*, p. 67
Lawsuit in which Utḫap-tae son of Zike accuses Urḫi-Tešup of falsely claiming a debt concerning horses against him. Urḫi-Tešup is fined an ox.

EN 9/1 397 SMN 1066 A 34 *CPN*, p. 140
Court case in which Ulmi-Tilla, a shepherd, charges Akiya with improperly imprisoning him in the city of Zirra. Because his herd was left unattended, 30 goats were lost. Ulmi-Tilla produced witnesses and Akiya was fined.

EN 9/1 398 SMN 852 A 34 *CPN*, p. 164
Court case in which Ḫumpape successfully charges Ḫerika and Ar-tašenni with the theft of grain. Šimanni the scribe.

EN 9/1 399 SMN 1450 A 26 *CPN*, p. 153
Court case in which Šilwa-Tešup DUMU LUGAL successfully sues Iriri-Tilla son of Arik-k[ur]we for the return of a missing slave girl. Tarmi-Tešup the scribe.

EN 9/1 400 SMN 3501 F 24
Lawsuit in which Kuššuya son of Sîn-bani and Akip-šenni son of Niḫri[ya], the guarantor of Ḫamanna, go to court concerning the transfer of the wife and children of Ḫamanna who has defaulted on his debt.

EN 9/2 401 SMN 2248 N 120 *SCTN* 2:71
Statement (*umma*) of Azzina son of Tešup-nirari before judges in court in a lawsuit with [Ar-tura] son of Kuššiya. Zini the scribe.

EN 9/3 402 SMN 3603 G 29
Deposition of Mušuya [son of . . . .] before judges. Eḫli-Tešup the scribe.

EN 9/1 403 SMN 3477 F 16 *CPN*, p. 65
Court case before the judges of the city of Nuzi in which Niḫriya son of Ekurra charges Zike son of Akip-šarri with the theft of a sheep and is awarded 12 sheep as compensation. [d]AK-DINGIR.RA the scribe.

EN 9/1 404 SMN 3611 G 29
Lawsuit in which Utḫap-tae son of Zike and Iriš-kenu go to court concerning a *rakib narkabti*. Taya the scribe.

EN 9/1 405 SMN 3388 D 6 *CPN*, p. 164
Lawsuit in which Akip-tašenni accuses three men of the theft of straw from the palace granary for which each is fined 2 oxen, 2 asses, and 20 sheep. Ḫašip-Tilla the scribe.

EN 9/1 406 SMN 1656
Lawsuit in which Ikkiya goes to court with Urḫi-Tilla son of Aštar-Tilla concerning the theft of property of Šilwa-Tešup DUMU LUGAL.

EN 9/3 407 SMN 3584 G 29
Ṭuppi tamgurti of Šar-tae son of Zizzi and Ḫerši son of Ḫaniku concerning a *titennūtu* contract. [. . .]-*e* the scribe.

EN 9/1 408 SMN 2707 *SCTN* 2:236; *CPN*, p. 150
Taya son of Ḫerpani and Utḫap-še son of Šukriya go to court concerning a dispute over the return of a kid.

EN 9/1 409 SMN 3763
Lawsuit in which Ilaya son of Ḫabira and Tatau the LÚ.DAM.GÀR go to court concerning payment for a "two cubit" slave girl purchased by Ilaya. Emuša the scribe.

EN 9/1 410 SMN 2772
Ṭuppi tamgurti by which Turar-Tešup son of [. . . .] and Eḫli-Tešup son of Taya make an agreement concerning the payment of sheep. Tablet written in Nuzi.

EN 9/1 411 SMN 3100 C 28 *CPN*, p. 170
Lawsuit in which Šukriya accuses Tanaya of the theft of a hide which was made into a pair of shoes. Tanaya is fined 1 ox.

EN 9/3 412 SMN 3509 F 16 *LDN*, pp. 125–26 as *EN* 9 373
Statement (*umma*) of Šeḫal-Tešub son of Tauka and Teḫip-šarri son of [Akip]-šarri concerning the repayment? of silver belonging to Teḫip-šarri. Ḫe[rr]ikanni son of [. . .]-nirari the scribe.

EN 9/1 413 SMN 3110 C 28
Ṭuppi taḫsilti in which Tišam-mušni claims that Akap-tae son of Ar-zizza seized 10 ANŠE of fields given to him by the king. Teḫip-Tilla the scribe.

EN 9/1 414 SMN 672 A 26 *CPN*, p. 114
Lawsuit in which Nupanani son of Ward-Šamaš forces Naiš-tuni *warad ekalli* to redeem 6 GIŠ.APIN of fields in the city of Tašenni by returning one garment and n MA.NA of copper in fulfillment of a *titennūtu* contract. The fields belong to Artirwe. Ḫutiya son of ^{d}UTA.MA.AN.SUM the scribe.

EN 9/1 415 SMN 699 A 14
Fragmentary court case.

EN 9/1 416 SMN 2636 P 465 *SCTN* 2:201
Damaged lawsuit by which Ḫampizi son of Ar-šatuya sues Šenni son of Kulmeya. [Te]šup-atal the scribe.

EN 9/1 417 SMN 1423 C 81 *CPN*, p. 166
Court case in which Maḫiya charges 3 men with the theft of an ox for which each is fined 2 oxen. Iniya the scribe.

EN 9/1 418 SMN 3152 C 28
Fragmentary lawsuit in the city of Artiḫe between Akitta son of Akiya and Tarmi-Tešup son of Šaua concerning a field given *ana titennūtu* to Tarmi-Tešup's father.

EN 9/2 419 SMN 2309 S 124 *SCTN* 2:81
Lawsuit between Puḫi-šenni son of Muš-apu and Ḫatarte son of Atanaḫ-ili and Teḫiya son of Ukur-atal concerning 26 MA.NA 30 GÍN of bronze the two owed Puḫi-šenni. [. . . .]-*ab-ba* the scribe.[11]

EN 9/1 420 SMN 1455 A 15 *CPN*, p. 106
Lawsuit in which Ezira, corroborated by witnesses, accuses Šarrukili with misappropriating land and houses which had been given to Ezira upon his adoption by Kurišu.

EN 9/2 421 SMN 2178 S 112 *SCTN* 2:14.
Fragmentary [*ṭuppi mārūti*] text. Sîn-liqiš the scribe.

EN 9/3 422 SMN 2394 S 132 *SCTN* 2:114
Fragmentary court case. Kel-[. . .] the scribe.[12]

EN 9/1 423 SMN 3478 F 16
Fragmentary lawsuit between Ka-ilu and Ḫutanni. dUTU.PAB the scribe.

EN 9/1 424 SMN 3607 G 29 *CPN*, p. 57
Lawsuit in which Uzimpalitu son of Taḫirišti successfully charges Arik-kanari DUMU LUGAL with having falsely denied receiving a herd of sheep from him. Arik-kanari is condemned to pay 180 sheep. See also *EN* 9/1 431 and 448. Teḫi-[. . .] the scribe.

EN 9/1 425 SMN 2514 S 151 *SCTN* 2:151–52
Lawsuit by which Utḫap-tae son of Zike recovers 30 shekels of silver from Ḫutiya son of Kalmaš-šura for the sale of a horse. See also *EN* 9/1 431.

EN 9/1 426 SMN 2607 P 401 *SCTN* 2:180–81; *CPN*, p. 59
Statement (*umma*) of the judges of the city of Ašḫušši concerning a lawsuit by Ḫašip-turi daughter of [. . . .] who brings new evidence against Umpiya son of Eḫliya and has a prior decision reversed. Aḫ-ummiša the scribe.

EN 9/1 427 SMN 2647 P 466 *SCTN* 2:205
Ṭuppi tamgurti by which Ḫampizi son of Ar-šatuya agrees to pay the equivalent of the fine he was assessed to Ḫurazzi son of Alkiya. dAK-DINGIR.RA son of Sîn-napšir the scribe.

[11] So according to *SCTN* 2:81.

[12] *SCTN* 2:114 reads dIM-X-X DUB.SAR here.

EN 9/3 428 SMN 3493
Fragmentary [*titennūtu*] agreement wherein a 2 ANŠE field is given to Niḫriya by two or more individuals. Balṭu-kašid the scribe.

EN 9/3 429 SMN 3530
Fragmentary [*titennūtu*] agreement with Akkul-enni and Ar-tešše as principals.

EN 9/1 430 SMN 3053 C 28 *CPN*, p. 45
Lawsuit in which Šar-Tešup son of Utḫap-tae charges Teššuya with having failed to return an ass previously loaned to him and receives an ass as an indemnity after Teššuya failed the river ordeal.

EN 9/1 431 SMN 3097 C 28 *CPN*, p. 147
Memorandum concerning a lawsuit in which Utḫap-tae charges Ḫutiya with having failed to pay for a horse previously sold to him. See also *EN* 9/1 425 in which the suit is resolved. Amumi-Tešup the scribe.

EN 9/1 432 SMN 3098 C 28 *CPN*, p. 58; *STPPKA*, p. 19
Appeal before the king by Arik-kanari DUMU LUGAL of an earlier decision concerning the delivery of 180 sheep to Azipalitu son of Taḫirišti. The appeal is denied and a penalty of 1 slave girl is assessed. See also *EN* 9/1 424 and 448.

EN 9/1 433 SMN 3103 C 28
Ṭuppi tamgurti between Šurki-Tilla son of Amur-rabi and Teḫip-zizza son of Ar-nuzu. Teḫip-zizza has been sentenced to pay one ox for a loss that Šurki-Tilla has incurred. He has paid thirty shekels of silver, so Šurki-Tilla declares himself satisfied and releases his claim to the remaining silver. Sîn-šaduni son of Amur-šarri the scribe.

EN 9/1 434 SMN 3102 C 28 *CPN*, p. 150
Lawsuit in which Šar-Tešup son of Utḫap-tae charges Arip-šarri son of Kun[tani] with converting three GIŠ.APIN of emmer deposited with him for three years. Arip-šarri is penalized 30 GIŠ.APIN of emmer wheat and 3 bundles of straw. Tu-[. . . .] son of [. . . .] the scribe.

EN 9/1 435 SMN 3119 C 28
Legal text involving an ineritance? dispute involving Ḫutiya, Saua, Akitta. Ḫaiš-Tešup the scribe.

EN 9/1 436 SMN 3117 C 28 *CPN*, p. 149
Lawsuit in which Šar-Tešup son of Utḫap-tae sues Palteya for money owed on the sale of a horse. Akkul-enni son of MU-DIRI the scribe.

EN 9/1 437 SMN 736 *CPN*, pp. 31,66,160
Court case in which Ḫui-Tilla is accused by Kikkiya of stealing two *sassuku* trees from the orchard of Ḫišmi-Tešup in the city of Artiḫe and fined 2 MA.NA (of silver) the equivalent of 4 oxen, 4 asses, and 40 sheep. Ṣilliya the scribe.

EN 9/1 438 SMN 3764
Lawsuit between Pai-Tešup son of [. . . .] and Tae concerning a field. ^{d}IŠKUR.MA.AN.SUM the scribe.

EN 9/1 439 SMN 1671
Legal? text involving a dispute over a loan? payment. Ari-waltie a principal.

EN 9/2 440 SMN 2372 S 132 *SCTN* 2:103; *CPN*, pp. 148–49
Lawsuit between Pašši-Tilla son of Pula-ḫali and Ḫupita and Alki-Tilla sons of Akitte concerning the debt of Tultukka son of Akitte. Case tried in Tupšarriniwe. Akkul-enni the scribe.

EN 9/2 441 SMN 2374 S 132 *SCTN* 2:104
Statement (*umma*) of Urḫi-Tešup son of Yanzi-mašu before judges concerning a lawsuit between him and Palteya son of Puḫi-šenni over the payment of a servant woman owed to him. Ari-ḫamanna the scribe.

EN 9/3 442 SMN 3632 G 29
Statement (*umma*) of Ḫutte son of Turari, Zike son of Zilip-Tilla, Akiptašenni son of Ikkiya, Kammiya son of Šimika-atal, Šakup-šenni son of Zilteya, and Paya son of [. . . .], all of the city of Šuriniwe concerning a legal dispute.

EN 9/1 443 SMN 3147 C 28
Court case involving Taḫirišti son of Ipša-ḫalu and Arik-kanari son of Šašibutil.

EN 9/1 444 SMN 3588
Court case involving Krib-šerri son of Ḫut-Tešup and Qaya son of Šaš-tae.

EN 9/1 445 SMN 3137 C 28
Statement (*umma*) of Kipi-šenni concerning an agreement over horses with Šar-Tešup son of Utḫap-tae. Tablet written after the *šudutu* in the gate of the Temple of ^{d}Ḫurpaḫi in Nuzi. Sîn-šaduni the scribe.

EN 9/3 446 SMN 3764
Fragmentary text.

EN 9/3 447 SMN 3684? H 15
Fragmentary text.

EN 9/1 448 SMN 3604 G 29 *CPN*, p. 57
Appeal by Arik-kanari DUMU LUGAL of the decision rendered by the judges of the city of Kurri concerning the penalty assessed in an earlier decision. The appeal is denied and the penalty is confirmed. See also *EN* 9/1 424 and 432.

EN 9/3 449 SMN 1225
Letter to ^{f}Ašta-ḫuta [daughter of . . . .] from Ar-Tešup.

EN 9/2 450 SMN 2127 S 110 *LDN*, p. 127 as *EN* 9 375; *STPPKA*, p. 119
Loan of Ḫišma-apu son of Tarmiya who borrows grain from Utḫap-tae son of Ar-tura. Tarmi-Tešup the scribe.

EN 9/3 451 SMN 1023 *LDN*, p. 127 as *EN* 9 376
Antichretic loan contract wherein Impurtu son of Akiya borrows 13 MA.NA 30 GÍN of tin from Wur-Tešup son of Tarmi-Tešup to be repaid in the month of Šeḫali of Tešup. Kaluppani the scribe. Collated.

EN 9/2 452 SMN 2351 S 132 *SCTN* 2:92–93. *LDN*, p. 122 as *EN* 9 362
Ṭuppi taḫsilti concerning various quantities of tin for a total of 18 MA.NA 55 GÍN borrowed from Waḫḫura by different individuals.

EN 9/3 453 SMN 2057
"Turar-Tešup of the city of Ameriya." Possibly a scribal practice text.

EN 9/3 454 SMN 2734 *SCTN* 2:253; *LDN*, p. 111 as *EN* 9 334
Interest-bearing loan contract wherein Ulmi-Till son of Akip-šenni borrows [11] ANŠE of grain from Akip-apu son of Šennaya to be repaid with interest after the harvest.

EN 9/2 455 SMN 2526 S 151 *SCTN* 2:157
Fragmentary loan text wherein Ḫašinna borrows an ox from Puḫi-šenni.

EN 9/3 456 SMN 2792
Fragmentary text. [. . .]-*ni*?-[. . .] scribe.

EN 9/3 457 SMN 2835
Fragmentary text. SAG.AN.KI the scribe.

EN 9/2 458 SMN 2174 S 112 *SCTN* 2:13
Fragmentary lawsuit with the testimony of a number of men concerning property.

EN 9/3 459 SMN 1543
Fragmentary loan? text concerning shepherds and their wives?.

EN 9/3 460 SMN 3526 F 24
Statement (*umma*) of Paip-purni son of Nul-zaḫi concerning the purchase of a donkey from Teḫip-šarri for 7 MA.NA of tin. Ḫutiya the scribe.

EN 9/1 461 SMN 2525 S 151 *SCTN* 2:157
Fragment of a loan text wherein Šaḫlu[ya son of] Tuliya borrows n GUN and 31 MA.NA of [. . . .] from Šimika-atal.

EN 9/1 462 SMN 2222 N 120 *SCTN* 2:42–43; *CPN*, p. 14
Two groups of three men are designated as *manzaduḫlu* officials.

EN 9/1 463 SMN 686
21 MA.NA of bronze belonging to Šilwa-Tešup DUMU [LUGAL] and 2 *sasinnu*, given to Ili-ma-aḫi to be made into 31 *za-aq-qí-t*[*ú*?].

EN 9/1 464 SMN 2211 N 120 *SCTN* 2:31
List of palace personnel.

EN 9/3 465 SMN 3418 D 6
Declaration (*lišānu*) of Aḫuiya son of Akap-šenni concerning the payment of an interest-bearing loan of grain which he borrowed from Utḫap-tae, repaid with interest after the harvest. Ili-ma-aḫi the scribe.

EN 9/1 466 SMN 3468 F 6
Damaged list of names and various amounts of barley.

EN 9/1 467 SMN 888
Fragmentary [declaration (*lišānu*)] before witnesses by fWatila daughter of Pui-tae concerning 6 sheep for her daughter Elḫim-nuzu and 1 ox for Wurmakiri.

EN 9/3 468 SMN 2071
List of 19 witnesses to fAnirše being given as a wife to Ḫanatu by fTulpunnaya. [Šer]šiya the scribe.

EN 9/3 469 SMN 2252 N 120 *SCTN* 2:72
[*Ṭuppi*] *aḫḫuti* wherein Ad-mati-il(u) was taken into brothership by Akiya son of dAK-DINGIR.RA. Tablet written after the *šudutu* [in the Great Gate of. . . .] by Sîn-iqiša the scribe.

EN 9/1 470 SMN 855 *CPN*, p. 176
Court case in which Ḫutiya accuses Kušši-ḫarpe of accepting an *ilku* payment of 2 sheep and of improperly giving fields to Kišteya. Kušši-ḫarpe acknowledges the payment of the *ilku* as *irana* for the fields of Zapaki but denies the charge. Balṭu-kašid the scribe.

EN 9/3 471 SMN 1048
Fragmentary statements (*umma*) of Adad-šarri and Peški-ilišu concerning a goat. Transliteration published by Speiser as *AASOR* 16, p. 20 no. 14.

EN 9/3 472 SMN 3266 D 3
Fragmentary statements (*umma*) of Umpiya, Akaya, and others concerning oxen from various towns (Kunatu, Tarmiyawe, Intašwe, Ilabra) brought by Assyrians.

EN 9/3 473 SMN 3265 D 3
Statement (*umma*) of Ḫapir-Tilla son of Ninkiya concerning his daughter fA-šil-lumti whom he gave as a wife to Ḫut-tirta the servant of [Kub]i-nari. Tablet written after the *šudutu* of the palace in the gate of the city of Zizza by [. . . .]la the scribe.

EN 9/3 474 SMN 3531
Fragmentary text.

EN 9/3 475 SMN 1140
[n GUN] 7 MA.NA of bronze, the *ḫamussu*-tax (see *CAD* Ḫ 73 s.v.) of the palace which Taizi son of Nan-teya for Elḫip-Tilla, the *šakin biti*, received and to Karmiša he delivered in Al-Ilani.

EN 9/3 476 SMN 941 A 23
Receipt of 35 sheep and goats which Šilwa-Tešup gave to Ḫutip-apu son of Elḫip-apu.

EN 9/2 477 SMN 2391 S 132 *SCTN* 2:113
Record of the sale of a horse by Eteš-šenni son of Ḫabira to Puya son of Ḫašiya for a fine mature ox, 30 MA.NA of [tin], 7 GÍN of bronze, etc. Seal of the scribe.

EN 9/2 478 SMN 2357 S 132 *SCTN* 2:95.
Record of 16 horses received by men of Kipali the LÚ.DAM.GÀR.

EN 9/3 479 SMN 2084
List of 7 witnesses in the city of Ḫalmaniwe. [*Šumu*[!]*-l*]*ib*[!]*-ši* son of Taya the scribe among the witnesses.

EN 9/3 480 SMN 3532
Statement (*umma*) of [Š]aten-šuḫ son of Ḫutip-Tilla concerning 20 ANŠE of *tabtu* which he had exchanged for 20 ANŠE of *šeʾu* with Ḫašip-Tilla and Naniya sons of Kip-ukur.

EN 9/3 481 SMN 3158 C 36
Fragmentary [*titennūtu*?] agreement. [. .]anamuḫi the scribe.

EN 9/3 482 SMN 997x
Document concerning the *ilku* of houses of various individuals. Urḫi-Tilla, Ḫašip-Tilla, and Ḫašiya are the principals. Seal of the scribe. Same SMN number as *EN* 5 38 but different text.

EN 9/3 483 SMN 3598 G 29
Fragmentary legal record before the judges. 7 witnesses appear.

EN 9/1 484 SMN 3723
Fragmentary legal text. Nai-teya son of Ikkinna appears before judges in a dispute over a field.

EN 9/1 485 SMN 3138 C 28
Fragmentary text concerning surveying. Some personal names preserved.

EN 9/3 486 SMN 3458
Fragmentary statement (*umma*) of Ziluma son of Ak[ap]-šenni concerning [. . . .] daughter of Aštena and a fine *tulmapu* cow which he gave to Akuiya at the beginning of the month of Saputi. Aitt[ara] the scribe.

EN 9/3 487 SMN 867/1039 *EN* 7 201
Record of numerous grain allotments received by numerous individuals in the city of Ṣilliyawa. Transliteration published as *EN* 7 201.

EN 9/3 488 SMN 3487 F 24
Fragmentary legal case wherein the judges in the city of Ulamme decide on a dispute over a sheep between Ataya and Akawa.

EN 9/3 489 SMN 2781
Fragmentary [*ṭuppi mārūti*] text. Ḫupita the scribe.

EN 9/2 490 SMN 2333 S 127/9 *SCTN* 2:87; *LDN*, p. 108 as *EN* 9 323
Šurki-Tilla son of Tampi-kutatti borrows grain from Urḫi-kušuḫ DUMU LUGAL.

EN 9/3 491 SMN HM 8403
Receipt of 8 containers of oil (DAL Ì.MEŠ) given to the MÍ.LUGAL of Nuzi.

EN 9/3 492 SMN 3111 C 28
[Declaration (*lišānu*)[?]] wherein Ḫerri-šarri states that he paid for 40 GÍN of silver to Utḫap-tae son of Zike. Uta-andul the scribe.

EN 9/2 493 SMN 2308 S 124 *SCTN* 2:80
Loan of Urḫi-kutu son of Šeḫurni who borrows grain from Puḫi-šenni son of Muš-apu. Elḫip-Tilla the scribe son of [Kel]-Tešup.

EN 9/3 494 SMN 2090
Statement (*umma*) of I[riri]-Tilla son of [. . . .] concerning [. .]-rannu of the palace which had been given to Wan[tiya] son of Eḫlip-apu. Furthermore, a gift for the king was delivered in the city of Turša.

EN 9/3 495 SMN 938
Paddle shaped tablet (tag?) with hole through handle. Statement (*umma*) of Tiyampera.

EN 9/3 496 SMN 3533
Paddle shaped tablet (tag?) with hole through handle. Record of 480 DAL 2 SÌLA of oil.

EN 9/1 497 SMN 2643 P 460–66 *SCTN* 2:203
Loan text by which Tuliya borrows 15 MA.NA of tin from Tešup-mati son of Šerta-ma-ilu. Tur-šenni the scribe.

EN 9/1–3 498 SMN 974 *CPN*, p. 150
Court case in which Uantari (= Wantari) son of Šukriya accuses Ezira of the theft of grain. Ezira successfully countersues claiming ownership of the field. Copy of reverse was left out in *EN* 9/1 and appeared in *EN* 9/3. Šamaš-ura the scribe.

EN 9/3 499 SMN 3722
Declaration [*lišānu*] of Pai-Tilla son of Ziliya concerning a lawsuit. Šeriš-atal the scribe.

EN 9/1 500 SMN 2239 N 120 *SCTN* 2:67
Lawsuit in which ᶠTulpun-naya daughter of Šeltunaya sues Arik-kanari son of Tulpi-šenni over an orchard.

EN 9/3 501 SMN 2343 S 130 *SCTN* 2:89–90
Statement (*umma*) of Paya son of [Elḫip]-šarri concerning Tešup-nirari son of Bel-šaduni and a slave given? to Puḫi-šenni son of Muš-apu. Appa the scribe son of Intiya.

EN 9/3 502 SMN 3648
Fragmentary legal case with Šukri-Tešup the principal party who sues Ḫašiya, Taya, Šarteya, and Marilitiya. Akiya the scribe.

EN 9/3 503 SMN 3534
Fragmentary statement (*umma*) of ᶠAš[. . . .] daughter of [. . . .]. Šimanni son of Nabu-ila the scribe.

EN 9/3 504 SMN 3535
Fragmentary text.

EN 9/2 505 SMN 2373 S 132 *SCTN* 2:103
Statement (*umma*) of Tupkin-a[tal] son of Ḫapiašu concerning the receipt of two road horses that were owed to him by Pašši-Tilla son of Pula-ḫali. Tablet written at the gate of Al-Ilani by Ḫu[t-Tešup] the scribe.

EN 9/3 506 SMN 2632 P 465 *SCTN* 2:199
Statement (*umma*) of Šuki[. .] son of Sîn-nadin-[aḫḫi] wherein he states that he bought 1 *naḫlaptu* from Ilikiša for 25 *qa* of grain. Tukkani the scribe.

EN 9/3 507 SMN 3536
Fragmentary declaration (*lišānu*) of Beliya son of Za[. . .]ya concerning a field in the *ugāru* of the city of Kipri. Seal of the scribe.

EN 9/3 508 SMN 3469
Fragmentary text concerning a dispute? over a house of Ḫut[. . .].

EN 9/3 509 SMN 1134
Fragmentary text.

EN 9/3 510 SMN 3537
Fragmentary list of men assigned to various individuals.

EN 9/1 511 SMN 2602 P 400 *SCTN* 2:179
Fragmentary *titennūtu*? transaction whereby Šekar-Tilla gives a field to the sons of Taya. Nanna-adaḫ the scribe.

EN 9/2 512 SMN 3538
Fragmentary loan of bronze made by Pašši-Tilla son of Pula-ḫali.

EN 9/2 513 SMN 2405 S 132 *SCTN* 2:119
Loan text wherein Itḫ-apiḫe son of [Zil]ip-erwi borrows bronze from Pašši-Tilla. Šamaš-naṣir [the scribe].

EN 9/3 514 SMN 2200/3539 S 113?
Fragmentary text. List of witnesses partially preserved. [. . .]-*ni*-x the scribe.

EN 9/2 515 SMN 2250 S 120 *SCTN* 2:72
Fragmentary text involving Pašši-Tilla and payment, perhaps for doors. Tablet written at the Tupšarriniwe gate by Šamaš-naṣir.

EN 9/3 516 SMN 3540
Fragmentary statement (*umma*) concerning transactions of wool and oil. [. . . .] the scribe.

EN 9/3 517 SMN 3663
Fragmentary statement (*um*[*ma*]).

EN 9/3 518 SMN 2356 S 132 *SCTN* 2 95
Transaction whereby Paši-Tilla son of [Pula-ḫali] provides grain to Ḫutiya son of En[. . . .] for which Ḫutiya promises to repay 4000 bricks in the month of Impurtani. Enna-[mati] the scribe.

EN 9/3 519 SMN 3541
Fragmentary text.

EN 9/3 520
No text.

EN 9/3 521 SMN 1232
Fragmentary text.

EN 9/3 522 SMN 3542
Fragmentary text. Possibly a tin loan.

EN 9/3 523 SMN 2524 S 151 *SCTN* 2:156
Fragmentary [*ṭuppi titennūti*]. Below is a transliteration based on a collation combined with *SCTN* 2:156 which reflects a slightly better state of preservation. Turar-Tešup son of Itḫ-apiḫe the scribe.

(1) [. . . .]-*rí*? DUMU *it-ḫi-ip*-LUGAL (2) [. . . .] (3) [. . . . *a*-]*na ti-te*-[*en-nu-ti* . . .] (4) [*a-na*] [I]*še-ka*$_4$*-ru-um* DUMU *šú*[*k-ri-ia*] (5) [*at-t*]*a-din ù i-na*-[*an-na*] (6) [. . .x] *mi a*[*r*? . . .] (7) [*a-na ti*]-*te-en-nu-t*[*i* . . .] (rest of obverse destroyed) l.e. (8) *an-nu-ú* [*it-ti-šu* . . .] rev. (9) *ú-ta-ar* (10) NA$_4$.KIŠIB DUB.SAR-*rù* (11) [IGI *a*]-*kip-ta-še-en-ni* DUMU *še*?-*e*[*l*-. .] (12) [IGI *n*]*i-zu-uk* DUMU *pu-ri-ki* (13) [IGI] *a-ri-ip-ḫur-ra* DUMU *a-k*[*a*?-. . .] (14) IGI *tu-ra-ar-te-šup* DUB.S[AR] (15) DUMU *it-ḫa-pí-ḫé* 16) NA$_4$ *ni-zu-uk* (17) NA$_4$ *a-ri-ip*-[*ḫur-ra*] (remainder destroyed)

EN 9/2 524 SMN 1448
Part of a *ṭuppi titennūtu* by which Akiya gives the sons of Pula-ḫali a field.

EN 9/2 525 SMN 3543
Fragment of a *ṭuppi mārūti* by which Elḫip-apu son of Abe[ya] adopts Puḫi-šenni son of Muš-apu.

EN 9/2 526 SMN 2304 S 124 *SCTN* 2:79
Ṭuppi titennūti by which Muš-apu son of Purna-zini receives fields from Pui[-tae?] son of Ikkiya.

EN 9/2 527 SMN 2320 S 124 *SCTN* 2:85
Fragmentary record of goods Puḫi-šenni [son of Muš-apu] paid, perhaps for property.

EN 9/2 528 SMN 2506 S 151 *SCTN* 2:147
Fragmentary text. Šimikatal and Tarmiya [lú][*ḫazannu*?] mentioned.

EN 9/2 529 SMN 3620 S 133 *SCTN* 2:127
Loan of tin with interest of [Pa]šši-Tilla son of Pula-[ḫali]. [Enna]-mati the scribe. *SCTN* 2:127 where it is listed as SMN 2446 (now assigned to *EN* 9/1 372).

Cumulative SMN Index to *Excavations at Nuzi* 9

SMN	*EN*
657	*EN* 9/1 306
662	*EN* 9/1 305
672	*EN* 9/1 414
679	*EN* 9/1 304
686	*EN* 9/1 463
699	*EN* 9/1 415
721	*EN* 9/3 69
723	*EN* 9/1 25
736	*EN* 9/1 437
739	*EN* 9/3 276
753	*EN* 9/1 370
755	*EN* 9/1 139
773	*EN* 9/1 376
776	*EN* 9/1 308
780	*EN* 9/1 303
793[1]	EN 9/1 368
798	*EN* 9/3 231
817	*EN* 9/1 365
822	*EN* 9/3 90
825	*EN* 9/1 162
835	*EN* 9/3 88
843+1293	*EN* 9/3 80
845	*EN* 9/3 100
852	*EN* 9/1 398
855	*EN* 9/1 470
858	*EN* 9/1 121
867[2]	*EN* 9/3 487
879	*EN* 9/1 317
888	*EN* 9/1 467
905(+1779)	*EN* 9/3 71
914	*EN* 9/1 314
929	*EN* 9/1 369
934	*EN* 9/3 394
938	*EN* 9/3 495
941[3]	*EN* 9/3 476
954	*EN* 9/1 307
973	*EN* 9/1 368
974	*EN* 9/1 498
997	*EN* 9/3 482
998	*EN* 9/3 173
1010	*EN* 9/3 318
1023	*EN* 9/3 451
1025	*EN* 9/1 245
1039[4]	*EN* 9/3 487
1042	*EN* 9/3 78
1043	*EN* 9/3 169
1045	*EN* 9/1 116
1048[5]	*EN* 9/3 471
1062	*EN* 9/3 164
1066	*EN* 9/1 397
1067	*EN* 9/1 165
1071	*EN* 9/1 366
1074	*EN* 9/3 361
1083	*EN* 9/3 70
1089	*EN* 9/3 271
1090	*EN* 9/1 12
1101[6]	*EN* 9/1 131
1109	*EN* 9/1 13
1134	*EN* 9/3 509
1140	*EN* 9/3 475
1151[7]	*EN* 9/1 138
1158	*EN* 9/3 89

Introductory Note: This cumulative list is included to facilitate the use of *EN* 9, allowing the reader to know in which part, 9/1–3, a particular text is to be found.

[1] Published as SMN 973 in *EN* 9/1.

[2] Transliteration, *EN* 7 201. Index in that volume lists SMN number as 867, but on page 62 of that volume the SMN number is listed as 1039. Possibly a join is involved here. In any case, it is the same text as *EN* 9/3 487.

[3] Copy by Pfeiffer of the same text appeared as *EN* 2 60.

[4] See above note to SMN 867.

[5] Transliteration, *AASOR* 16 14.

[6] Published in *SCCNH* 2 as SMN 2264, which actually is *EN* 6 47. This number corrected on the basis of a Lacheman manuscript.

[7] Not SMN 1154 as published in *SCCNH* 2 (1987), p. 363, catalogue entry for *EN* 9/1 138.

1166	*EN* 9/1 367	2041	*EN* 9/3 218
1167	*EN* 9/1 335	2047	*EN* 9/1 151
1168	*EN* 9/1 8	2051	*EN* 9/3 288
1176	*EN* 9/3 232	2052	*EN* 9/3 86
1204	*EN* 9/1 309	2057	*EN* 9/3 453
1212	*EN* 9/1 240	2068	*EN* 9/1 30
1218	*EN* 9/3 383	2071	*EN* 9/3 468
1219	*EN* 9/1 313	2075	*EN* 9/2 384
1225	*EN* 9/3 449	2077	*EN* 9/2 329
1232	*EN* 9/3 521	2079	*EN* 9/2 340
1237	*EN* 9/1 310	2081	*EN* 9/2 342
1245	*EN* 9/1 312	2083	*EN* 9/2 20
1247	*EN* 9/1 320	2084	*EN* 9/3 479
1263	*EN* 9/3 315	2090	*EN* 9/3 494
1276	*EN* 9/1 375	2091	*EN* 9/2 22
1293+843	*EN* 9/3 80	2095	*EN* 9/2 21
1300	*EN* 9/3 174	2100	*EN* 9/3 82
1415+1708	*EN* 9/1 26	2102	*EN* 9/2 152
1418	*EN* 9/1 147	2107	*EN* 9/2 262
1421	*EN* 9/3 66	2108	*EN* 9/2 363
1423	*EN* 9/1 417	2109	*EN* 9/3 254
1435	*EN* 9/1 319	2112	*EN* 9/2 186
1448	*EN* 9/2 524	2113	*EN* 9/2 336
1450	*EN* 9/1 399	2114	*EN* 9/2 67
1451	*EN* 9/3 255	2116	*EN* 9/2 353
1454	*EN* 9/1 14	2124	*EN* 9/2 297
1455	*EN* 9/1 420	2125+2476	*EN* 9/2 176
1542	*EN* 9/1 178	2126	*EN* 9/2 83
1543	*EN* 9/3 459	2127	*EN* 9/2 450
1592	*EN* 9/1 149	2128	*EN* 9/2 16
1593	*EN* 9/1 141	2132	*EN* 9/2 172
1596	*EN* 9/3 208	2133	*EN* 9/2 29
1598	*EN* 9/1 265	2136	*EN* 9/3 65
1633	*EN* 9/3 382	2137	*EN* 9/1 95
1635	*EN* 9/1 148	2138	*EN* 9/1 191
1669	*EN* 9/3 249	2139	*EN* 9/1 192
1671	*EN* 9/1 439	2142	*EN* 9/2 343
1684	*EN* 9/2 128	2143	*EN* 9/2 200
1705	*EN* 9/1 300	2144	*EN* 9/1 154
1708+1415	*EN* 9/1 26	2150	*EN* 9/1 389
1711	*EN* 9/3 261	2157	*EN* 9/2 322
1849	*EN* 9/1 243	2158	*EN* 9/2 354
1998	*EN* 9/3 287	2160	*EN* 9/1 351
1999	*EN* 9/1 123	2161	*EN* 9/2 359
2001	*EN* 9/2 360	2162	*EN* 9/2 338
2002	*EN* 9/2 188	2167	*EN* 9/2 321
2004	*EN* 9/2 184	2168+?	*EN* 9/2 28
2007	*EN* 9/2 19	2173+2316	*EN* 9/2 77
2010	*EN* 9/3 72	2174	*EN* 9/2 458
2011	*EN* 9/2 298	2178	*EN* 9/2 421
2012	*EN* 9/2 393	2179	*EN* 9/2 142
2013	*EN* 9/2 156	2180	*EN* 9/2 341
2015	*EN* 9/1 9	2193	*EN* 9/2 27

2194	*EN* 9/2 163	2354	*EN* 9/2 93
2200	*EN* 9/3 520	2356	*EN* 9/3 518
2208	*EN* 9/2 125	2357	*EN* 9/2 478
2211	*EN* 9/1 464	2358	*EN* 9/2 324
2212	*EN* 9/1 379	2358X	*EN* 9/2 371
2216[8]	*EN* 9/1 353	2359	*EN* 9/2 339
2217	*EN* 9/1 381	2361	*EN* 9/2 111
2221	*EN* 9/2 250	2362	*EN* 9/2 31
2222	*EN* 9/1 462	2363	*EN* 9/2 337
2239	*EN* 9/1 500	2365	*EN* 9/2 292
2240	*EN* 9/3 159	2366	*EN* 9/2 32
2242	*EN* 9/3 91	2367	*EN* 9/2 157
2245	*EN* 9/2 166	2368	*EN* 9/2 209
2246	*EN* 9/2 391	2370	*EN* 9/2 291
2248	*EN* 9/2 401	2371	*EN* 9/2 387
2250	*EN* 9/2 515	2372	*EN* 9/2 440
2251	*EN* 9/3 205	2373	*EN* 9/2 505
2252	*EN* 9/3 469	2374	*EN* 9/2 441
2264X[9]	*EN* 9/1 131	2376	*EN* 9/2 33
2301	*EN* 9/2 189	2377	*EN* 9/2 207
2302	*EN* 9/2 17	2379	*EN* 9/2 374
2303	*EN* 9/2 327	2380	*EN* 9/2 102
2304	*EN* 9/2 526	2381	*EN* 9/2 344
2307+2433	*EN* 9/2 23	2382	*EN* 9/2 347
2308	*EN* 9/2 493	2384	*EN* 9/2 346
2309	*EN* 9/2 419	2385	*EN* 9/1 134
2311	*EN* 9/2 175	2387	*EN* 9/2 325
2312	*EN* 9/2 171	2388	*EN* 9/1 233
2313	*EN* 9/2 143	2390	*EN* 9/2 10
2314	*EN* 9/2 74	2391	*EN* 9/2 477
2315	*EN* 9/2 334	2392	*EN* 9/1 350
2316+2173	*EN* 9/2 77	2393	*EN* 9/2 364
2319+2321	*EN* 9/2 146	2394	*EN* 9/3 422
2320	*EN* 9/2 527	2401	*EN* 9/2 283
2321+2319	*EN* 9/2 146	2405	*EN* 9/2 513
2323	*EN* 9/2 49	2414	*EN* 9/2 356
2333	*EN* 9/2 490	2418	*EN* 9/2 289
2334	*EN* 9/2 323	2423	*EN* 9/2 268
2335	*EN* 9/2 362	2426	*EN* 9/2 212
2336	*EN* 9/2 358	2433+2307	*EN* 9/2 23
2337	*EN* 9/2 73	2434	*EN* 9/2 348
2338	*EN* 9/2 158	2438	*EN* 9/2 110
2343	*EN* 9/3 501	2439	*EN* 9/2 97
2345	*EN* 9/2 236	2443	*EN* 9/2 224
2349	*EN* 9/2 352	2445	*EN* 9/2 349
2350	*EN* 9/2 331	2446	*EN* 9/1 372
2351	*EN* 9/2 452	2474	*EN* 9/2 38
2352	*EN* 9/2 357	2475	*EN* 9/2 129

[8] Transliteration, *AASOR* 16 22.

[9] SMN 2264 is also listed as *EN* 6 47, which is a different tablet. To further complicate matters, the same number was previously associated with SMN 2713 in a handwritten note in Lacheman's copy of *SCTN* 2, p. 239.

2476+2125	*EN* 9/2 176
2479	*EN* 9/2 187
2481	*EN* 9/2 392
2485	*EN* 9/2 34
2487	*EN* 9/2 101
2488	*EN* 9/2 35
2490	*EN* 9/2 234
2493	*EN* 9/2 153
2495	*EN* 9/2 395
2497	*EN* 9/2 36
2498	*EN* 9/2 76
2499	*EN* 9/2 273
2500	*EN* 9/2 204
2501	*EN* 9/2 40
2504	*EN* 9/2 106
2505	*EN* 9/2 130
2506	*EN* 9/2 528
2510	*EN* 9/2 103
2511	*EN* 9/2 177
2512	*EN* 9/2 96
2513	*EN* 9/2 279
2514	*EN* 9/1 425
2517	*EN* 9/2 39
2518	*EN* 9/2 185
2519	*EN* 9/2 145
2520	*EN* 9/2 206
2524	*EN* 9/3 523
2525	*EN* 9/1 461
2526	*EN* 9/2 455
2557	*EN* 9/3 211
2568	*EN* 9/1 181
2572	*EN* 9/1 114
2574	*EN* 9/1 196
2579	*EN* 9/1 99
2580	*EN* 9/1 41
2582	*EN* 9/1 197
2583	*EN* 9/1 389
2584	*EN* 9/1 42
2587	*EN* 9/1 126
2591	*EN* 9/1 193
2593	*EN* 9/1 373
2596	*EN* 9/1 225
2602	*EN* 9/1 511
2607	*EN* 9/1 426
2608	*EN* 9/1 183
2613	*EN* 9/1 15
2614	*EN* 9/3 92
2619	*EN* 9/1 390
2620	*EN* 9/2 301
2622	*EN* 9/1 194
2627	*EN* 9/1 75
2628	*EN* 9/1 198
2629	*EN* 9/1 24
2630	*EN* 9/1 8
2631	*EN* 9/1 203
2632	*EN* 9/3 506
2633	*EN* 9/1 248
2635	*EN* 9/1 332
2636	*EN* 9/1 416
2642	*EN* 9/1 135
2643	*EN* 9/1 497
2644	*EN* 9/1 285
2645	*EN* 9/1 47
2646	*EN* 9/1 199
2647	*EN* 9/1 427
2649	*EN* 9/1 195
2650	*EN* 9/1 43
2658	*EN* 9/1 252
2660	*EN* 9/1 213
2674	*EN* 9/2 326
2680	*EN* 9/2 333
2681	*EN* 9/2 299
2684	*EN* 9/1 4
2690	*EN* 9/2 345
2696	*EN* 9/1 201
2700+?	*EN* 9/2 18
2703	*EN* 9/1 251
2706	*EN* 9/2 81
2707	*EN* 9/1 408
2708	*EN* 9/2 264
2712	*EN* 9/1 244
2713	*EN* 9/1 45B[10]
2716	*EN* 9/3 50
2719	*EN* 9/3 230
2720	*EN* 9/1 44
2732	*EN* 9/1 247
2733	*EN* 9/2 45
2734	*EN* 9/3 454
2737	*EN* 9/1 113
2769	*EN* 9/3 274
2772	*EN* 9/1 410
2773	*EN* 9/2 267
2774	*EN* 9/3 53
2775+2779+	*EN* 9/3 52A+B+C
2777	*EN* 9/2 275
2778	*EN* 9/3 150
2779+2775+	*EN* 9/3 52A+B+C
2781	*EN* 9/3 489
2782	*EN* 9/3 54
2792	*EN* 9/3 456
2803	*EN* 9/2 144
2815	*EN* 9/3 161

[10] See *SCCNH* 2 (1987), p. 363, catalogue description to *EN* 9/1 131 and note to SMN 2264 above.

2818	*EN* 9/1 257
2821	*EN* 9/2 168
2823	*EN* 9/3 278
2835	*EN* 9/3 457
2847	*EN* 9/3 237
2910	*EN* 9/1 311
2920	*EN* 9/1 256
2925	*EN* 9/1 241
2950	*EN* 9/3 280
2993	*EN* 9/3 259B
2994	*EN* 9/1 239
2996	*EN* 9/3 266
2997	*EN* 9/3 270
2998	*EN* 9/3 281
2999	*EN* 9/3 282
3001	*EN* 9/3 108
3004	*EN* 9/3 98
3053	*EN* 9/1 430
3056	*EN* 9/3 385[11]
3082	*EN* 9/1 1
3083	*EN* 9/1 117
3085	*EN* 9/3 330
3094	*EN* 9/1 2
3097	*EN* 9/1 431
3098	*EN* 9/1 432
3100	*EN* 9/1 411
3101	*EN* 9/1 3
3102	*EN* 9/1 434
3103	*EN* 9/1 433
3104	*EN* 9/1 377
3105	*EN* 9/1 94
3107	*EN* 9/1 85
3109	*EN* 9/1 396
3110	*EN* 9/1 413
3111	*EN* 9/3 492
3113	*EN* 9/1 286
3117	*EN* 9/1 436
3119	*EN* 9/1 435
3129	*EN* 9/1 258
3137	*EN* 9/1 445
3138	*EN* 9/1 485
3147	*EN* 9/1 443
3150	*EN* 9/1 59
3153[12]	*EN* 9/1 418
3157	*EN* 9/3 284
3158	*EN* 9/3 481
3164[13]	*EN* 9/1 438
3175	*EN* 9/1 124
3179	*EN* 9/3 105
3238	*EN* 9/3 295
3265	*EN* 9/3 473
3266	*EN* 9/3 472
3356	*EN* 9/1 112
3388	*EN* 9/1 405
3418	*EN* 9/3 465
3458	*EN* 9/3 486
3464	*EN* 9/3 87
3468	*EN* 9/1 466
3469	*EN* 9/3 508
3472	*EN* 9/1 170
3475	*EN* 9/3 60
3476	*EN* 9/1 214
3477	*EN* 9/1 403
3478	*EN* 9/1 423
3481	*EN* 9/3 378
3483	*EN* 9/2 46
3485	*EN* 9/1 226
3487	*EN* 9/3 488
3491	*EN* 9/3 56
3492	*EN* 9/1 160
3493	*EN* 9/3 428
3495	*EN* 9/1 219
3496	*EN* 9/1 355
3497	*EN* 9/1 253
3499	*EN* 9/3 190
3501	*EN* 9/1 400
3506	*EN* 9/3 109
3508	*EN* 9/3 380
3509	*EN* 9/3 412
3510	*EN* 9/1 269
3515	*EN* 9/3 293
3519	*EN* 9/1 296
3520	*EN* 9/1 386
3526	*EN* 9/3 460
3527	*EN* 9/3 277
3528	*EN* 9/3 290
3529	*EN* 9/3 294
3530	*EN* 9/3 429
3531	*EN* 9/3 474
3532	*EN* 9/3 480
3533	*EN* 9/3 496
3534	*EN* 9/3 503
3535	*EN* 9/3 504
3536	*EN* 9/3 507

[11] Transliteration, *EN* 7 452.

[12] SMN 3152 was the published number for this text in *SCCNH* 2 (1987), p. 374, catalogue entry for *EN* 9/1 418, but it is also the number for *EN* 5 11. The correct number is SMN 3153.

[13] Published number in *SCCNH* 2 (1987), p. 376 under catalogue entry for *EN* 9/1 418 should be corrected to read SMN 3164, not 3764.

3537	*EN* 9/3 510
3538	*EN* 9/2 512
3539	*EN* 9/3 514
3540	*EN* 9/3 516
3541	*EN* 9/3 519
3542	*EN* 9/3 522
3543	*EN* 9/2 525
3557	*EN* 9/1 140
3560	*EN* 9/1 6
3562	*EN* 9/3 316
3564	*EN* 9/1 137
3567	*EN* 9/1 119
3576	*EN* 9/3 84
3580	*EN* 9/3 210
3582	*EN* 9/1 115
3584	*EN* 9/3 407
3585	*EN* 9/3 227
3586	*EN* 9/3 259
3587	*EN* 9/1 155
3588	*EN* 9/1 444
3589	*EN* 9/3 57
3590	*EN* 9/3 221
3591	*EN* 9/3 58
3592	*EN* 9/3 407
3594	*EN* 9/3 216
3595	*EN* 9/1 5
3597	*EN* 9/3 220
3598	*EN* 9/3 483
3599	*EN* 9/3 222
3600	*EN* 9/3 223
3601	*EN* 9/3 182
3602	*EN* 9/1 302
3603	*EN* 9/3 402
3604	*EN* 9/1 448
3606	*EN* 9/3 51
3607	*EN* 9/1 424
3609	*EN* 9/3 215
3610	*EN* 9/1 37
3611	*EN* 9/1 404
3613	*EN* 9/3 217
3614	*EN* 9/3 202
3617	*EN* 9/3 263
3619	*EN* 9/3 61
3620	*EN* 9/2 529
3622	*EN* 9/3 55
3627	*EN* 9/3 229
3628	*EN* 9/3 64
3629	*EN* 9/3 179
3631	*EN* 9/3 104
3632	*EN* 9/3 442
3645	*EN* 9/1 242
3648	*EN* 9/3 502
3650	*EN* 9/1 133
3652	*EN* 9/3 63
3657	*EN* 9/2 118
3663	*EN* 9/3 517
3665	*EN* 9/3 180
3666	*EN* 9/1 48
3684	*EN* 9/3 447
3705	*EN* 9/3 238[14]
3719	*EN* 9/1 260
3722	*EN* 9/3 499
3723	*EN* 9/1 484
3748	*EN* 9/3 328
3753	*EN* 9/3 79
3755	*EN* 9/3 272
3760	*EN* 9/3 62
3762	*EN* 9/3 246
3763	*EN* 9/1 409
3764	*EN* 9/3 446
3775	*EN* 9/3 272
8400(HM)	*EN* 9/1 122
8401(HM)	*EN* 9/3 68
8402(HM)	*EN* 9/3 107
8403(HM)	*EN* 9/3 491

[14] Transliteration, *EN* 7 432.

Cumulative Room List to *Excavations at Nuzi* 9

Room No.	*Tablet No.*	*SMN No.*
None	*EN* 9/1 4	2684
	EN 9/1 7	2015
	EN 9/1 14	1454
	EN 9/2 45	2733
	EN 9/3 50	2716
	EN 9/3 52A,B,C	2775+2779+?
	EN 9/3 53	2774
	EN 9/3 55	2782
	EN 9/3 62	3760
	EN 9/3 66	1421
	EN 9/3 68	HM 8401
	EN 9/3 72	2010
	EN 9/3 79	3753
	EN 9/2 81	2706
	EN 9/3 98	3004
	EN 9/3 100	845
	EN 9/3 107	HM 8402
	EN 9/3 108	3001
	EN 9/1 122	HM 8400
	EN 9/2 128	1684
	EN 9/1 144	2803
	EN 9/2 144	2803
	EN 9/1 149	1592
	EN 9/2 152	2102
	EN 9/1 152	2102
	EN 9/1 154	2144
	EN 9/3 161	2815
	EN 9/3 164	1062
	EN 9/1 165	1067
	EN 9/3 167	1707
	EN 9/2 168	2821
	EN 9/3 173	998
	EN 9/3 174	1300
	EN 9/1 178	1542
	EN 9/2 184	2004
	EN 9/2 188	2002
	EN 9/3 190	703
	EN 9/1 192	2139
	EN 9/2 200	2143
	EN 9/1 201	2696
	EN 9/3 208	1596
	EN 9/3 210	3580
	EN 9/3 218	2041
	EN 9/3 230	2719
	EN 9/3 231	798
	EN 9/3 232	1176
	EN 9/3 237	2847
	EN 9/3 238	3705
	EN 9/1 239	2994
	EN 9/1 241	2925
	EN 9/1 243	1849
	EN 9/1 244	2712
	EN 9/3 246	3762
	EN 9/1 247	2732
	EN 9/1 248	2633
	EN 9/3 249	1669
	EN 9/1 251	2703
	EN 9/3 254	2109
	EN 9/3 255	1451
	EN 9/1 256	2920
	EN 9/1 257	2818
	EN 9/3 259B	2993
	EN 9/1 260	3719
	EN 9/3 261	1711
	EN 9/2 264	2708
	EN 9/1 265	1598
	EN 9/3 266	2996
	EN 9/2 267	2773
	EN 9/3 270	2997
	EN 9/3 272	3755
	EN 9/3 274	2769
	EN 9/2 275	2777
	EN 9/3 277	3527
	EN 9/3 278	2823
	EN 9/3 280	2950
	EN 9/3 281	2998
	EN 9/3 282	2999
	EN 9/3 287	1998
	EN 9/3 288	2051
	EN 9/3 290	3528
	EN 9/3 294	3529
	EN 9/3 318	1010
	EN 9/3 330	3085
	EN 9/2 343	2142
	EN 9/2 345	2690
	EN 9/3 382	1633

Room No.	*Tablet No.*	*SMN No.*
	EN 9/3 394	934
	EN 9/1 396	3109
	EN 9/1 406	1656
	EN 9/1 408	2707
	EN 9/1 409	3763
	EN 9/1 410	2772
	EN 9/3 428	3493
	EN 9/3 429	3530
	EN 9/1 437	736
	EN 9/1 444	3588
	EN 9/3 446	3764
	EN 9/3 449	1225
	EN 9/3 451	1023
	EN 9/3 453	2057
	EN 9/3 454	2734
	EN 9/3 456	2792
	EN 9/3 457	2835
	EN 9/3 459	1543
	EN 9/1 461	2525
	EN 9/1 463	686
	EN 9/1 467	888
	EN 9/3 468	2071
	EN 9/1 470	855
	EN 9/3 471	1048
	EN 9/3 474	3531
	EN 9/3 475	1140
	EN 9/3 479	2084
	EN 9/3 480	3532
	EN 9/3 482	997
	EN 9/1 484	3723
	EN 9/3 486	3458
	EN 9/3 487	867/1039
	EN 9/3 489	2781
	EN 9/3 491	HM 8403
	EN 9/3 494	2090
	EN 9/3 495	938
	EN 9/3 496	3533
	EN 9/1 498	974
	EN 9/3 499	3722
	EN 9/3 502	3648
	EN 9/3 503	3534
	EN 9/3 504	3535
	EN 9/3 506	2632
	EN 9/3 507	3536
	EN 9/3 508	3469
	EN 9/3 509	1134
	EN 9/3 510	3537
	EN 9/2 512	3538
	EN 9/3 514	3539
	EN 9/2 515	2250
	EN 9/3 516	3540
	EN 9/3 517	3663
	EN 9/3 518	2356
	EN 9/3 519	3541
	EN 9/3 520	2200
	EN 9/3 521	1232
	EN 9/3 522	3542
	EN 9/2 524	1448
	EN 9/2 525	3543
A 10	*EN* 9/3 78	1042
A 11	*EN* 9/3 169	1043
	EN 9/3 276	739
A 14	*EN* 9/3 271	1089
	EN 9/1 304	679
	EN 9/1 307	954
	EN 9/1 366	1071
	EN 9/1 367	1166
	EN 9/1 368	793
	EN 9/1 369	929
	EN 9/3 383	1218
	EN 9/1 415	699
A 15	*EN* 9/1 420	1455
A 23	*EN* 9/1 245	1025
	EN 9/3 361	1074
	EN 9/1 375	1276
	EN 9/3 476	941
A 26	*EN* 9/1 25	723
	EN 9/3 70	1083
	EN 9/3 80	843+1293
	EN 9/3 89	1158
	EN 9/1 162	825
	EN 9/1 303	780
	EN 9/1 305	662
	EN 9/1 308	776
	EN 9/1 309	1204
	EN 9/1 310	1237
	EN 9/1 312	1245
	EN 9/1 319	1435
	EN 9/1 370	753
	EN 9/1 399	1450
	EN 9/1 414	672
A 30	*EN* 9/1 11	906
	EN 9/3 69	721
	EN 9/3 71	905
	EN 9/1 147	1418

Room No.	*Tablet No.*	*SMN No.*
A 33	*EN* 9/1 317	879
A 34	*EN* 9/1 240	1212
	EN 9/1 397	1066
	EN 9/1 398	852
C 28	*EN* 9/1 1	3082
	EN 9/1 2	3094
	EN 9/1 3	3101
	EN 9/1 59	3150
	EN 9/1 85	3107
	EN 9/1 94	3105
	EN 9/1 117	3083
	EN 9/1 124	3175
	EN 9/1 258	3129
	EN 9/1 286	3113
	EN 9/1 377	3104
	EN 9/1 411	3100
	EN 9/1 413	3110
	EN 9/1 418	3152
	EN 9/1 430	3053
	EN 9/1 431	3097
	EN 9/1 432	3098
	EN 9/1 433	3103
	EN 9/1 434	3102
	EN 9/1 435	3119
	EN 9/1 436	3117
	EN 9/1 443	3147
	EN 9/1 445	3137
	EN 9/1 485	3138
	EN 9/3 492	3111
C 36	*EN* 9/3 105	3175
	EN 9/3 284	3157
	EN 9/3 481	3158
C 81	*EN* 9/1 417	1423
D 3	*EN* 9/3 295	3238
	EN 9/3 472	3266
	EN 9/3 473	3265
D 6	*EN* 9/1 112	3356
	EN 9/1 405	3388
	EN 9/3 465	3418
D 20	*EN* 9/3 87	3464
F 6	*EN* 9/1 466	3468
F 16	*EN* 9/3 60	3475
	EN 9/1 170	3472
	EN 9/1 214	3476
	EN 9/1 403	3477
	EN 9/3 412	3509
	EN 9/1 423	3478
F 24	*EN* 9/2 46	3483
	EN 9/3 56	3491
	EN 9/3 109	3506
	EN 9/1 160	3492
	EN 9/1 219	3495
	EN 9/1 226	3485
	EN 9/1 253	3497
	EN 9/1 269	3519
	EN 9/3 293	3515
	EN 9/1 355	3496
	EN 9/3 378	3481
	EN 9/3 380	3508
	EN 9/1 386	3520
	EN 9/1 400	3501
	EN 9/3 460	3526
	EN 9/3 488	3487
F 25	*EN* 9/1 6	3560
	EN 9/1 140	3557
	EN 9/3 316	3562
F 26	*EN* 9/3 84	3576
F 38	*EN* 9/1 115	3582
G 23	*EN* 9/3 259	3586
G 29	*EN* 9/1 5	3595
	EN 9/3 51	3606
	EN 9/1 37	3610
	EN 9/3 55	3622
	EN 9/3 57	3589
	EN 9/3 58	3591
	EN 9/3 61	3619
	EN 9/3 64	3628
	EN 9/3 104	3631
	EN 9/1 155	3587
	EN 9/3 179	3629
	EN 9/3 182	3601
	EN 9/3 202	3614
	EN 9/3 215	3609
	EN 9/3 216	3594
	EN 9/3 217	3613
	EN 9/3 220	3597
	EN 9/3 221	3590

Room No.	*Tablet No.*	*SMN No.*
	EN 9/3 222	3599
	EN 9/3 223	3600
	EN 9/3 227	3585
	EN 9/3 229	3627
	EN 9/1 242	3645
	EN 9/3 263	3617
	EN 9/1 302	3602
	EN 9/3 402	3603
	EN 9/1 404	3611
	EN 9/3 407	3584
	EN 9/1 424	3607
	EN 9/3 442	3632
	EN 9/1 448	3604
	EN 9/3 483	3598
G 53	*EN* 9/3 63	3652
	EN 9/3 180	3665
G 73	*EN* 9/1 48	3666
	EN 9/2 118	3657
H 15	*EN* 9/3 447	3684
K 197	*EN* 9/3 211	2557
K 465	*EN* 9/1 24	2629
M 79	*EN* 9/1 335	1167
N 120	*EN* 9/1 30	2068
	EN 9/2 67	2114
	EN 9/3 82	2100
	EN 9/3 86	2052
	EN 9/3 91	2242
	EN 9/2 125	2208
	EN 9/1 151	2047
	EN 9/3 159	2240
	EN 9/2 166	2245
	EN 9/3 205	2251
	EN 9/2 250	2221
	EN 9/2 262	2107
	EN 9/2 336	2113
	EN 9/2 353	2116
	EN 9/1 379	2212
	EN 9/1 381	2217
	EN 9/2 391	2246
	EN 9/2 401	2248
	EN 9/1 401	2248
	EN 9/1 462	2222
	EN 9/1 464	2211
	EN 9/3 469	2252
	EN 9/1 500	2239
P 357	*EN* 9/1 114	2572
	EN 9/1 181	2568
P 382	*EN* 9/1 41	2580
	EN 9/1 42	2584
	EN 9/1 99	2579
	EN 9/1 126	2587
	EN 9/1 197	2582
	EN 9/1 389	2583
P 400	*EN* 9/1 193	2591
	EN 9/1 225	2596
	EN 9/1 373	2593
	EN 9/1 511	2602
P 401	*EN* 9/1 15	2613
	EN 9/1 183	2608
	EN 9/1 426	2607
P 401-456!	*EN* 9/1 390	2619
P 428!	*EN* 9/2 301	2620
P 456!	*EN* 9/1 301	2620
P 460-466	*EN* 9/1 135	2642
	EN 9/1 497	2643
P 465	*EN* 9/1 8	2630
	EN 9/1 75	2627
	EN 9/1 191	2138
	EN 9/1 194	2622
	EN 9/1 198	2628
	EN 9/1 203	2631
	EN 9/1 248	2633
	EN 9/2 326	2674
	EN 9/1 332	2635
	EN 9/1 416	2636
P 466	*EN* 9/1 43	2650
	EN 9/1 47	2645
	EN 9/1 95	2137
	EN 9/1 195	2649
	EN 9/1 199	2646
	EN 9/1 285	2644
	EN 9/1 427	2647
P 470	*EN* 9/3 65	2136

Room No.	*Tablet No.*	*SMN No.*
P 480	*EN* 9/2 333	2680
P 485	*EN* 9/1 213	2660
	EN 9/1 252	2658
	EN 9/2 299	2681
R 76	*EN* 9/3 90	822
Rm. 130	*EN* 9/3 501	2343
Rm. 151	*EN* 9/3 523	2524
S 019	*EN* 9/3 385	3056
S 110	*EN* 9/2 322	2157
S 112	*EN* 9/2 20	2083
	EN 9/2 28	2168+?
	EN 9/2 142	2179
	EN 9/2 186	2112
	EN 9/2 321	2167
	EN 9/2 338	2162
	EN 9/2 341	2180
	EN 9/2 354	2158
	EN 9/2 359	2161
	EN 9/2 363	2108
	EN 9/2 421	2178
	EN 9/2 450	2127
	EN 9/2 458	2174
S 113	*EN* 9/2 18	2700+?
	EN 9/2 27	2193
	EN 9/2 156	2013
	EN 9/1 156	2013
	EN 9/2 163	2194
	EN 9/2 360	2001
	EN 9/2 393	2012
S 124	*EN* 9/2 17	2302
	EN 9/2 19	2007
	EN 9/2 23	2307
	EN 9/2 49	2323
	EN 9/2 74	2314
	EN 9/2 77	2173+2316
	EN 9/2 143	2313
	EN 9/2 146	2319+2321
	EN 9/2 171	2312
	EN 9/2 175	2311
	EN 9/2 189	2310
	EN 9/2 327	2303
	EN 9/2 334	2315

Room No.	*Tablet No.*	*SMN No.*
	EN 9/2 419	2309
	EN 9/1 419	2309
	EN 9/2 493	2308
	EN 9/2 530	2304
	EN 9/2 531	2320
S 127/9	*EN* 9/2 490	2333
S 129	*EN* 9/2 21	2095
	EN 9/2 22	2091
	EN 9/2 73	2337
	EN 9/2 158	2338
	EN 9/2 323	2334
	EN 9/2 358	2336
	EN 9/2 362	2335
S 130	*EN* 9/2 83	2126
	EN 9/2 236	2345
	EN 9/2 297	2124
S 131	*EN* 9/2 298	2011
S 132	*EN* 9/2 10	2390
	EN 9/2 31	2362
	EN 9/2 32	2366
	EN 9/1 93	2354
	EN 9/2 93	2354
	EN 9/2 102	2380
	EN 9/1 102	2380
	EN 9/2 111	2361
	EN 9/1 134	2385
	EN 9/2 145	2519
	EN 9/2 157	2367
	EN 9/2 207	2377
	EN 9/2 209	2368
	EN 9/1 233	2388
	EN 9/2 283	2401
	EN 9/2 289	2418
	EN 9/2 291	2370
	EN 9/2 292	2365
	EN 9/2 324	2358
	EN 9/2 325	2387
	EN 9/2 329	2077
	EN 9/2 331	2350
	EN 9/2 337	2363
	EN 9/2 339	2359
	EN 9/2 340	2079
	EN 9/2 342	2081
	EN 9/2 344	2381
	EN 9/2 346	2384
	EN 9/2 347	2382

Room No.	Tablet No.	SMN No.
	EN 9/2 352	2349
	EN 9/2 356	2414
	EN 9/2 357	2352
	EN 9/2 364	2393
	EN 9/2 371	2358A
	EN 9/1 371	2358
	EN 9/2 374	2379
	EN 9/2 384	2075
	EN 9/2 387	2371
	EN 9/3 422	2394
	EN 9/1 440	2372
	EN 9/2 440	2372
	EN 9/2 441	2374
	EN 9/2 452	2351
	EN 9/2 477	2391
	EN 9/2 478	2357
	EN 9/2 505	2373
	EN 9/2 513	2405
S 133	*EN* 9/2 97	2439
	EN 9/2 110	2438
	EN 9/2 212	2426
	EN 9/2 224	2443
	EN 9/2 268	2428
	EN 9/2 348	2434
	EN 9/2 349	2445
S 136	*EN* 9/2 129	2475
	EN 9/2 176	2125+2476
S 151	*EN* 9/2 16	2128
	EN 9/1 29	2133
	EN 9/2 29	2133
	EN 9/2 34	2485
	EN 9/2 35	2488
	EN 9/2 36	2497
	EN 9/2 38	2474
	EN 9/2 39	2517
	EN 9/2 40	2501
	EN 9/2 76	2498
	EN 9/2 96	2512
	EN 9/2 101	2487
	EN 9/2 103	2510
	EN 9/2 106	2504
	EN 9/2 130	2505
	EN 9/2 153	2493
	EN 9/1 153	2493
	EN 9/2 177	2511
	EN 9/2 185	2518
	EN 9/2 187	2479
	EN 9/2 204	2500
	EN 9/2 206	2520
	EN 9/2 234	2490
	EN 9/2 273	2499
	EN 9/2 279	2513
	EN 9/2 392	2481
	EN 9/2 395	2495
	EN 9/1 425	2514
	EN 9/1 444	2525
	EN 9/2 455	2526
	EN 9/1 461	2525
	EN 9/2 528	2506
S 152	*EN* 9/2 33	2376
	EN 9/2 172	2132
T 18	*EN* 9/1 320	1247
	EN 9/3 328	3748
T 19	*EN* 9/3 88	835
	EN 9/1 314	914
	EN 9/3 315	1263
	EN 9/1 365	817
U 374/365!	*EN* 9/1 196	2574
V 428	*EN* 9/3 92	2614

Cumulative List of Scribes to *Excavations at Nuzi* 9

A[. . . .]	*EN* 9/3 217
Abi-ilu	*EN* 9/2 184
Abi-ilu son of Nabu-ila	*EN* 9/1 123; *EN* 9/2 349
AD-I-PAL[?]	*EN* 9/1 48[1]
A-ummiša	*EN* 9/1 426
Aḫa-ay-amši	*EN* 9/2 363
Aittara	*EN* 9/3 [385]; 486
Akap-šenni	*EN* 9/3 78; *EN* 9/1 225
Akap-šenni son of Šukriya	*EN* 9/2 177
Akap-tae	*EN* 9/3 179
Akaya	*EN* 9/1 317
^{d}AK-DINGIR.MEŠ *see* Tešup-nirari	
^{d}AK-DINGIR.RA (Nabu-ila)	*EN* 9/1 30; 296; *EN* 9/2 393; *EN* 9/1 403
^{d}AK-DINGIR.RA son of Sîn-napšir	*EN* 9/1 25; *EN* 9/2 31 (witness); *EN* 9/1 139; 427
Akip-Tilla	*EN* 9/1 136
A[kipta]-šenni	*EN* 9/2 166
Akipta-šenni son of Tešup-atal	*EN* 9/3 57; 61
Akiya	*EN* 9/3 502
Akiya son of Šumu-libši (MU-DIRI)	*EN* 9/1 253
Akkul-enni	*EN* 9/2 440
Akkul-enni son of Šumu-libši	*EN* 9/1 436 (lib[!]-[ši[?]])
Amumiya	*EN* 9/2 17; [38][2]
Amumi-Tešup	*EN* 9/3 217 (Amu[mi-Tešup]);[3] *EN* 9/1 431
Amumi-Tešup son of Sîn-nadin-šumi	*EN* 9/3 271; 274[4]
Apil-Sîn	*EN* 9/1 1; 2; 3

Introductory Note: This list was augmented and corrected thanks to the efforts of Paola Negri Scafa, whose work on the graphemic analysis of the Nuzi texts allowed for numerous refinements and identifications of scribes in damaged or fragmentary contexts. Mr. Richard Wright was most helpful in the rechecking of the references. This listing supersedes previous scribe lists for *EN* 9/1–2 and revises the respective catalogue entries.

[1] If the third sign is BALA, the name might be read AD-*i-pal*, hitherto unattested.

[2] So according to graphemic analysis of text.

[3] Assigned on the basis of graphemic analysis to this scribe and not to Amumiya.

[4] There are difficulties with this text. Amumi-Tešup and Sîn-nadin-šumi are both mentioned. One possible reading would be Amumi-Tešup [scribe] son[!] of Sîn-nadin-šumi. But the sign before Sîn-nadin-šumi does not appear to be a DUMU. Furthermore, there is a NA_4 before Amumu-Tešup where a ŠU is expected if he were the scribe in this trial text. Therefore its scribal attribution is offered with great reservation until the text can be subjected to additional graphemic analysis and collation.

Appa son of Intiya	*EN* 9/3 501
Ariḫ-ḫamanna	*EN* 9/2 331; 441
Arim-matka	*EN* 9/1 15; 75; *EN* 9/2 35
Arip-šarri	*EN* 9/3 60; *EN* 9/1 170; 183; 244; *EN* 9/2 [10]; 186; 187; *EN* 9/3 261? *EN* 9/2 262; *EN* 9/3 378
Ar-purusa	*EN* 9/2 34; *EN* 9/3 231
Ar-Tešup son of Turari	*EN* 9/1 140
Balṭu-kašid	*EN* 9/3 428; *EN* 9/1 470
Balṭu-kašid son of Apil-Sîn	*EN* 9/1 43; *EN* 9/3 71 (witness); *EN* 9/2 392
Belam-nirari	*EN* 9/3 104
Bel-ili?	*EN* 9/2 324
Beliya-utu? (be-li-[i]a-ú-tu)	*EN* 9/3 277
Bi[. . .]e/ia son of Sa?[. . .]pu	*EN* 9/1 219
Dayyan-beli	*EN* 9/3 55; *EN* 9/1 150
DI.KU$_5$-EN *see* Dayyan-beli	
DUGUD-EN-li *see* Kabtu-beli	
Eḫli-Tešup	*EN* 9/1 389; *EN* 9/3 402
Eḫli-Tešup son of Tešup-[. . . .]	*EN* 9/3 263
Elḫip-Tilla (= son of Kel-Tešup)	*EN* 9/2 19; 20; 21; 22; 23; [74]; 77; 146; 163; 188; [310][5]; 323; 329; [327]?; [333]; 329; 336; 358; 362
Elḫip-Tilla son of Kel-Tešup	*EN* 9/2 171; 493
Emuqa	*EN* 9/1 409
Emuqa son of Balṭu-kašid	*EN* 9/3 382
Enna-mati	*EN* 9/2 101 *EN* 9/3 [518]; *EN* 9/2 529
Enna-mati son of Puḫi-šenni	*EN* 9/2 189
Ḫašip-tašenni	*EN* 9/1 [149]; *EN* 9/3 232
Ḫašip-Tilla	*EN* 9/2 387; *EN* 9/1 405
Ḫeltip-kušu⟨ḫ⟩	*EN* 9/2 67
Ḫerrikanni son of [. . .]-nirari	*EN* 9/3 412
Ḫupita	*EN* 9/3 64; *EN* 9/1 132; *EN* 9/3 489
Ḫurpi-Tešup	*EN* 9/1 165
Ḫutip-apu	*EN* 9/2 359
Ḫutiya	*EN* 9/1 386; *EN* 9/3 290; 293; 460
Ḫutiya son of Uta-mansum	*EN* 9/1 414
Ḫut-Tešup	*EN* 9/2 292; 505 (Ḫu[t-Tešup])
Ila-nišu	*EN* 9/1 131
Ila-rabi (DINGIR.A.GAL)	*EN* 9/1 181
Ili-ma-aḫi	*EN* 9/3 465
Iniya	*EN* 9/3 56; 180; 190; *EN* 9/1 417
Ipša-ḫalu	*EN* 9/3 169; 249; *EN* 9/2 322
Iriri	*EN* 9/1 154; 233

[5] In Owen, *LDN*, p. 99, this text is assigned to Teḫiya. But DUB.SAR in rev. 45 is written close to both Teḫiya and [Elḫip]-Tilla. It is assigned to the latter as a result of graphemic analysis.

^{d}IŠKUR.MA.AN.SUM	*EN* 9/3 68([IŠKUR/^{d}UTA-MA.AN].SUM); 107; *EN* 9/1 366; 368; 369; 438
^{d}IŠKUR.MA.AN.SUM son of ^{d}UTA.[AN.DÙL]	*EN* 9/1 178; 365; *EN* 9/3 383
Kabtu-beli	*EN* 9/3 69; 70
Kaluppani	*EN* 9/3 451
Kaluppani son of Aḫu-šini	*EN* 9/2 234
Kel-Tešup	*EN* 9/1 117; *EN* 9/2 326; *EN* 9/3 422 (possibly Kel[teya])
Kel-Tešup son of Sîn-ibni	*EN* 9/3 205$^{?}$; *EN* 9/2 364 (witness)
Kelteya	*EN* 9/2 338 (possibly Kel-[Tešup])
Kinniya	*EN* 9/1 41
Kip-talili	*EN* 9/3 272
Maliya	*EN* 9/2 209
[Man]nu-[tari]ssu	*EN* 9/2 97
Mukiya	*EN* 9/3 211
Muš-Tešup son of Ḫupita	*EN* 9/2 118
Mušteya	*EN* 9/2 339
Nabu-ila *see* ^{d}AK-DINGIR.RA	
Nanna-adaḫ	*EN* 9/1 196; *EN* 9/2 111; *EN* 9/1 366 (witness); *EN* 9/1 511
^{d}NANNA-MA.AN.SUM	*EN* 9/1 14; *EN* 9/2 81; 279$^{?}$
Niḫriya	*EN* 9/2 273
Ninkiya	*EN* 9/2 374
Nirari son of Taya	*EN* 9/3 65 ([ni-ra]-ri); *EN* 9/1 160; (cf. also *EN* 9/1 381)
Nirḫi-Tilla	*EN* 9/1 151; 379
Pui-tae	*EN* 9/2 152
Qaqqadu	*EN* 9/2 212
Rim-Sîn	*EN* 9/2 76
SAG.AN.KI	*EN* 9/2 168; 172; 298$^{!}$[6]; *EN* 9/1 377; *EN* 9/3 457
^{d}Sîn(30)-KUR-ni *see* Sîn-šaduni	
^{d}Sîn(30)-ŠEŠ-SUM-na *see* Sîn-aḫḫa-iddina	
Sîn-aḫḫa-iddina	*EN* 9/1 11[7]
Sîn-iqiša	*EN* 9/1 9 (^{d}30-qí-ša); *EN* 9/3 86; *EN* 9/1 126; *EN* 9/3 469
Sîn-liqiš	*EN* 9/2 421
Sîn-mušal	*EN* 9/3 80
Sîn-šaduni	*EN* 9/1 44; *EN* 9/3 218; *EN*9/2 264; *EN* 9/1 445
Sîn-šaduni son of Amur-šarri	*EN* 9/3 182; 276; *EN* 9/1 433
Sîn-šarri	*EN* 9/1 319
Šamaš-naṣir	*EN* 9/2 207; 283; 337; 340; 341; 344; 345$^{?}$; 352; 353; 360; 513

[6] Previous reading Kase was incorrect.

[7] So instead of Sîn-nadin-aḫḫe.

Šamaš-naṣir son of Akiya	*EN* 9/2 224; *EN* 9/3 230; *EN* 9/2 250; 299; *EN* 9/1 423; *EN* 9/1 515
Šamaš-nuri (^{d}UTU.IZI.GAR)	*EN* 9/1 191
Šamaš-ura	*EN* 9/1 498
Šamaš-uraššu son of Ṣilliya	*EN* 9/2 29
Šaršiya *see* Šeršiya	
Šar-Tilla son of Iluya	*EN* 9/1 95; 193; 198; 199 (patronym to be restored); *EN* 9/3 288
Šeriš-atal	*EN* 9/3 499
Šeršiya	*EN* 9/3 62; *EN* 9/1 127[8]; *EN* 9/2 395; *EN* 9/3 468
Šimanni	*EN* 9/1 398; *EN* 9/2 185
Šimanni son of Nabu-ila	*EN* 9/2 40; *EN* 9/3 503
ŠU.^{d}IŠKUR (=? Šar-Tešup)	*EN* 9/2 33
Šukriya	*EN* 9/3 280
[Šuk$^{?}$/A$^{?}$]ri-Tešup	*EN* 9/3 50
[*Šumu*$^{!}$-*l*]*ib*$^{!}$-*ši* son of Taya	*EN* 9/3 479 (witness)
Tae	*EN* 9/3 167
Taika	*EN* 9/3 58
Takki	*EN* 9/1 265
Taknak-ilu	*EN* 9/2 321
Tampi-Tilla	*EN* 9/1 226
Tarmi-Tešup	*EN* 9/1 399; *EN* 9/2 450
Tarmi-Tešup son of Šarru-muštal(AD.GI.GI)	*EN* 9/3 254
Tarmi-Tilla	*EN* 9/2 157; 342; 343
Tarmiya	*EN* 9/1 195; 203
Tarmiya son of Kuari	*EN* 9/1 192; 213; 251; *EN* 9/2 176
Taya	*EN* 9/2 27; 28;[9] 31; 46; *EN* 9/1 404
Taya son of Apil-Sîn	*EN* 9/3 71 (witness) *EN* 9/1 147; *EN* 9/2 32
Te-x-[. . .]	*EN* 9/1 413
Teḫip-Tilla	*EN* 9/2 297; 384
Teḫi-[. .]	*EN* 9/1 424
Teḫiya	*EN* 9/2 301; *EN* 9/1 367
Tešup-nirari(^{d}AK-DINGIR.MEŠ)	*EN* 9/3 330
Tu[. . .] son$^{?}$ of G/Zi[. . .]	*EN* 9/1 434
Tuḫmiya	*EN* 9/1 373
Tukkani	*EN* 9/3 506
Tukulti-beli	*EN* 9/1 260
Turari	*EN* 9/1 122; 147
Turar-Tešup	*EN* 9/1 314; 332; 351
Turar-Tešup son of Itḫ-apiḫe	*EN* 9/1 5; *EN* 9/3 523
Turar-Tešup son of Kel-Tešup	*EN* 9/1 8; *EN* 9/2 16
Tur-šenni	*EN* 9/3 63; *EN* 9/1 497
Unuku	*EN* 9/3 82

[8] According to graphemic anlysis, Šarwiya in this text is an error for Šar/Šer-ši$^{!}$-ia.

[9] Traces in the copy of 28:25 do not agree with the reading Taya and appear to be [. . .]-ia.

Urḫi-Tešup	*EN* 9/1 321; *EN* 9/2 364
^{d}UTA-AN.DÙL *see* Uta-andul	
Uta-andul	*EN* 9/3 492
Uta-andul son of Taya	*EN* 9/1 355
^{d}UTA-AN.GAL	*EN* 9/1 6
^{d}UTA-ḪE.GAL	*EN* 9/3 66
[^{d}UTA/IŠKUR-MA.AN].SUM	*EN* 9/3 68
^{d}UTA-PAB *see* Šamaš-naṣir	
Utḫap-tae	*EN* 9/1 155 *EN* 9/3 216; 221; 223; 227; 229; 246
Utḫap-tae son of En-šukru	*EN* 9/3 222
Wur-Tešup	*EN* 9/3 84
Zini	*EN* 9/1 47; *EN* 9/3 164; *EN* 9/2 401
Zinni son of Kiyannipu	*EN* 9/1 194
[x]-*a-gal* son of Sîn-iluya	*EN* 9/2 45
[. . .]-*a-ka*	*EN* 9/1 269[10]
[x]-*an-na-mu-ḫi*	*EN* 9/3 481
[. .]-*an-ni*	*EN* 9/1 285
[. .-*a/i*]*p*-apu son of [. . . .]-šenni	*EN* 9/1 214
[. . .]-*e*	*EN* 9/3 407
[. .]-*el*-Tešup	*EN* 9/1 59
[. .]-*ia*	*EN* 9/2 28; 279
[. . .]-*i*$^{?}$-Tilla	*EN* 9/3 318
[. .]-*la*	*EN* 9/3 473
[. . . .]-*ni*-[. . . .]	*EN* 9/2 371
[. . . .]-*ni*$^{?}$-[. . . .]	*EN* 9/3 456
[. . . .]-*nu*	*EN* 9/2 354
[. .]-RI	*EN* 9/3 255
[. .]-*ša*	*EN* 9/1 24
[. .]-*ši-ia*	*EN* 9/3 468
[. .]-*ši-ip*-Tilla$^{?}$	*EN* 9/1 390
[. . .]-X-*ta-e*	*EN* 9/3 167

[10] Possibly name of the scribe's father.

50

OBVERSE

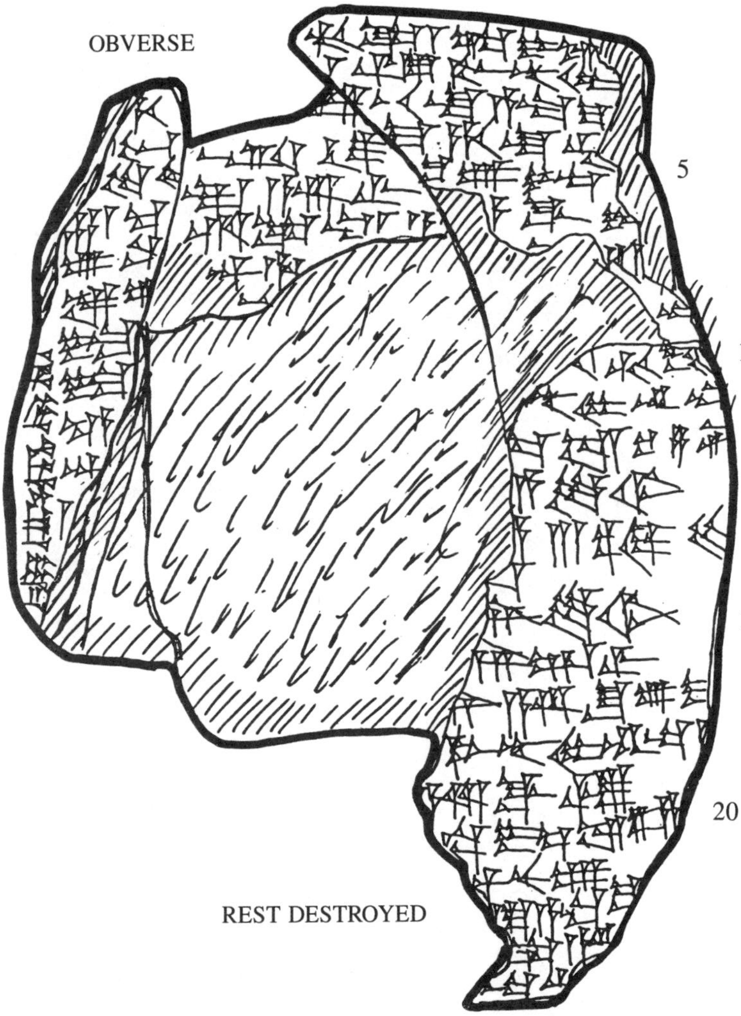

REST DESTROYED

51

OBVERSE

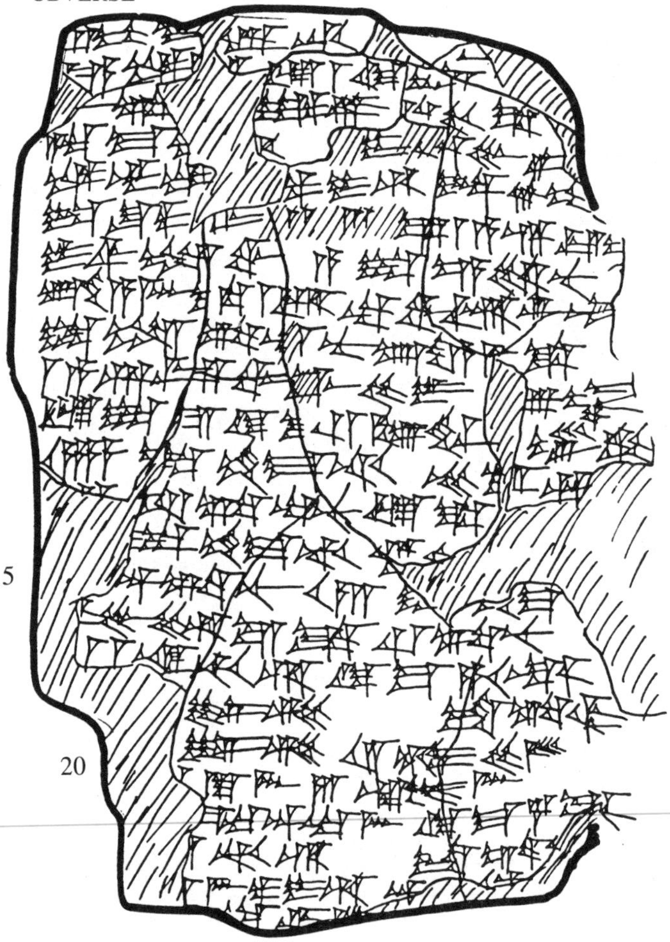

51

LOWER EDGE

REVERSE

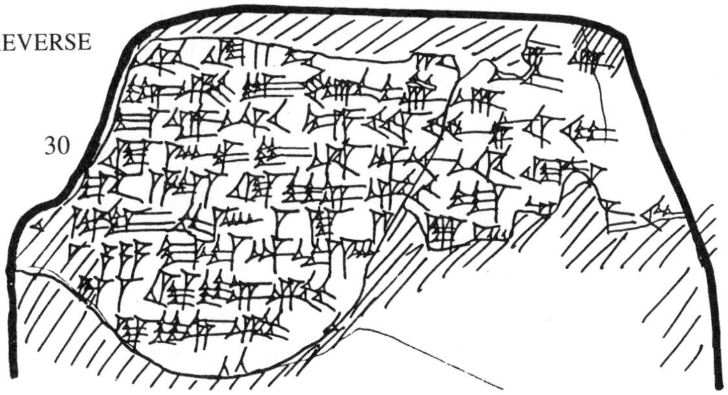

REST OF REVERSE DESTROYED

LEFT EDGE

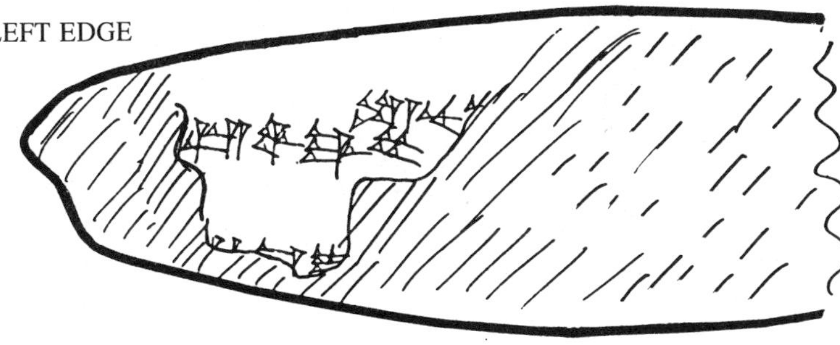

52

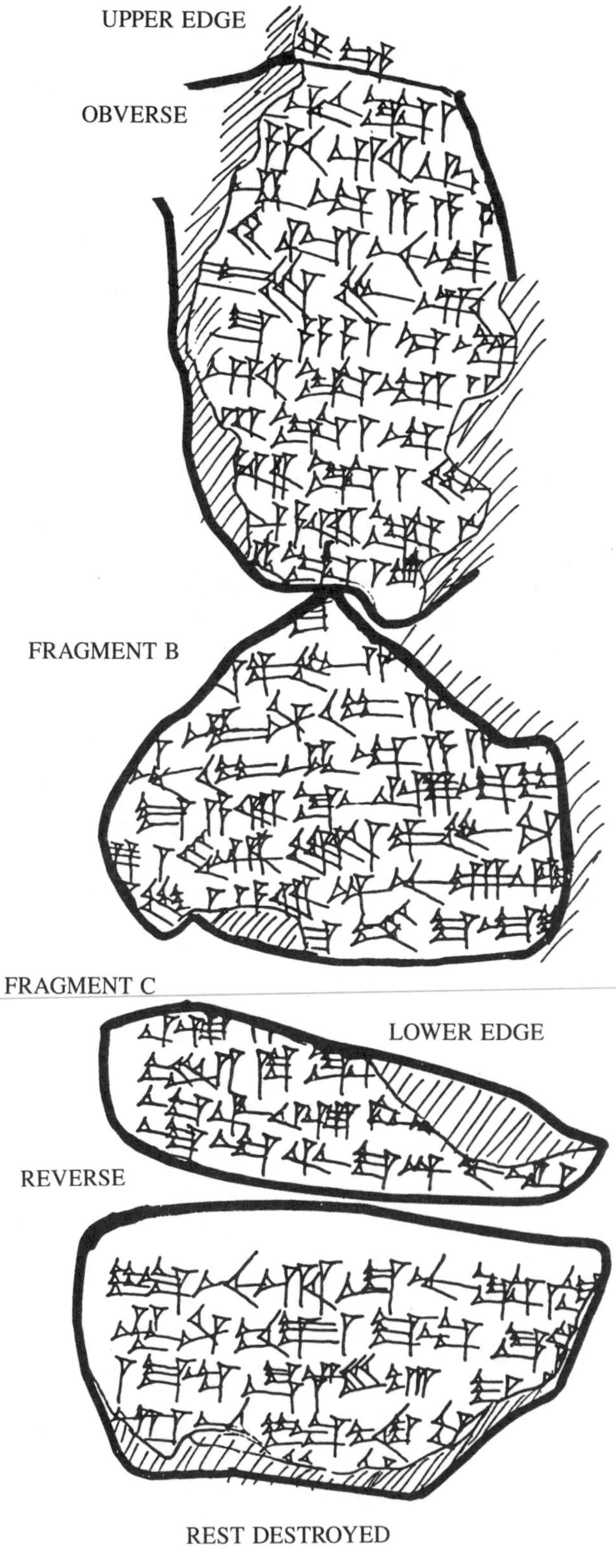
UPPER EDGE
OBVERSE
FRAGMENT B
FRAGMENT C
LOWER EDGE
REVERSE
REST DESTROYED

53

BEGINNING OF OBVERSE DESTROYED

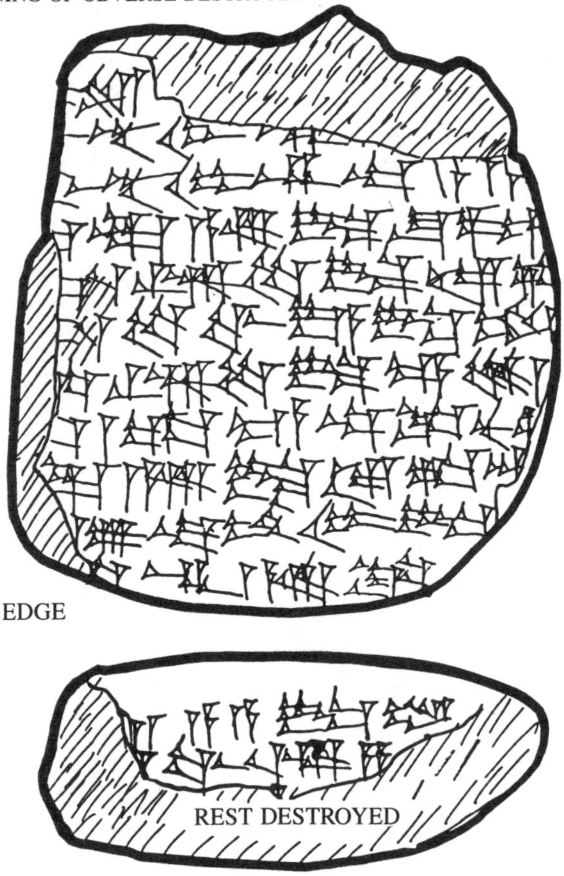

LOWER EDGE

REST DESTROYED

54

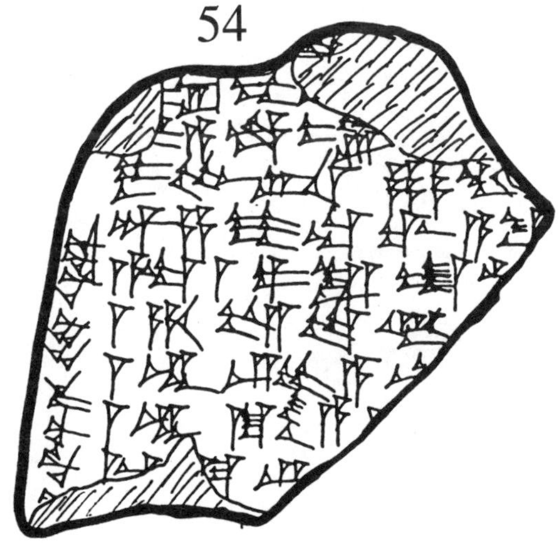

REST DESTROYED

55

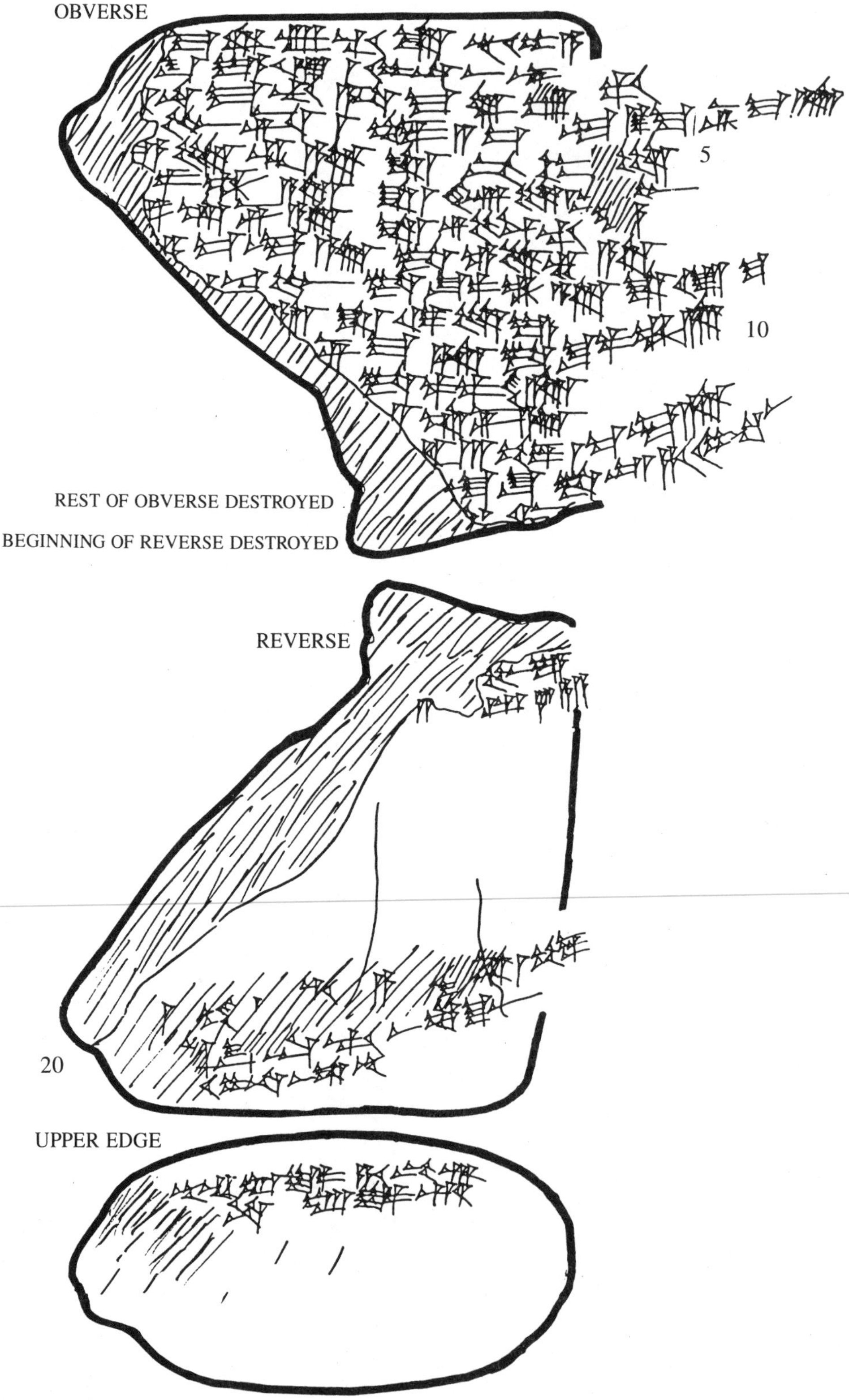
OBVERSE
5
10
REST OF OBVERSE DESTROYED
BEGINNING OF REVERSE DESTROYED
REVERSE
20
UPPER EDGE

56

OBVERSE

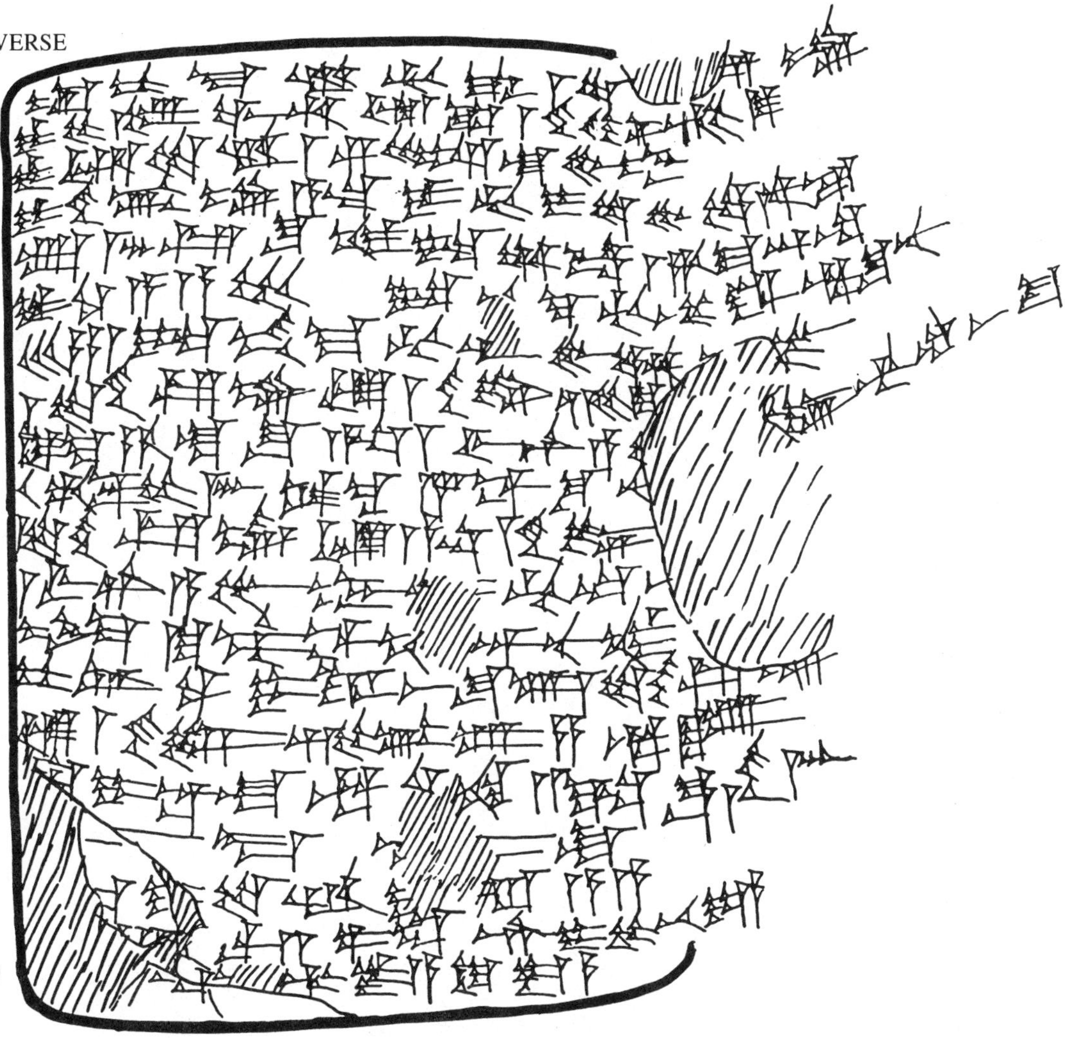

LOWER EDGE

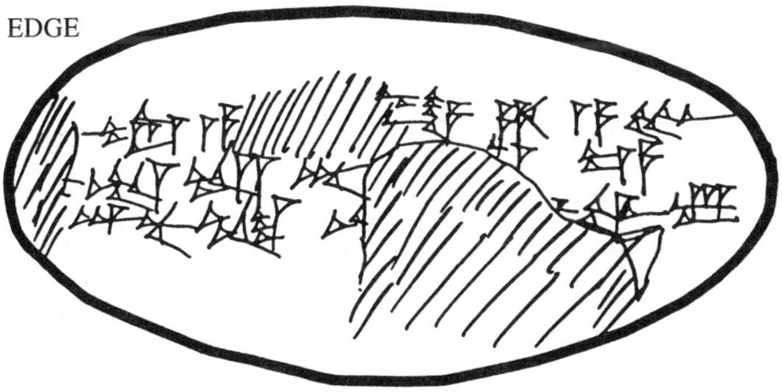

56

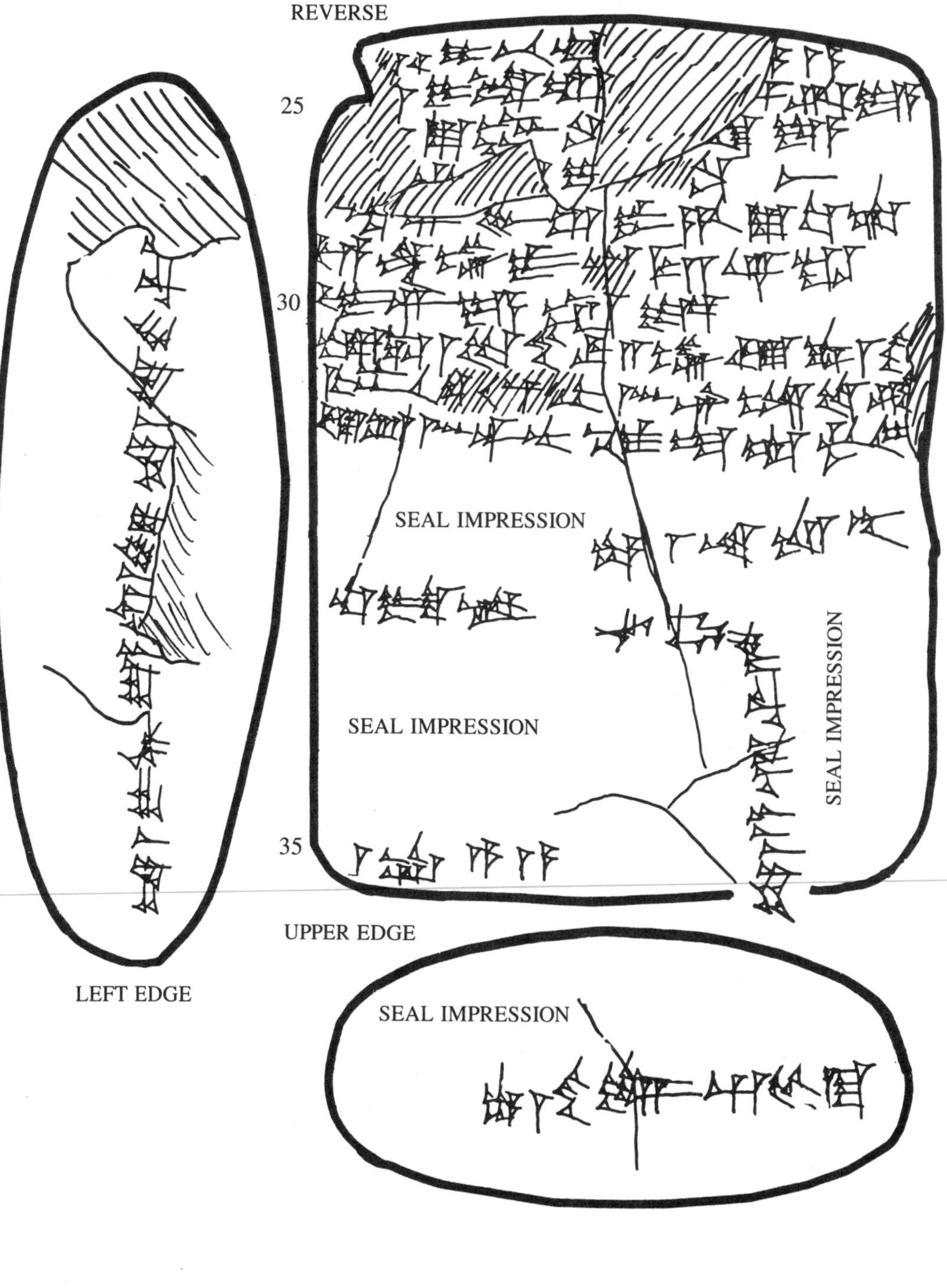
REVERSE
25
30
SEAL IMPRESSION
SEAL IMPRESSION
SEAL IMPRESSION
35
UPPER EDGE
LEFT EDGE
SEAL IMPRESSION

57

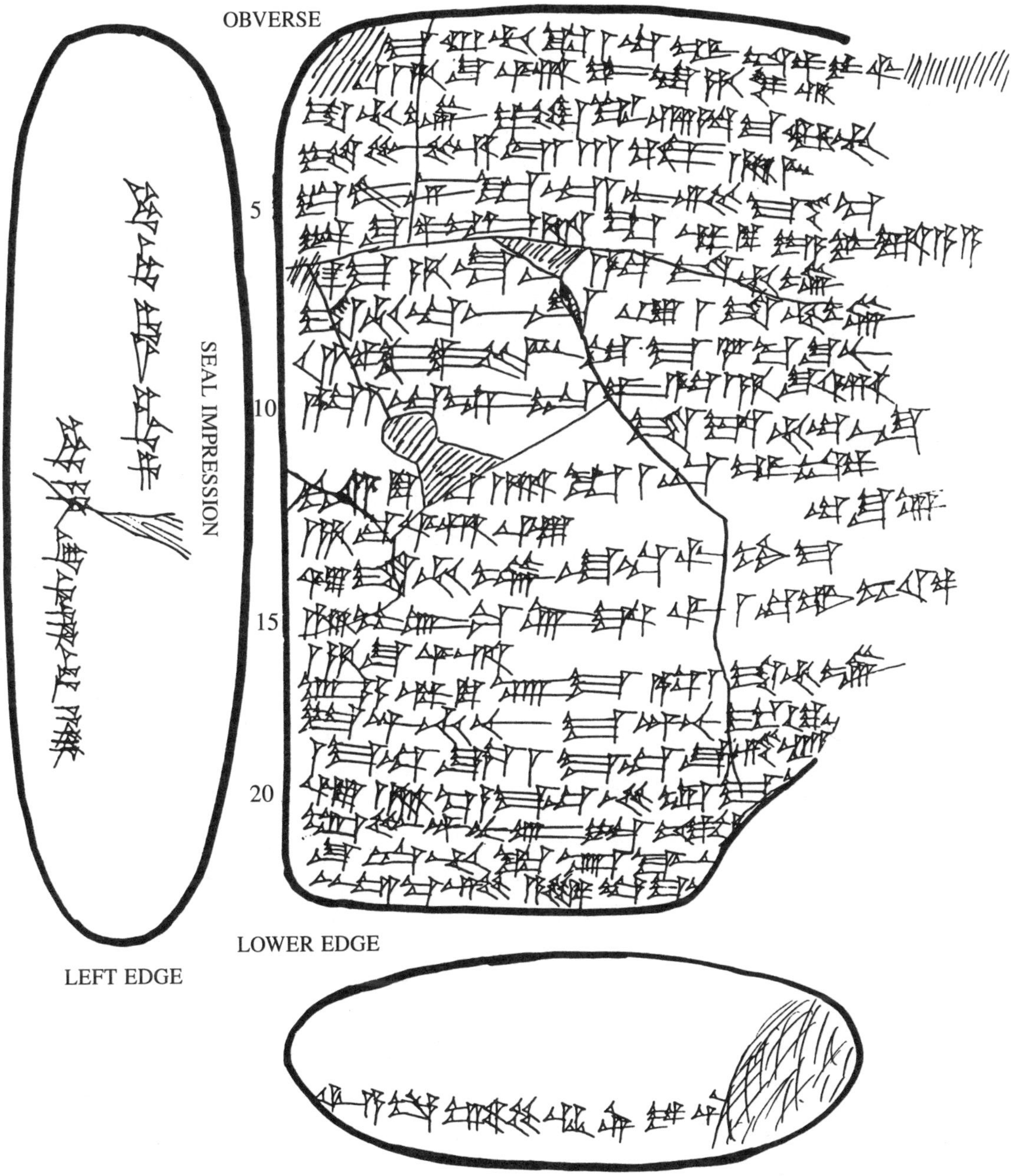

57

REVERSE

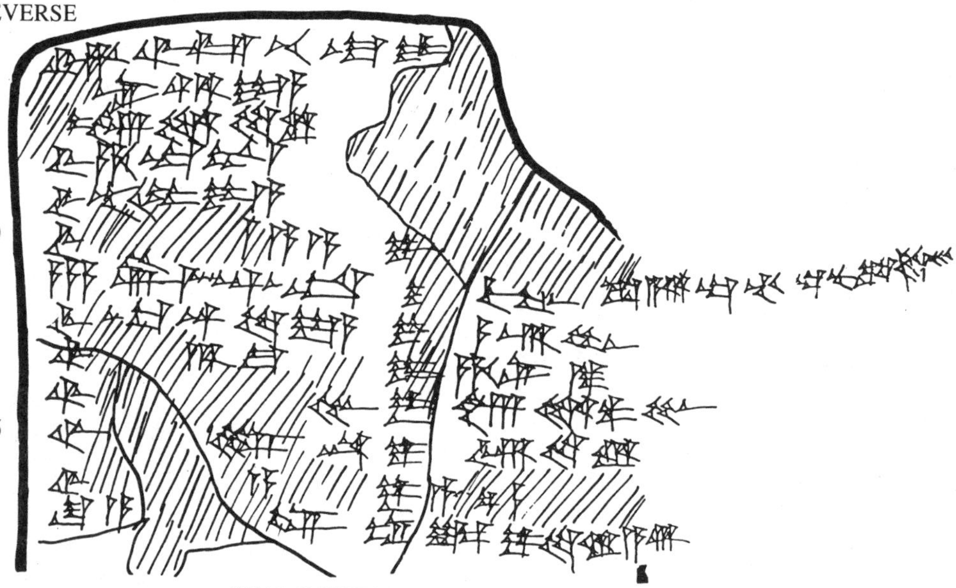

SEAL IMPRESSION

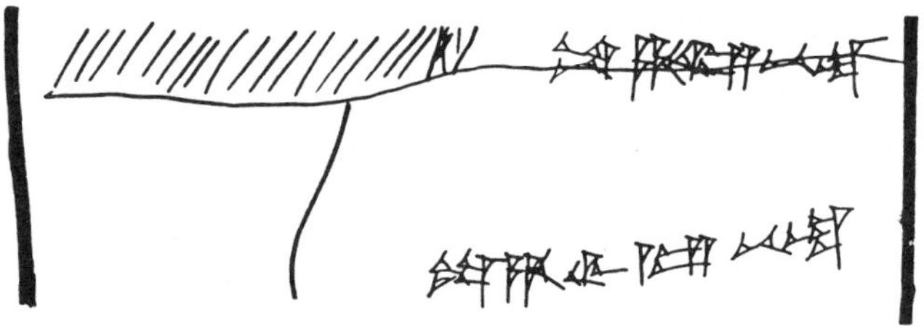

UPPER EDGE

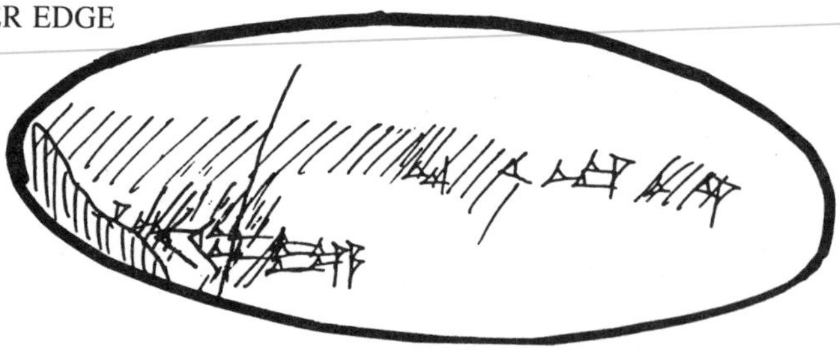

58

OBVERSE

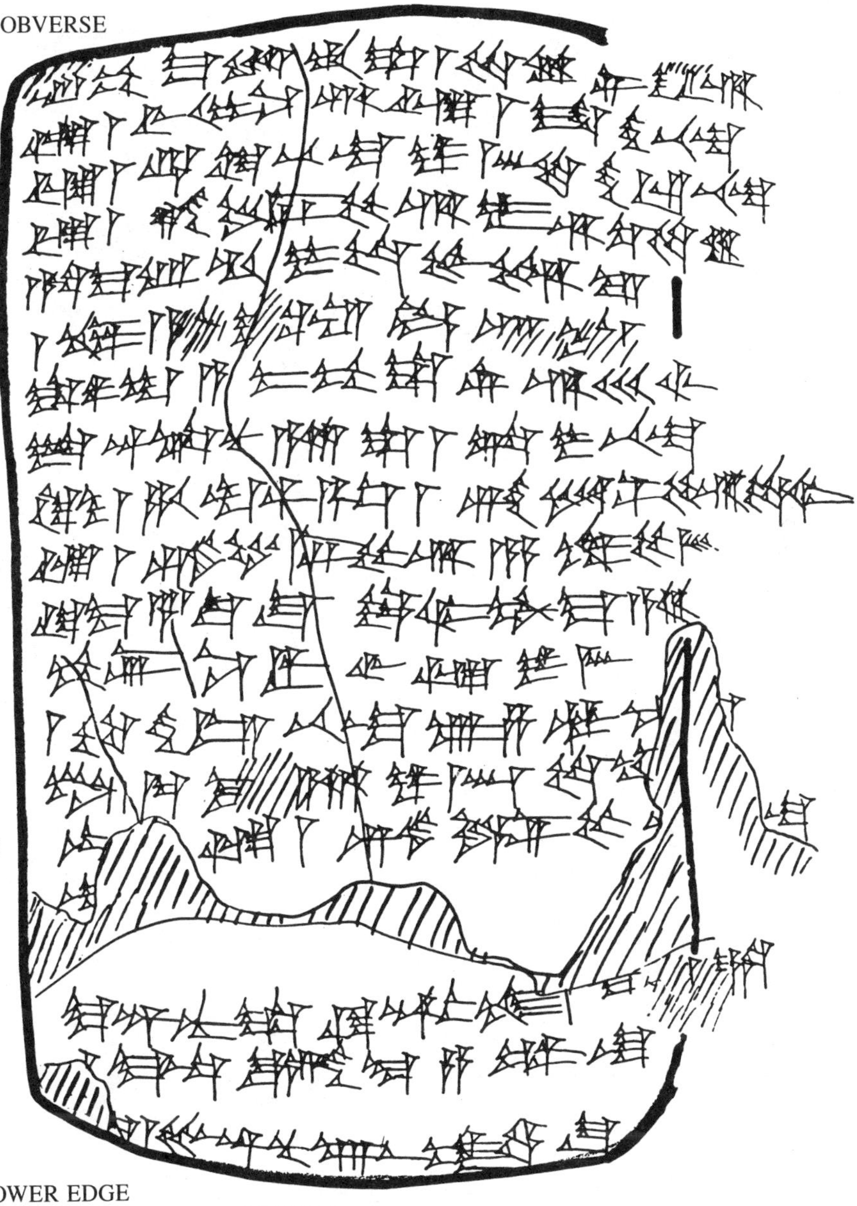

LOWER EDGE

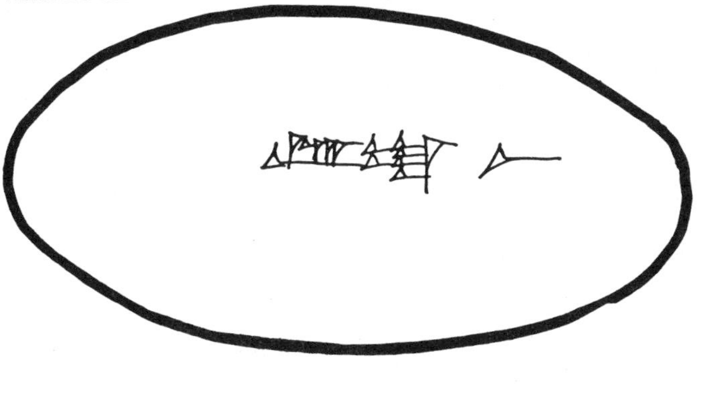

58

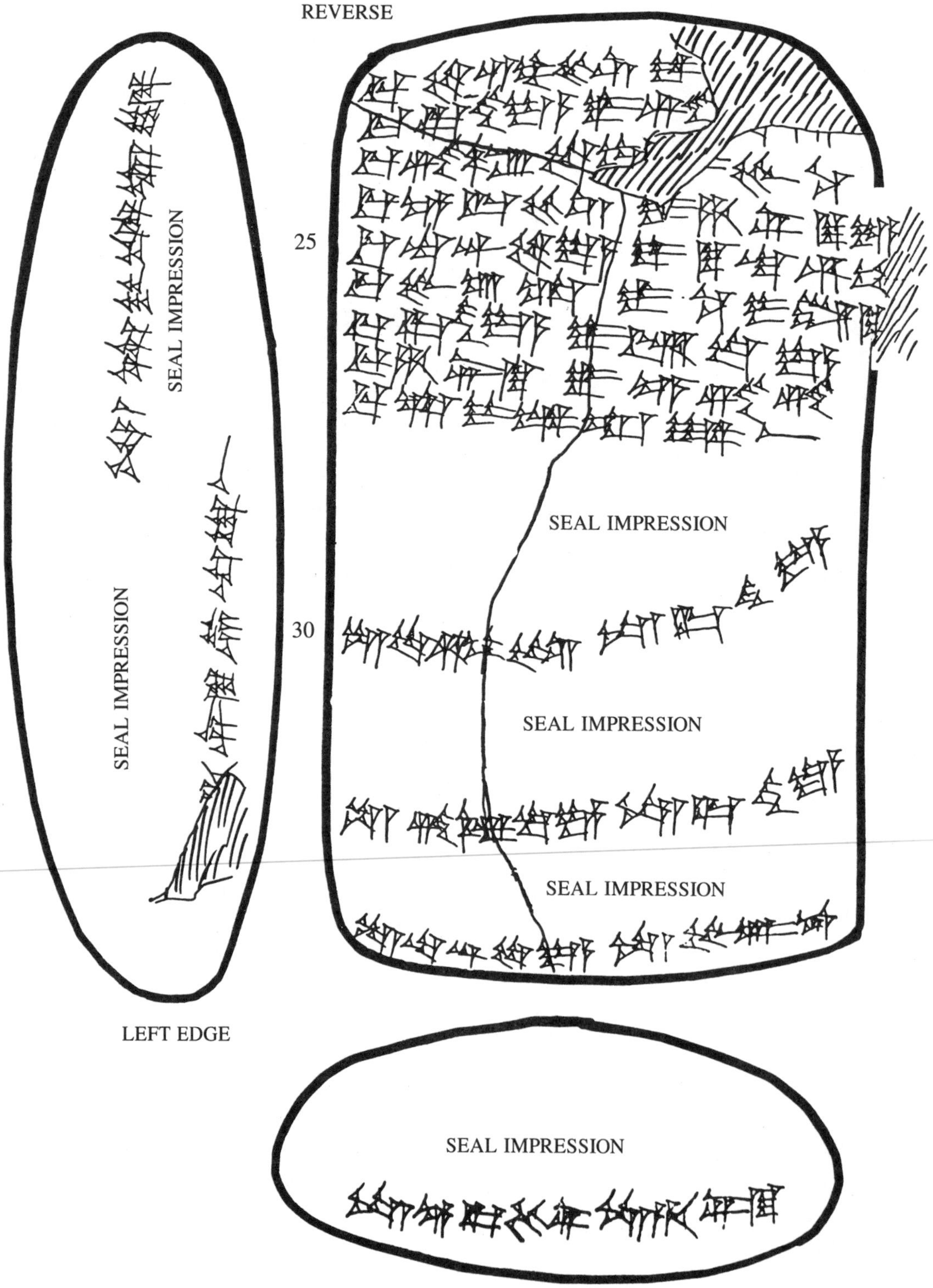
REVERSE
SEAL IMPRESSION
SEAL IMPRESSION
SEAL IMPRESSION
SEAL IMPRESSION
SEAL IMPRESSION
LEFT EDGE
SEAL IMPRESSION

60

OBVERSE

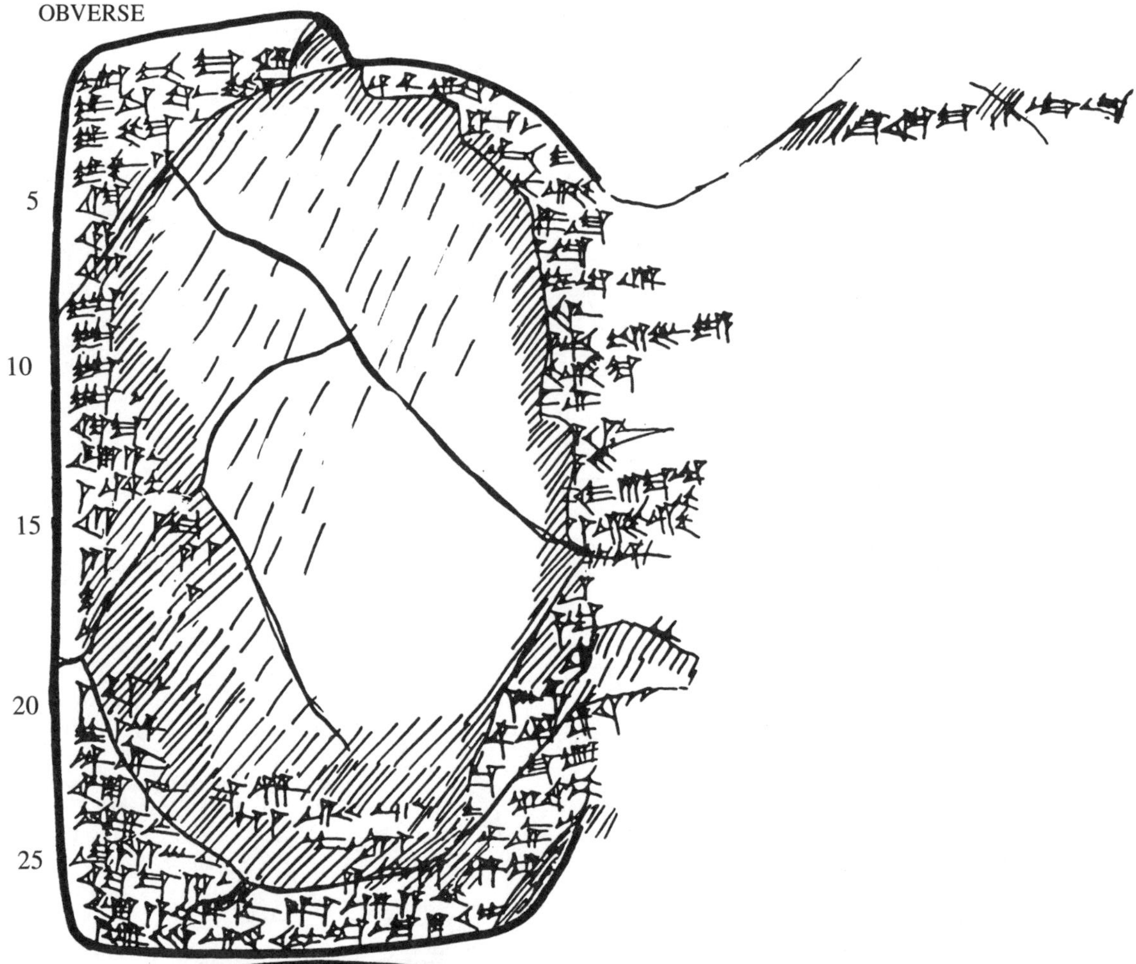

LOWER EDGE

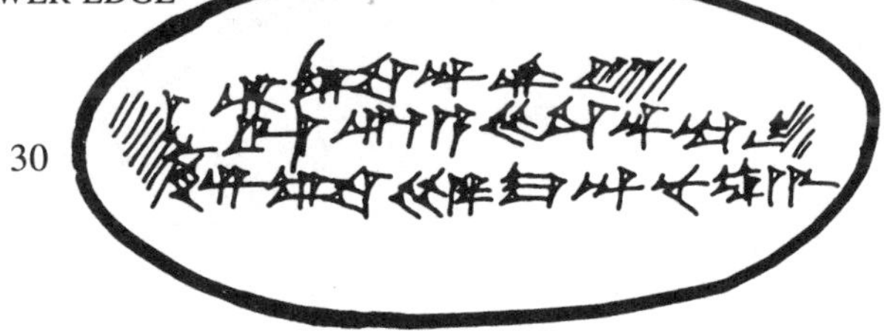

60

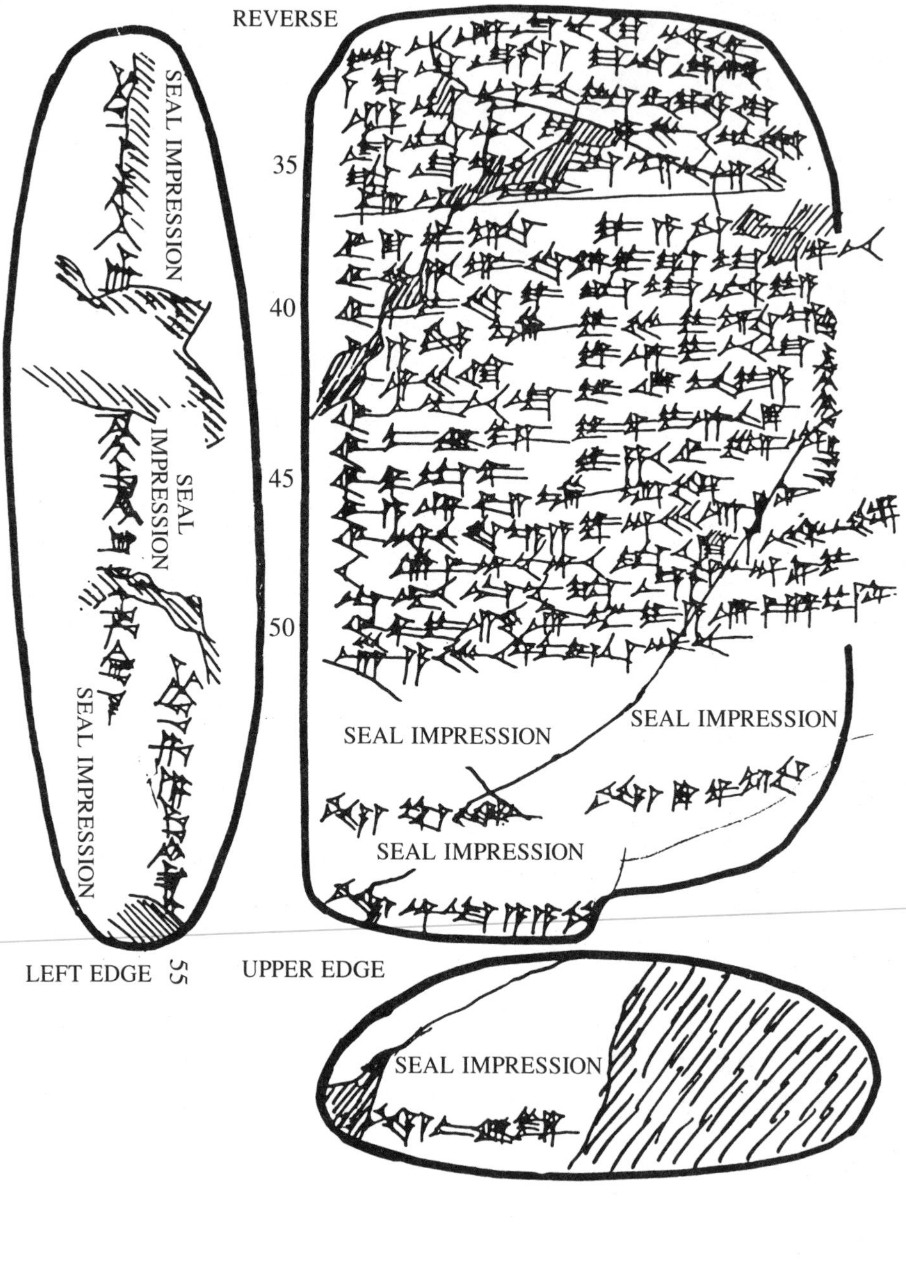
REVERSE
35
40
45
50
SEAL IMPRESSION
SEAL IMPRESSION
SEAL IMPRESSION
SEAL IMPRESSION
SEAL IMPRESSION
SEAL IMPRESSION
LEFT EDGE
55
UPPER EDGE
SEAL IMPRESSION

61

OBVERSE

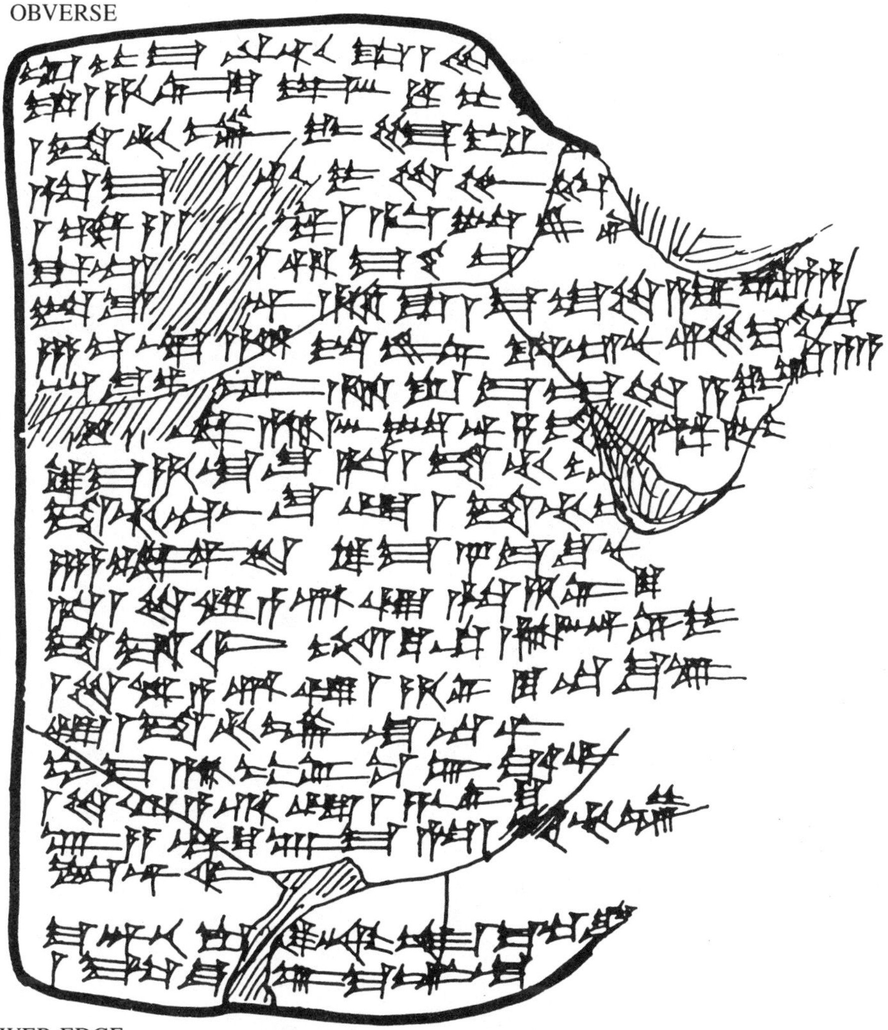

LOWER EDGE

61

REVERSE

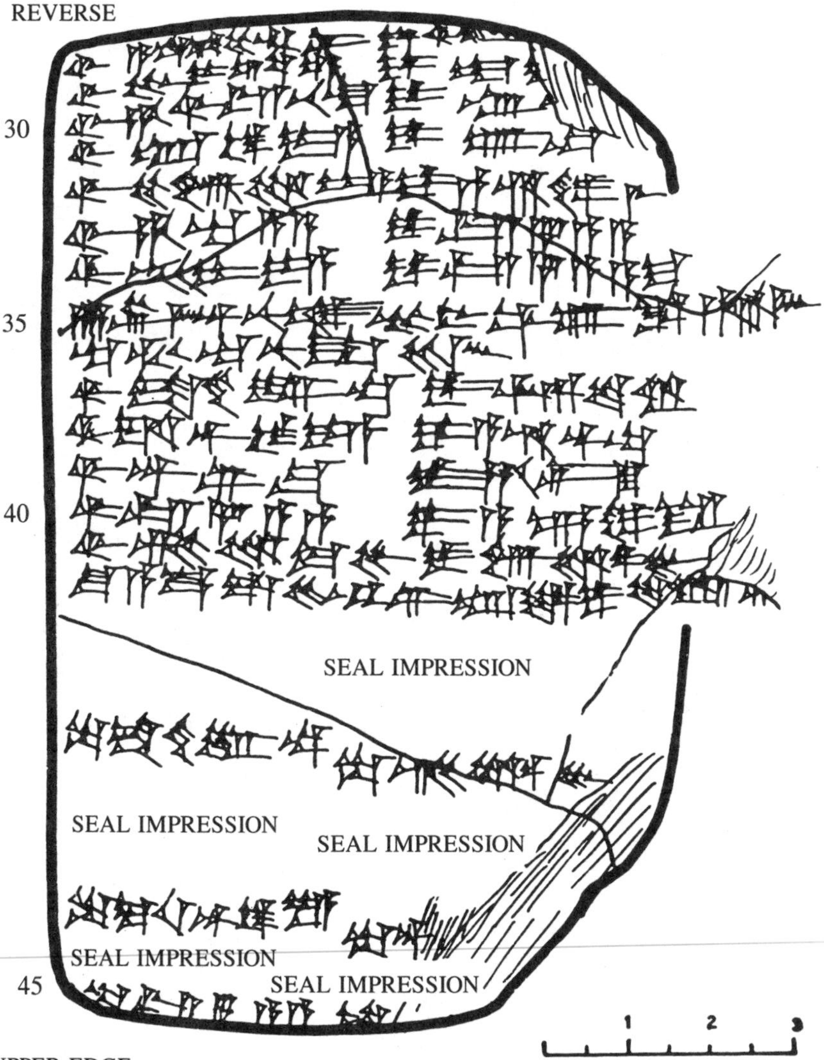

LEFT EDGE

UPPER EDGE

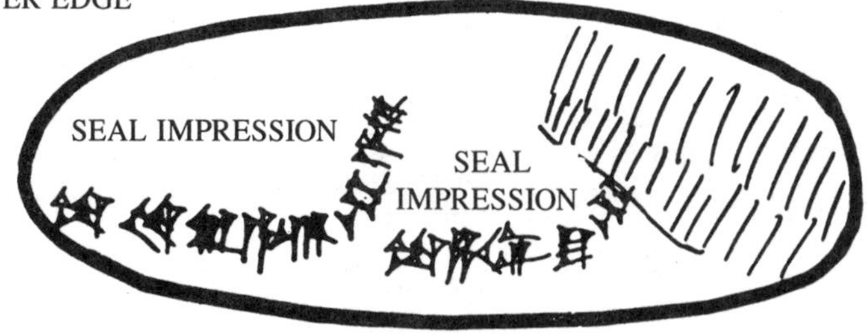

62

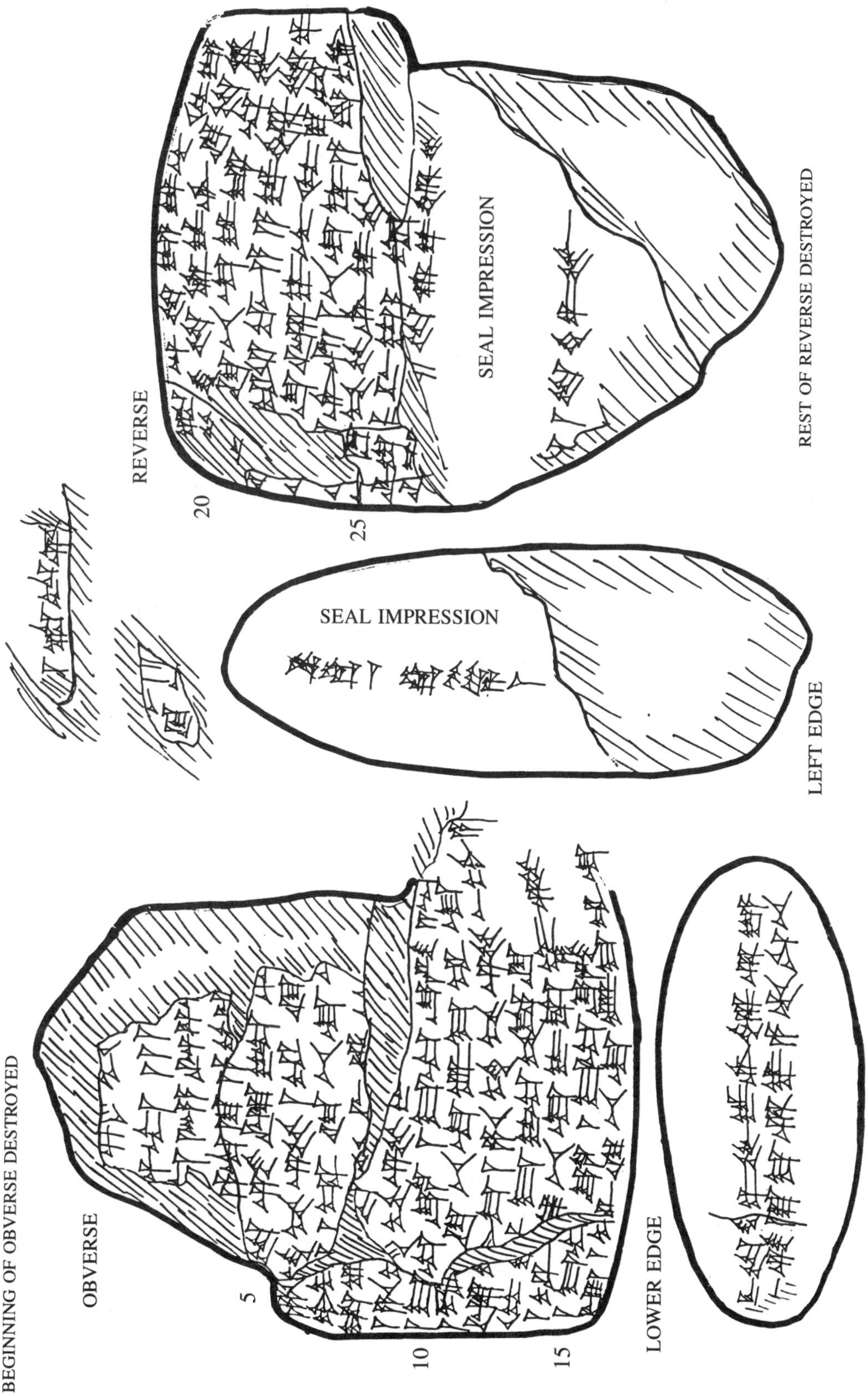
BEGINNING OF OBVERSE DESTROYED
OBVERSE
LOWER EDGE
LEFT EDGE
SEAL IMPRESSION
REVERSE
SEAL IMPRESSION
REST OF REVERSE DESTROYED

63

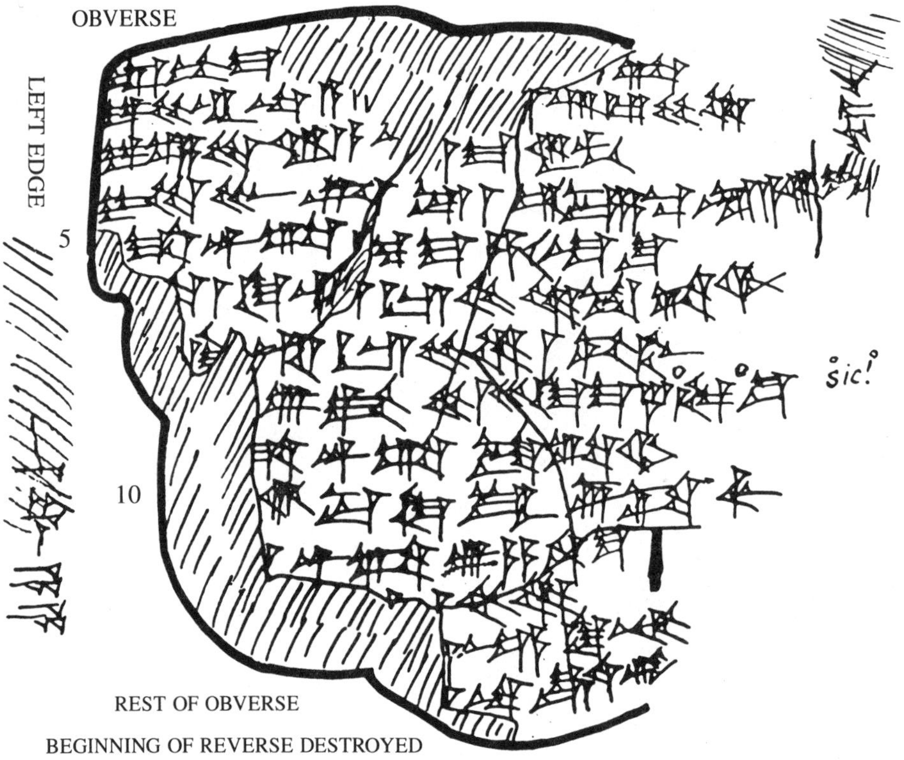
OBVERSE
LEFT EDGE
5
10
sic!
REST OF OBVERSE
BEGINNING OF REVERSE DESTROYED

63

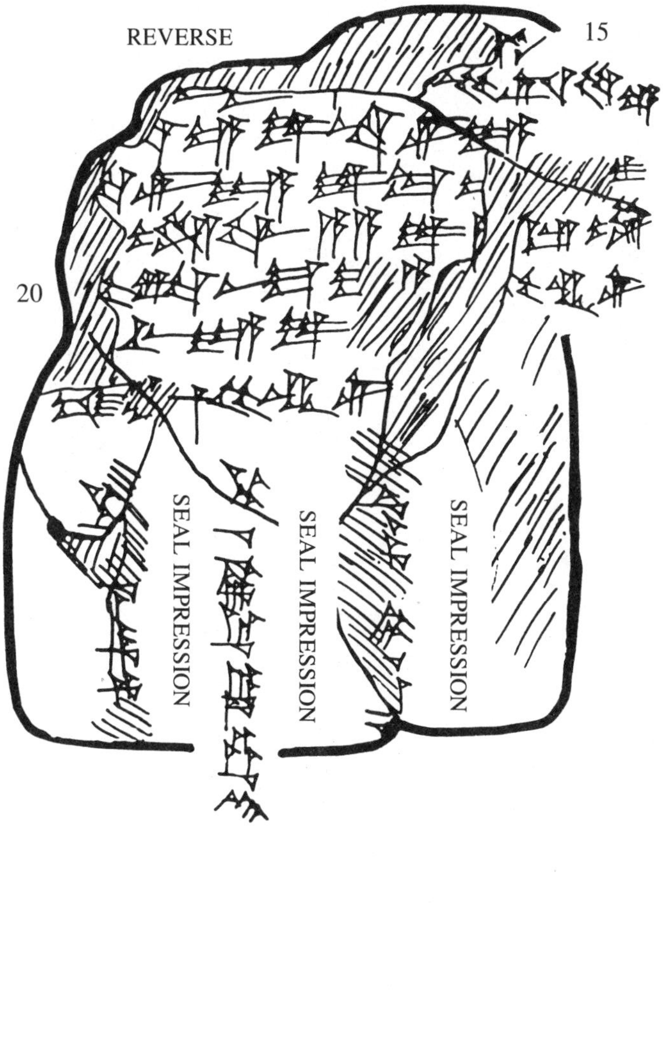
REVERSE
15
20
SEAL IMPRESSION
SEAL IMPRESSION
SEAL IMPRESSION

64

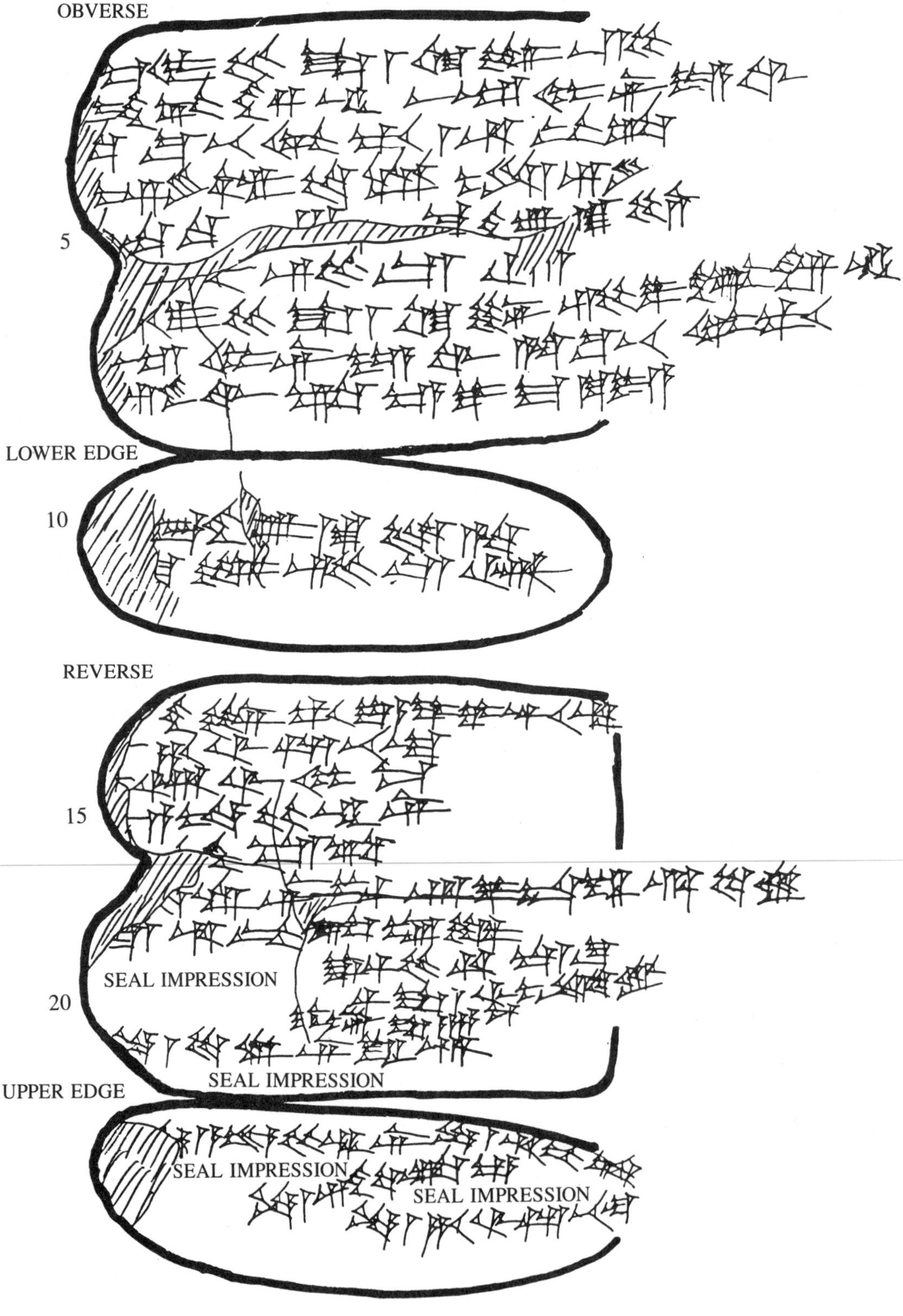
OBVERSE
LOWER EDGE
REVERSE
SEAL IMPRESSION
SEAL IMPRESSION
UPPER EDGE
SEAL IMPRESSION
SEAL IMPRESSION

65

OBVERSE

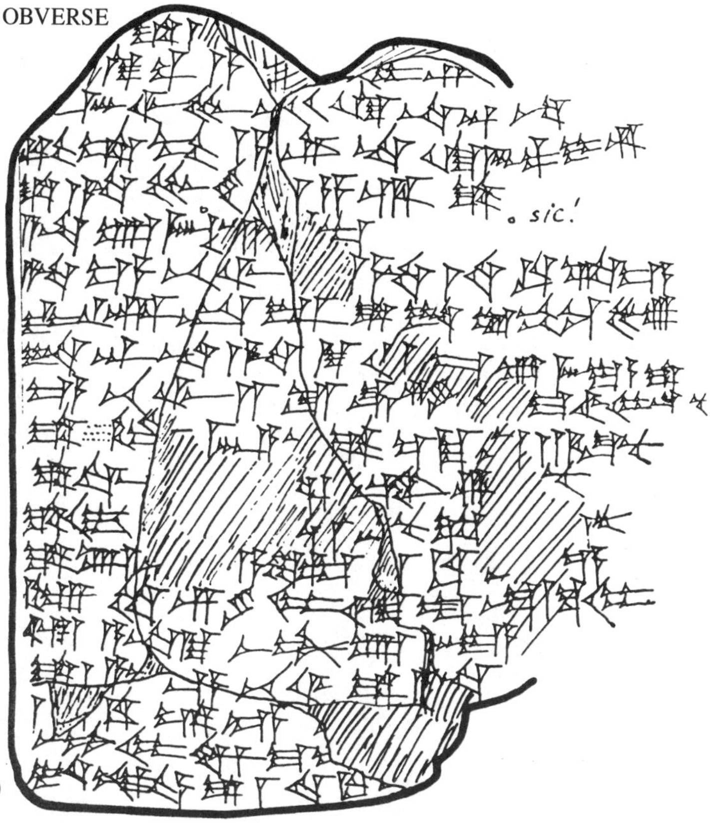

ADD TO L. 4

LOWER EDGE

65

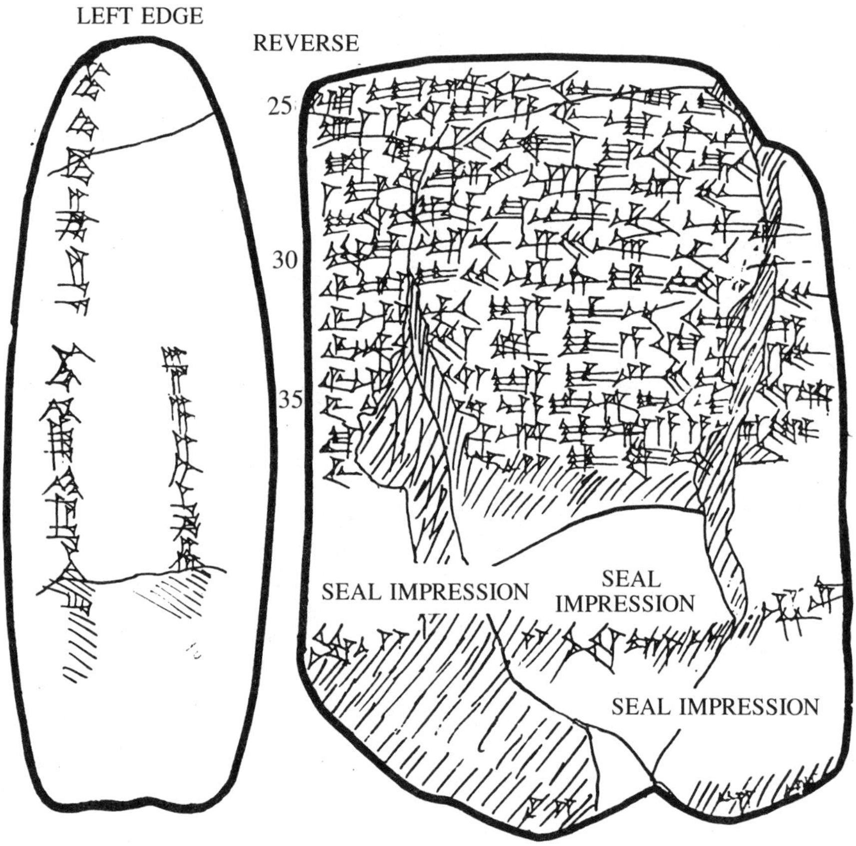
LEFT EDGE
REVERSE
25
30
35
SEAL IMPRESSION
SEAL IMPRESSION
SEAL IMPRESSION

66

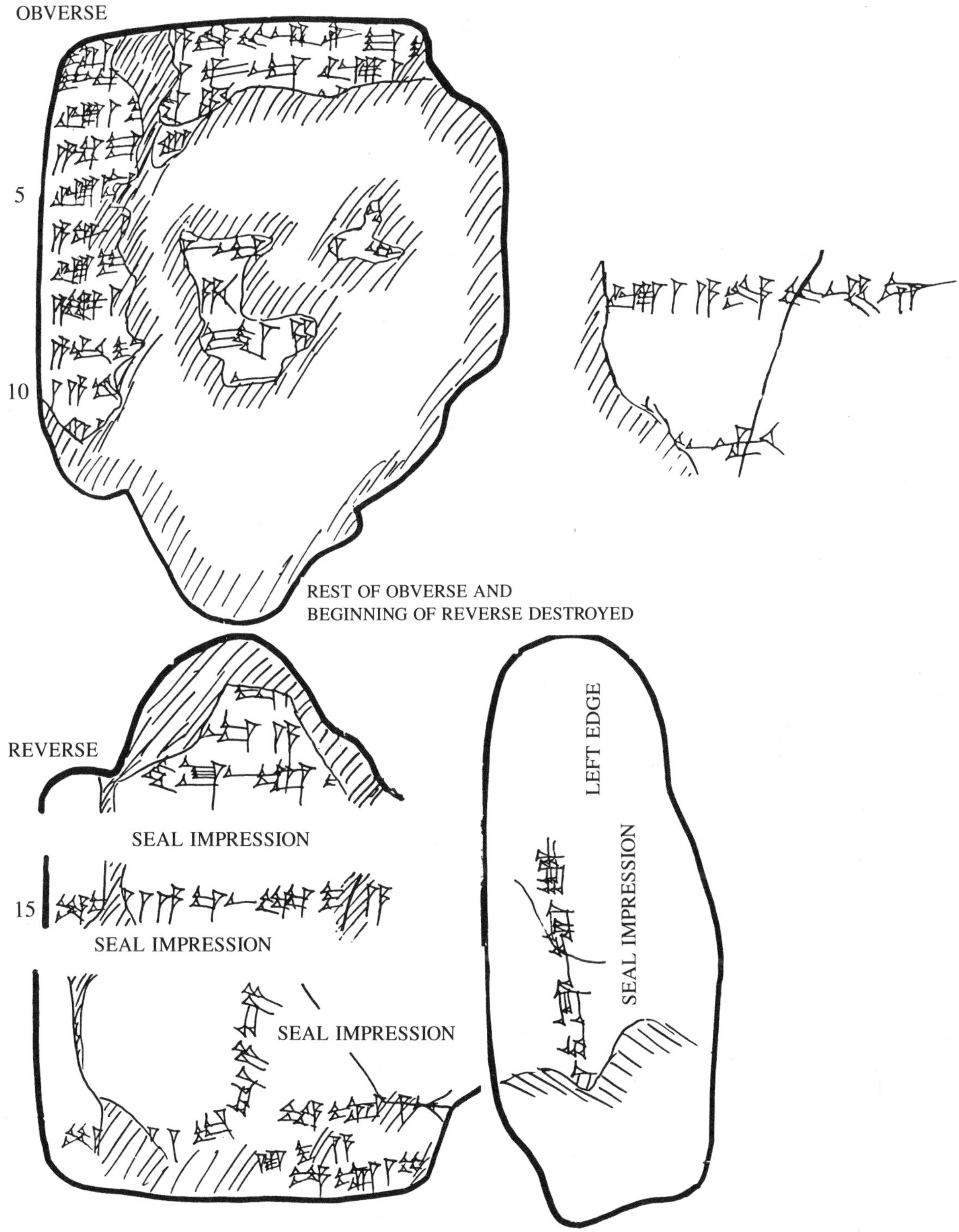
OBVERSE
REST OF OBVERSE AND
BEGINNING OF REVERSE DESTROYED
REVERSE
SEAL IMPRESSION
SEAL IMPRESSION
SEAL IMPRESSION
LEFT EDGE
SEAL IMPRESSION

68

OBVERSE

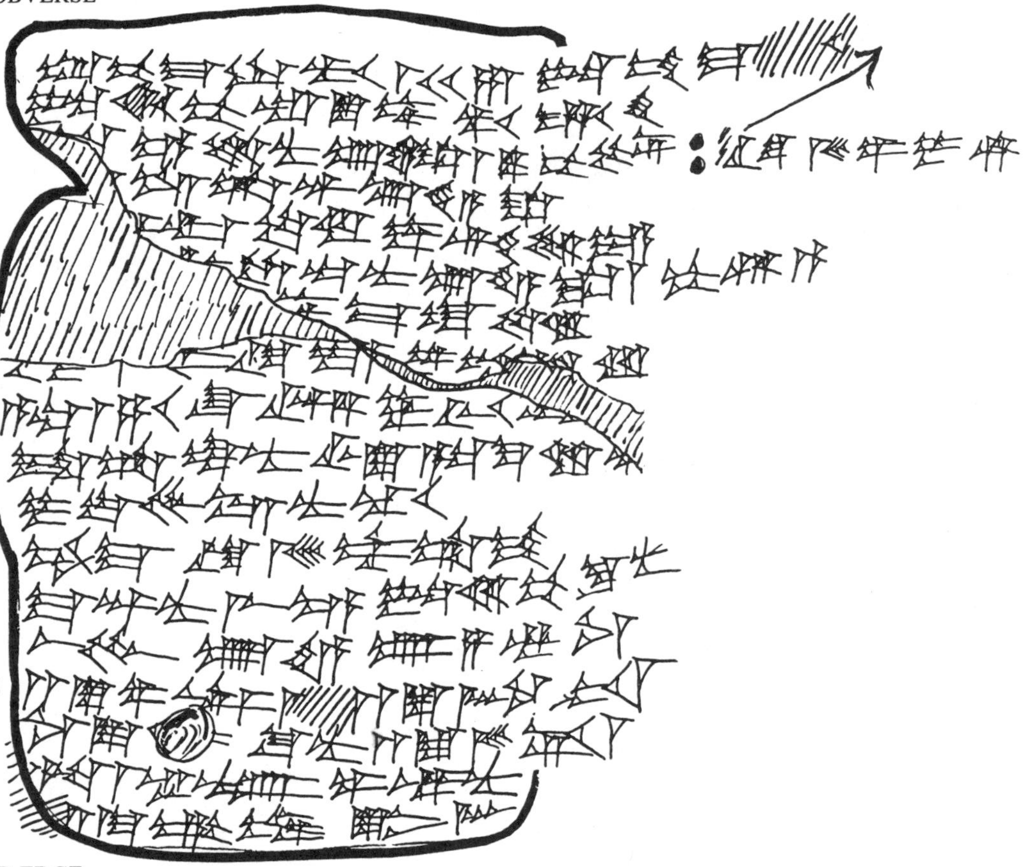

LOWER EDGE

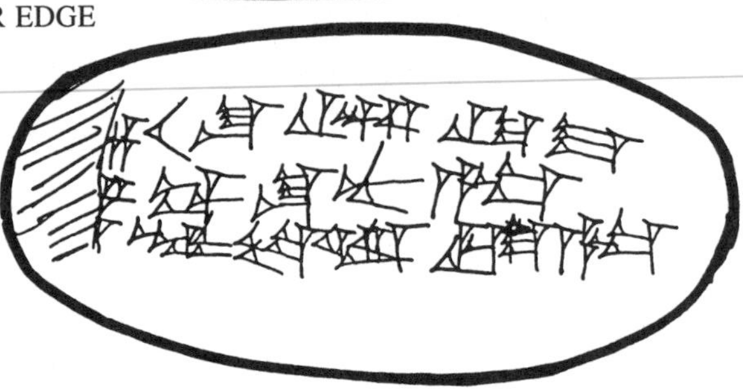

68

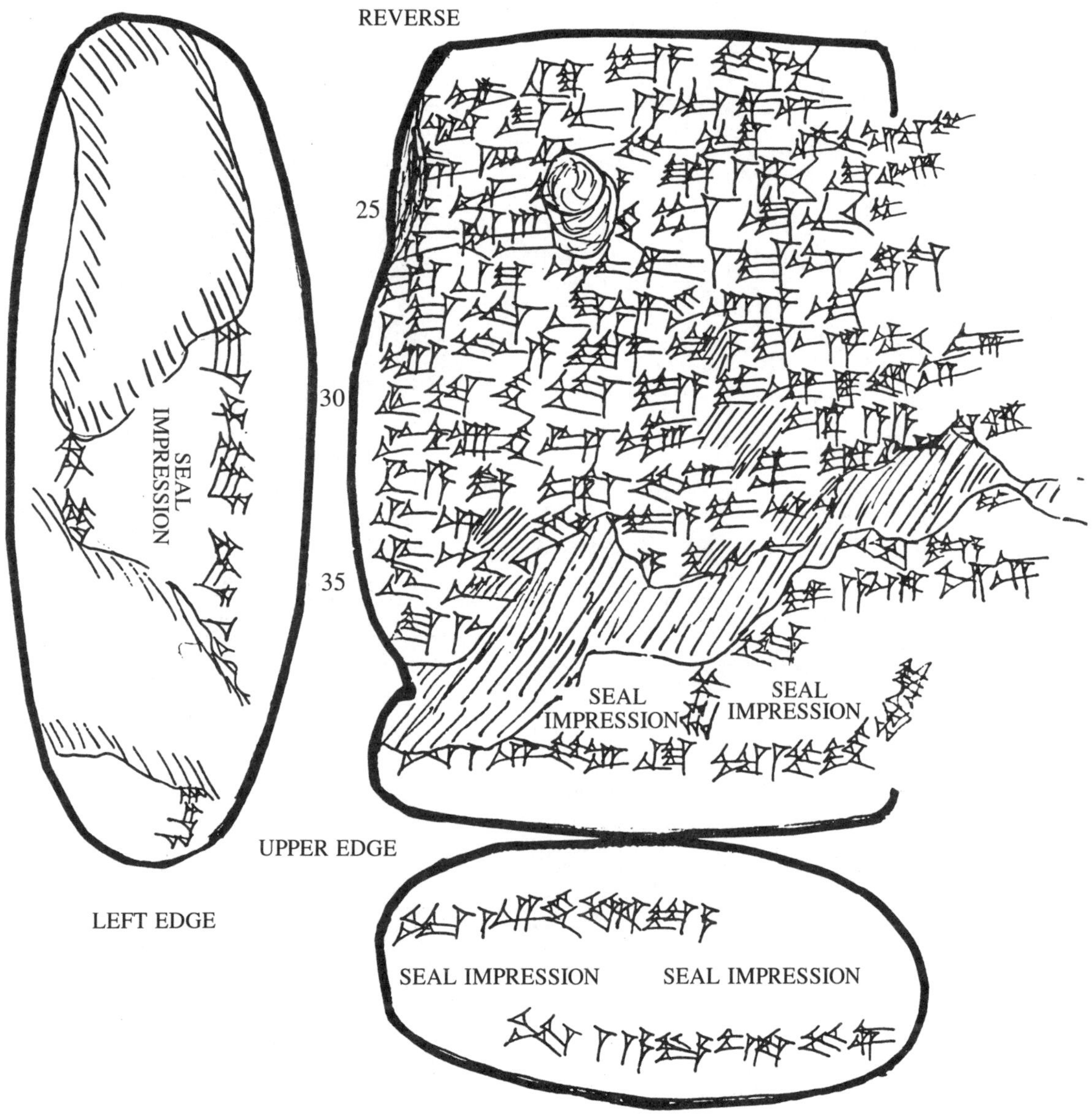
REVERSE
LEFT EDGE
SEAL IMPRESSION
SEAL IMPRESSION
SEAL IMPRESSION
UPPER EDGE
SEAL IMPRESSION
SEAL IMPRESSION

69

OBVERSE

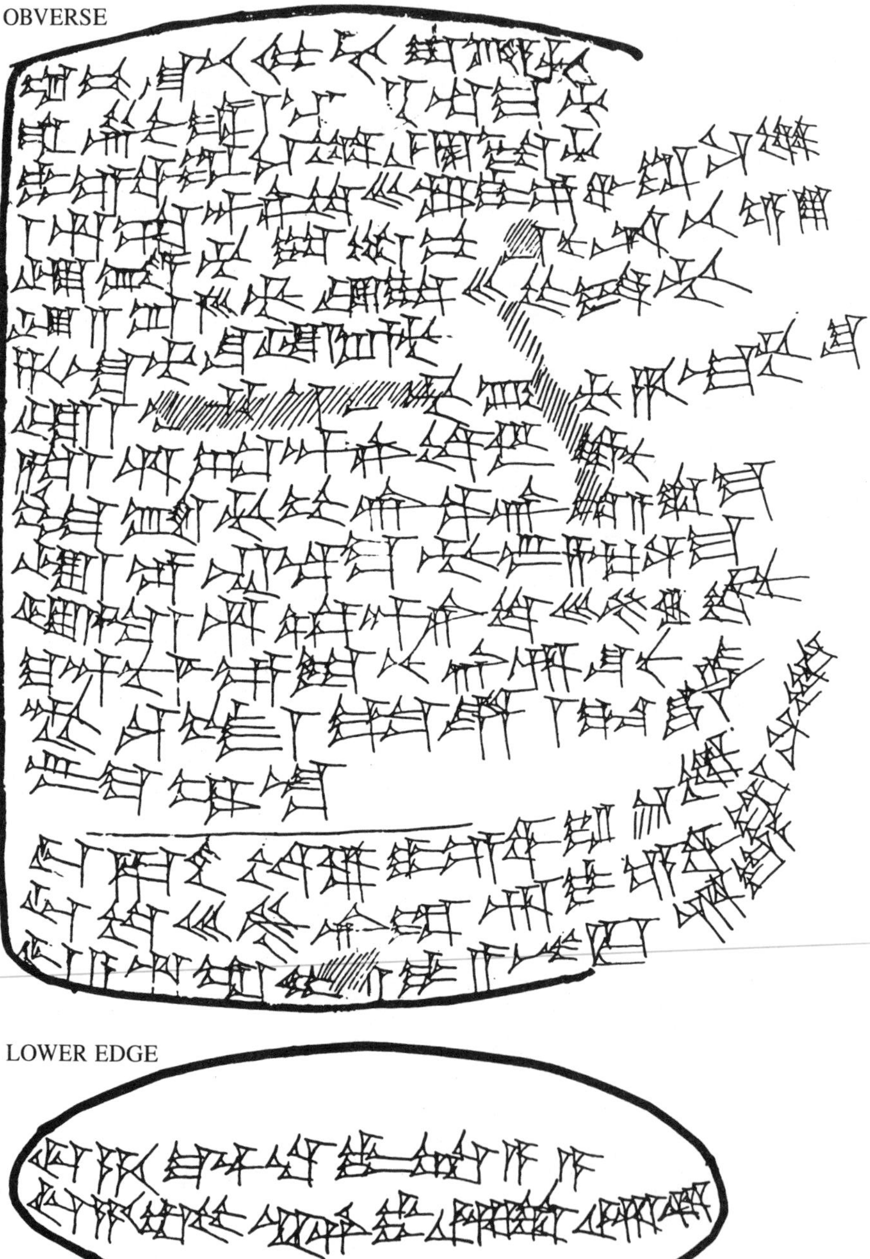

LOWER EDGE

69

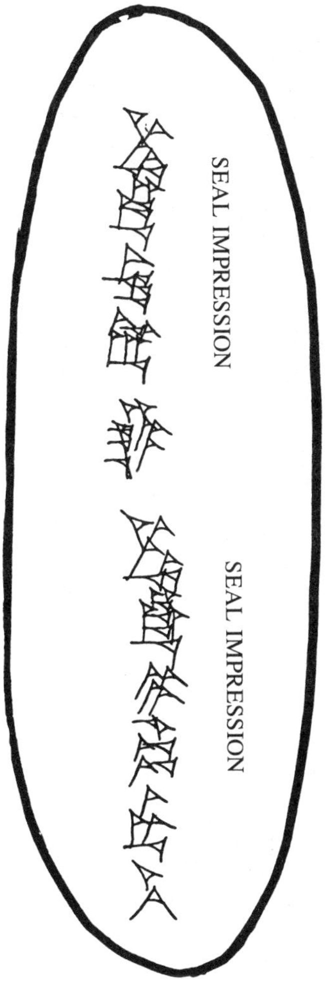

REVERSE

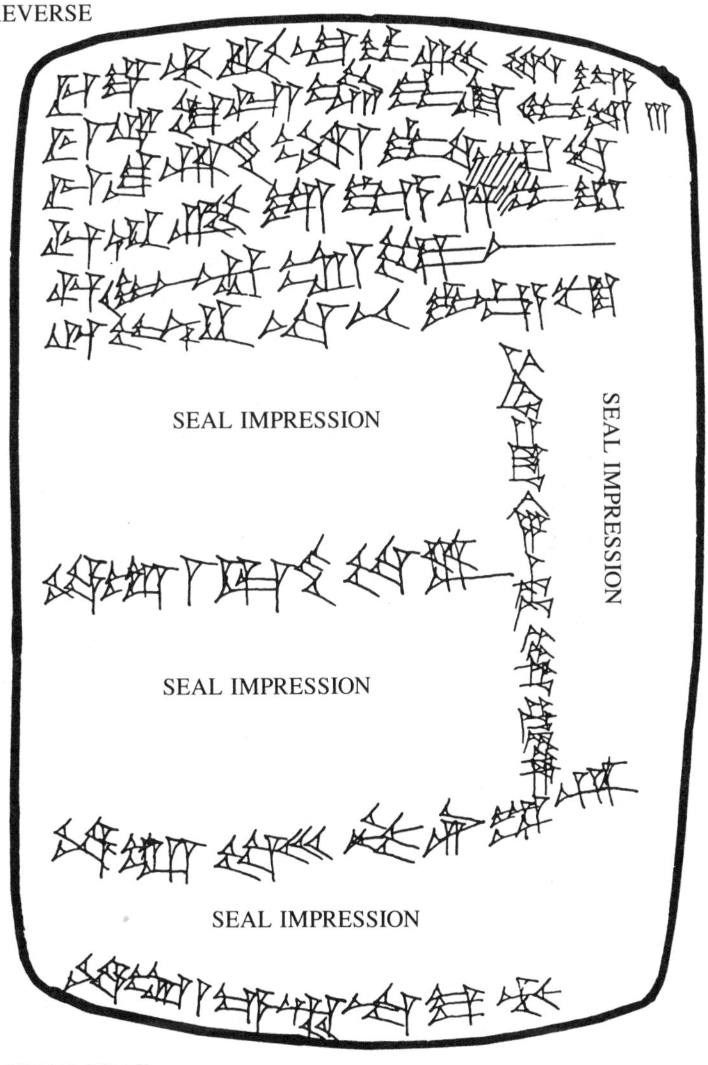

UPPER EDGE

70

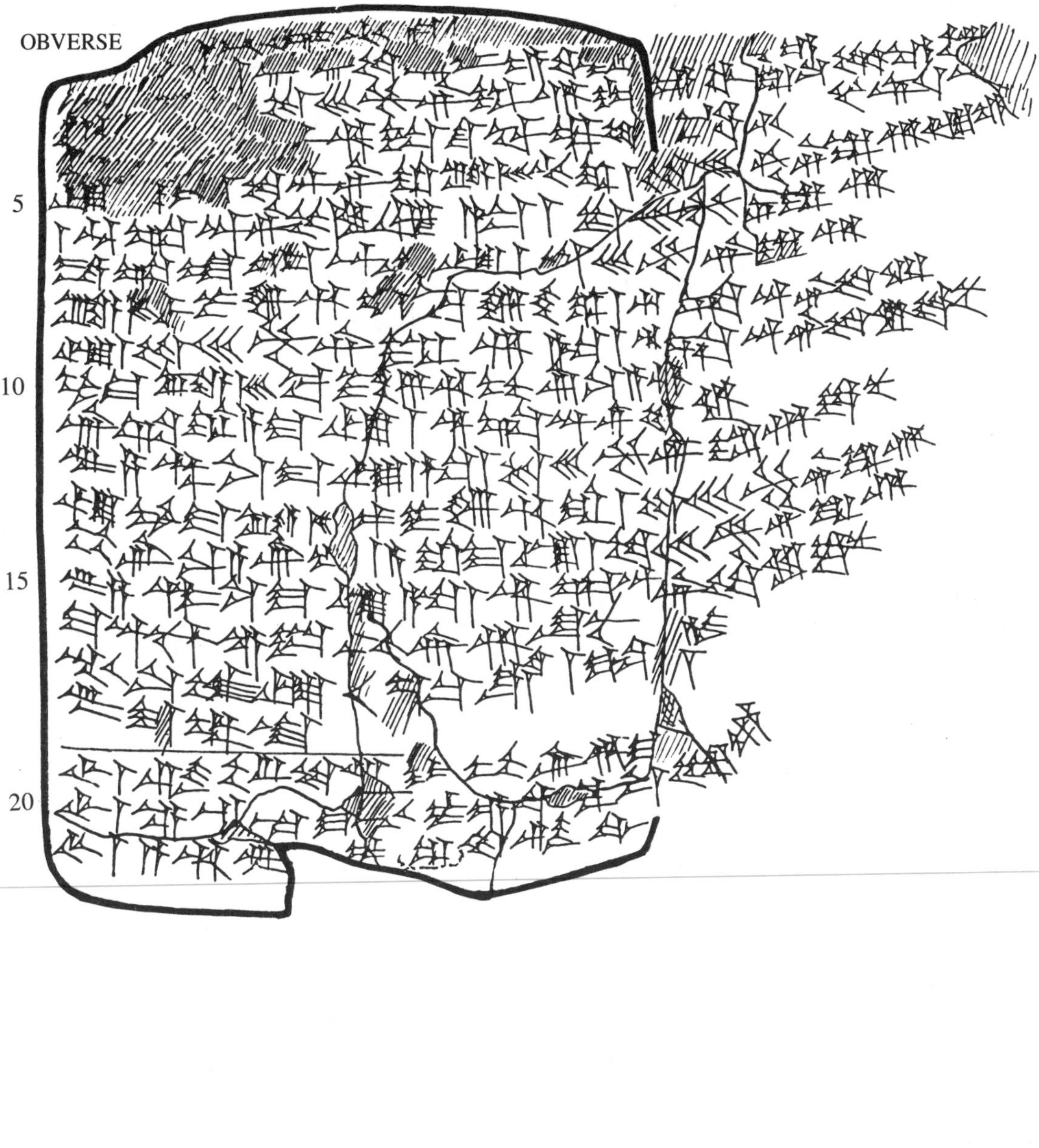

70

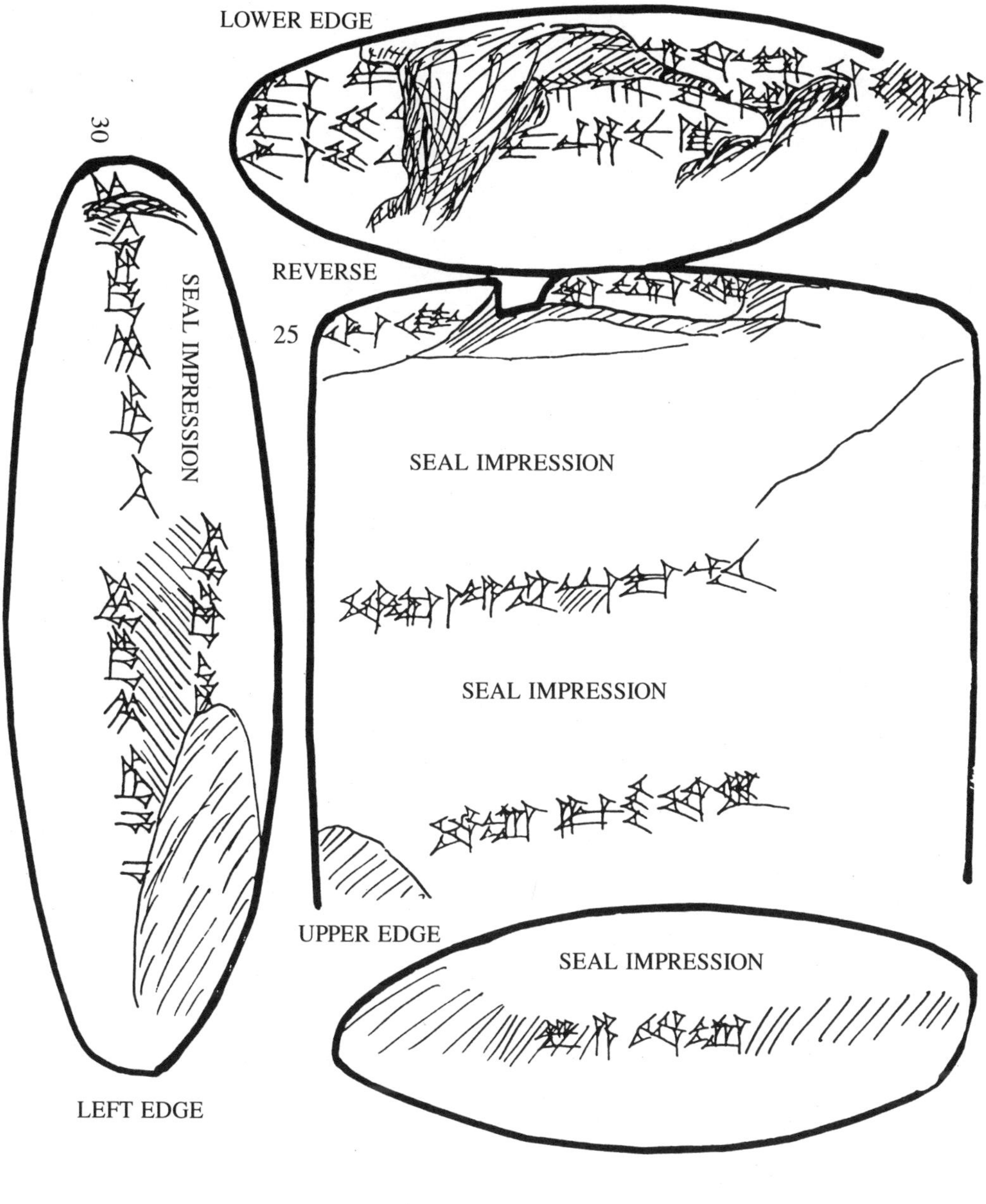
LOWER EDGE
30
REVERSE
25
SEAL IMPRESSION
SEAL IMPRESSION
SEAL IMPRESSION
UPPER EDGE
SEAL IMPRESSION
LEFT EDGE

71

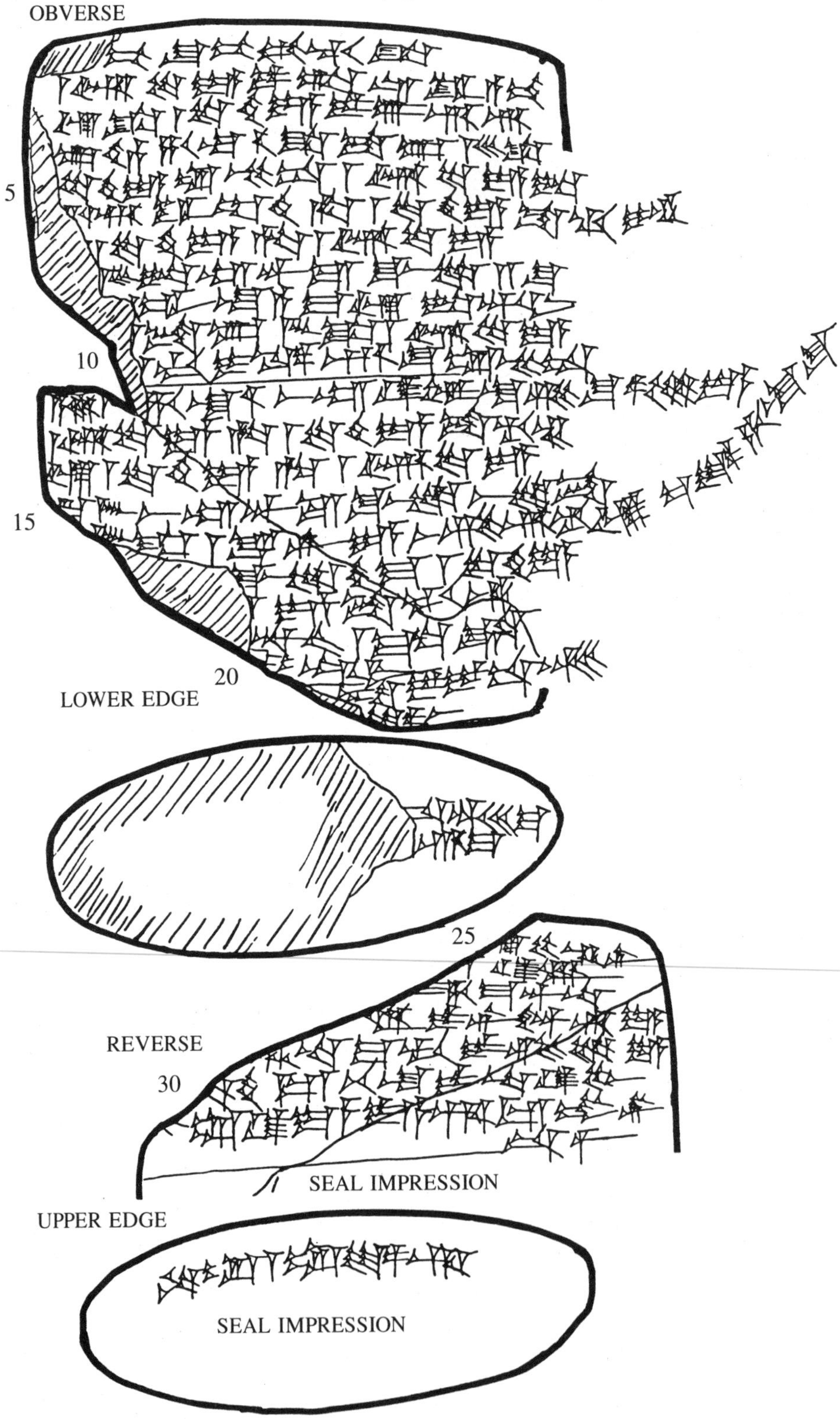
OBVERSE
LOWER EDGE
REVERSE
SEAL IMPRESSION
UPPER EDGE
SEAL IMPRESSION

72

OBVERSE

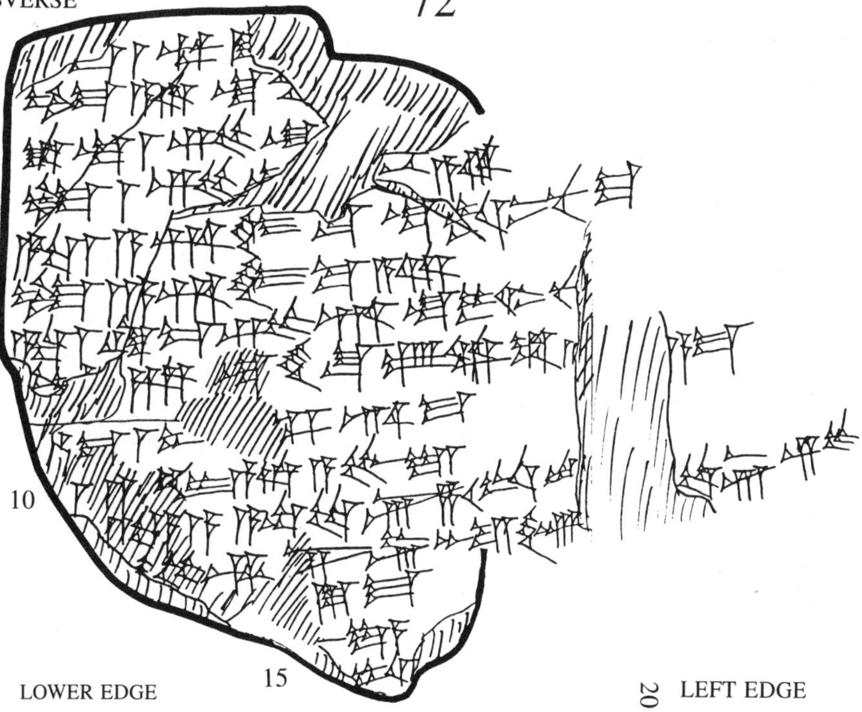

LOWER EDGE

REST OF OBVERSE AND BEGINNING OF REVERSE DESTROYED

LEFT EDGE

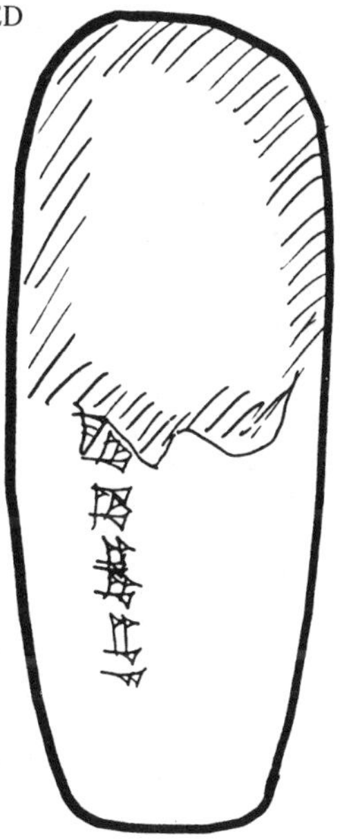

REVERSE

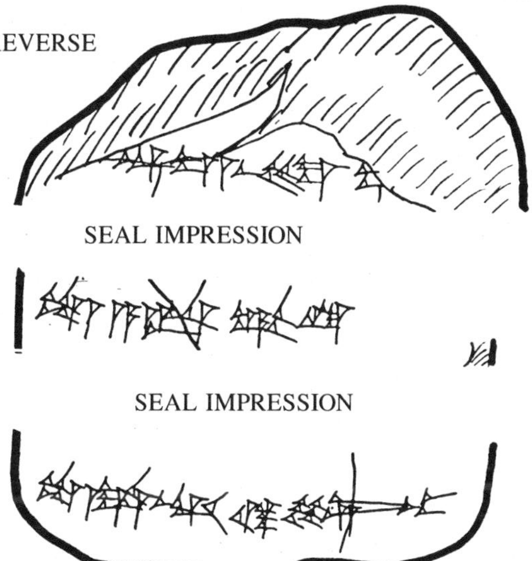

UPPER EDGE

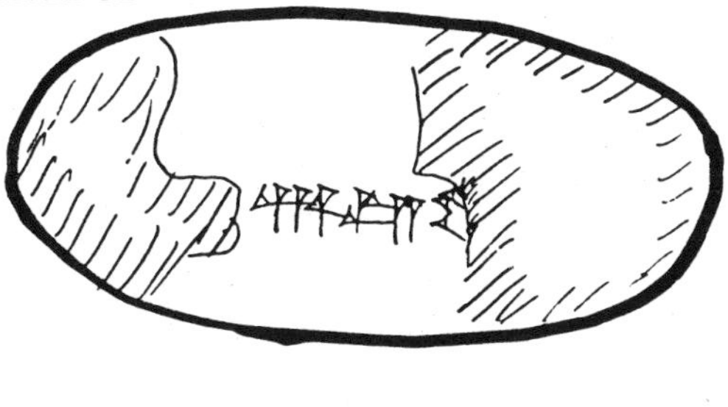

78

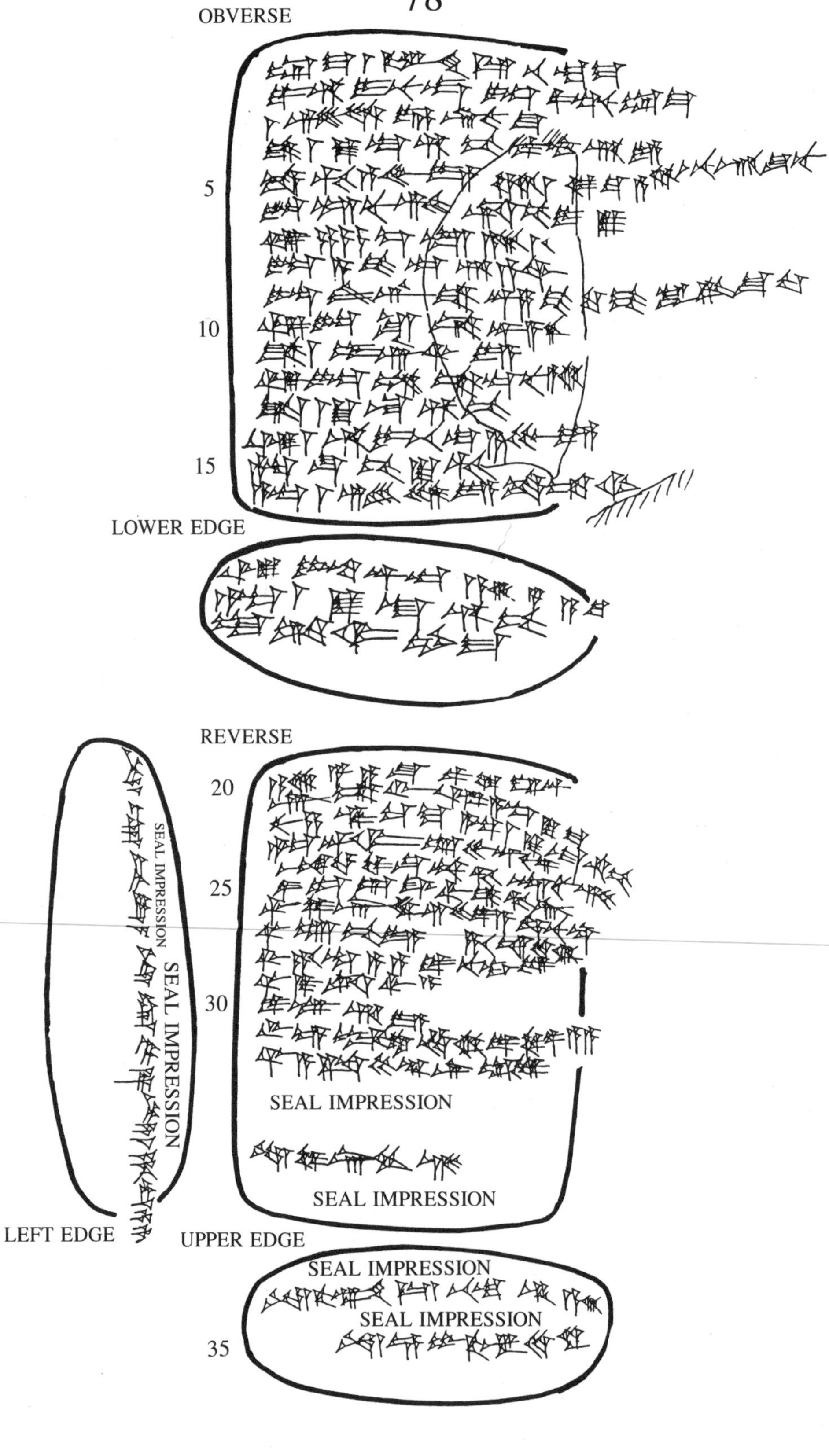
OBVERSE
LOWER EDGE
REVERSE
SEAL IMPRESSION
SEAL IMPRESSION
SEAL IMPRESSION
SEAL IMPRESSION
LEFT EDGE
UPPER EDGE
SEAL IMPRESSION
SEAL IMPRESSION

79

OBVERSE

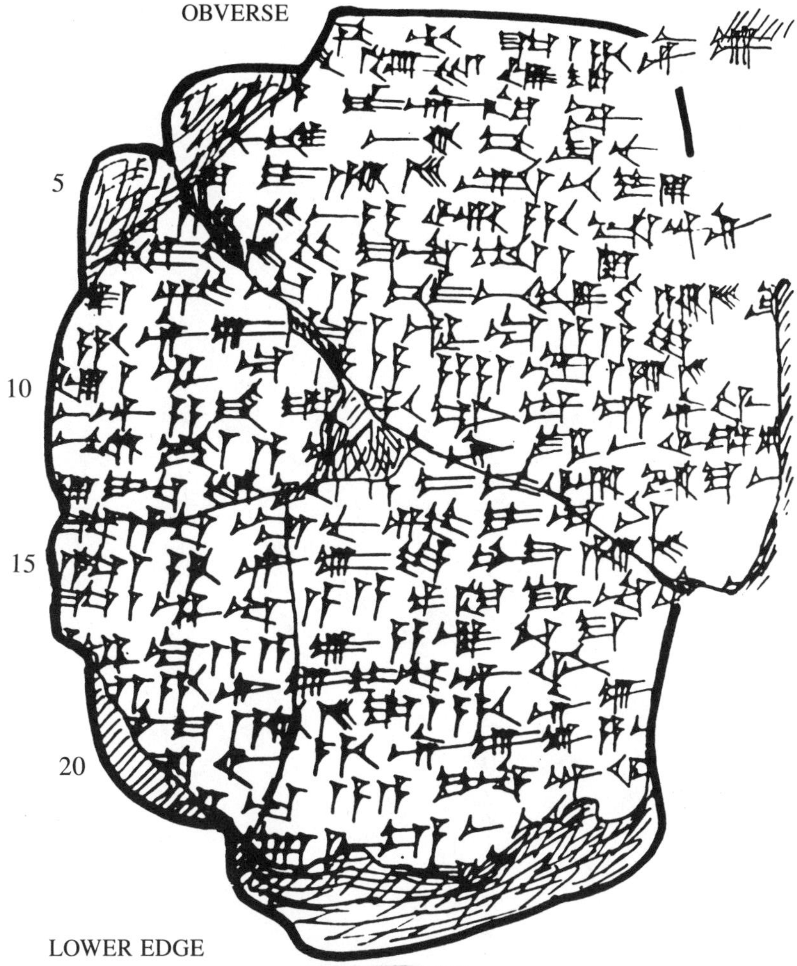

LOWER EDGE

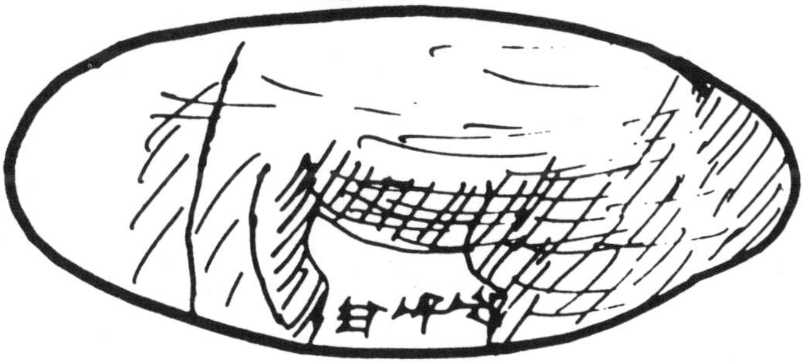

79

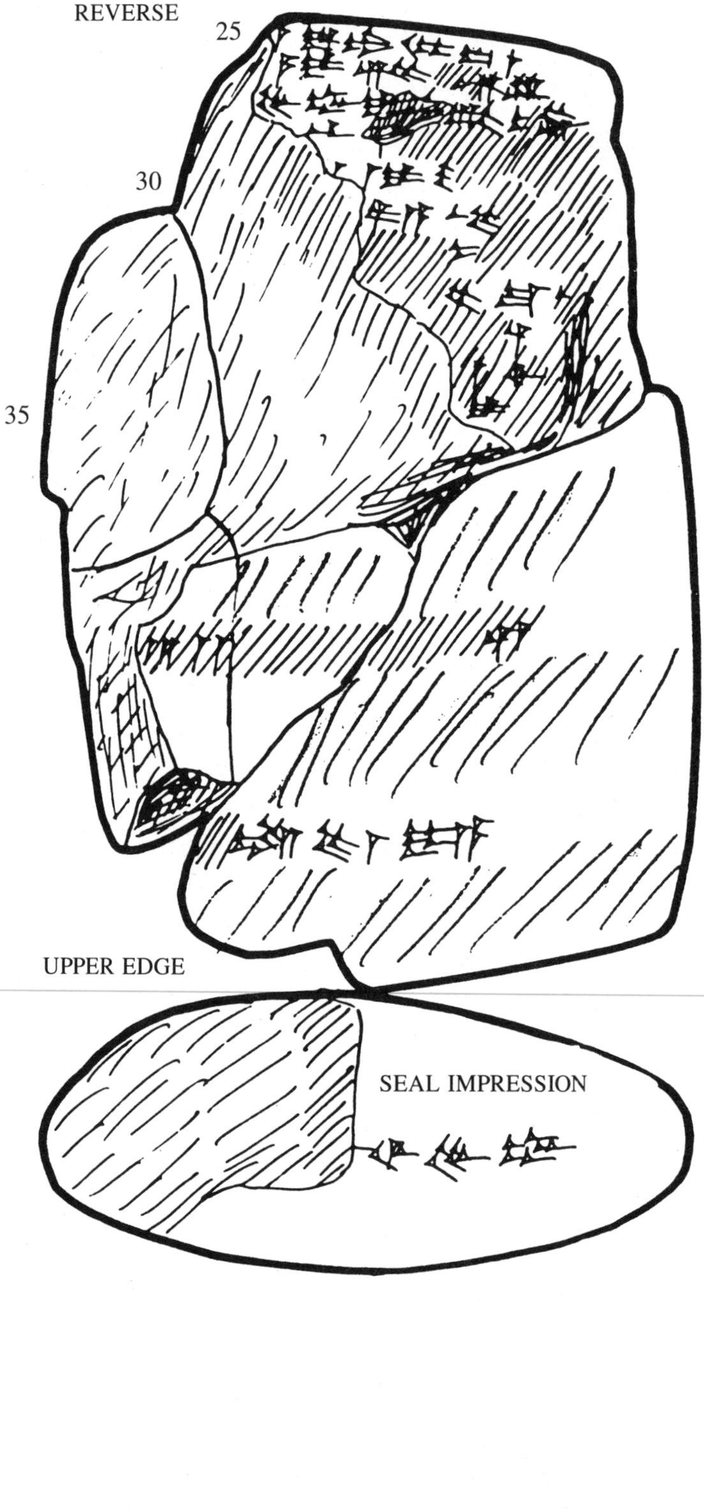

80

OBVERSE

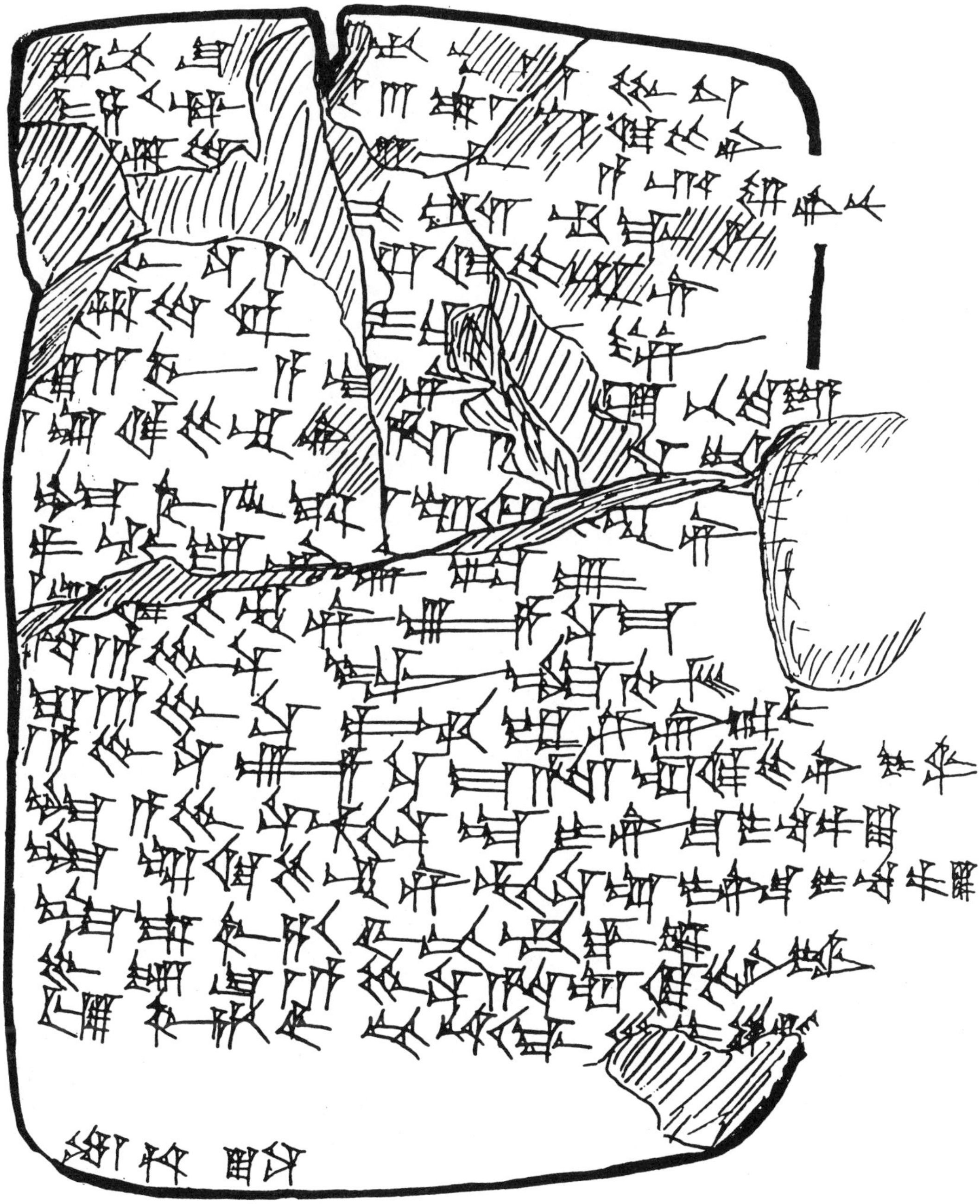

80

REVERSE

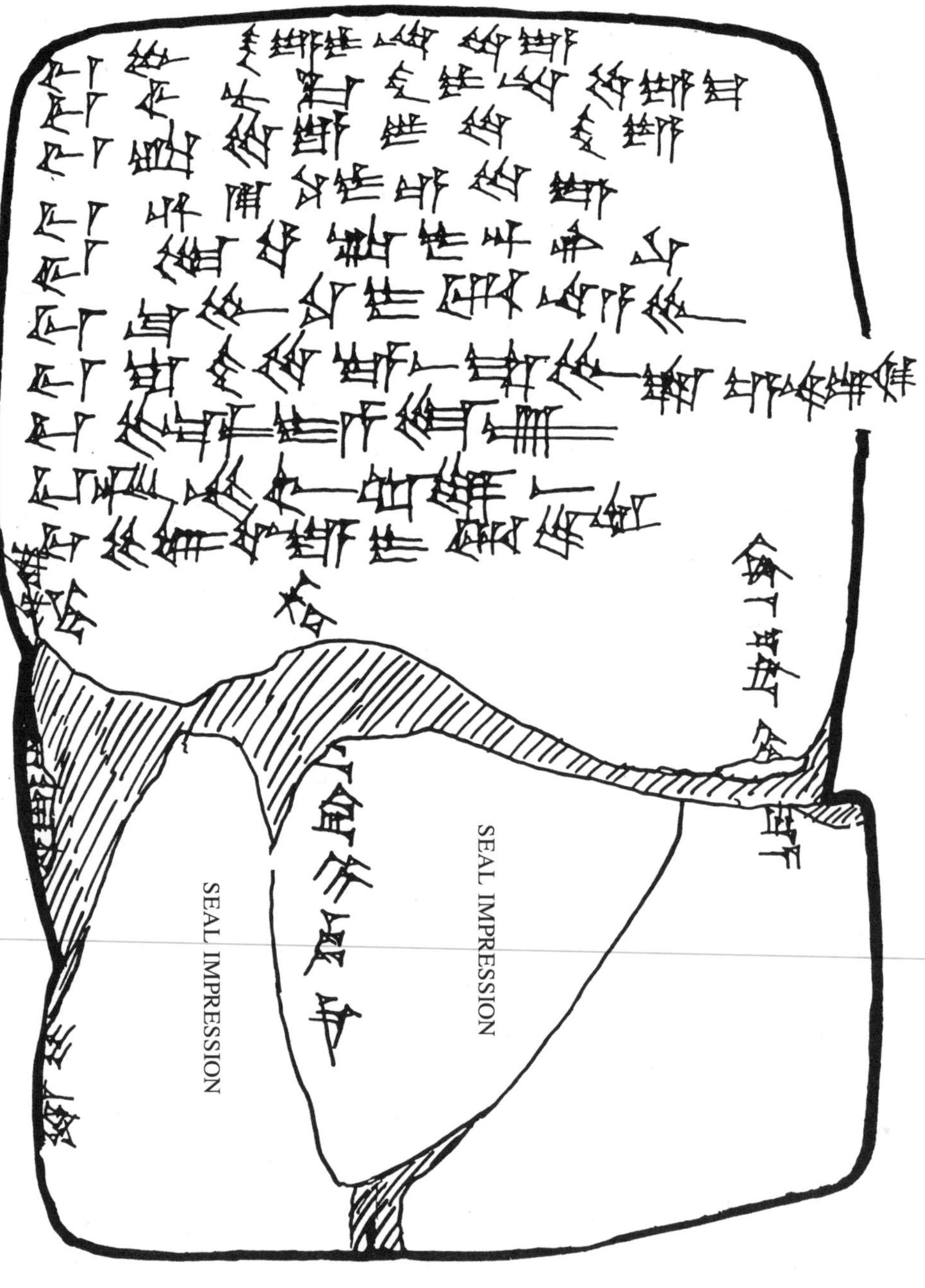

82

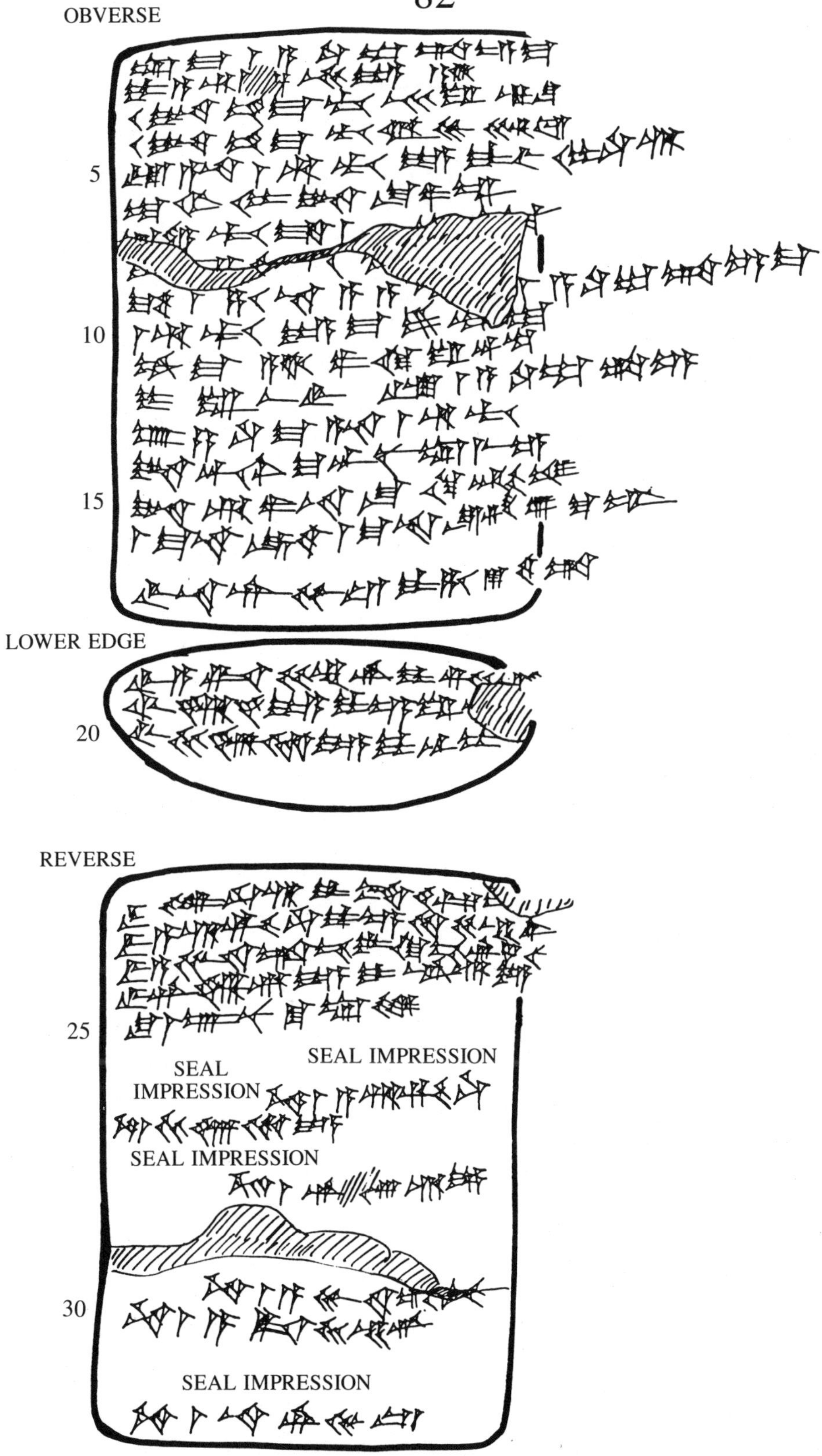
OBVERSE
LOWER EDGE
REVERSE
SEAL IMPRESSION
SEAL
IMPRESSION
SEAL IMPRESSION
SEAL IMPRESSION

84

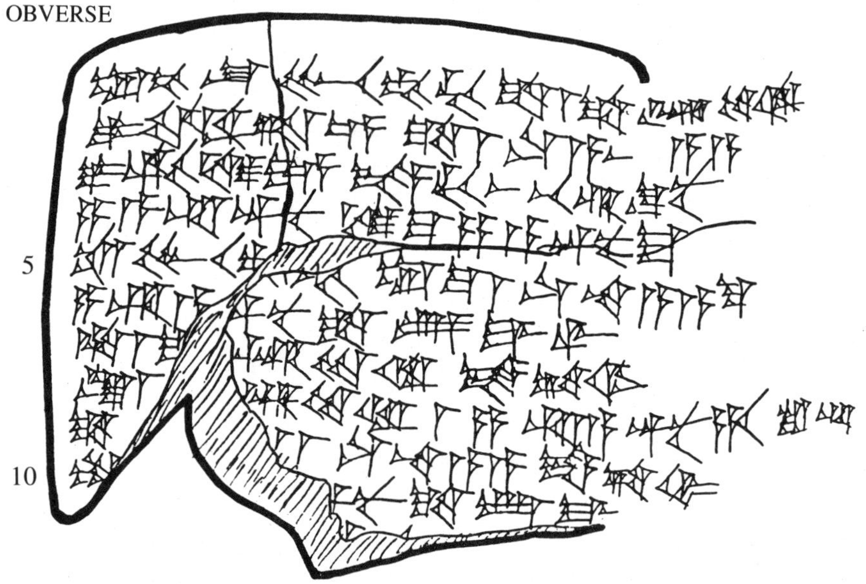

REST OF OBVERSE AND BEGINNING OF REVERSE DESTROYED

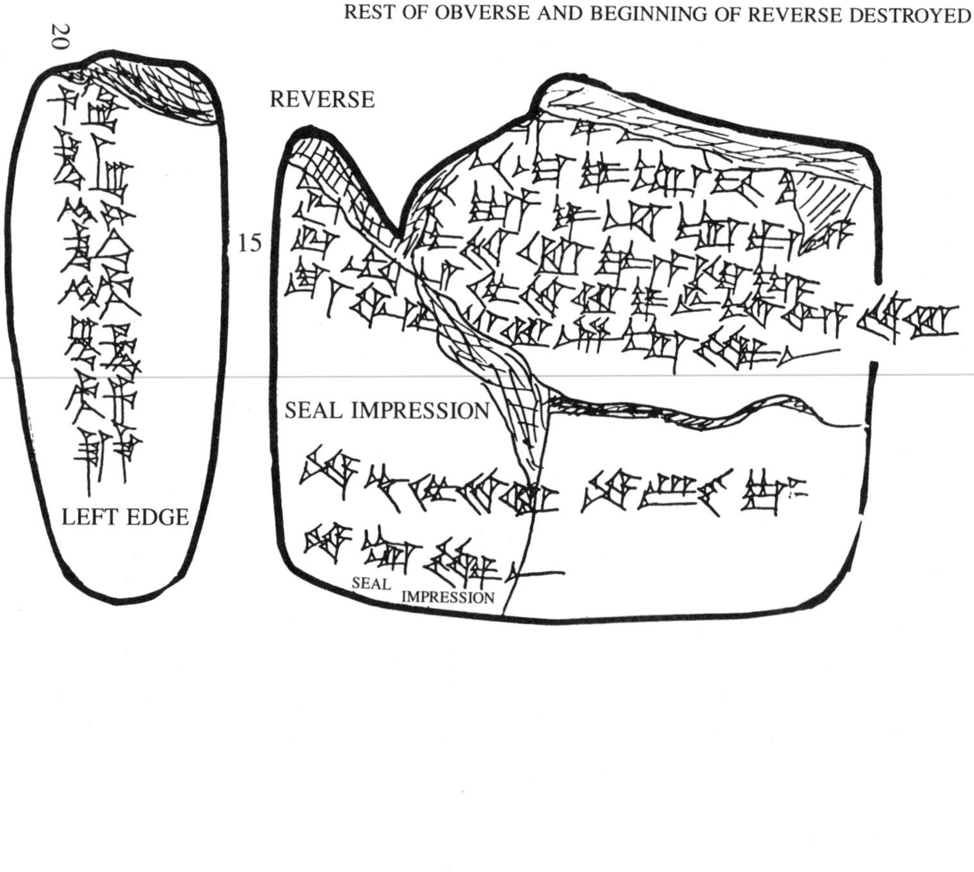

86

OBVERSE

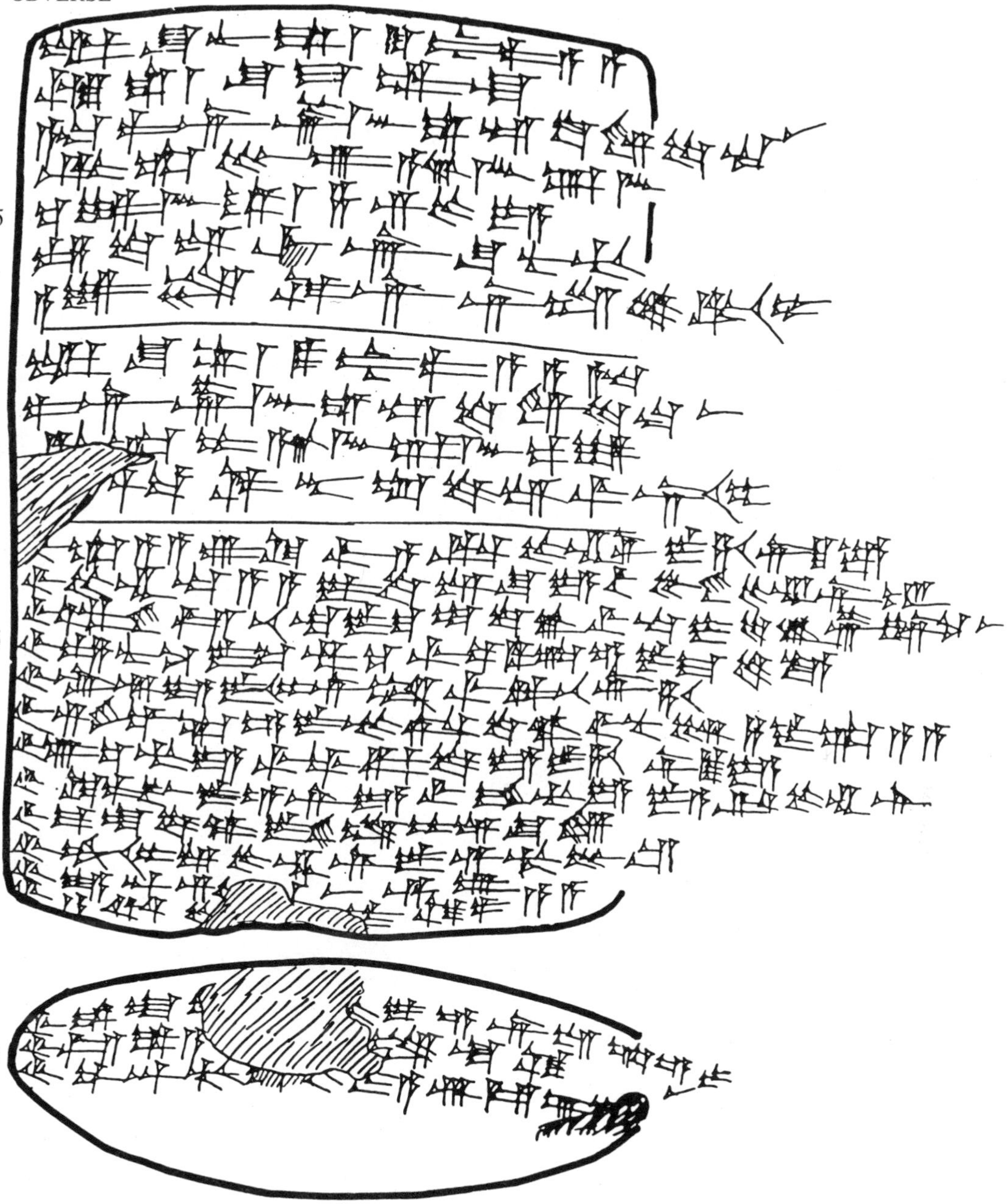

86

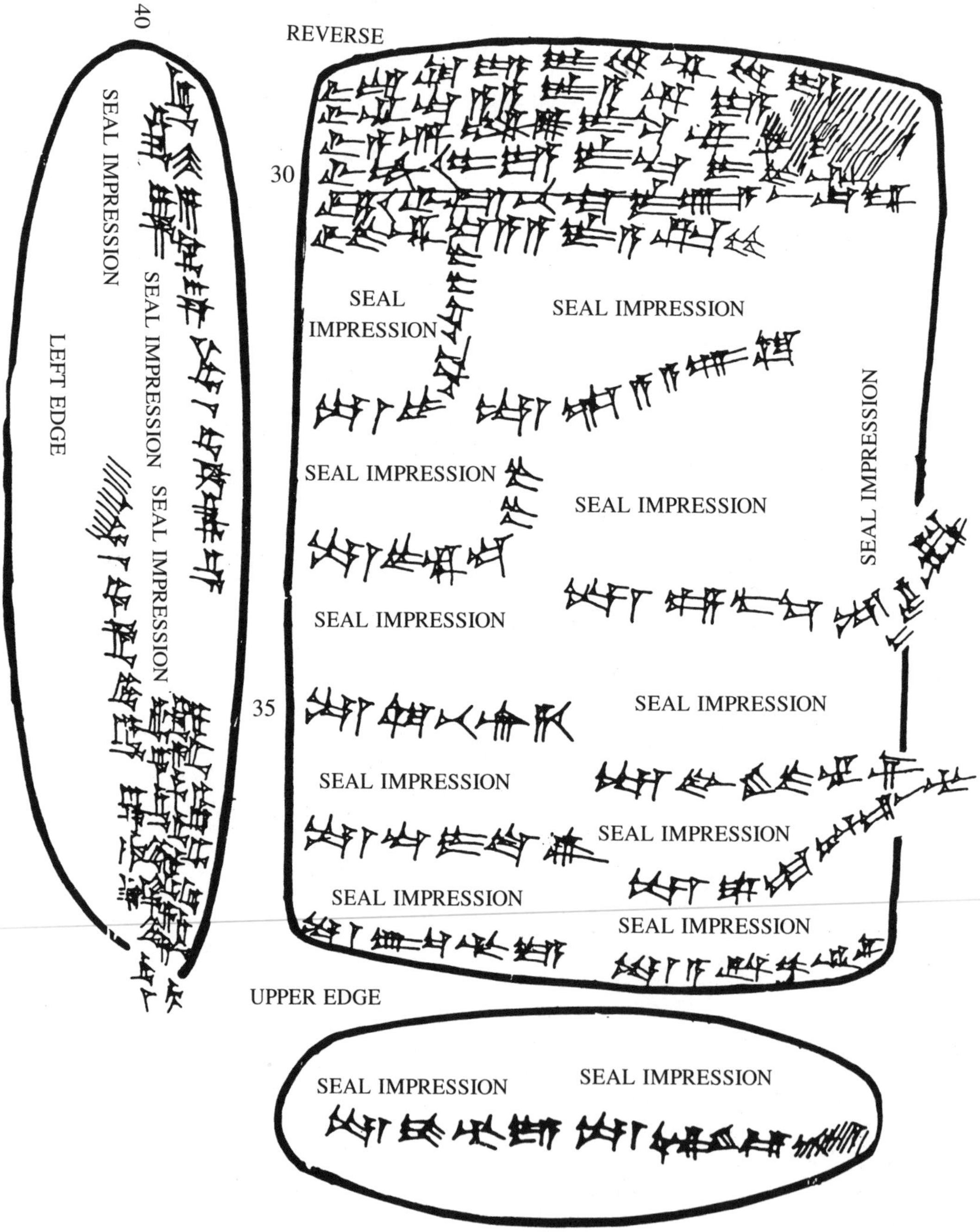
REVERSE
30
SEAL IMPRESSION
SEAL IMPRESSION
SEAL IMPRESSION
SEAL IMPRESSION
SEAL IMPRESSION
SEAL IMPRESSION
35
SEAL IMPRESSION
SEAL IMPRESSION
SEAL IMPRESSION
SEAL IMPRESSION
SEAL IMPRESSION
SEAL IMPRESSION
40
LEFT EDGE
SEAL IMPRESSION
SEAL IMPRESSION
SEAL IMPRESSION
UPPER EDGE
SEAL IMPRESSION
SEAL IMPRESSION

87

OBVERSE

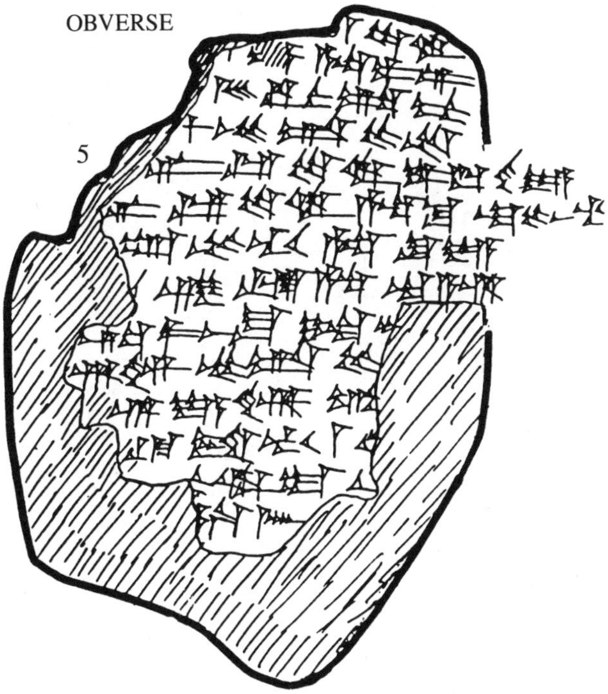

REST OF OBVERSE DESTROYED

REVERSE BEGINNING OF REVERSE DESTROYED

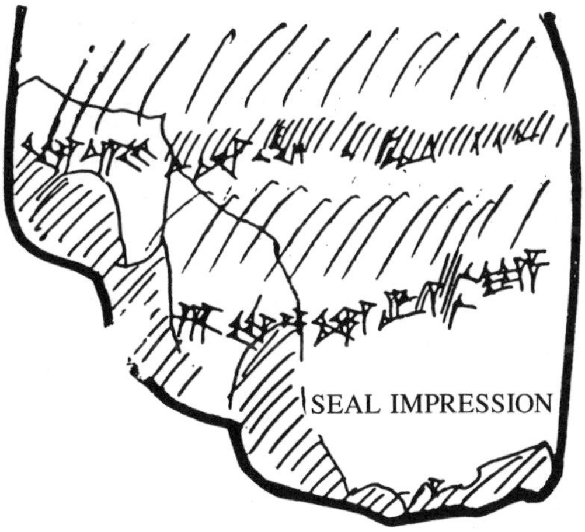

88

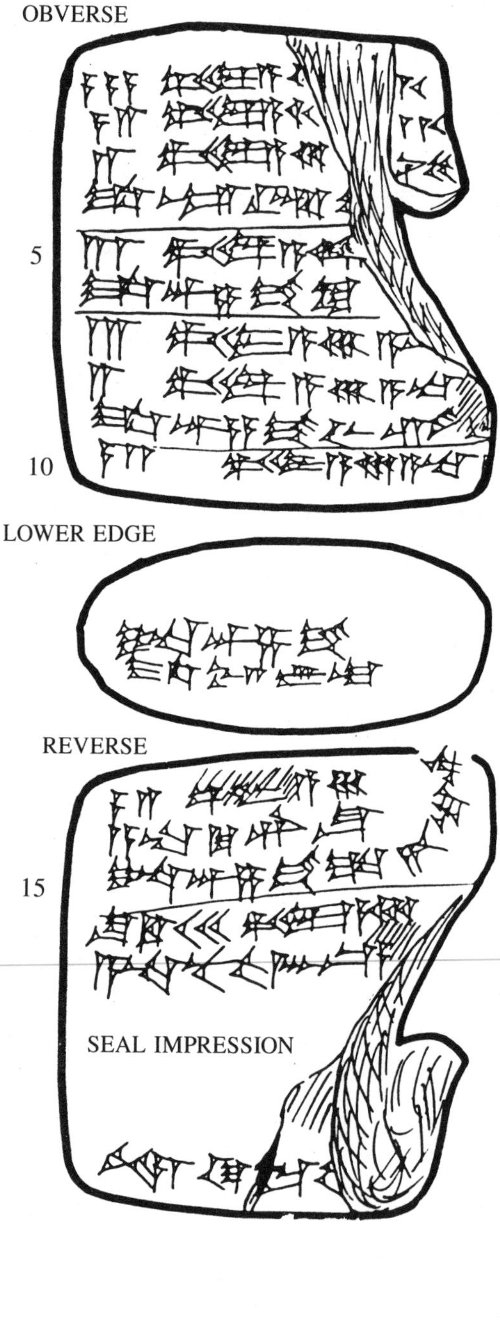

89

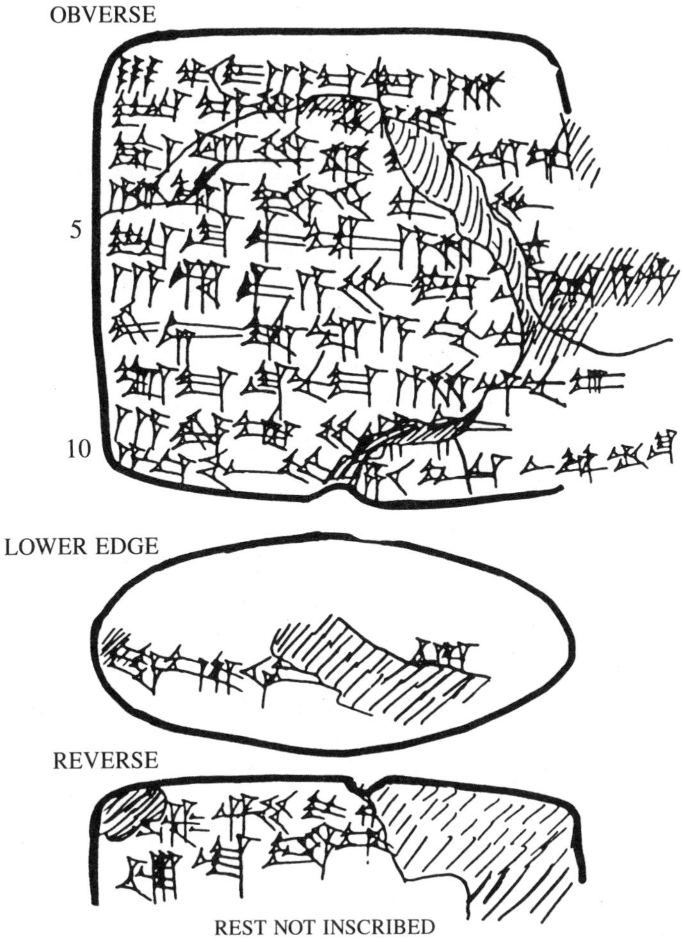

90

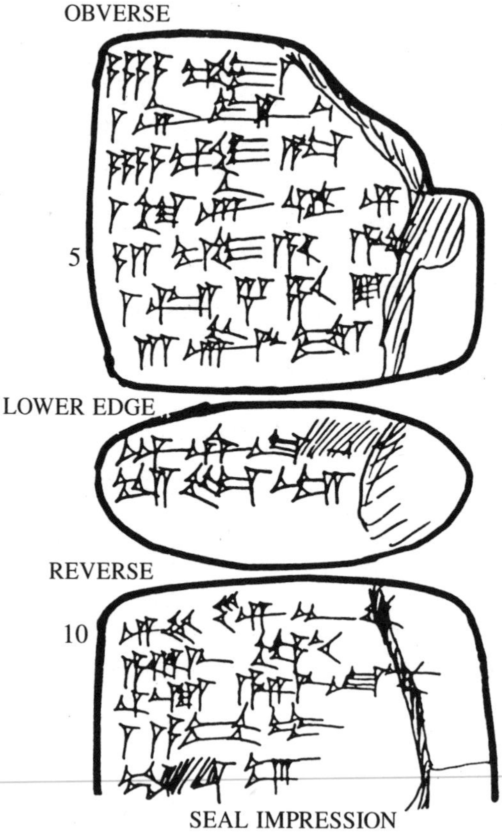

91

OBVERSE

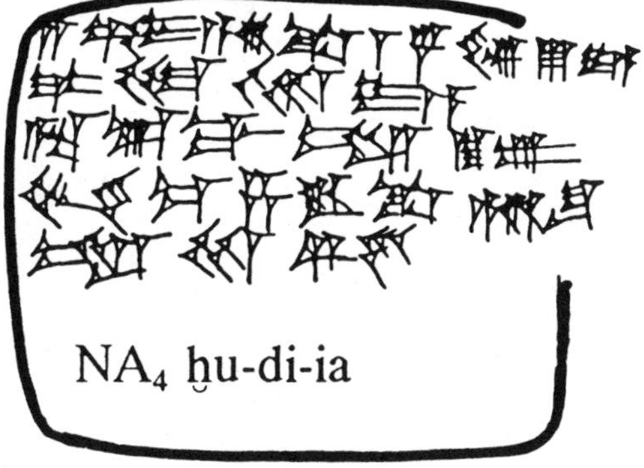

REST NOT INSCRIBED

92

OBVERSE

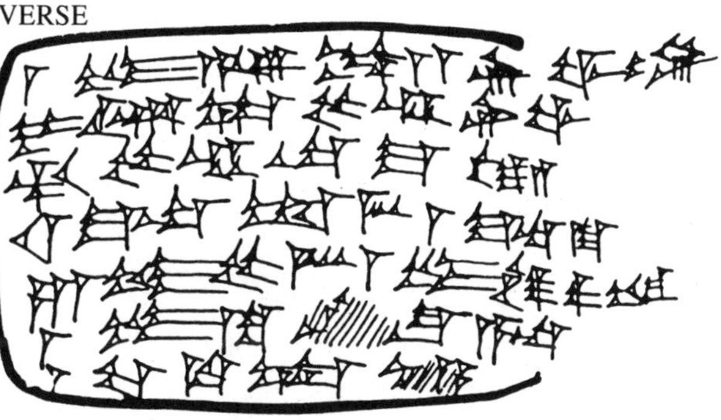

LOWER EDGE

REST NOT INSCRIBED

98

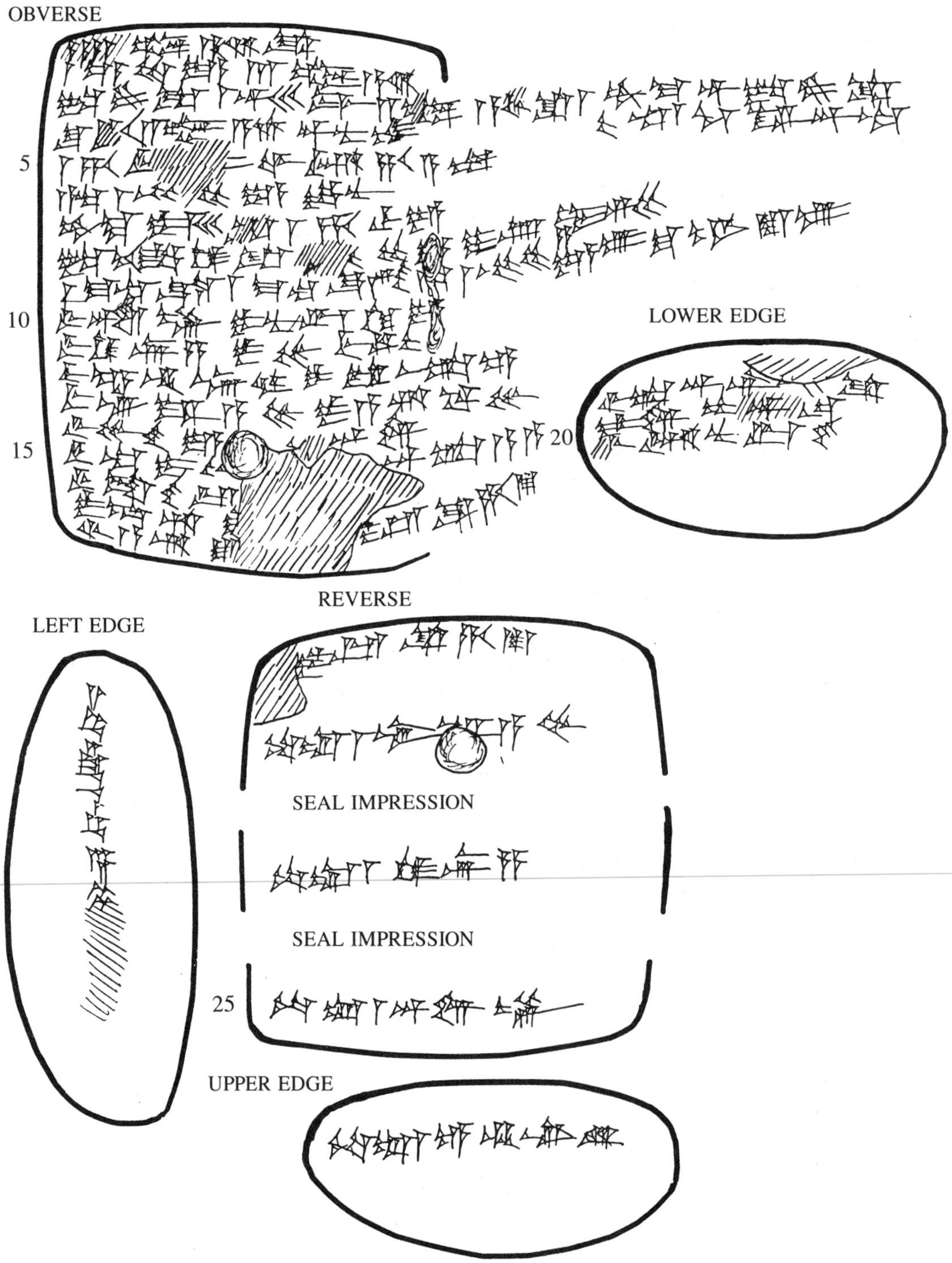
OBVERSE
LOWER EDGE
REVERSE
LEFT EDGE
SEAL IMPRESSION
SEAL IMPRESSION
UPPER EDGE

100

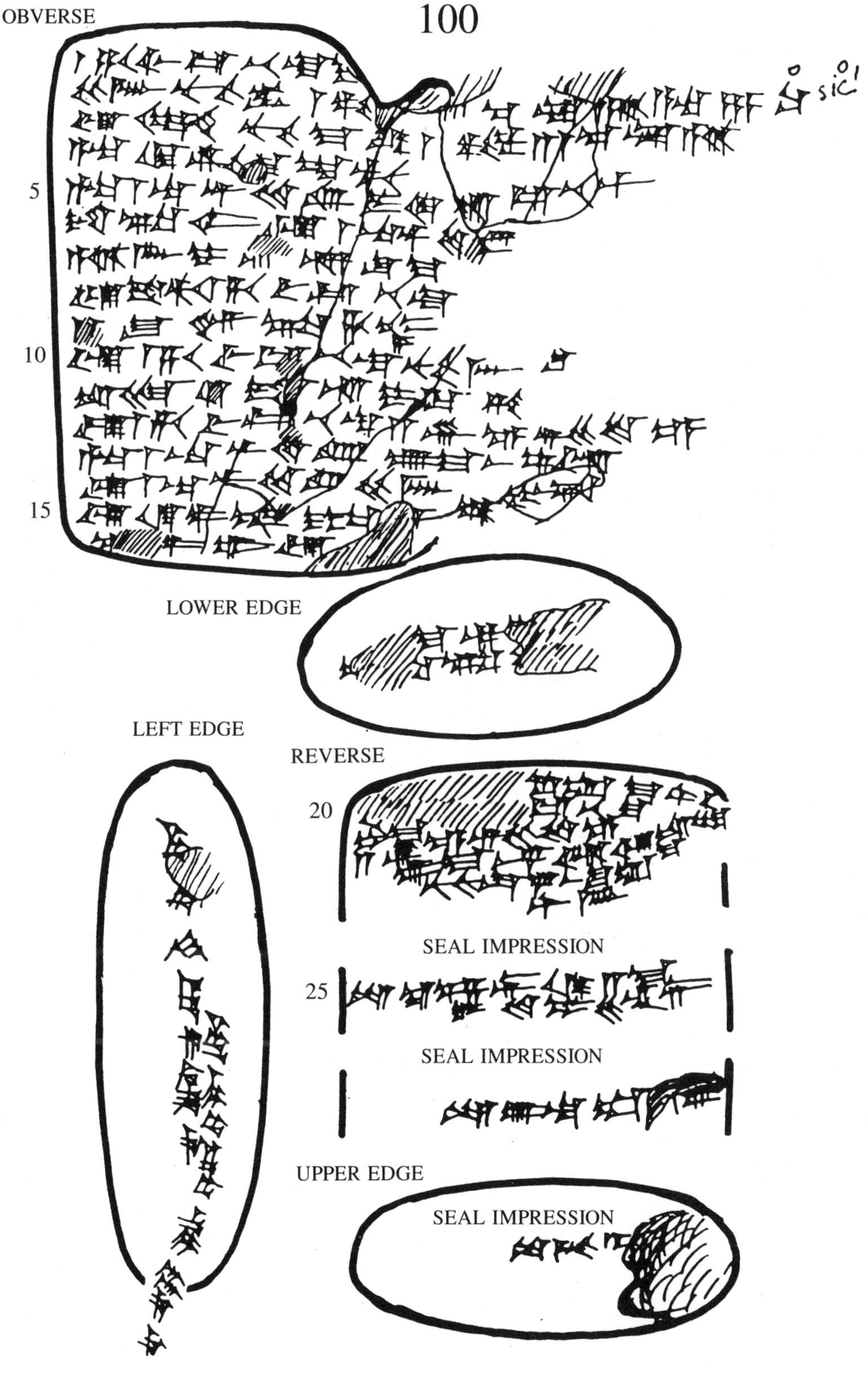
OBVERSE
sic!
5
10
15
LOWER EDGE
LEFT EDGE
REVERSE
20
SEAL IMPRESSION
25
SEAL IMPRESSION
UPPER EDGE
SEAL IMPRESSION

104

BEGINNING OF OBVERSE DESTROYED

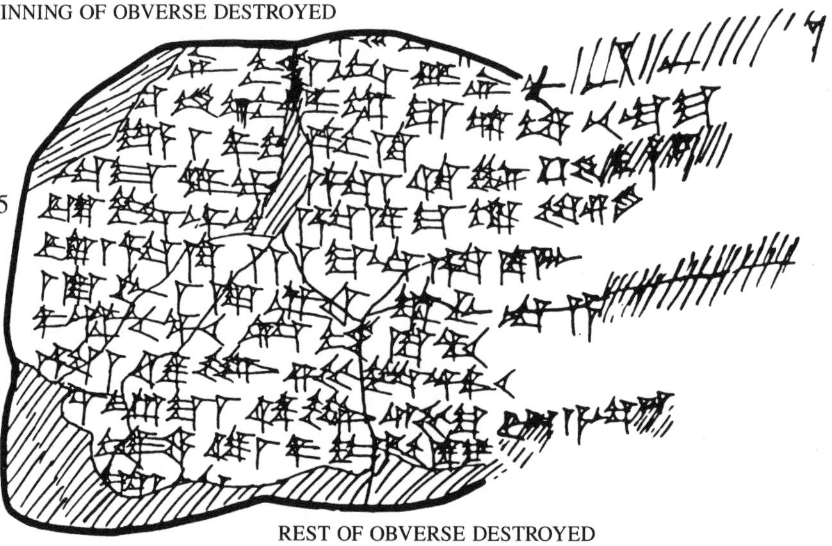

REST OF OBVERSE DESTROYED

BEGINNING OF REVERSE DESTROYED

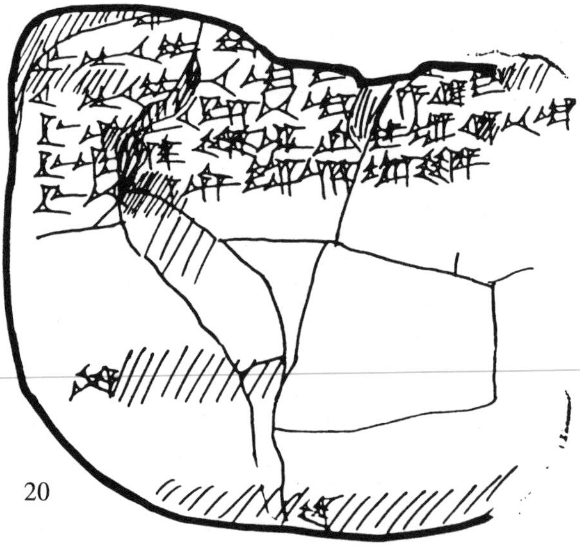

REST OF REVERSE DESTROYED

LEFT EDGE

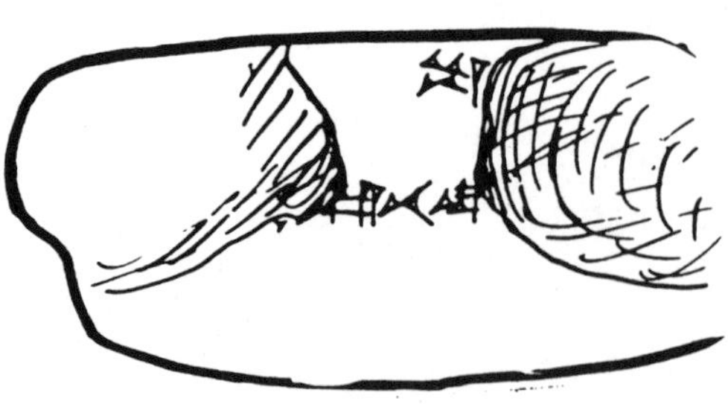

105

OBVERSE

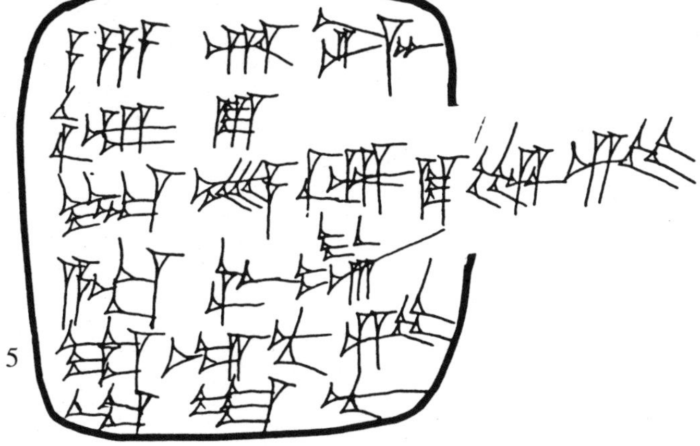

REST NOT INSCRIBED

107

OBVERSE

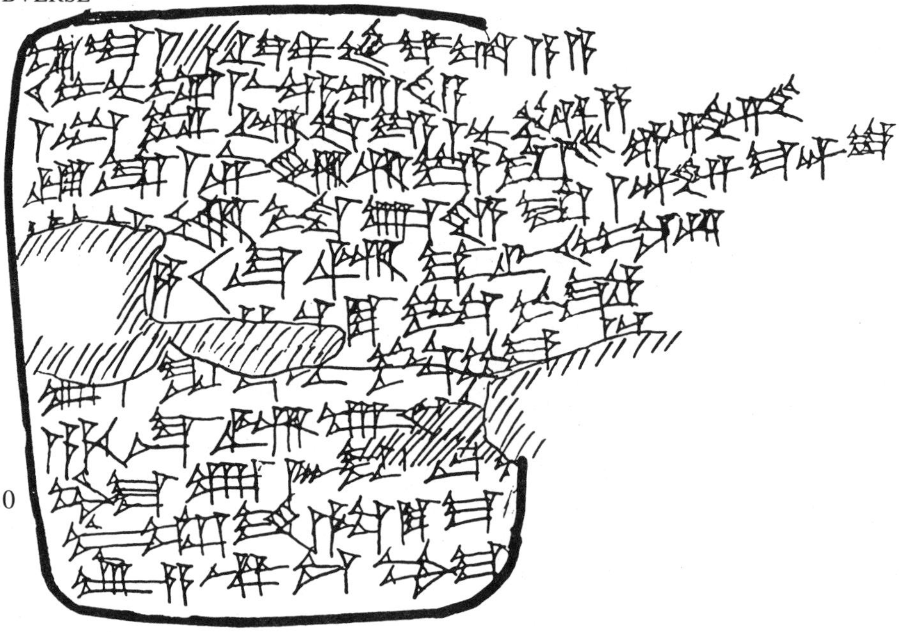

LOWER EDGE

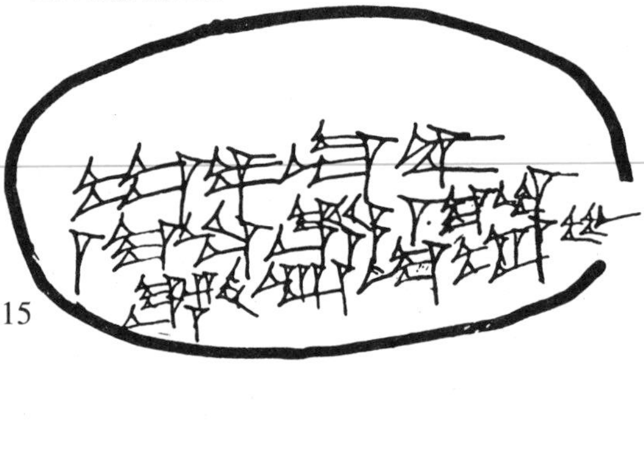

107

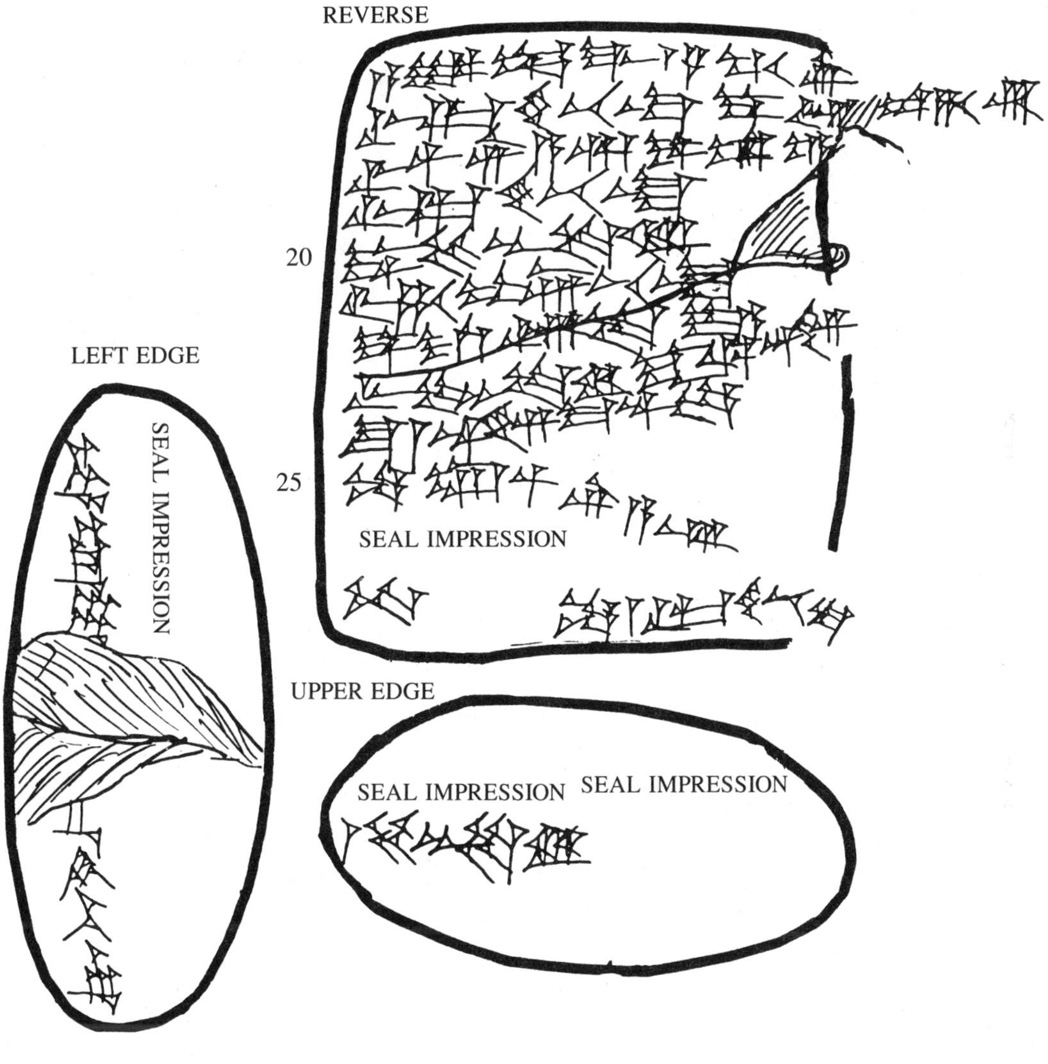
REVERSE
20
25
SEAL IMPRESSION
LEFT EDGE
SEAL IMPRESSION
UPPER EDGE
SEAL IMPRESSION
SEAL IMPRESSION

108

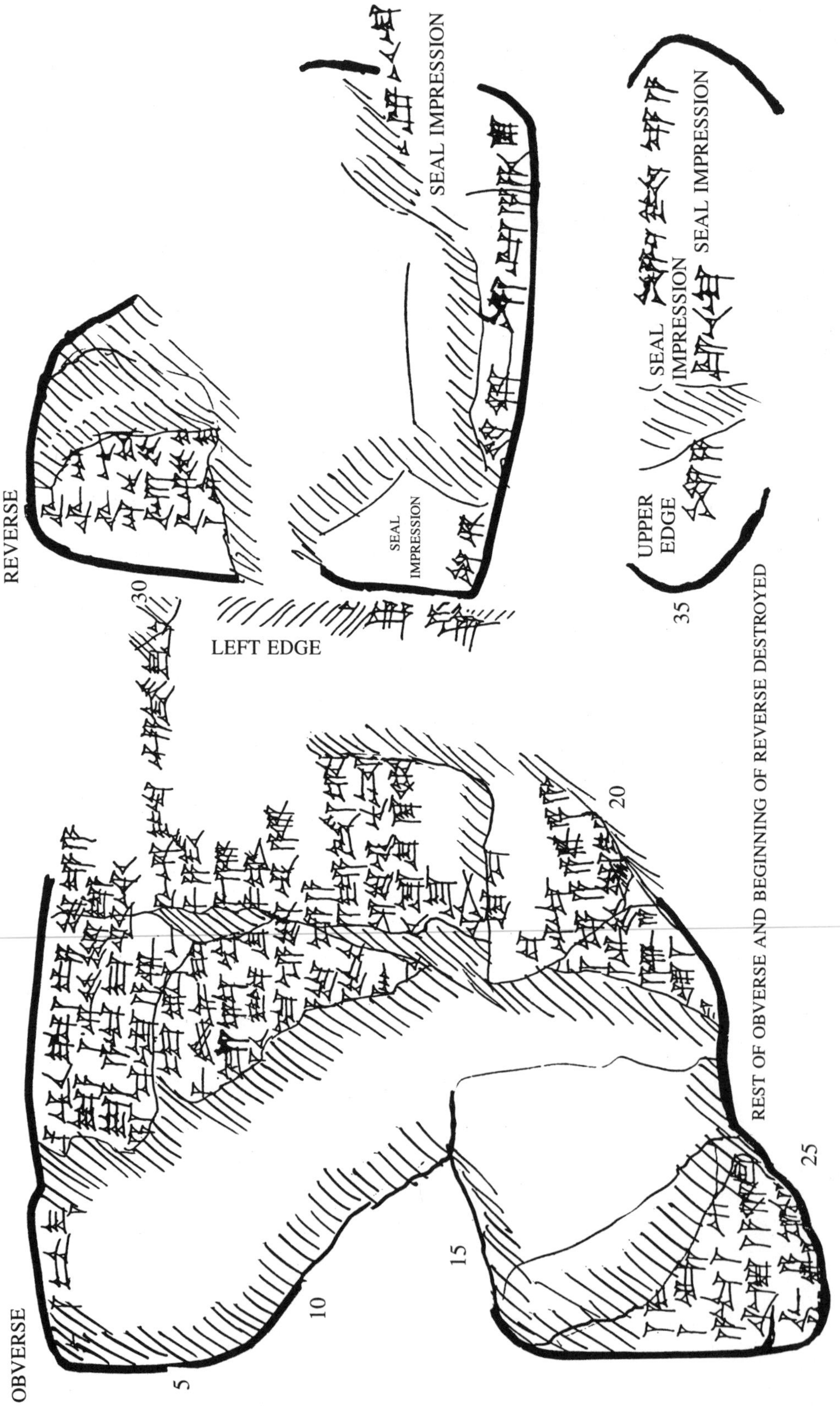
OBVERSE
REVERSE
LEFT EDGE
SEAL IMPRESSION
SEAL IMPRESSION
UPPER EDGE
SEAL IMPRESSION
SEAL IMPRESSION
REST OF OBVERSE AND BEGINNING OF REVERSE DESTROYED

109

OBVERSE

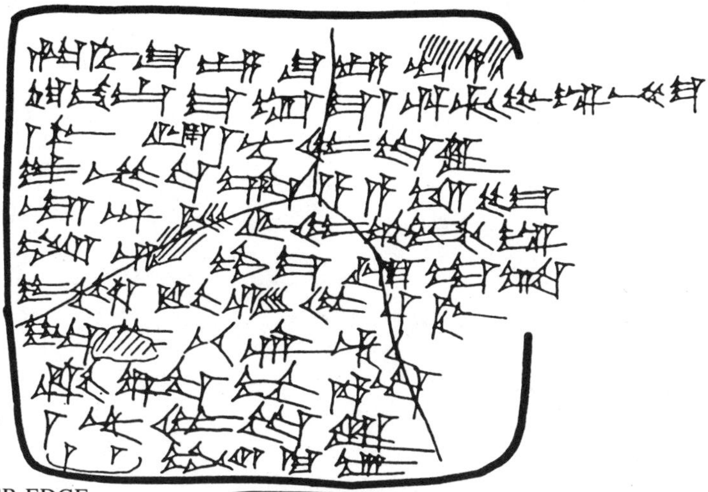

LOWER EDGE

REVERSE

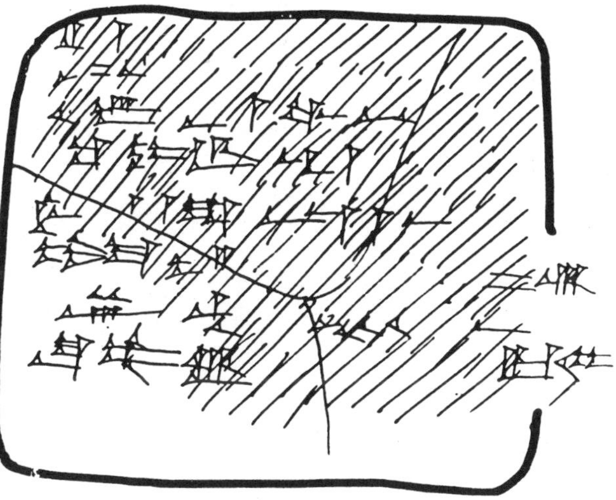

159

OBVERSE

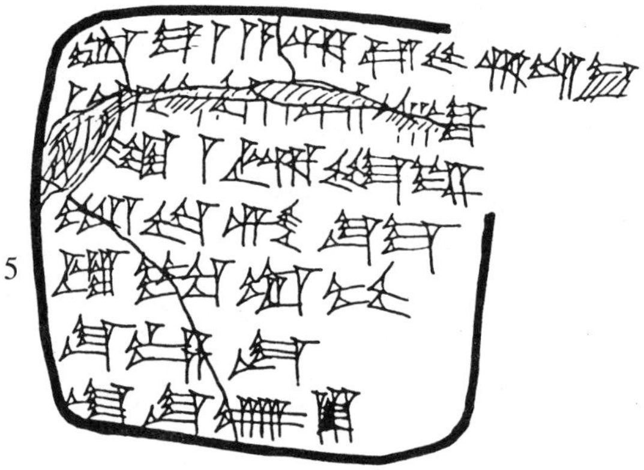

REVERSE

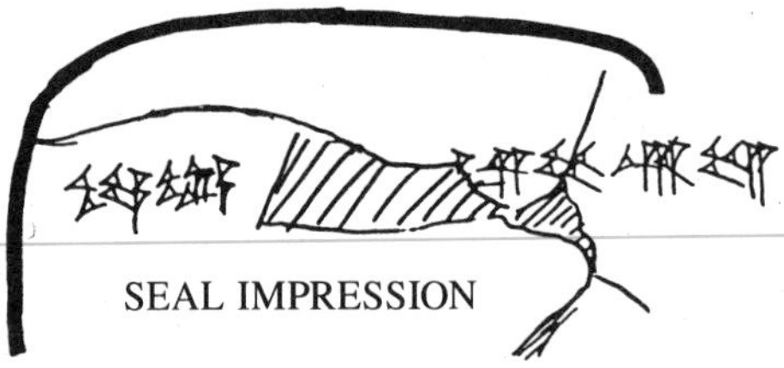

161

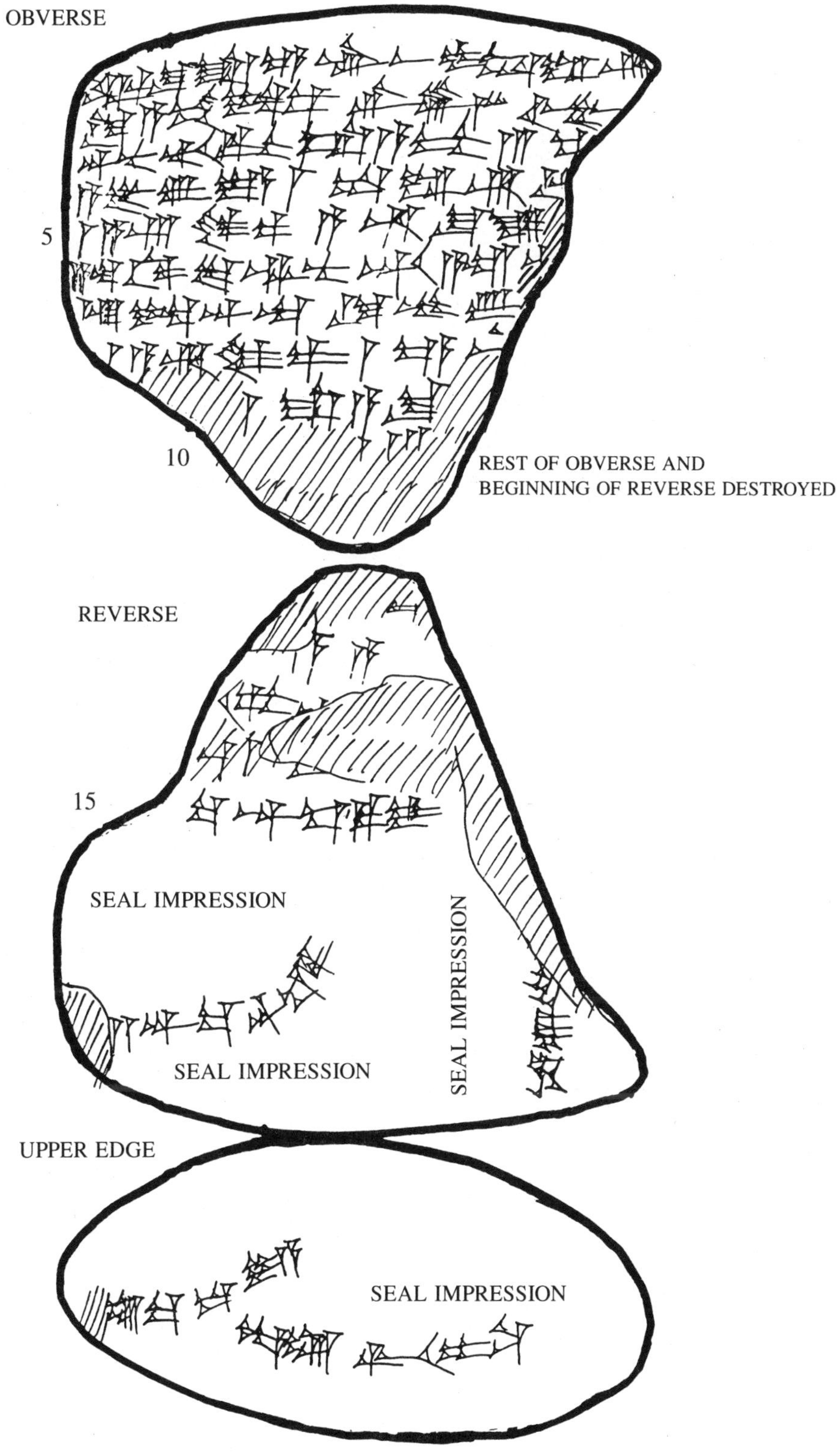
OBVERSE
5
10
REST OF OBVERSE AND
BEGINNING OF REVERSE DESTROYED
REVERSE
15
SEAL IMPRESSION
SEAL IMPRESSION
SEAL IMPRESSION
UPPER EDGE
SEAL IMPRESSION

164

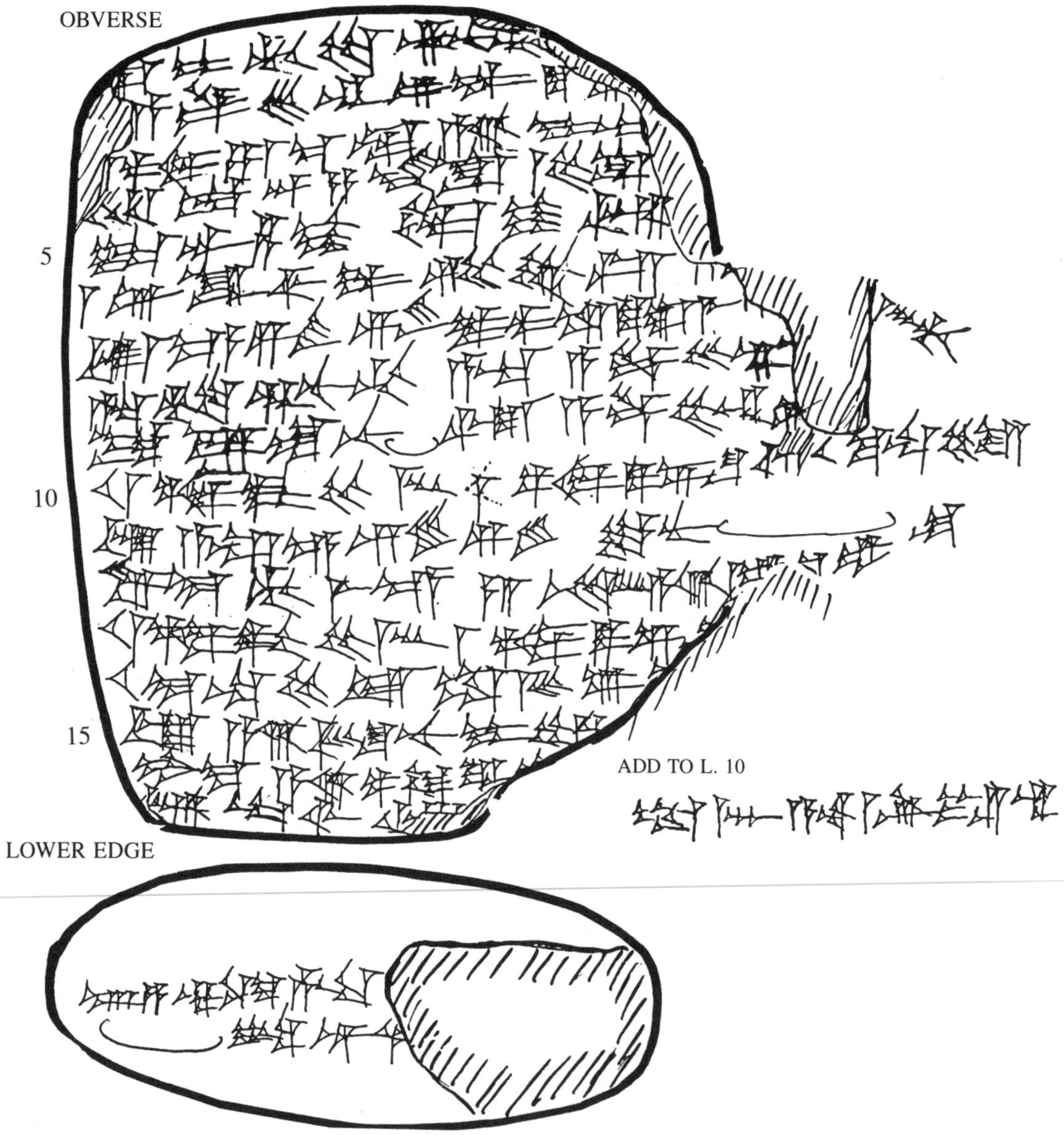
OBVERSE
5
10
15
ADD TO L. 10
LOWER EDGE

164

REVERSE

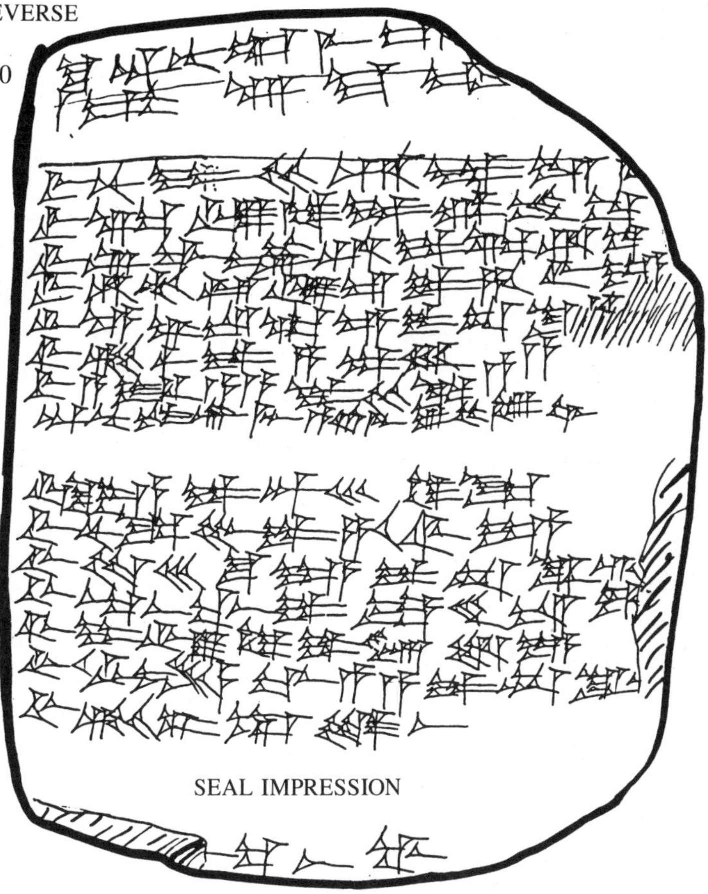

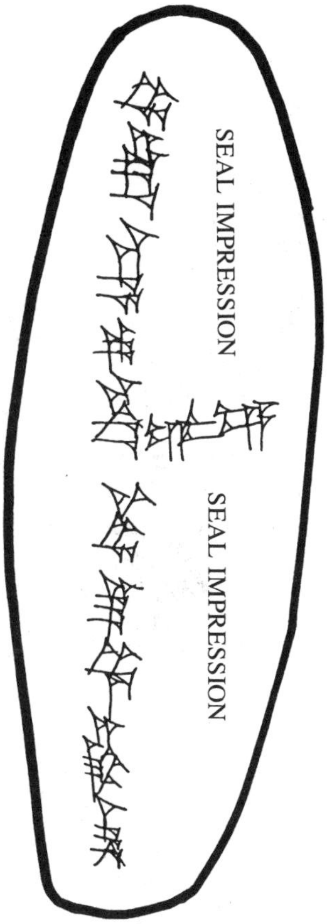

LEFT EDGE

UPPER EDGE

167

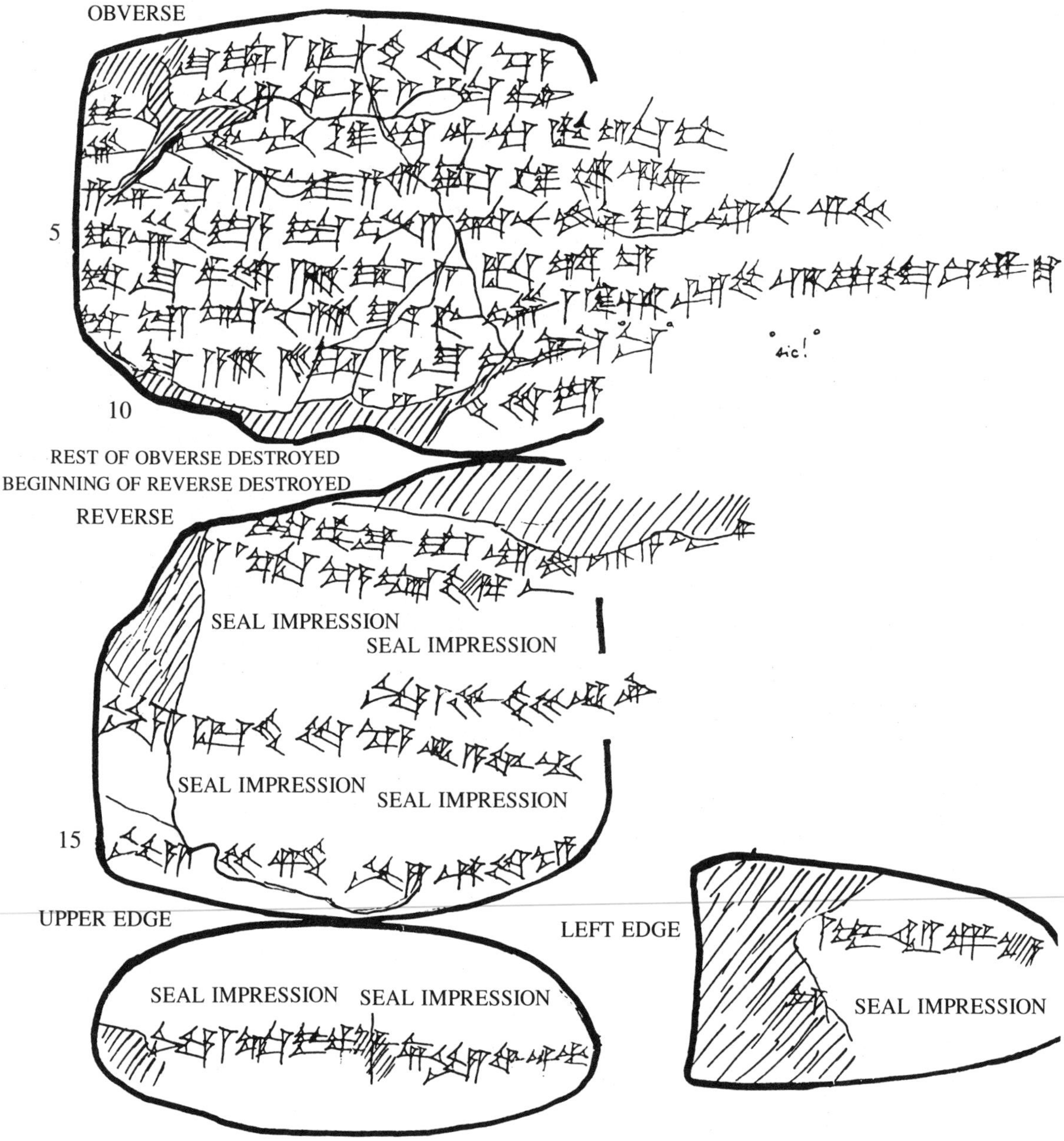
OBVERSE
5
sic!
10
REST OF OBVERSE DESTROYED
BEGINNING OF REVERSE DESTROYED
REVERSE
SEAL IMPRESSION
SEAL IMPRESSION
SEAL IMPRESSION
SEAL IMPRESSION
15
UPPER EDGE
SEAL IMPRESSION
SEAL IMPRESSION
LEFT EDGE
SEAL IMPRESSION

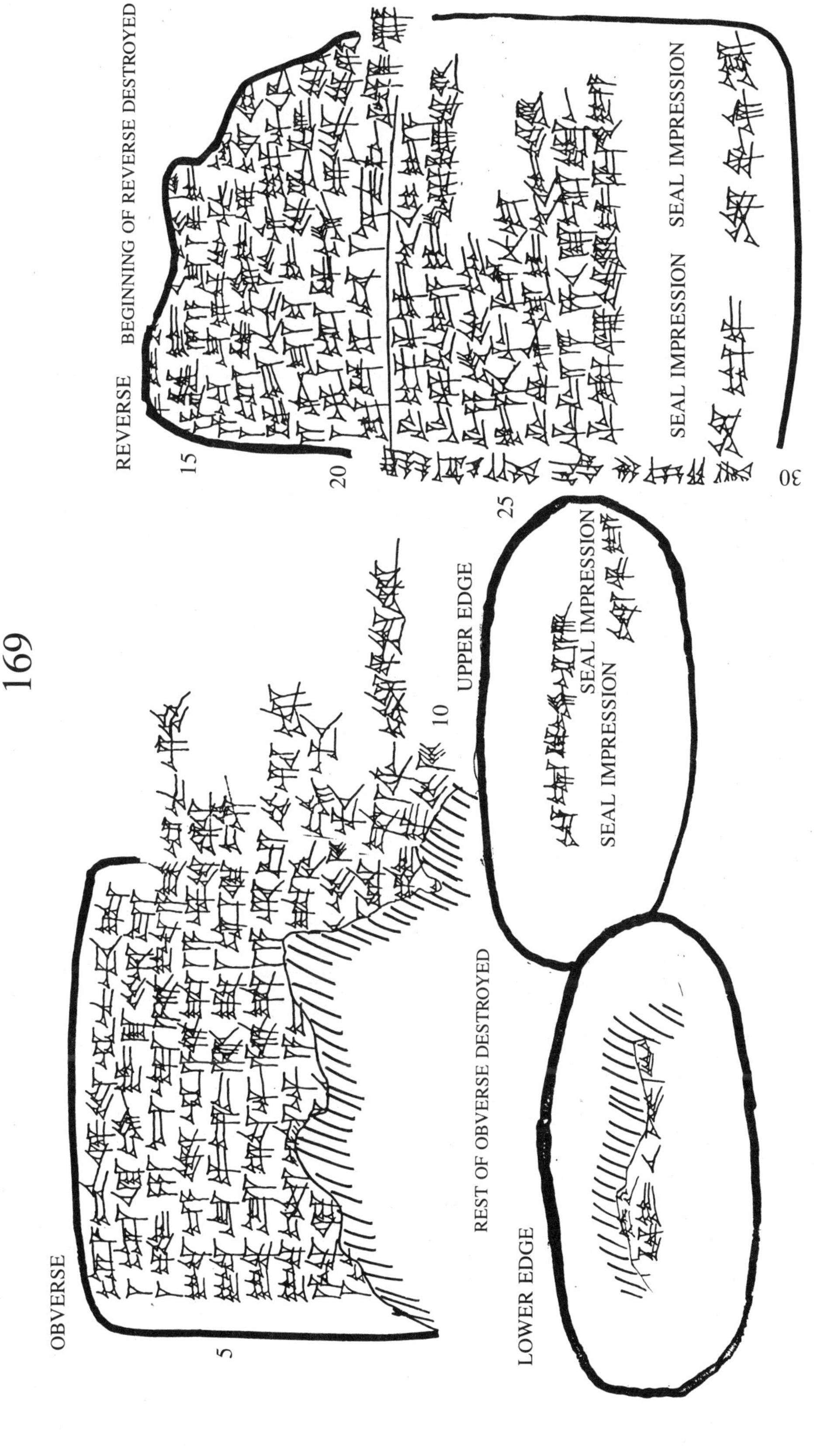
169
OBVERSE
5
10
REST OF OBVERSE DESTROYED
UPPER EDGE
SEAL IMPRESSION
SEAL IMPRESSION
LOWER EDGE
REVERSE
BEGINNING OF REVERSE DESTROYED
15
20
25
30
SEAL IMPRESSION
SEAL IMPRESSION
SEAL IMPRESSION

173

OBVERSE

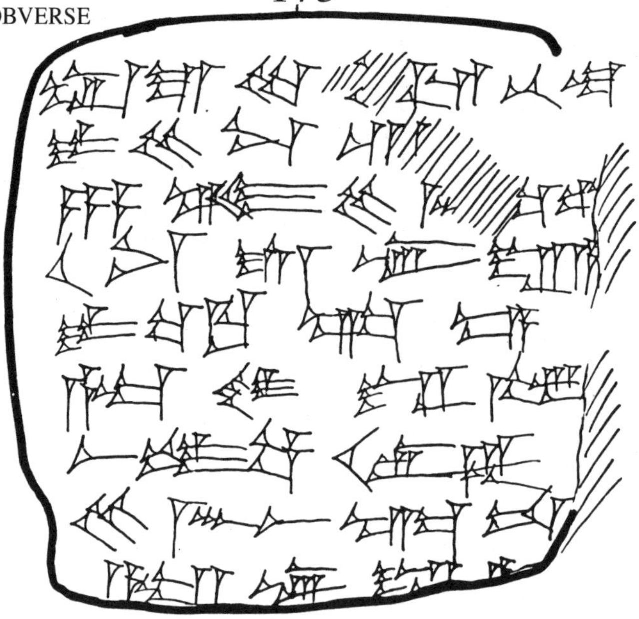

BEGINNING OF REVERSE DESTROYED

REVERSE

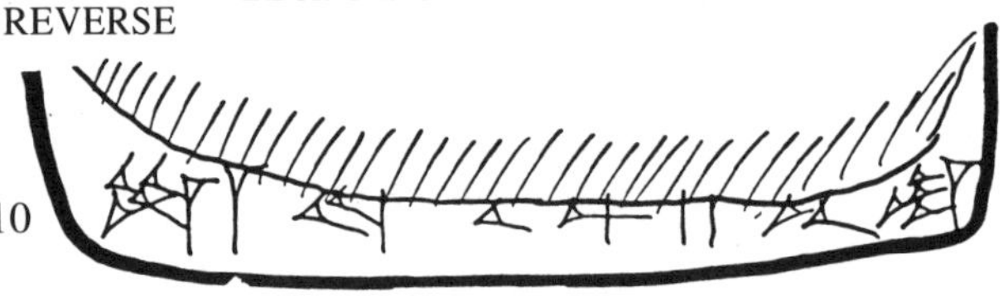

174

BEGINNING OF OBVERSE DESTROYED

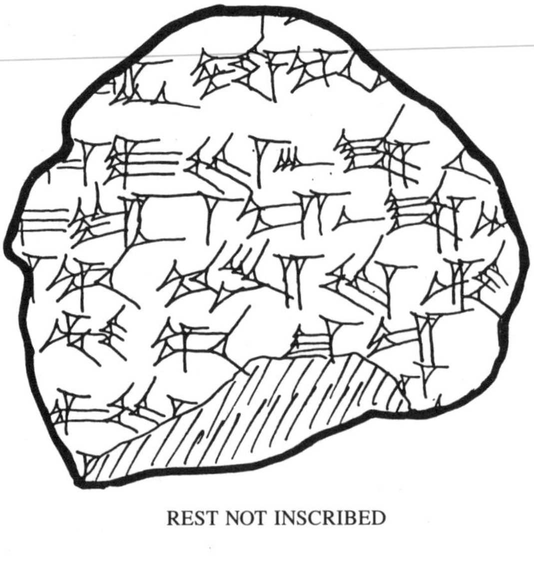

REST NOT INSCRIBED

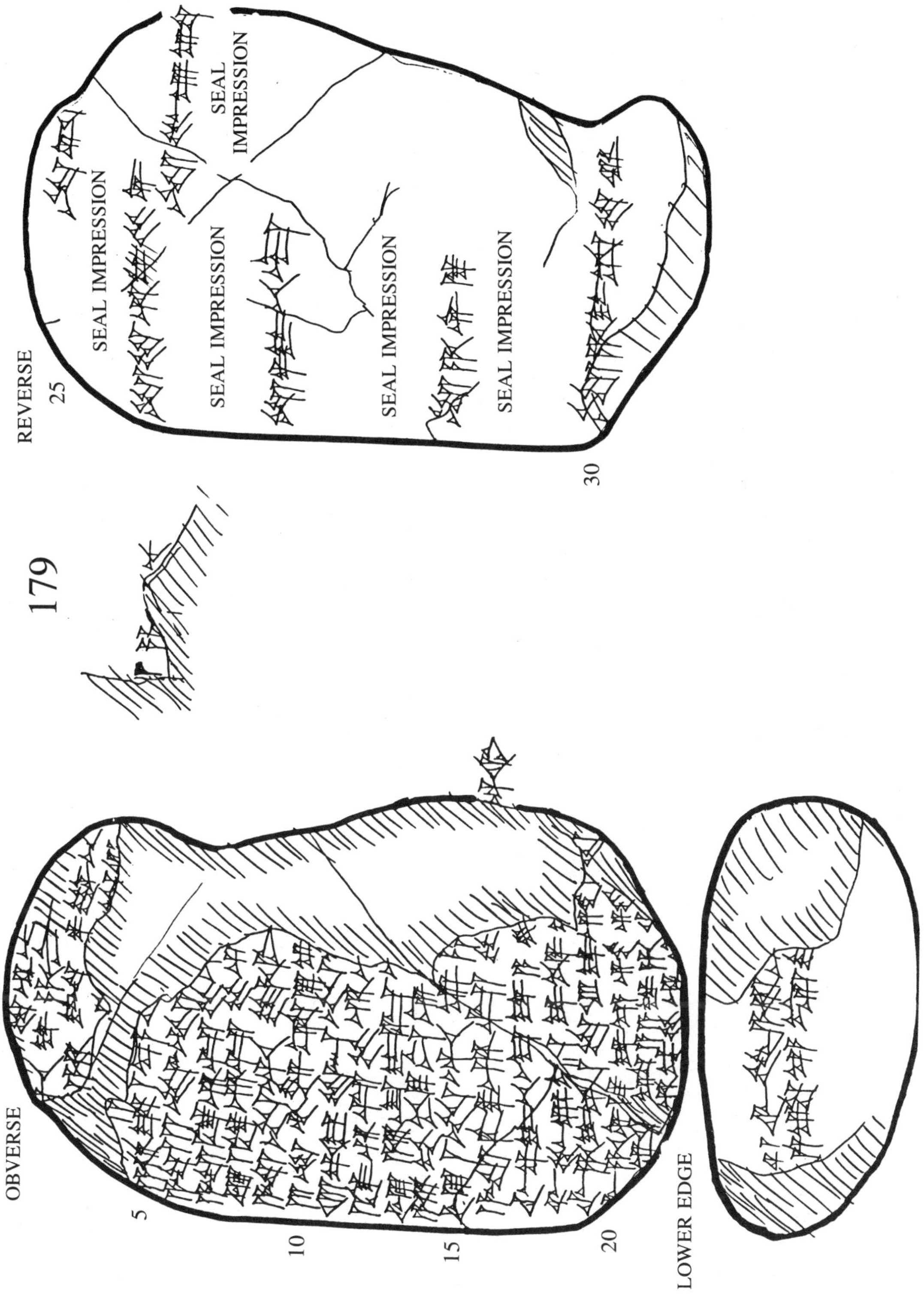
179
REVERSE
25
SEAL IMPRESSION
SEAL IMPRESSION
SEAL IMPRESSION
SEAL IMPRESSION
SEAL IMPRESSION
30
OBVERSE
5
10
15
20
LOWER EDGE

180

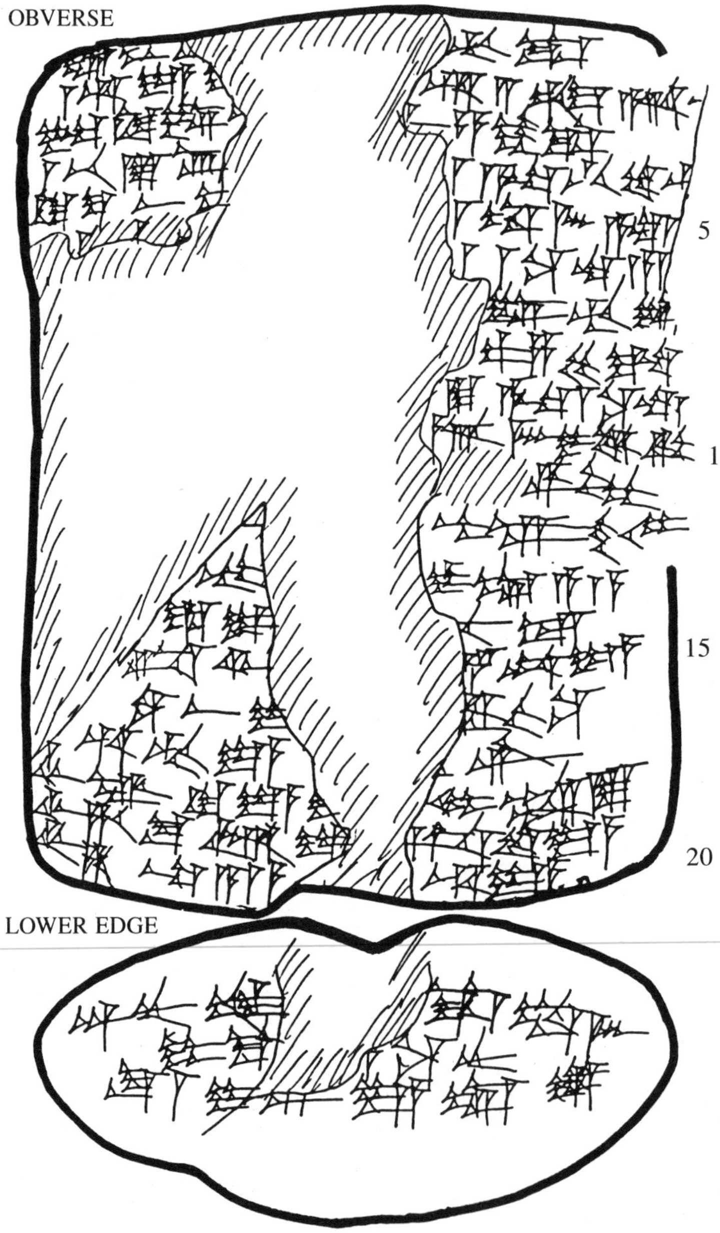

180

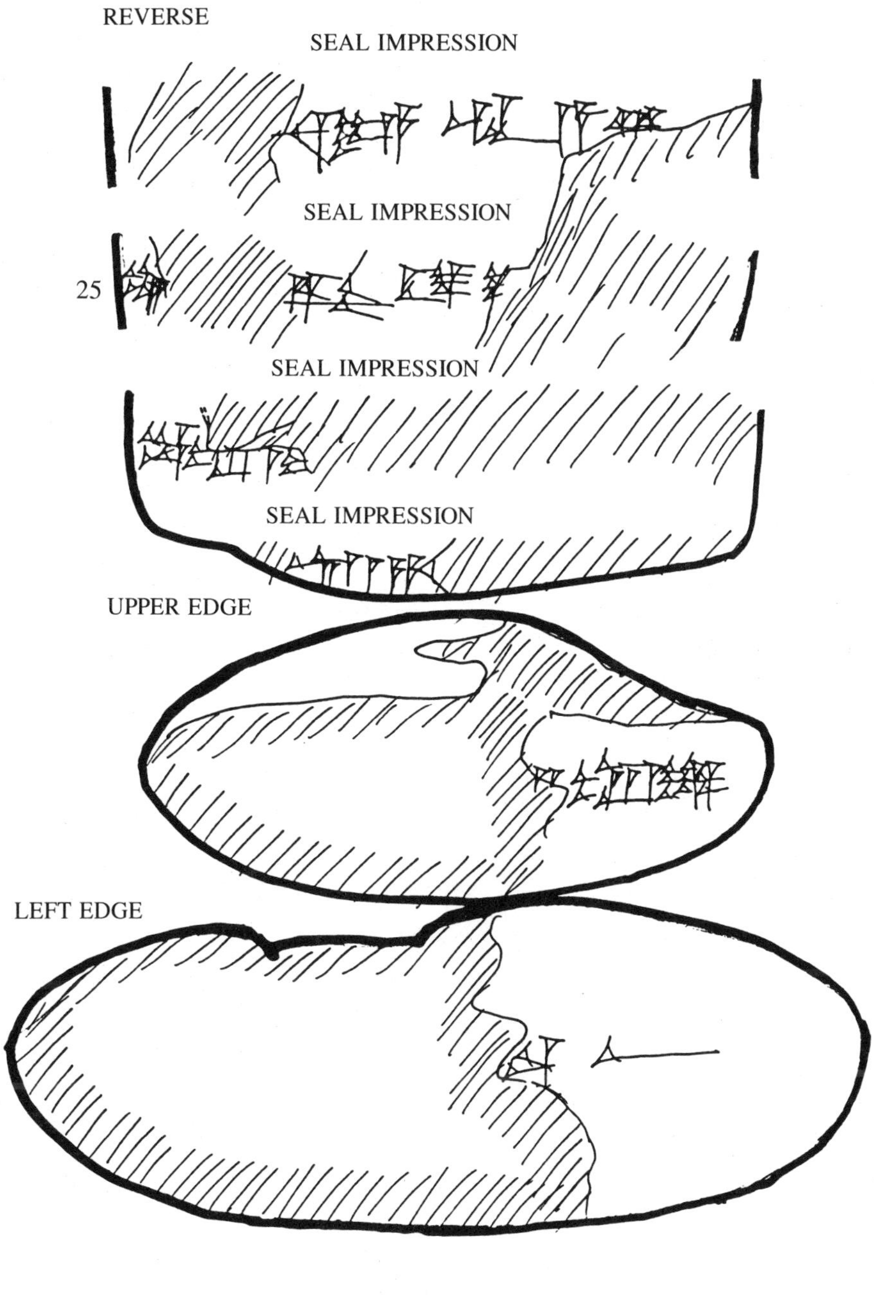
REVERSE
SEAL IMPRESSION
SEAL IMPRESSION
25
SEAL IMPRESSION
SEAL IMPRESSION
UPPER EDGE
LEFT EDGE

182

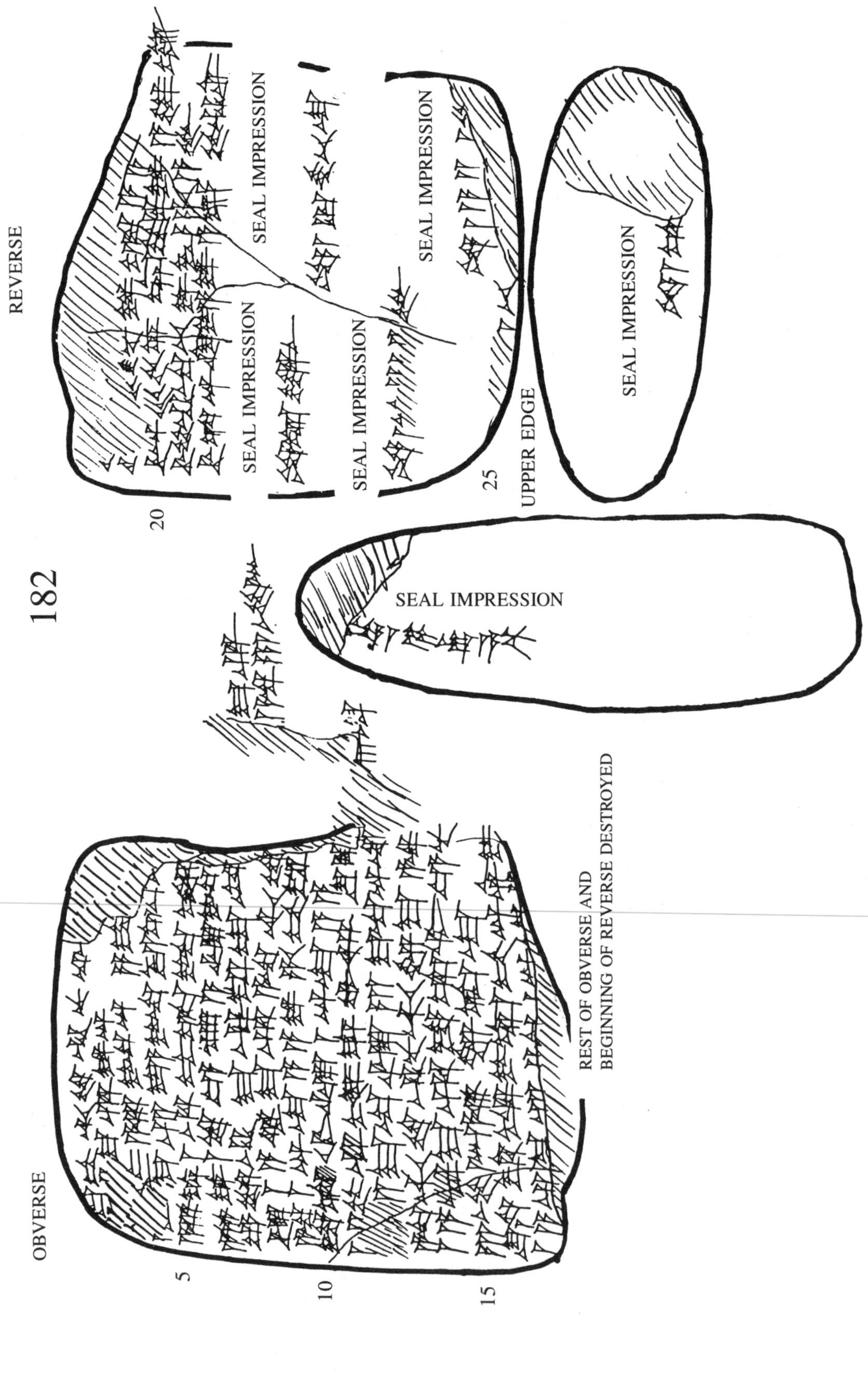
OBVERSE
REVERSE
SEAL IMPRESSION
SEAL IMPRESSION
SEAL IMPRESSION
SEAL IMPRESSION
SEAL IMPRESSION
SEAL IMPRESSION
UPPER EDGE
REST OF OBVERSE AND BEGINNING OF REVERSE DESTROYED
5
10
15
20
25

190

OBVERSE

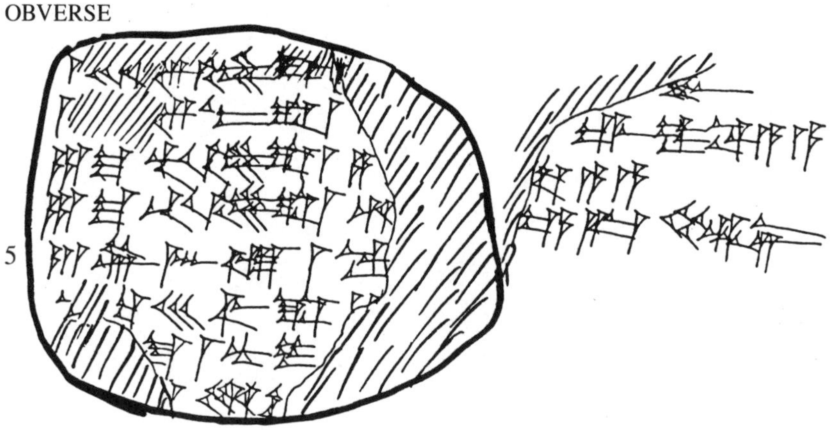

REVERSE

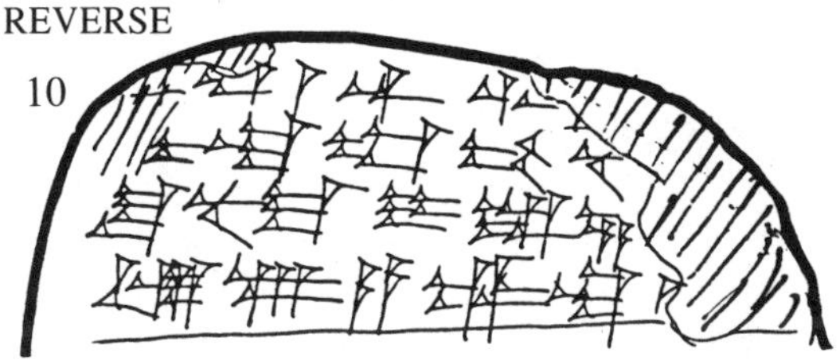

REST NOT INSCRIBED

202

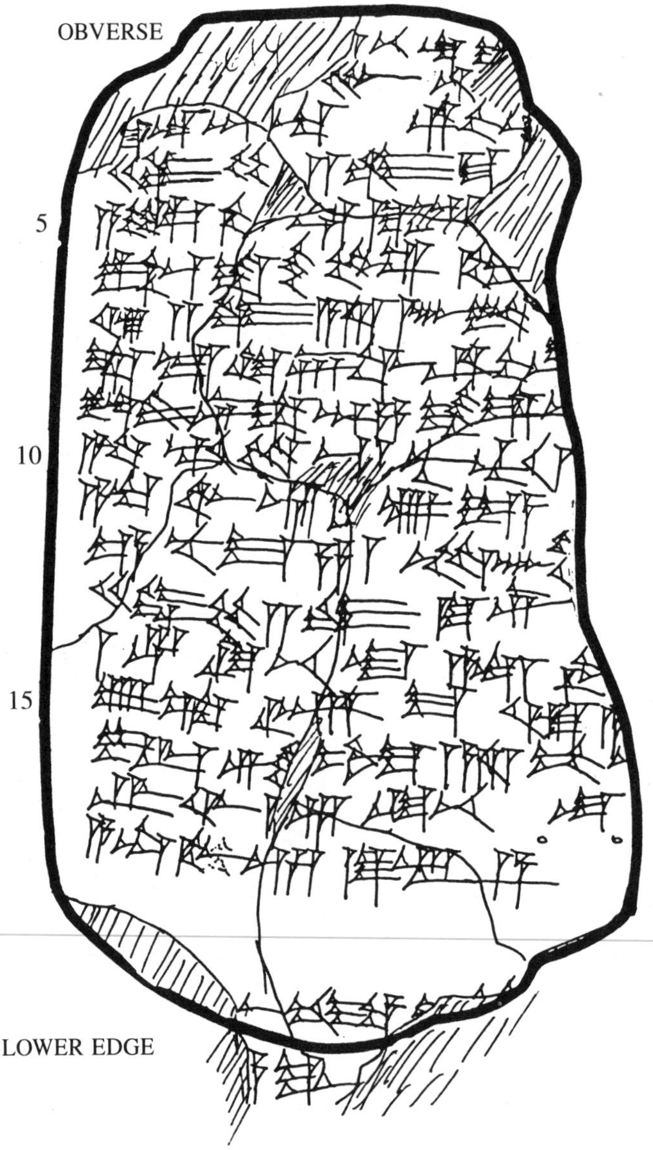

202

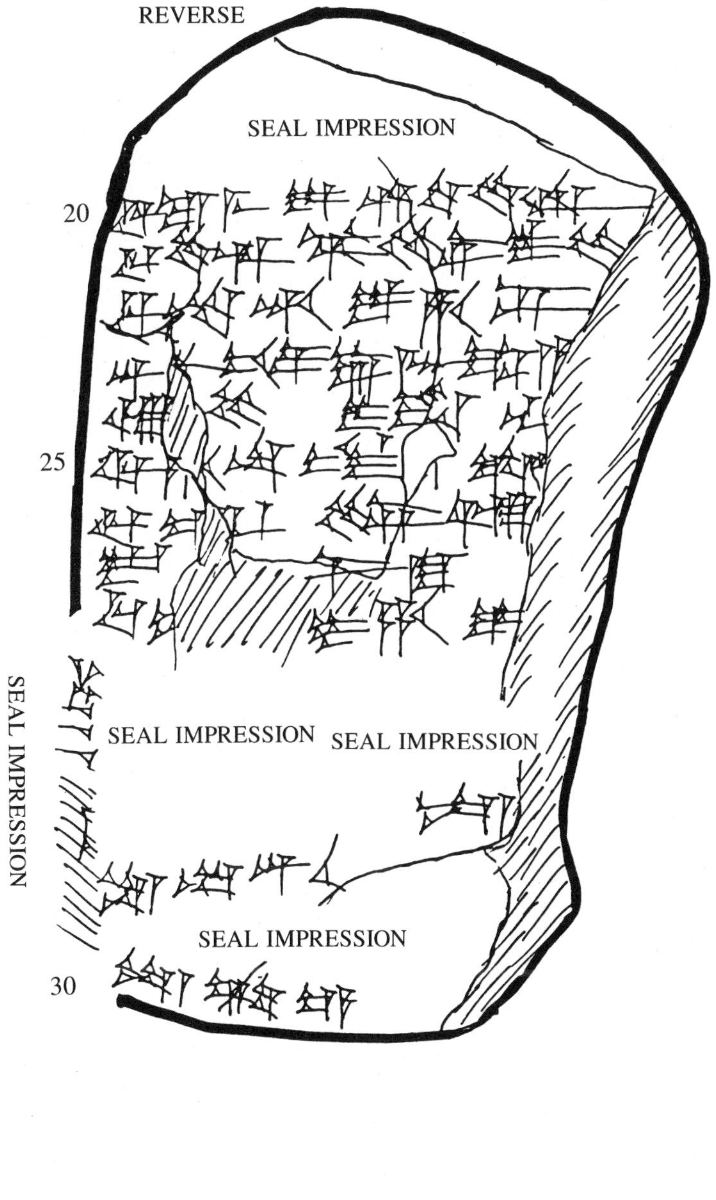
REVERSE
SEAL IMPRESSION
20
25
SEAL IMPRESSION
SEAL IMPRESSION
SEAL IMPRESSION
SEAL IMPRESSION
30

205

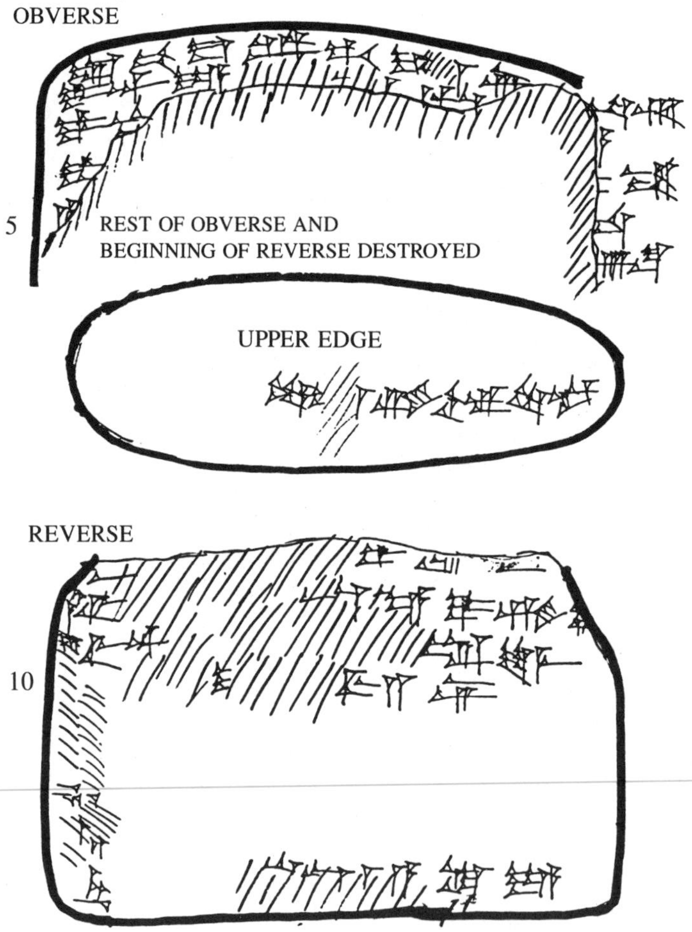
OBVERSE
REST OF OBVERSE AND
BEGINNING OF REVERSE DESTROYED
UPPER EDGE
REVERSE

208

OBVERSE

BEGINNING OF OBVERSE DESTROYED

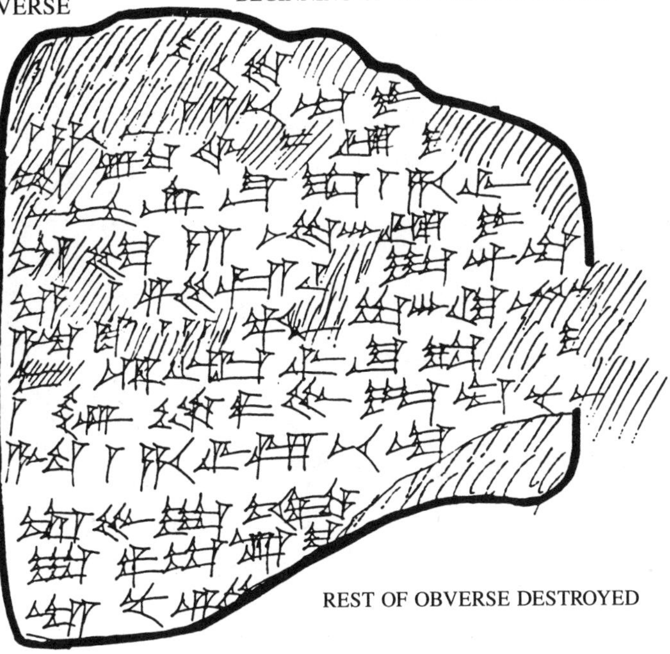

REST OF OBVERSE DESTROYED

REVERSE

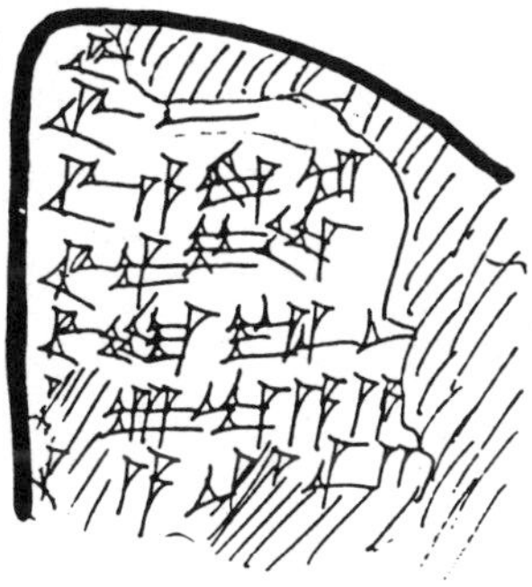

REST DESTROYED

210

OBVERSE

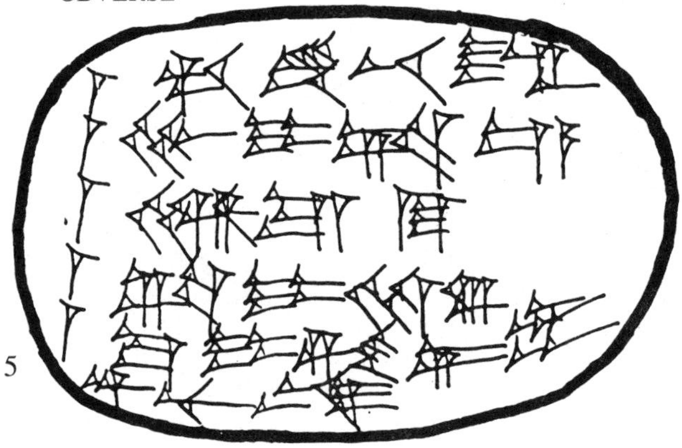

REVERSE

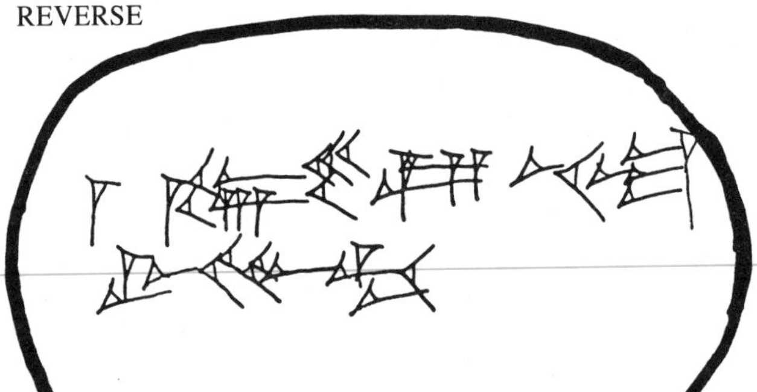

211

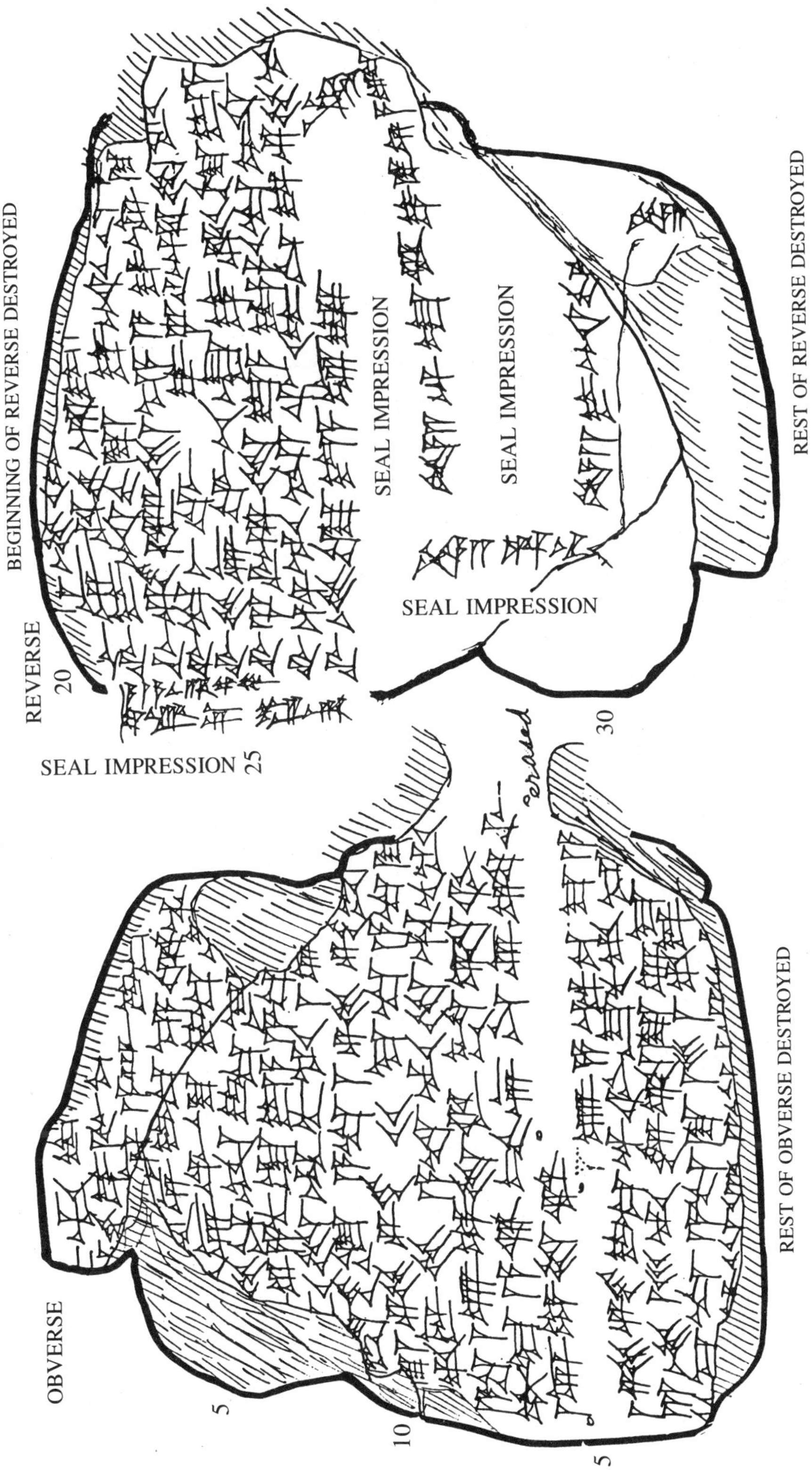
BEGINNING OF REVERSE DESTROYED
REVERSE
SEAL IMPRESSION
SEAL IMPRESSION
SEAL IMPRESSION
SEAL IMPRESSION
REST OF REVERSE DESTROYED
erased
OBVERSE
REST OF OBVERSE DESTROYED

215

OBVERSE

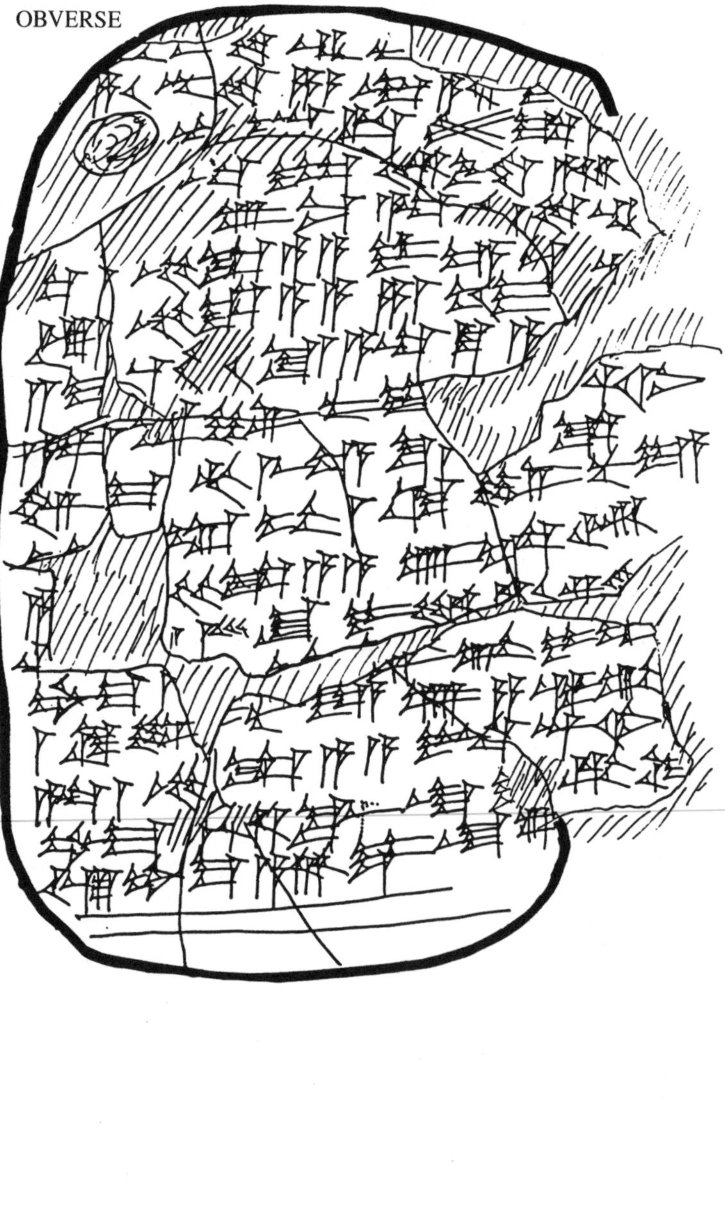

215

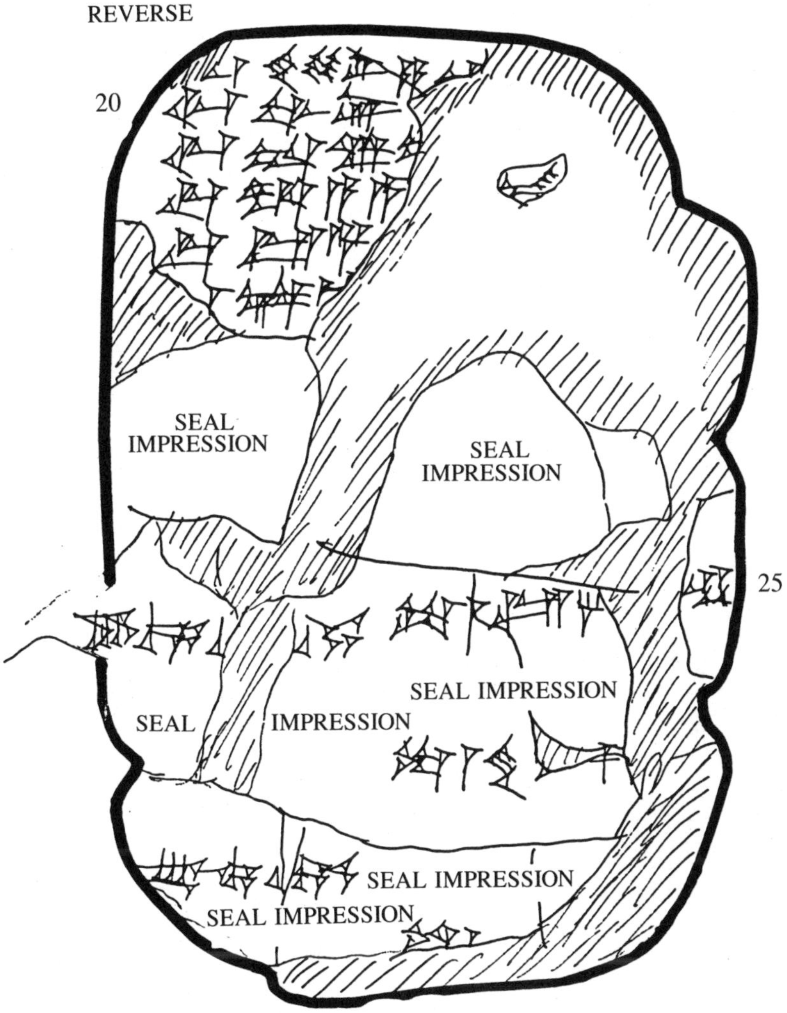
REVERSE
20
SEAL IMPRESSION
SEAL IMPRESSION
25
SEAL IMPRESSION
SEAL
IMPRESSION
SEAL IMPRESSION
SEAL IMPRESSION

216

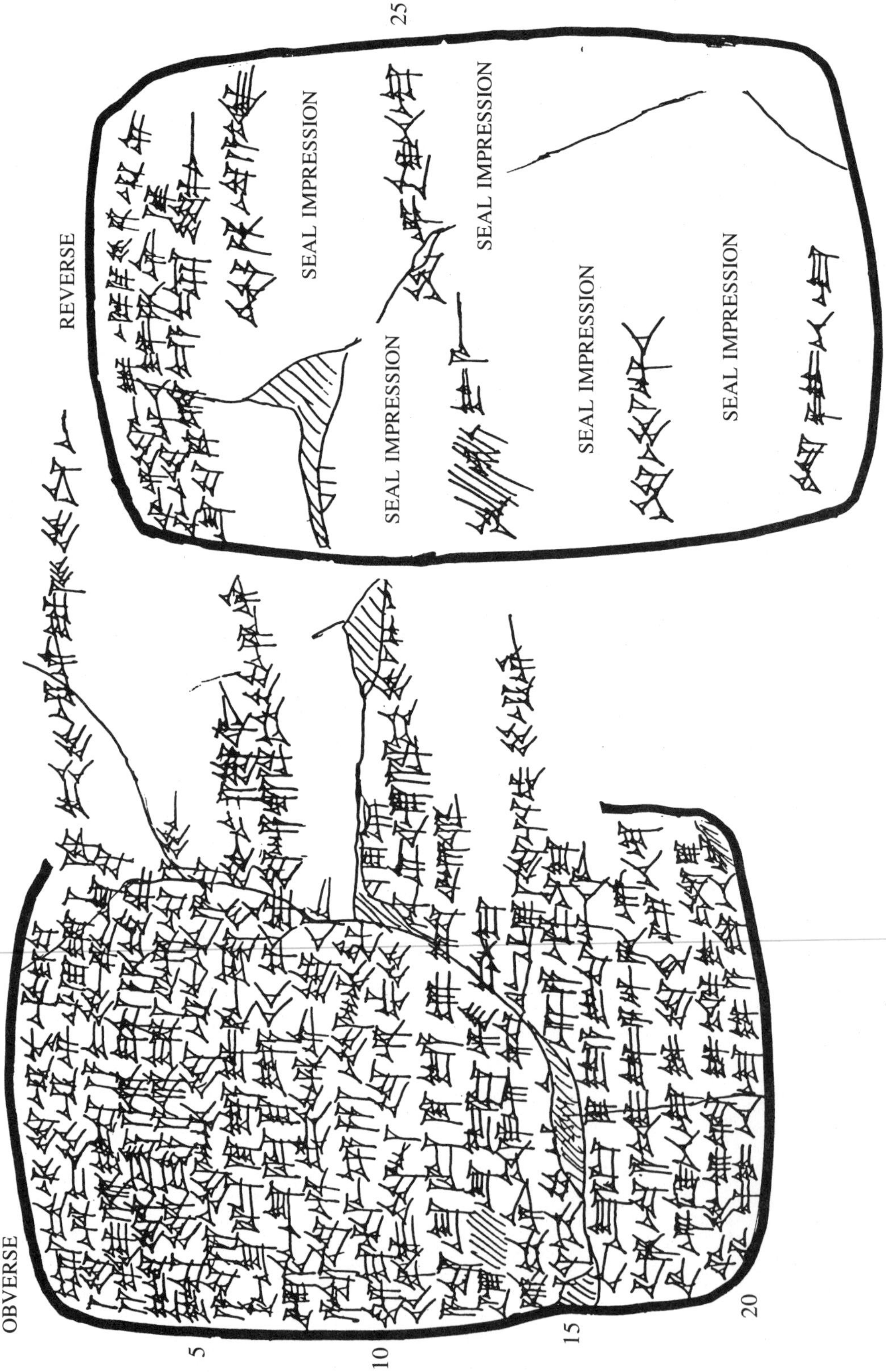
OBVERSE
5
10
15
20
REVERSE
25
SEAL IMPRESSION
SEAL IMPRESSION
SEAL IMPRESSION
SEAL IMPRESSION
SEAL IMPRESSION

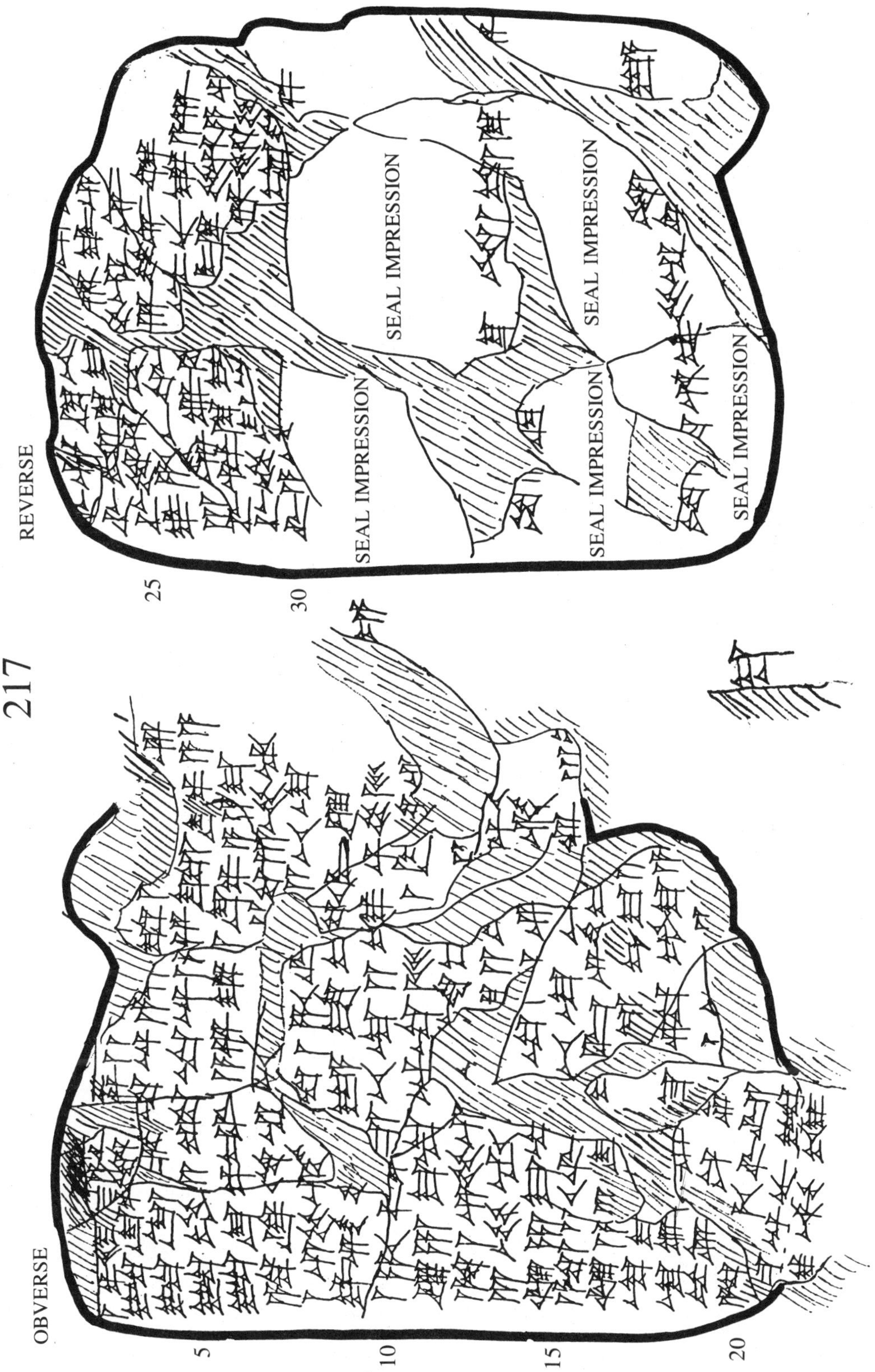
217
OBVERSE
REVERSE
SEAL IMPRESSION
SEAL IMPRESSION
SEAL IMPRESSION
SEAL IMPRESSION
SEAL IMPRESSION

218

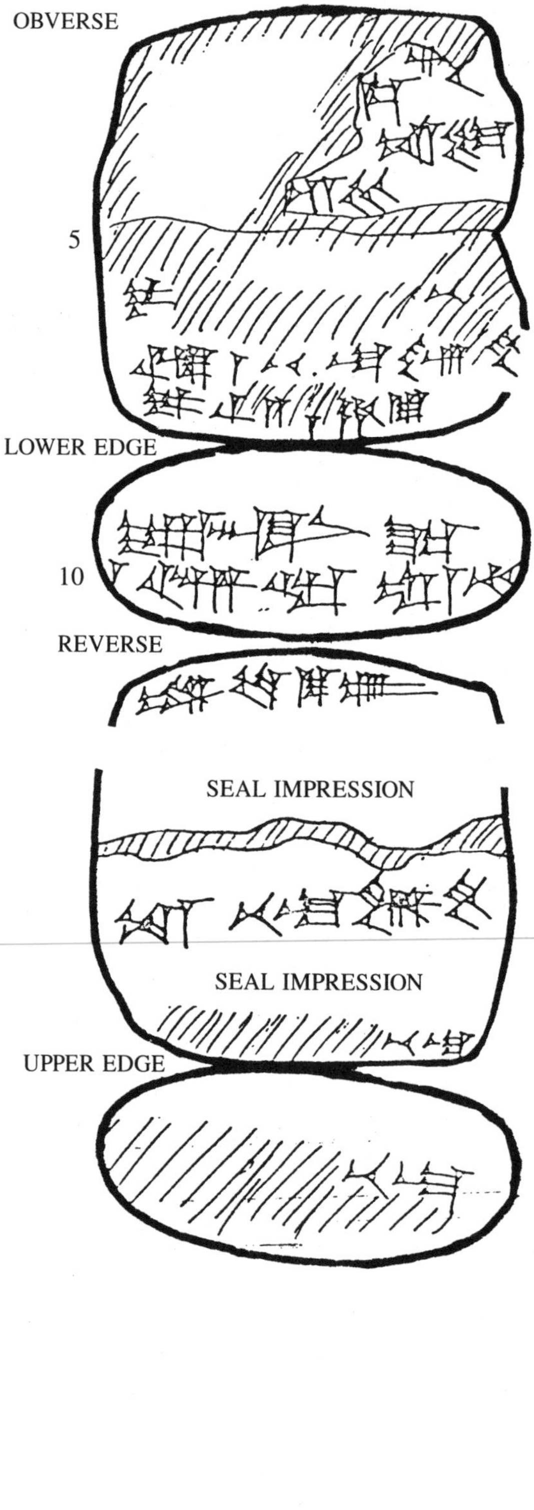
OBVERSE
5
LOWER EDGE
10
REVERSE
SEAL IMPRESSION
SEAL IMPRESSION
UPPER EDGE

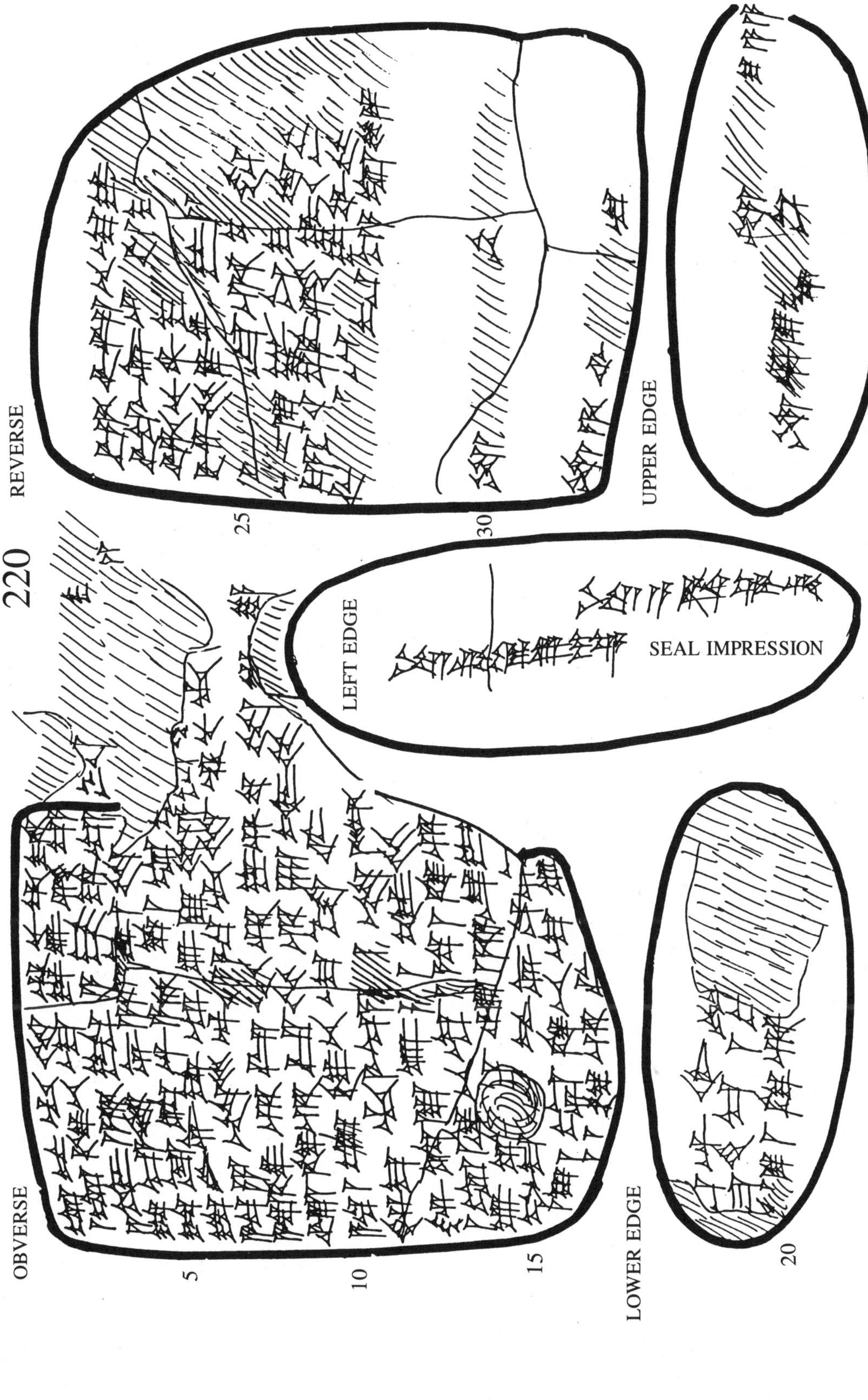
220
OBVERSE
REVERSE
LEFT EDGE
SEAL IMPRESSION
UPPER EDGE
LOWER EDGE

221

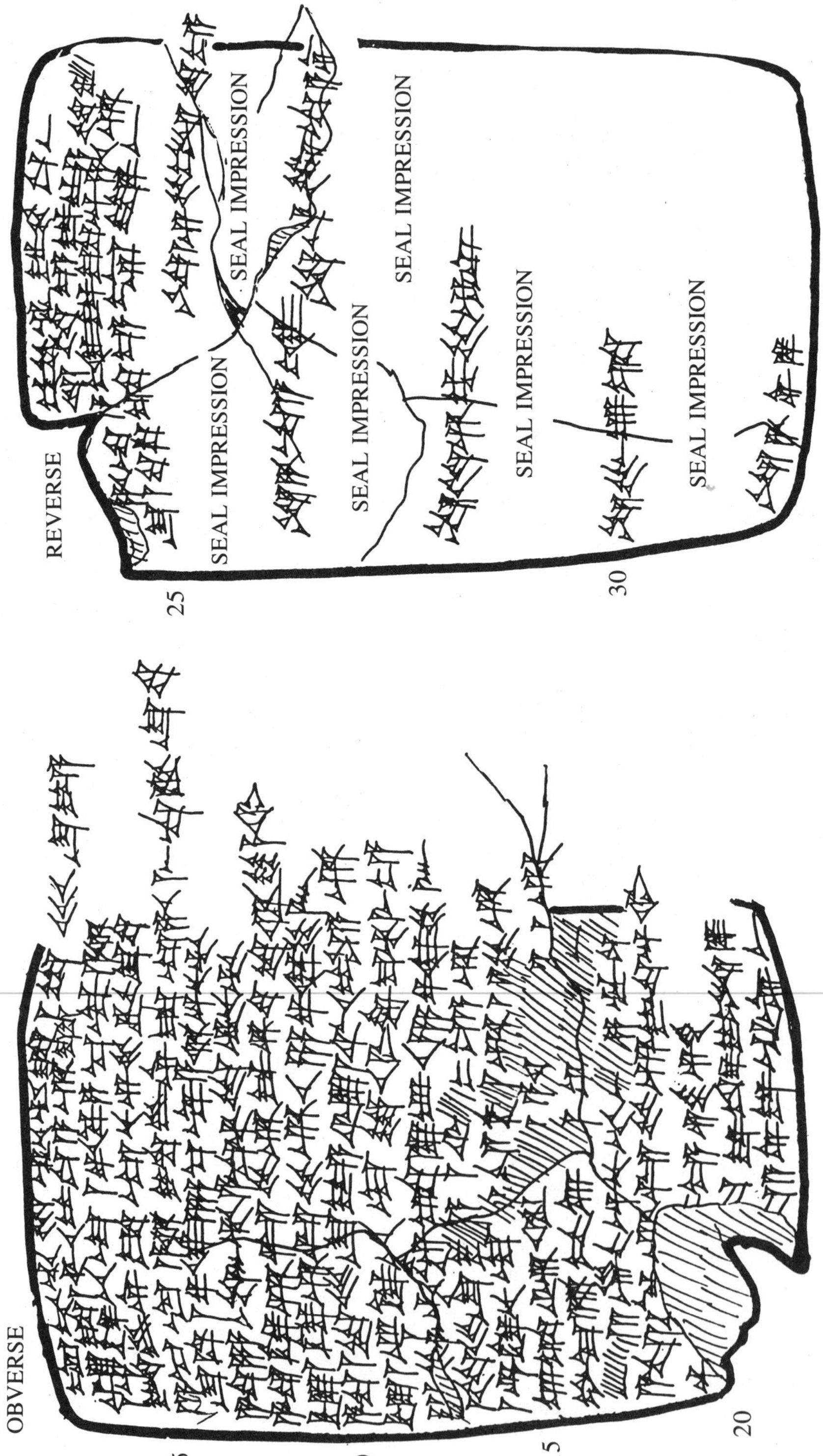
OBVERSE
REVERSE
SEAL IMPRESSION
SEAL IMPRESSION
SEAL IMPRESSION
SEAL IMPRESSION
SEAL IMPRESSION
SEAL IMPRESSION

222

OBVERSE

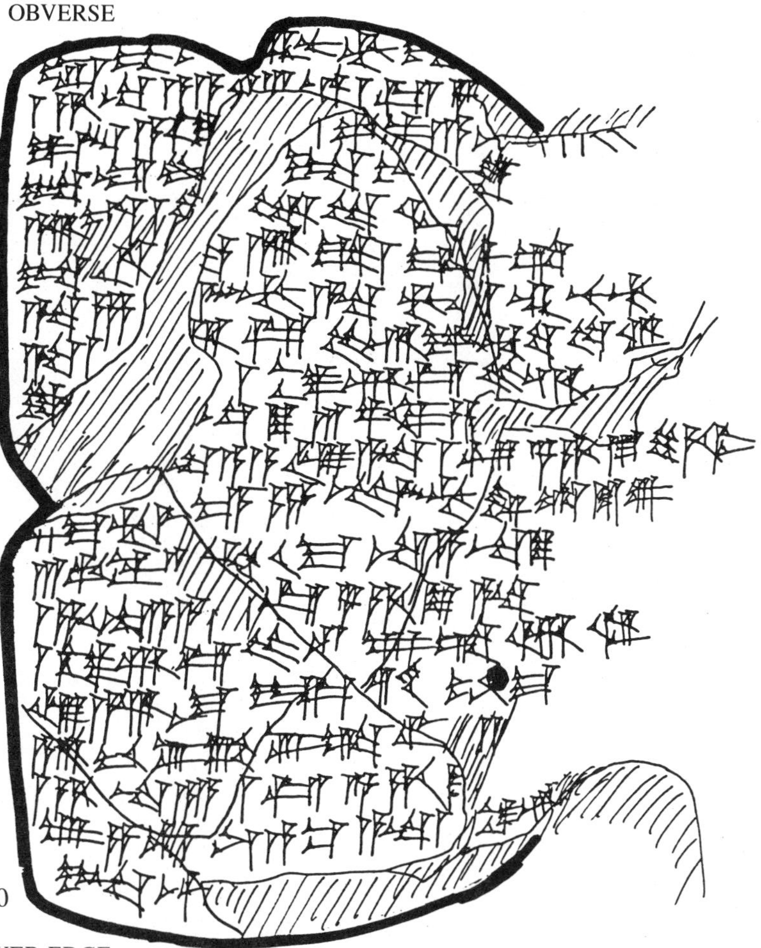

LOWER EDGE

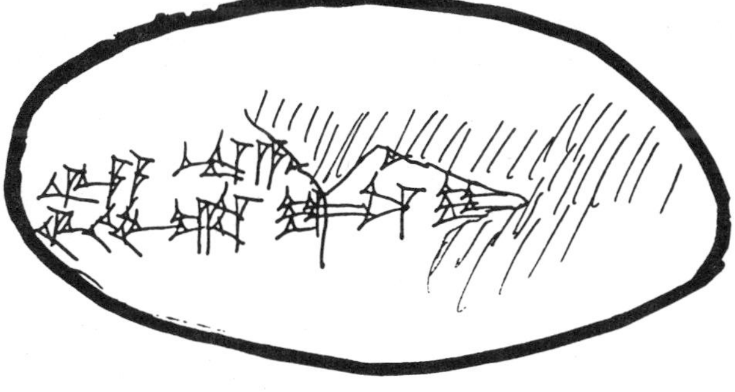

222

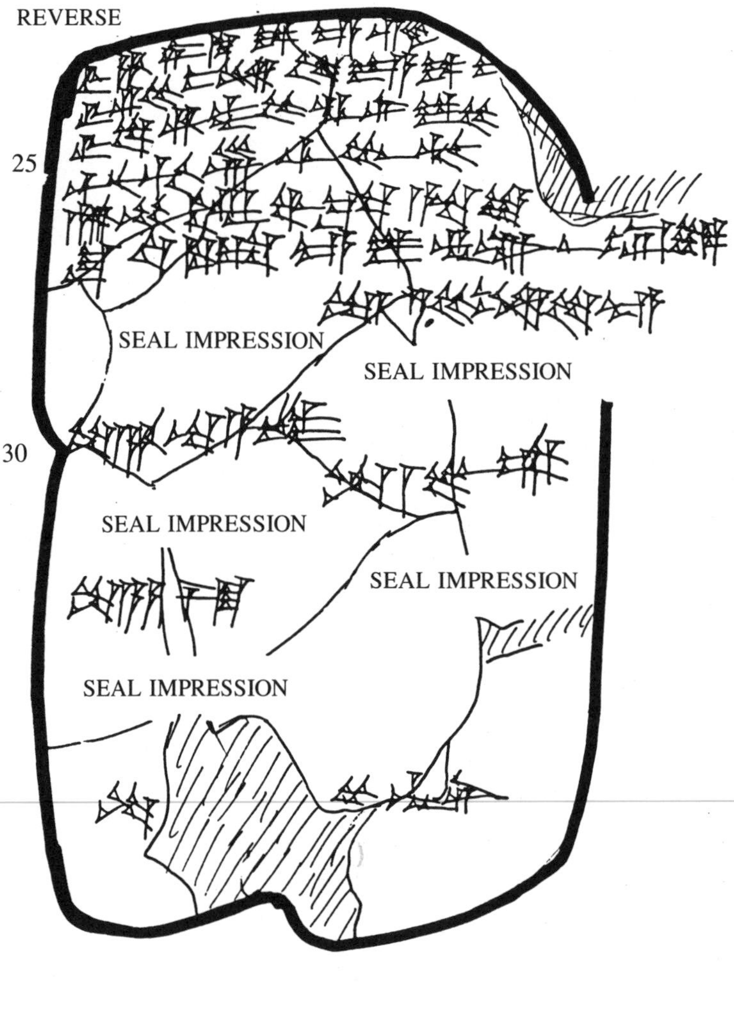
REVERSE
SEAL IMPRESSION
SEAL IMPRESSION
SEAL IMPRESSION
SEAL IMPRESSION
SEAL IMPRESSION

223

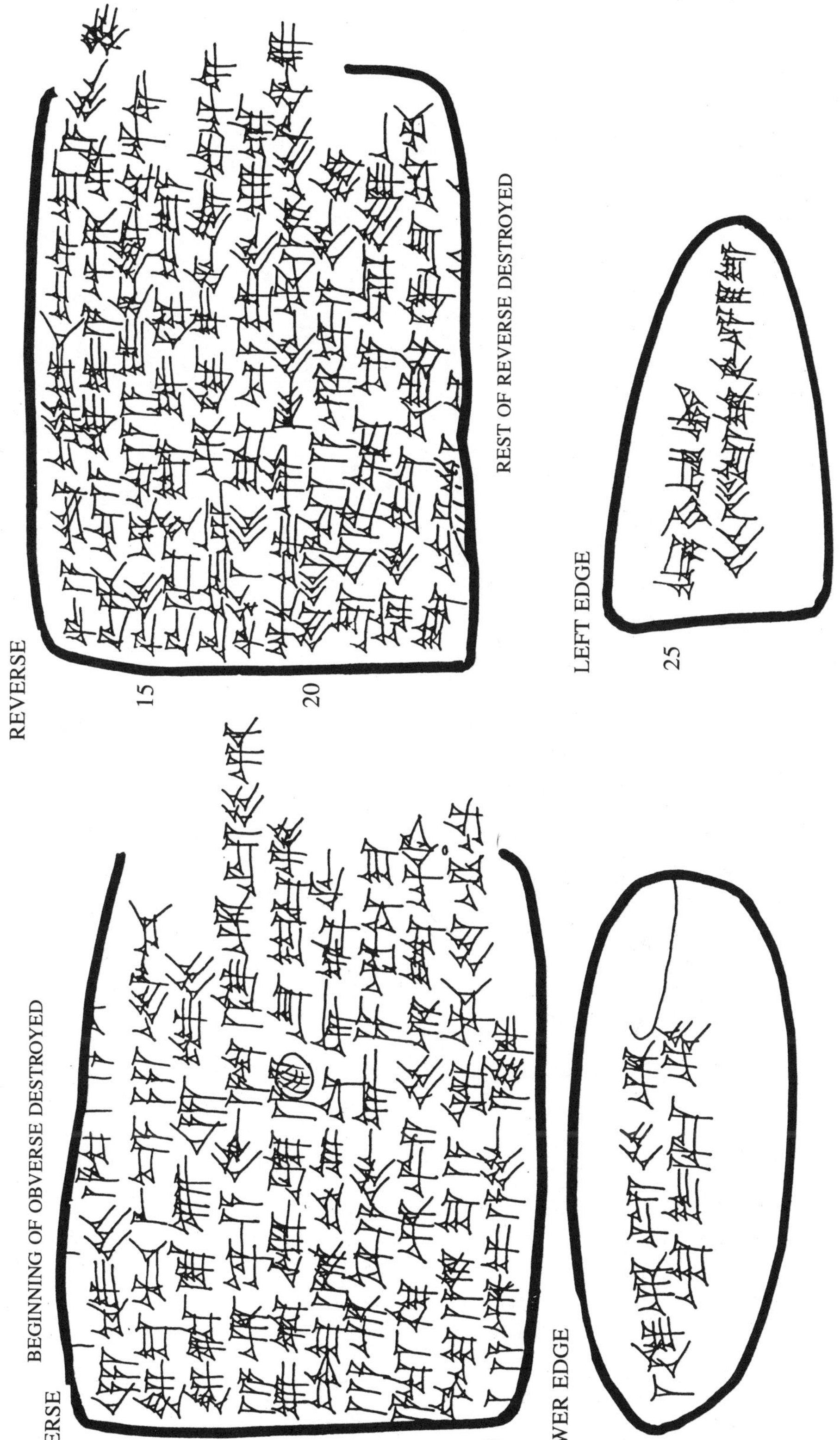
OBVERSE
BEGINNING OF OBVERSE DESTROYED
5
10
LOWER EDGE
REVERSE
15
20
REST OF REVERSE DESTROYED
LEFT EDGE
25

227

OBVERSE

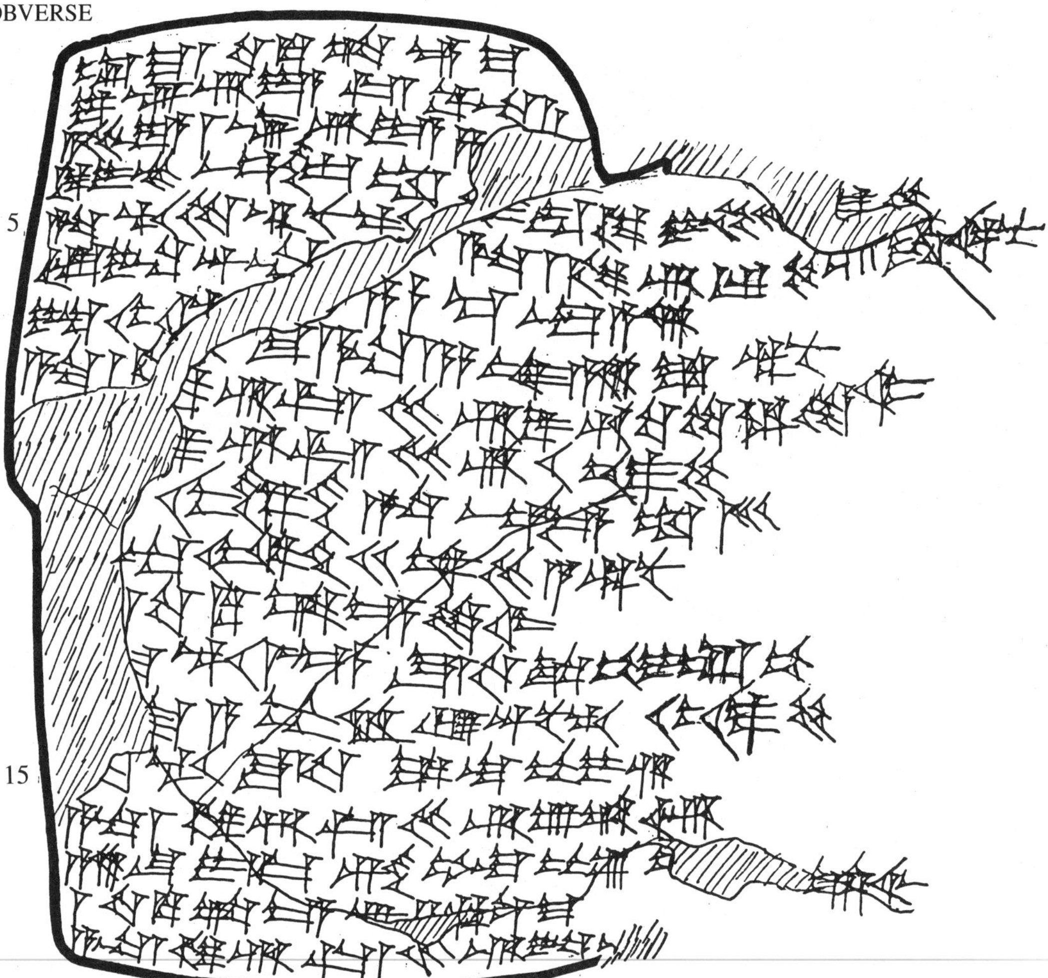

LOWER EDGE

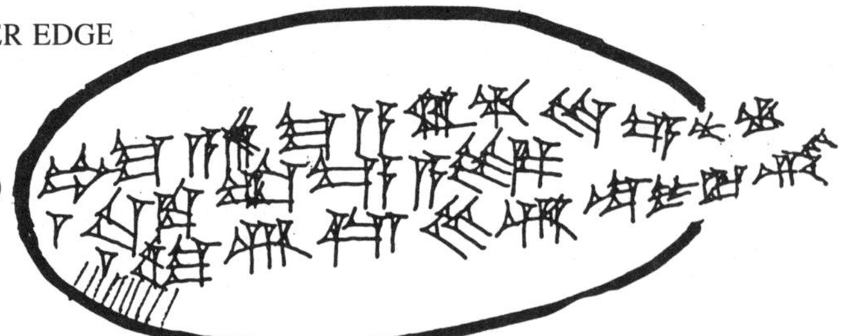

227

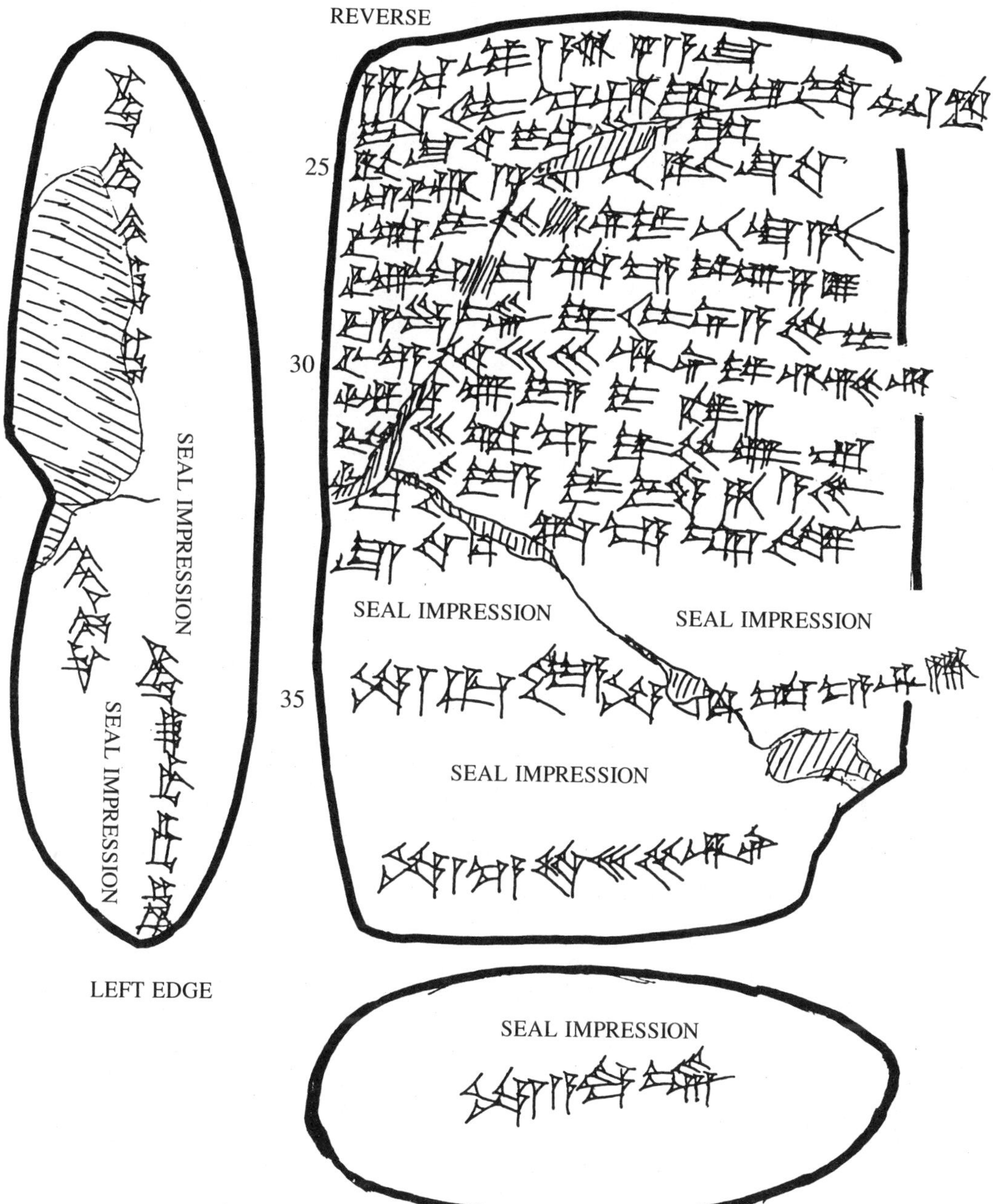
REVERSE
SEAL IMPRESSION
SEAL IMPRESSION
SEAL IMPRESSION
SEAL IMPRESSION
SEAL IMPRESSION
LEFT EDGE
SEAL IMPRESSION

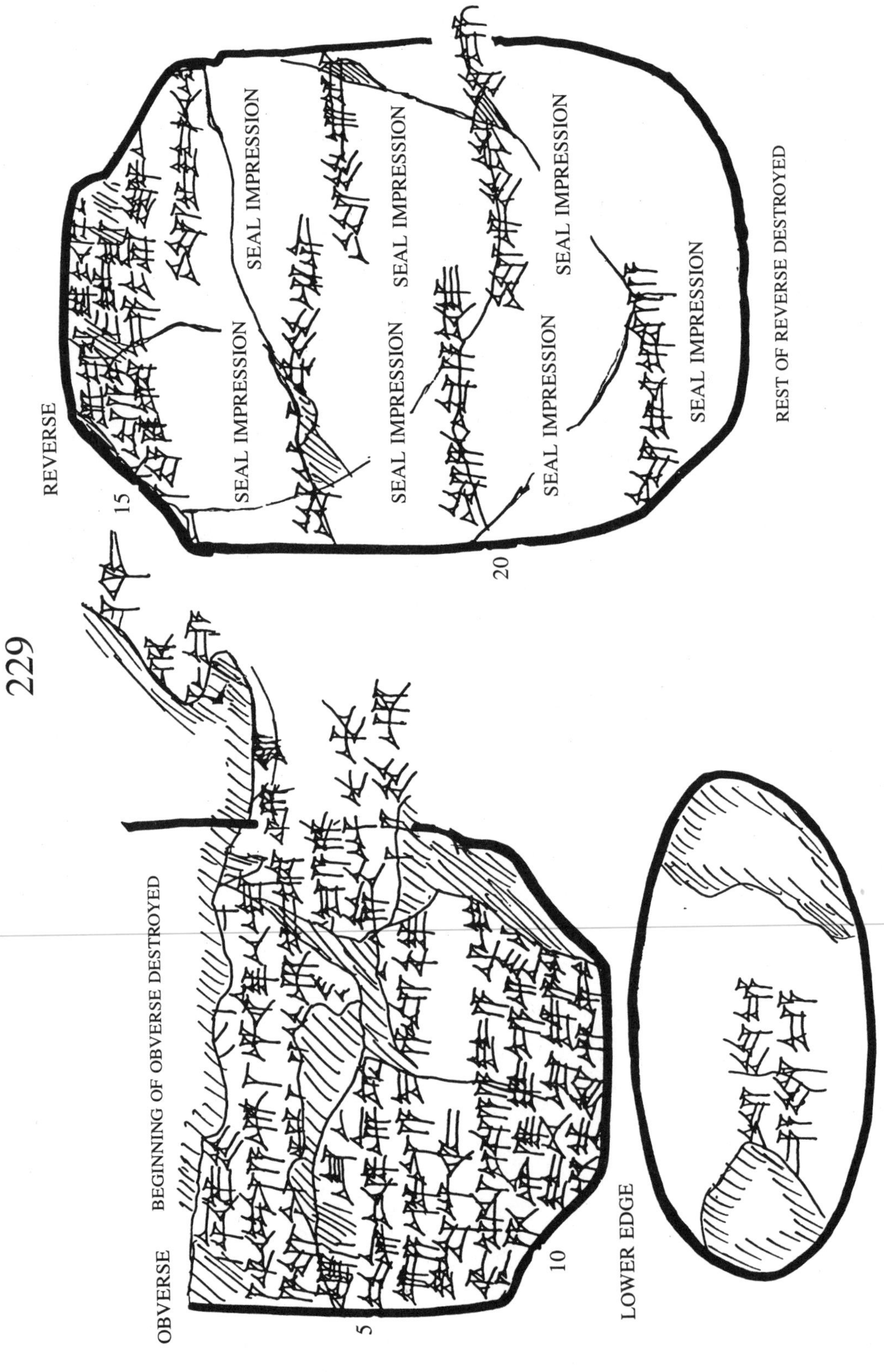
229
OBVERSE
BEGINNING OF OBVERSE DESTROYED
LOWER EDGE
REVERSE
SEAL IMPRESSION
SEAL IMPRESSION
SEAL IMPRESSION
SEAL IMPRESSION
SEAL IMPRESSION
SEAL IMPRESSION
SEAL IMPRESSION
REST OF REVERSE DESTROYED

230

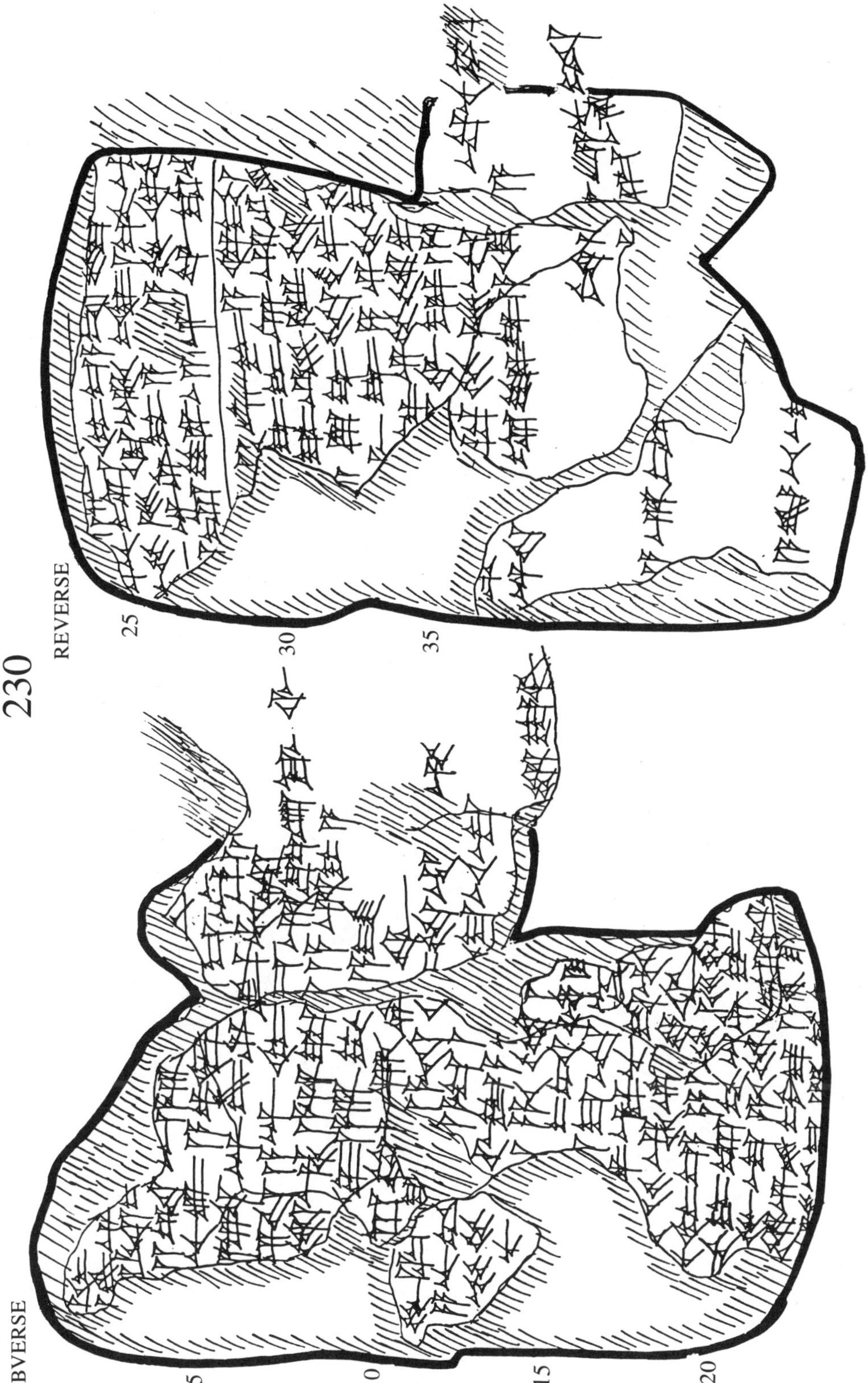

231

OBVERSE

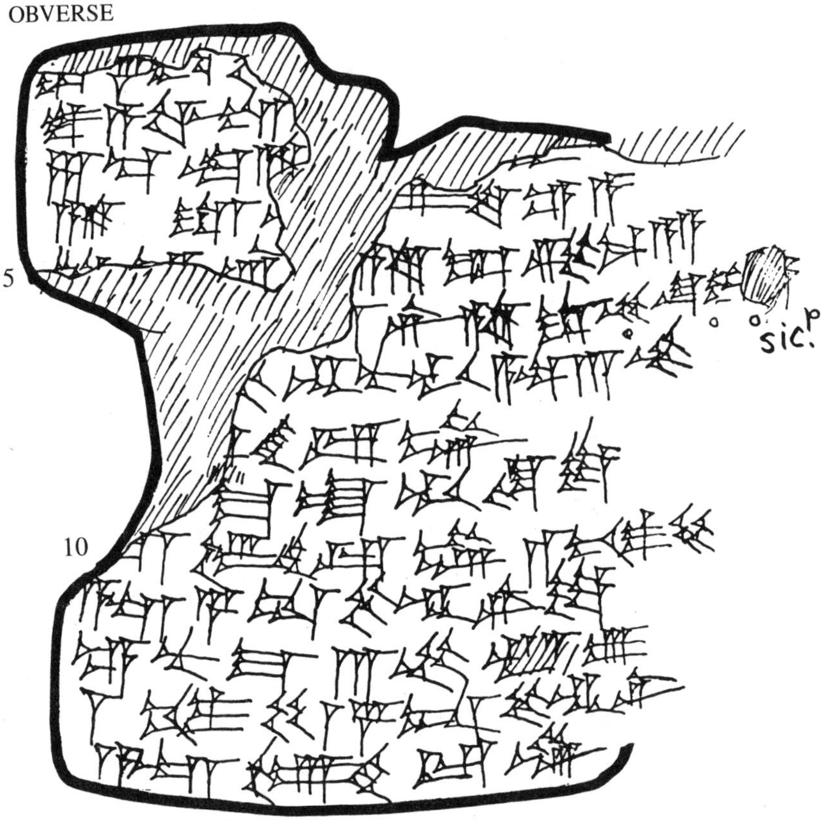

LOWER EDGE

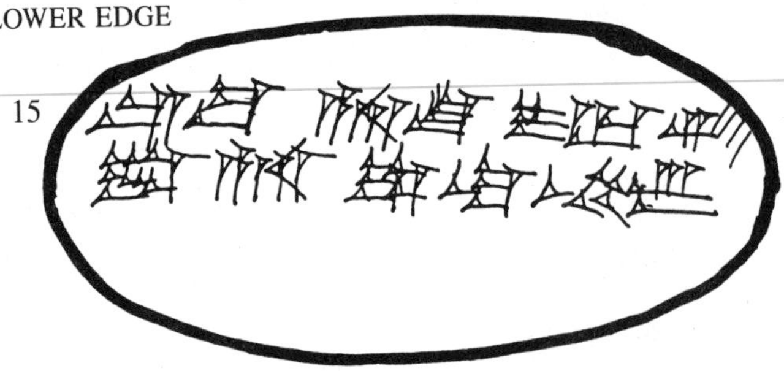

231

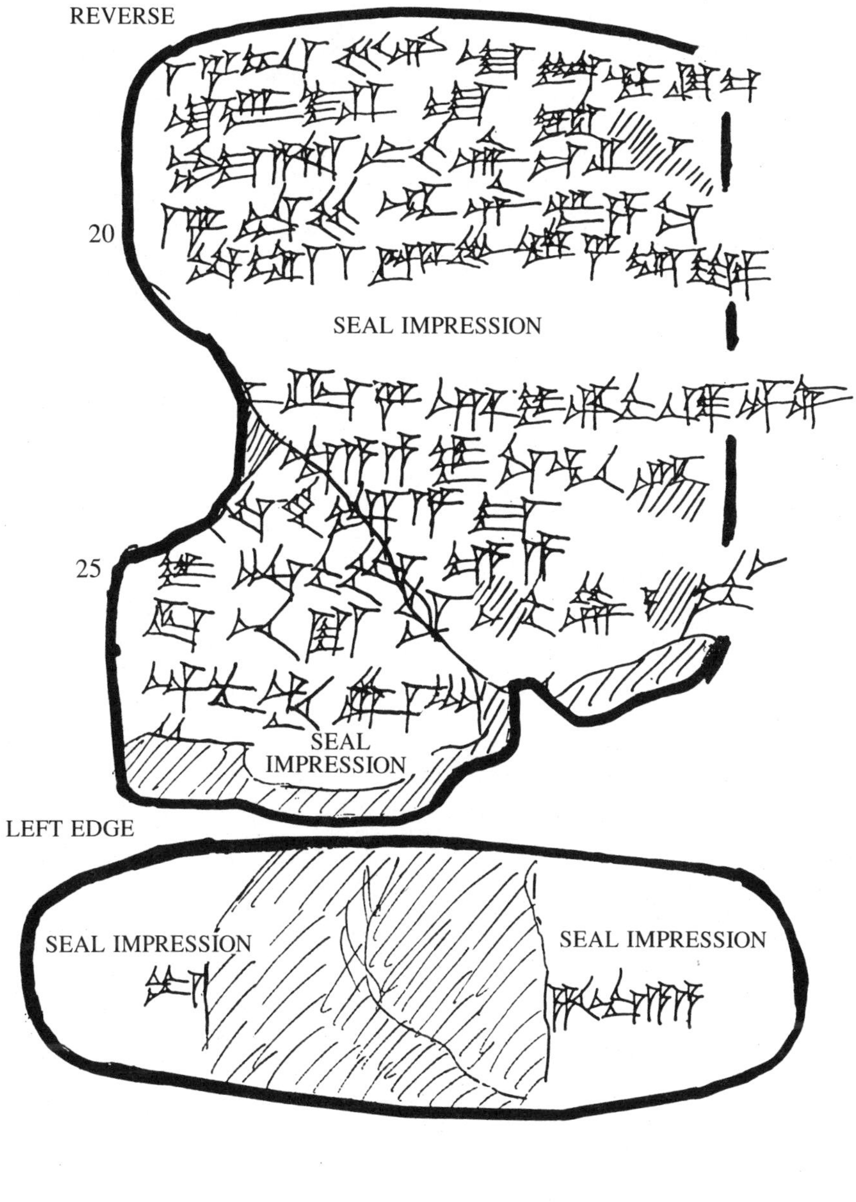
REVERSE
20
SEAL IMPRESSION
25
SEAL IMPRESSION
LEFT EDGE
SEAL IMPRESSION
SEAL IMPRESSION

232

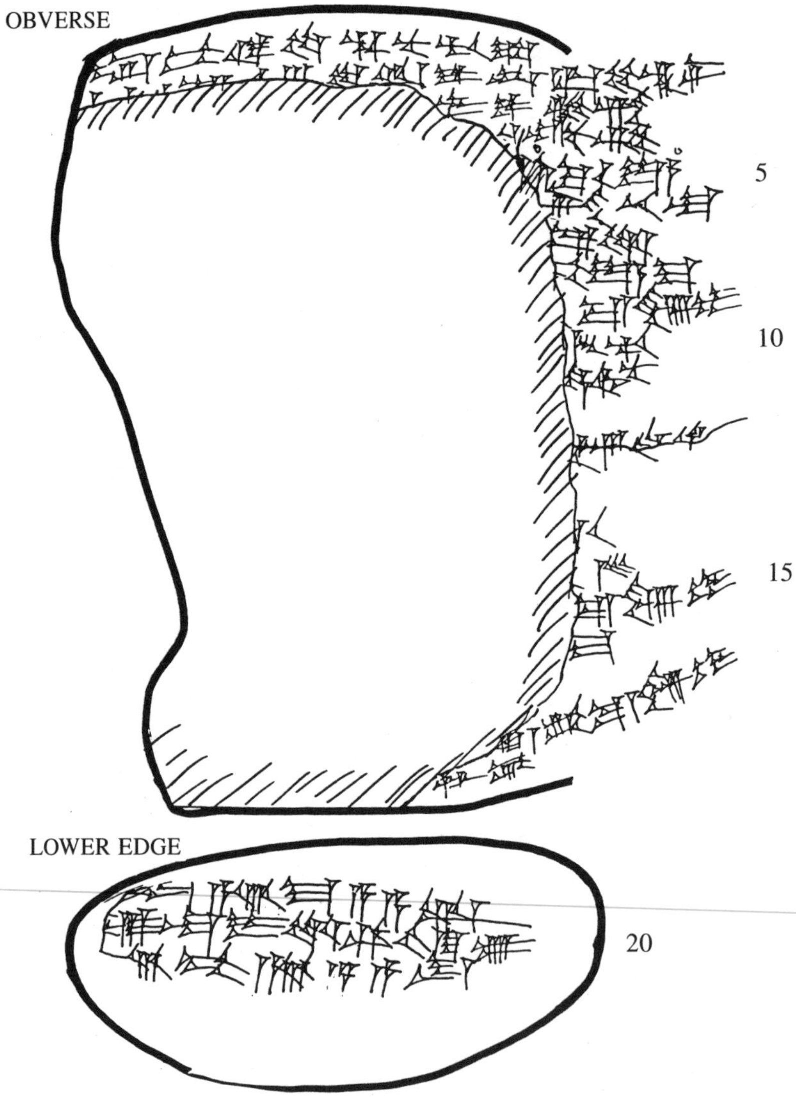

232

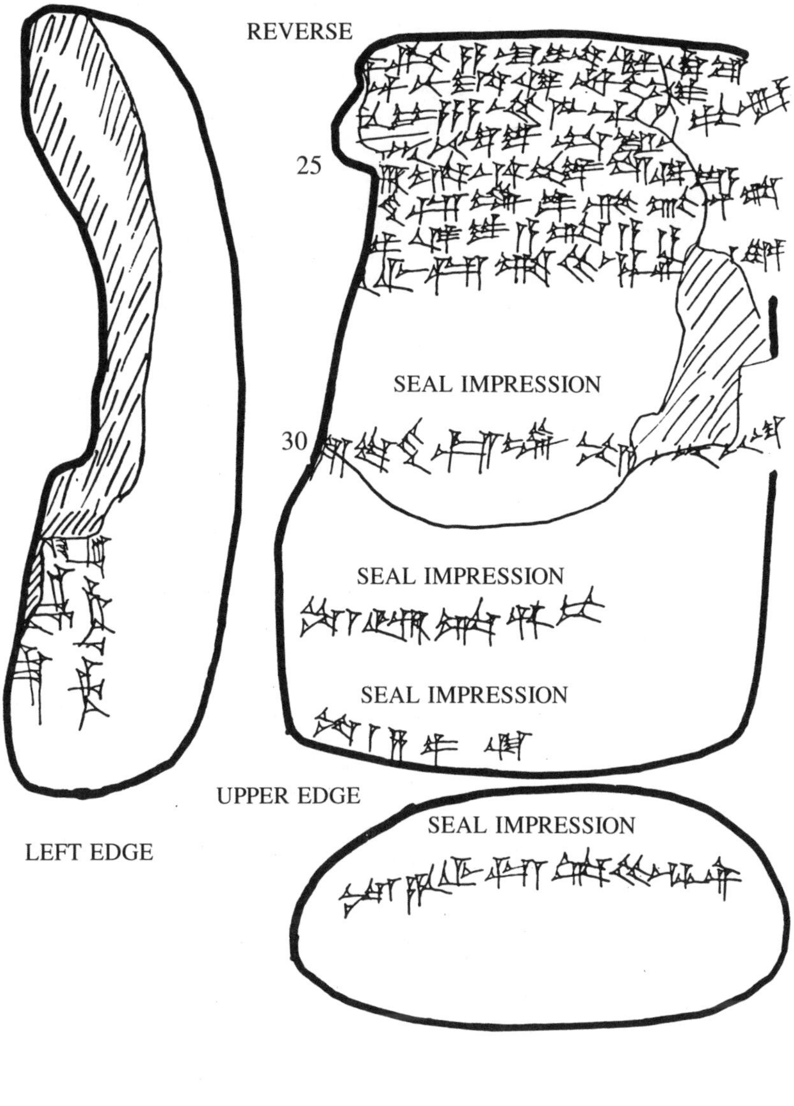
REVERSE
25
SEAL IMPRESSION
30
SEAL IMPRESSION
SEAL IMPRESSION
UPPER EDGE
SEAL IMPRESSION
LEFT EDGE

237

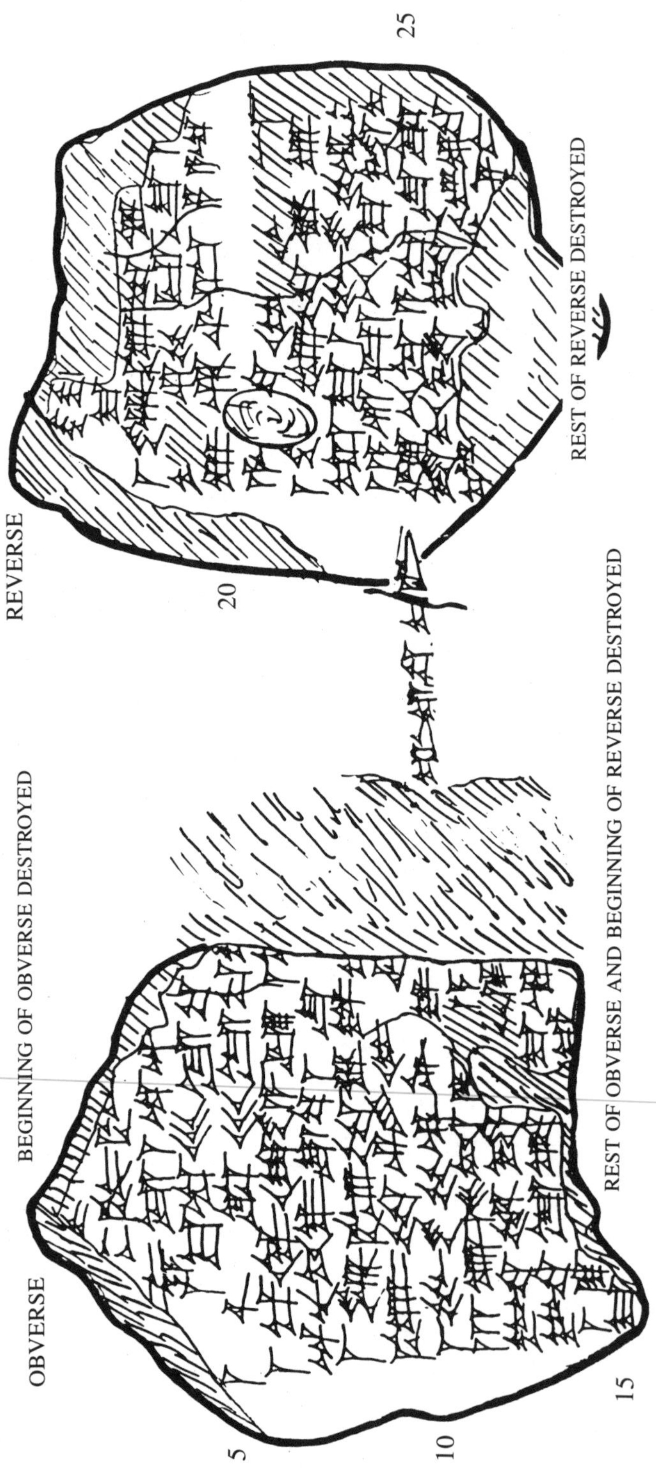
OBVERSE
BEGINNING OF OBVERSE DESTROYED
REST OF OBVERSE AND BEGINNING OF REVERSE DESTROYED
REVERSE
REST OF REVERSE DESTROYED

238

OBVERSE

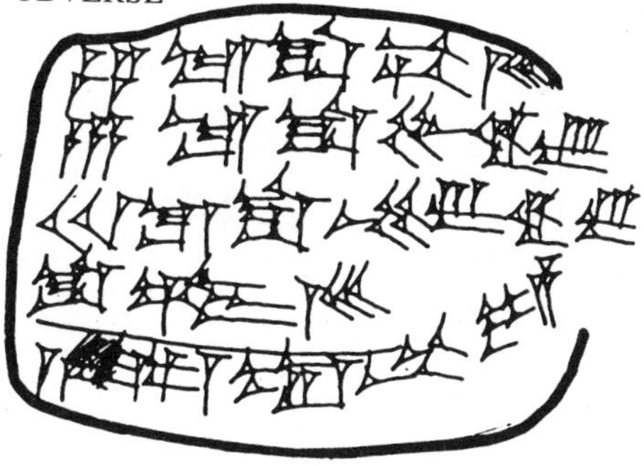

LOWER EDGE

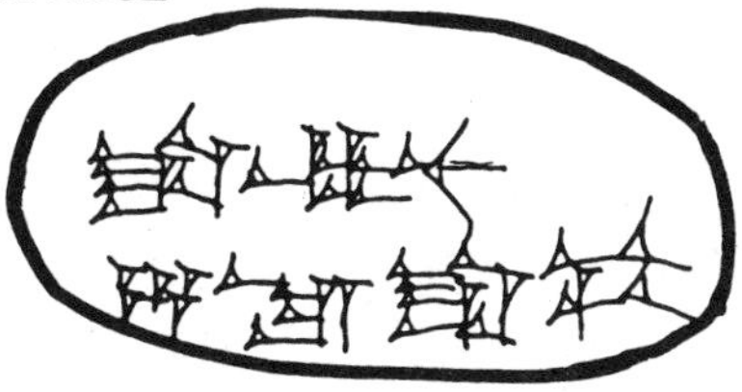

REVERSE

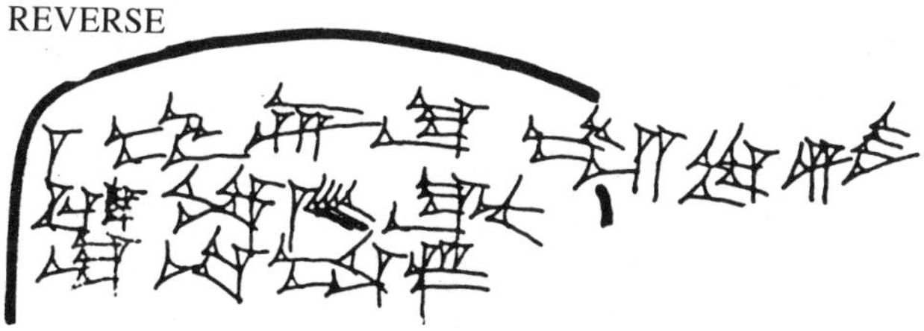

SEAL IMPRESSION

246

OBVERSE

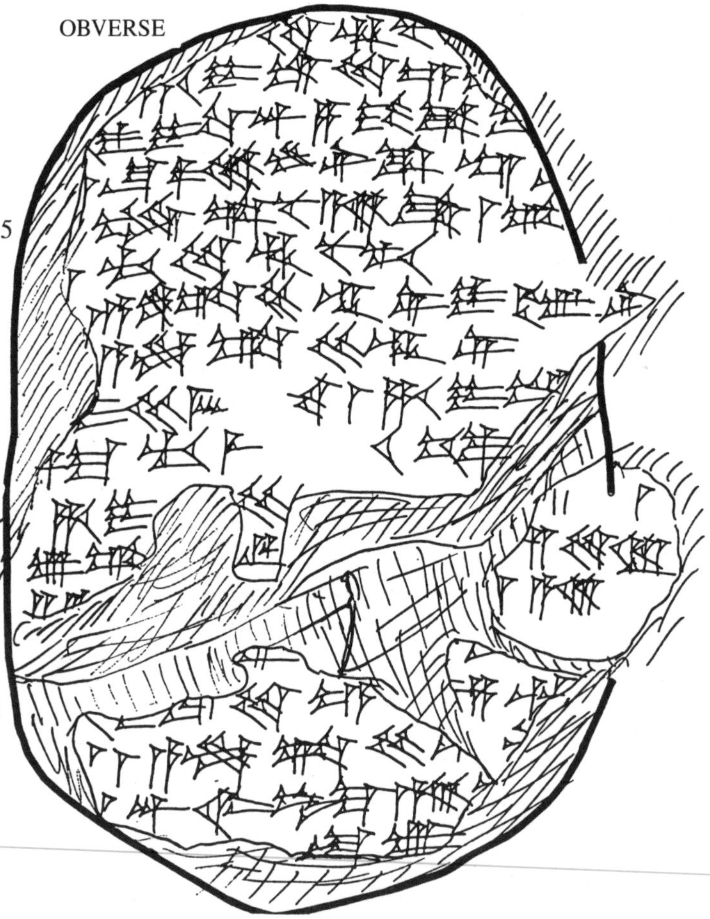

REST OF OBVERSE AND BEGINNING OF REVERSE DESTROYED

246

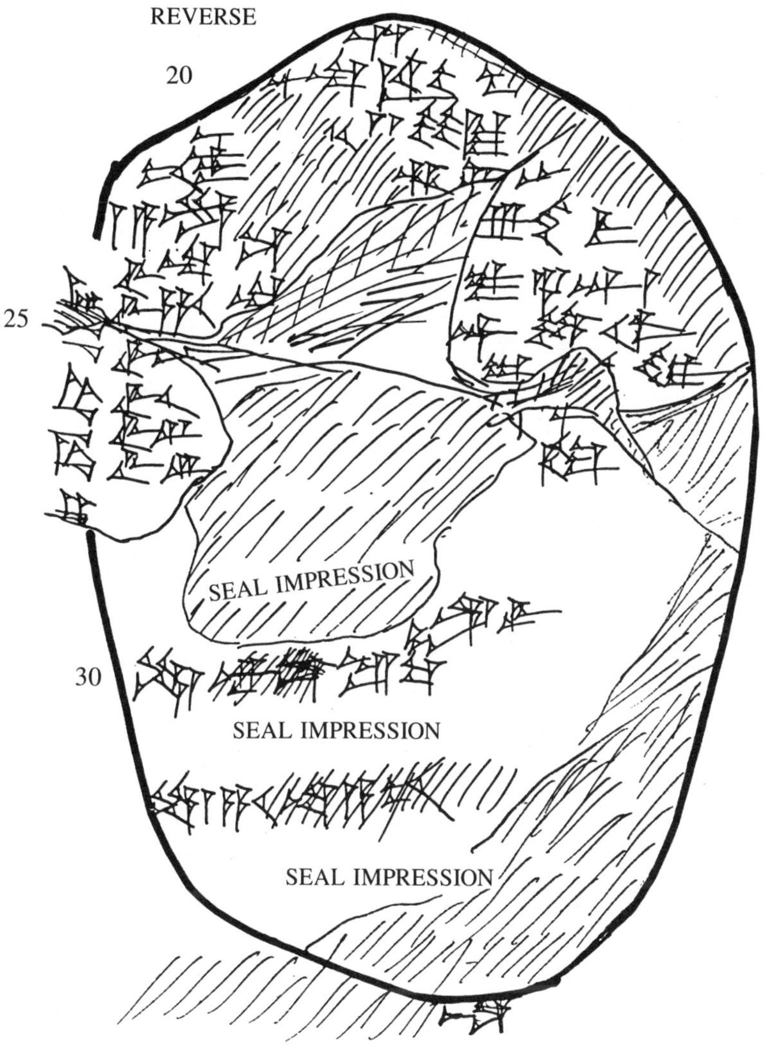
REVERSE
20
25
SEAL IMPRESSION
30
SEAL IMPRESSION
SEAL IMPRESSION

249

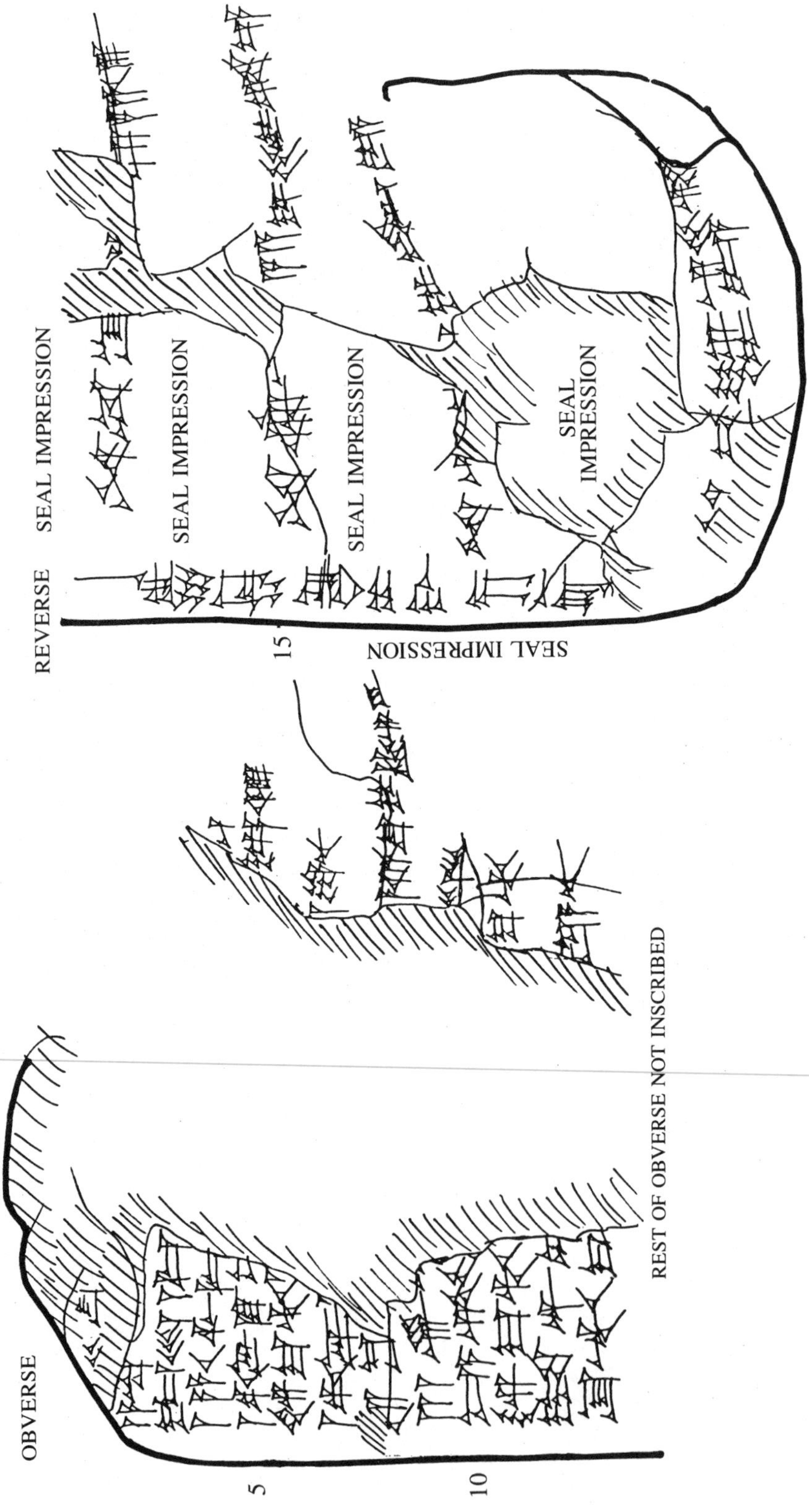
OBVERSE
REST OF OBVERSE NOT INSCRIBED
REVERSE
SEAL IMPRESSION
SEAL IMPRESSION
SEAL IMPRESSION
SEAL IMPRESSION
SEAL IMPRESSION

254

OBVERSE

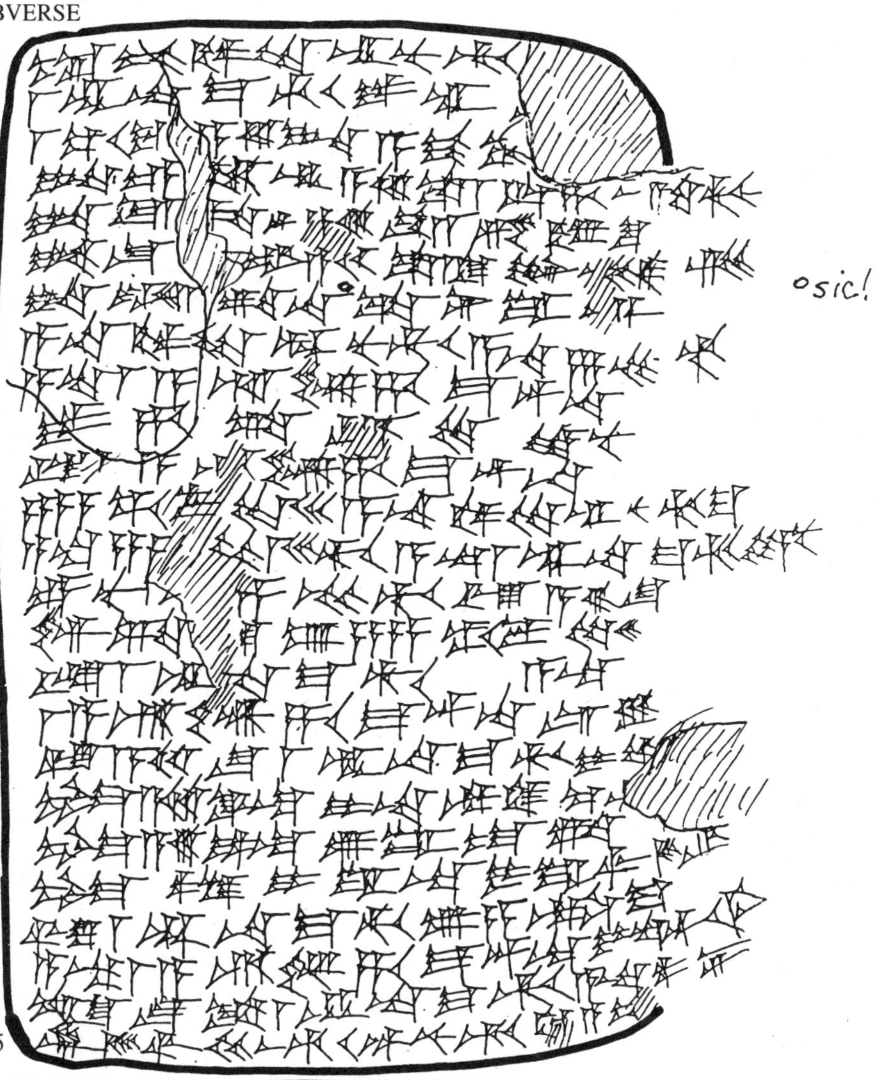

LOWER EDGE

254

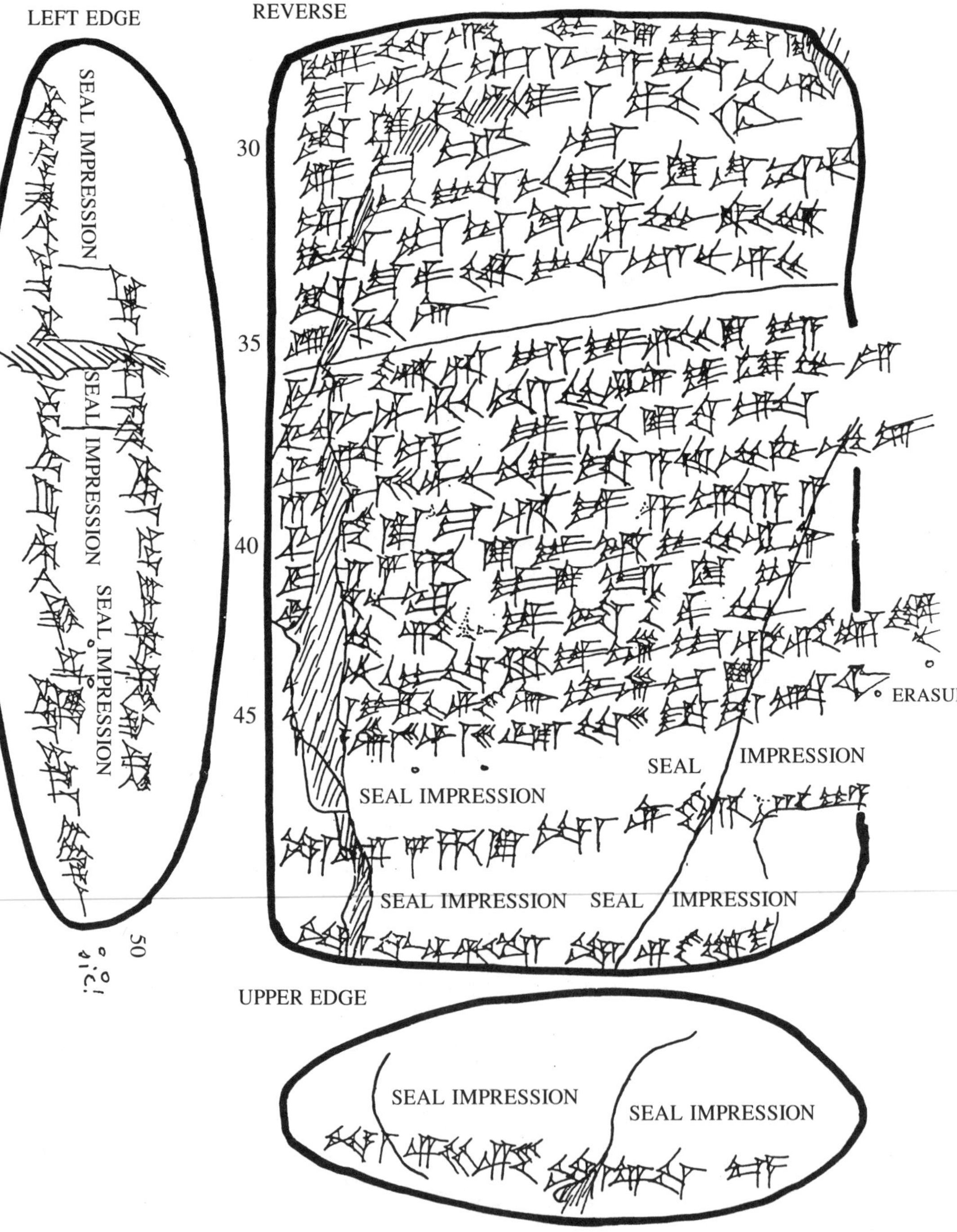
LEFT EDGE
SEAL IMPRESSION
SEAL IMPRESSION
SEAL IMPRESSION
50
REVERSE
30
35
40
45
ERASURE
SEAL
IMPRESSION
SEAL IMPRESSION
SEAL IMPRESSION
SEAL
IMPRESSION
UPPER EDGE
SEAL IMPRESSION
SEAL IMPRESSION

255

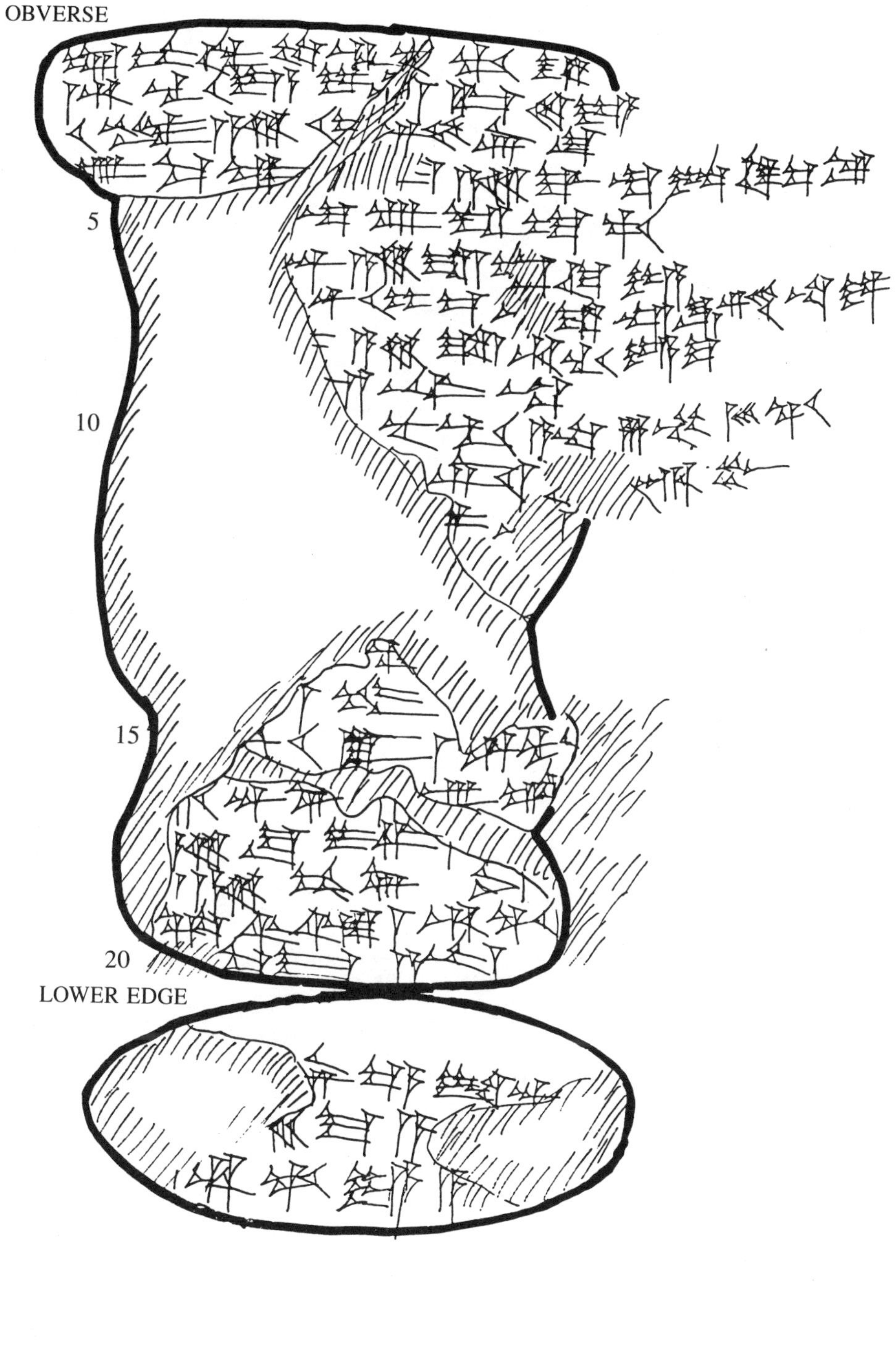

255

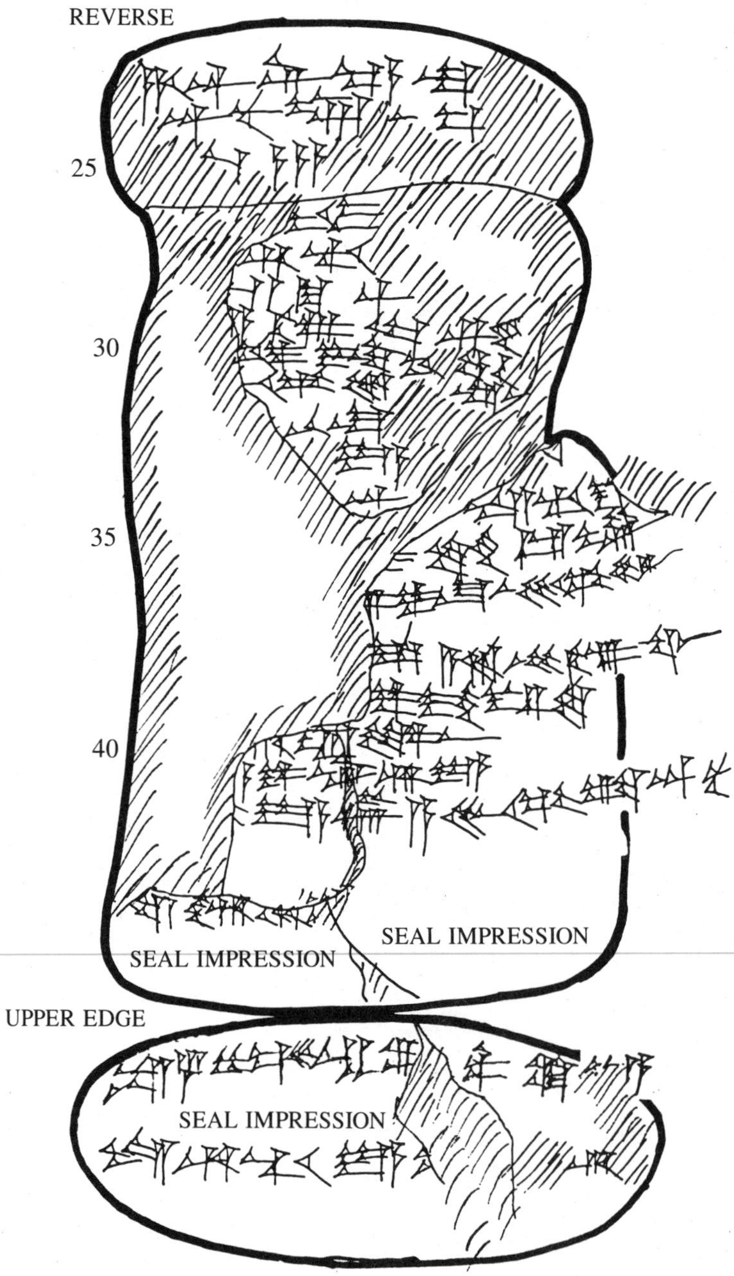
REVERSE
25
30
35
40
SEAL IMPRESSION
SEAL IMPRESSION
UPPER EDGE
SEAL IMPRESSION

259

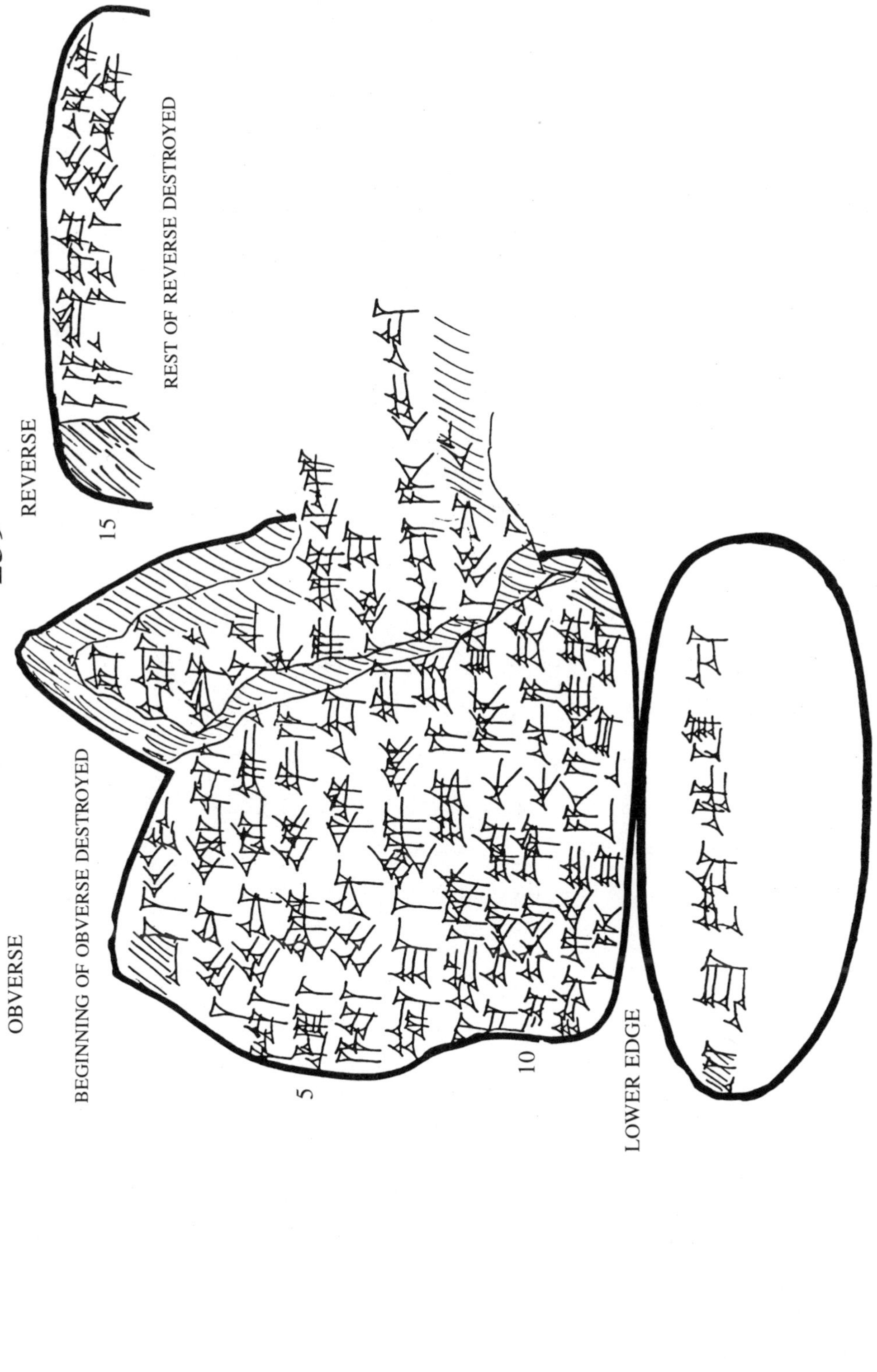
OBVERSE
BEGINNING OF OBVERSE DESTROYED
LOWER EDGE
REVERSE
REST OF REVERSE DESTROYED

261

OBVERSE

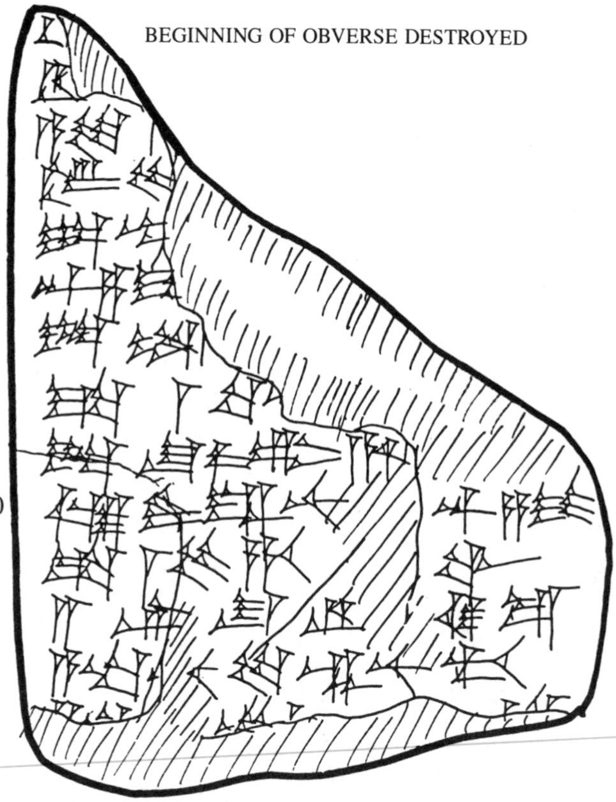

REST OF OBVERSE AND BEGINNING OF REVERSE DESTROYED

261

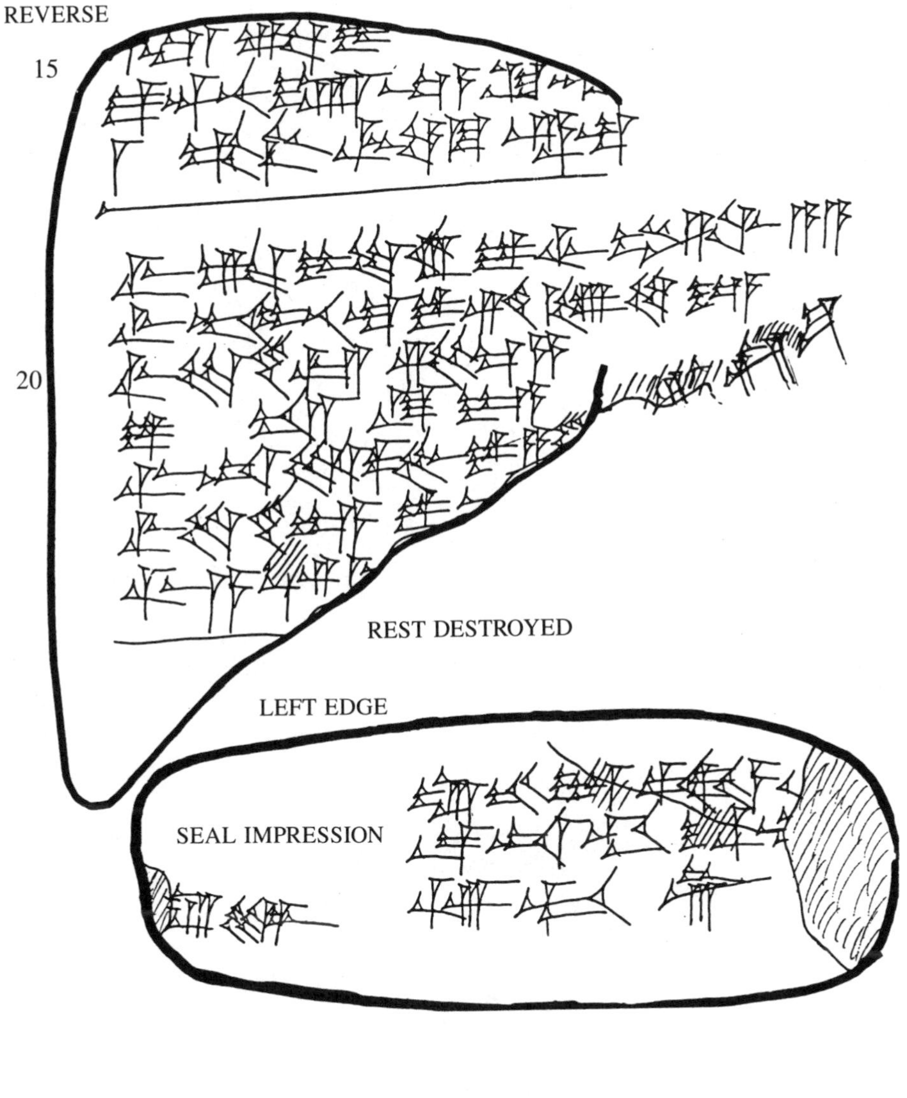

263

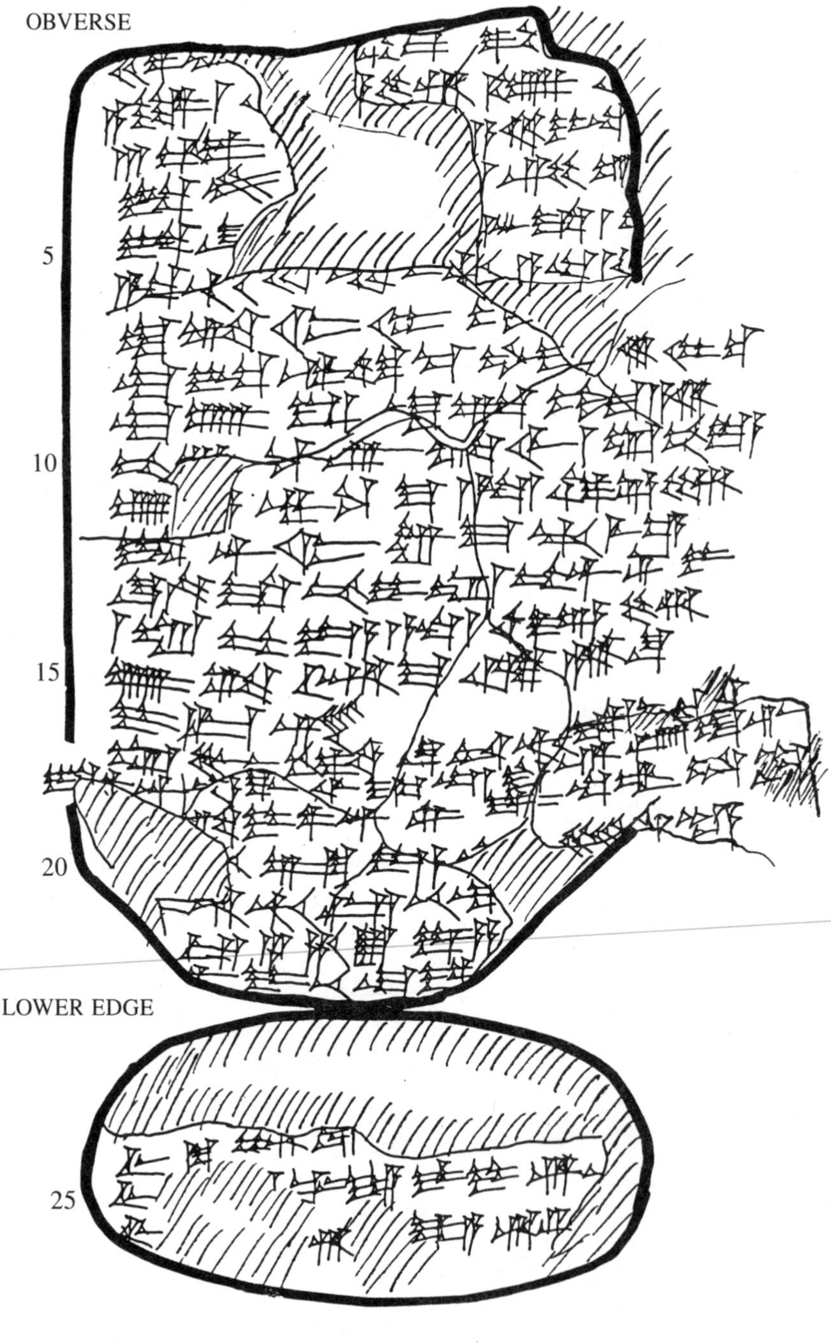

263

REVERSE

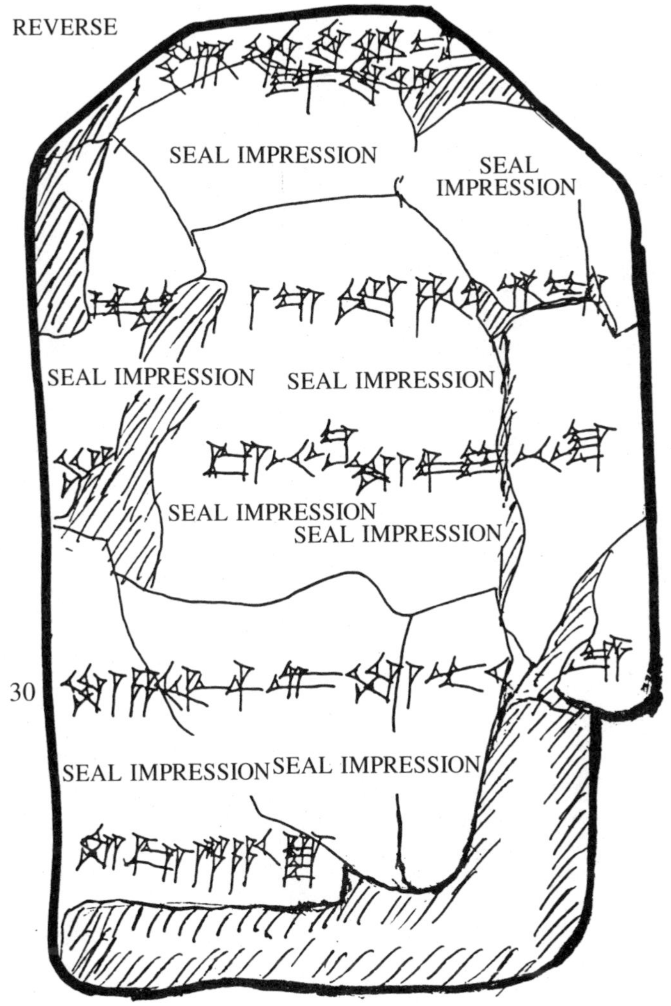
SEAL IMPRESSION
SEAL IMPRESSION
SEAL IMPRESSION
SEAL IMPRESSION
SEAL IMPRESSION
SEAL IMPRESSION
30
SEAL IMPRESSION
SEAL IMPRESSION

266

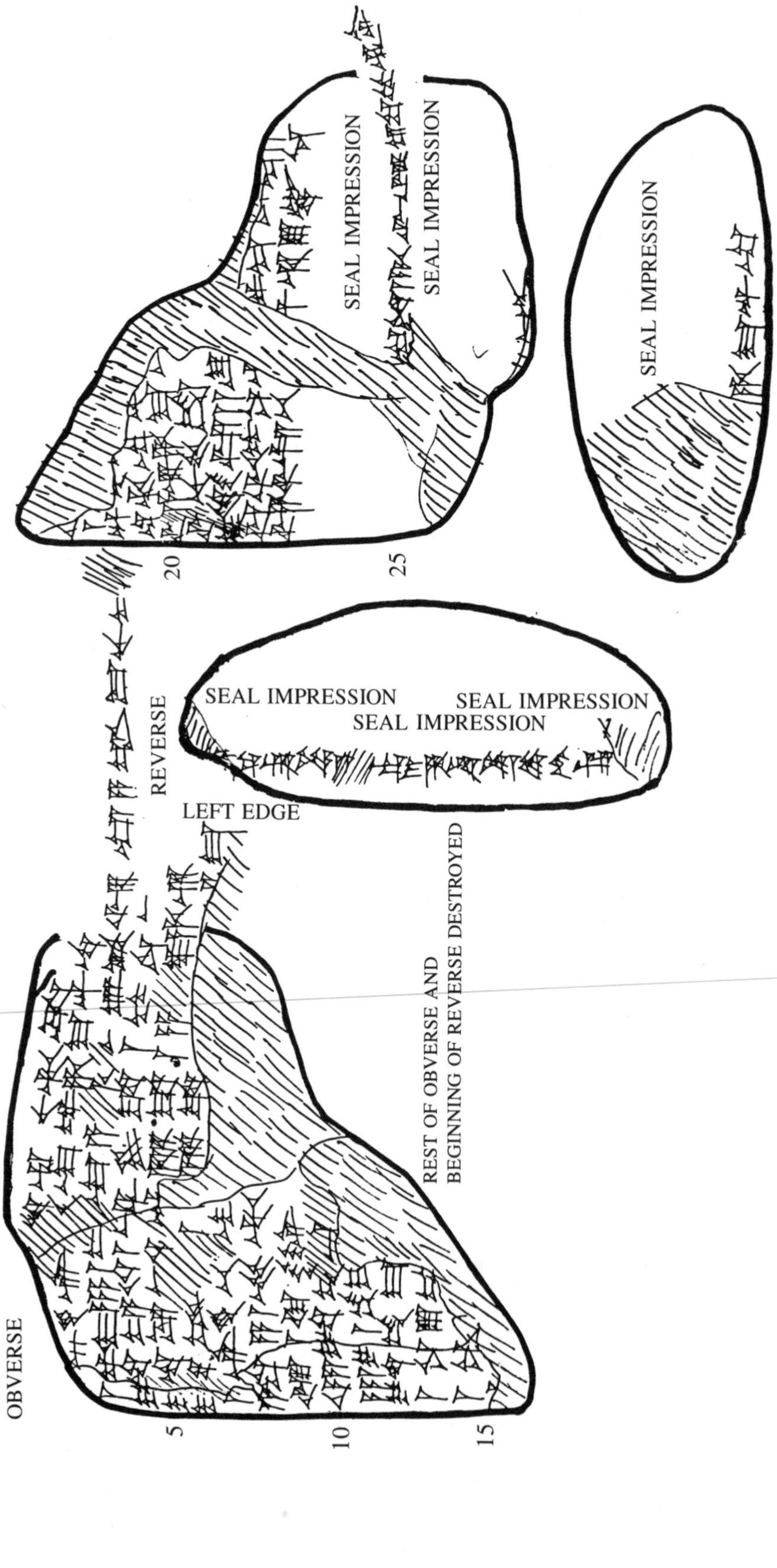
OBVERSE
REST OF OBVERSE AND
BEGINNING OF REVERSE DESTROYED
LEFT EDGE
REVERSE
SEAL IMPRESSION
SEAL IMPRESSION
SEAL IMPRESSION
SEAL IMPRESSION
SEAL IMPRESSION
SEAL IMPRESSION

270

270

REVERSE

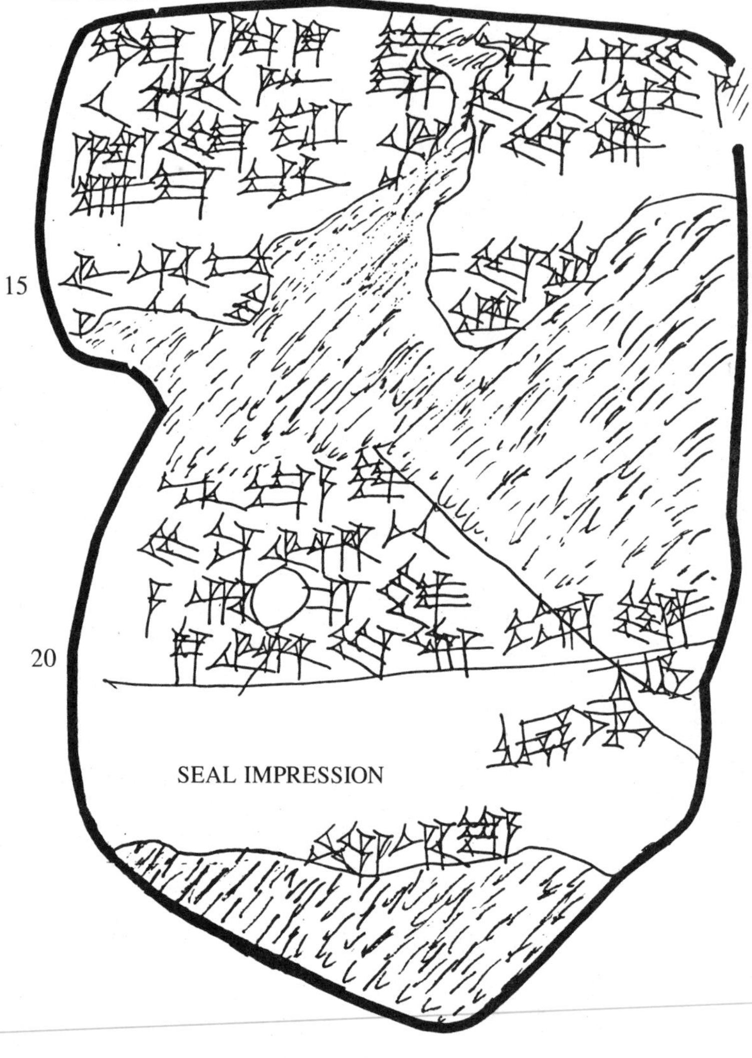

LEFT EDGE

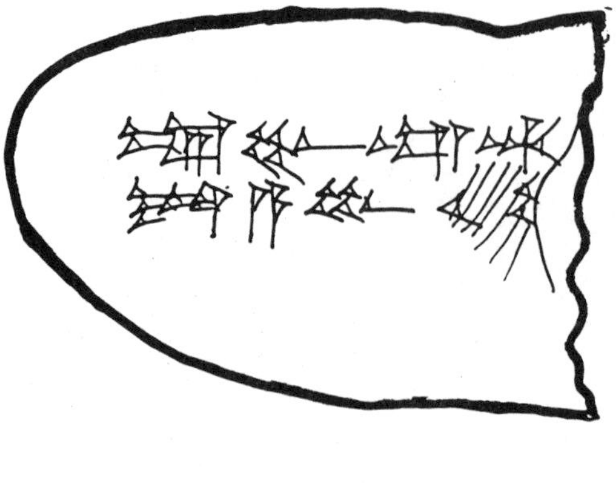

271

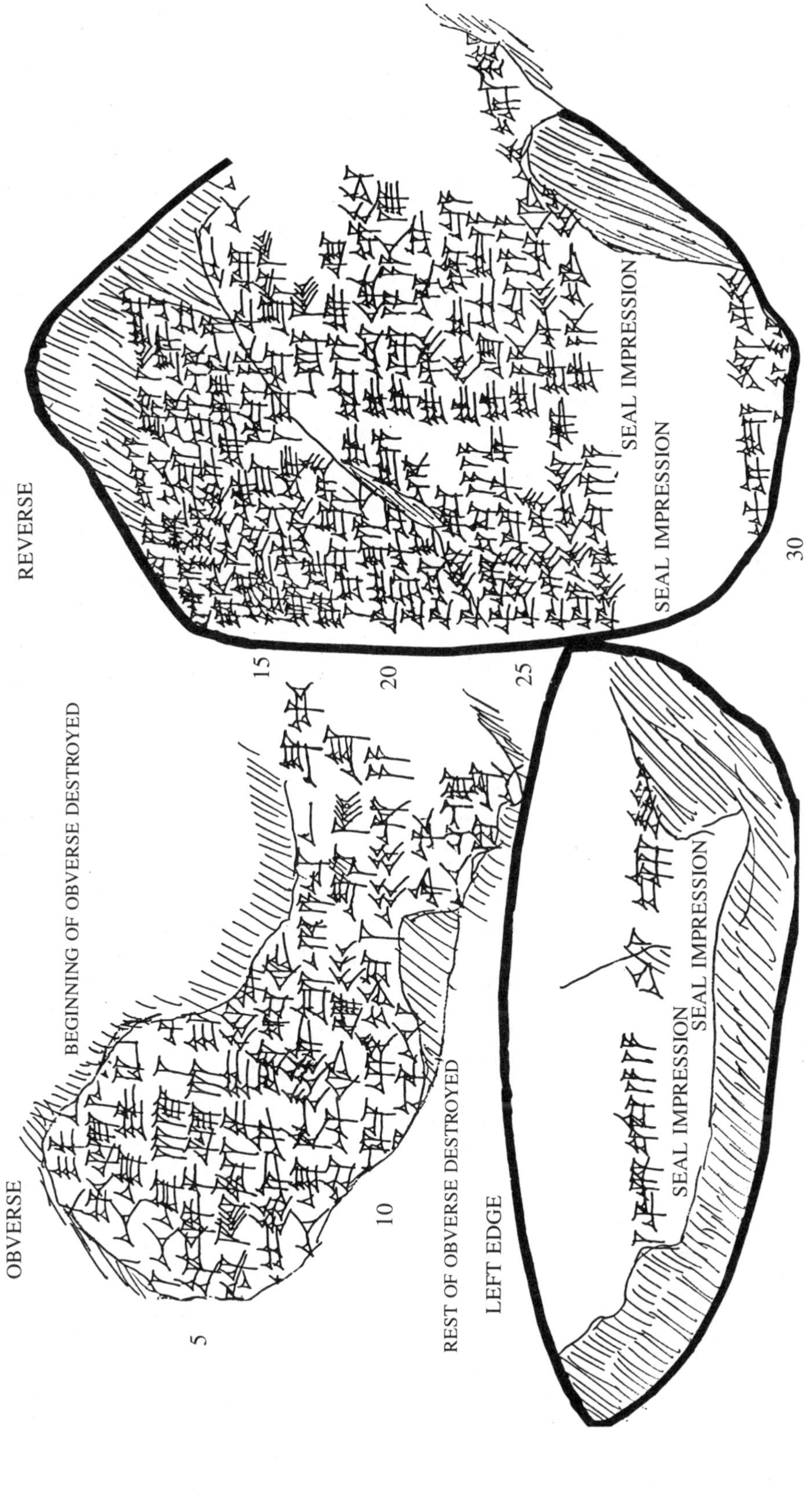

OBVERSE
BEGINNING OF OBVERSE DESTROYED
REST OF OBVERSE DESTROYED
REVERSE
SEAL IMPRESSION
SEAL IMPRESSION
LEFT EDGE
SEAL IMPRESSION
SEAL IMPRESSION
SEAL IMPRESSION

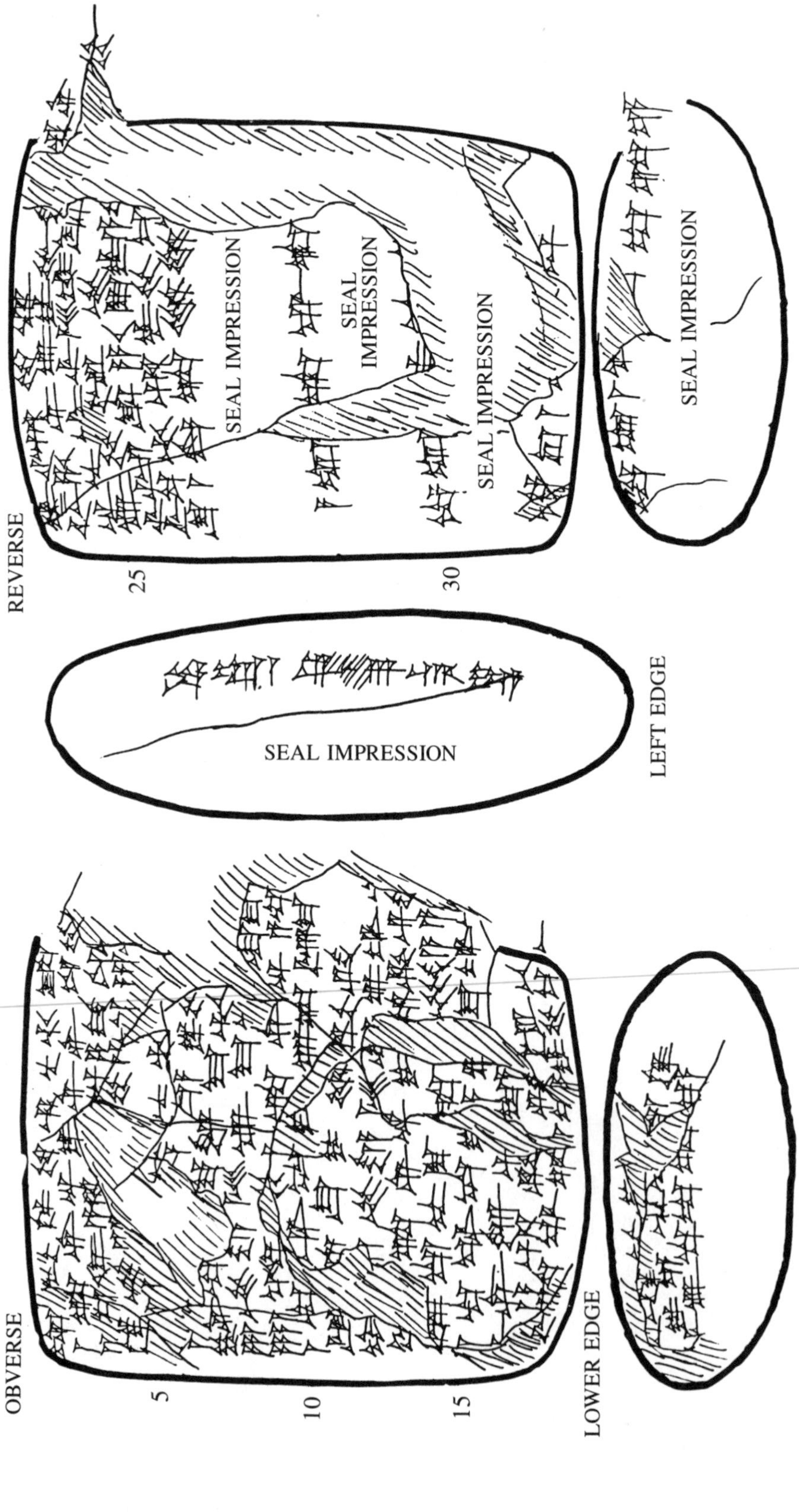
272
OBVERSE
LOWER EDGE
LEFT EDGE
SEAL IMPRESSION
REVERSE
SEAL IMPRESSION
SEAL IMPRESSION
SEAL IMPRESSION
SEAL IMPRESSION
5
10
15
25
30

274

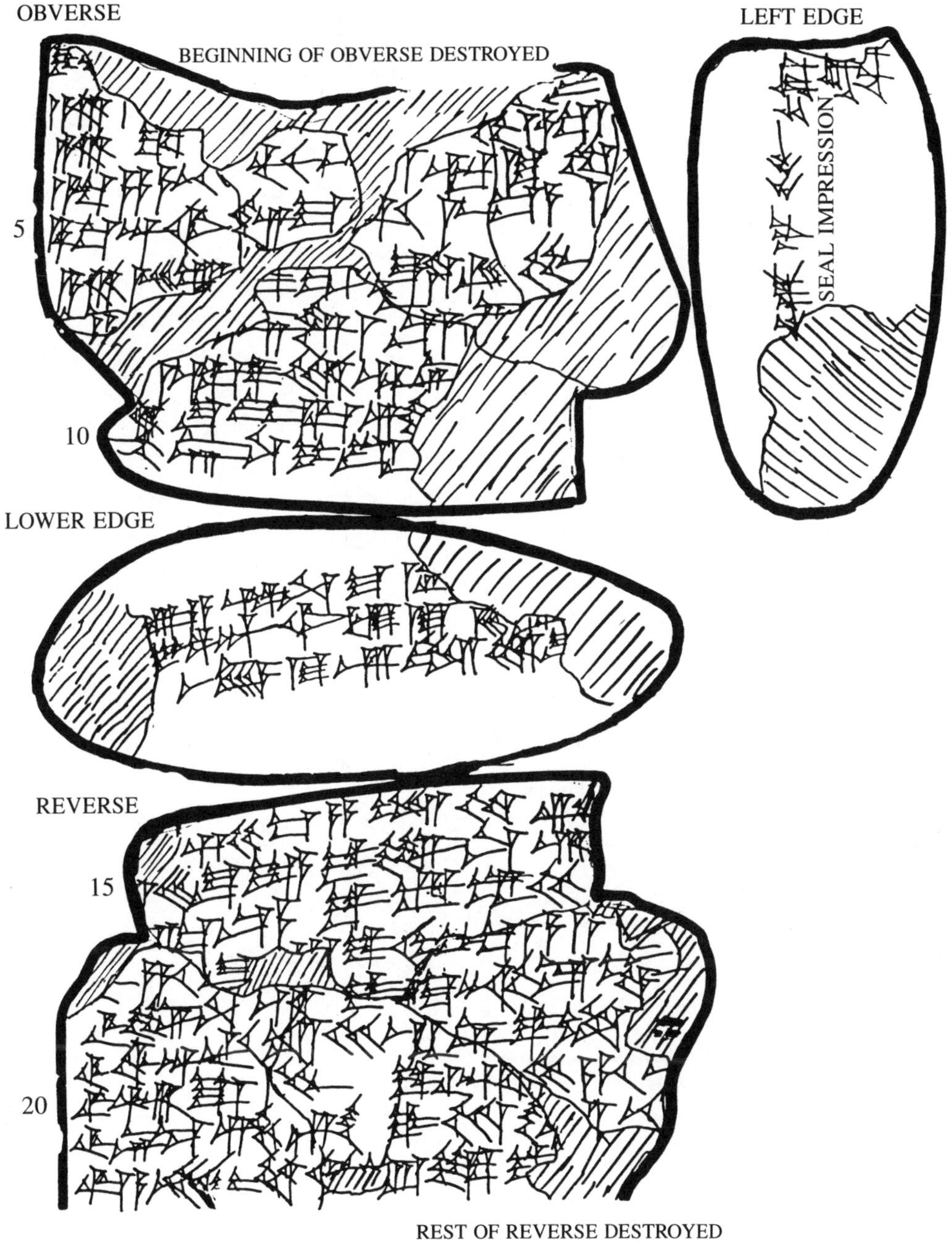
OBVERSE
BEGINNING OF OBVERSE DESTROYED
LEFT EDGE
SEAL IMPRESSION
LOWER EDGE
REVERSE
REST OF REVERSE DESTROYED

276

OBVERSE

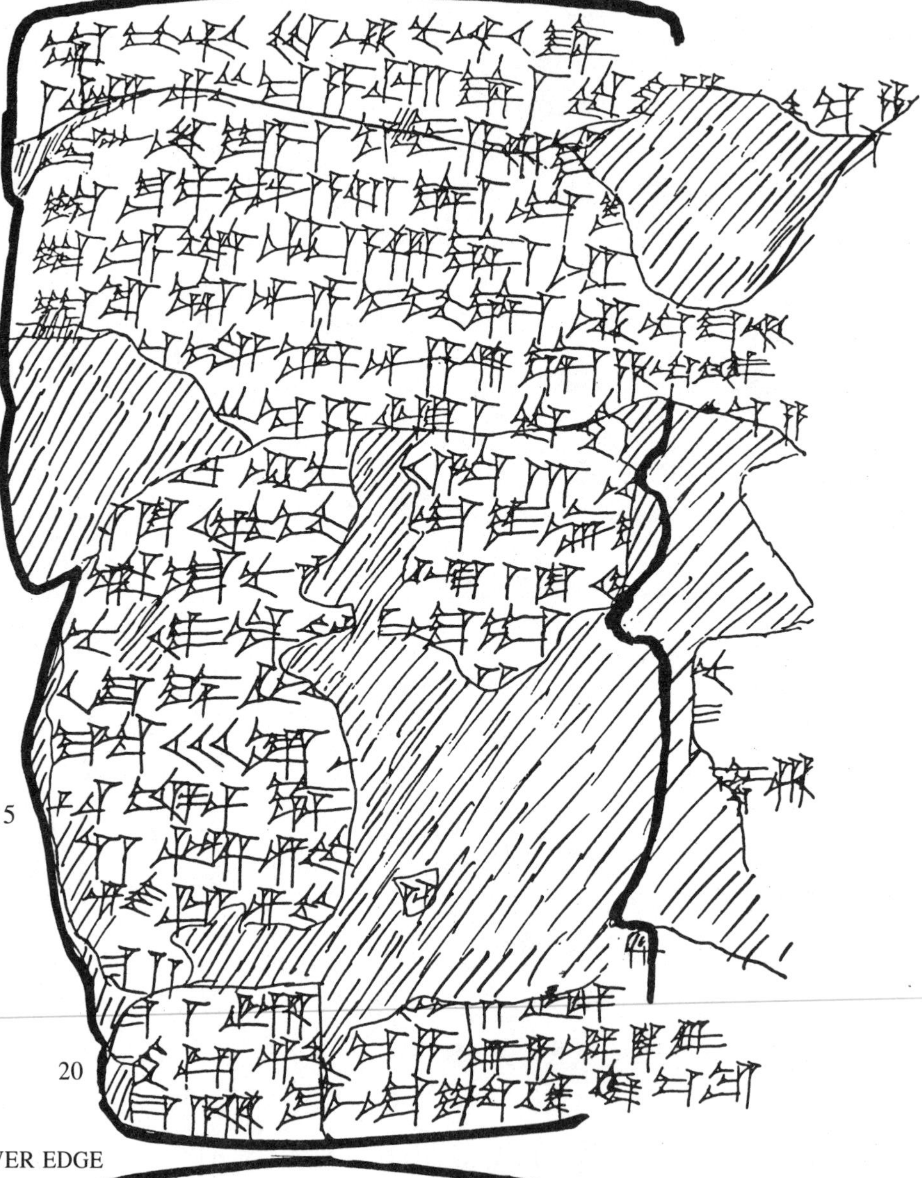

LOWER EDGE

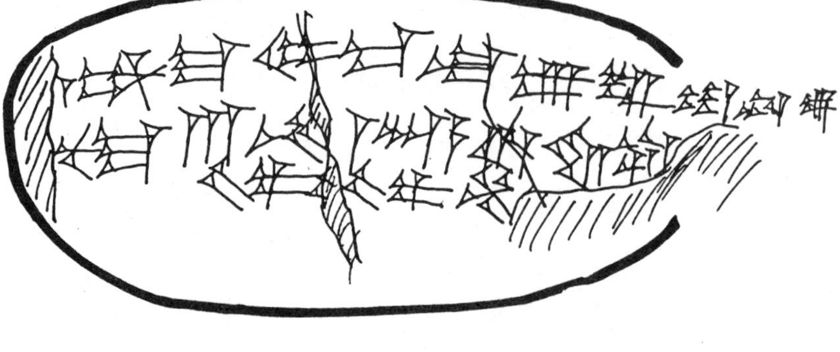

276

REVERSE

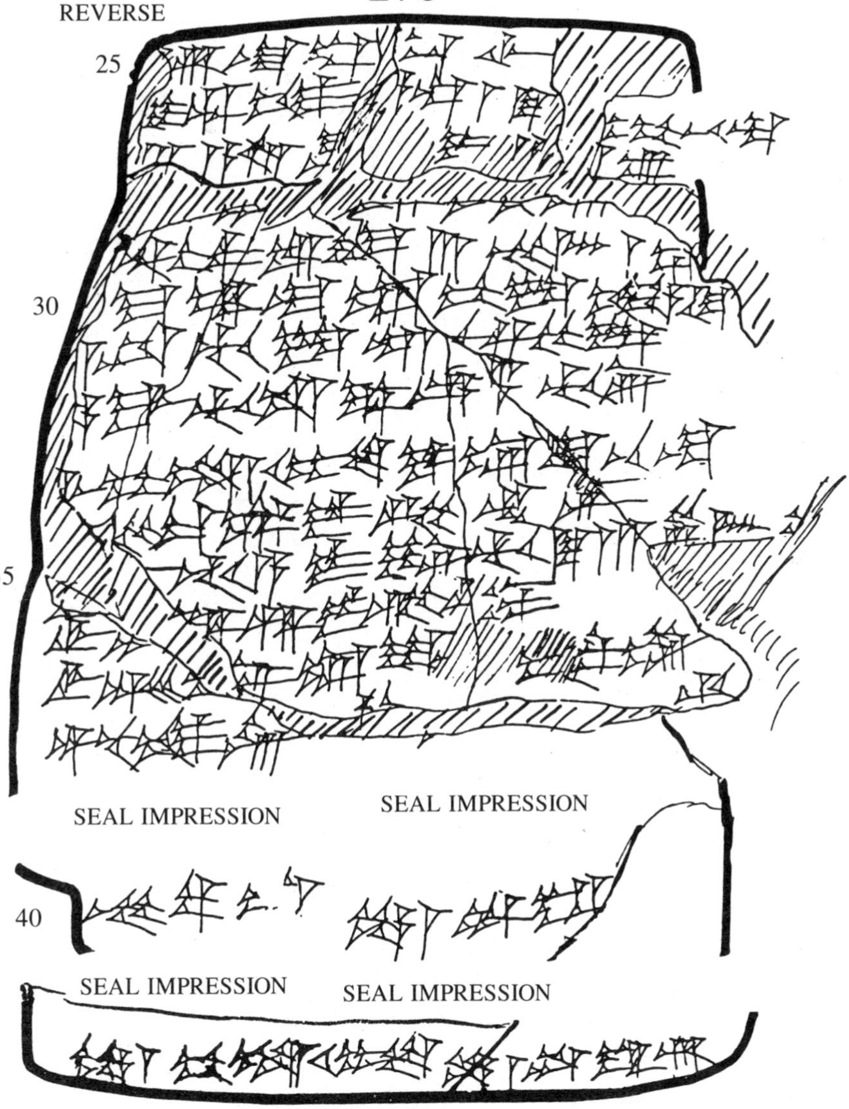

UPPER EDGE

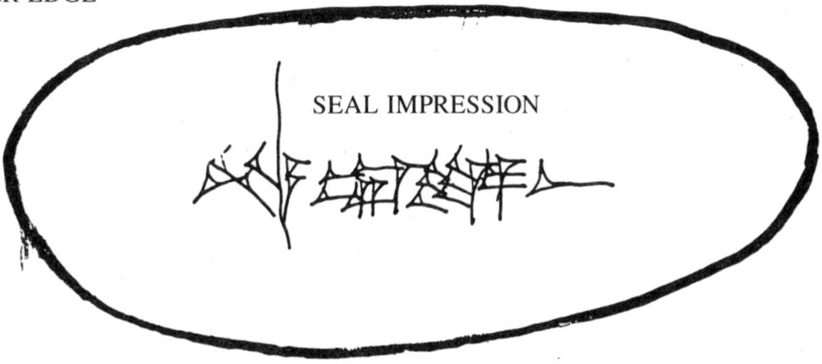

277

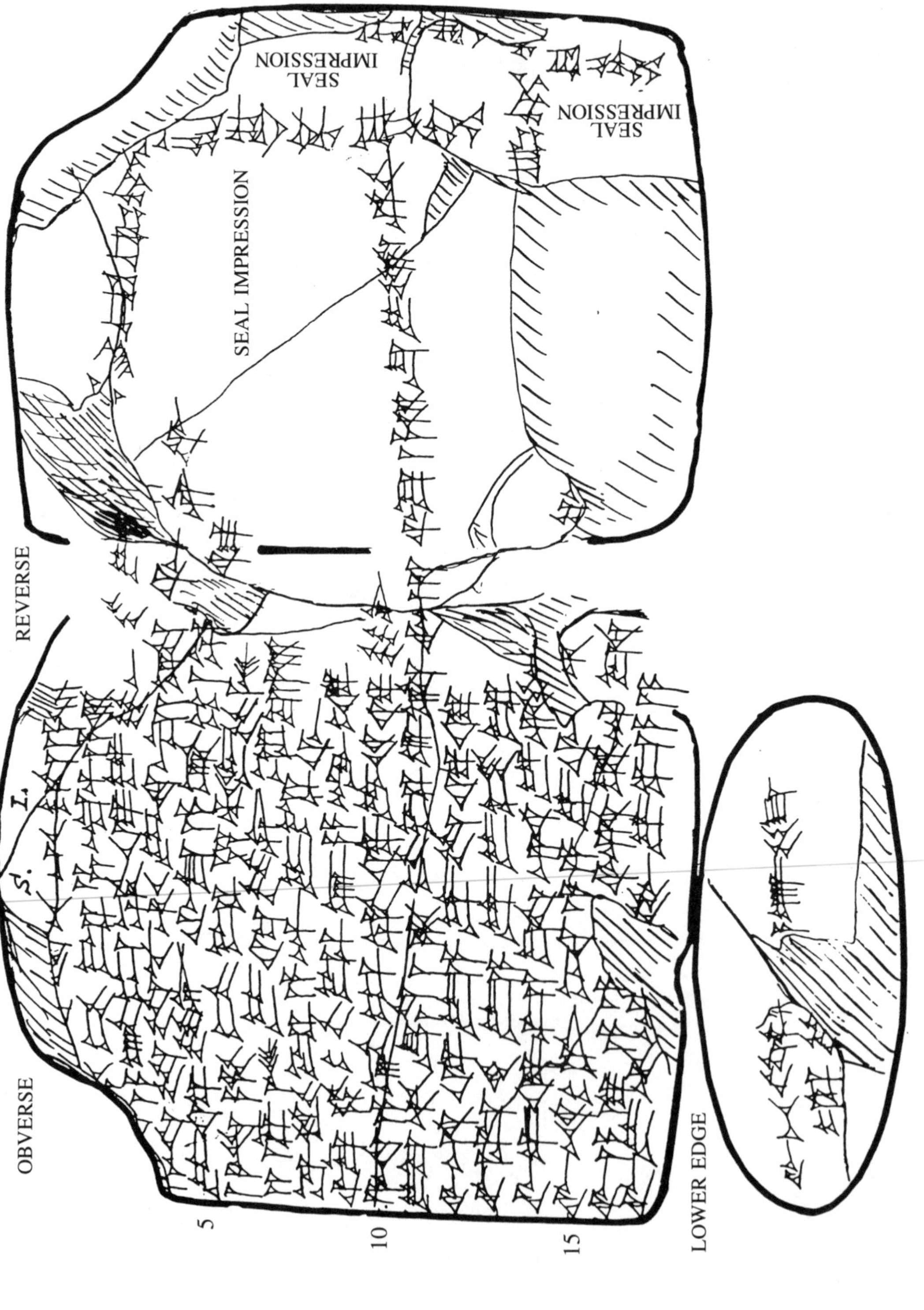
REVERSE
SEAL IMPRESSION
SEAL IMPRESSION
SEAL IMPRESSION
OBVERSE
LOWER EDGE

278

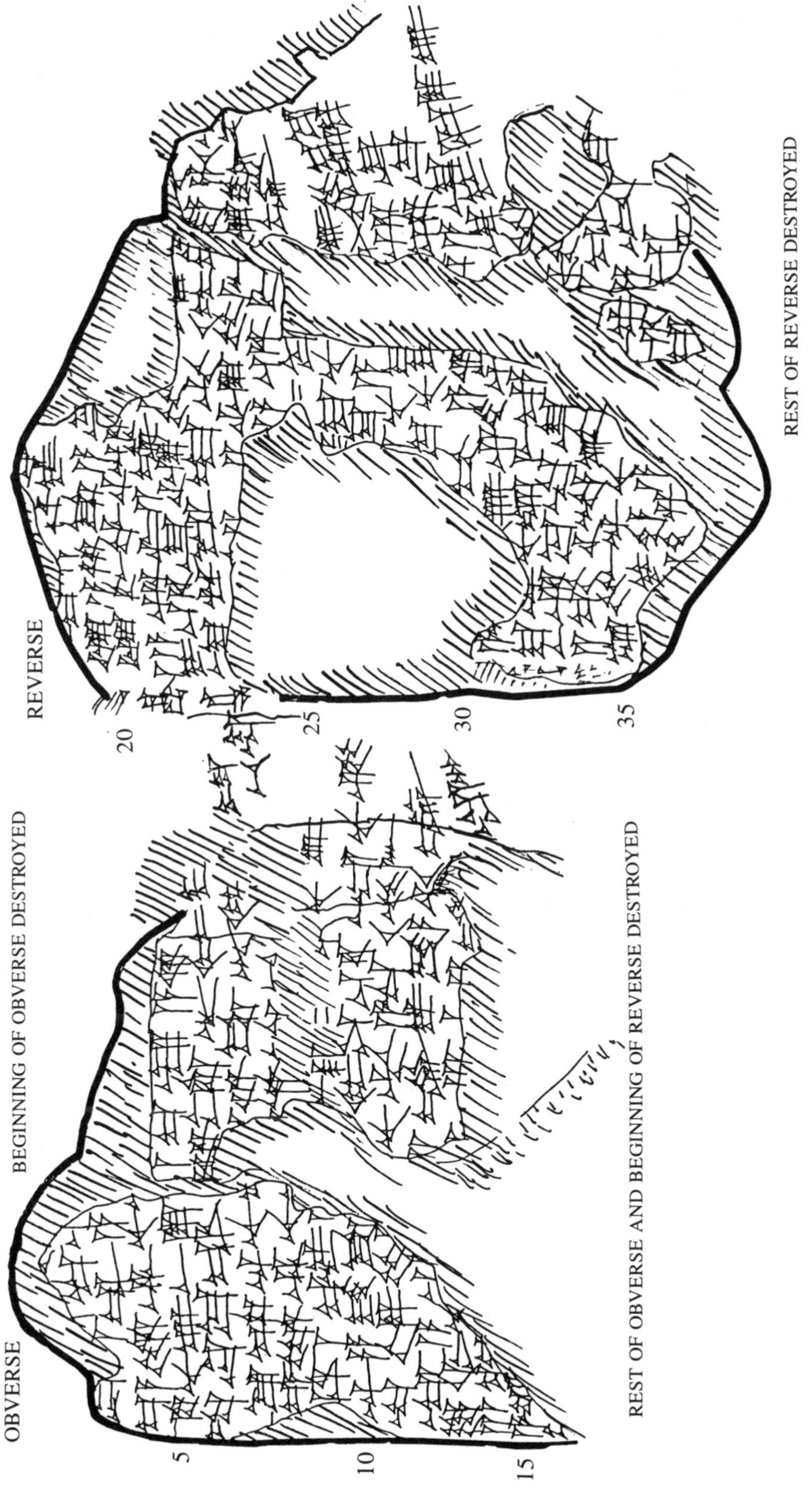
OBVERSE
BEGINNING OF OBVERSE DESTROYED
REST OF OBVERSE AND BEGINNING OF REVERSE DESTROYED
5
10
15
REVERSE
REST OF REVERSE DESTROYED
20
25
30
35

280

OBVERSE

BEGINNING OF OBVERSE DESTROYED

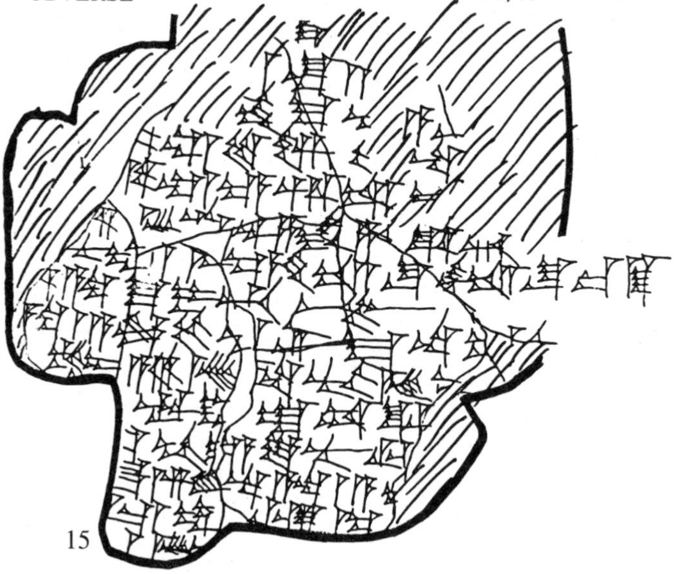

REST OF OBVERSE AND BEGINNING OF REVERSE DESTROYED

REVERSE

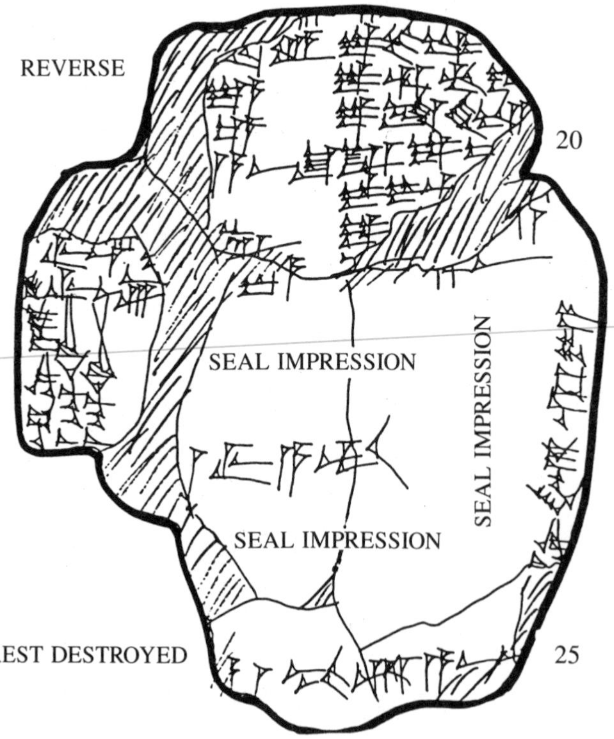

REST DESTROYED

281

BEGINNING OF OBVERSE DESTROYED

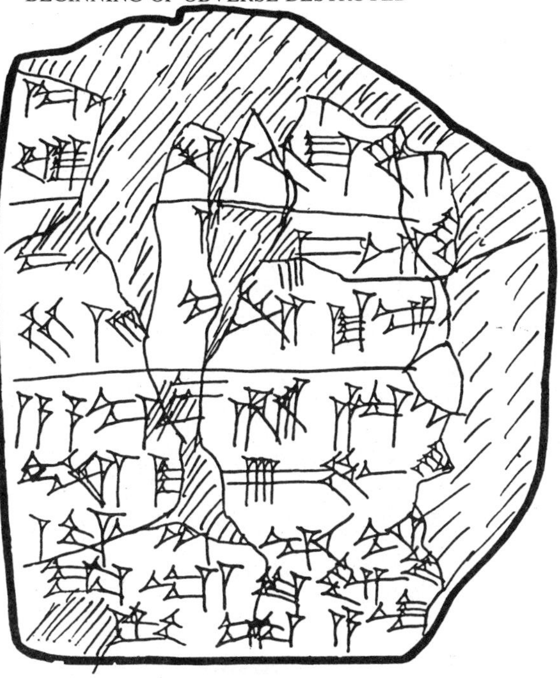

REST NOT INSCRIBED

282

BEGINNING OF OBVERSE DESTROYED

OBVERSE

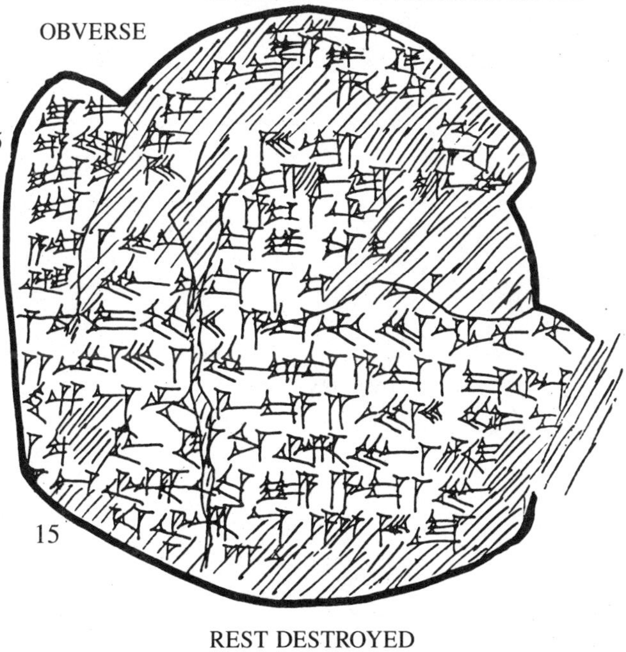

REST DESTROYED

284

OBVERSE

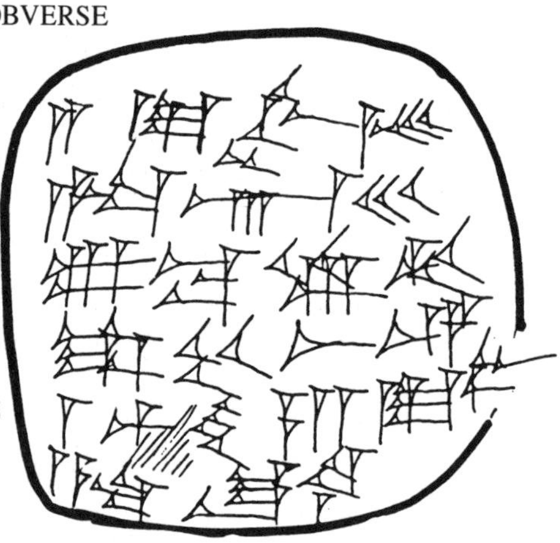

LOWER EDGE

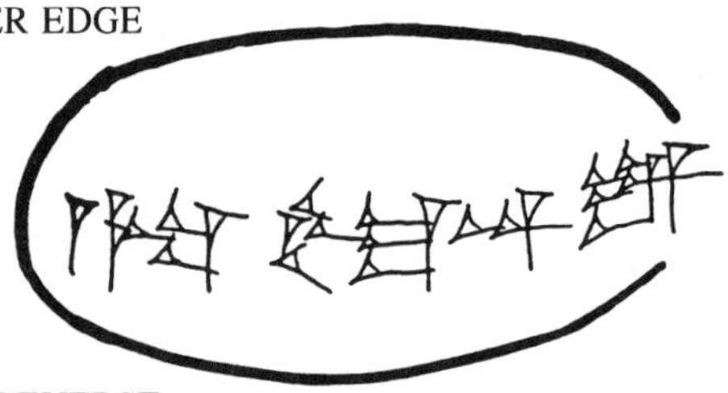

REVERSE

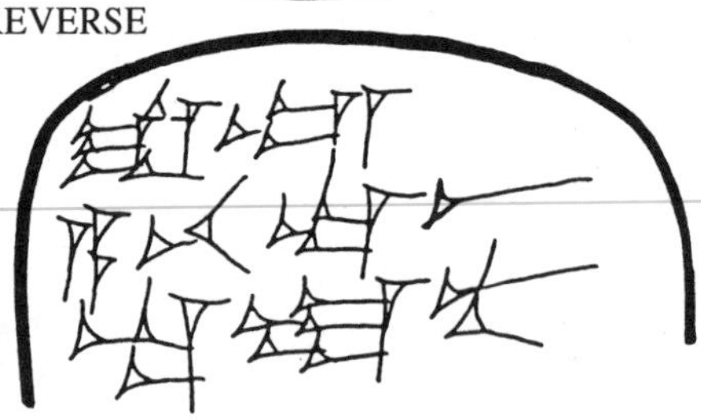

REST NOT INSCRIBED

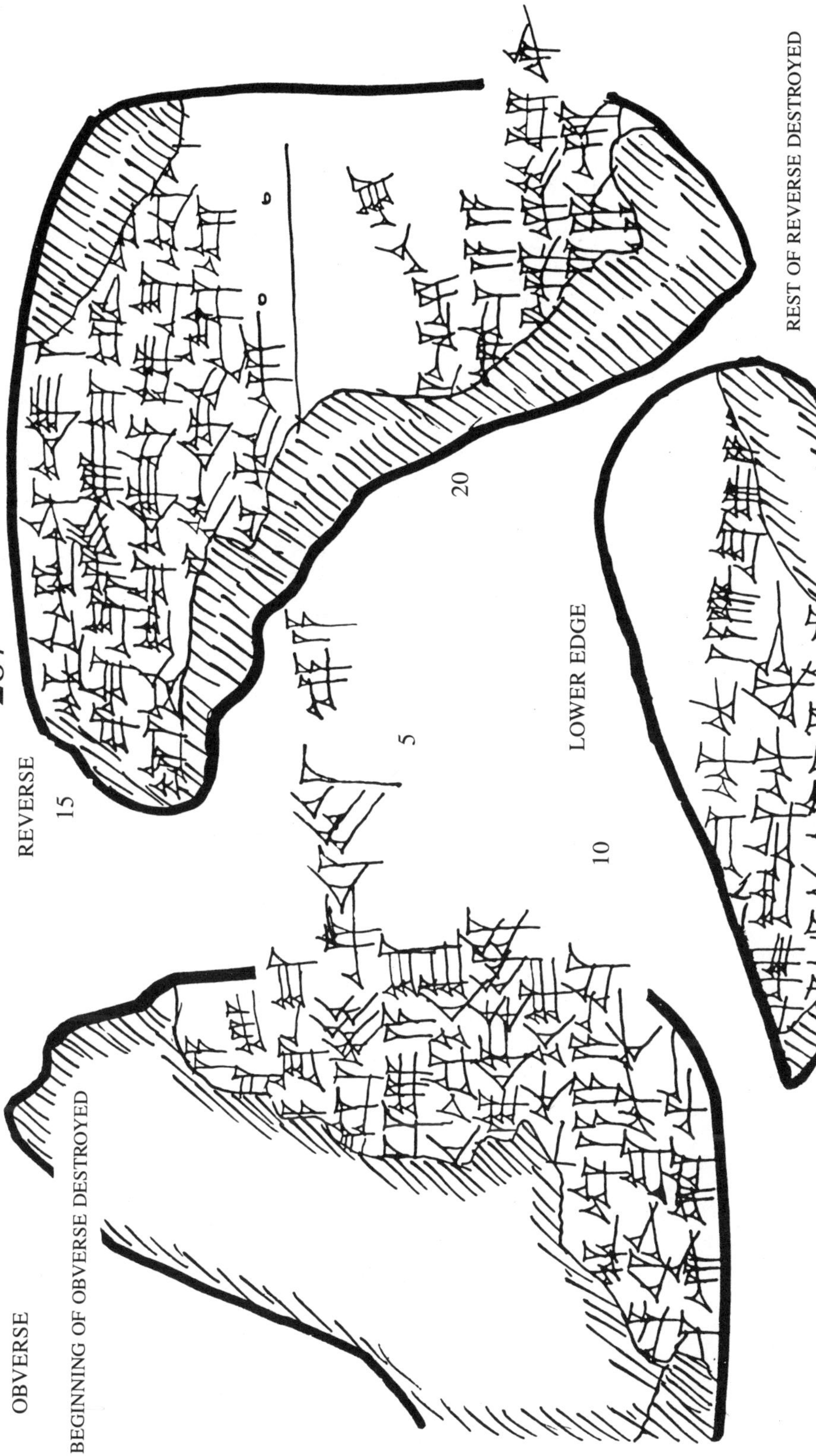
287
OBVERSE
BEGINNING OF OBVERSE DESTROYED
5
10
LOWER EDGE
REVERSE
15
20
REST OF REVERSE DESTROYED

288

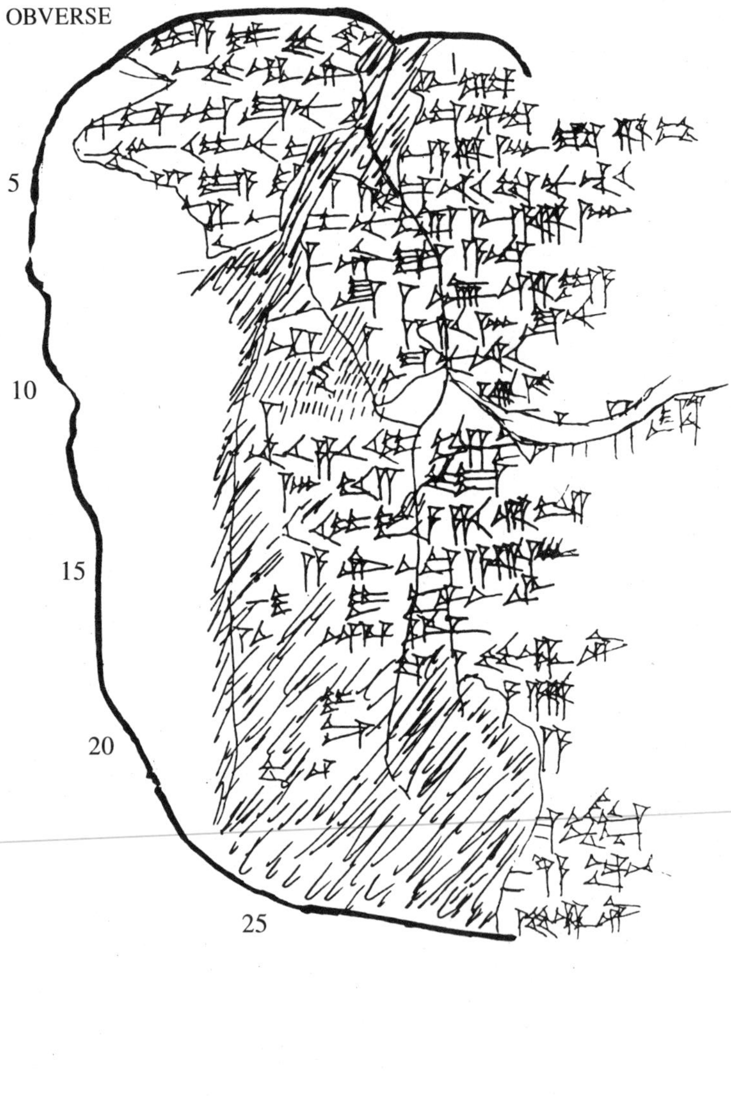

288

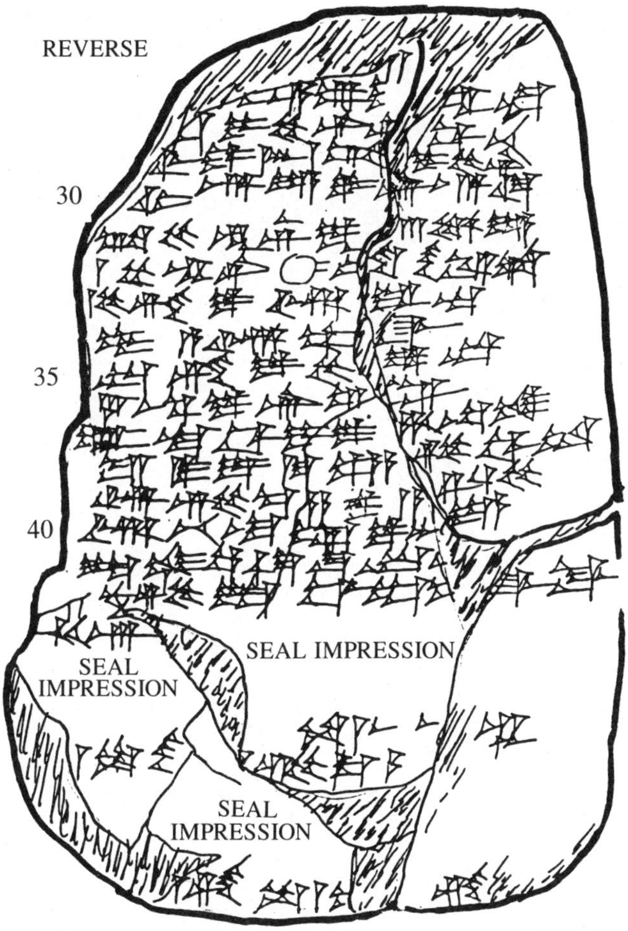

UPPER EDGE

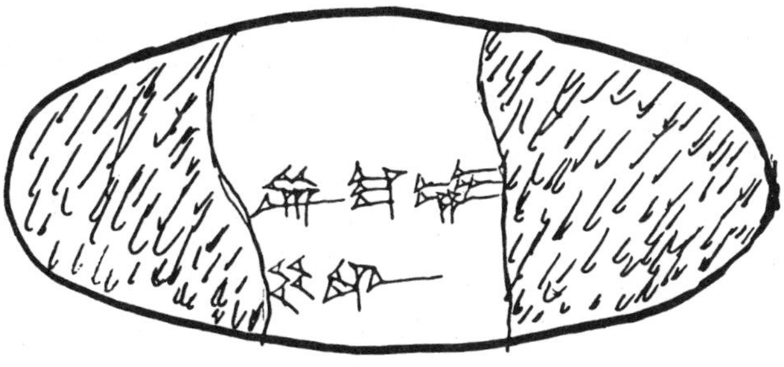

290

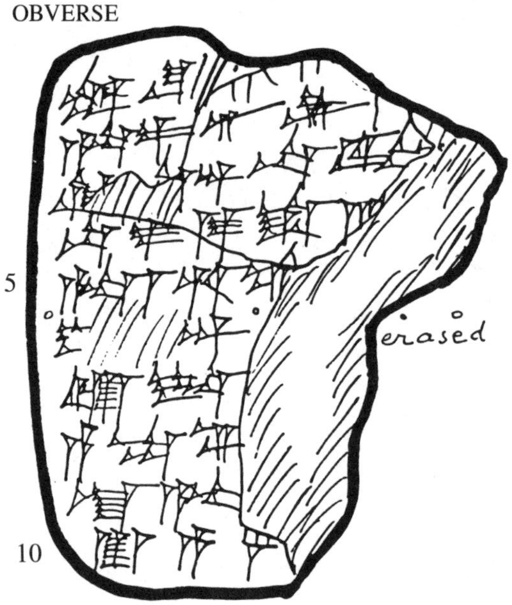
OBVERSE
5
10
erased

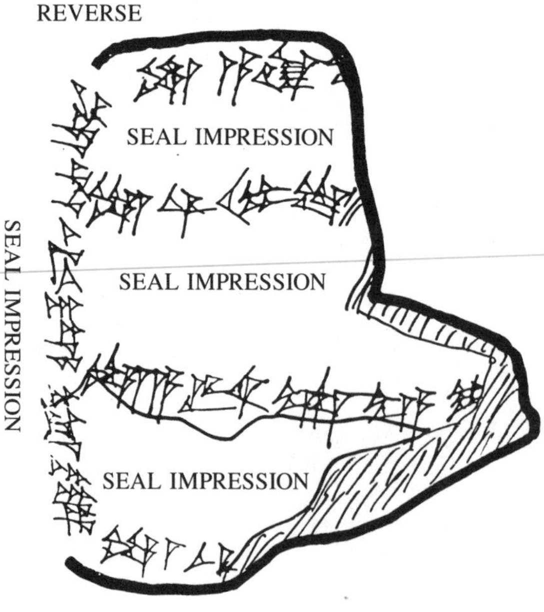
REVERSE
SEAL IMPRESSION
SEAL IMPRESSION
SEAL IMPRESSION
SEAL IMPRESSION

293

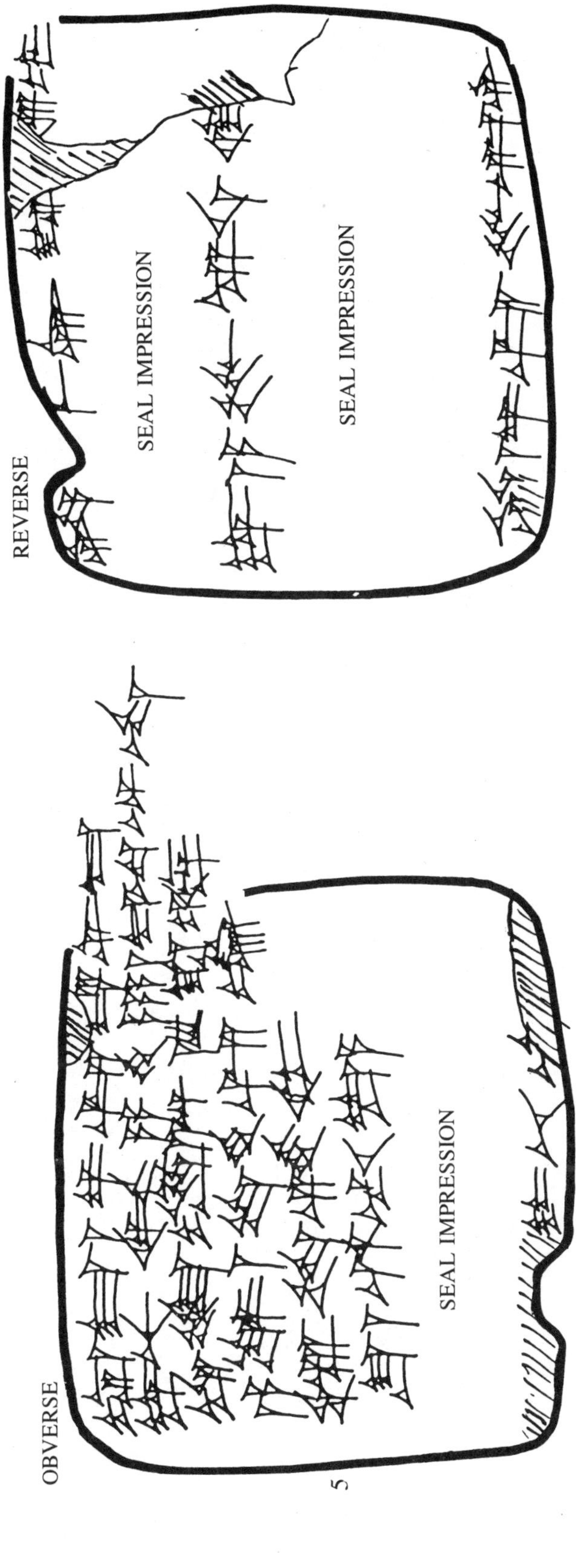
REVERSE
SEAL IMPRESSION
SEAL IMPRESSION
OBVERSE
SEAL IMPRESSION

294

REVERSE

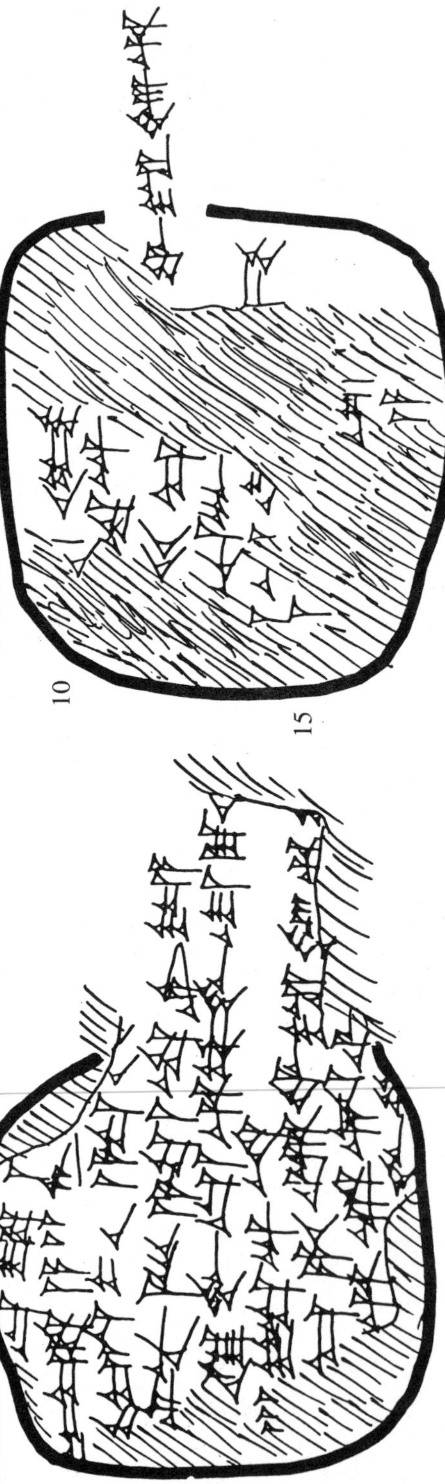

OBVERSE

295

OBVERSE

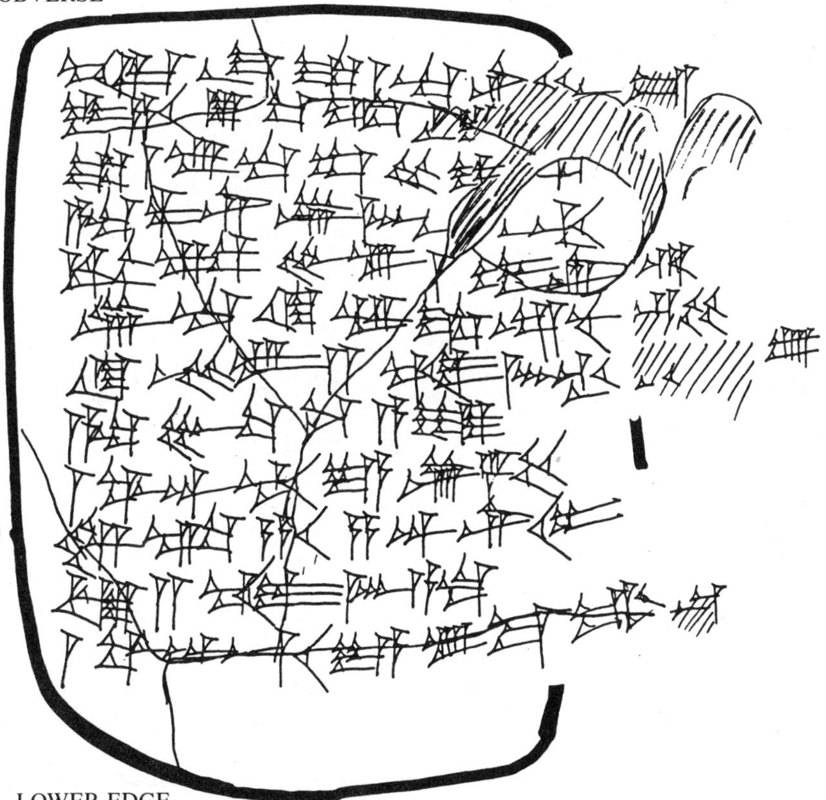

LOWER EDGE

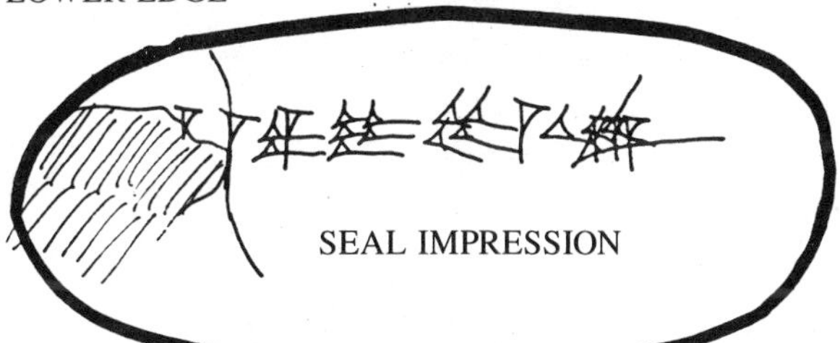

295

REVERSE

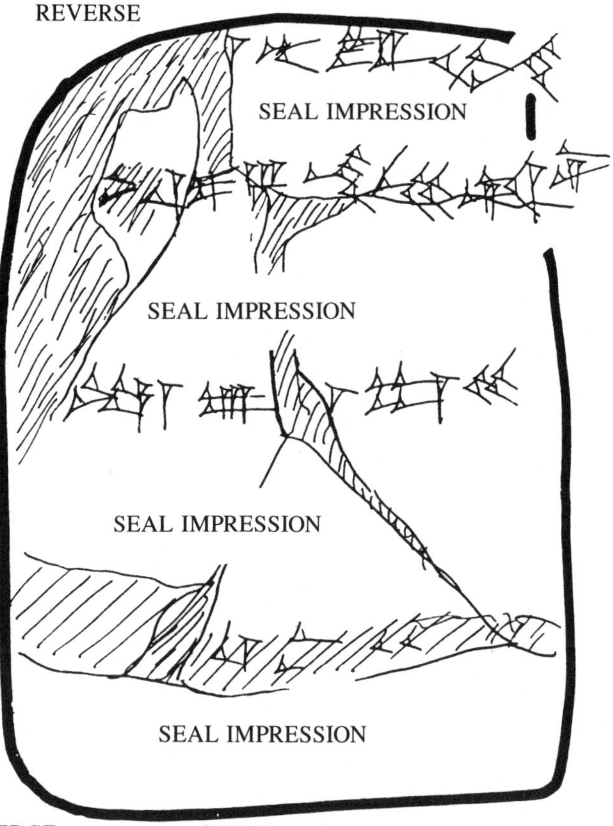

UPPER EDGE

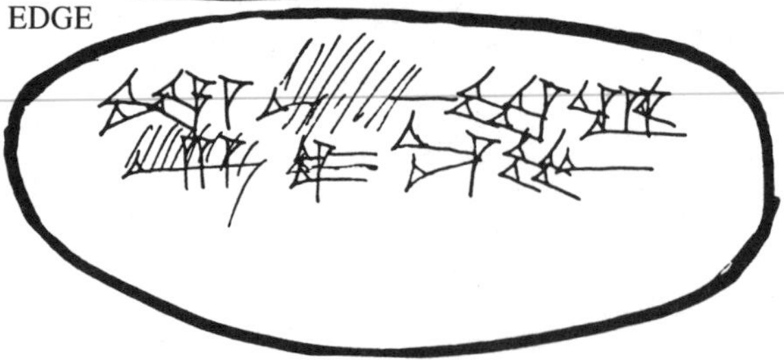

315

OBVERSE

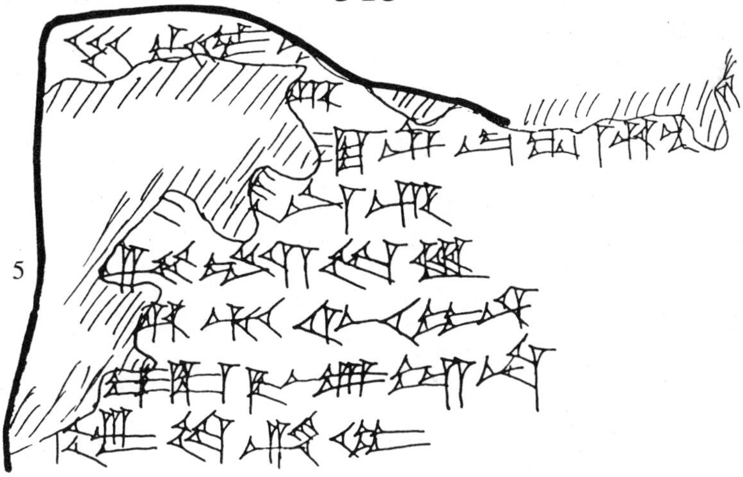

REVERSE SEAL IMPRESSION

316

OBVERSE

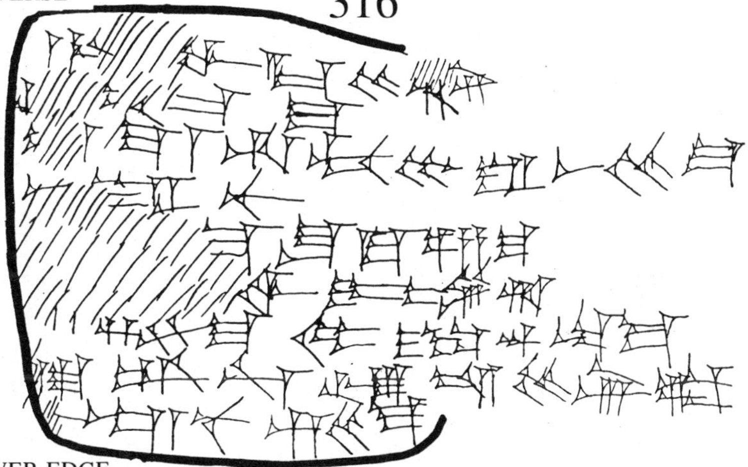

LOWER EDGE

REST NOT INSCRIBED

318

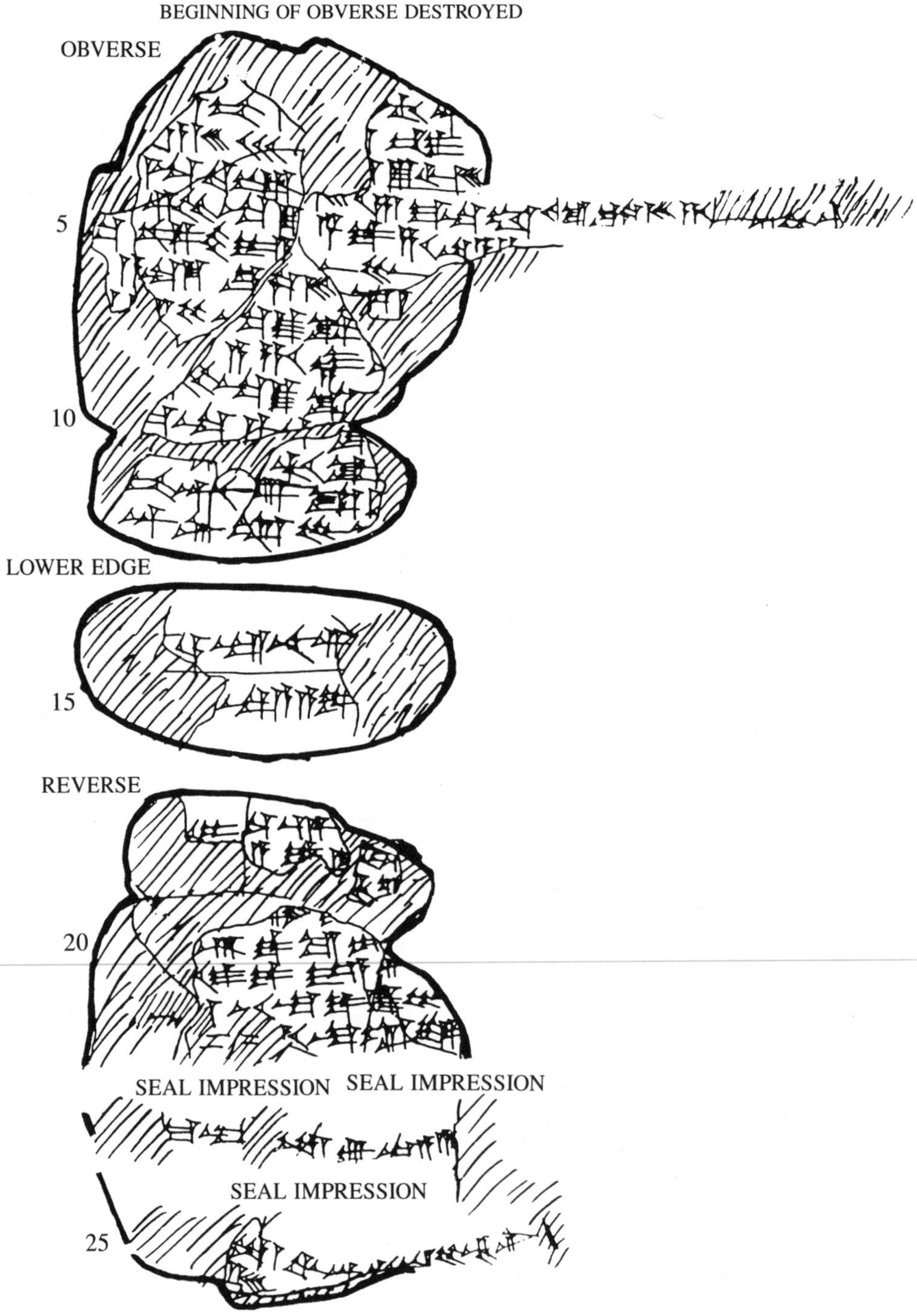
BEGINNING OF OBVERSE DESTROYED
OBVERSE
LOWER EDGE
REVERSE
SEAL IMPRESSION
SEAL IMPRESSION
SEAL IMPRESSION

328

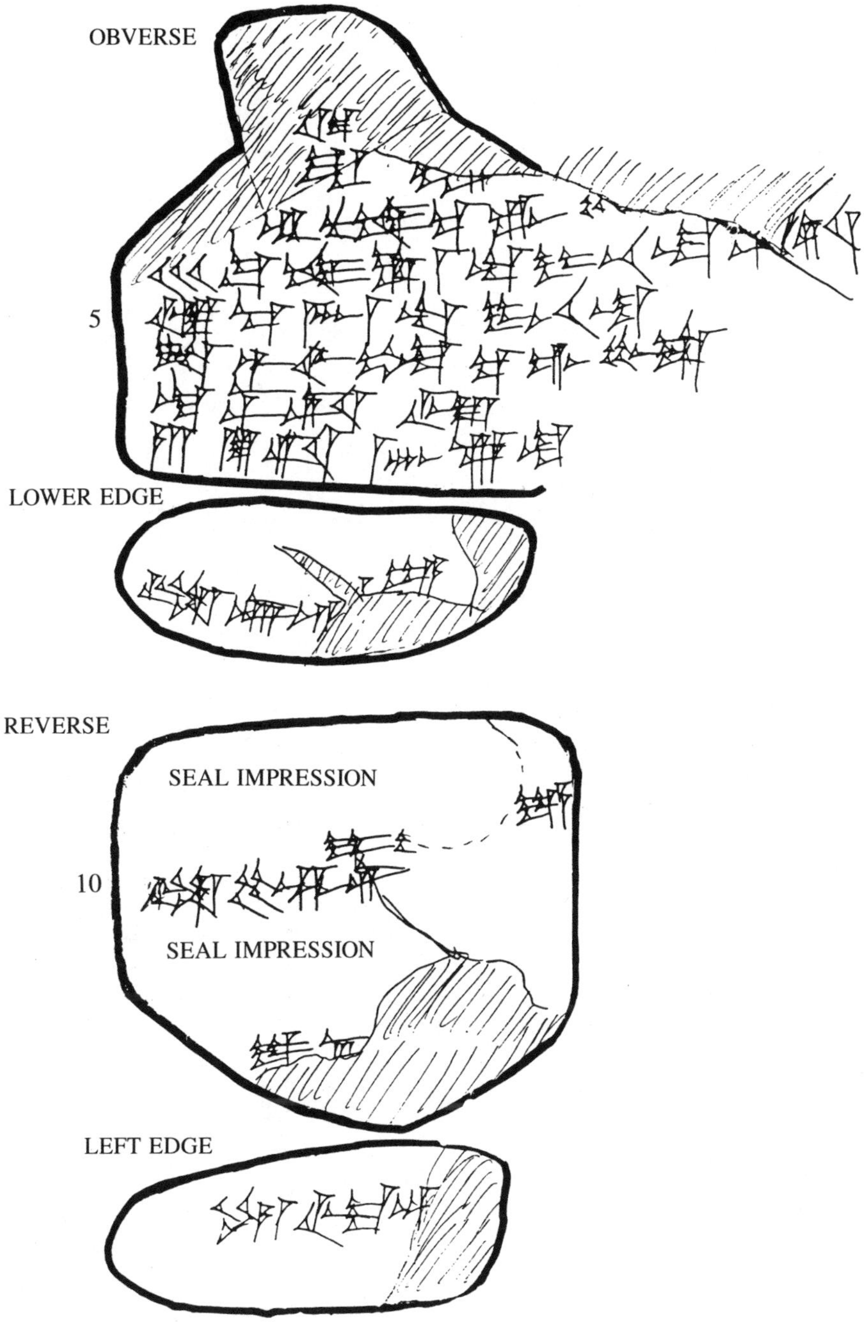
OBVERSE
5
LOWER EDGE
REVERSE
SEAL IMPRESSION
10
SEAL IMPRESSION
LEFT EDGE

330

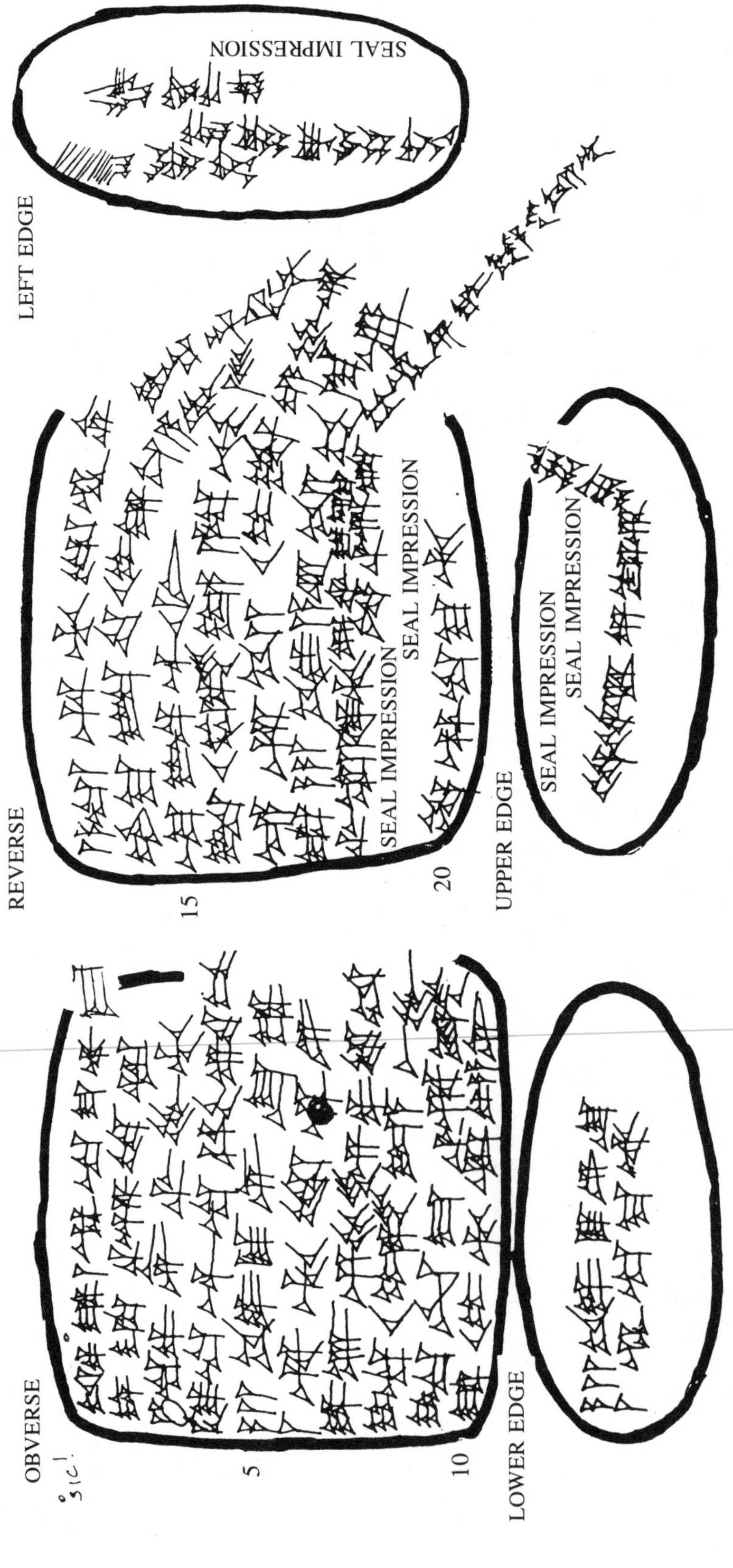
OBVERSE
LOWER EDGE
REVERSE
UPPER EDGE
LEFT EDGE
SEAL IMPRESSION
SEAL IMPRESSION
SEAL IMPRESSION
SEAL IMPRESSION
SEAL IMPRESSION
SEAL IMPRESSION

361

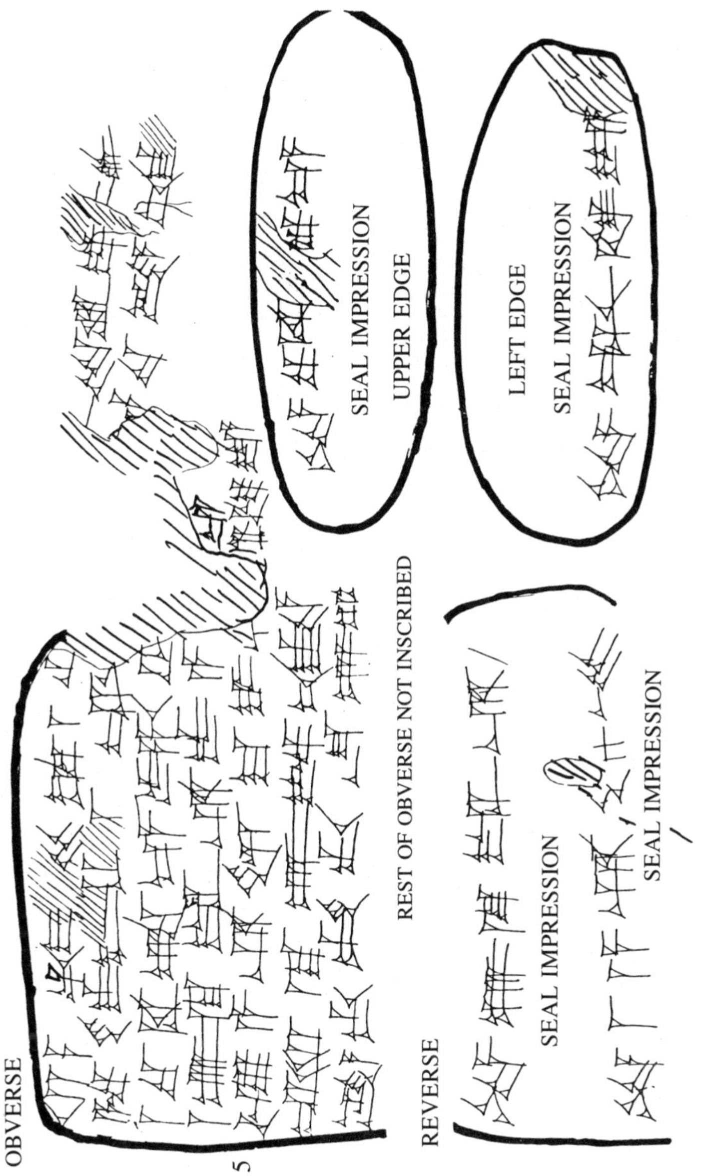
OBVERSE
5
REST OF OBVERSE NOT INSCRIBED
REVERSE
SEAL IMPRESSION
SEAL IMPRESSION
SEAL IMPRESSION
SEAL IMPRESSION
UPPER EDGE
LEFT EDGE
SEAL IMPRESSION

378

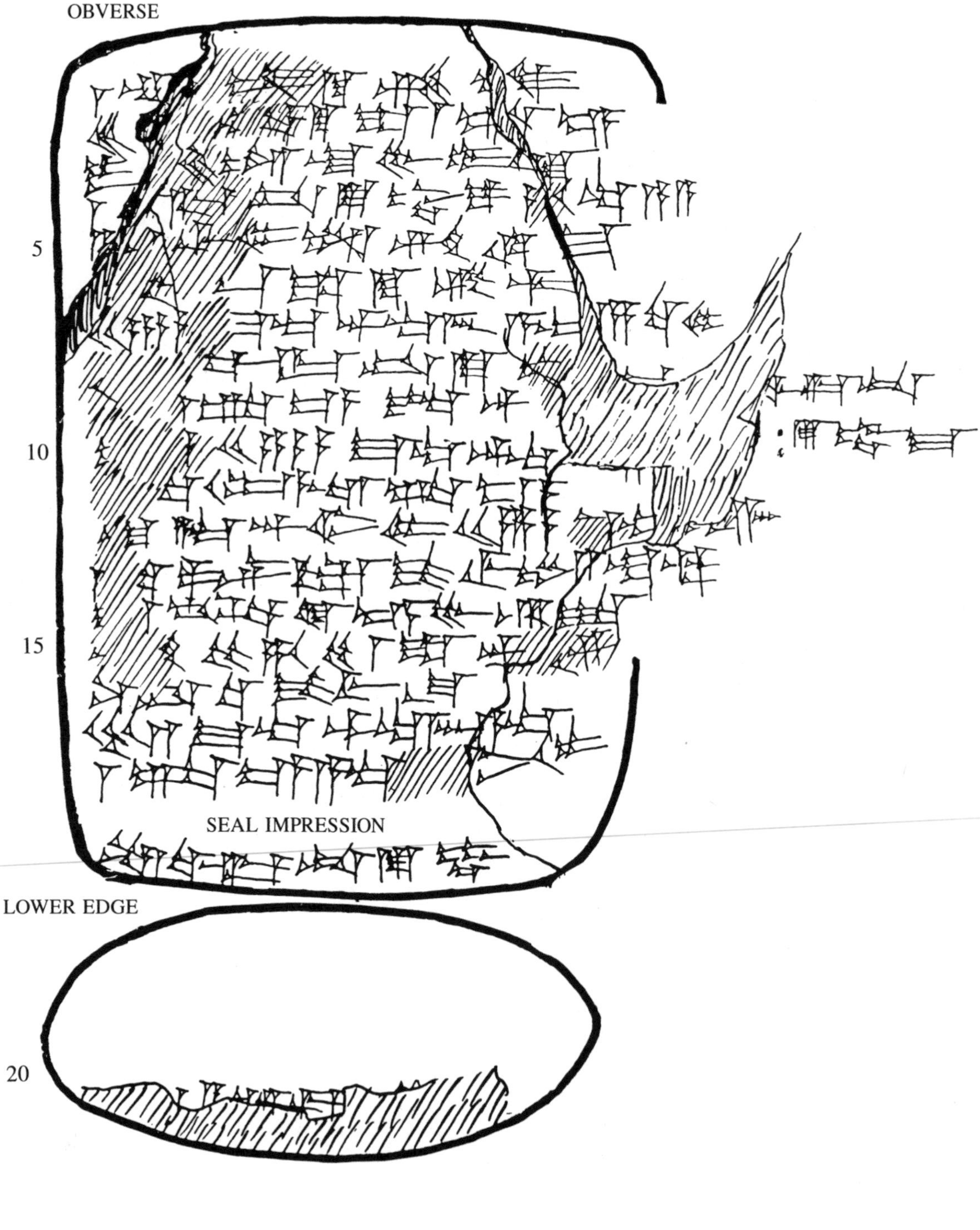

378

REVERSE

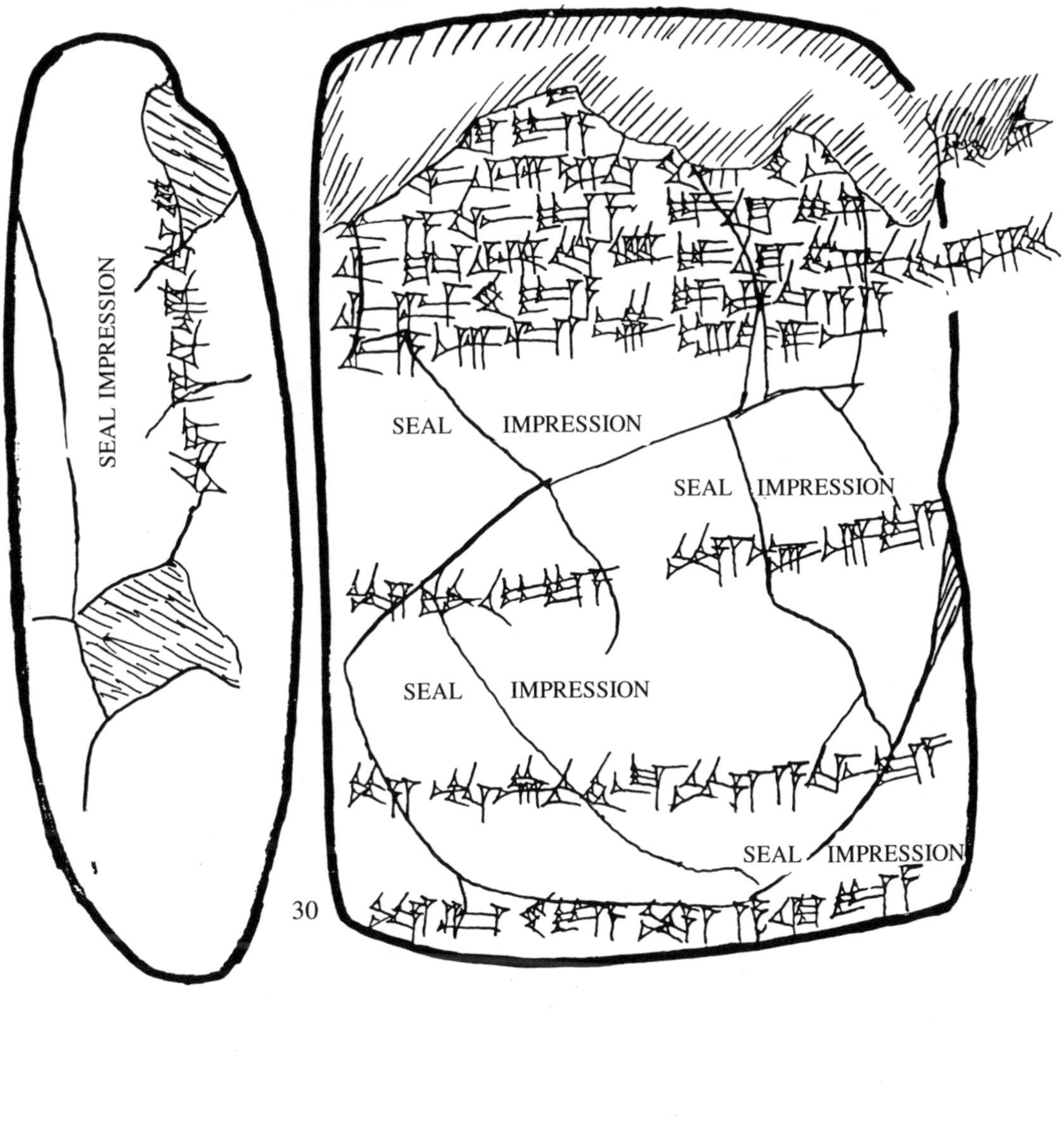
SEAL IMPRESSION
25
SEAL IMPRESSION
SEAL IMPRESSION
SEAL IMPRESSION
SEAL IMPRESSION
30

380

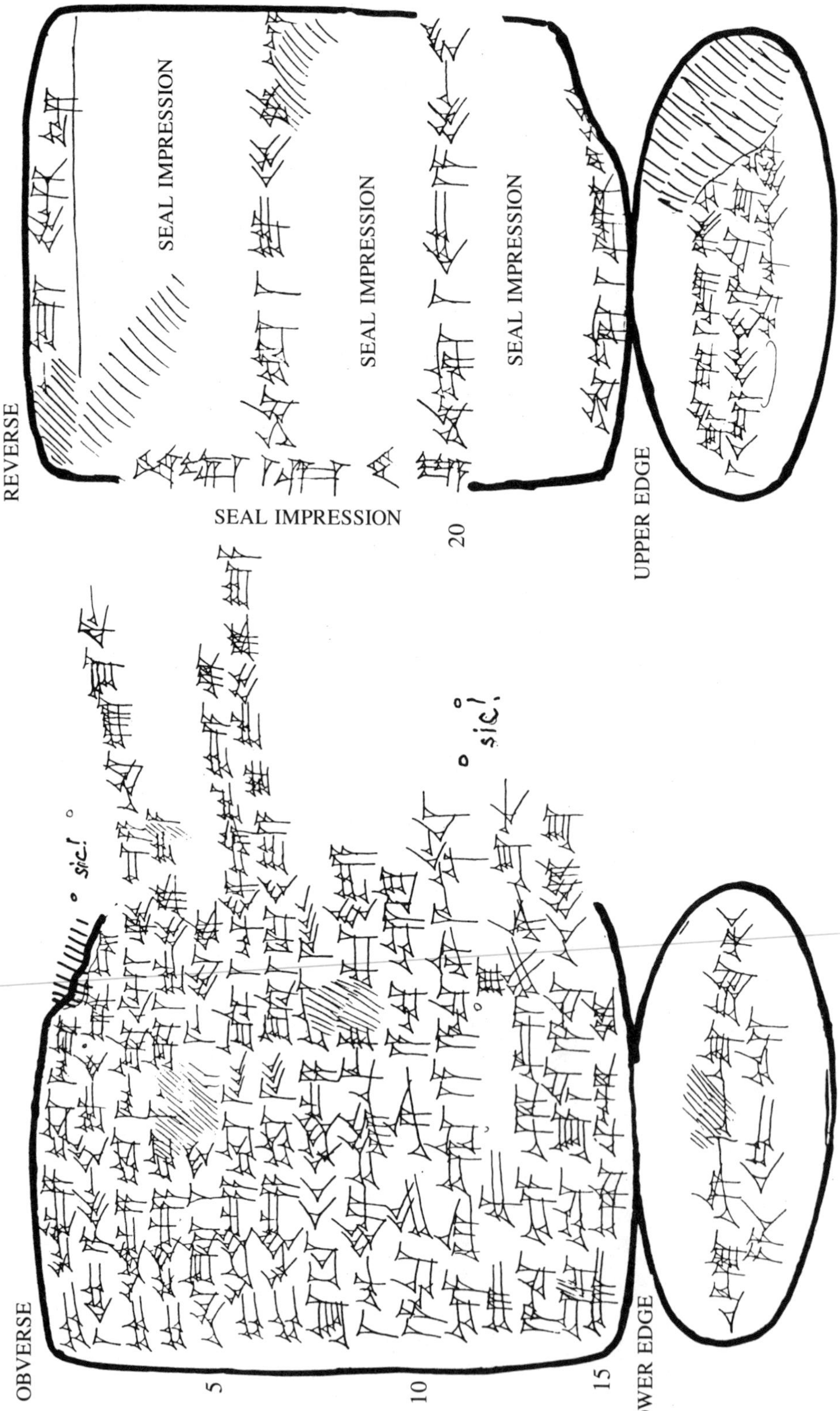
REVERSE
SEAL IMPRESSION
SEAL IMPRESSION
SEAL IMPRESSION
SEAL IMPRESSION
UPPER EDGE
OBVERSE
sic!
sic!
LOWER EDGE

382

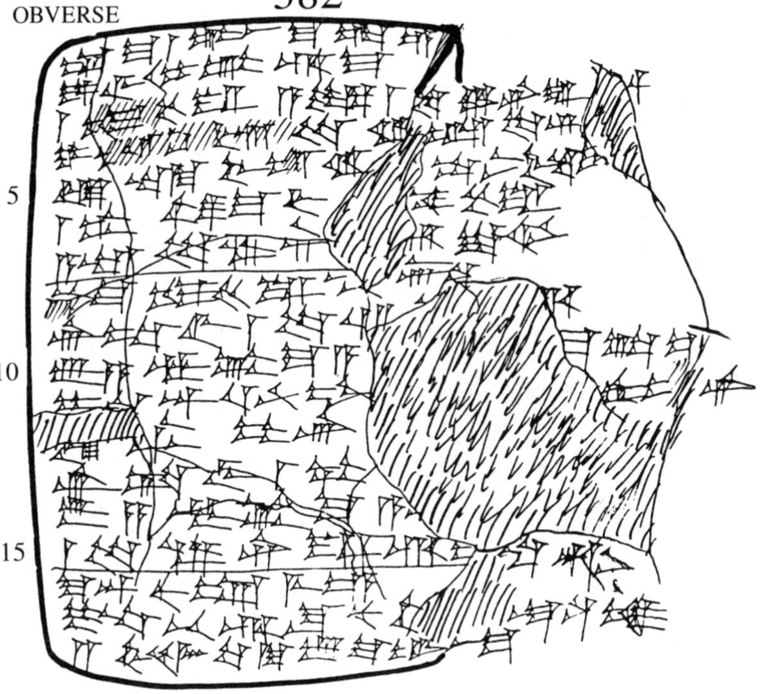
OBVERSE

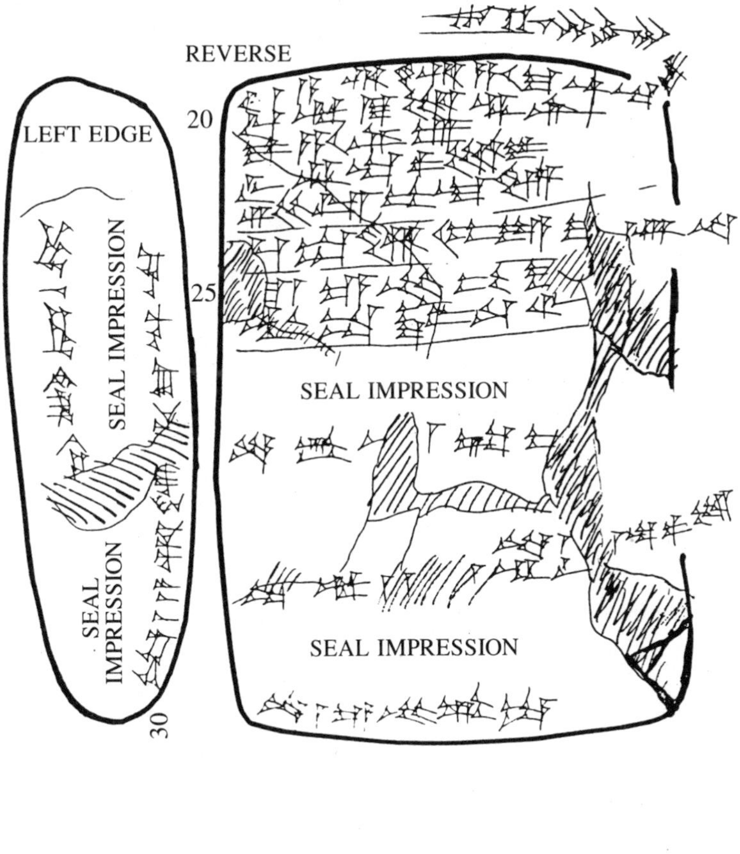
REVERSE
LEFT EDGE
SEAL IMPRESSION
SEAL IMPRESSION
SEAL IMPRESSION
SEAL IMPRESSION

383

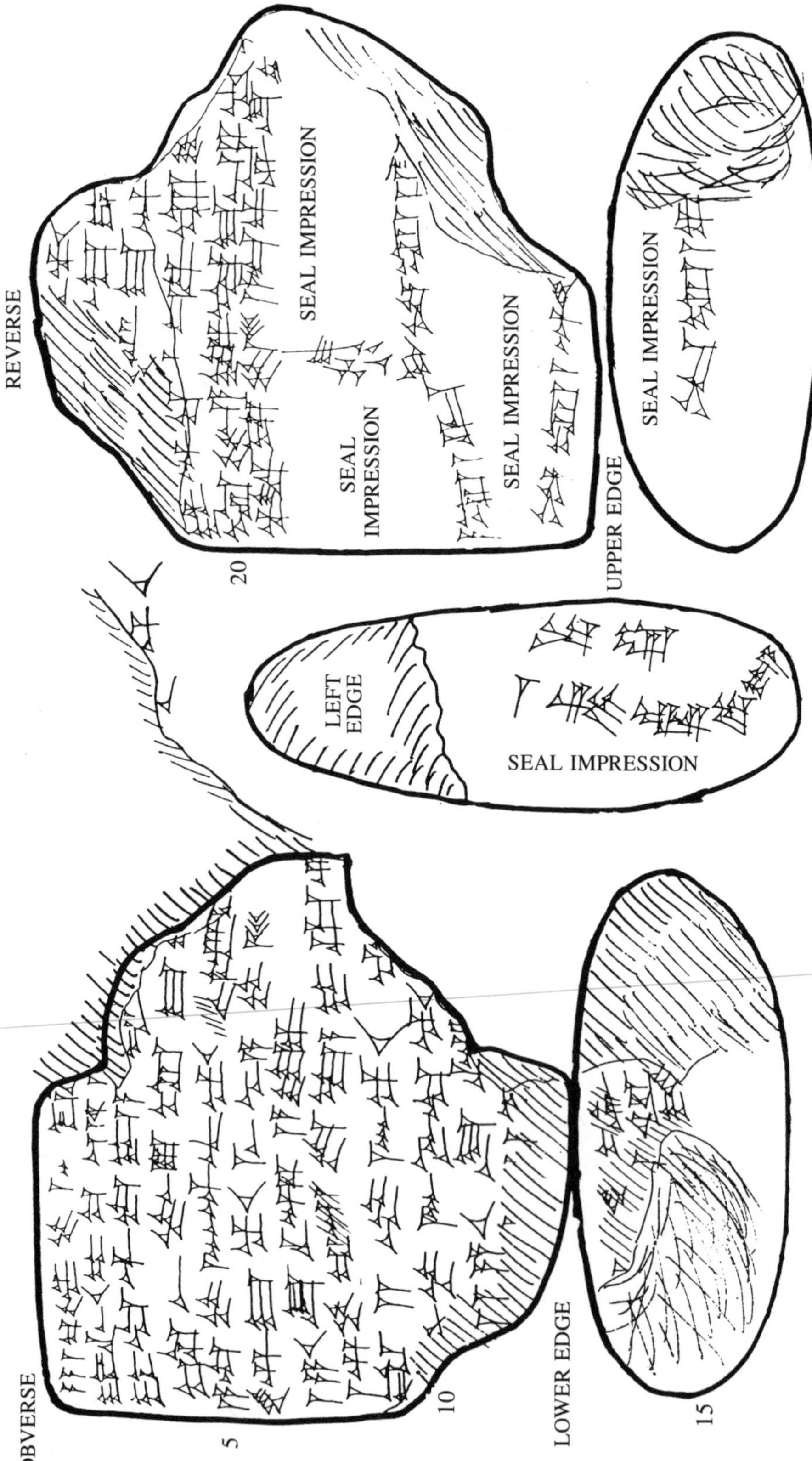
OBVERSE
LOWER EDGE
REVERSE
UPPER EDGE
LEFT EDGE
SEAL IMPRESSION
SEAL IMPRESSION
SEAL IMPRESSION
SEAL IMPRESSION
SEAL IMPRESSION

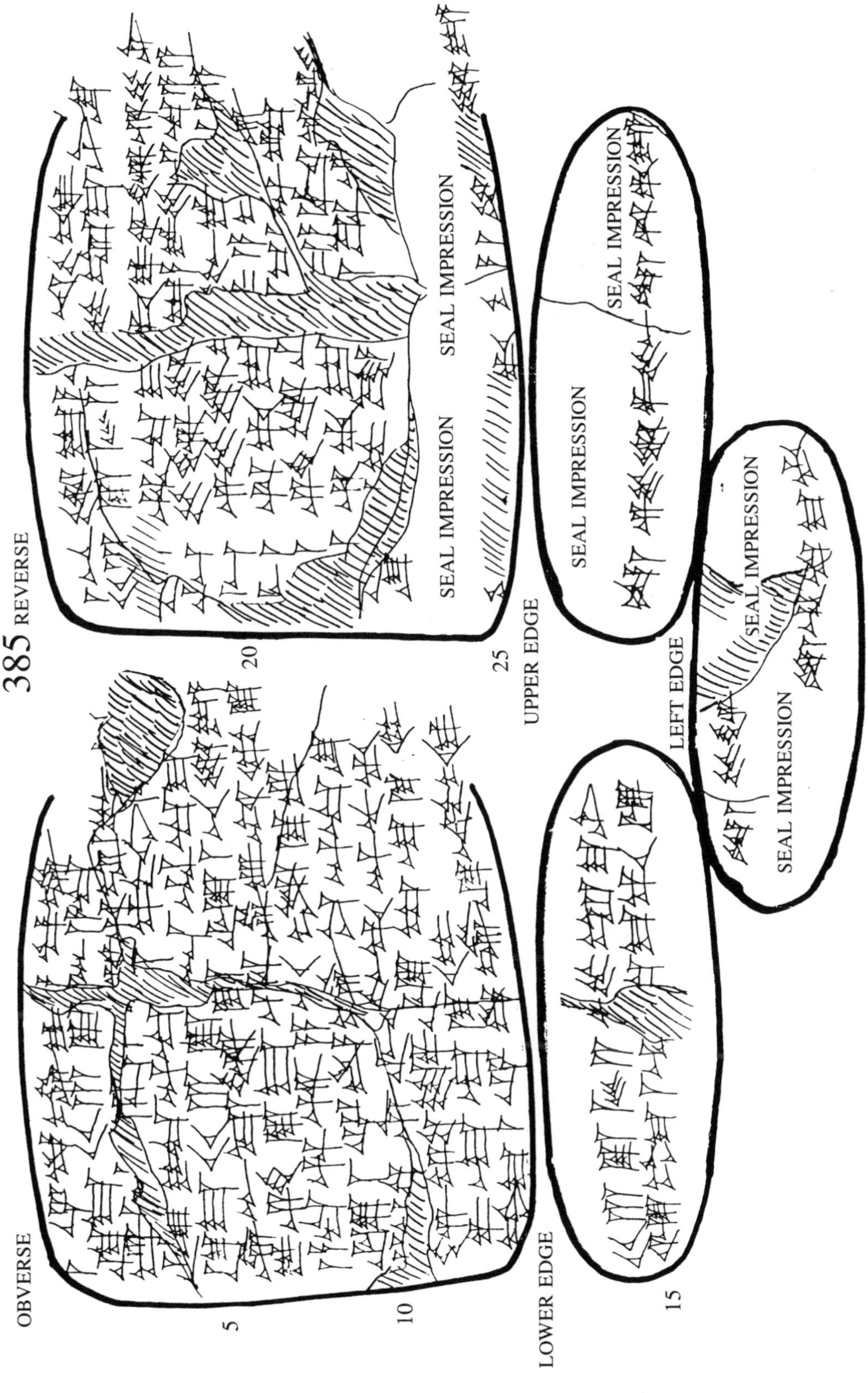
385
OBVERSE
5
10
LOWER EDGE
15
REVERSE
20
25
UPPER EDGE
LEFT EDGE
SEAL IMPRESSION
SEAL IMPRESSION
SEAL IMPRESSION
SEAL IMPRESSION
SEAL IMPRESSION
SEAL IMPRESSION
SEAL IMPRESSION

394

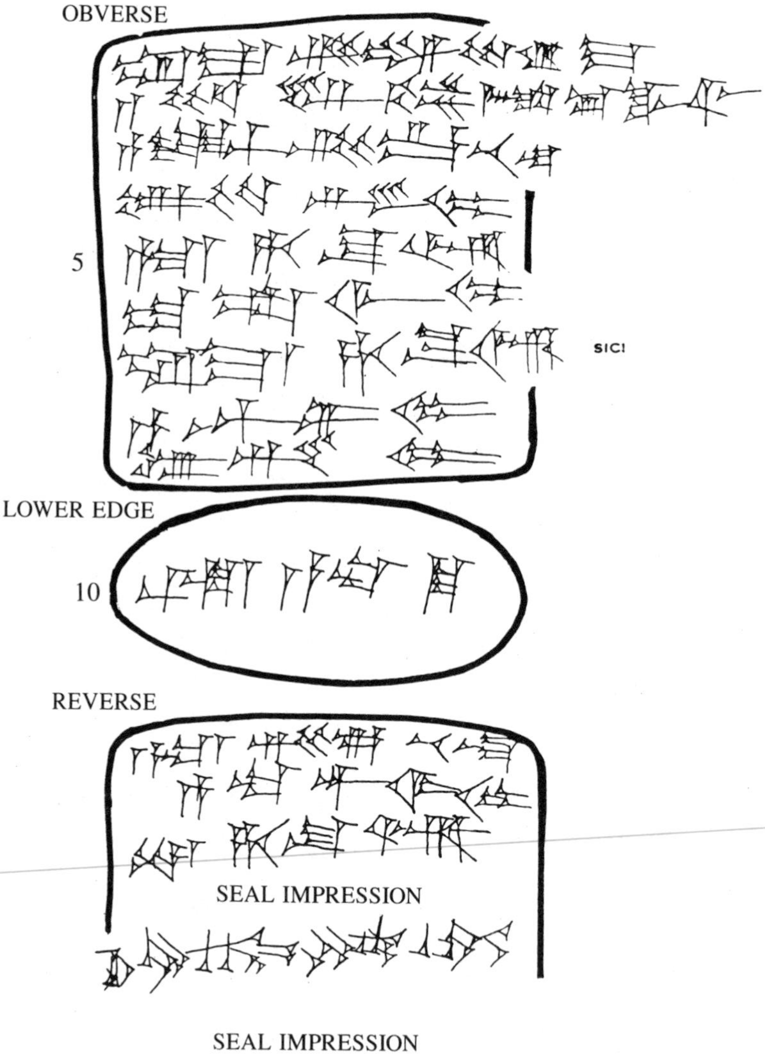
OBVERSE
SIC!
LOWER EDGE
REVERSE
SEAL IMPRESSION
SEAL IMPRESSION

402

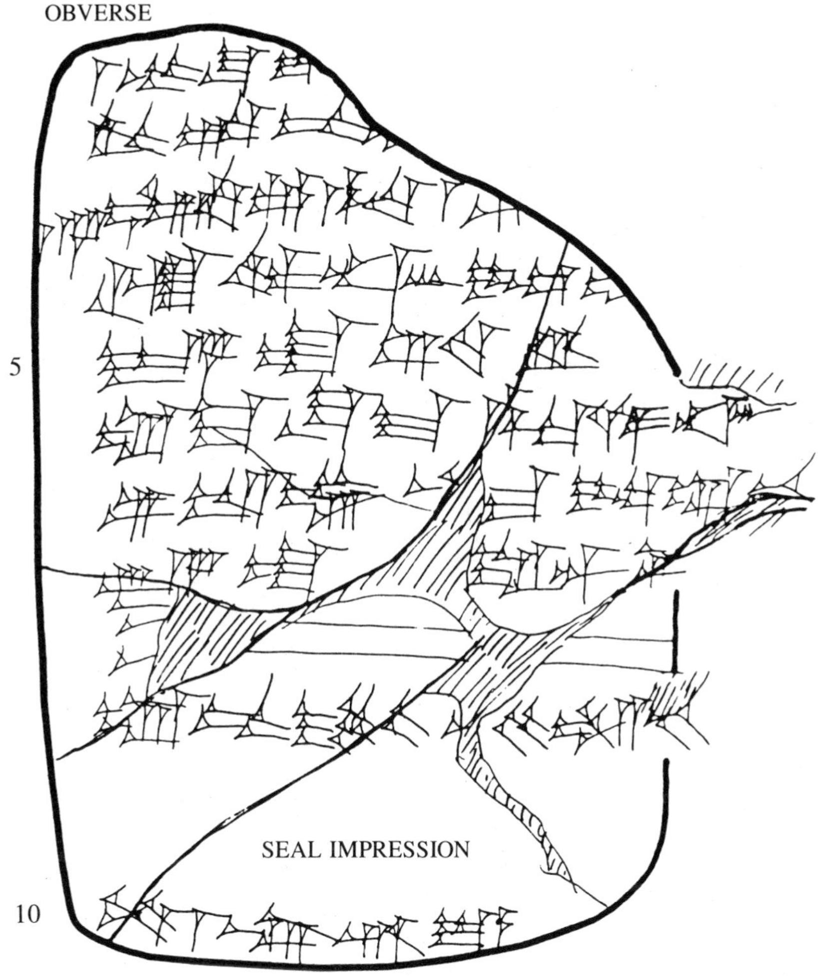

402

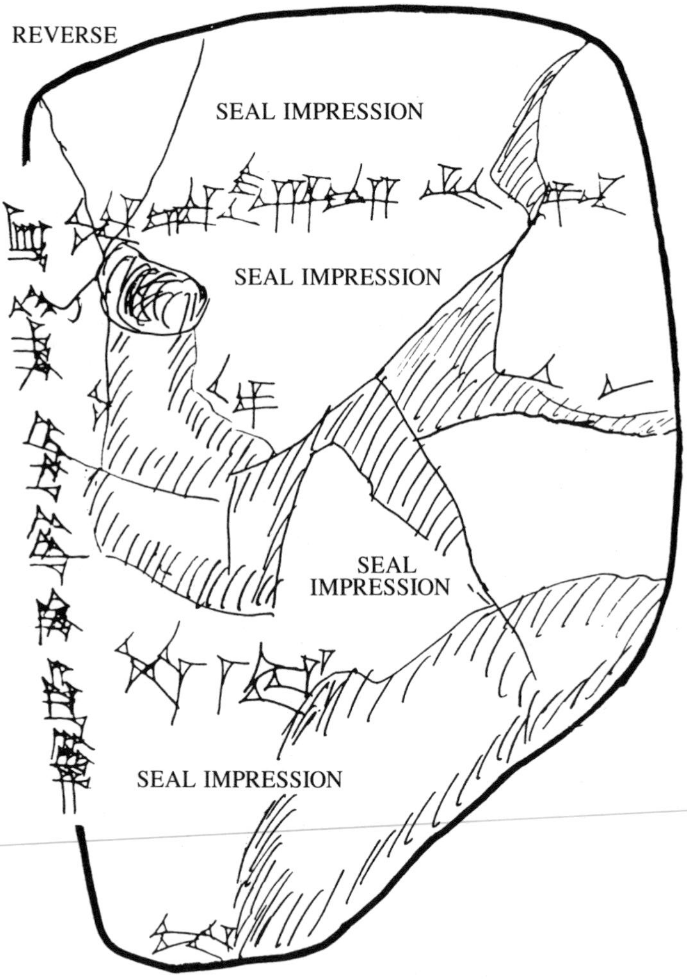
REVERSE
SEAL IMPRESSION
SEAL IMPRESSION
SEAL IMPRESSION
SEAL IMPRESSION

407

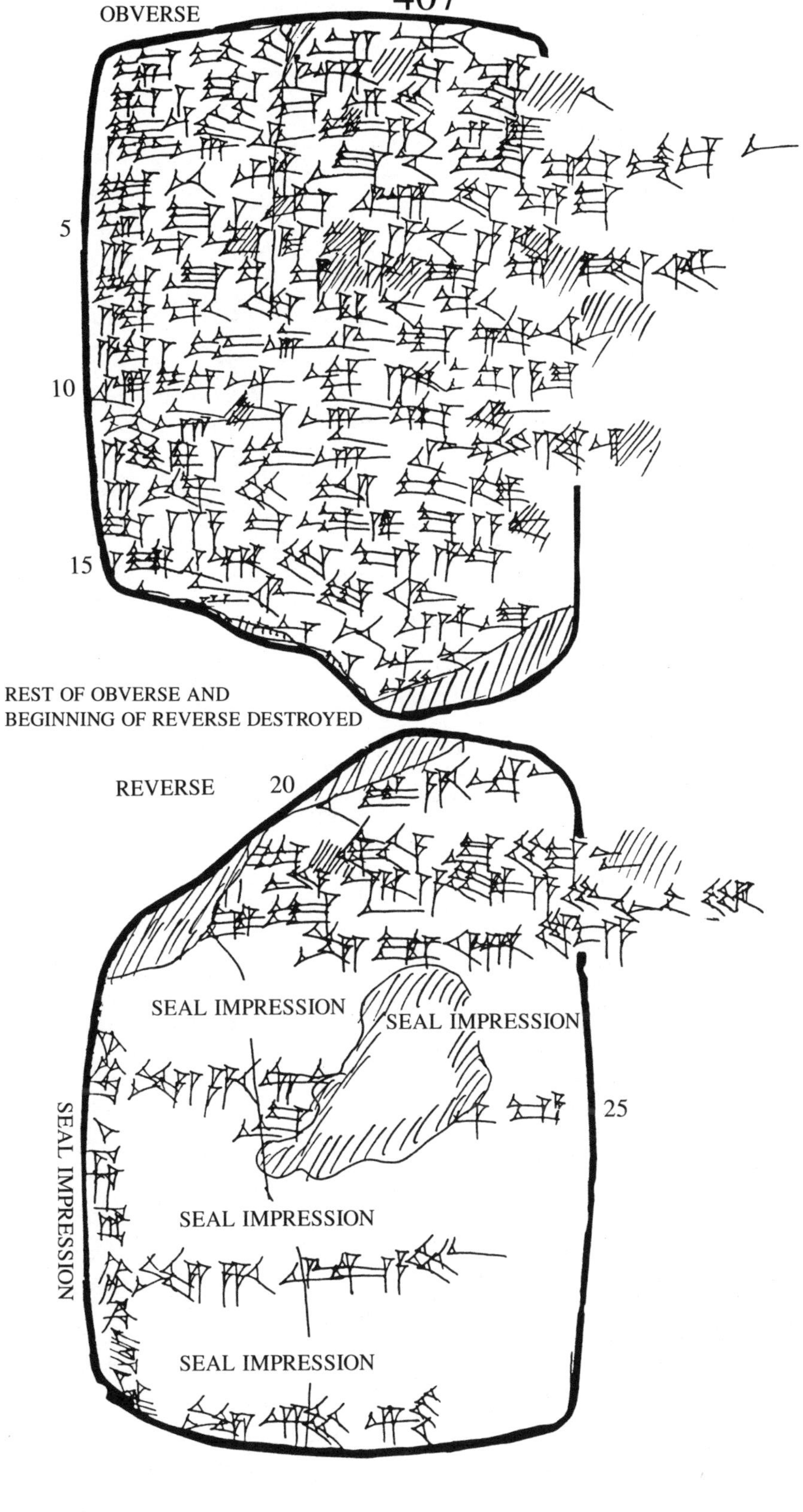
OBVERSE
5
10
15
REST OF OBVERSE AND
BEGINNING OF REVERSE DESTROYED
REVERSE
20
SEAL IMPRESSION
SEAL IMPRESSION
25
SEAL IMPRESSION
SEAL IMPRESSION
SEAL IMPRESSION

412

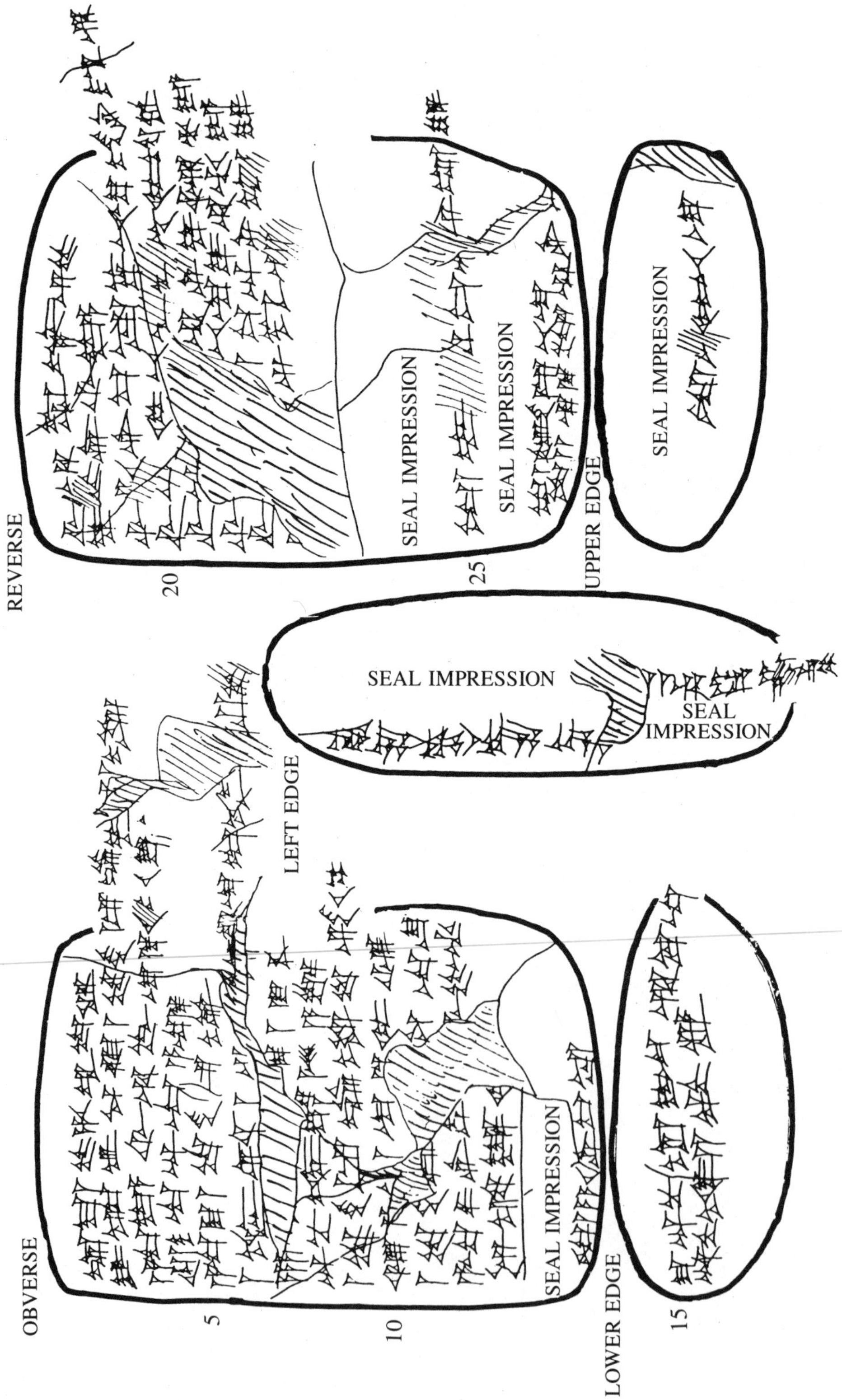
OBVERSE
5
10
SEAL IMPRESSION
LOWER EDGE
15
REVERSE
20
25
SEAL IMPRESSION
SEAL IMPRESSION
UPPER EDGE
SEAL IMPRESSION
LEFT EDGE
SEAL IMPRESSION
SEAL IMPRESSION

422

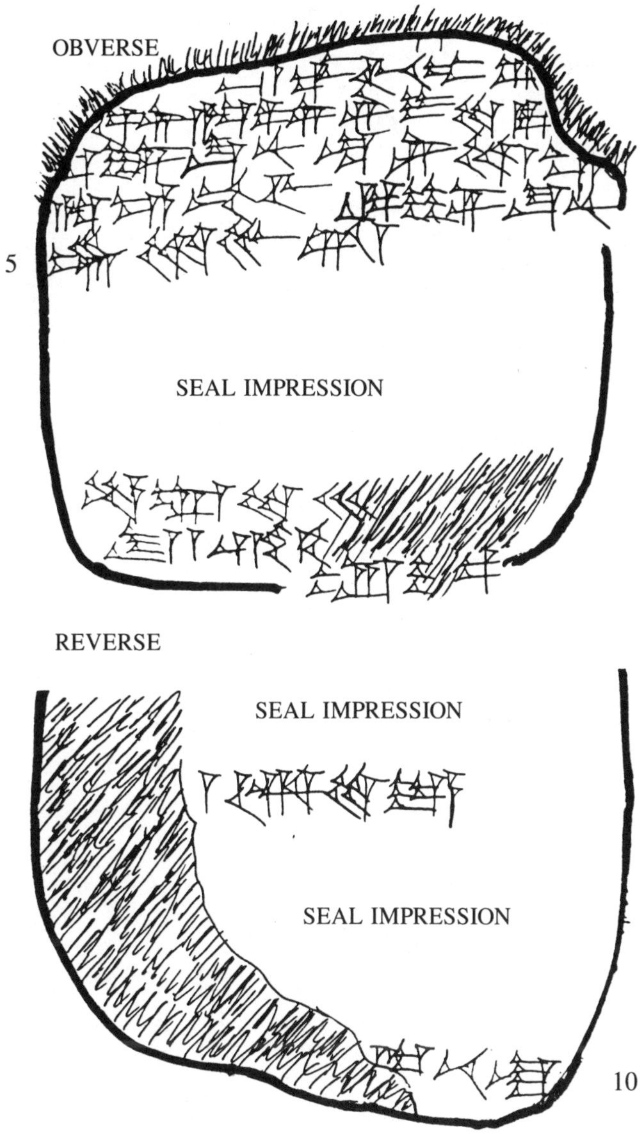
OBVERSE
5
SEAL IMPRESSION
REVERSE
SEAL IMPRESSION
SEAL IMPRESSION
10

428

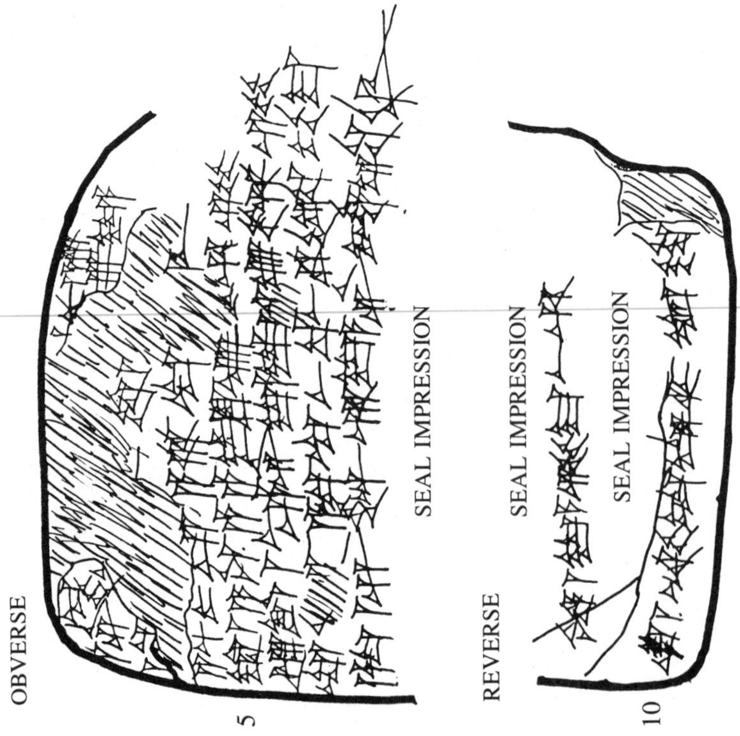
OBVERSE
5
SEAL IMPRESSION
REVERSE
SEAL IMPRESSION
SEAL IMPRESSION
10

429

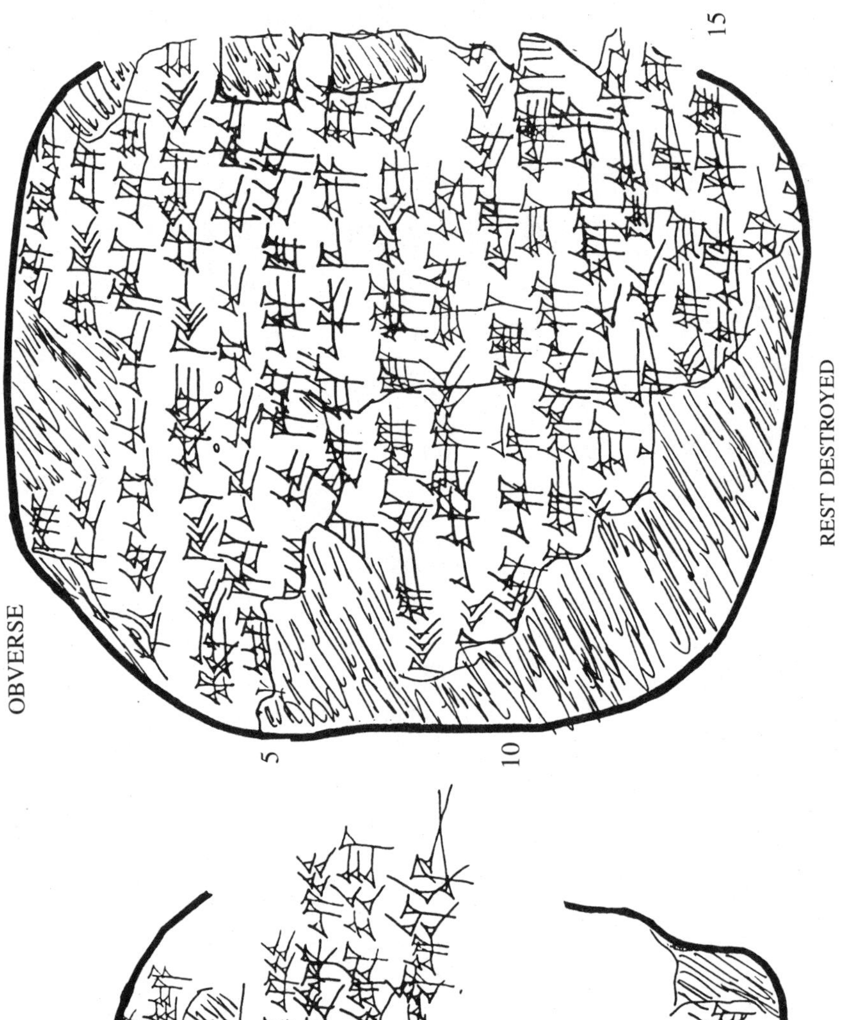
OBVERSE
5
10
15
REST DESTROYED

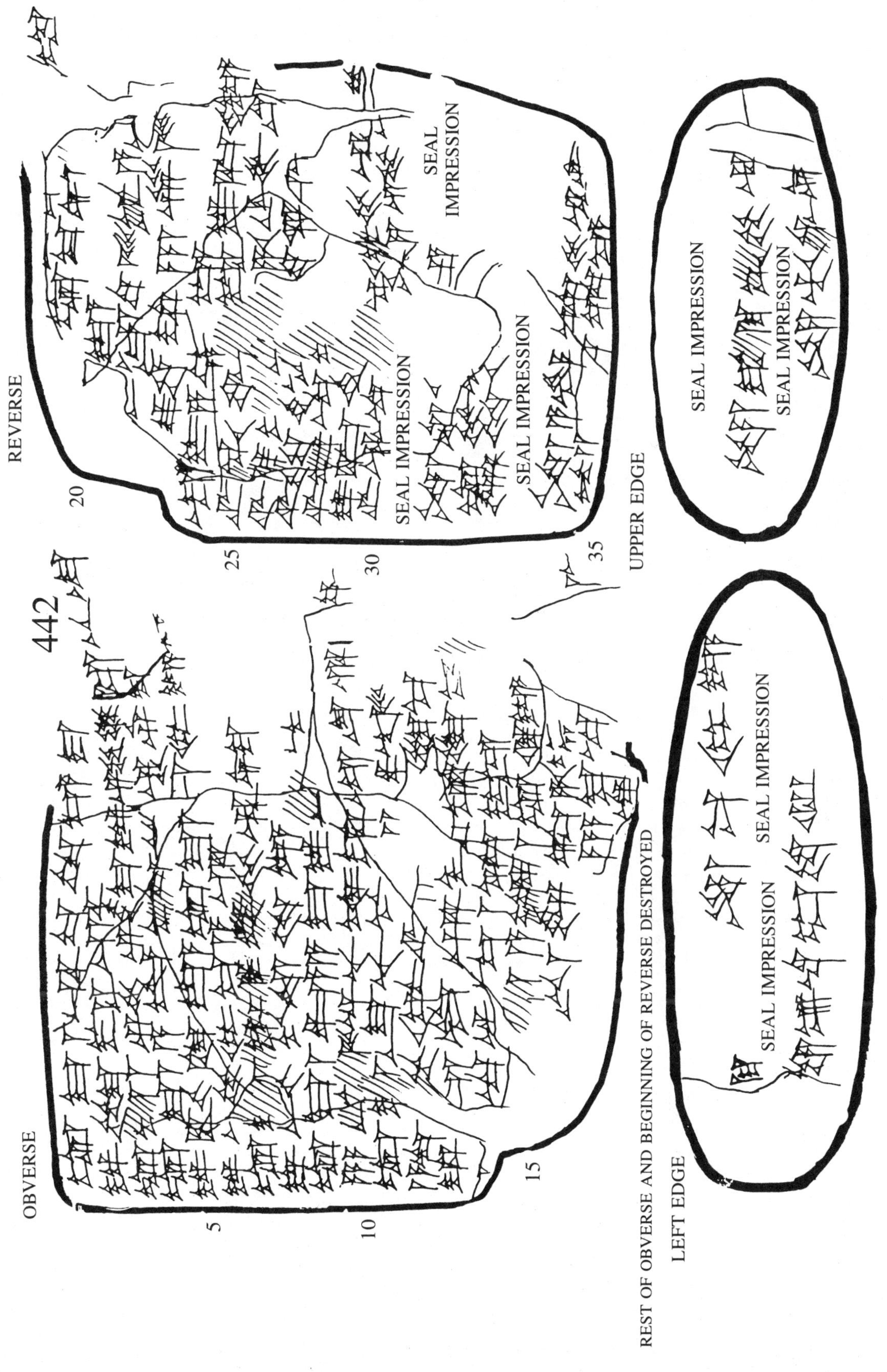
442
OBVERSE
REVERSE
SEAL IMPRESSION
SEAL IMPRESSION
SEAL IMPRESSION
UPPER EDGE
REST OF OBVERSE AND BEGINNING OF REVERSE DESTROYED
LEFT EDGE
SEAL IMPRESSION
SEAL IMPRESSION
SEAL IMPRESSION
SEAL IMPRESSION

446

OBVERSE

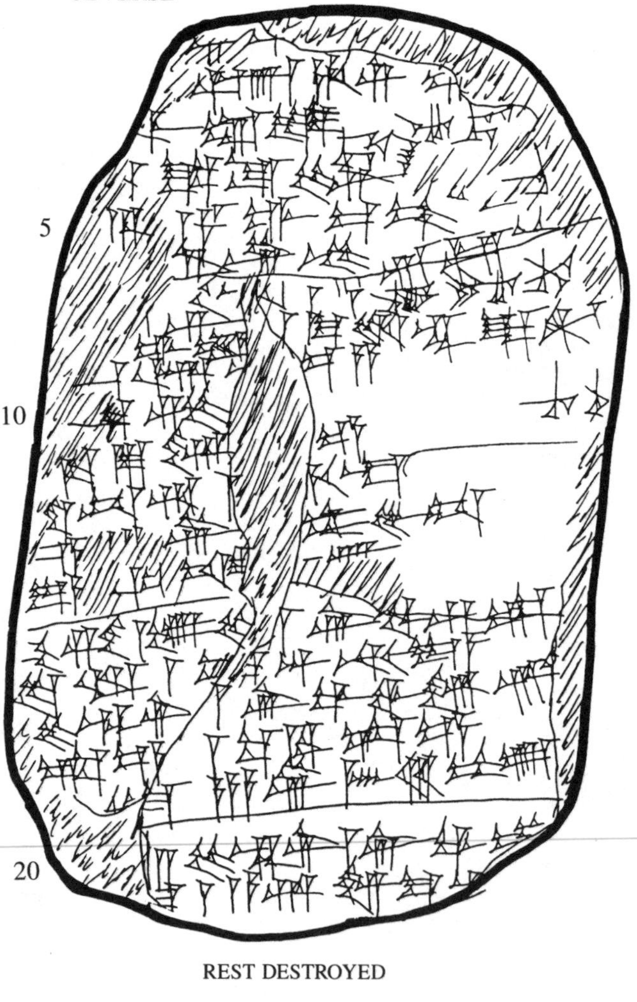

REST DESTROYED

447

OBVERSE

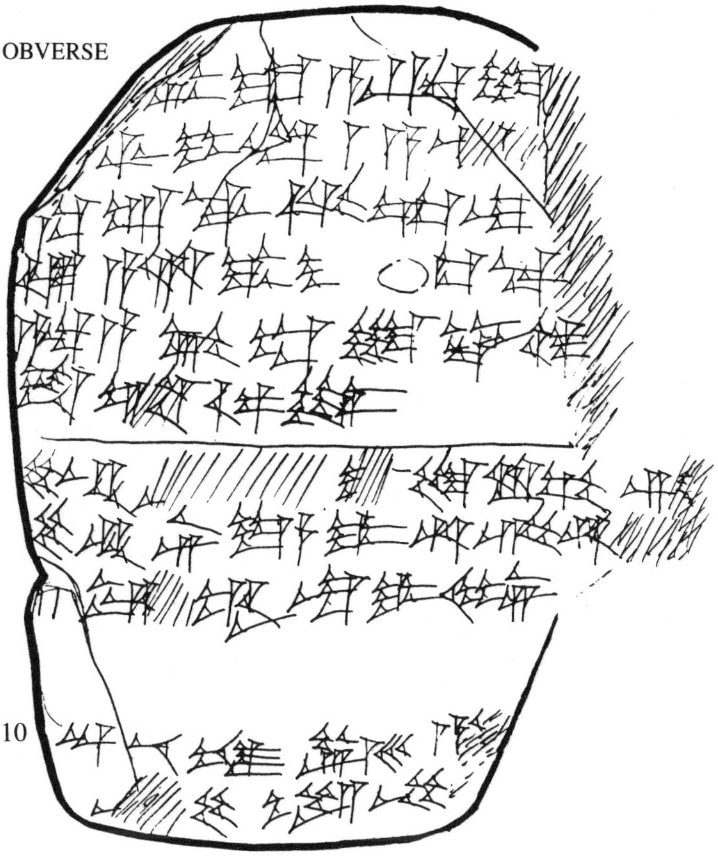

REVERSE DESTROYED

449

OBVERSE

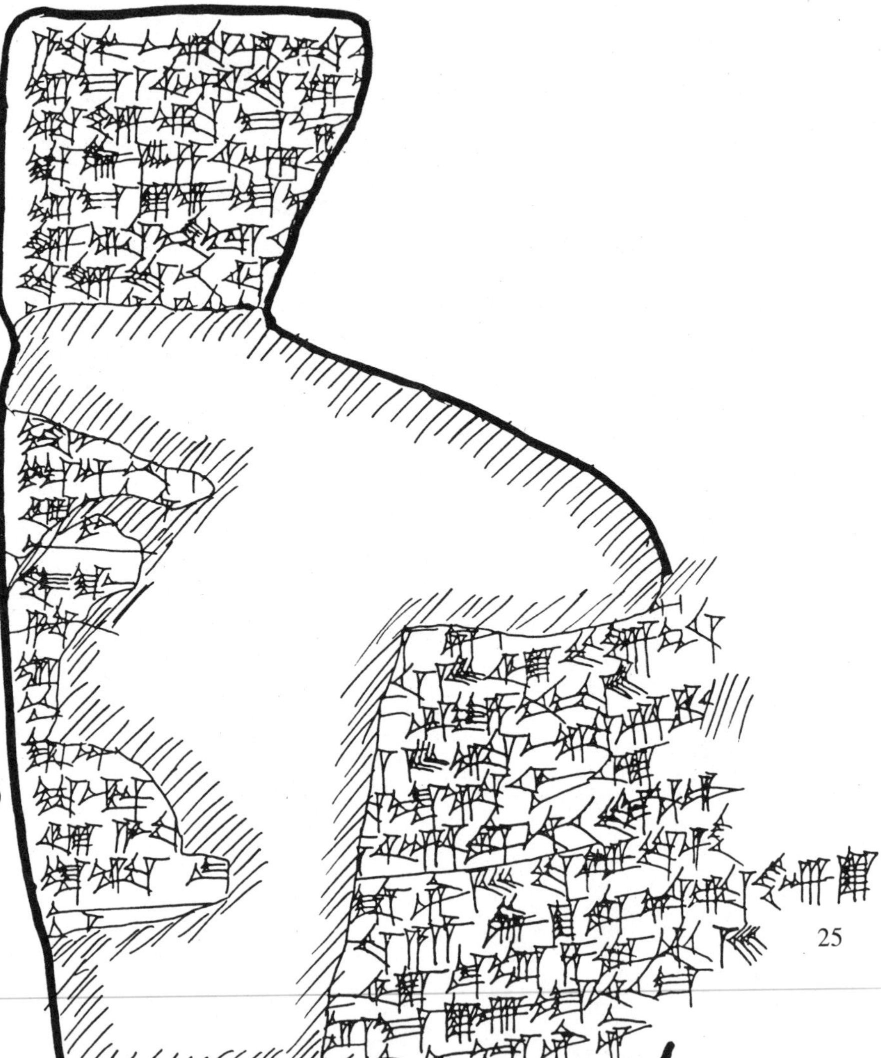

LOWER EDGE

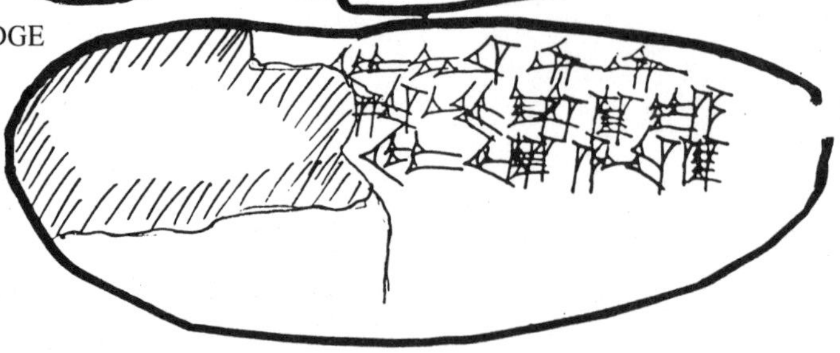

449

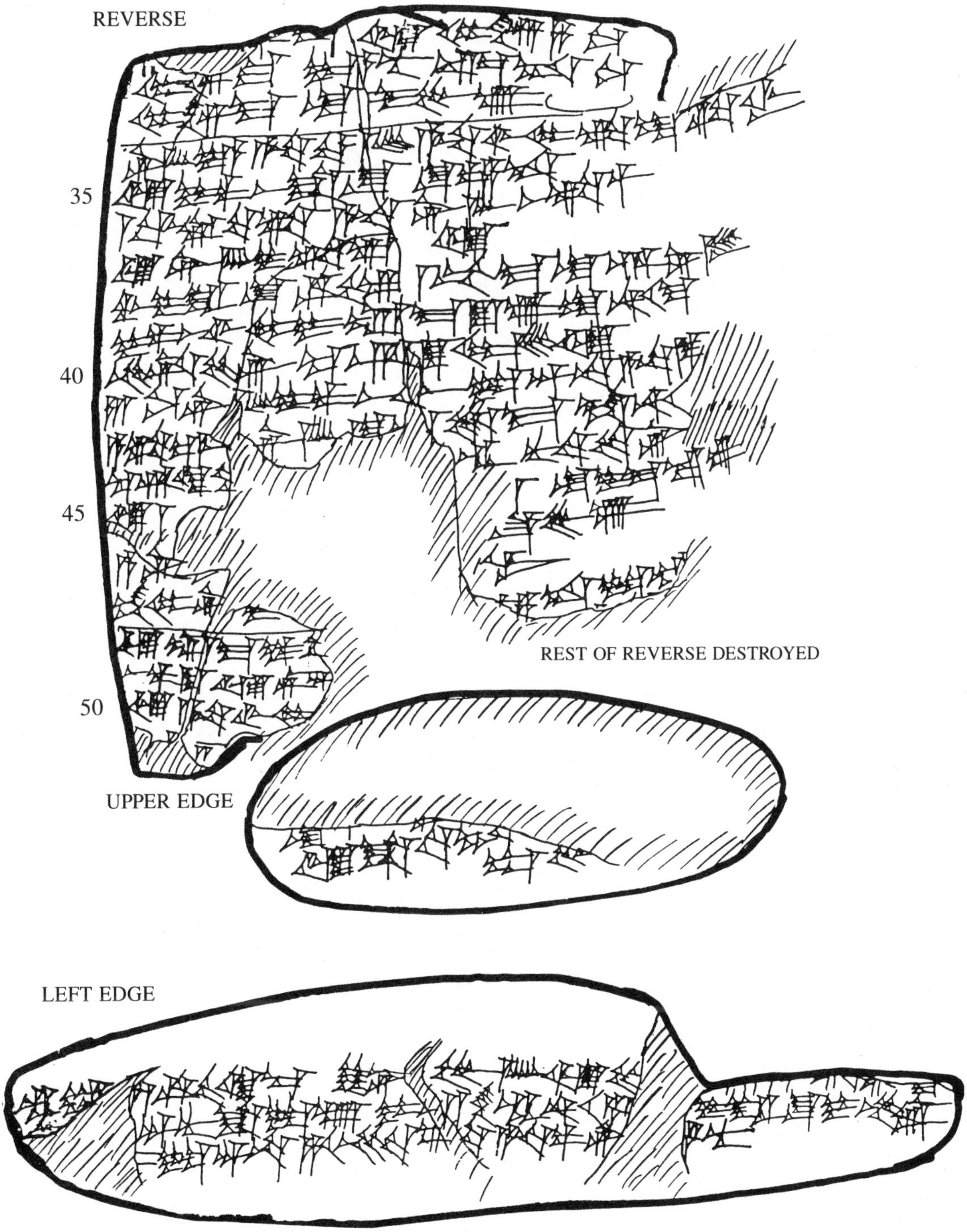

302

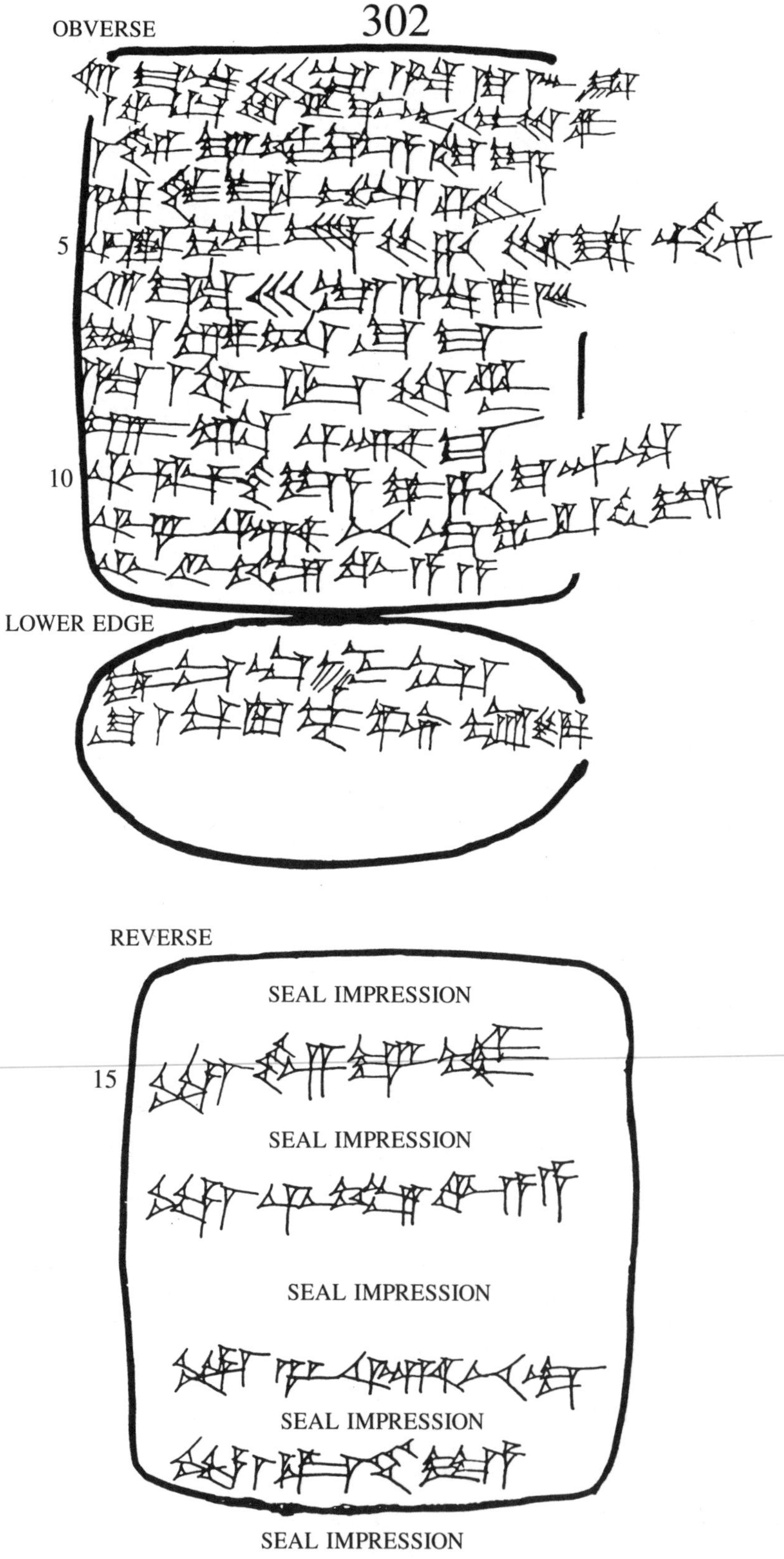
OBVERSE
LOWER EDGE
REVERSE
SEAL IMPRESSION
SEAL IMPRESSION
SEAL IMPRESSION
SEAL IMPRESSION
SEAL IMPRESSION

453

OBVERSE

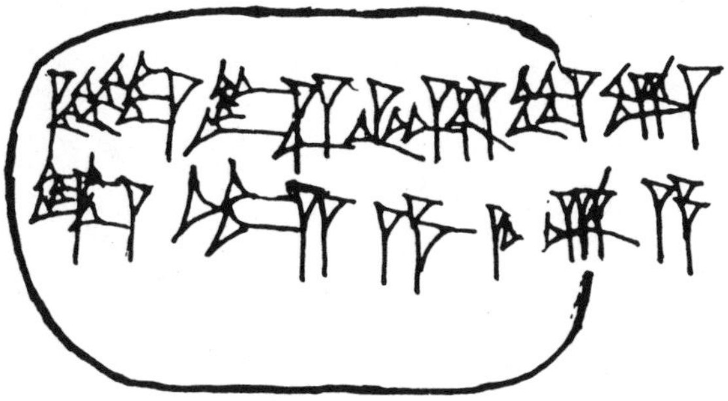

REST NOT INSCRIBED

454

OBVERSE

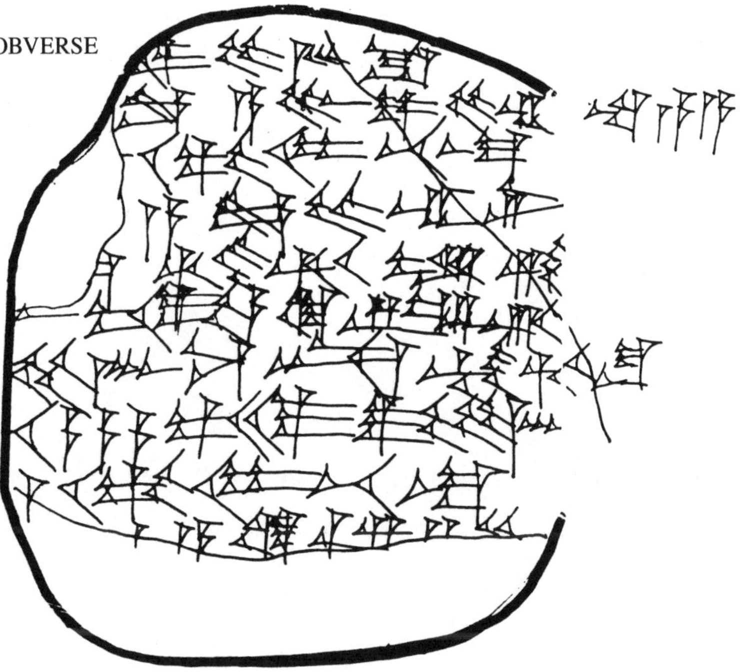

REST DESTROYED

456

OBVERSE

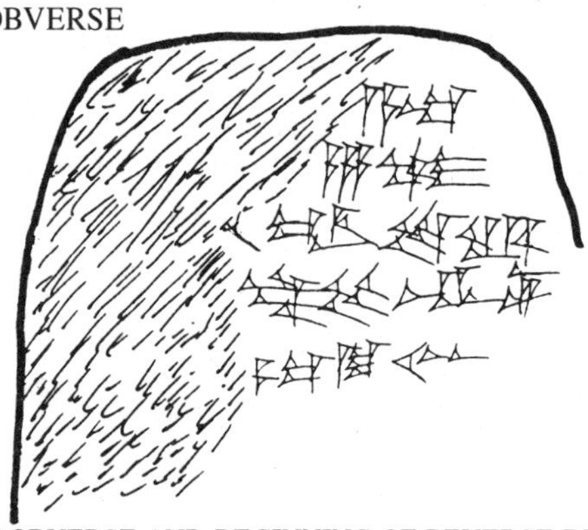

REVERSE

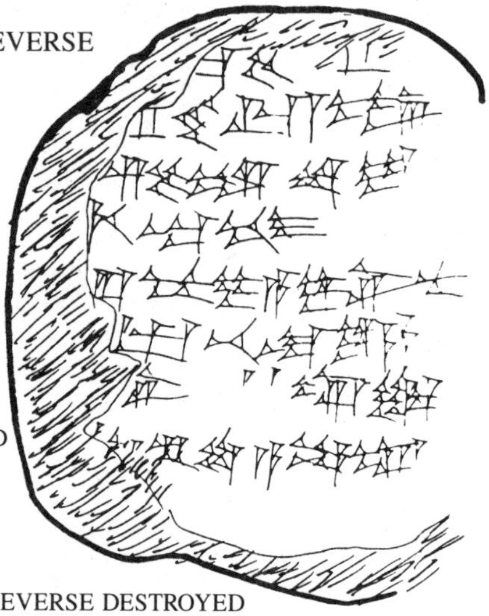

REST OF OBVERSE AND BEGINNING OF REVERSE DESTROYED

REST OF REVERSE DESTROYED

457

OBVERSE

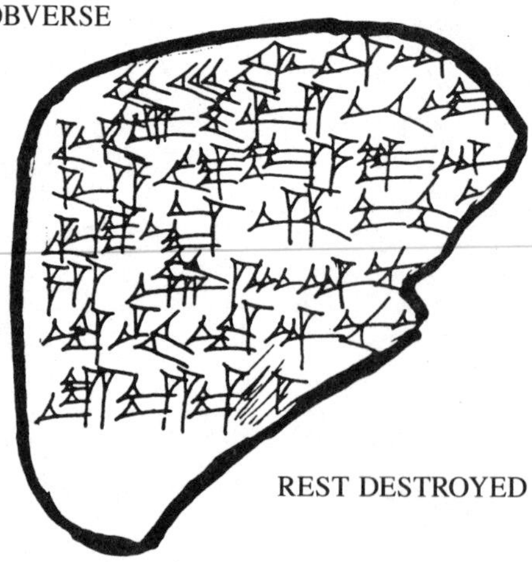

REST DESTROYED

459

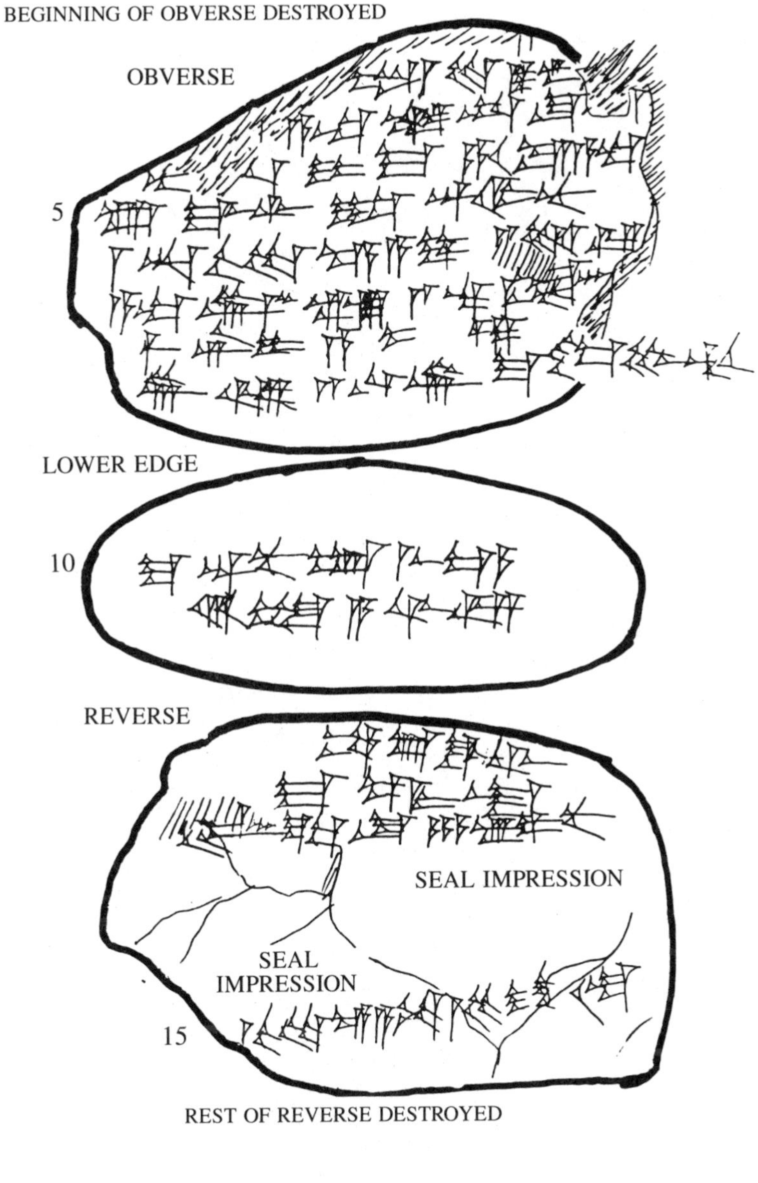
BEGINNING OF OBVERSE DESTROYED
OBVERSE
LOWER EDGE
REVERSE
SEAL IMPRESSION
SEAL
IMPRESSION
REST OF REVERSE DESTROYED

460

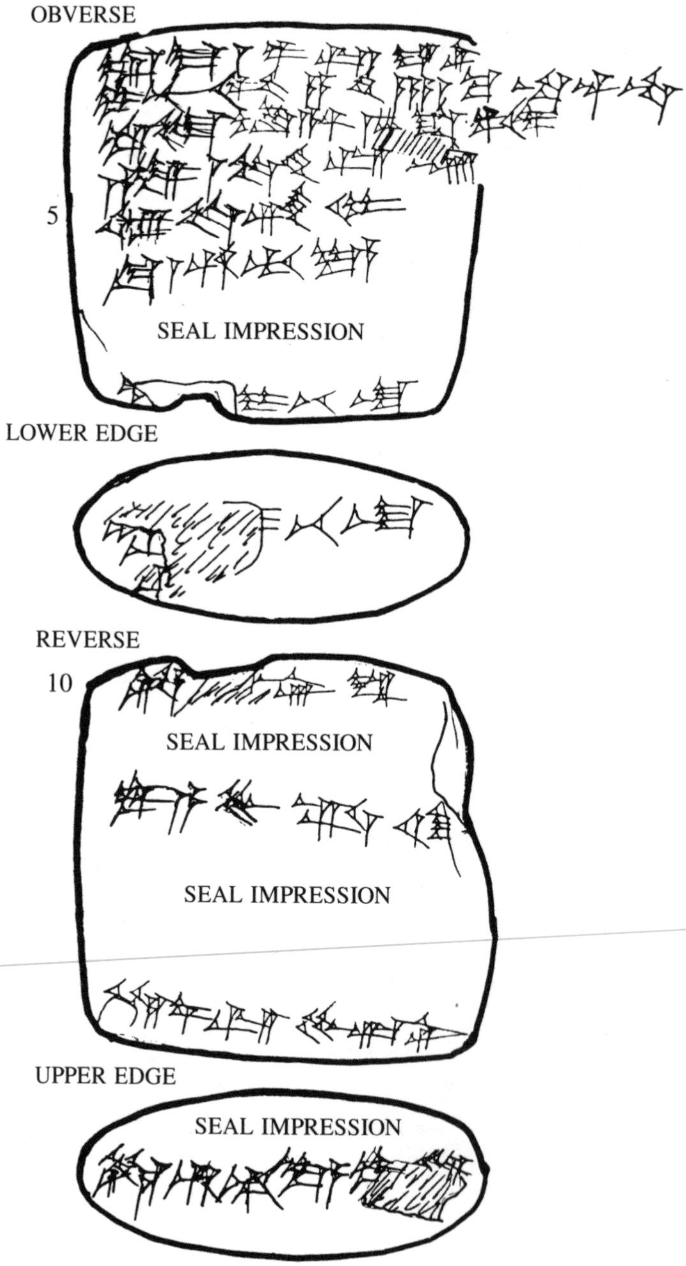
OBVERSE
SEAL IMPRESSION
LOWER EDGE
REVERSE
SEAL IMPRESSION
SEAL IMPRESSION
UPPER EDGE
SEAL IMPRESSION

465

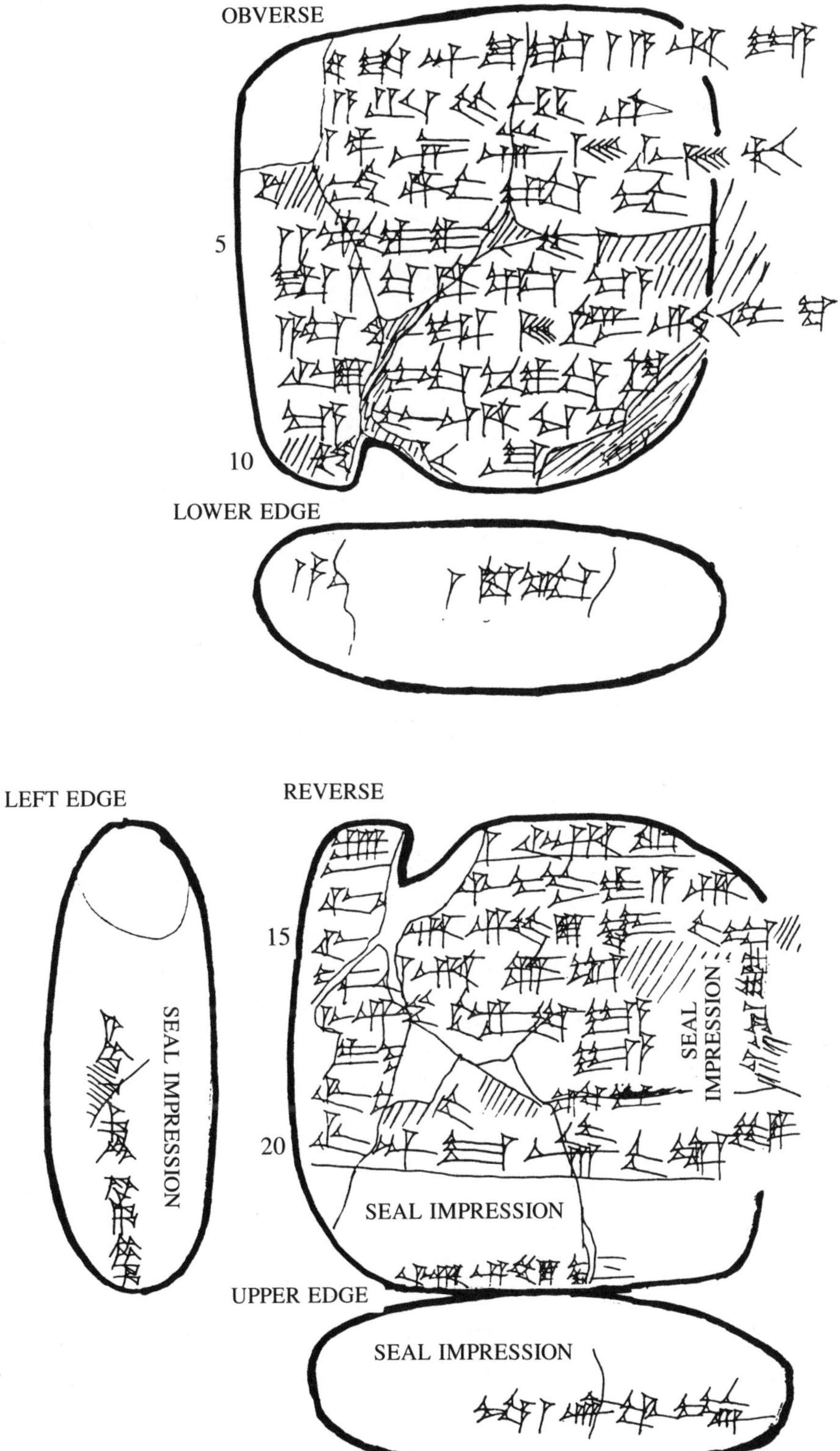
OBVERSE
LOWER EDGE
LEFT EDGE
REVERSE
SEAL IMPRESSION
SEAL IMPRESSION
SEAL IMPRESSION
UPPER EDGE
SEAL IMPRESSION

468

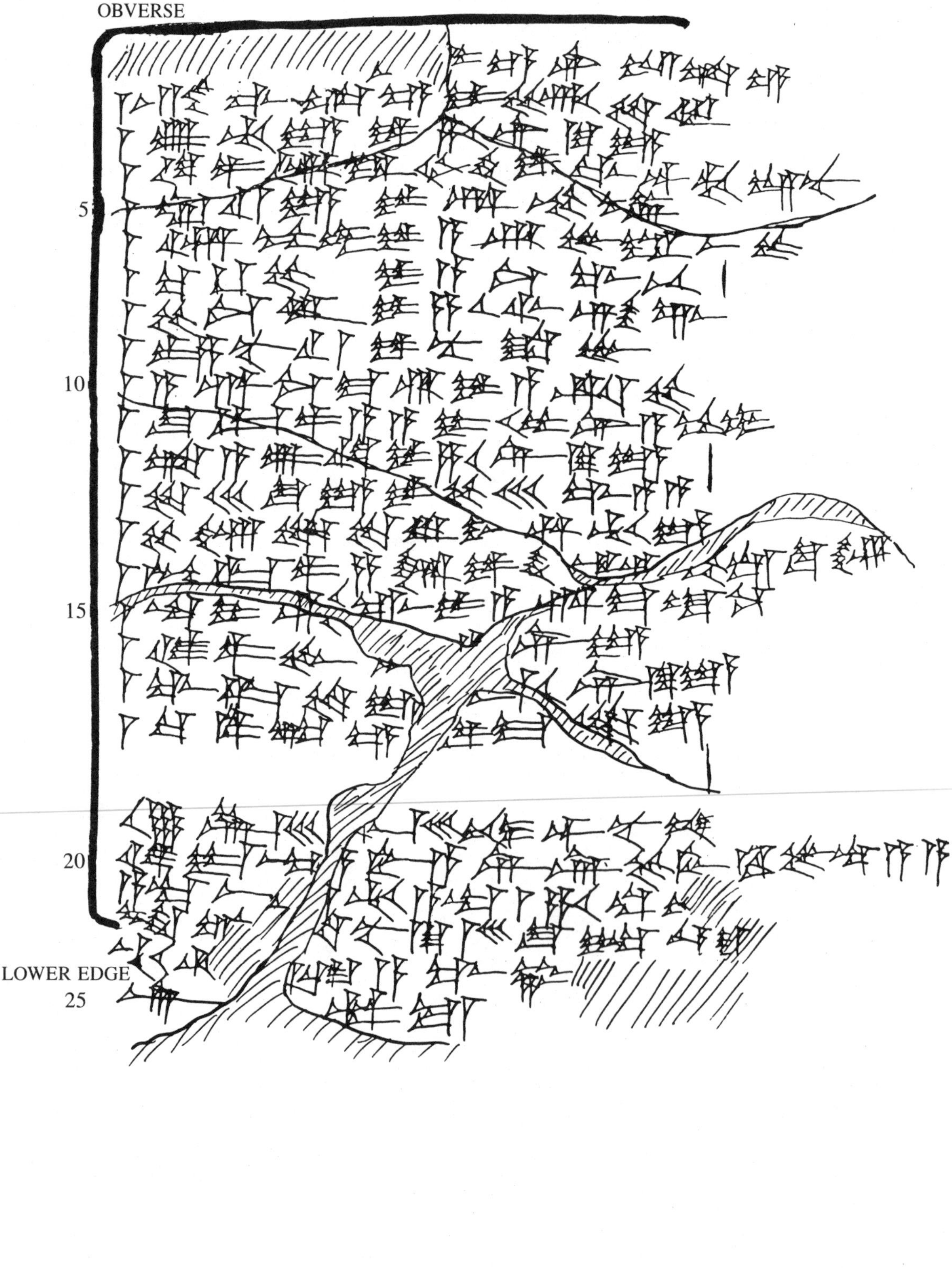

468

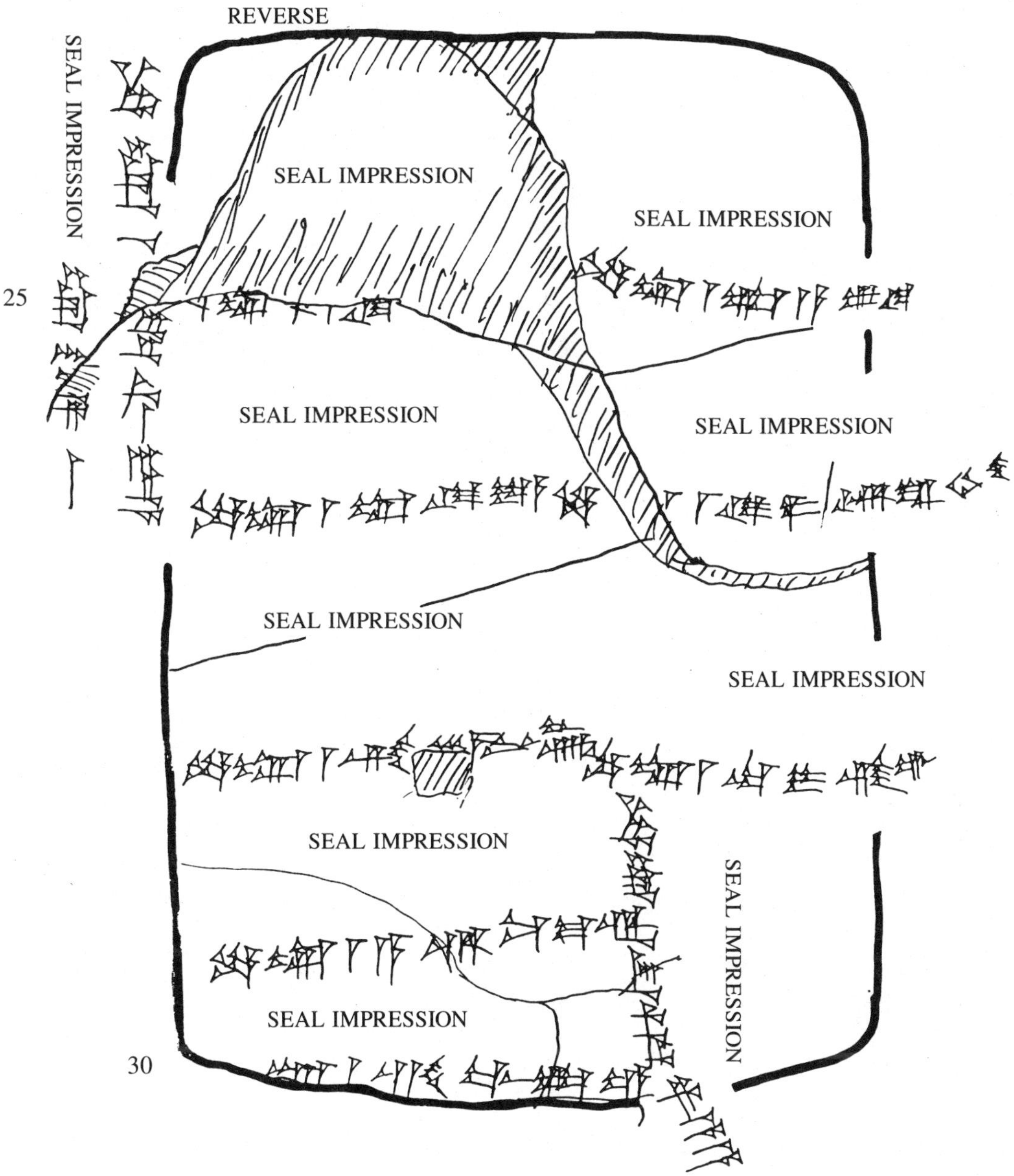
REVERSE
SEAL IMPRESSION
SEAL IMPRESSION
SEAL IMPRESSION
25
SEAL IMPRESSION
SEAL IMPRESSION
SEAL IMPRESSION
SEAL IMPRESSION
SEAL IMPRESSION
SEAL IMPRESSION
SEAL IMPRESSION
30

469

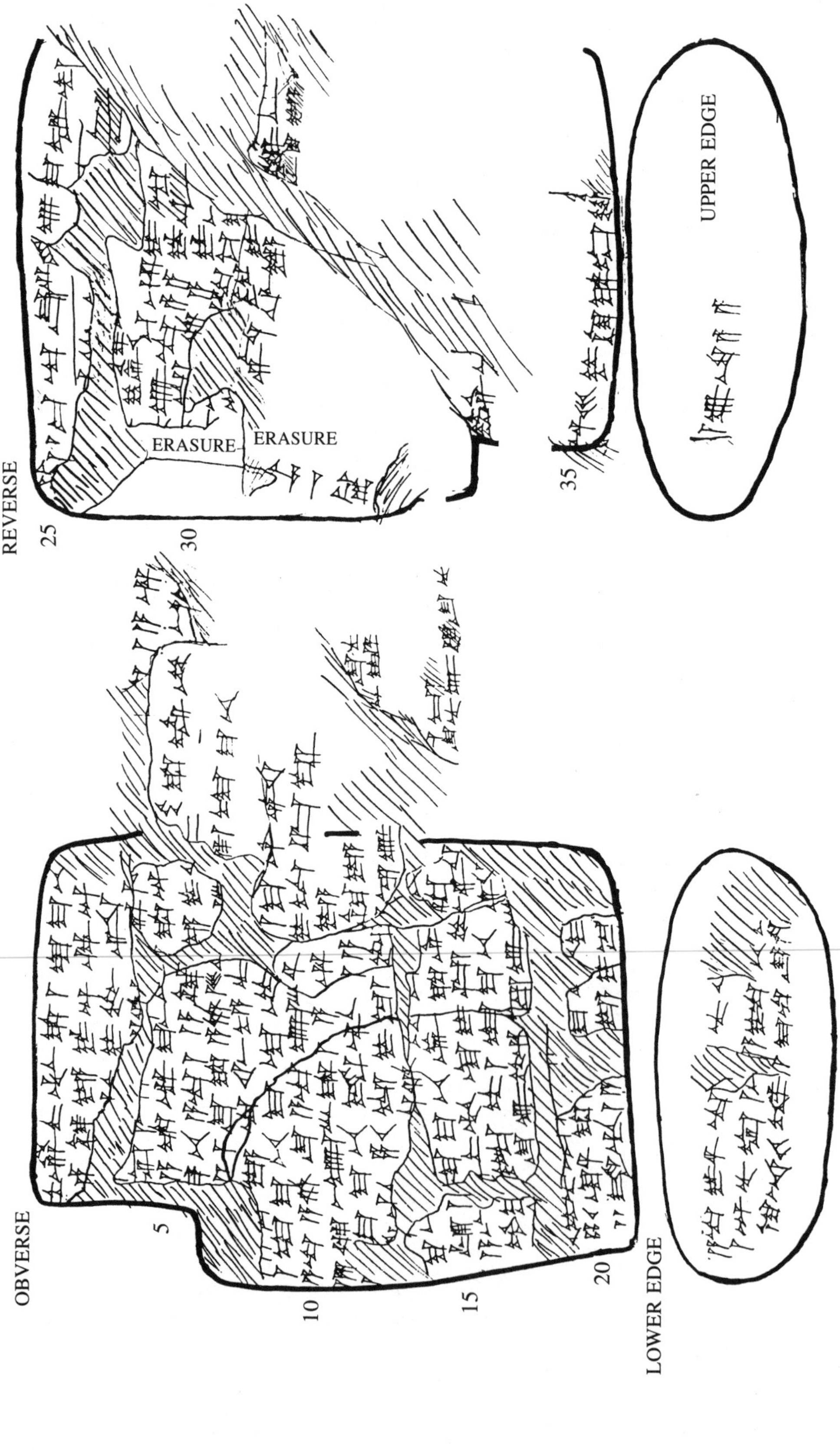

471

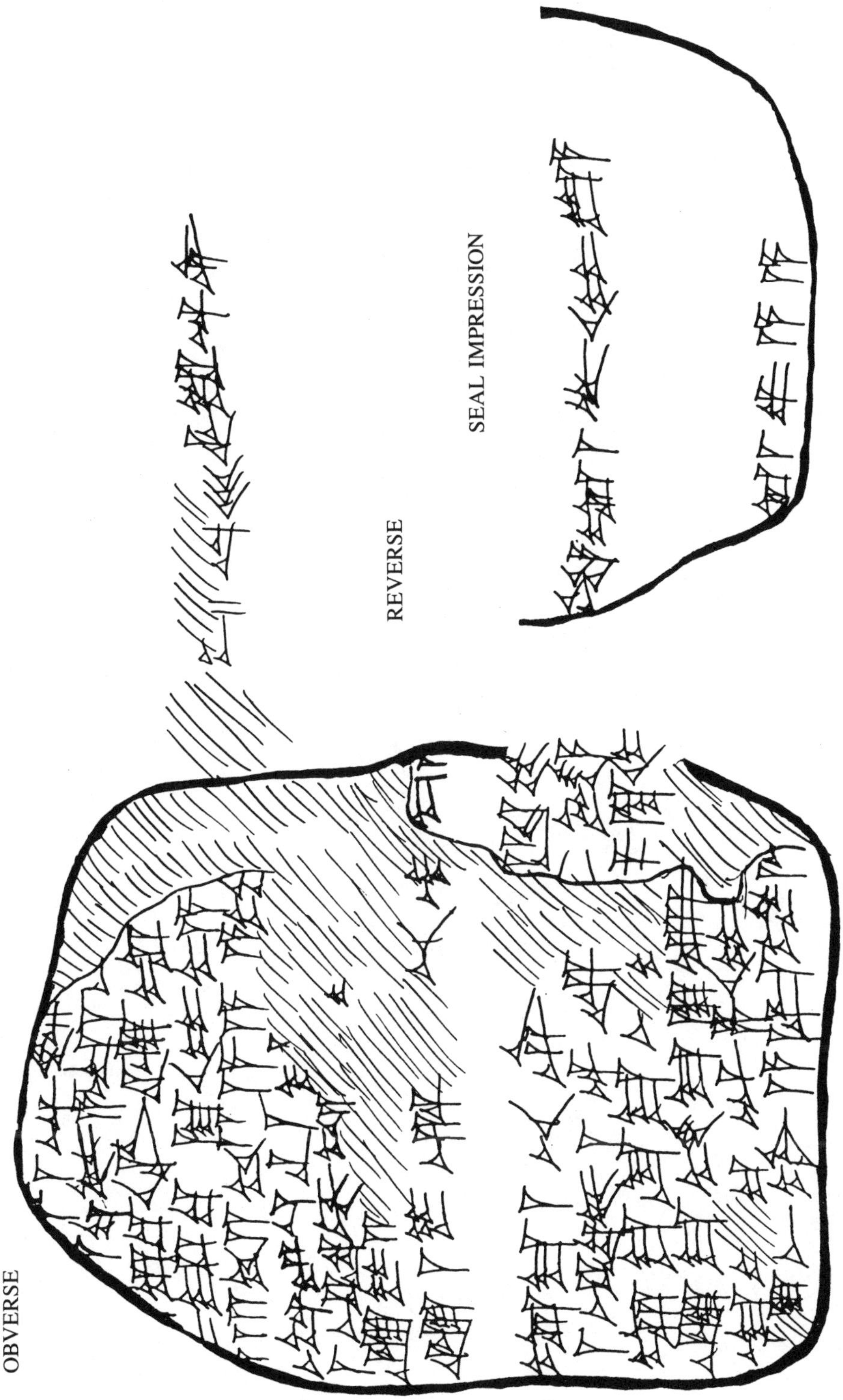

472

OBVERSE

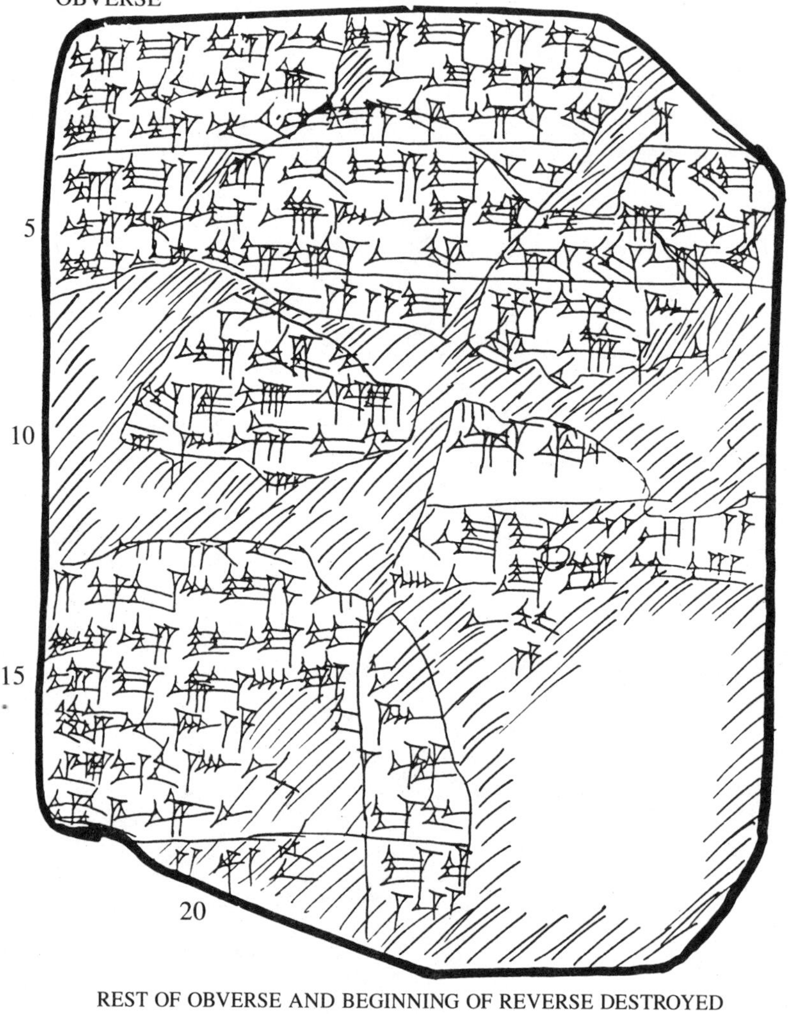

REST OF OBVERSE AND BEGINNING OF REVERSE DESTROYED

REVERSE

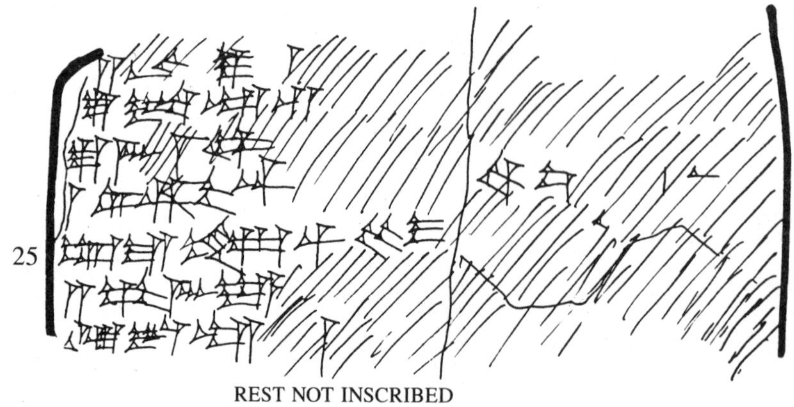

REST NOT INSCRIBED

473

OBVERSE

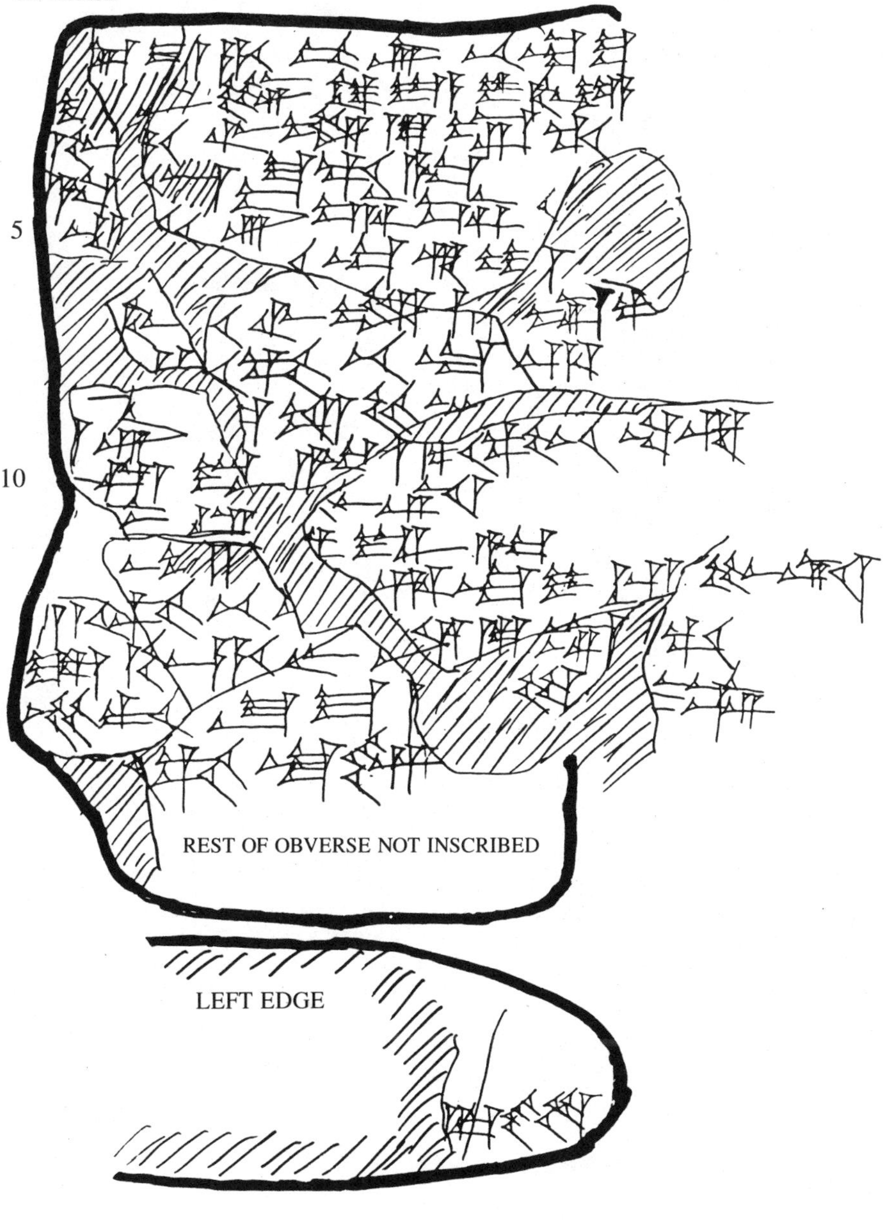

473

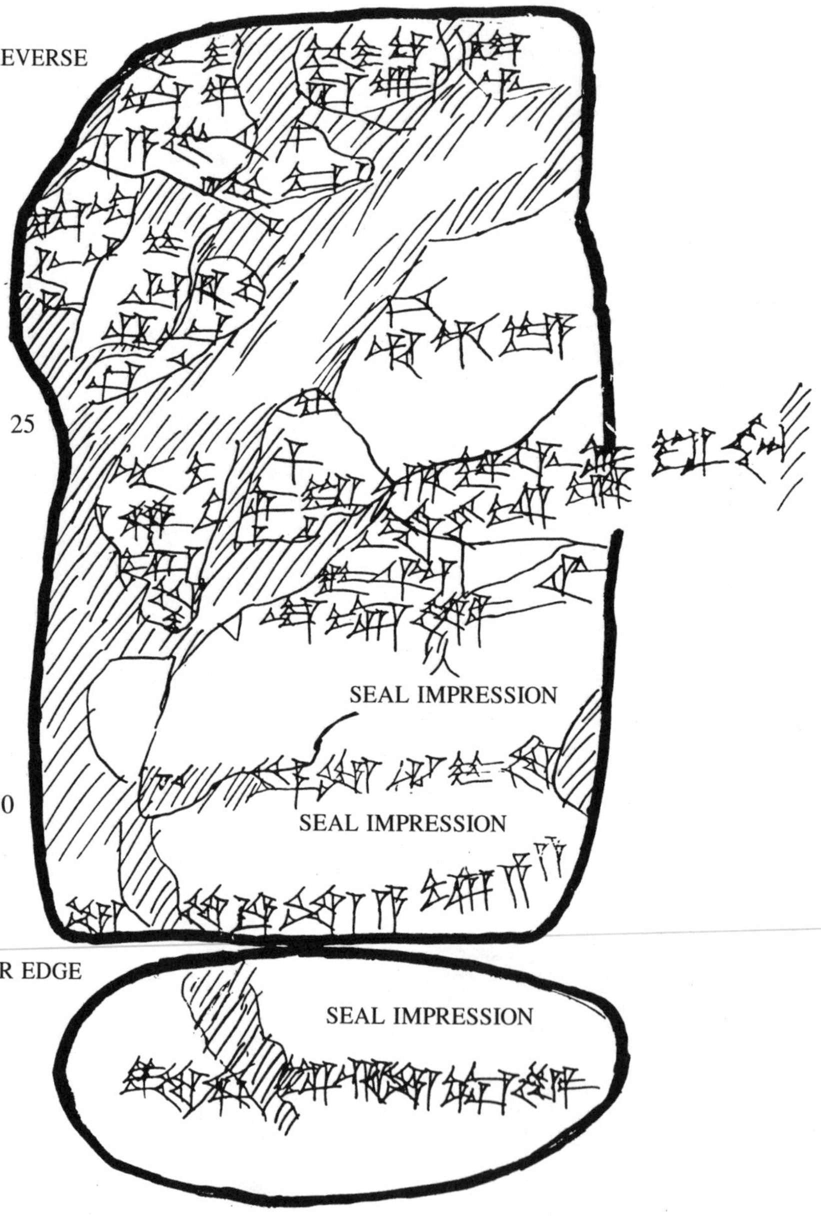
REVERSE
SEAL IMPRESSION
SEAL IMPRESSION
UPPER EDGE
SEAL IMPRESSION

474

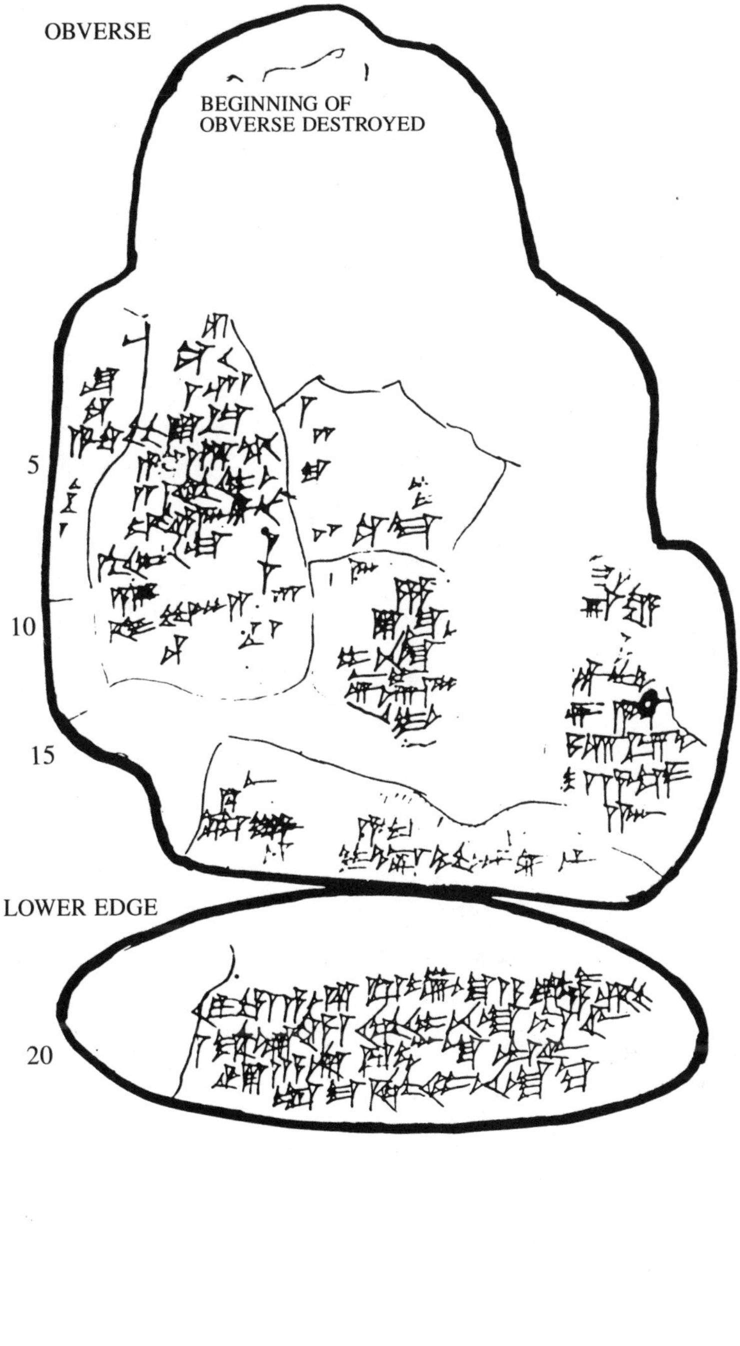

474

REVERSE

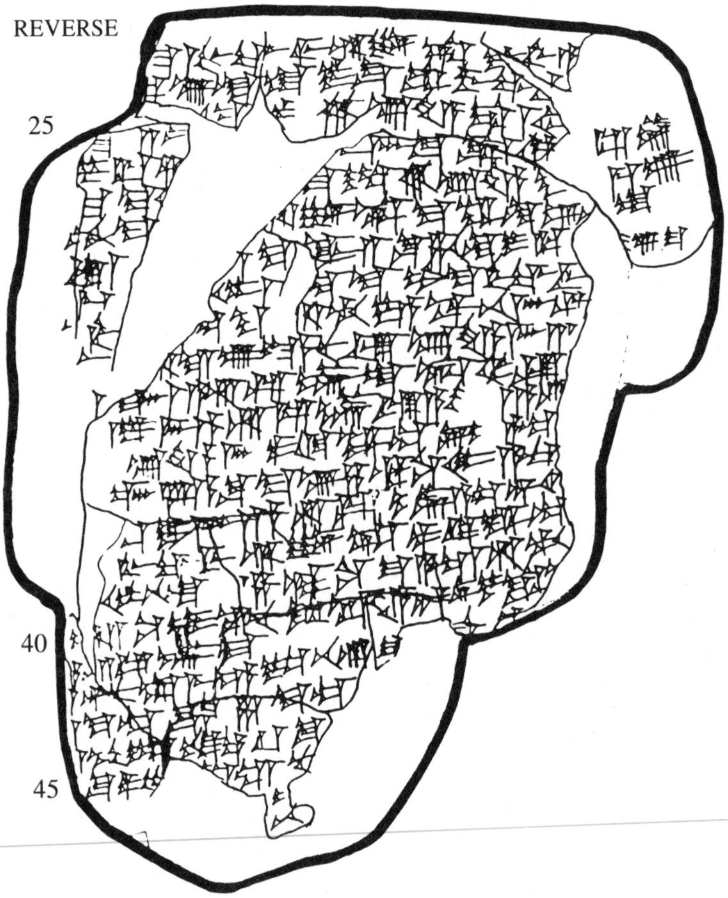

REST OF REVERSE DESTROYED

475

OBVERSE

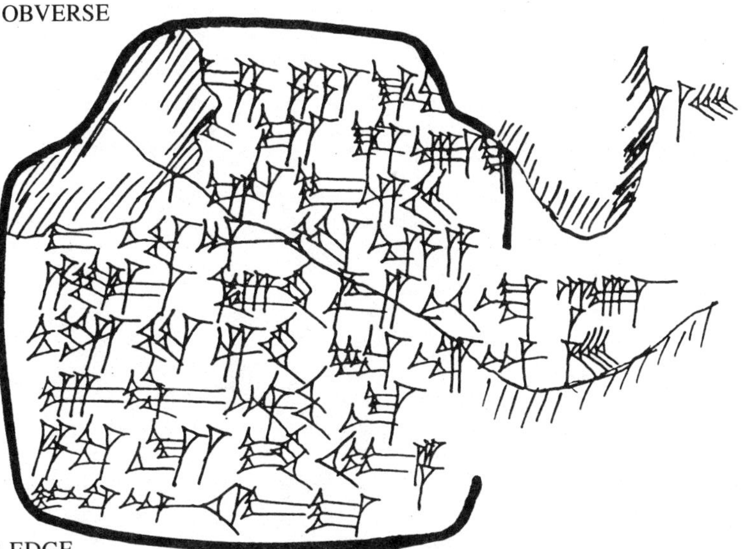

LOWER EDGE

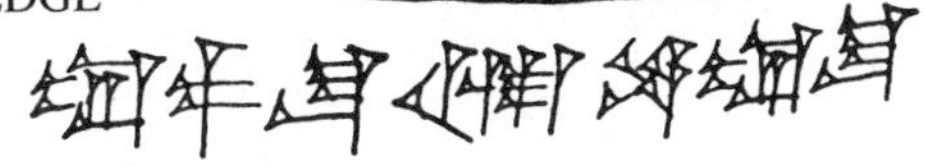

REVERSE

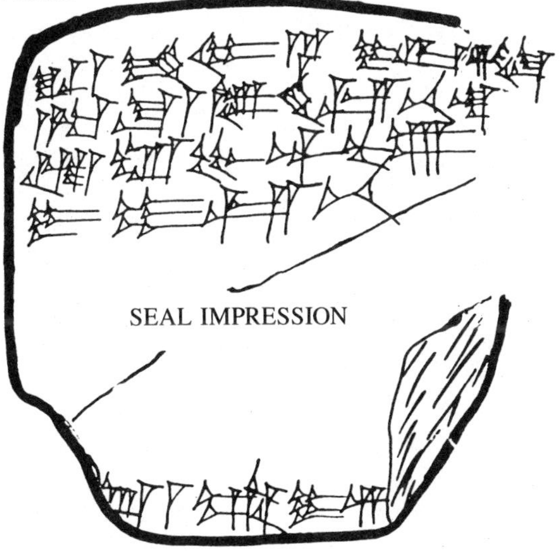

476

OBVERSE

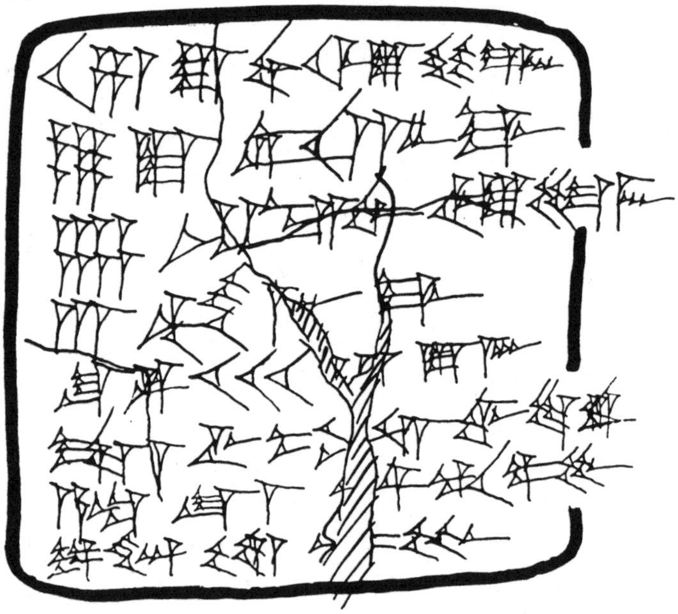

REVERSE

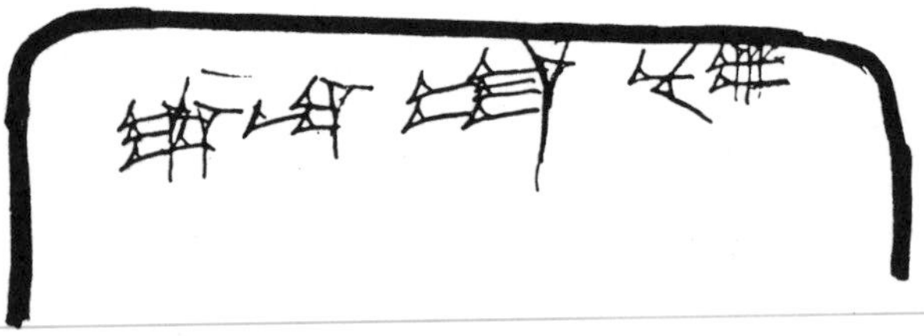

SEAL IMPRESSION

479

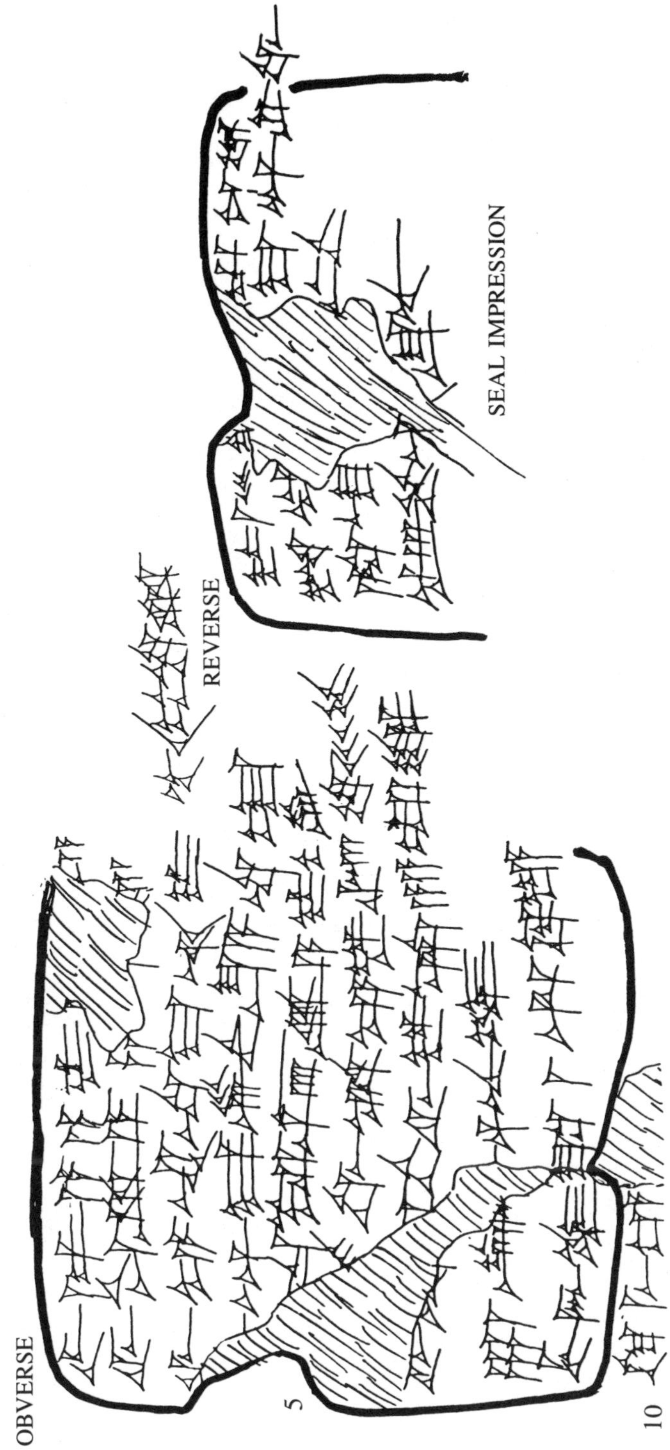

479

OBVERSE

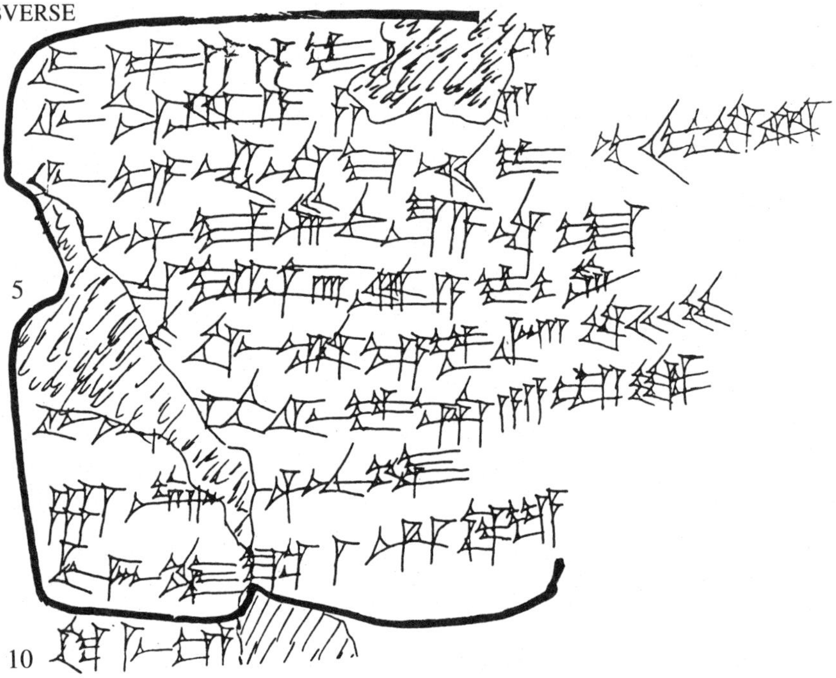

REVERSE

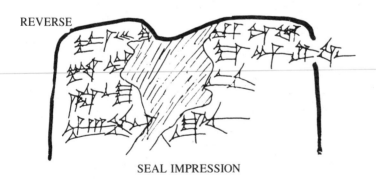

SEAL IMPRESSION

480

OBVERSE

REVERSE

SEAL IMPRESSION

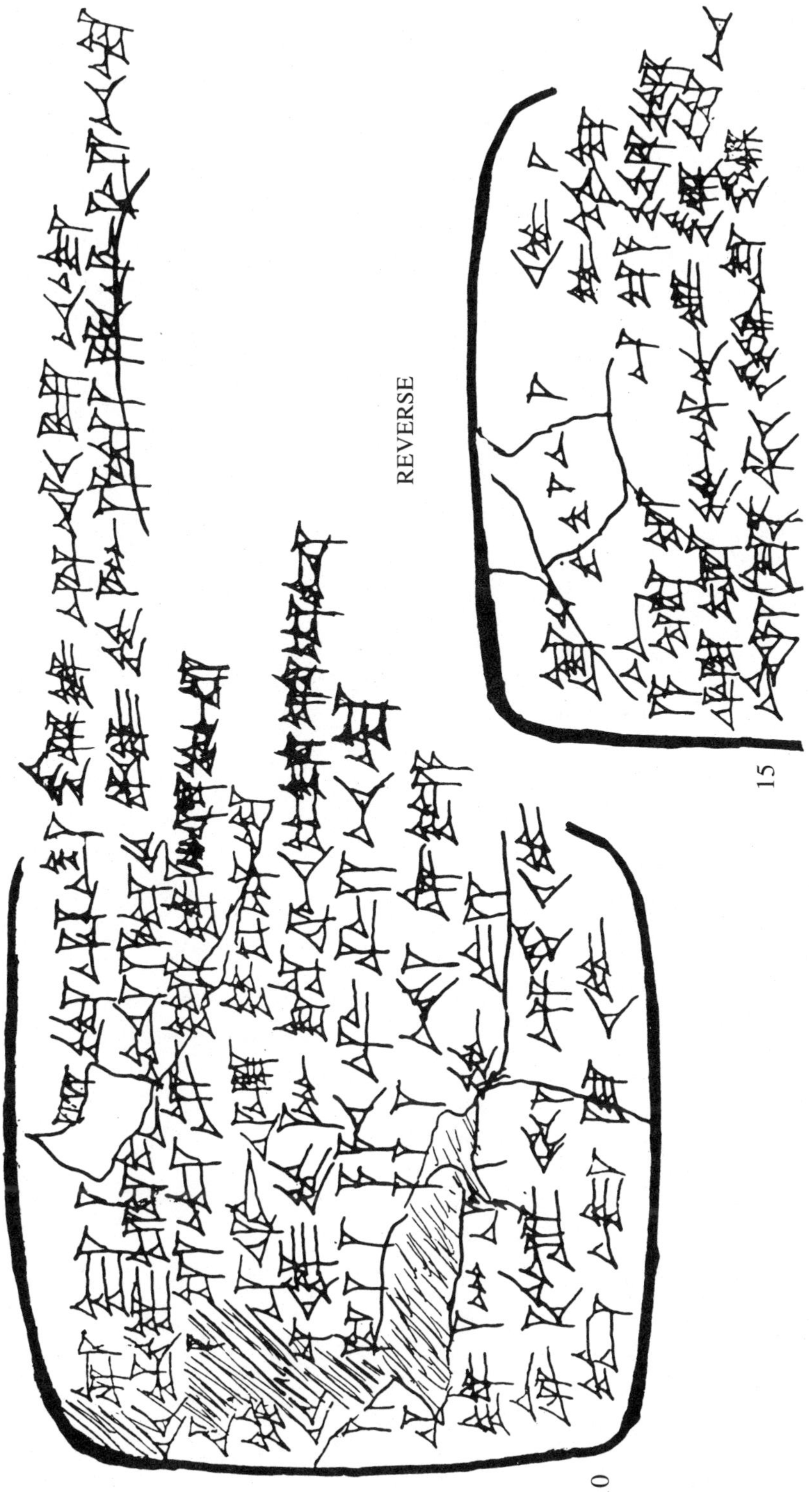

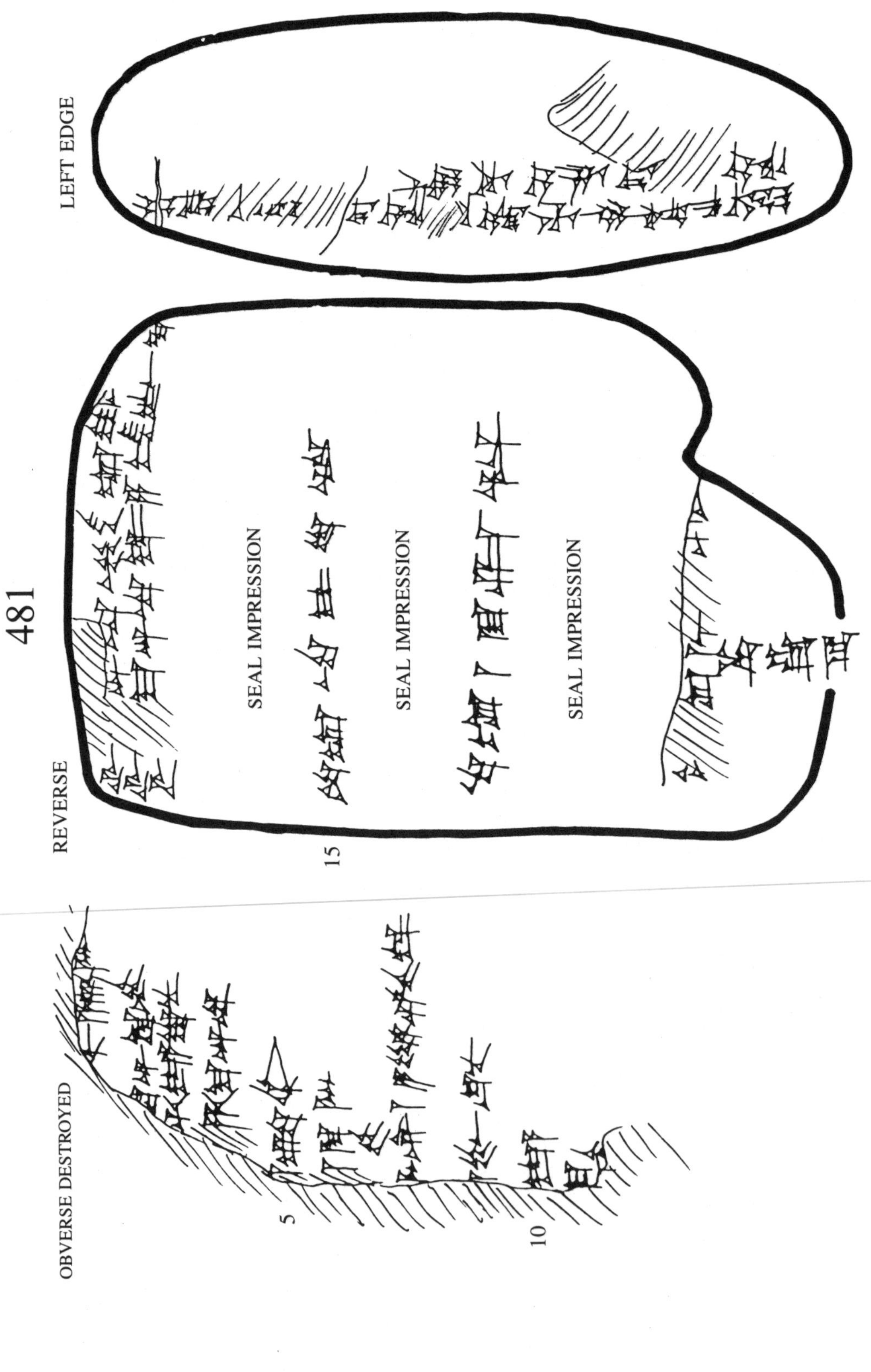
481
OBVERSE DESTROYED
REVERSE
LEFT EDGE
SEAL IMPRESSION
SEAL IMPRESSION
SEAL IMPRESSION

482

OBVERSE

BEGINNING OF OBVERSE DESTROYED

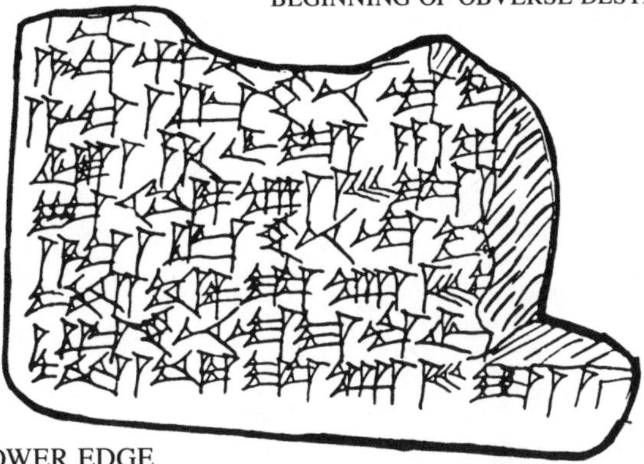

LOWER EDGE

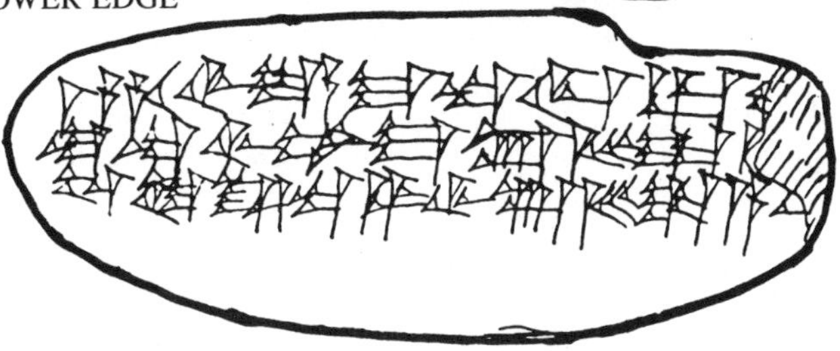

LEFT EDGE

REVERSE

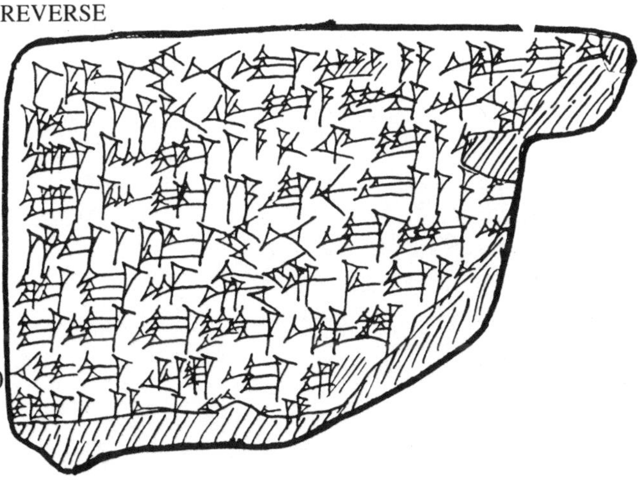

REST OF REVERSE DESTROYED

483

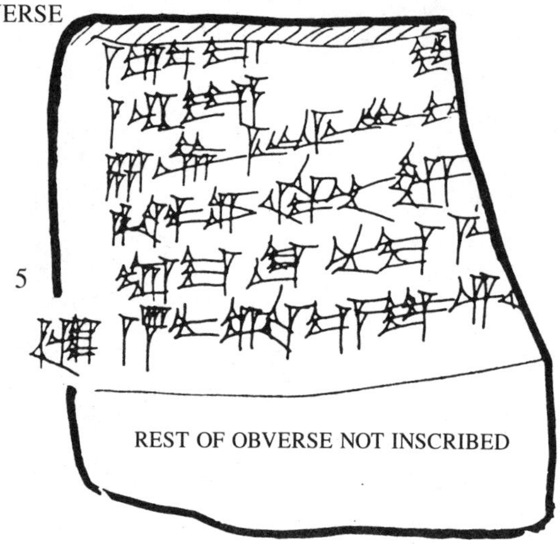
BEGINNING OF OBVERSE DESTROYED
OBVERSE
5
REST OF OBVERSE NOT INSCRIBED

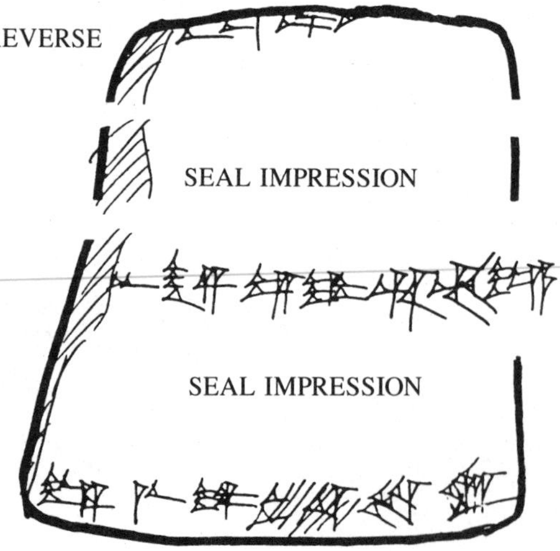
BEGINNING OF REVERSE DESTROYED
REVERSE
SEAL IMPRESSION
SEAL IMPRESSION
SEAL IMPRESSION

486

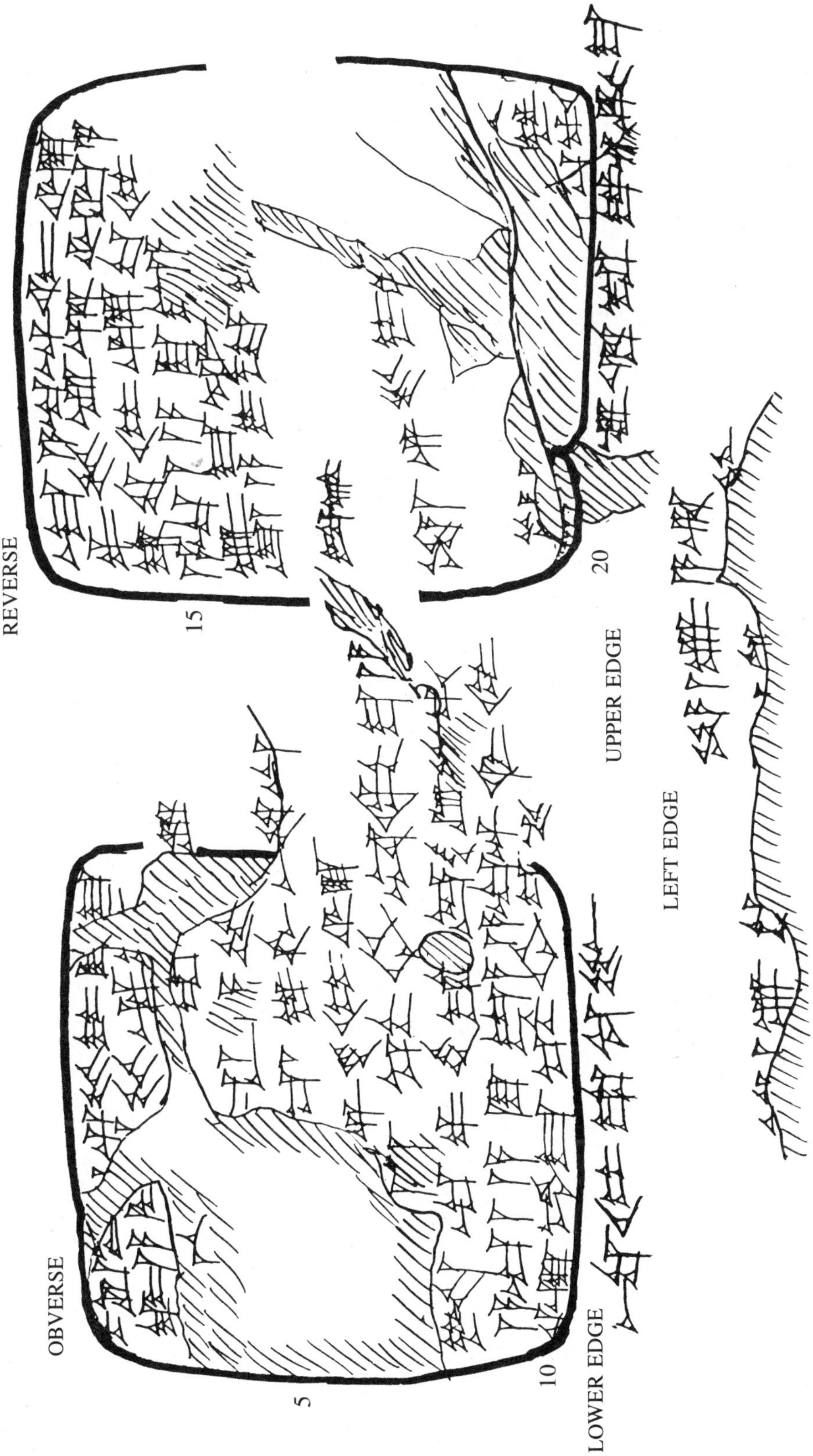

487

OBVERSE

BEGINNING OF OBVERSE DESTROYED

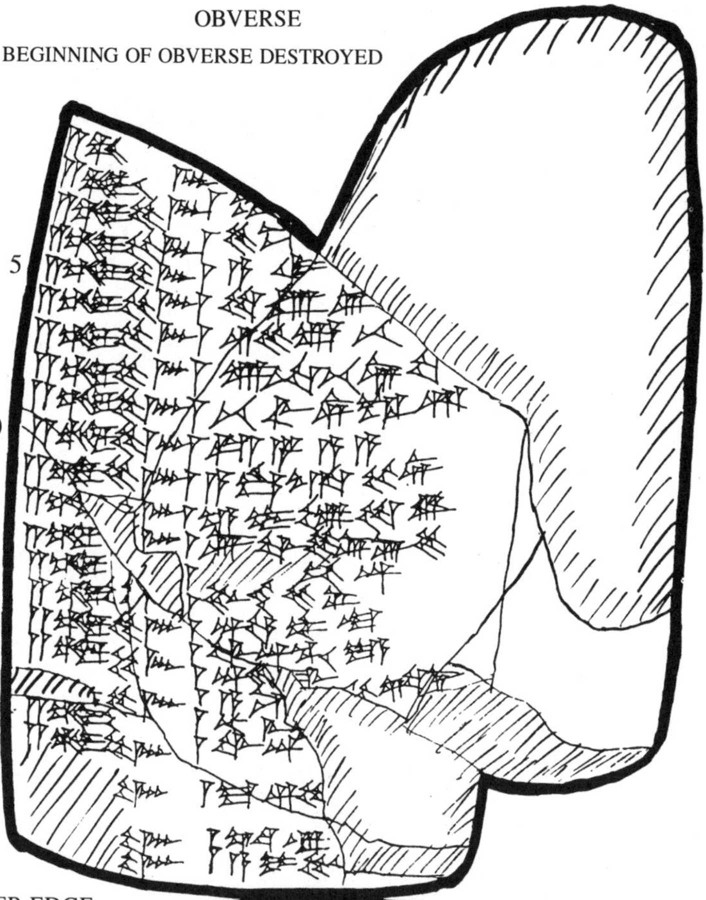

LOWER EDGE

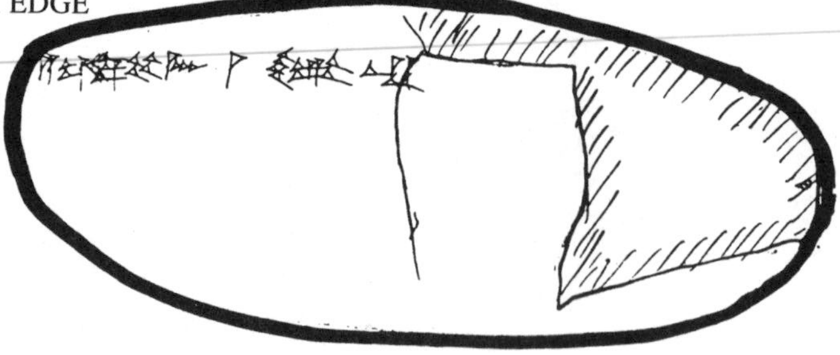

487

REVERSE

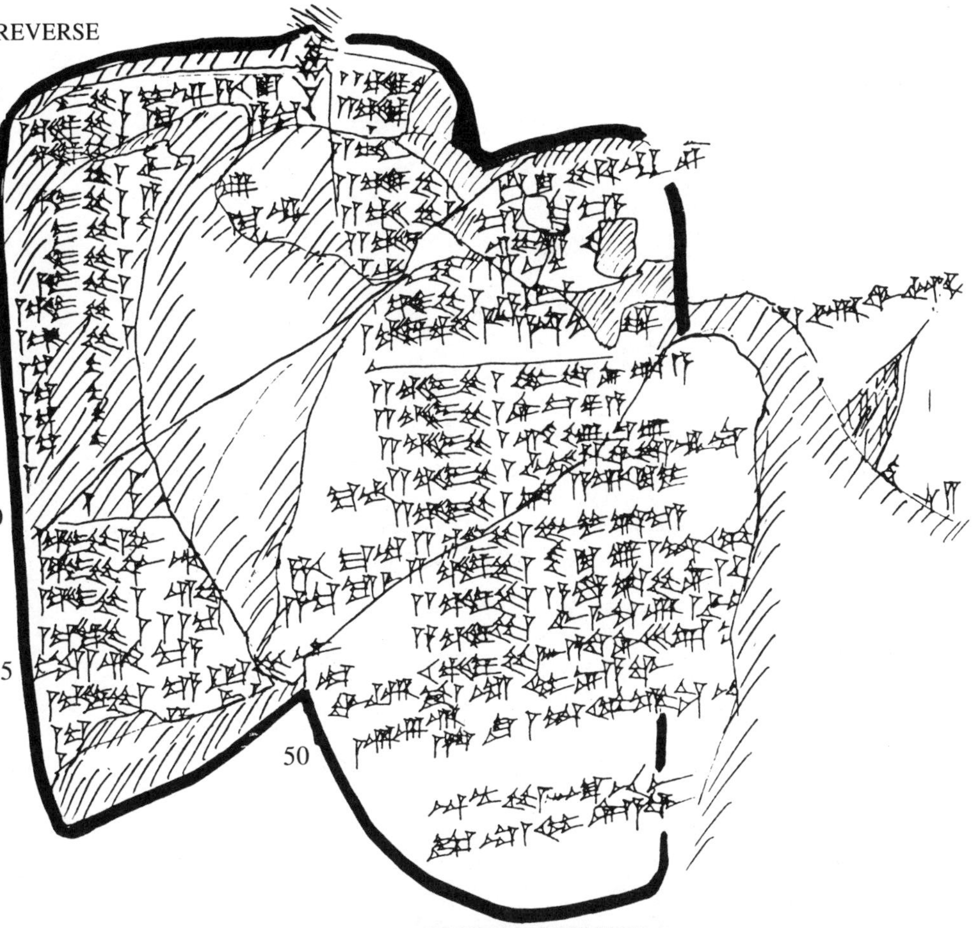

LEFT EDGE

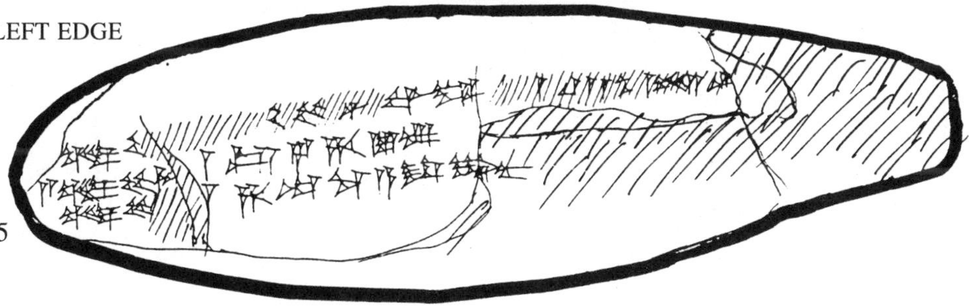

488

OBVERSE

BEGINNING OF OBVERSE DESTROYED

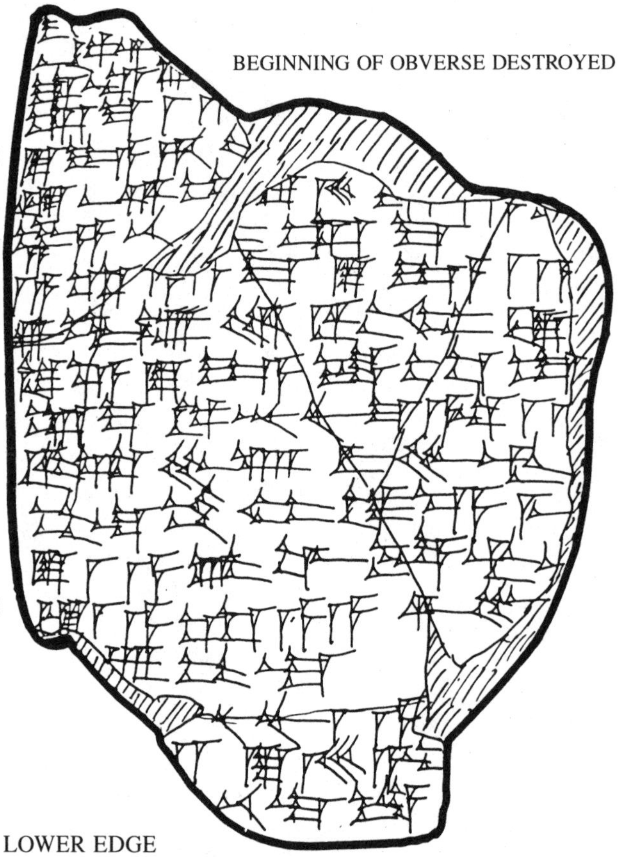

LOWER EDGE

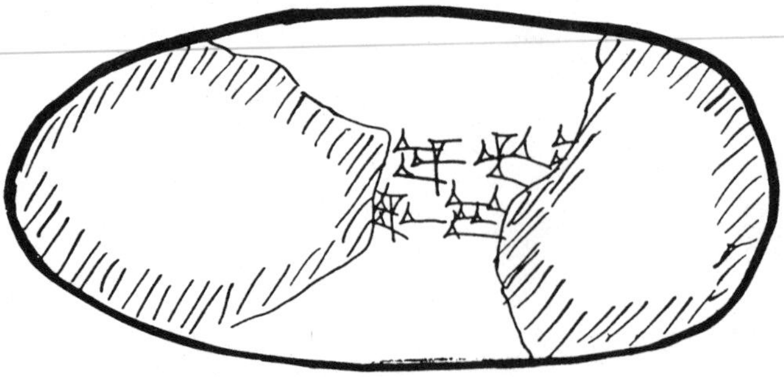

488

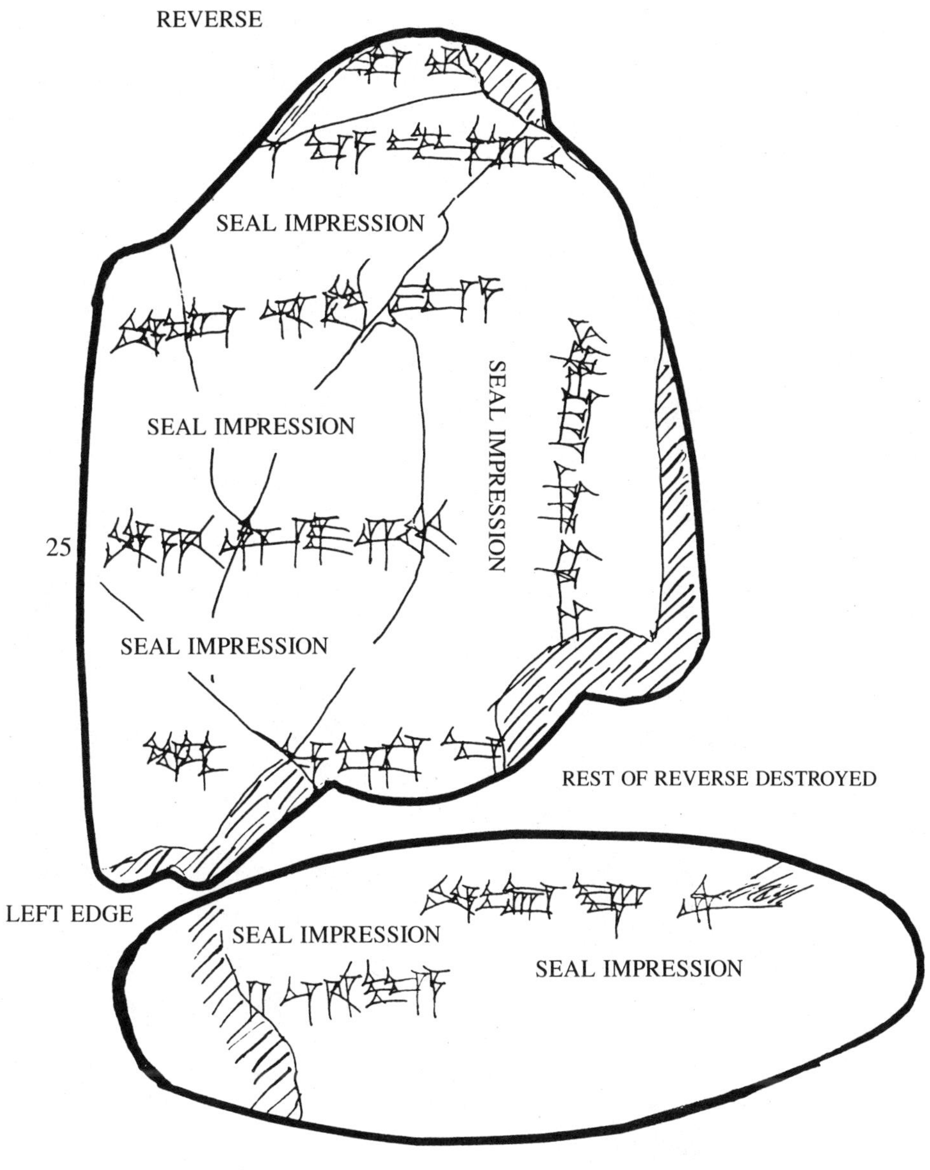
REVERSE
SEAL IMPRESSION
SEAL IMPRESSION
SEAL IMPRESSION
25
SEAL IMPRESSION
REST OF REVERSE DESTROYED
LEFT EDGE
SEAL IMPRESSION
SEAL IMPRESSION

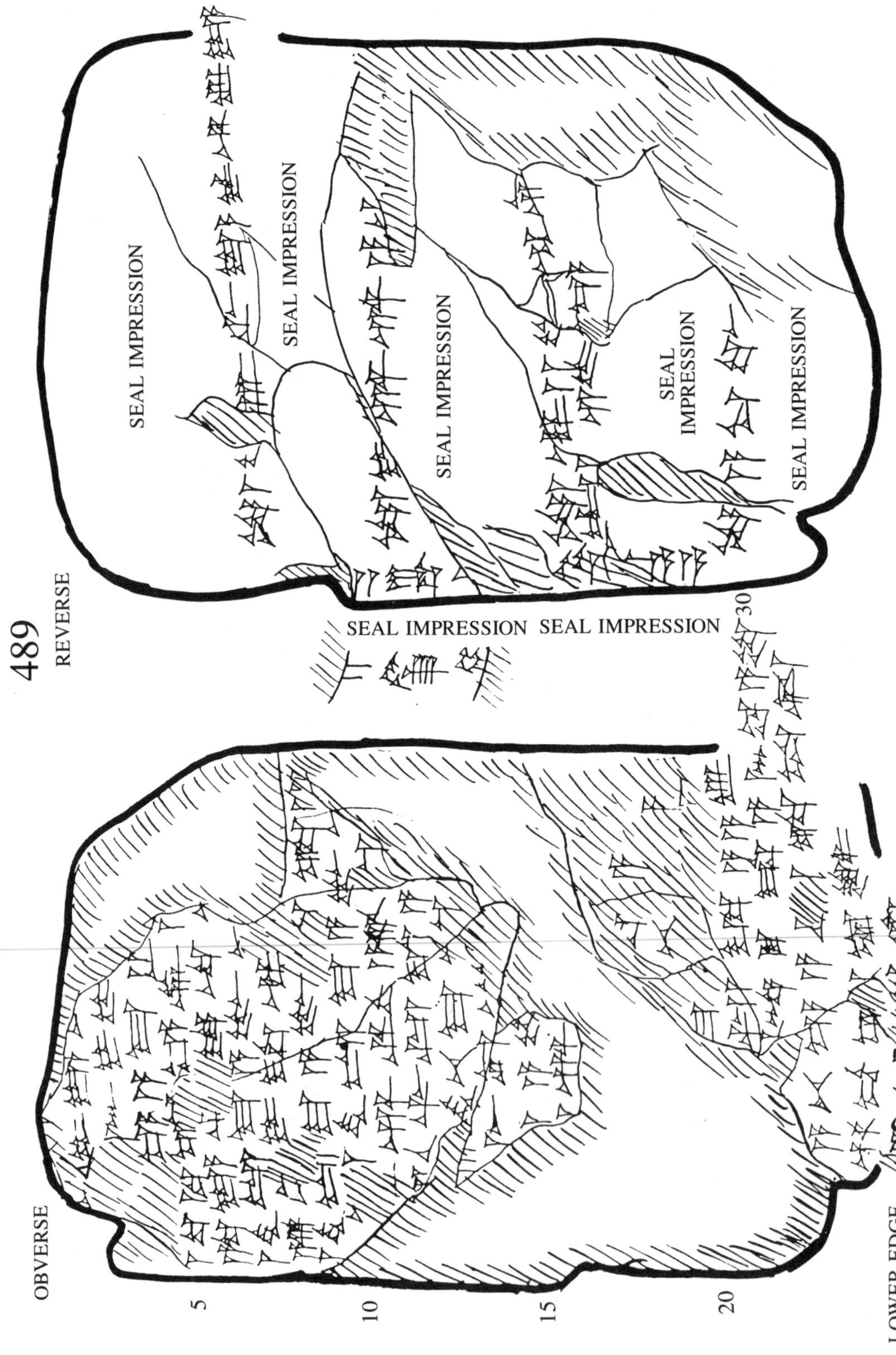
489
REVERSE
SEAL IMPRESSION
SEAL IMPRESSION
SEAL IMPRESSION
SEAL IMPRESSION
SEAL IMPRESSION
SEAL IMPRESSION SEAL IMPRESSION
OBVERSE
LOWER EDGE

491

OBVERSE

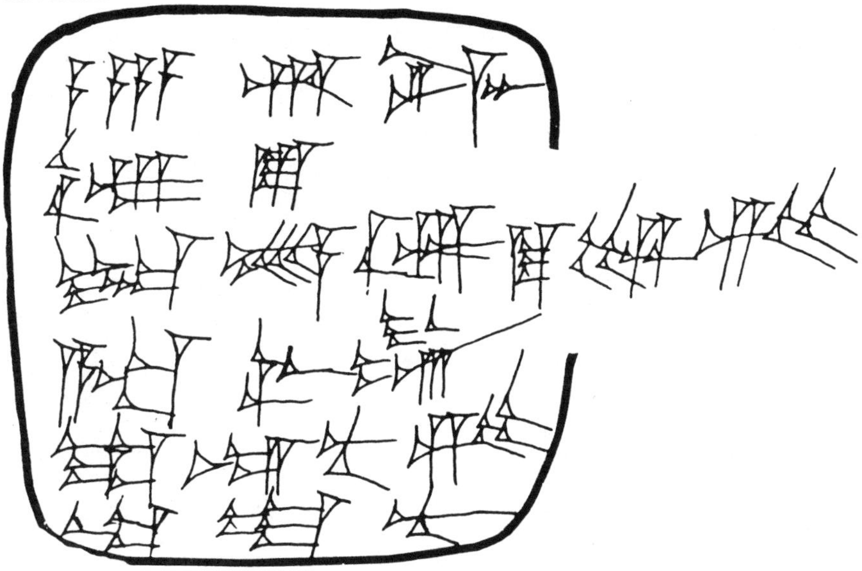

REST NOT INSCRIBED

492

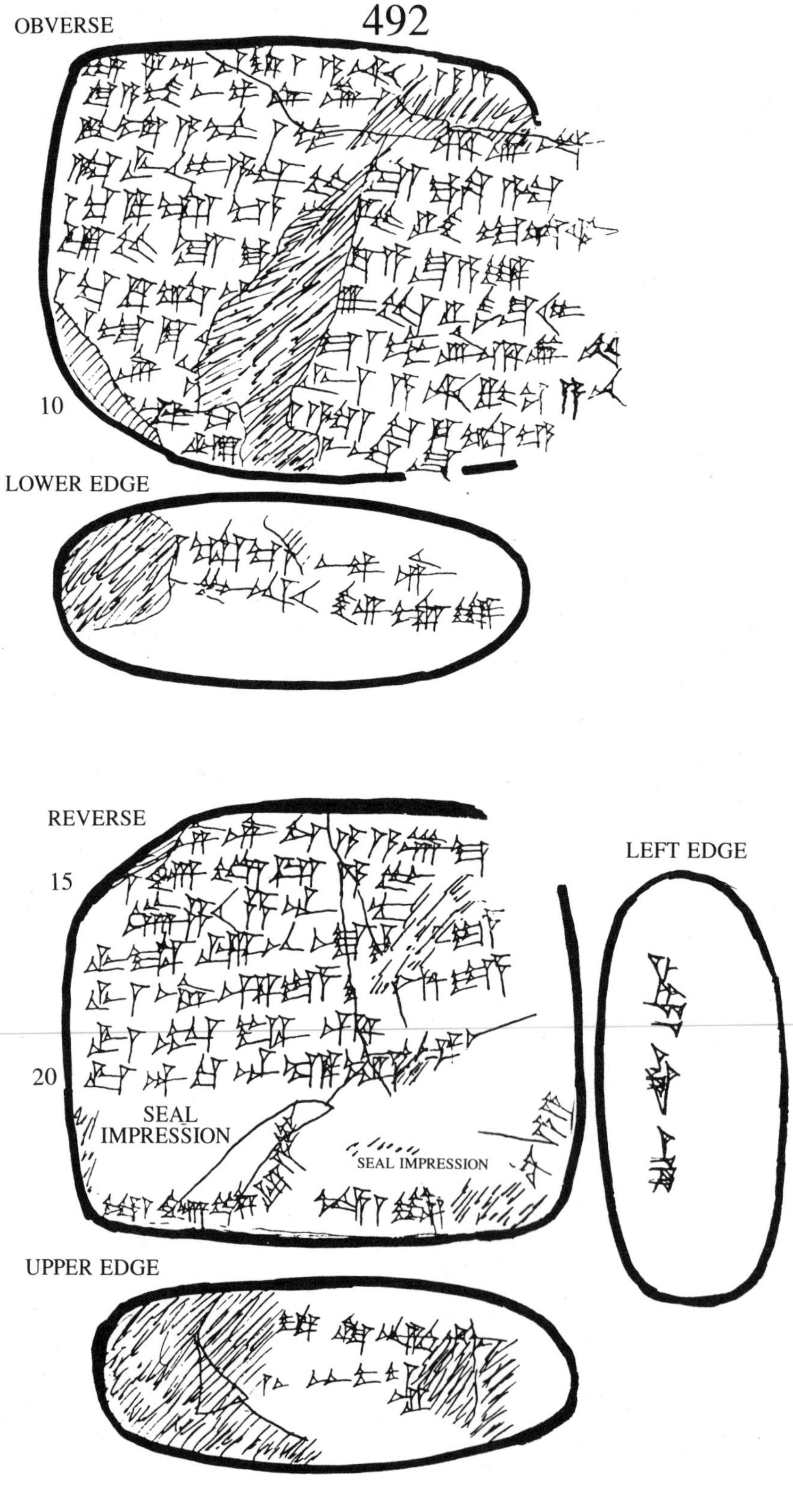
OBVERSE
10
LOWER EDGE
REVERSE
15
20
SEAL IMPRESSION
SEAL IMPRESSION
LEFT EDGE
UPPER EDGE

494

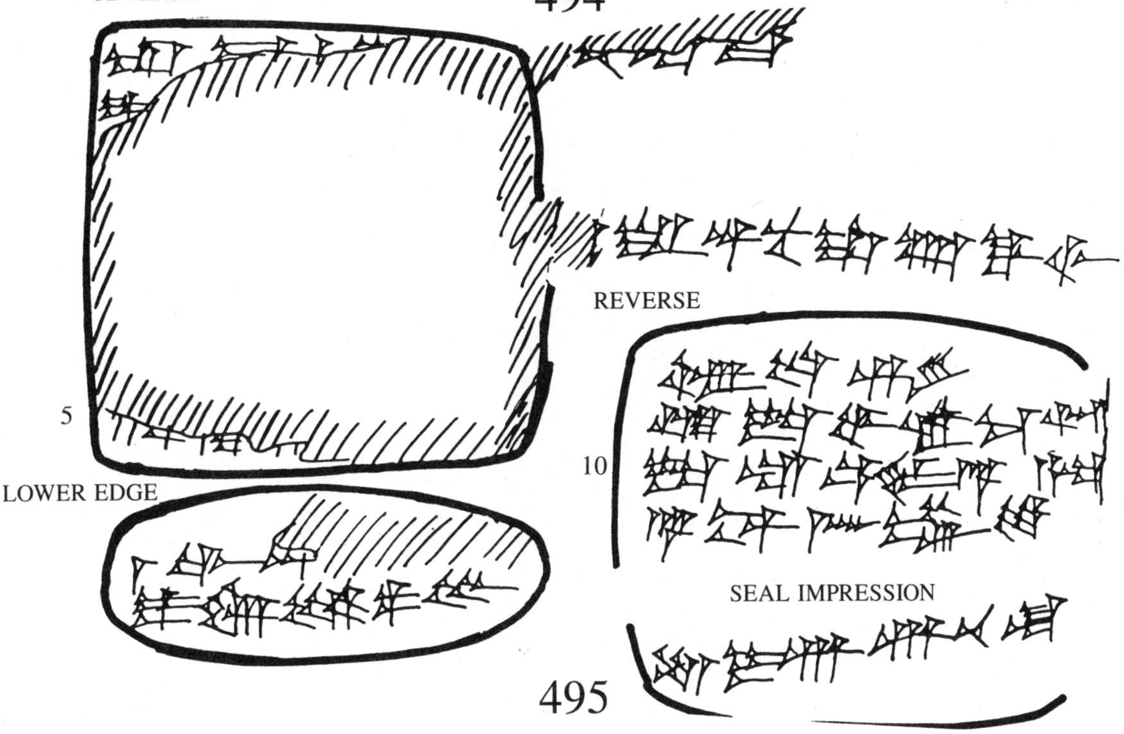
OBVERSE
LOWER EDGE
REVERSE
SEAL IMPRESSION

495

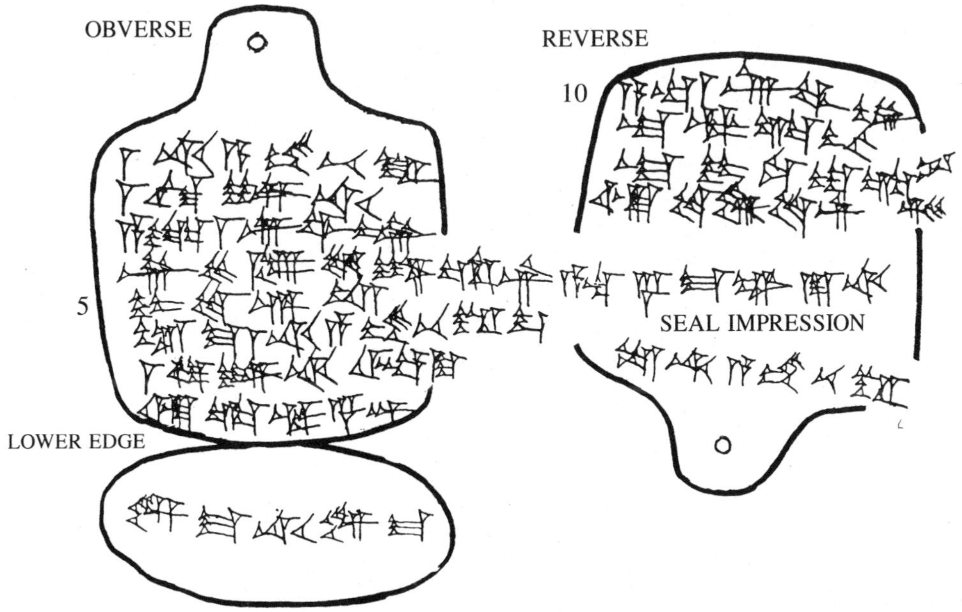
OBVERSE
REVERSE
LOWER EDGE
SEAL IMPRESSION

496

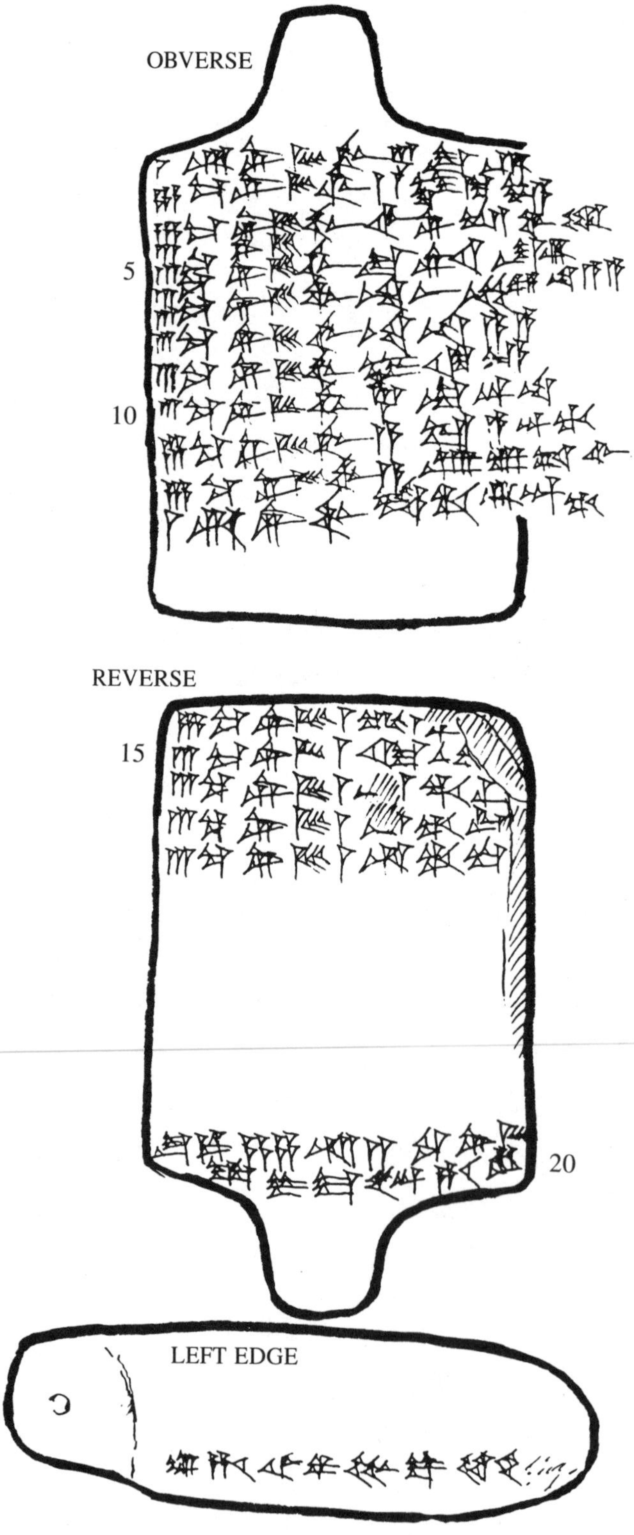

498

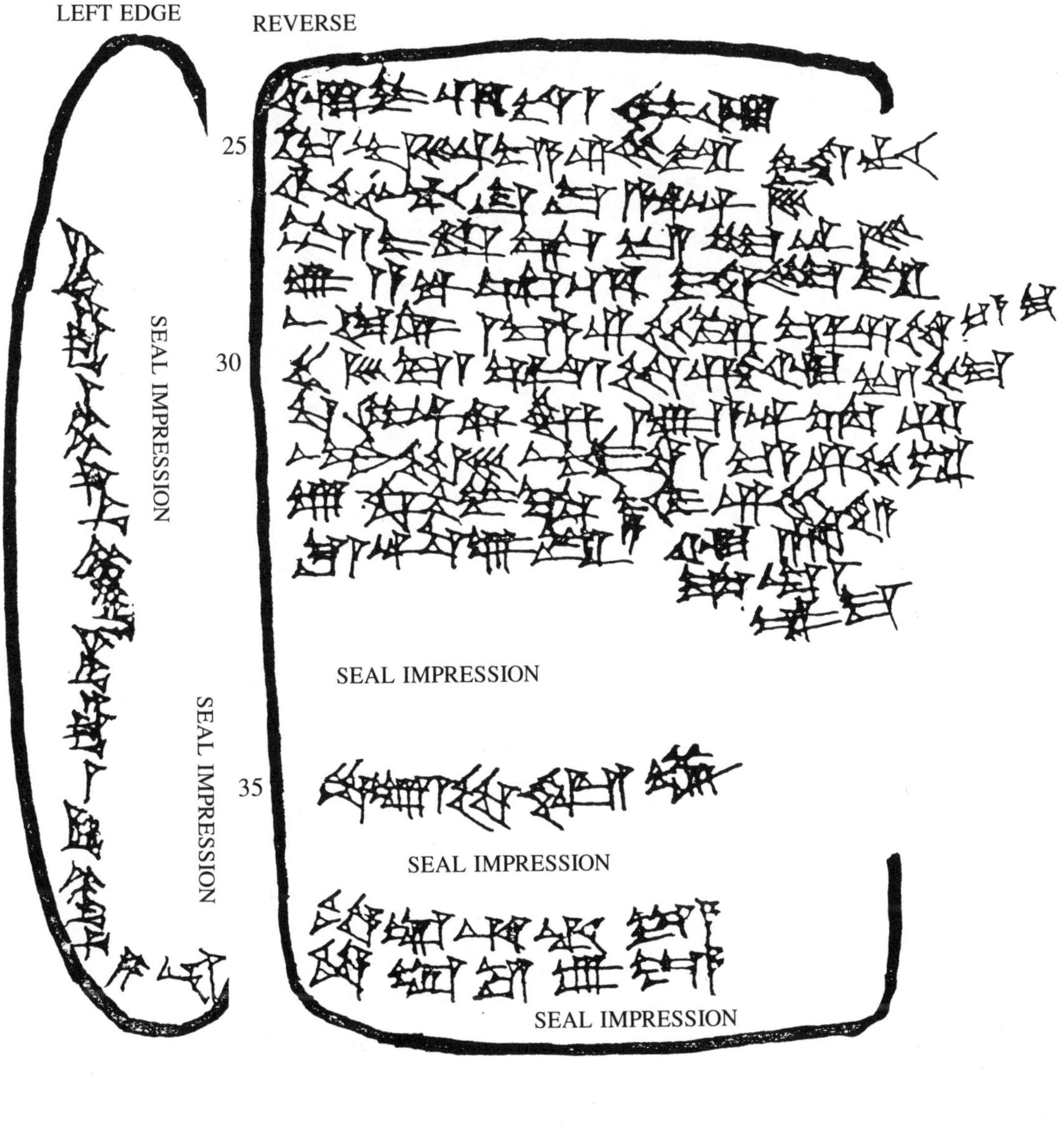
LEFT EDGE
REVERSE
25
30
35
SEAL IMPRESSION
SEAL IMPRESSION
SEAL IMPRESSION
SEAL IMPRESSION
SEAL IMPRESSION

499

OBVERSE

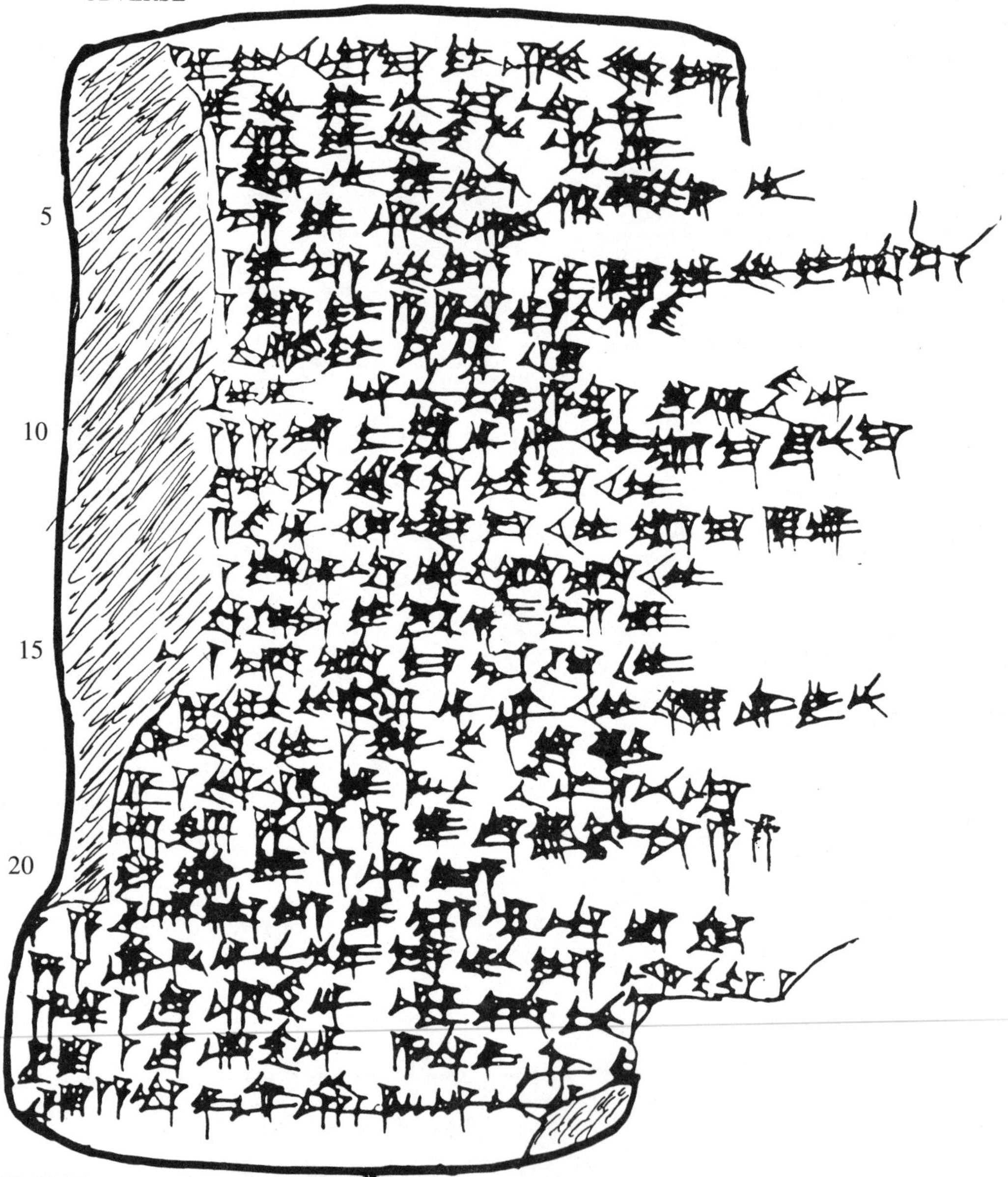

LOWER EDGE

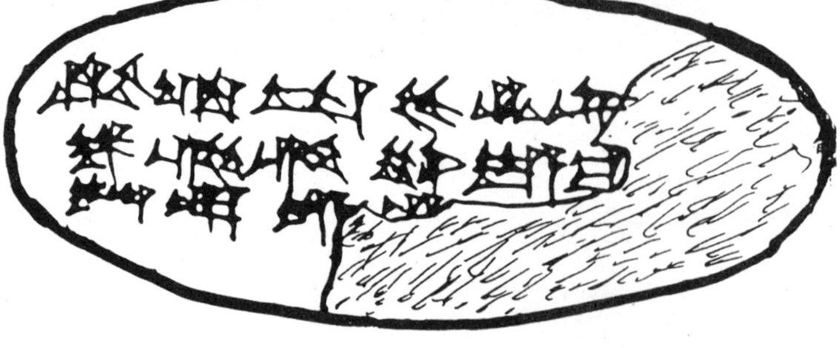

499

REVERSE

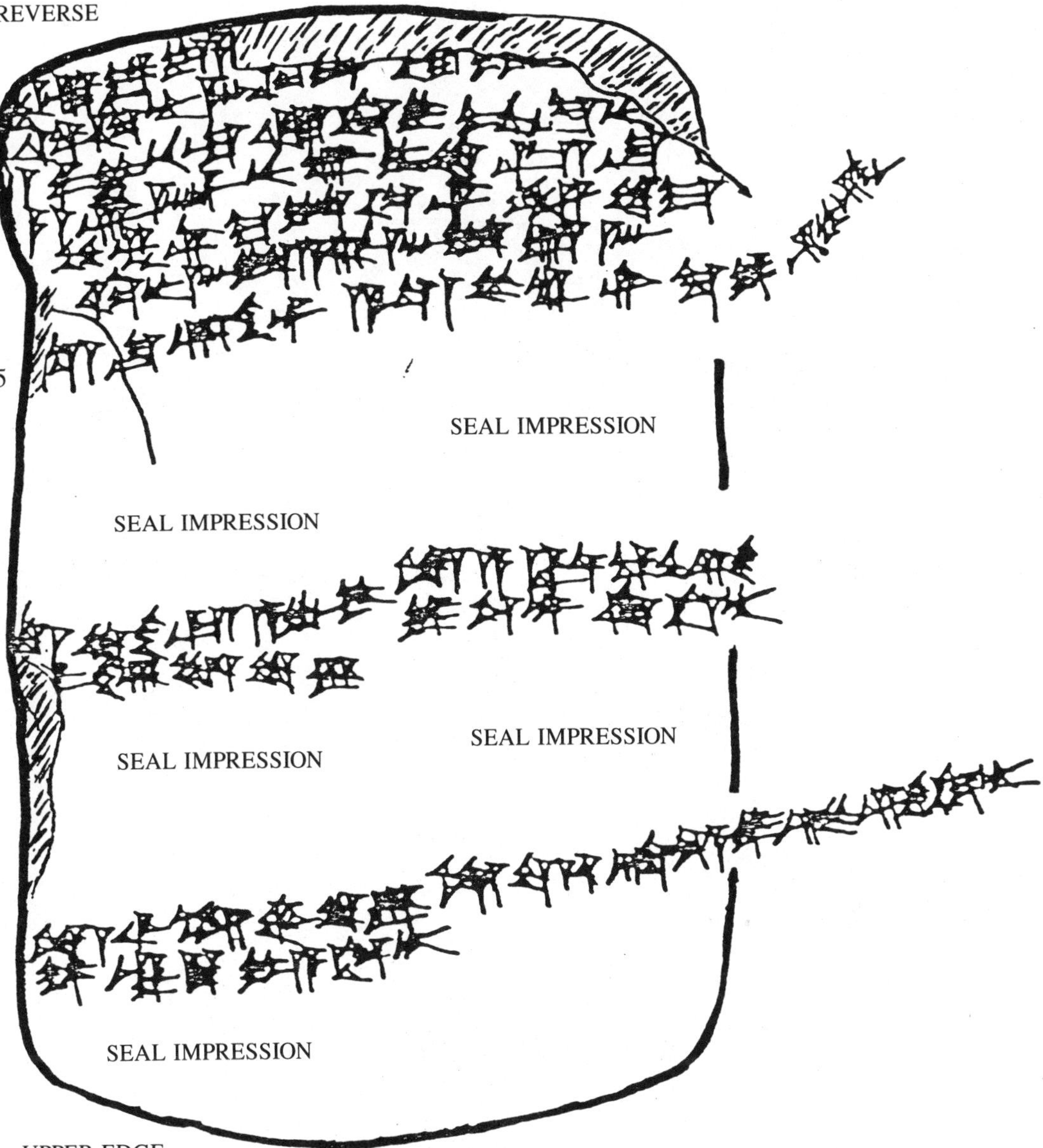

UPPER EDGE

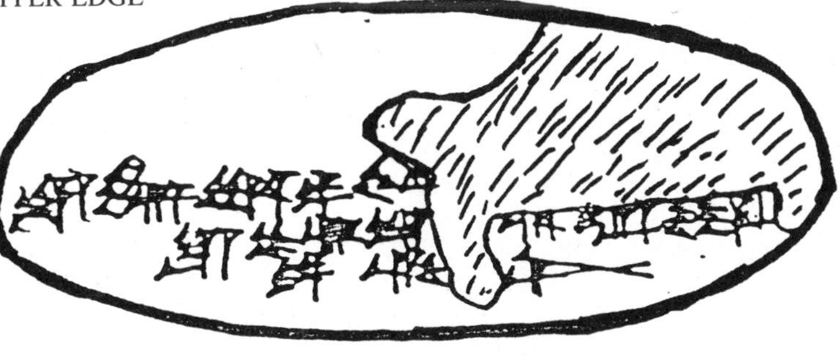

501

OBVERSE

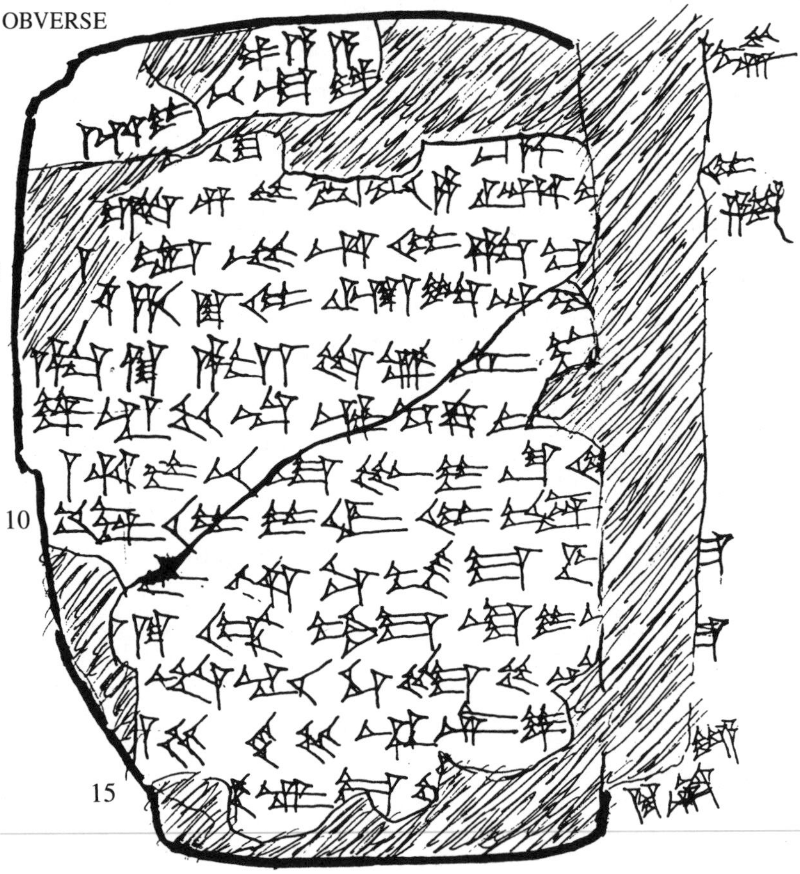

501

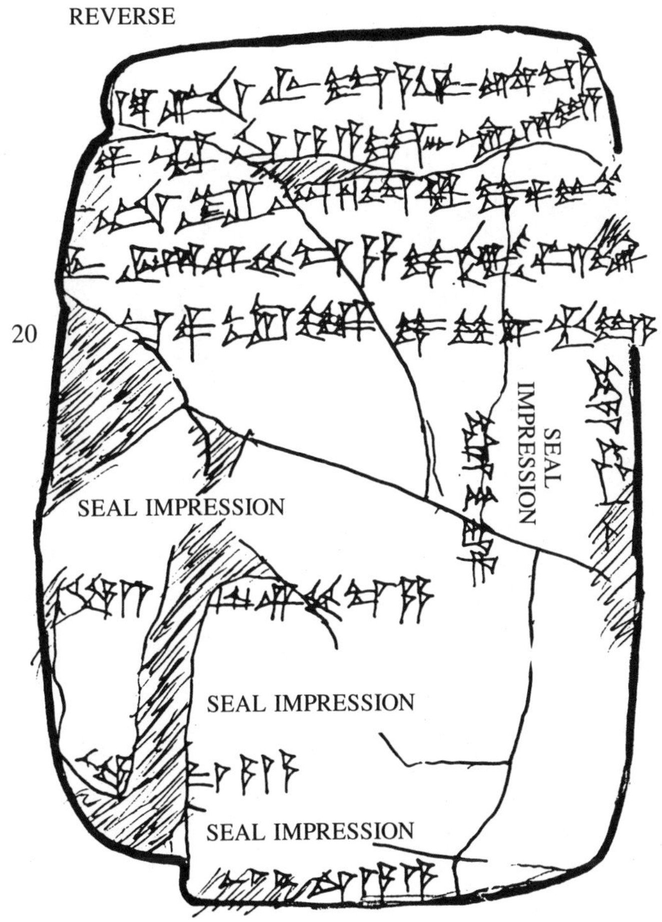
REVERSE
20
SEAL IMPRESSION
SEAL IMPRESSION
SEAL IMPRESSION
SEAL IMPRESSION

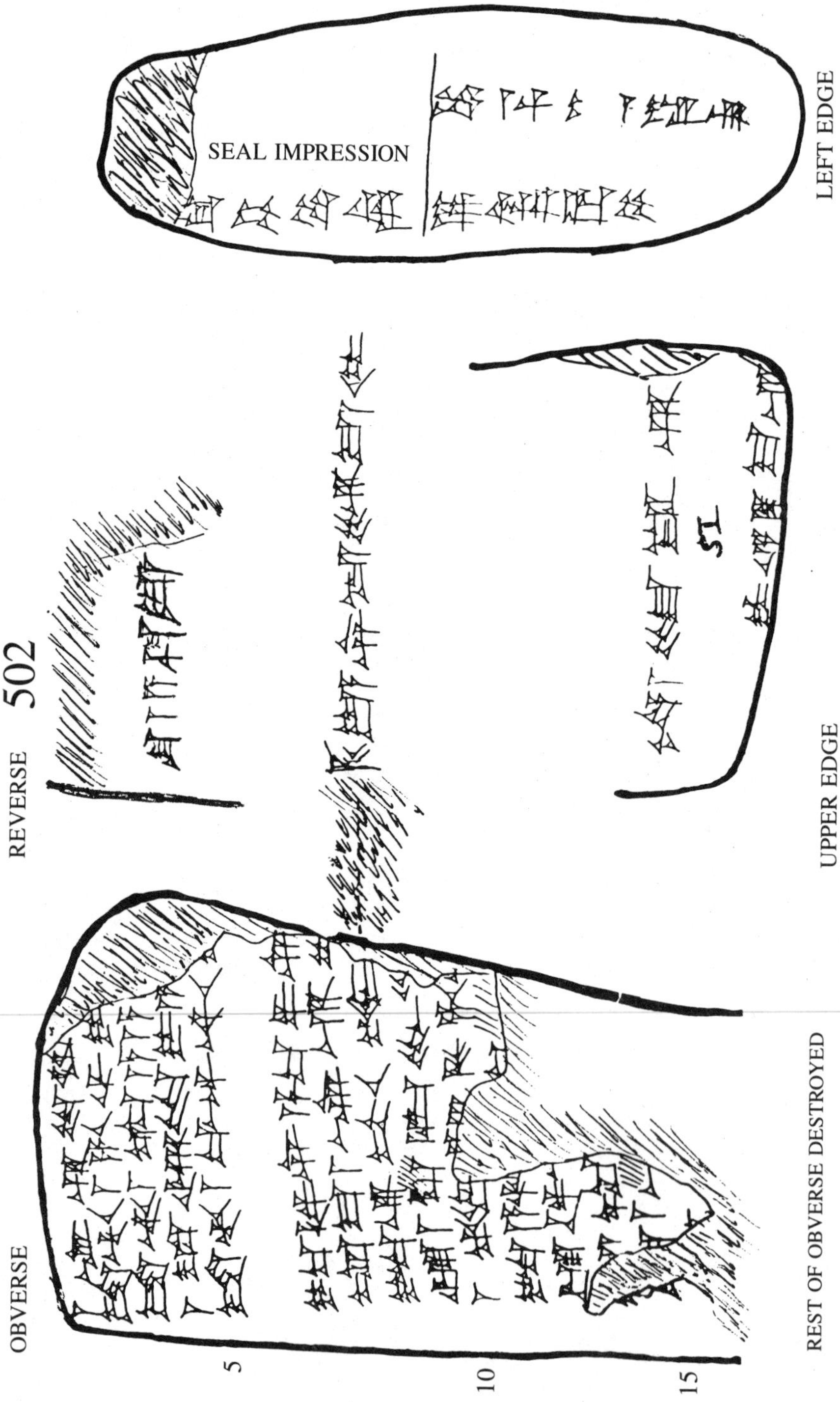
502
OBVERSE
REVERSE
REST OF OBVERSE DESTROYED
UPPER EDGE
LEFT EDGE
SEAL IMPRESSION
SEAL IMPRESSION

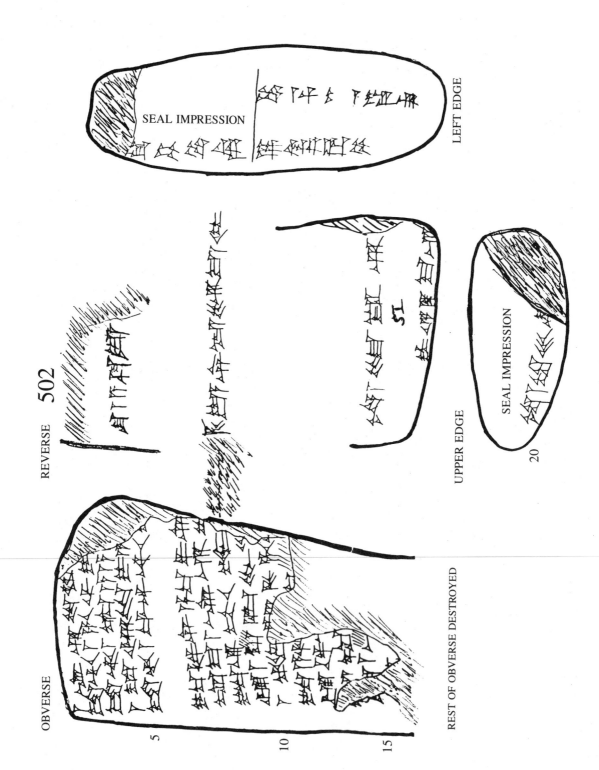

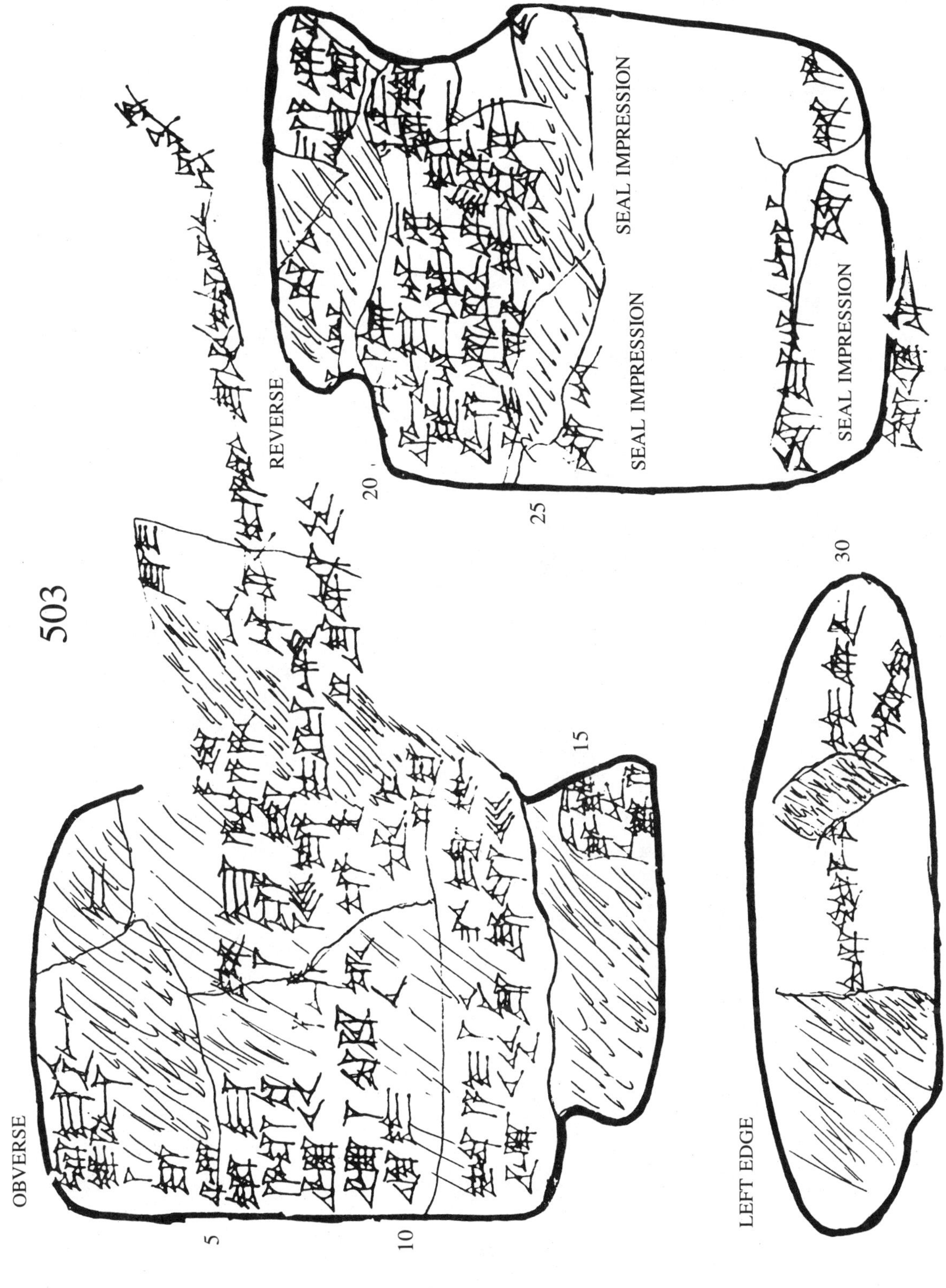
503
OBVERSE
REVERSE
SEAL IMPRESSION
SEAL IMPRESSION
SEAL IMPRESSION
LEFT EDGE

504

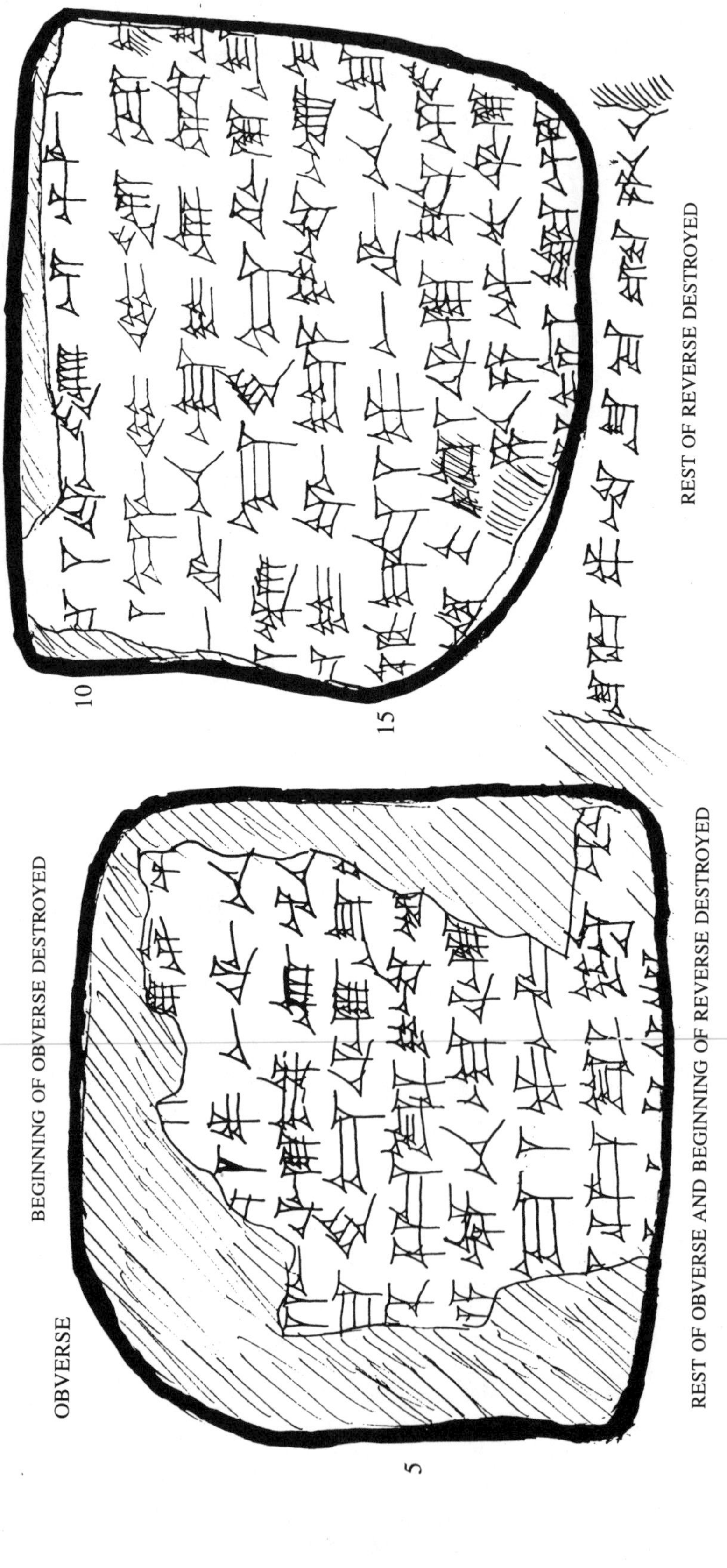
REVERSE
BEGINNING OF REVERSE DESTROYED
10
15
REST OF REVERSE DESTROYED
OBVERSE
BEGINNING OF OBVERSE DESTROYED
5
REST OF OBVERSE AND BEGINNING OF REVERSE DESTROYED

506

OBVERSE

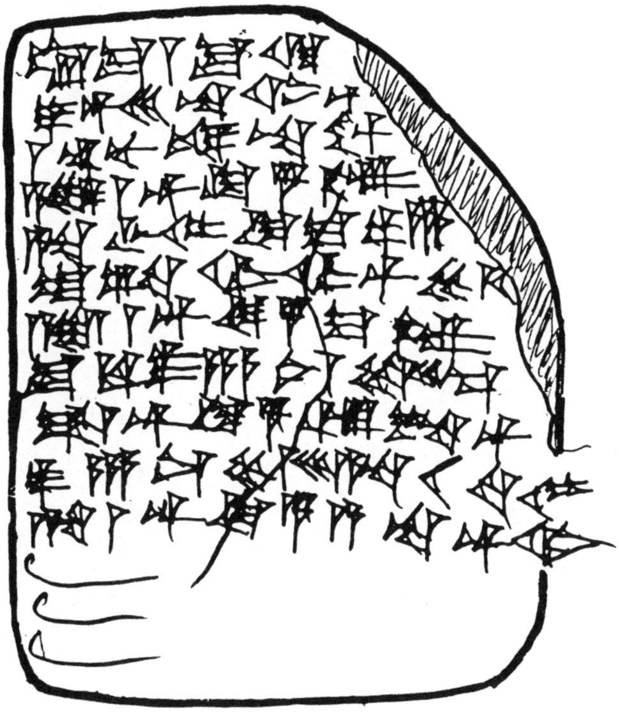

REVERSE

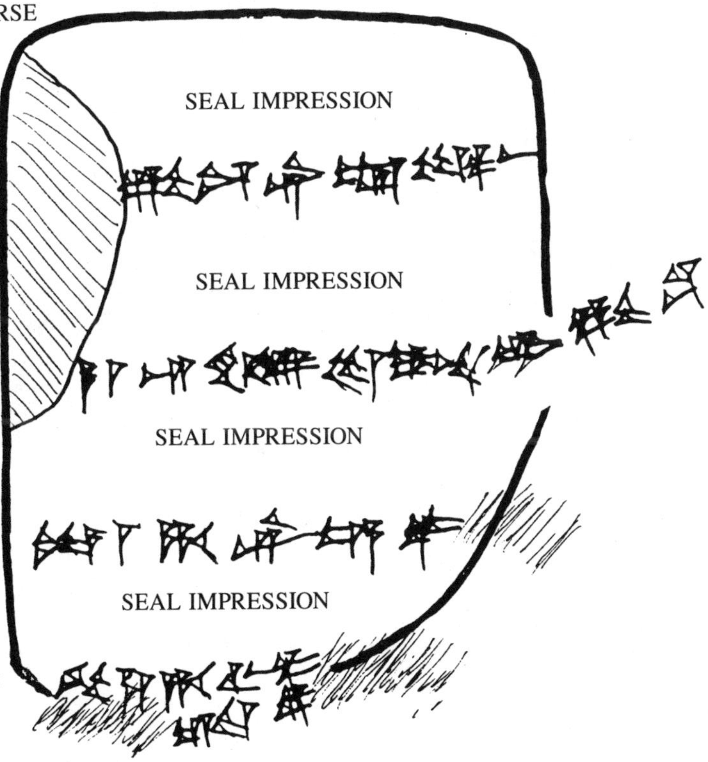

507

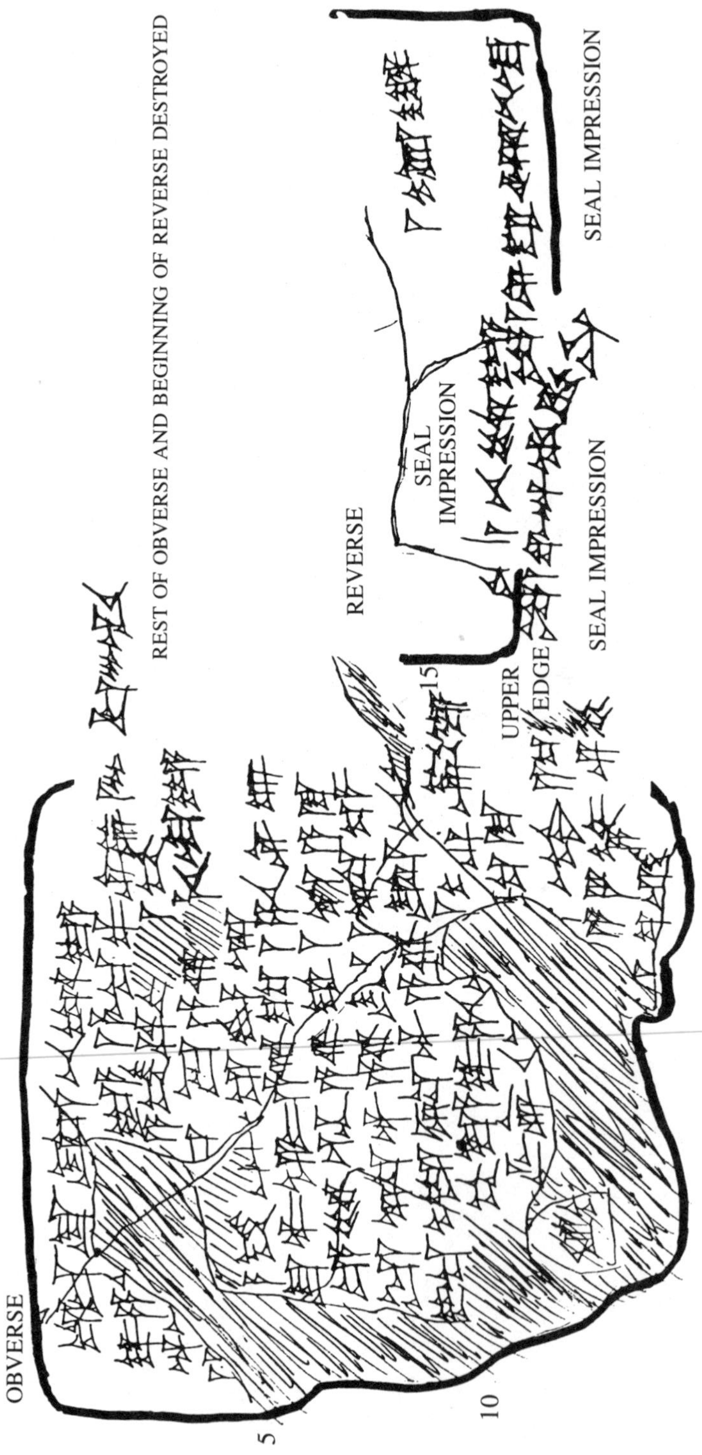
OBVERSE
5
10
15
REST OF OBVERSE AND BEGINNING OF REVERSE DESTROYED
REVERSE
SEAL IMPRESSION
UPPER EDGE
SEAL IMPRESSION
SEAL IMPRESSION

508

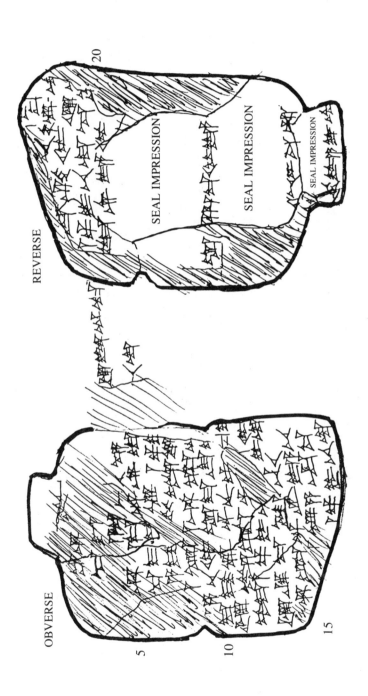

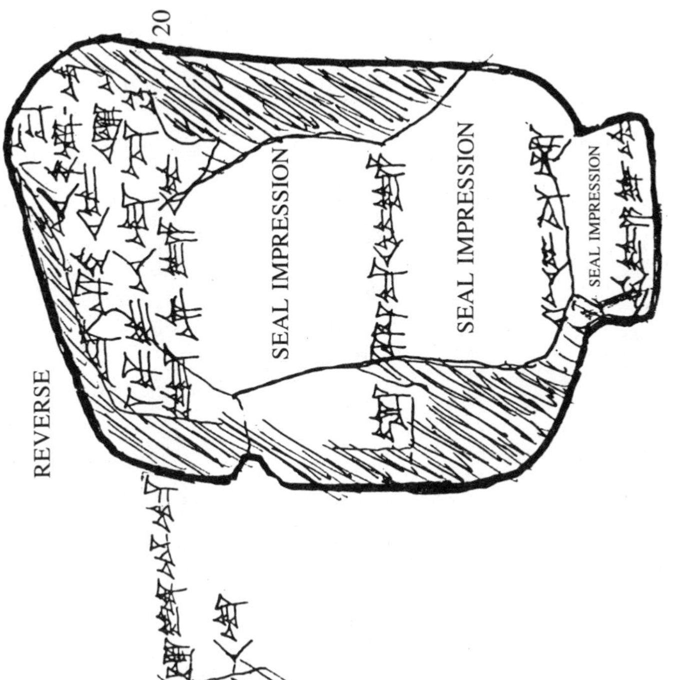
OBVERSE
REVERSE
SEAL IMPRESSION
SEAL IMPRESSION
SEAL IMPRESSION

509

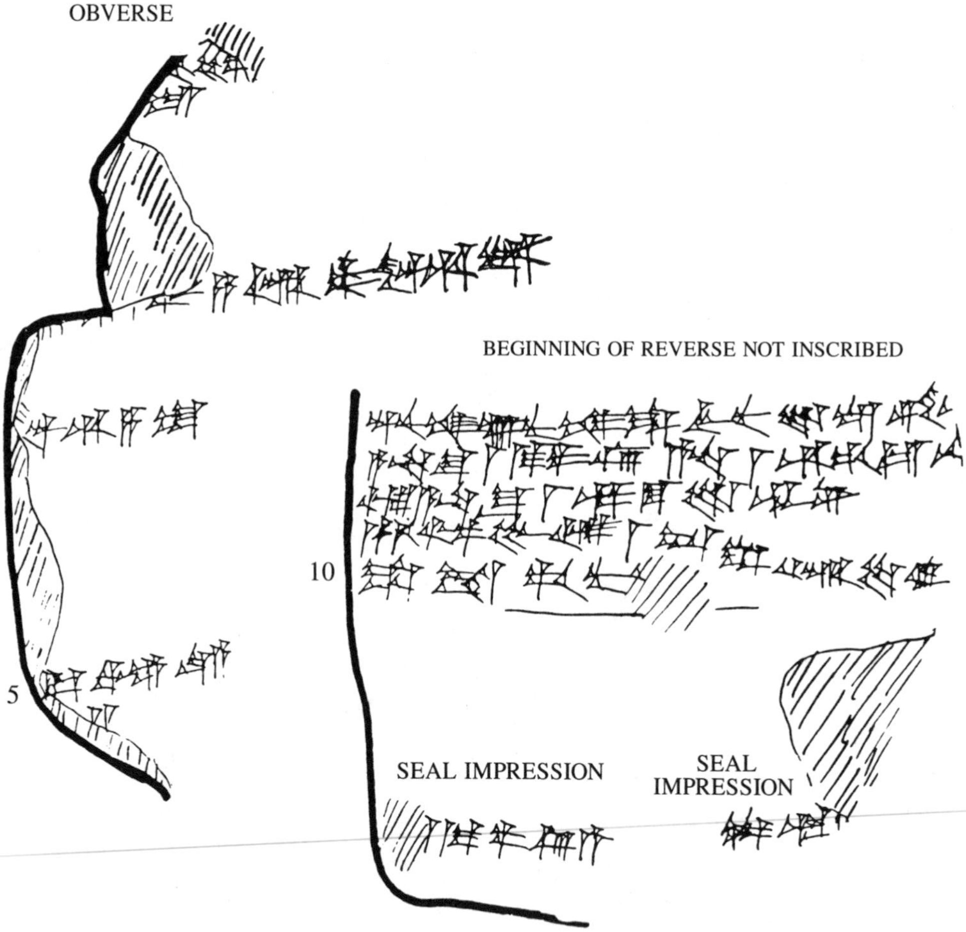
OBVERSE
5
BEGINNING OF REVERSE NOT INSCRIBED
10
SEAL IMPRESSION
SEAL IMPRESSION

510

OBVERSE

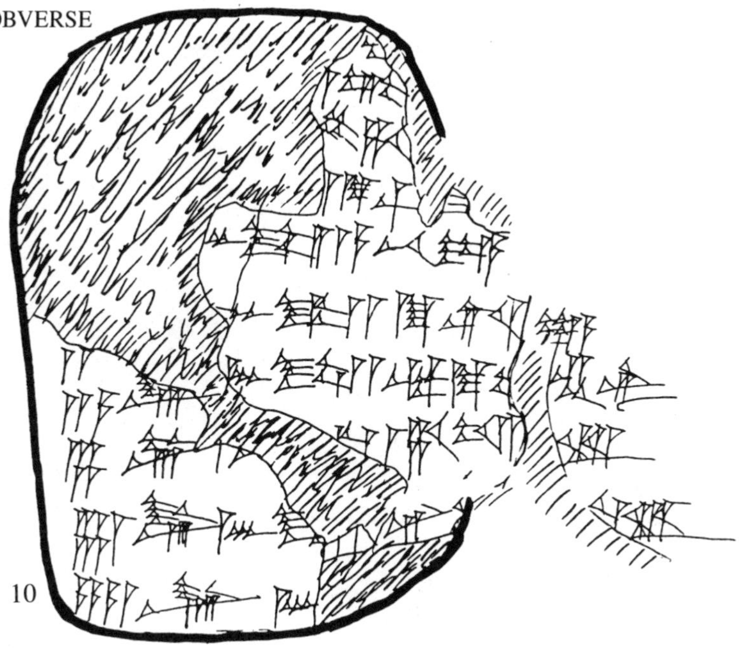

LOWER EDGE

REVERSE

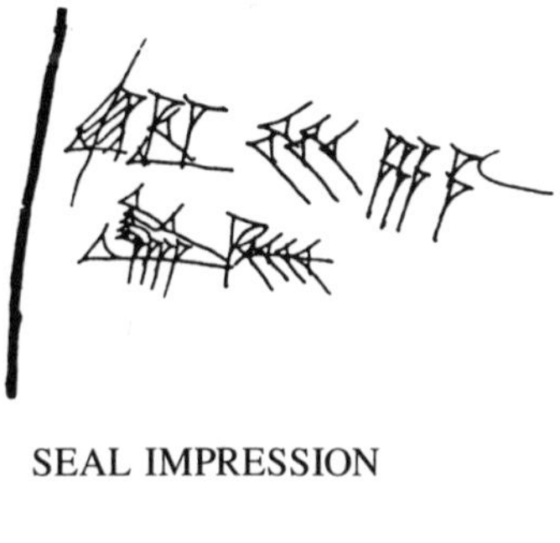

SEAL IMPRESSION

514

OBVERSE

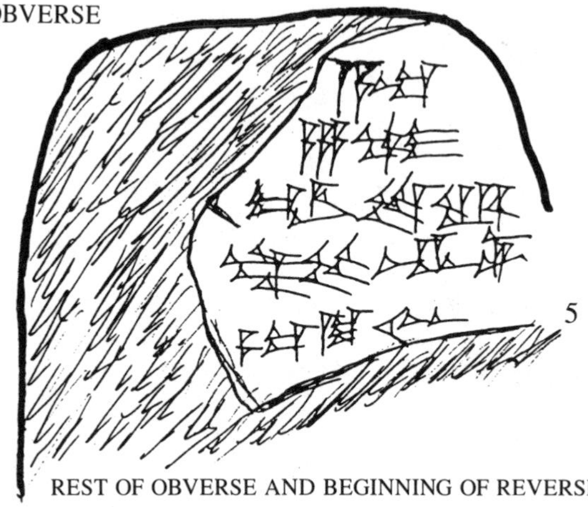

REST OF OBVERSE AND BEGINNING OF REVERSE DESTROYED

REVERSE

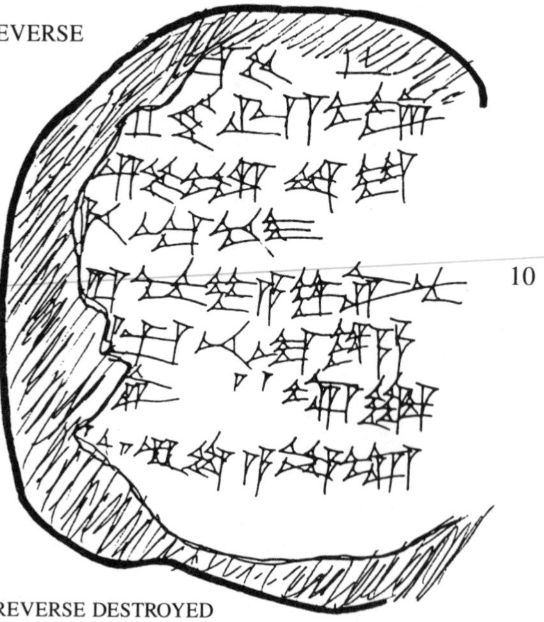

REST OF REVERSE DESTROYED

516

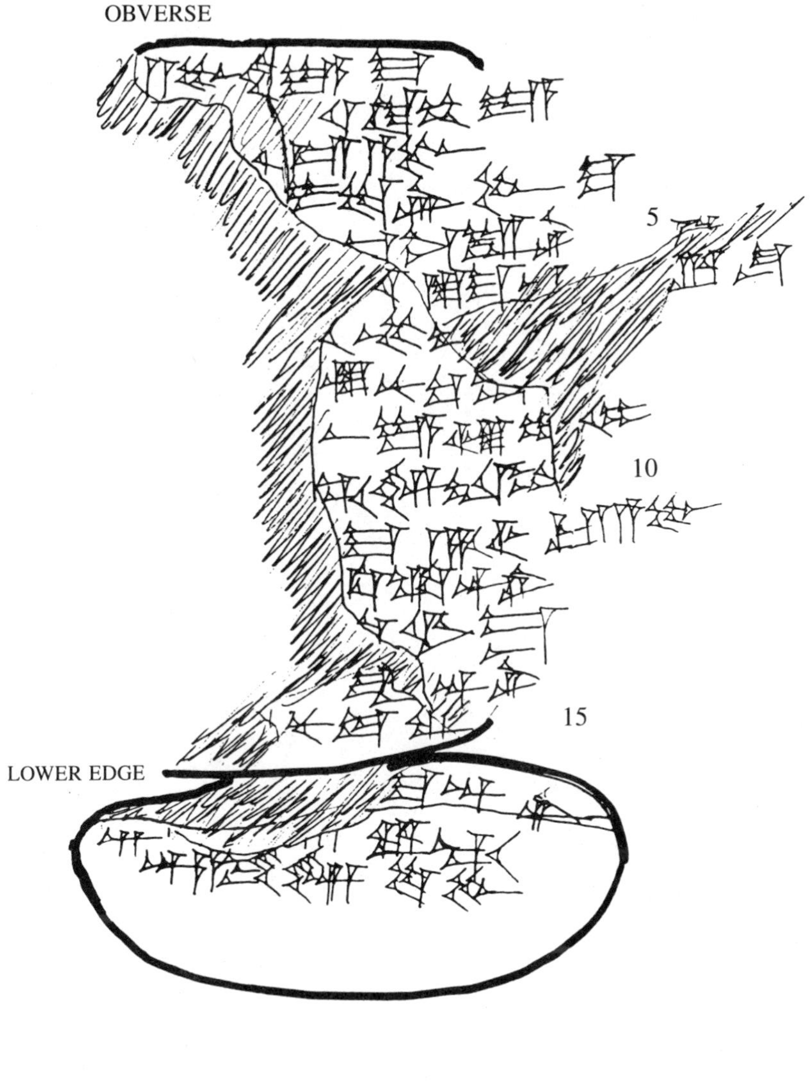

516

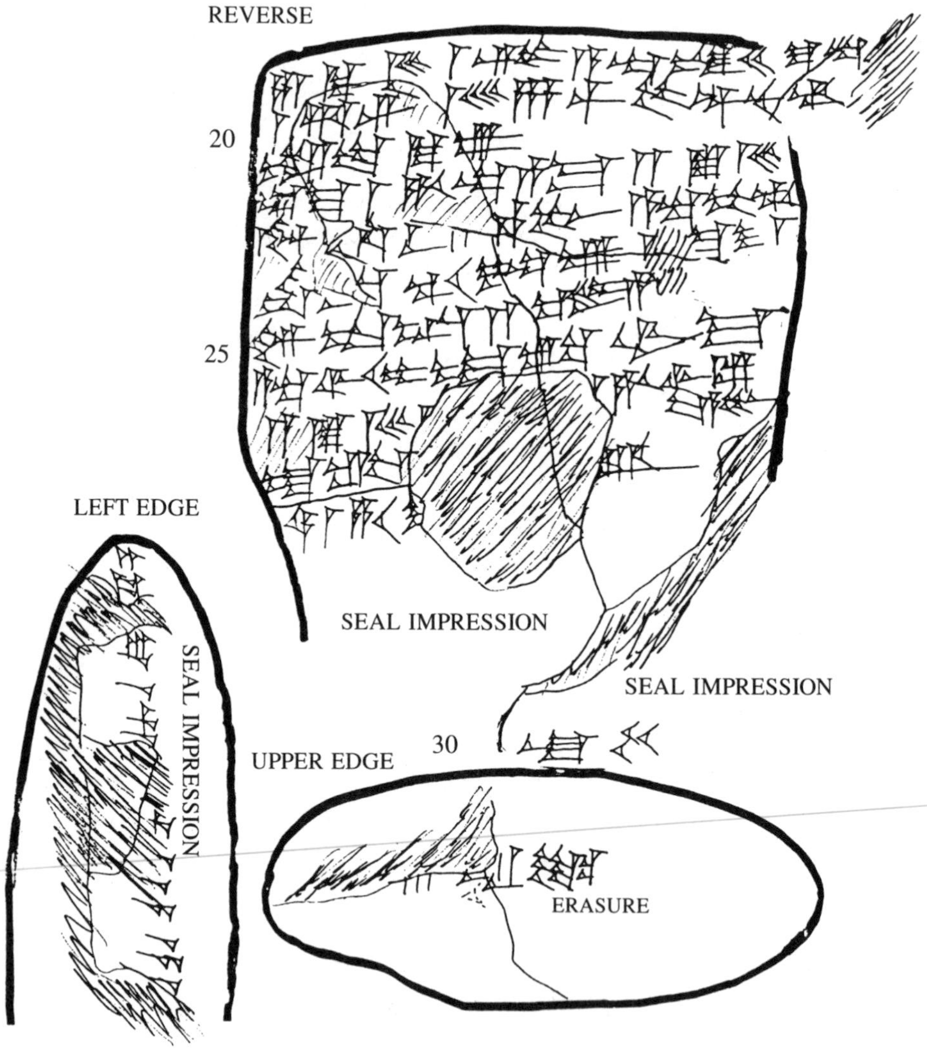

REVERSE
20
25
SEAL IMPRESSION
SEAL IMPRESSION
30
LEFT EDGE
SEAL IMPRESSION
UPPER EDGE
ERASURE

517

LEFT EDGE

OBVERSE

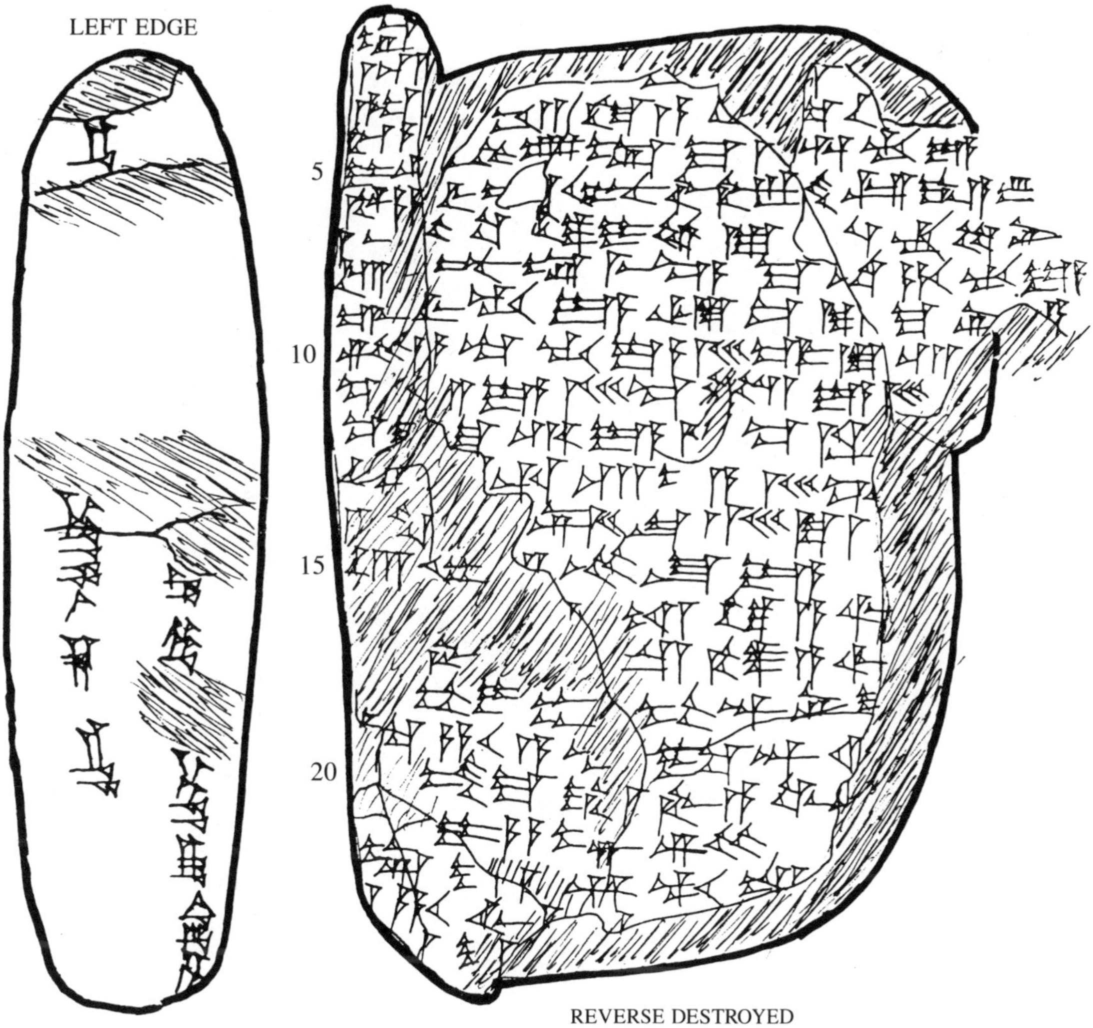

REVERSE DESTROYED

518

OBVERSE

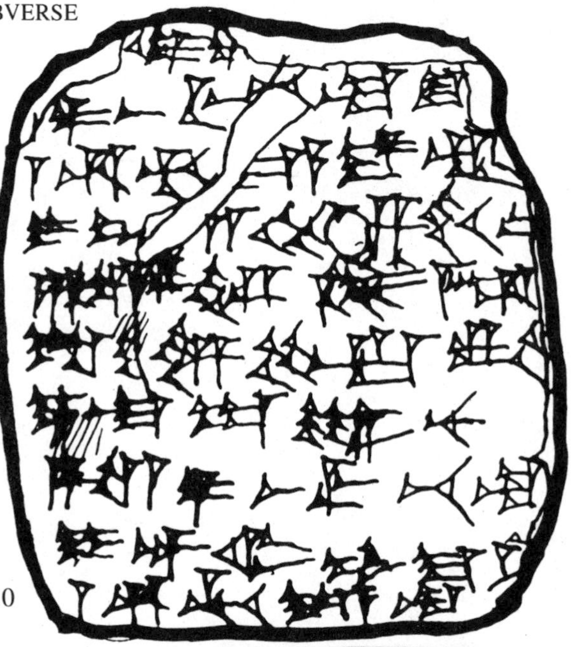

LOWER EDGE

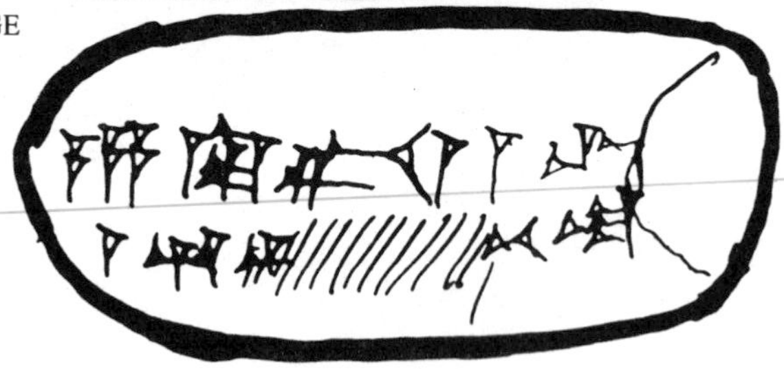

518

REVERSE

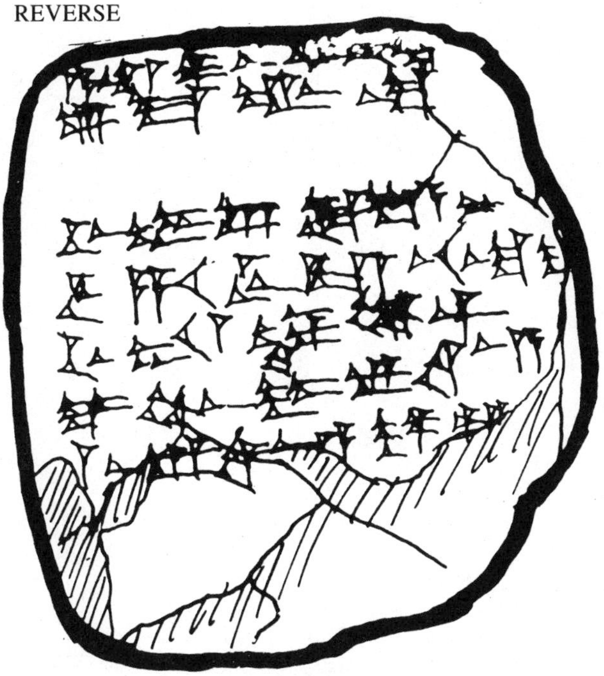

LEFT EDGE

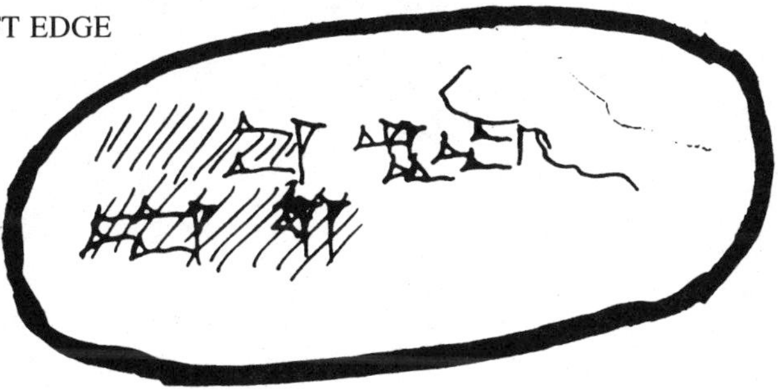

519

OBVERSE

BEGINNING OF OBVERSE DESTROYED

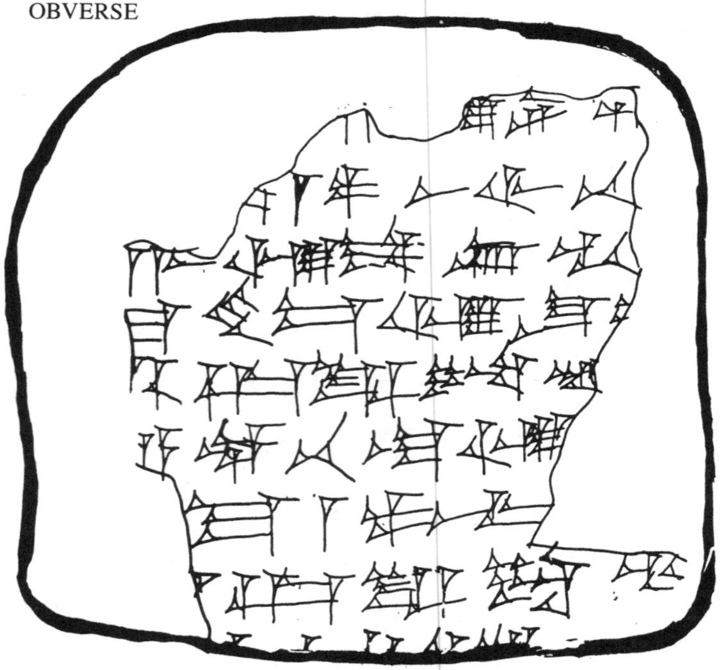

REST OF OBVERSE AND BEGINNING OF REVERSE DESTROYED

REVERSE

BEGINNING OF REVERSE DESTROYED

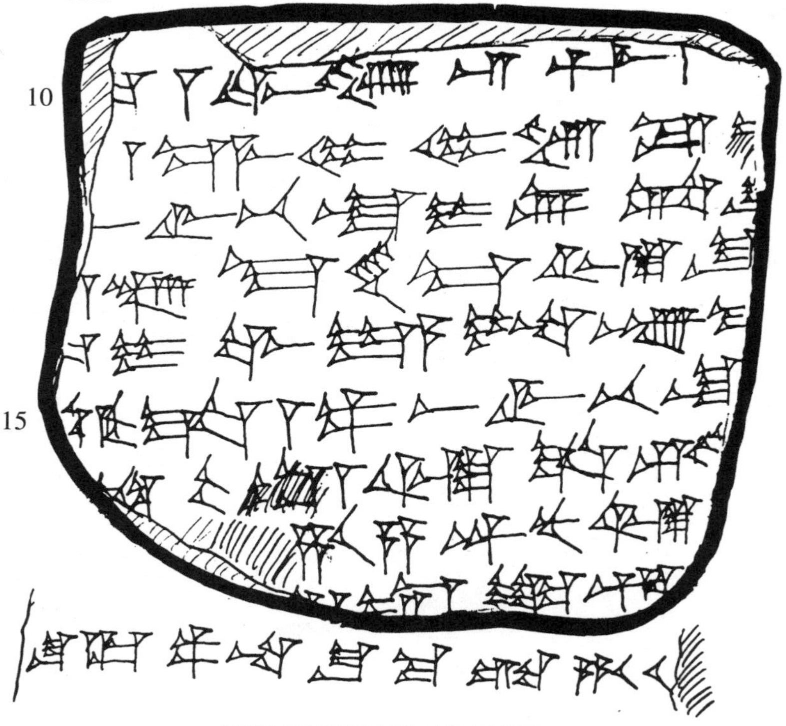

REST OF REVERSE DESTROYED

521

OBVERSE

BEGINNING OF OBVERSE DESTROYED

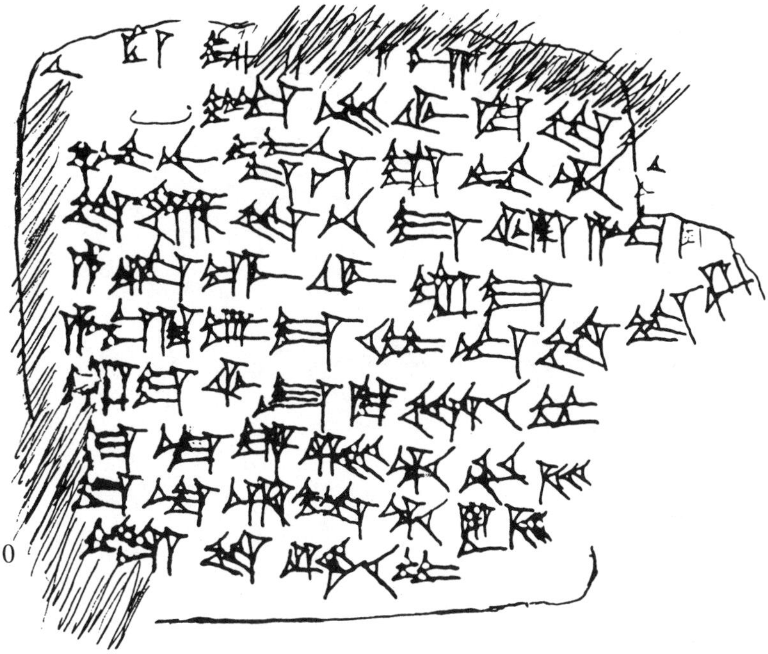

REVERSE

SEAL IMPRESSION

522

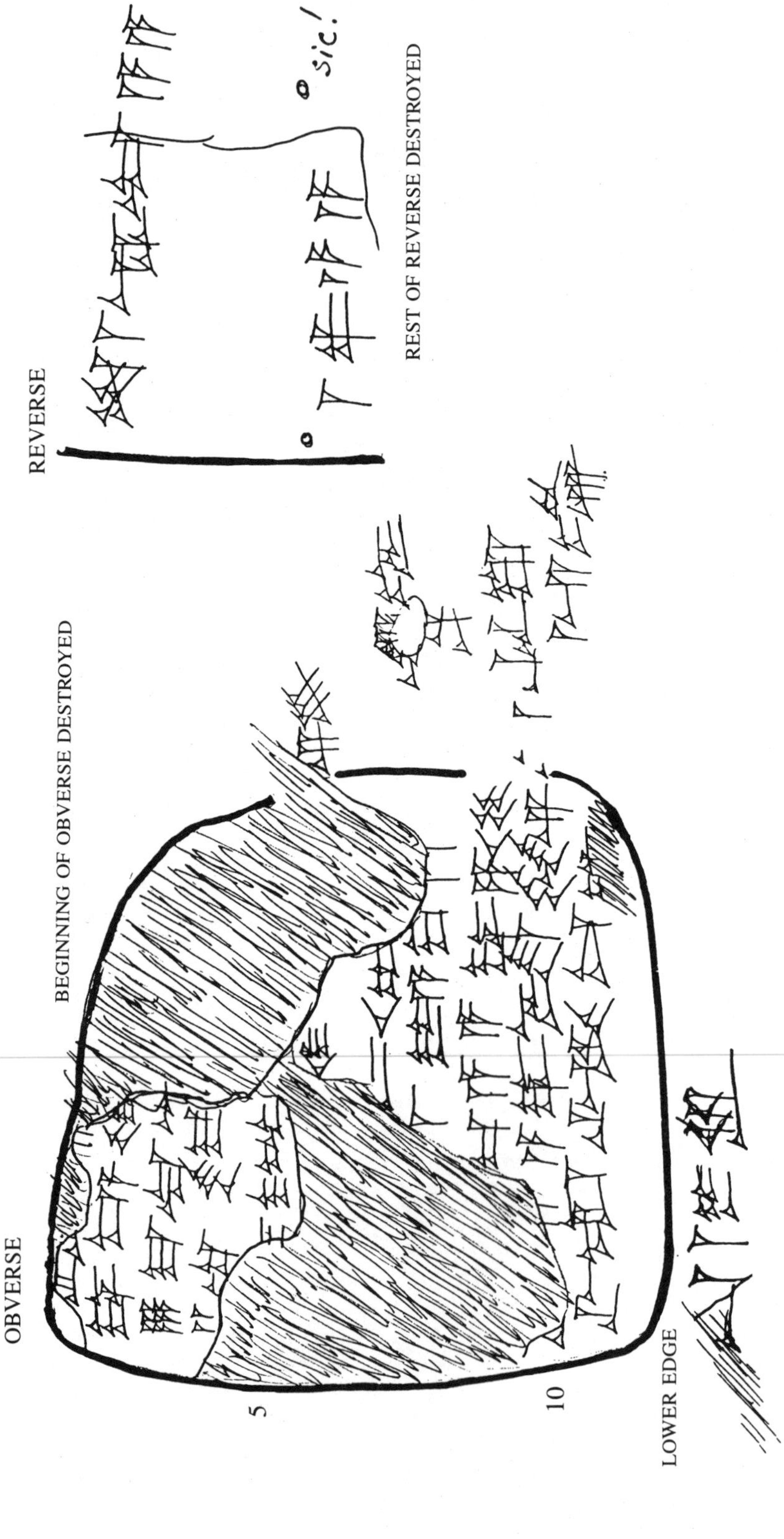
OBVERSE
BEGINNING OF OBVERSE DESTROYED
5
10
LOWER EDGE
REVERSE
sic!
REST OF REVERSE DESTROYED

523

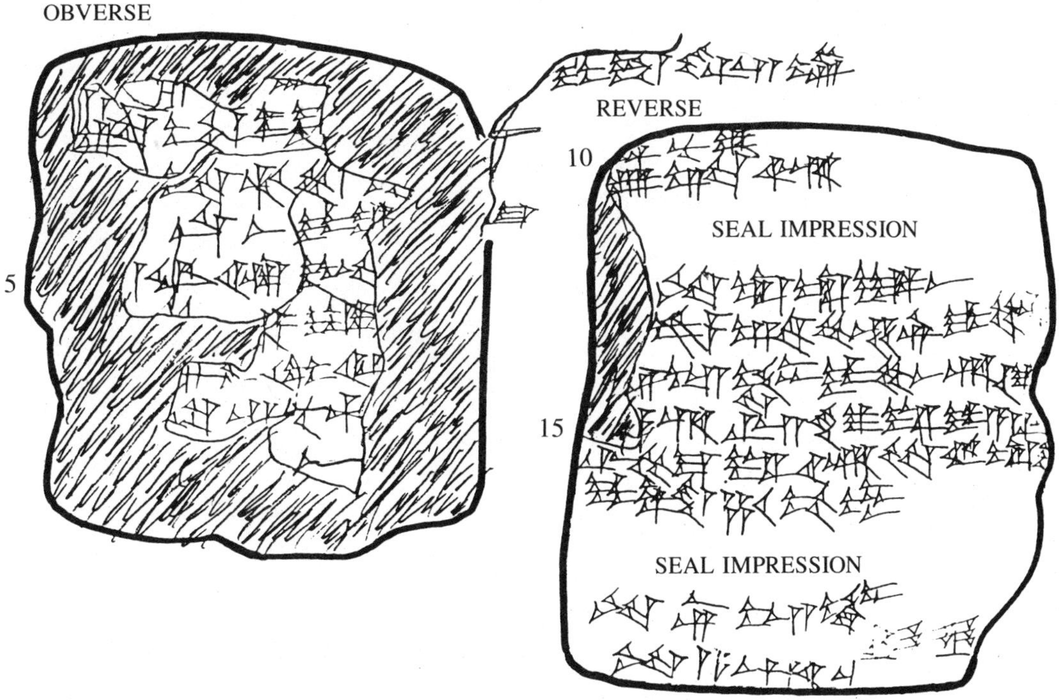